EVER CLOSER UNION

SECOND EDITION

EVER CLOSER UNION

AN INTRODUCTION TO EUROPEAN INTEGRATION

DESMOND DINAN

BOULDER
LONDON

Published in the United States of America in 1999 by
Lynne Rienner Publishers, Inc.
1800 30th Street, Boulder, Colorado 80301

Library of Congress Cataloging-in-Publication Data
Dinan, Desmond, 1957–
Ever closer union : an introduction to European integration / Desmond Dinan. — 2nd ed.
p. cm.
Includes bibliographical references and index.
ISBN 1-55587-739-7 (pbk. : alk. paper)
1. European Economic Community. 2. European federation. I. Title.
HC241.2.D476 1999
337.1'42—dc21 99-11101
CIP

Printed and bound in the United States of America

The paper used in this publication meets the requirements of the American National Standard for Permanence of Paper for Printed Library Materials Z39.48-1984.

5 4 3 2 1

To Cian and Cliona,
our new editions

Contents

PART 2 INSTITUTIONS

PART 3 POLICIES

Tables and Figures

Preface

A lot has happened in the European Union (EU) since the first edition of this book was published in 1994. So much, indeed, that the second edition is substantially different from the first. I trimmed the original Part 1 in order to include an additional chapter in the new Part 1 covering key developments since the mid-1990s, notably the 1995 enlargement, the 1996–1997 intergovernmental conference and ensuing Amsterdam Treaty, and preparations for the next enlargement. The launch of the euro—another key development since the first edition appeared—is dealt with in a radically revised chapter in Part 3 on Economic and Monetary Union. As well as extensive revisions in each of the chapters on institutions and policies, the second edition also includes a new final chapter on U.S.-EU relations.

A lot has been published on and by the EU since the first edition came out. The rapid evolution of the Internet—another post–first edition development—has greatly helped scholarship on the EU by making it easier to track official and unofficial publications and by providing immediate access to key documents and up-to-the-minute information. *Europa,* the EU website, is an invaluable resource for anyone interested in European integration. It contains a wealth of information on EU institutions, policies, and programs, as well as links to other important websites such as those of the EU presidency and of leading academic associations. I advise readers who want to update this book—for instance, with the results of elections to the European Parliament or the composition of a new European Commission—to do so by visiting the *Europa* website at www.europa.eu.int.

A lot of people have helped me to produce this new edition. In particular I would like to thank my publisher, Lynne Rienner, and her colleagues—Sally Glover (assistant to Lynne), Lesli Brooks Athanasoulis (project editor), and Diane Hess (copyeditor)—for their assistance and support.

—*D. D.*

INTRODUCTION

The European Union (EU) is a unique international entity that directly affects the daily lives of its 375 million citizens. People move frequently and freely between most of its member states; when traveling "abroad," they carry burgundy EU passports. Students participate in EU-sponsored university exchange programs. Farms depend on the Common Agricultural Policy (CAP) for their livelihoods. Businesspeople examine the latest rules and regulations from the EU's headquarters in Brussels before devising manufacturing and marketing strategies. Millions of unemployed people take EU-funded training courses, while may of them blame the EU's economic policies for their plight. Throughout the EU women enjoy equality in the workplace because of landmark decisions in the European Court of Justice.

Public awareness of European integration grew dramatically in the late 1980s, when the then European Community (EC) implemented a program to establish a single market—in which goods, people, capital, and services could move freely across member states' frontiers—by the end of 1992. The single market program, in turn, revived interest in Economic Monetary Union (EMU), a long-cherished objective. Events in 1989 and 1990—revolution in Central and Eastern Europe, the collapse of the Berlin Wall, and German unification—focused attention also on European Political Union (EPU), including efforts to integrate member states' foreign and security policies. By incorporating both EMU and EPU, the Treaty on European Union (TEU) of February 1992 was a decisive step on the road to "ever closer union," an aspiration first expressed in the Treaty of Rome (1957), the EC's founding charter that is better known today as the Treaty Establishing the European Community (TEC).

The European Union, established by the TEU, is based on three pillars:

- *First Pillar:* the EC, embracing the European Coal and Steel Community, the European Economic Community, and the European Atomic Energy Community. Of the three communities, the European

Figure 0.1 Names and Numbers

The European Union (EU) did not come into existence until November 1993, when it subsumed, but did not replace, the European Community (EC). Nevertheless, in this book (as in everyday conversation) the name EU is used when referring generally to events before 1993 and to policies that, legally, belong to the EC.

The EU's founding treaties—the Treaty Establishing the European Community (TEC) and the Treaty on European Union (TEU)—have been chopped and changed many times with numerous articles added, altered, or deleted. In an effort to simplify the treaties after so many revisions, the Treaty of Amsterdam (1997) renumbered the articles in the TEC and TEU. The new numbers are used in this book except when referring specifically to pre-Amsterdam versions of the treaties. In cases where treaty articles are still widely known by their old numbers, those numbers are also given, preceded by a "formerly." A "conversion" table, with the old and new numbers, is included in Appendixes 2 and 3 at the end of this book.

Economic Community is by far the most important. Moreover, the TEU officially substituted the more familiar-sounding "European Community" for the more cumbersome "European Economic Community." The EC forms the core of the EU.

- *Second Pillar:* the Common Foreign and Security Policy (CFSP).
- *Third Pillar:* police and judicial cooperation in criminal matters.

The EU's pervasiveness tends to obscure its uniqueness and relative newness. The voluntary sharing of sovereignty by nation-states—a step toward the ever closer union envisioned in the EC and the TEU—is unprecedented in modern history. Before World War II, the kind of European integration with which we are so familiar today was a pipe dream. Nations jealously guarded their sovereignty (national authority) and cooperated solely on the basis of intergovernmental agreement. Only sixty years ago, France and Germany were implacable enemies.

The change in political opinion and behavior that brought the EC into existence owed much to the destructiveness of World War II and the virulent nationalism that preceded it, as well as to the complexity of economic, social, and political life that followed. To a great extent, the EC was a security system for Western Europe. Its first manifestation, the European Coal and Steel Community (ECSC), emerged in 1952 in response to an urgent need both to rehabilitate defeated Germany and to allay understandable French security concerns, all in a radically altered international environment. Coal and steel lay at the core of both countries' economic systems and war-making potential. By establishing a supranational entity to manage the coal and steel sectors, the ECSC's six member states (France, Germany, Italy, Belgium, the Netherlands, and Luxembourg) became so closely intertwined that a future war between any of them soon appeared unthinkable and impossible.

For Jean Monnet, a senior French official who pioneered the idea of sectoral economic integration, the ECSC was not an end in itself but part of a process that would culminate in a European federation transcending the nation-state. Such a goal was inherent in the word "community," which distinguished the new arrangement from traditional forms of intergovernmental collaboration and international organization. The ECSC was supranational as well as transnational: It engaged in activities that cut across national boundaries and included a High Authority (the forerunner of the Commission) with power to make decisions at a level above that of national governments.

Integration indeed progressed. The functionally broader European Economic Community followed in the wake of the ECSC, and initially it prospered politically as well as economically. But French president Charles de Gaulle's inflexible opposition to supranationalism caused a reassessment of earlier, optimistic thinking about the supposedly inexorable nature of European integration. Ideological and political battles in the mid-1960s emphasized an apparent dichotomy between intergovernmentalism and supranationalism, between the supposed decline of the nation-state and the putative rise of a European federation.

In reality, intergovernmentalism and supranationalism are not irreconcilable; rather, they jointly characterize the EU system. Member states are willing to share sovereignty in certain areas because, quite simply, it is in their national interest to do so. Put negatively, in an age of rapid technological and commercial change, national governments are unable to act independently to maximize their citizens' welfare. Thus governments are willing to share sovereignty, but their desire to retain as much political control as possible leads to the EU's peculiar institutional and decision-making structure: The Commission has only a modicum of supranational authority; in some cases government ministers are willing to be outvoted in the Council, and in others they retain a national veto over proposed EU legislation; the directly elected European Parliament is increasingly powerful and influential, although its members are motivated by national as well as supranational considerations.

The Single European Act (SEA) of 1986 is a striking example of how member states reconcile intergovernmentalism and supranationalism in relation to the EU's functional scope and institutional structure. By the mid-1980s, the EC had enlarged from the original six ECSC member states to include also Britain, Denmark, Ireland, Greece, Portugal, and Spain. Earlier in the decade, ideological, technological, and economic developments convinced member states to achieve a single, barrier-free market by the end of 1992, buttressed by stronger European-level social, environmental, and industrial policies. Although the SEA broadened the EC's functional scope, it did not extend the EC's activities much beyond the objectives implicit in the original TEC. Similarly, member states agreed to enhance the EC's limited supranational authority only to the extent necessary to achieve the SEA's goals.

The TEU saw a major extension of Community competence, notably in the area of EMU. Most member states considered EMU a corollary of the successful single market program and wanted to end de facto German dominance of the existing European Monetary System (EMS). Their response was a federal structure for monetary policymaking: a European system of central banks that includes a European central bank.

By contrast, the Common Foreign and Security Policy (CFSP) enshrined in the TEU clearly showed the limits of supranationalism. Not least because of German unification, governments agreed in the run-up to the TEU on the urgency of closer foreign policy and security cooperation but were unwilling to share national sovereignty in these areas. Accordingly, the high political issues of foreign, security, and, ultimately, defense cooperation were consigned to a separate "pillar" outside the Community system, subject to intergovernmental agreement.

The fate of the TEU also demonstrated the limits of European integration. By 1993 the single market was almost fully in place. Yet growing popular concern about further loss of sovereignty and about secretive and undemocratic decisionmaking in Brussels—compounded by creeping economic recession, the high cost of German unification, and intense frustration over the EC's inability to broker a lasting cease-fire in Bosnia—shattered the permissive consensus that had hitherto characterized European integration. Failure to ratify the TEU by the end of 1992 epitomized for many a deep crisis of confidence in Europe's future.

At the heart of the TEU ratification crisis lay doubts about the EU's relevance in the post–Cold War world. What was the EU's feasibility and utility in a radically altered international environment? From the outset, the EC had considered itself synonymous with Europe. With the Cold War over, could the EU foster pan-European solidarity and a genuinely all-European integration? The enlargement of the EU in 1995 to include Austria, Finland, and Sweden raised the perennial question of whether "wider" would also mean "weaker," a question that assumed added salience when enlargement negotiations began with five Central and Eastern European countries, plus Cyprus, in 1998.

Table 0.1 The Ever Deeper Union

1951	Treaty of Paris establishes the European Coal and Steel Community
1957	Treaties of Rome establish the European Economic Community and the European Atomic Energy Community
1962	Launch of the Common Agricultural Policy
1968	Completion of the customs union
1970	Launch of European Political Cooperation (foreign policy coordination)
1975	Launch of the European Council
1979	Launch of the European Monetary System
1986	The Single European Act launches the single market program and extends Community competence in the fields of environmental policy, economic and social cohesion, research and technology policy, and social policy
1989	Extension of Commission responsibility for competition policy
1992	The Treaty on European Union sets the EU on the road to Economic and Monetary Union, transforms European Political Cooperation into the Common Foreign and Security Policy, and launches intergovernmental cooperation on Justice and Home Affairs
1997	The Treaty of Amsterdam extends Community competence over certain aspects of Justice and Home Affairs and sets a target date for completion of "an area of freedom, security, and justice"
1999	Launch of a common monetary policy and a single currency (the euro)

Table 0.2 The Ever Wider Union

Original Member States (1958)	First Enlargement (1973)	Second Enlargement (1981)	Third Enlargement (1986)	Fourth Enlargement (1995)
Belgium	Britain	Greece	Spain	Austria
France	Denmark		Portugal	Finland
Germany	Ireland			Sweden
Italy				
Luxembourg				
Netherlands				

Table 0.3 The Impact of Enlargement

	1958	1973	1981	1986	1995
Area (000km)	1,167	1,524	1,658	2,252	3,234
Population (million)	185	273	287	338	370
Member states	6	9	10	12	15
Official languages	4	6	7	9	11
Commissioners	9	13	14	17	20
Members of the European Parliament	142	198	434	518	626
Qualified majority voting (qualified majority/ total number of votes in the Council)	12/17	41/58	45/63	54/76	62/87

It is easy to exaggerate the EU's difficulties in the post-Maastricht period, although serious problems undoubtedly persist. Yet the notion of an EU in crisis could be misleading and need not be entirely disadvantageous. The history of the EU's development is a history of overcoming crises: the crisis of German reconstruction in the late 1940s, leading to the European Coal and Steel Community; the European Defense Community crisis in the mid-1950s, leading to the relaunch of European integration; the crisis of declining competitiveness and decisionmaking paralysis in the 1970s and early 1980s, leading to the SEA; and the crisis of German unification in the late 1980s, leading to the TEU.

If only because the EU had already reached an advanced stage of political and economic development, the TEU ratification crisis was unlikely to trigger the kind of revival and transformation that followed other crises in the history of European integration. At the very least, the ratification crisis and the general malaise that followed it failed to stop the EMU juggernaut, which gathered speed in the late 1990s. Nor was there talk of dismantling the single market or of systematically rolling back existing levels of integration. Although the Amsterdam Treaty disappointed proponents of deeper integration and bold innovation (a dwindling band in any case), its provisions to allow further integration among fewer than the full complement of member states and to establish "an area of freedom, security, and justice" within five years of the treaty's implementation are not unimportant.

The main challenges ahead lie in the realization of EMU and enlargement. Will EMU work in the medium to long term? Can it be sustained? How will it affect the EU's role in the world? How will the EU manage enlargement? Will it make the necessary institutional and policy adjustments? What effect will enlargement have on relations among existing member states, and on the EU's role in the world?

In view of these and other challenges, will there be an ever closer union among the peoples of Europe, as advocated by the treaties? Even if people feel more "European," will they feel a greater affinity for the EU? Will the benefits of integration be enjoyed reasonably equally by all member states, and by all social groups? Or will European integration engender a sense of alienation and exclusion among the less advantaged? In some respects Europeans are closer than ever before; economic and technological changes are pushing, in any case, in that direction. But in terms of identity, affinity, and solidarity, the catchphrase "ever closer union" could still warrant a question mark, although not necessarily in the title of this book—in contrast to the first edition.

Part 1

History

1

Reconstruction, Reconciliation, and Integration, 1945–1957

A famous poster commemorating the birth of European integration depicts two men, Jean Monnet and Robert Schuman, standing together "at the beginning of the European Community (9 May 1950)." The date in parentheses is the day on which Schuman, then foreign minister of France, announced an unprecedented plan to place "the whole of Franco-German coal and steel production under a common High Authority, within the framework of an organization open to the participation of the other countries of Europe."[1] Monnet, a senior French official, was the brains behind the novel initiative.

It is difficult to appreciate today the boldness and prescience of Schuman's proposal. The intervening decades have virtually obliterated our awareness not only of the depth of distrust toward Germany in the immediate postwar years but also of the importance of coal and steel for European prosperity at that time. Schuman's short, simple statement outlined a strategy to reconcile German economic recovery and French national security. By accepting the recently established Federal Republic of Germany as an economic equal and handing over responsibility for both countries' coal and steel industries to a supranational authority, the Schuman Plan gave substance to the hitherto vague notion of European unity and integration. Fleshing out the Schuman Declaration resulted first in the European Coal and Steel Community (ECSC) and later in the European Atomic Energy Community (Euratom) and the European Economic Community (EEC)—better known as the European Community (EC). Schuman Day is celebrated annually on May 9 in Brussels, Luxembourg, and Strasbourg as the birthday of what is now known as the EU.

Celebration of Schuman Day and solemnization of the Schuman Plan bolster what can be called the "official history" of European integration, which depicts Monnet and Schuman as visionaries soaring above the squalor and squabbles of postwar Europe, pointing the way to the promised land of peace and prosperity along the prudent path of economic

Table 1.1 Chronology, 1945–1957

Year	Month	Event
1945	May	End of World War II in Europe
1946	September	Churchill's "United States of Europe" speech
1947	March	Truman Doctrine announced; Britain and France sign Dunkirk Treaty (defensive alliance)
	June	Marshall Plan announced
	July	Organization for European Economic Cooperation established
	October	General Agreement on Tariffs and Trade (GATT) launched
	December	International Committee of the Movements for European Unity established in Paris
1948	January	Benelux customs union launched
	March	Brussels Treaty (defensive alliance of France, Britain, and Benelux) signed
	April	Organization for Economic Cooperation and Development (OECD) established
	May	Congress of Europe held in The Hague
	June	Berlin blockade begins
1949	April	NATO treaty signed in Washington, D.C.; International Ruhr Authority established; Federal Republic of Germany (West Germany) established
	May	Council of Europe launched; end of Berlin blockade
1950	May	Schuman Declaration
	June	Negotiations begin to establish the European Coal and Steel Community (ECSC)
	October	Pleven Plan for a European Defense Community (EDC)
	November	European Convention for the Protection of Human Rights and Fundamental Freedoms signed in Rome
1951	April	Treaty establishing the ECSC signed in Paris
1952	May	Treaty establishing the EDC signed in Paris
	August	ECSC launched in Luxembourg
	September	ECSC Assembly holds first session in Strasbourg
1954	August	French National Assembly rejects EDC treaty
	October	Brussels Treaty amended to establish Western European Union
1955	May	Germany joins NATO
	June	Messina Conference to relaunch European integration; Spaak Committee meets for first time
1956	May	Venice Conference: Spaak Committee recommends a European Economic Community (EEC) and a European Atomic Energy Community (Euratom)
	June	Intergovernmental conference to negotiate EEC and ECSC treaties opens in Brussels
	October-November	Suez crisis
1957	January	The Saar rejoins Germany
	March	Treaties of Rome (establishing the EEC and Euratom) signed

and political integration. Without doubt, Monnet and Schuman were men of vision who sincerely believed in the virtues of integration and the necessity of European unity. But the declaration of May 9 owed as much to narrowly defined national interest as to broadly based international altruism and was rooted as much in the experience of the interwar years as in the unique circumstances of the postwar world. Just as the Schuman Declaration was itself the product of clever political calculation, the institutions to which it ultimately gave rise were the result of intense intergovernmental bargaining.

JEAN MONNET AND THE EUROPEAN MOVEMENT

At the time of the Schuman Declaration, Monnet was director of the French Modernization Plan. As its name implies, the plan was designed to overhaul the French economy, which had shown signs of serious sickness well before World War II. General Charles de Gaulle, leader of the provisional government formed immediately after the liberation, realized that France could never become great again barring a radical economic revitalization. Without improving its performance and competitiveness, France would be unable to satisfy the domestic demands for economic growth on which the postwar political consensus rested; nor would it be able to play a leading role in the emerging international order. Keenly aware of the need to increase national production, improve productivity, boost foreign trade, maximize employment, and raise living standards, de Gaulle charged Monnet with promoting these formidable objectives at the head of the newly established Economic Planning Office.[2]

Despite his unconventional background, Monnet was an ideal choice. Then in his late fifties, he had spent a lifetime working in the private and public sectors in France and abroad. Monnet's experience as a senior Allied administrator during both world wars convinced him of the potential of peacetime economic planning. Nor was he encumbered by political baggage. Atypically for a Frenchman who had lived through the intensely ideological 1920s and 1930s, Monnet had no party affiliation. Inasmuch as he was politically motivated, it was by the remorseless ideology of efficiency.[3]

Monnet came to the conclusion early in World War II that economic integration was the only means by which conflict in Europe could be avoided. In a note in August 1943 to the French Committee of National Liberation in Algiers, Monnet claimed that there would be no peace in Europe "if States reestablished themselves on the basis of national sovereignty with all that this implies by way of prestige politics and economic protectionism." Instead, Monnet argued, "the States of Europe must form a federation or a 'European entity,' which will make them a single economic entity."[4]

Although such sentiments may seem radical in retrospect, they were by no means unusual at the time. On the contrary, during and immediately after World War II public figures and political pundits on both sides of the Atlantic outdid themselves in their advocacy of European integration. Repugnance against the slaughter of two European civil wars in as many generations and the economic depression and political extremism of the intervening years fueled popular support for a reorganization of the international system. Words such as "integration," "union," and even "supranationalism" were bandied about as panaceas for Europe's ills. The popular and political mood gave rise in the late 1940s to the European movement, a loose collection of individuals and interest groups ranged across the political spectrum, from the non-Communist left to the discredited far right, that shared advocacy of European unity.[5]

The intellectual ancestry of the European movement may have stretched into antiquity, but its immediate roots lay in the interwar years. In 1923 an Austro-Hungarian aristocrat, Count Richard Coudenhove-Kalergi, buoyed by the success the previous year of his book *Pan-Europa*, launched an organization of the same name. Inspired as much by the devastation of the Great War as by the emergence during it of a powerful United States and a menacing Soviet Union, Pan-Europa quickly acquired an ardent following, not least among influential politicians. The zenith of the pan-European movement was a stirring speech by French foreign minister Aristide Briand at the League of Nations in 1929. But the lofty ideals of European unity were soon swept aside by the flood tide of fascism in the 1930s. It took the bitter experience of defeat and occupation in 1939 and 1940 for pan-European ideas to revive and flourish in European minds.[6]

The resistance movement, itself a loose collection of individuals and groups opposed to Axis occupation, took up the cause of European unity as one plank of a proposed radical reorganization of postwar politics, economics, and society. Resistance literature, secretly circulated in occupied Europe, espoused the goal of international cooperation and integration as a basis for future peace and prosperity. Altiero Spinelli, a fervent federalist and a leading player in what eventually became the European Community, drafted a manifesto in 1940 and 1941 for a "free and united Europe" while imprisoned on the Italian island of Ventotene. Following his release after Mussolini's ouster, Spinelli traveled secretly to Switzerland for a meeting of European resistance representatives. Out of that meeting, held in Geneva in June and July 1944, came the "Draft Declaration of the European Resistance," which included a call for a "Federal Union among the European peoples."[7]

The legacy of the prewar Pan-Europa and the wartime resistance movements generated a groundswell of support for European unity in the early postwar years. Politicians of all persuasions espoused the cause of economic and political integration. One above all others came to personify the European movement: Winston Churchill, then Europe's best known and most respected statesman. Renowned especially for his inspiring oratory, which had boosted British spirits during the dark days of 1940 and 1941, Churchill raised European morale by calling for a "United States of Europe" in a speech in Zurich in September 1946.[8]

But Churchill advocated a far more limited and cautious form of European integration than did many of his Continental colleagues. The United Europe Movement, which Churchill launched in May 1947, promoted what became known as the "unionist" position, as distinct from the more radical "federalist" position of Spinelli and his Union of European Federalists. Differences between the unionists and federalists, based on political, geographical, and cultural considerations, came to the fore at the Congress of Europe, a glittering gathering of over 600 influential Europeans from sixteen countries held in The Hague in May 1948. Both sides agreed only on the desirability of European unity and on the need to institutionalize that ideal by establishing an international organization with a parliamentary body. For the unionists, that body would be merely a consultative assembly bound to defer to a committee of government ministers. For the federalists, by contrast, it would be a constituent assembly charged with drafting a constitution for the United States of Europe.

What emerged from the acrimonious Hague congress and from follow-up negotiations had the appearance of a compromise but was in fact a capitulation to the unionist position. The ensuing Council of Europe was a far cry from what the federalists had initially wanted. Although pledged "to achieve a closer union between its members in order to protect and promote the ideals and principles which constitute their common heritage and to further their economic and social progress," the Council of Europe did little more than exchange ideas and information on social, legal, and cultural matters.[9] Only in one important area, that of human rights, did the Council of Europe stand out. Its Court of Human Rights, often confused with the EU's Court of Justice, became a bulwark for the protection of civil liberties throughout Europe. More broadly, the Council of Europe enjoyed a brief resurgence in 1989 during the revolution in Central and Eastern Europe when public attention once again focused, as it had forty years earlier, on the possibility of establishing pan-European institutions.

The Council of Europe had a direct impact on the future EC. Its member states wanted to locate the council away from a national capital to symbolize European reconciliation, and they settled on Strasbourg, a frequently fought-over city on the border between France and Germany. Later, the EC placed its parliament there also. As the European Community revived and flourished in the 1980s, many members of the European Parliament (EP) regretted the choice of Strasbourg, nearly 300 miles from the Commission and the Council secretariat in Brussels, as the EP's seat. For them, Strasbourg came to symbolize not Franco-German reconciliation but the obscurity and relative unimportance of their own institution.

Almost alone among influential Europeans at the time, Monnet stood aloof from the European movement and from the Council of Europe that emerged from it. Monnet's detachment was due not to doubts about European unity but to disdain for the populism of the movement and its constituent parts. Monnet was an elitist and a pragmatist. His road to European unity would follow the unglamorous path of functional integration. Close cooperation between countries in specific economic sectors, Monnet believed, held the key to overcoming national sovereignty and ultimately achieving European federation. Decisions to implement functional economic cooperation would be taken not by 600 delegates at the Congress of Europe but by powerful politicians in the privacy of their government ministries.

Monnet loved aphorisms. "Nothing is possible without men; nothing is lasting without institutions" was one of his favorites. Another one—"People only accept change when they are faced with necessity, and only recognize necessity when a crisis is upon them"—offers a clue to Monnet's modus operandi.[10] At a decisive moment during World War II, Monnet saw a unique opportunity to act. With France on the verge of military defeat and political capitulation in June 1940, Monnet proposed to Churchill an "indissoluble union" between both countries. By offering common citizenship, forming a joint government, and pursuing a single war strategy, Monnet hoped to strengthen the French government's flagging position, encourage French forces in North Africa to continue the war alongside Britain, and lay the foundation for future European union.[11]

The failure of this extraordinary initiative was, Monnet thought, a huge opportunity lost. The lessons were obvious: Only great crises move politicians to act against their cautious instincts; only a future crisis would provide the necessary push for European integration. The episode also taught Monnet something about Churchill. Although he had brought the offer to the British cabinet's attention, the prime minister had been skeptical, if not hostile, from the outset. It must have irritated Monnet to see Churchill emerge after the war as the mouthpiece of the European movement. That alone might have convinced Monnet to find other ways to pursue his cherished goal of European integration.

Uninvolved in the federalist or unionist movements, Monnet devoted his considerable energy to drafting the French Modernization Plan. Given his conviction that Europe could not be united unless France was resurgent, the plan was an indispensable component of Monnet's strategy for European integration. Monnet toiled with a troupe of young disciples to transform the ailing French economy. Based on lengthy consultations with employers, workers, and consumers, Monnet's team set production targets, foreign trade goals, and employment objectives. Few were ever met, but the plan instilled badly needed confidence that helped France achieve an enviable economic recovery (although not by later German standards).

No catalytic crisis had occurred so far to allow Monnet to take a bold initiative on the European stage, although two ominous developments greatly alarmed European governments and boosted the European movement. The first was the state of the European economy after six years of invasion and occupation, blitzkrieg and aerial bombardment. World War II was the most costly conflict in modern history, and its destructiveness has been well documented. Perhaps the most surprising aspect of the war, however—precisely because of the technological and strategic innovations unleashed during it—was that six years of incessant fighting had not caused even greater destruction. The war's major material impact was less on industrial plant than on infrastructure, compounded by shortages of raw materials and skilled labor. Both Monnet and his assistant Robert Marjolin mention in their memoirs that there was less material destruction in France in 1945 than either had expected to find on their return from exile.[12] Wartime demolition of roads, bridges, canals, dikes, and docks posed a more formidable challenge to postwar planners than did the destruction of factories.

The task of economic recovery was doubtless daunting, but it could be undertaken without undermining the authority of the nation-state. Although the unprecedented extent of material destruction during World War II was certainly a factor in the growth of the postwar movement for European integration, it was not, Monnet realized, serious enough to trigger a political reaction of the kind that would cause European countries to pool their sovereignty in a unique, supranational entity. Nor was the collapse of the Grand Alliance and the emergence of the Cold War sufficient by itself to produce the desired result.

Like the destructiveness of World War II, the origins and development of the Cold War are well known. As hostility between the erstwhile Allies intensified, Western European governments grew increasingly alarmed, not as much about the prospect of direct Soviet attack as about the more realistic prospect of internal Communist subversion. Communist parties were popular in Western Europe immediately after the war and fared well in early postwar elections, especially in Italy and France. They owed their popularity to the corresponding unpopularity of capitalism—a reaction against the economic depression and the outbreak of war at either end of the 1930s. More important, Communist parties reaped the electoral rewards of their participation in, and often leadership of, the wartime resistance movement. So, too, did they benefit from wartime admiration in Europe and the United States of the Soviet Union's heroic stand against Nazi Germany, a struggle led by the indomitable "Uncle Joe" Stalin.

In 1946 and 1947, the French Communist Party shared power with the Christian Democrats and the Socialists, and the Italian Community Party seemed on the verge of an outright election victory. As relations between the Soviet Union and the Western powers deteriorated, relations between indigenous Communist parties and their non-Communist counterparts similarly degenerated. In May 1947 Paul Remadier, the French premier, ousted the Communists from government; in Italy, U.S. money and Christian Democratic scaremongering helped keep the Communists in opposition. Although communism remained popular with large numbers of people, electoral support waned as the Cold War intensified, notably after the February 1948 Communist coup in Czechoslovakia and during the Berlin blockade of 1948–1949. Nevertheless, the economic consequences of the war, exacerbated by a summer drought in 1946 and an ice-bound winter in 1947, seemed to offer ideal conditions for Communist parties to exploit.

The emergence of the Cold War and its domestic political repercussions contributed to the growth of the European movement, whose rhetoric stressed the need for the countries of Europe, once at the center of the international system, to join together to assert their position in an increasingly rigid bipolar world. As the Cold War intensified and the Iron Curtain descended abruptly to divide the continent, integration became a means by which Western Europe could defend itself, in close collaboration with the United States, against external Soviet aggression and threat and internal Communist subversion. Western Europe's relative economic weakness and supposed political vulnerability drew the United States deeper into the continent's affairs and turned Washington into a zealous champion of European integration.

THE MARSHALL PLAN AND EUROPEAN INTEGRATION

Probably the best-known U.S. international initiative ever, the Marshall Plan was the main instrument used by the United States to encourage European integration.[13] But the Marshall Plan—or the European Recovery Program, as it was formally called—had many origins and objectives, all of them interconnected. One was humanitarian. William L. Clayton, U.S. assistant secretary of state for economic affairs, painted a harrowing picture of devastated Europe upon his return from a mission in May 1947. Famine and starvation appeared imminent, especially in occupied Germany, where economic recovery had barely begun. Elsewhere in Europe the situation was by no means as bad, but Clayton understandably concentrated on the worst cases he had witnessed. Clayton's report led directly to a far more famous event: General George Marshall's Harvard commencement speech of June 5, 1947, in which the U.S. secretary of state pledged wholehearted U.S. support for European postwar reconstruction.[14]

Healthy economic and political self-interest also guided the U.S. undertaking. Fear of an imminent economic recession, similar to that which followed the cessation of hostilities in 1918, was one such motivation.

Without economic growth in Europe, U.S. exports would stagnate and decline, and the United States itself would follow Europe into depression. But the U.S. economy depended much less on exports to Europe in the late 1940s than it does today. Thus, the export argument alone would not have sufficed to convince a skeptical Congress to give substance to Marshall's speech in the form of massive financial assistance.

A less immediate but nonetheless palpable concern about economic security, coupled with powerful political and strategic arguments, finally made the difference. Twice in the previous thirty years the United States had become involved militarily in Europe's wars, and hundreds of thousands of American lives had been lost. Despite its strong emotional appeal, isolationism had patently failed. Apart from the emerging consensus that postwar U.S. security depended on increasing international involvement, the onset of the Cold War provided a powerful incentive for the United States to play a leading part in European affairs. A future resurgent Germany, however unlikely in 1947, may have posed a serious threat to U.S. security, but the immediate danger seemed to come from the Red Army in the East and local Communist parties in the West.

Americans and Europeans agreed about the problem and the prescription. The direct Soviet threat could best be countered by immediate U.S. intervention—as in Greece in 1947—and military alliance building and leadership—as in the case of NATO two years later. The indirect Communist danger, by contrast, could best be defused by restoring Western Europe to sound economic health. The United States would play the role of pharmacist, dispensing large doses of drugs in the form of badly needed dollars. On both sides of the Atlantic, the prescription emphasized the importance of integration for future peace and prosperity in Europe.

The lessons of the interwar years had led U.S. officials and policymakers, like their European counterparts, to endorse postwar integration. A small number of influential Americans had been swayed by the teaching and writing of Coudenhove-Kalergi, who spent World War II at New York University.[15] Others, who would play a pivotal role in the formulation and implementation of U.S. policy toward Western Europe in the late 1940s and early 1950s, became close friends of Monnet when he worked in Washington, D.C., in the early 1940s. With Monnet, "the eminence grise of the Wise Men of American foreign policy," they discussed the limits of national sovereignty and advantages of supranationality.[16] Also, they applied to war-torn Europe the lessons of modern U.S. history. Just as the United States had grown strong and prosperous by promoting interstate commerce and establishing a single market, so, too, could Europe. In that simple, straightforward way, European integration became an essential part "of a grand design for remaking the Old World in the likeness of the New."[17]

The Marshall Plan occupies a special place in the historiography of the Cold War. Some revisionist historians see in it an effort by the United

States to acquire an empire in Europe by design; others argue that Europe's economic weakness allowed the United States to acquire an empire there by default. For their part, many contemporary Europeans were well aware of the dangers of relying too much on U.S. economic largess and military protection and perceived European integration as a means of asserting the continent's independence. Similarly, perhaps paradoxically, many contemporary Americans looked to European integration, which the Marshall Plan was supposed to enhance, as a way of obviating the necessity for future U.S. intervention in the Old World.

Disputes about the significance of the Marshall Plan for postwar U.S. foreign policy are related to an equally important question: What part did the Marshall Plan play in fostering European integration? The accepted view is that the Marshall Plan failed to break down national barriers. Neither Marshall's stricture that aid recipients had to act together and present a common recovery program nor the enormous influence and wealth of the United States could overcome the reluctance of European governments to cooperate closely, let alone share sovereignty. By effectively excluding the Soviet Union and its satellite countries in Eastern Europe, the Marshall Plan at least ensured that integration would be confined to Western Europe. But the degree of integration attained was far from what U.S. planners had sought.

For all their platitudes about integration, European governments were unwilling to turn rhetoric into reality. To meet the prerequisite for Marshall Plan assistance they established the Organization for European Economic Cooperation (OEEC), an umbrella body to solicit U.S. funds. But the OEEC was too large and diverse to act as an institutional instrument of integration. Its eighteen members varied greatly in size, population, and economic well-being. Perhaps more important, widely differing political cultures and wartime experiences made the prospect of agreement on integration extremely remote. Thus, the OEEC failed to live up to its foster parents' expectations. Instead, shortly after the EEC began functioning in 1958, the OEEC turned into the Organization for Economic Cooperation and Development (OECD), the Paris-based body for international economic research and analysis.[18]

Like the contemporaneous Congress of Europe, the OEEC triggered debate on European integration, but it produced a paucity of tangible results. For all their interest in integration and European unity, governments were reluctant to take concrete steps to surrender some of their sovereignty. Yet the Marshall Plan indirectly caused the cataclysmic crisis that Monnet knew was necessary to prompt the French government to act. Because it involved the reconstruction of Western Germany as part of the reconstruction of Western Europe, the Marshall Plan set the stage for a series of diplomatic decisions that would gradually rehabilitate the former enemy, much to the consternation of Germany's neighbor to the west. The threat to France's own economic recovery and security was immense. Here was a crisis that Monnet could exploit to the full.

Even as the United States and Britain revised their harsh policies toward Germany, France stuck stubbornly to a number of severe strictures. Germany would be demilitarized, decentralized, and deindustrialized. France had suffered grievously from German militarism and expansionism, far more than either Britain or the United States. The humiliation and horror of World War II—defeat and occupation, deportation and enslavement, pillage and destruction—would not quickly be forgotten. France had salvaged some of its honor through the resistance movement and by raising an army in 1944 that participated in the final stages of the national liberation and the subsequent invasion of Germany. Denied a place at the negotiating table in Yalta and Potsdam, France at least won the right to occupy a small part of the vanquished Third Reich. The gradual softening of British and U.S. occupation policy served only to strengthen French determination to stick to a rigid course. Not surprisingly, France refused to merge its occupation zone into the newly established Anglo-American "Bizonia" in May 1947.[19]

For all his remonstrations about integration and reconciliation, even Monnet was not unaffected by the rampant Germanophobia that swept France at the time. After all, Monnet had predicated his plan for French economic modernization upon a punitive policy toward Germany. Coal and steel, the two key industrial sectors in mid-twentieth-century Europe, lay at the heart of the Modernization Plan. Postwar French policy toward Germany sought both to win control over the coal-rich Saar, which France then occupied, and to prevent the economic recovery of the Ruhr. Not only had the Ruhr become a synonym for the evil German military-industrial complex but its resuscitation would threaten France's own economic revival. Monnet based his economic planning squarely on the assumption that Ruhr coal would be available to fuel French steel mills, whose increased output would find buyers in displaced German markets. German economic rehabilitation, if it came before full implementation of the Monnet Plan, would greatly imperil France's economic fortunes and, by extension, France's international stature.

As long as the Soviet Union was somehow involved in formulating Allied policy toward Germany, France had a good chance of thwarting Britain's and the United States' increasingly benign approach. Although there had never truly been four-power cooperation on Germany, the Western Allies were reluctant to break openly with the Soviet Union, hoping perhaps to avert an irrevocable collapse of the Grand Alliance. To try to negotiate a postwar settlement or at least to maintain the fiction of Allied unity, the foreign ministers of Britain, France, the United States, and the Soviet Union met periodically. The breakdown of the Moscow meeting of foreign ministers in March 1947 proved decisive. Thereafter, the Anglo-Americans increasingly acted unilaterally in the West and the Soviet Union pursued its own policy in the East.

French difficulty in adhering to a repressive policy came to a head in early 1948. The Ruhr lay within the British zone of occupation, and France was not party to Anglo-American planning in Germany. As long as France remained outside Bizonia, Paris could only watch angrily as London and Washington gradually loosened the Ruhr's economic shackles. Pragmatism briefly triumphed when France agreed to cooperate with Bizonia in an effort to influence Anglo-American policy from within. During the subsequent London Conference of the Western Allies, which led eventually to the merger of the French zone and Bizonia into the Federal Republic of Germany, France supported the establishment of the International Ruhr Authority as a vehicle of controlling industrial production there.

The Federal Republic of Germany, conceived in the Western Allies conference and born in September 1949, lacked many attributes of sovereignty. Apart from accepting limits on foreign policy and a complete absence of defense policy, the new German state had to acquiesce in the existence and operation of the International Ruhr Authority. But French hopes that the authority would serve French interests by maintaining strict controls on Ruhr production soon proved unrealistic. Realizing that the Ruhr was the industrial heartland (or, to use the metaphor current at the time, the "spark plug") of Europe,[20] the United States pushed more and more for German industrial recovery as a vital prerequisite for European economic recovery. By the same token, the United States appreciated the implication of that policy for Paris and understood the need to involve France fully in bringing about a durable European economic and strategic settlement. Accordingly, Washington and London pressed Paris to devise a mutually acceptable solution to the Ruhr problem and to take the initiative in proposing a new Allied policy toward the Federal Republic.

By the end of 1949, therefore, France faced the failure of its restrictive Ruhr policy. The International Ruhr Authority, a body intended to perpetuate French control over the area under the guise of Allied cooperation with the fledgling Federal Republic, had made little headway. French officials gradually grasped the fact that policy toward Germany would have to be revised, not least in order to salvage the all-important and closely related Modernization Plan. Thus in the months ahead, French officials searched for a strategy that would satisfy their country's overriding concern with security, meet its industrial demands for adequate supplies of coal and markets for steel, and relieve U.S. pressure for a policy compatible with growing German economic capability.[21]

Monnet himself had the most to gain—and the most to lose—from this challenge. After all, the Modernization Plan, now at risk, was his plan. Apart from a vested personal interest in the plan's success, Monnet bore primary responsibility in the French civil service for efforts to overcome exacting economic obstacles. The particular set of problems facing France in 1949 and 1950 offered Monnet a unique opportunity to act. Capitalizing on the growing sentiment in official French circles that policy toward Germany should in future be based on economic association rather than antagonism, he approached Schuman with the imaginative idea of a supranational coal and steel community. Thus the lifting of Allied restrictions on German steel production and the prospect of a reversal to the status quo ante of Franco-German relations had provided the crisis that, Monnet was certain, would force his government to take a dramatic step on the road to Franco-German reconciliation and European integration.

THE SCHUMAN PLAN

In his memoirs, Monnet describes the melodrama surrounding the Schuman Declaration.[22] Monnet sent his proposal for a coal and steel community to both René Pleven, the French prime minister, and Schuman. Pleven failed to act immediately, thus allowing Schuman to take the initiative that subsequently bore his name. Schuman's background lent poignancy to the coal and steel proposal. Coming from the disputed province of Lorraine, where he had suffered personally from the incessant conflict between France and Germany, Schuman sought above all else to promote reconciliation between both countries.[23] As a Christian Democrat, Schuman held political principles that reinforced his personal convictions. Constrained by the climate of retribution toward Germany that pervaded postwar France and by a natural reserve and inhibition, Schuman had hitherto refrained from taking any conciliatory steps in the direction of the erstwhile enemy. Now, emboldened by Monnet's suggestion and by the swing in official French opinion toward economic accord with Germany, Schuman floated the fateful proposal with secrecy and speed.

Before the proposal could be made public, Monnet and Schuman needed the approval of three key parties: the French, German, and U.S. governments. On May 9, 1950, Schuman simultaneously placed the proposal before his own cabinet in Paris and brought it to Chancellor Konrad Adenauer's attention in Bonn. The German leader responded enthusiastically. Like Schuman, Adenauer had a strong personal yearning for Franco-German reconciliation. Moreover, keenly aware of the depth of French distrust toward the new Federal Republic, Adenauer realized that shared sovereignty pointed the way to Germany's international rehabilitation. Only by integrating closely with neighboring countries could Germany hope to remove the remaining controls on its domestic and foreign policy. Three months previously, Adenauer had taken the initiative by floating the idea of a full Franco-German union. Although Adenauer's trial balloon had alarmed nervous French officials, it clearly indicated the chancellor's receptiveness to a proposal for integration of any kind.[24]

Monnet had earlier alerted U.S. officials to the French initiative. Secretary of State Dean Acheson had arrived in Paris on May 7, en route to London for a meeting of British, French, and U.S. foreign ministers to discuss German economic issues. Taking advantage of Acheson's presence, Monnet and Schuman quickly took him into their confidence. Acheson, they knew, strongly supported not only European integration but also the necessity of French efforts to bring it about. The previous October, Acheson had shared with Schuman his belief that "our policy in Germany, and the development of a German Government which can take its place in Western Europe, depends on the assumption by your country of leadership in Europe on these problems."[25]

Not surprisingly, Acheson endorsed the Schuman Plan and drafted a statement of support for President Truman to release once the plan became public. Yet Acheson's immediate reaction was cautious and pointed to what would become a persistent source of tension between the United States and the EU. At first, Acheson feared that the Schuman Plan was a clever cover for "a gigantic European cartel." Acheson drafted the presidential statement of support partly to allay his "apprehension that upon receiving partial information, the Antitrust Division in the Department of Justice might stimulate some critical comments, which would have been damaging at that stage."[26] U.S. suspicion of the EU's commitment to international economic competition would deepen in the years ahead, and the Department of Justice would lose none of its misgivings.

The good fortune of Acheson's presence in Paris suggests that Monnet and Schuman would not otherwise have advised him in advance of their coal and steel proposal. But U.S. support was too important to have been jeopardized by their waiting to inform Washington until after a public announcement. In the event, Monnet's assiduous and prolonged cultivation of the U.S. establishment now bore fruit as he astutely lined up support by drawing on close friendships with key U.S. policymakers such as John McCloy, high commissioner in Germany. Within a month the United States set up the special Working Group on the Schuman Proposal in its Paris embassy. The working group soon became "a hotbed of Monnet enthusiasts [with] the thinking of Monnet and the young American integrationists . . . often so similar as to be indistinguishable."[27]

Buoyed by Acheson's endorsement and Adenauer's approval, Schuman had little difficulty convincing his cabinet colleagues to support the scheme. A public announcement immediately followed at a hastily convened press conference in the French foreign ministry. The result was "a public relations coup of heroic proportions."[28] Although French officials had been moving in the direction of Franco-German economic association for some time, the Schuman Declaration had all the appearance of a dramatic reversal of policy. Instead of trying to keep the traditional enemy down, France would build a new Europe on the basis of equality with Germany. Coal and steel, the two key sectors of industrial production and war-making potential, would be removed from national control and placed under a single, supranational authority. As Monnet put it, "If . . . the victors and the vanquished agreed to exercise joint sovereignty over part of their joint resources . . . then a solid link would be forged between them, the way would be wide open for further collective action, and a great example would be given to the other nations of Europe."[29]

Schuman's offer to open the proposed organization "to the participation of the other countries of Europe" was not as generous as it seemed. For one thing, the countries of Eastern Europe were automatically excluded by the onset of the Cold War. For another, the Scandinavian countries had shown, during the Congress of Europe and subsequently in the Council of Europe, their skepticism about supranationalism. For Schuman and Monnet, European integration meant, essentially, Franco-German integration. Germany was the traditional enemy, the economic powerhouse of Europe, and the country that posed the greatest threat to France. Franco-German reconciliation, by means of "European" integration, apparently offered the only opportunity to avoid a repetition of the disastrous conflict that had characterized the first five decades of the twentieth century. Schuman's image of "the other countries of Europe" meant, in reality, the neighboring countries of Belgium, the Netherlands, and Luxembourg to the north and Italy to the south.

Britain was most conspicuous by its absence from the French view of this "new" Europe. After all, as France's traditional twentieth-century ally, Britain was surely the first country to which France would look for support of an international initiative to come to terms with postwar Germany. Indeed, Monnet's first proposal for European integration, the dramatic offer of Anglo-French union, had centered on Britain. Similarly, during the war itself, Robert Marjolin, Monnet's deputy, had stated his "profound conviction" that "the key to any politico-economic reorganization in continental Europe has to be sought in Franco-British relations."[30] Even as late as 1948, "Western European integration without Britain was unacceptable in Washington," where the ultimate decision about Europe's future would be made.[31] By 1950, however, both France and the United States had dropped Britain from their plans for European integration. Britain's obvious reluctance to involve itself in European integration, despite Churchill's memorable endorsement of a United States of Europe, convinced Washington and Paris that progress would have to be made without British support.

Britain preferred to remain aloof because of a political culture that emphasized national sovereignty and abhorred supranationality; a long history of infrequent direct involvement in continental European affairs and the unique wartime experience of having escaped invasion also contributed. In addition, Britain saw itself as an intermediary between the United States and continental Europe, an aspect of the Anglo-American "special relationship" that London feared would be endangered by participation in European integration despite Washington's assertions to the contrary. British officials also thought that too close an involvement in the process of European integration would jeopardize London's strong political and economic orientation toward the declining empire and emerging commonwealth.[32]

Schuman's decision to give the British government no more than a few hours notice of his groundbreaking declaration vividly illustrates French indifference to London's involvement in the future coal and steel community. British foreign minister Ernest Bevin was furious, doubly so when he discovered that Acheson had known all about the impending declaration when he had arrived in London the day before Schuman's press conference.[33] Any French embarrassment at slighting Bevin rapidly dissipated when the British government belittled the plan. The governing Labour Party delayed publication of an important policy paper on Europe in order to include an assessment of the French proposal. When it appeared in June 1950, the paper explicitly stated Britain's objections to participation in European integration and barely disguised the government's hostility to the Schuman Plan.

Yet the French government held open the door to British participation in the coal and steel negotiations. Other prospective member states, especially the Benelux countries, hoped that Britain would take the decisive step. But in order to cross the threshold, all participants had to accept the principle of shared sovereignty, whatever that would turn out to mean in practice. Monnet stuck to the position that if the principle of supranationality itself was debatable, the proposed organization would soon go the way of the ineffectual OEEC. Following a series of cabinet meetings and diplomatic exchanges with France, the British government reached a predictable but discouraging conclusion. At the definitive cabinet meeting, "there seems to have been a general, resentful agreement to give a negative answer [to France]."[34]

THE ECSC AND THE EDC

With understandable artistic license, Theodore White wrote in retrospect that "Monnet's prestige in French politics was akin to that of George Marshall in American politics. . . . Watching Monnet thread his suggestion [the Schuman Declaration] through the bureaucracies and foreign ministries of Europe was to take delight in his political art."[35] Monnet's standing may indeed have been high, but his proposal for a coal and steel community by no means sailed easily through the relevant government departments of the six negotiating states: France, Germany, Italy, Belgium, the Netherlands, and Luxembourg. John Gillingham, author of an authoritative history of the Schuman Plan, entitled his chapter on the ECSC negotiations "From Summit to Swamp."[36] The summit was the high point of the declaration itself, made in the glare of publicity and self-congratulation; the swamp was the low point of intergovernmental squabbling as each country jockeyed for advantage in pursuit of its own interests. Monnet thought the negotiations, which began in June 1950, would be over by the end of the summer; in the event, they began in earnest only in August 1950 and eventually ended in April 1951. Ratification by the member states' parliaments took nearly another year. The European Coal and Steel Community finally began operating in August 1952.

Monnet negotiated for France and prevailed upon Adenauer to appoint Walter Hallstein, a law professor, state secretary in the foreign office, and later the Commission's first president, as Germany's representative. The main agenda items were the proposed community's competence, institutions, and decisionmaking procedures. Based on a French document, the negotiators gradually gave substance and shape to the new organization. What emerged was a supranational High Authority, the institutional depository of shared national sovereignty over the coal and steel sectors. The High Authority would be responsible for formulating a common market in coal and steel and for supervising such related issues as pricing, wages, investment, and competition. As Monnet saw it, the purpose of the community was not "to substitute the High Authority for private enterprise, but . . . to make possible real competition throughout a vast market, from which producers, workers and consumers would all gain."[37] Sensitive especially to U.S. concerns, doubly so in view of Acheson's first reaction, Monnet also wove into the treaty a number of antitrust provisions.

Because of the High Authority's small size, national bureaucracies would have to cooperate closely with it to implement community legislation. A separate institution, the Court of Justice, would adjudicate disputes and ensure member states' compliance with the terms of the treaty. In a move that was to have important repercussions for the future of European integration, the other negotiators forced Monnet to accept the Council of Ministers (generally known as the Council) in the institutional framework. Initially intended to be advisory and intermediary, as the embodiment of the member states' interests the Council would increasingly act as a brake on supranationalism within the community. Finally, a Common Assembly consisting of delegates of the national parliaments would give the ECSC the appearance of direct democratic accountability.

The contemporaneous controversy over German remilitarization at first imperiled the coal and steel negotiations but ultimately saved them to a great extent. Faced with U.S. demands for German rearmament following the outbreak of the Korean War, French prime minister Pleven announced in October 1950 a plan for German remilitarization under the aegis of a European defense community, just as Schuman had earlier proposed German reindustrialization under the aegis of a coal and steel community. Monnet was the architect of both ideas. His advocacy of the European Defense Community (EDC) grew directly out of his championing of the Schuman Plan. Fierce French hostility to German remilitarization, even in the face of Anglo-American pressure and the seriousness of the Cold War, caused Adenauer to doubt France's commitment to Franco-German reconciliation and European integration. If shared sovereignty was good enough for German industry, Adenauer asked, why was it not also acceptable for German rearmament? Faced with possible German recalcitrance in the coal and steel talks, Monnet pressed Pleven to pursue the parallel idea of a supranational organization for European defense.[38]

Negotiations to form the EDC, in which German units would be integrated into a European army, began in February 1951. Five of the six nations negotiating a treaty to establish the European Coal and Steel Community simultaneously participated in these discussions (the Netherlands, the odd country out, delayed taking part until October 1951). Although Monnet was not directly involved in the EDC talks, he again used his influence behind the scenes to win powerful U.S. support for the Pleven Plan. Based on a deep distrust of supranationalism, Britain resisted U.S. entreaties to enter the EDC talks. Despite British aloofness the Six persevered in their negotiations. After complex and hard bargaining, they signed the EDC treaty on May 27, 1952, in Paris.

The EDC negotiations spawned another initiative that raised federalists' hopes for the future of European integration. Article 38 of the Paris Treaty called for the establishment of a supranational political authority to direct the EDC. Deferring to domestic parliamentary opinion, in September 1952 the foreign ministers of the Six acted on a resolution passed by the Council of Europe's Assembly, calling on them to entrust a parliamentary body with the task of implementing Article 38 by drafting the statute for the supranational European Political Community. Reflecting, perhaps, the six governments' indifference toward the proposed political community and doubts that it would ever come to anything, the foreign ministers asked a special committee of the newly established ECSC Common Assembly to draft a treaty.[39]

The so-called constitutional committee lost little time in drawing up plans for a political community that would not only encompass the EDC and ECSC but also embrace foreign, economic, and monetary policy coordination. The result would have been an organization more advanced along the road of European integration than the most optimistic EC member states hoped would come out of the 1991 intergovernmental conferences that resulted in the Treaty on European Union. Even in the extraordinary climate of the early 1950s, with the Korean War and the attendant acceptance of German rearmament acting as a spur to greater European integration, the Six balked at the constitutional committee's extravagant recommendations. At a series of intergovernmental meetings in 1953 and early in 1954, the Six successfully diluted the more far-reaching institutional and supranational aspects of the draft treaty establishing the political community. Much to the member states' relief, the proposed community soon withered away, a casualty of its stillborn sibling, the EDC.

Having survived the penultimate negotiating stage, the EDC foundered on the rock of ratification. Gaullist hostility to sharing sovereignty over sacrosanct national defense policy, coupled with implacable Communist opposition to German rearmament, resulted in August 1954 in defeat of the EDC treaty in the French parliament. It was paradoxical that the EDC failed in France, where the original initiative had been taken in 1950 and the treaty had been signed in 1952. In the interim, Stalin's death and the end of hostilities in Korea had lessened Cold War tensions and made the issue of German remilitarization far less urgent. Moreover, in the early 1950s Paris had become increasingly preoccupied with a dissipating colonial conflict in Indochina (later Vietnam).[40]

The genie of German rearmament could not be stuffed back in the bottle. With the collapse of the EDC, Anthony Eden, Britain's prime minister, proposed instead that Germany join with Britain, France, Italy, and the Benelux countries in the Western European Union (WEU), a new defense organization intended as a vehicle to facilitate German entry into the North Atlantic Treaty Organization (NATO). As expected, Germany joined NATO via the WEU in May 1955. Thus in a fitting finale to the EDC debacle, France acquiesced in German membership in NATO, a prospect that five years previously had filled Paris with fright.

The EDC left an interesting legacy. Having marked the high point of European federalist aspirations, the failed proposal quickly acquired the aura of a great opportunity lost. As the EC struggled through the political setbacks of the 1960s, the economic difficulties of the 1970s, and a belated revival in the 1980s, supporters of supranationalism harked back to the early 1950s as the European movement's golden age. If only the EDC and related political community had been ratified, the argument goes, European integration would have reached a level considered unattainable in later years. Yet the collapse of both proposals and the failure of subsequent initiatives along similar lines clearly indicate the limits on European integration in the 1950s and beyond. It was no historical accident that the EDC fell at the final hurdle of French ratification or that the political community languished in the wings. Only with great reluctance had the Six confronted the question of a defense community and the equally daunting challenge of a supranational political community. The outcome of both issues allowed them to concentrate instead on the kind of integration politically possible in the 1950s and for many years thereafter: functional economic integration.

As the epitome of functionalism, the ECSC survived the wreckage of the EDC. Together with lofty references to world peace and a "contribution . . . to civilization," the preamble of the ECSC treaty explicitly stated the organization's functionalist, ultimately federalist mission. By referring to the ECSC's role in rebuilding Europe, the preamble set the seal on Monnet's tendency to blur the distinction between Europe and Western Europe and to confine the geopolitical scope of the ECSC (and later the EC) to a core group of countries centered on the Rhine.

Concerned about the possible consequences of the EDC controversy for the Schuman Plan, Monnet pushed for early ratification of the ECSC treaty. In each prospective member state, the ratification debate was lively: Producer associations complained about the High Authority's ability to interfere in their affairs; labor groups fretted about the impact of keener competition; and nationalist politicians railed against the supposed onslaught of supranationalism. In the event, the ongoing EDC debacle channeled criticism of shared sovereignty away from the contemporaneous ECSC debate. While the EDC issue raged, the ECSC treaty was ratified in national parliaments with relatively little fanfare.

One of the issues still to be worked out, however, included the site of the institutions themselves. Despite Monnet's hope that a special area analogous to the District of Columbia would be set aside in the community, national governments eventually settled on Luxembourg as the site of the High Authority. It was there, in the capital of the small, sleepy Grand Duchy, that the ECSC began to function in August 1952.

The ECSC disappointed European federalists both in its conceptual framework and in its actual operation. It was an unglamorous organization that inadequately symbolized the high hopes of supranationalism in Europe. Yet the ECSC served a vital purpose in the postwar world in terms of Franco-German reconciliation and the related goal of European integration. To quote John Gillingham at some length, "A supranational authority had been created, a potential nucleus for a European federal system. It would serve in lieu of a peace treaty concluding hostilities between Germany and Western Europe. This was no grand settlement in the manner of Westphalia or Versailles. The agreement to create a heavy industry pool changed no borders, created no new alliances, and reduced only a few commercial and financial barriers. It did not even end the occupation of the Federal Republic. . . . By resolving the coal and steel conflicts that had stood between France and Germany since World War II, it did, however, remove the main obstacle to an economic partnership between the two nations."[41] These were by no means inconsiderable achievements.

THE EC AND EURATOM

A favorite metaphor of European federalists depicts the EU as a fragile, delicate craft constantly running aground on the treacherous shoals of national sovereignty and self-interest. With each repair and relaunch the ship is strengthened and streamlined, and navigational hazards are charted and exposed. Eventually, one supposes, the United States of Europe will resemble a supranational supertanker plying stormy economic, political, and security seas, invulnerable to the perils that lurk beneath the surface.

The first relaunch of the community concept took place immediately after the EDC foundered in 1954. But there was nothing inevitable or inexorable about the revival of European integration at that time. Certainly the ECSC continued to operate unabated, but it was not a striking success. The High Authority struggled in vain to formulate and implement effective pricing and competition policies and managed only with difficulty to regulate other aspects of the coal and steel sectors. Yet the political lessons of functional integration were not lost on the member states. Despite the bitterness engendered by the EDC debate, a willingness persisted at least to maintain, or even extend, functional economic cooperation for the sake of Franco-German cooperation and European integration.

A specific idea for economic integration, floated as part of the moribund European political community proposal, survived the defeat of the EDC. This called for the Six to abolish quotas and tariffs on trade among themselves, establish a joint external tariff, unify trade policy toward the rest of the world, devise common policies for a range of socioeconomic sectors, and organize a single internal market. Monnet thought this idea too ambitious, especially in the aftermath of the EDC debacle. Enamored as always of more definite and practical proposals, he continued to advocate the functional approach of sectoral integration. Even while the ECSC treaty was being negotiated, Monnet knew that coal was rapidly losing its position as the basis of industrial power and, by extension, military might. Atomic energy had already revolutionized strategic doctrine and seemed poised to replace coal and oil as the elixir of the future. Not surprisingly, Monnet now proposed a European atomic energy community, to be structured along the lines of the ECSC, in order both to achieve the immediate objectives of the ECSC itself and to promote the distant goal of European federation.

In November 1954, disappointed with the Coal and Steel Community's progress, concerned about the consequences for integration of the EDC's failure, and impatient to play a more active and aggressive role in advocating European unity, Monnet announced his intention to resign from the High Authority. As he explained to the ECSC Common Assembly in Strasbourg, "It is for Parliaments and Governments to decide on the transfer of new powers to the European institutions. The impulse must therefore come from without. [By resigning from the High Authority], I shall be able to join in the efforts of all those who are working to continue and enlarge what has been begun."[42] Monnet's vehicle for influencing "Parliaments and Governments . . . from without" would be the Action Committee for a United States of Europe, a small, "private supranational organization" of political party and trade union leaders.[43] Monnet envisioned the committee as a powerful pressure group to lobby for implementation of his new initiative.

Monnet's decision to resign took national governments by surprise. At a meeting in Messina in June 1955, ECSC foreign ministers discussed not only Monnet's replacement but also the future of European integration. Paul-Henri Spaak, Belgium's foreign minister, had prepared a memorandum on behalf of the Benelux countries suggesting further integration along the lines of Monnet's idea for an atomic energy community and the rival proposal for a common market. The foreign ministers asked Spaak to form a committee and write a report on future options. In later years, the Messina meeting came to be seen as a pivotal point for European integration.

Spaak was well suited by temperament and conviction to draft the necessary report. His enthusiasm for integration had already won him the nickname "Mr. Europe." As chairman of the conference that opened in Brussels later in 1955, Spaak steered the work of the various committees and subcommittees that drafted specific sections. The final report, presented to his fellow foreign ministers at a meeting in Venice in May 1956, proposed that the two objectives of sectoral (atomic energy) integration and wider economic integration (a common market) be realized in separate organizations with separate treaties. The Venice foreign ministers' meeting marked the opening of an intergovernmental conference (IGC) that culminated in the establishment of the European Atomic Energy Community (Euratom) and the European Economic Community (EEC).

The October-November 1956 Suez debacle—in which an Anglo-French military intervention ended in political disaster—turned the French government's attention squarely back to the Continent and made the prospect of a wider economic agreement with neighboring countries seem more important than before. As it was, Guy Mollet, the French prime minister, was staunchly in favor of integrating Europe. Until the Suez crisis cleared the air, however, Mollet refrained from pushing renewed efforts to do so, largely because of the bitter EDC bequest. French political opinion seemed well disposed toward Euratom, which offered an opportunity to share the exorbitant costs of atomic energy research and development while enjoying all the benefits. U.S. president Dwight Eisenhower's recent Atoms for Peace initiative increased Euratom's attraction. Not only was the United States willing to share nuclear technology for peaceful purposes, the State Department also recognized that "the most hopeful avenue for relaunching the movement toward European integration now appears to be the creation of a European common authority, along the lines of the Schuman Plan, to be responsible for the development of atomic energy for peaceful purposes."[44]

By contrast, reaction in France to the possible establishment of a common market was almost uniformly hostile. Robert Marjolin, who advised the French government on European affairs and subsequently participated in the Euratom and EEC negotiations, noted in his memoirs "*the hostility of almost the whole of French opinion to the removal, even gradual, of the protection which French industry enjoyed*" (original emphasis). That hostility led to intense confrontations between the negotiators in Brussels on the one hand and recalcitrant ministers and bureaucrats in Paris on the other. In addition to fighting for France in the IGC, Marjolin found himself waging a rear-guard action, what he called the "Battle of Paris."[45]

Marjolin and others argued the case for a customs union and common market on its own merits but bolstered their position with the assertion that France could not have the desirable atomic energy community without the undesirable economic community. With the exception of Britain, which participated in the EEC negotiations until November 1955, France's partners in the intergovernmental conference eagerly sought a common market in Europe. The advantage of a single market in industrial goods was obvious to Germany, although Ludwig Erhard, the finance minister, objected to the proposed community on the grounds that it would be protectionist and therefore would distort world trade. As for Euratom, the other countries in the negotiations did not share France's enthusiasm and doubted that the French government would exploit atomic energy only for civil projects.

A vote in the French parliament in July 1956 on whether to continue the Euratom negotiations resulted in an easy government victory. A similar vote on the EC negotiations, in January 1957, proved far more contentious. A vague desire to improve the country's image after the negative EDC vote of August 1954, a reaction against the Soviet Union and the French Communist Party in the wake of the invasion of Hungary in October 1956, the legacy of Suez, and a concern that France might permanently be left behind its more economically advanced neighbors undoubtedly contributed to the government's success. Yet the outcome was close. Only by guaranteeing clauses in the EEC treaty that favored France's overseas possessions and promising to include agriculture in the proposed common market did the government carry the day.

Having accepted these conditions during the parliamentary debate, the French government had to convince its partners in the IGC to incorporate them into the draft treaty. The other countries agreed to do so in part because of the benefits that would accrue to all from a common agricultural policy and in part because Belgium and the Netherlands would benefit as well from extending EC privileges to member states' overseas possessions. But the main reason for the other nations' acquiescence was the importance of including France in the Community. An EC without Britain was possible; an EC without France was impracticable. As Franco-German rapprochement lay at the core of the EC and the EC was the key to Germany's postwar rehabilitation, Adenauer would pay almost any price to placate Paris.

The IGC came to an end in a series of high-level meetings in February 1957. The outcome was two treaties, one for Euratom and the other for the EC. Both were signed at an elaborate ceremony in Rome on March 25. Although officially both are called the Treaties of Rome, in practice only the treaty establishing the EC—as the EEC came to be called—is known as the Treaty of Rome.

Only in France was there a serious problem with ratification, posed this time not by concerted Gaullist and Communist opposition but by the fall of Mollet's government during the early summer. Here Monnet's Action Committee was instrumental, if not decisive, in ensuring swift and successful ratification. First the committee pressed for early ratification in the German parliament. The committee's influence helped win the support of the Social Democratic Party (SPD), which had previously opposed both the ECSC and the EDC. With German ratification secure, the Action Committee turned its attention to the French parliament, where a comfortable majority endorsed the treaties on July 9, 1957.[46] By the end of the year, the Six had ratified the two treaties, allowing the two new communities to begin operating in January 1958.

On an ancillary issue, Monnet did not prevail. As he had done in the early 1950s during the launching of the ECSC, Monnet championed the cause of a special "European District" to house the new EC institutions in the late 1950s during the debate about Euratom and the EC. Following the flood of ECSC officials and associated personnel into the Grand Duchy, the Luxembourg government declined to host the new organizations. Almost by default, Brussels, site of the IGC that gave birth to the new communities, became their home.

By the time of the Brussels negotiations, held in the aftermath of the EDC debacle, "supranationality" was a term from which even the most ardent federalists recoiled. As Marjolin noted, "Nowhere did it appear in the documents drafted during the negotiations; no one so much as mentioned the word."[47] The preamble of the EEC treaty was far less flamboyant than its ECSC counterpart, referring only to the signatories' determination "to lay the foundations of an ever closer union among the peoples of Europe." The treaty itself outlined the essential principles of the common market: the free movement of goods, persons, services, and capital; a customs union and common external tariffs; and various community policies. Each new community's institutional framework emulated that of the ECSC but included a stronger Council and a correspondingly weaker Commission (because of the odium attached to "supranationalism" in the wake of the

EDC debacle, the name "Commission" replaced the more pretentious "High Authority" in the Treaty of Rome). In effect, "an institutional system was set up [in the communities] with the aim of doing justice to both the intergovernmental and supranational concepts."[48]

At first sight, the EC was an even greater disappointment than the ECSC. Neither organization realized the high hopes of advocates of European integration in the postwar period. Despite an apparent curtailment of supranationality in the Treaty of Rome, the EC's importance was nonetheless profound. In his memoirs, Robert Marjolin, who had fought hard in Brussels and Paris to make the EC possible, described the EC's significance in the following way: "I do not believe it is an exaggeration to say that this date [March 25, 1957] represents one of the greatest moments of Europe's history. Who would have thought during the 1930s, and even during the ten years that followed the war, that European states which had been tearing one another apart for so many centuries and some of which, like France and Italy, still had very closed economies, would form a common market intended eventually to become an economic area that could be linked to one great dynamic market?"[49]

NOTES

1. Pascal Fontaine, *Europe: A Fresh Start: The Schuman Declaration, 1950–90* (Luxembourg: Office for Official Publications of the European Communities, 1990), p. 44.
2. Jean Monnet, *Memoirs* (Garden City, NY: Doubleday, 1978), p. 239.
3. On Monnet's life and career, see Monnet, *Memoirs;* Douglas Brinkley and Clifford Hackett, eds., *Jean Monnet: The Path to European Unity* (New York: St. Martin's Press, 1991); and François Duchêne, *Jean Monnet: The First Statesman of Interdependence* (New York: Norton, 1994).
4. Monnet, *Memoirs*, p. 222.
5. For a comprehensive history of European integration and the European movement, see Walter Lipgens, *History of European Integration*, 2 vols. (London: Oxford University Press, 1981 and 1986); and Raymond Poidevin, ed., *Origins of European Integration: March 1948–May 1950* (Brussels: Bruylant, 1986).
6. On the pan-European idea and the origins of the European movement, see Richard Coudenhove-Kalergi, *Pan-Europa* (Vienna: Pan-Europa-Verlag, 1923); Arnold Zurcher, *The Struggle to Unite Europe, 1940–1958* (New York: New York University Press, 1958); and Peter Stirk, *European Unity in Context: The Interwar Period* (London: Pinter, 1989).
7. Altiero Spinelli, "European Union and the Resistance," in Ghita Ionescu, ed., *The New Politics of European Integration* (London: Macmillan, 1972), pp. 5–7.
8. Lipgens, *European Integration*, vol. 1, p. 319.
9. Pierre Gerbert, "The Origins: Early Attempts and the Emergence of the Six (1945–52)," in Roy Pryce, ed., *The Dynamics of European Union* (London: Croom Helm, 1987), pp. 40–44.
10. Monnet, *Memoirs*, pp. 286, 304–305.

11. Monnet's *Memoirs* opens with a description of the offer of Anglo-French union, pp. 17–35.

12. Monnet, *Memoirs*, p. 225; Robert Marjolin, *Architect of European Unity: Memoirs, 1911–1986* (London: Weidenfeld & Nicolson, 1989), pp. 228–229.

13. For an account of the Marshall Plan and its relationship to European integration, see Michael Hogan, *The Marshall Plan: America, Britain and the Reconstruction of Western Europe, 1947–1952* (Cambridge: Cambridge University Press, 1987); Alan Milward, *The Reconstruction of Western Europe* (London: Methuen, 1984); Forrest Pogue, *George C. Marshall*, vol. 4, *Statesman, 1945–1959* (New York: Viking Press, 1987); and Imanuel Wexler, *The Marshall Plan Revisited: The European Recovery Program in Economic Perspective* (Westport, CT: Greenwood Press, 1983).

14. Office of the Historian, *Foreign Relations of the United States* (hereafter cited as *FRUS*), vol. 3 (Washington, DC: U.S. Department of State, 1947), pp. 230–232, 237–239.

15. Zurcher, *Struggle to Unite Europe*, pp. 13–16.

16. Walter Isaacson, *The Wise Men: Six Friends and the World They Made* (New York: Simon & Schuster, 1986), p. 122.

17. Hogan, *Marshall Plan*, p. 52.

18. On the failure of the OEEC, see Milward, *Reconstruction*, pp. 466–469.

19. See John W. Young, *France, the Cold War, and the Western Alliance* (New York: St. Martin's Press, 1990); and F. Roy Willis, *France, Germany and the New Europe, 1945–1967* (Stanford: Stanford University Press, 1968), pp. 7–31.

20. Isaacson, *Wise Men*, p. 236.

21. On the change in French thinking that led to the Schuman Plan, see Milward, *Reconstruction*, p. 492, and Raymond Poidevin, *Robert Schuman: Homme d'Etat, 1866–1963* (Paris: Imprimerie Nationale, 1986), pp. 32–58.

22. Monnet, *Memoirs*, pp. 298–306. For an account of the historic declaration, see Roger Bullen and M. E. Pelly, *The Schuman Plan, the Council of Europe and Western European Integration* (London: Her Majesty's Stationery Office, 1986); William Diebold, "Imponderables of the Schuman Plan," in *Foreign Affairs* 29, no. 1 (October 1950): 114–129; and Mark Roseman, *Recasting the Ruhr, 1945–1958: Manpower, Economic Recovery, and Labor Relations* (New York: Berg, 1992).

23. On Schuman's life and career, see Poidevin, *Schuman*.

24. Konrad Adenauer, *Memoirs, 1945–1966* (Chicago: Henry Regnery, 1966), pp. 244–248. On Adenauer's commitment to European integration, see also Dennis Bark and David Gress, *A History of West Germany*, vol. 1, *1945–1963* (Oxford: Blackwell, 1989).

25. *FRUS*, 1949, vol. 3, p. 625.

26. Dean Acheson, *Present at the Creation: My Years in the State Department* (New York: Norton, 1969), pp. 383–384.

27. John Gillingham, *Coal, Steel and the Rebirth of Europe, 1945–1955: The Germans and French from Ruhr Conflict to Economic Community* (Cambridge: Cambridge University Press, 1991), p. 235.

28. Gillingham, *Coal, Steel*, p. 231.

29. Monnet, *Memoirs*, p. 293.

30. Marjolin, *Memoirs*, p. 126.

31. Milward, *Reconstruction*, p. 255.

32. For a discussion of British policy toward postwar Europe, see Alan Bullock, *The Life and Times of Ernest Bevin*, vol. 3, *Ernest Bevin: Foreign Secretary, 1948–1951* (London: Heinemann, 1983); Richard Ovendale, *Foreign Policy of the British Labour Government, 1945–1951* (London: Pinter, 1984); John Young, *Britain,*

France and the Unity of Europe, 1945–1951 (Leicester: Leicester University Press, 1984).

33. See Bullock, *Bevin*, vol. 3, pp. 731–733; and Dean Acheson, *Sketches from Life of Men I Have Known* (New York: H. Hamilton, 1961), pp. 38–41.

34. Milward, *Reconstruction*, p. 404.

35. Theodore White, *In Search of History: A Personal Adventure* (New York: Harper and Row, 1978), pp. 438–439.

36. Gillingham, *Coal, Steel*, p. 229.

37. Monnet, *Memoirs*, p. 329.

38. See Edward Fursdon, *The European Defense Community: A History* (New York: St. Martin's Press, 1980).

39. On the political community negotiations, see Rita Cardozo, "The Project for Political Union (1952–54)," in Pryce, *Dynamics*, pp. 49–77.

40. See Raymond Aron, *France Defeats EDC* (New York: F. A. Praeger, 1957).

41. Gillingham, *Coal, Steel*, pp. 297–298.

42. Monnet, *Memoirs*, p. 400.

43. Walter Yondorf, "Monnet and the Action Committee: The Formative Years of the European Communities," *International Organization* 19 (1965): 909; see also Pascal Fontaine, *Le Comité d'Action pour les Etats Unis d'Europe de Jean Monnet* (Lausanne: Centre de Recherches Européennes, 1974).

44. *FRUS*, 1955–1957, vol. 4, p. 323.

45. Marjolin, *Memoirs*, p. 284.

46. See Yondorf, "Action Committee," pp. 896–901.

47. Marjolin, *Memoirs*, p. 296.

48. Hanns-Jurgen Küsters, "The Treaties of Rome (1955–57)," in Pryce, *Dynamics*, p. 94.

49. Marjolin, *Memoirs*, p. 306.

2

The Decade of De Gaulle, 1958–1969

Three individuals, all French, have contributed most to shaping the EU. Yet if the EU ever built a pantheon for its heroes, only two of them would be buried there. The first, Jean Monnet, would have pride of place. The second, Jacques Delors, Commission president between 1985 and 1995, would repose beside Monnet in almost equal esteem. But the third, Charles de Gaulle, would never be considered for interment in the EU's hallowed ground. On the contrary, de Gaulle would be relegated to the rogues' gallery of EU villains. For in the popular opinion of European integrationists, de Gaulle's anachronistic championing of the nation-state destroyed the EC's development in the 1960s and stunted its institutional growth until the Single European Act of 1986 and the Treaty on European Union of 1992. In their view, de Gaulle belongs on the scrap heap.

Such an opinion reveals the intolerance of the ideologue. In fact, de Gaulle's contribution to the European integration was far from negative. The Common Agricultural Policy (CAP), subsequently denigrated as a drain on EU resources and an impediment to international trade accord, owes its existence to de Gaulle. In the 1960s, the CAP proved a vital instrument of Community solidarity and helped restructure declining Western European agriculture. More important, without the CAP there would not have been a community of any kind. Just as the French parliament had successfully insisted on agricultural provisions in the Treaty of Rome so, too, had de Gaulle demanded implementation of those provisions as a condition of implementing the treaty as a whole. The customs union and common external tariff (CET) came into being because of, not despite, the CAP.

De Gaulle is best known in the context of the EC for keeping Britain out and for curtailing the powers of the European Parliament (EP) and the Commission. Once again, both seem negative achievements. But allowing Britain to join in the early 1960s would in all likelihood have thwarted the CAP, undermined the Community, and turned the customs union into a broad free trade area. The difficulties of dealing with Britain in the EC, not

Table 2.1 Chronology, 1958–1969

Year	Month	Event
1958	January	Launch of the EC and Euratom
	May	Collapse of the French Fourth Republic
	June	Charles de Gaulle forms a provisional government
	July	A conference in Stresa, Italy, lays the foundations for the Common Agricultural Policy (CAP)
	September	A referendum endorses the establishment of the French Fifth Republic
	December	De Gaulle is elected president of France
1959	January	First stage of transition to a common market begins
1961	August	Britain applies to join the EC (followed by Denmark, Ireland, and Norway)
	November	France drafts a treaty for a political community (Fouchet Plan)
1962	January	Second stage of transition to a common market begins
	April	Fouchet Plan collapses
	July	U.S. president Kennedy outlines a "grand design" for U.S.-European relations
1963	January	De Gaulle vetoes Britain's EC membership application; de Gaulle and Adenauer sign the Elysée Treaty; accession negotiations with Britain (and Denmark, Ireland, and Norway) end
	July	Yaoundé Convention between the EC and seventeen African states and Madagascar is signed
1965	April	Merger Treaty, fusing the executives of the EC, ECSC, and Euratom, is signed
	July	Empty chair crisis begins
1966	January	EC enters the third and final stage of transition to a common market; agreement is reached on the Luxembourg Compromise, ending the empty chair crisis
1967	May	Britain applies a second time for EC membership (followed by Denmark, Ireland, and Norway)
	July	The Merger Treaty enters into force
	November	De Gaulle vetoes Britain's application a second time
	December	Accession negotiations with Britain (and Denmark, Ireland, and Norway) are suspended
1968	May	Student and worker riots in Paris
	July	The customs union is completed eighteen months ahead of schedule
1969	April	De Gaulle resigns
	July	The membership applications of Britain, Denmark, Ireland, and Norway are reactivated

only under Margaret Thatcher in the 1980s but also under previous and succeeding governments, seem to bear out de Gaulle's point. De Gaulle's stand against the Commission in 1965 epitomized his hostility to supranationalism. Yet intergovernmentalism, which de Gaulle so bluntly asserted during the empty chair crisis, laid the basis for the EC's survival in the 1970s and invigoration in the 1980s. Ironically, as Stanley Hoffmann has observed, the EU of the 1990s is "an improbable, yet not ineffectual, blend of de Gaulle and Monnet."[1]

FRANCE, GERMANY, AND THE EUROPEAN COMMUNITY

De Gaulle's first contribution to the EC was to bring France, then the politically and economically most important member state, back from the brink of catastrophe. Since the end of World War II a series of bitter colonial conflicts, first in Indochina and later in North Africa, had progressively undermined the already precarious Fourth Republic. In May 1958 a revolt by French army officers in Algiers, sparked by rumors of impending negotiations between the French government and the Algerian National Liberation Front, proved the last straw. Threatened by a right-wing coup and a left-wing countercoup, the government collapsed. Despite numerous new governments and cabinet reshuffles during the Fourth Republic's brief, unhappy history, the country's hitherto resourceful politicians seemed suddenly incapable of saving the regime.

Twice before at times of national crisis de Gaulle had come to the rescue: first when he rejected the armistice of June 1940 and set up the Free French Movement; second when he bridged deep political divisions and established a provisional government in newly liberated France in August 1944. Fourteen years later, only de Gaulle wielded the moral authority and commanded the national respect necessary once again to save the nation. Exploiting the legend of 1940 and the lessons of 1944, de Gaulle began negotiations with the political parties (minus the Communists) about forming not only a new government but a new regime. Few argued with his demand that the new republic possess a strong presidency insulated from parliamentary factionalism and having almost exclusive responsibility for foreign policy and defense. In September 1958, a grateful electorate ushered in the Fifth Republic by overwhelmingly endorsing de Gaulle's constitution. In 1962, having survived another army revolt and an attempted assassination because of his acquiescence in Algerian independence, de Gaulle held a referendum on direct elections for the presidency. The ensuing endorsement completed the constitutional construction of the Fifth Republic.

Monnet understood the importance for the EC of a politically stable France. In the run-up to the 1958 referendum, Monnet wrote that "to safeguard our future we must now put an end to the Algerian crisis and ensure governmental stability and authority. These two imperatives are linked." Similarly, Monnet voted yes in the referendum on direct elections for the presidency in order to "give the executive greater legitimacy and also facilitate the decisions required for the unification of Europe. For sovereignty to be relegated, authority must be well-established."[2] Of course de Gaulle was averse to surrendering any sovereignty whatsoever. For that reason Monnet voted against de Gaulle in that year's presidential election. But Monnet's point about a strong executive forming the necessary basis for the sharing of sovereignty was prescient, for it was precisely from such a position that President François Mitterrand advanced European integration so effectively in the mid- and late 1980s.

De Gaulle's concomitant financial and monetary reforms proved equally essential for the successful functioning of the EC. Without de Gaulle's drastic devaluation of the franc in 1958 and related government expenditure cuts and taxation hikes, the fragile French economy could not have survived intra-EC tariff reductions. Nor might the first round of tariff cuts, due to be implemented on January 1, 1959, have taken place had the French franc remained so grossly overvalued. There is some truth to de Gaulle's later assertion that when the EC came into being, "it was necessary—in order to achieve something—that we French put in order our economic, financial and monetary affairs. . . . From that moment the Community was in principle viable."[3]

EC membership may have provided a pretext to take financial and monetary measures that would otherwise have proved politically impossible (as was the case with a number of member states four decades later in the run-up to EMU). But the EC meant much more than that to de Gaulle. Despite its threat to French sovereignty, EC membership offered de Gaulle a valuable opportunity to promote two overriding objectives: economic modernization and an institutional framework in which to embed Franco-German rapprochement.

During the debate on economic integration in the mid-1950s, de Gaulle, then in the political wilderness, said little publicly. Privately, he reportedly told an associate that "we shall tear up [the Treaty of Rome] when we come to power."[4] When he *did* come to power, de Gaulle unequivocally supported key EC objectives on pragmatic political and economic grounds. Accordingly, the EC flourished in its early years not because de Gaulle reluctantly acquiesced in it—either for legal reasons or because his government depended on the support of the pro-EC parliamentarians or because he was preoccupied with Algeria—but because he strongly supported a certain amount of sectoral economic integration. As David Calleo noted at the time, "Of all the national governments, it is de Gaulle's France which has supported most vigorously and constantly . . . the creation of a genuinely integrated European economy."[5]

In his memoirs, Harold Wilson, Britain's prime minister in the mid-1960s and again in the mid-1970s, tells the story of de Gaulle dismissing the discipline of economics as "quartermaster stuff."[6] Despite his fashionable denunciation of the dismal science, de Gaulle appreciated the importance of good quartermasters for the successful functioning of a modern army. Although he had no formal training in economics, de Gaulle took a keen interest in financial and monetary affairs. In 1946 he appointed Monnet to head the new office of economic planning; in 1958 he resolved to make France a leading industrial power. As de Gaulle remarked in his own memoirs, "International competition . . . offered a lever to stimulate our business sector, to force it to increase productivity . . . hence my decision to promote the Common Market which was still just a collection of paper."[7] De Gaulle's main interest lay in the international arena, but he remained acutely aware that only if France were economically and socially stable could his foreign policy succeed. Paradoxically, it was economic weakness and social discord that blighted de Gaulle's foreign policy and ultimately prompted his resignation in 1969.

Apart from seeking industrial rejuvenation, de Gaulle saw in the EC a unique opportunity to modernize the large and cumbersome French agricultural sector. "How could we maintain on our territory more than two million farms," de Gaulle wondered, "three-quarters of which were too small and too poor to be profitable, but on which, nonetheless, nearly one-fifth of the French population live? How, in this day and age, could we leave the agricultural profession to stumble along, without the benefit of technical training, organized markets, and the support of a rational credit system required for it to be competitive?"[8] The solution lay in the proposed Common Agricultural Policy, which would provide an EC-wide outlet for French produce, guarantee high agricultural prices regardless of low prices on the world market, and subsidize the export of surplus produce outside the EC itself. In effect, de Gaulle sought to get the EC as a whole to prop up French agriculture. His quid pro quo was Germany's expected profit from the lowering and ultimate abandonment of intra-EC industrial tariffs. The negotiations ahead would be arduous and acrimonious, but the advantage for France was clear. Hence de Gaulle's admission that "if, on resuming control of our affairs, I indeed embraced the Common Market, it was as much because of our position as an agricultural country as for the progress it would impose on our industry. . . . The CAP was a sine qua non of [our] participation."[9]

Britain's proposal to establish a European free trade area to incorporate and possibly supplant the EC threatened to abort the embryonic CAP. Having decided not to join the EC, Britain sought instead to enjoy the benefits of free trade in Europe while eschewing a common external tariff, a common agricultural policy, and any form of economic integration. EC member states resented what they saw as Britain's efforts to undermine European integration by diluting the nascent EC in a wider free trade area. Robert Marjolin, a vice president of the new Commission, saw the proposal as "a great danger, that of being more or less sucked into a vast European free trade area in which [the Community] would have lost its individuality, and which might have prevented it from fully establishing itself according to the terms of the Treaty of Rome."[10]

De Gaulle especially feared the proposal's implications for agriculture, a sector specifically excluded from the free trade offer. Although talks about a possible free trade area had continued since the second half of 1956, de Gaulle brought them to an abrupt end soon after coming to power. Britain pressed ahead and, in November 1959, formed the European Free Trade Association (EFTA) with Austria, Denmark, Norway, Portugal, Sweden, and Switzerland. EC member states rejected an early EFTA overture for some kind of economic association, resolving instead to press ahead with closer integration. This proved so successful by the early 1960s that Britain applied for EC membership.

De Gaulle's position on the EC complemented his policy toward Germany. In September 1958 German chancellor Konrad Adenauer visited de Gaulle for the first time. Whereas de Gaulle had left the political stage in 1946 advocating a punitive policy toward a weak, divided Germany, he returned in 1958 to a radically altered European scene. With Germany reindustrialized and rearmed, de Gaulle abandoned his earlier position and espoused instead the then-orthodox French policy of reconciliation and rapprochement. The remarkably warm relationship that immediately blossomed between the octogenarian chancellor and septuagenarian president confirmed both leaders in the belief that their countries' future, and the future of Europe, depended above all on close Franco-German accord. At their second meeting, in November 1958, de Gaulle assured Adenauer of France's commitment to the Treaty of Rome and won German support for the CAP.

During the remaining years of Adenauer's tenure, neither leader allowed a myriad of political and economic issues to come between France and Germany. Key international developments in the late 1950s and early 1960s convinced Adenauer of the wisdom of sticking to the Franco-German course. For instance, when Soviet president Nikita Khrushchev threatened unspecified action unless the Western powers revised the status of Berlin, the divided former capital of Germany, de Gaulle immediately offered Adenauer his full support, a position from which France never wavered during the protracted Berlin crises of the coming years. Hans von der Groeben, a commissioner in the 1960s and later a historian of the EC, identified Khrushchev's ultimatum as being "of crucial importance to further political development and to the establishment of the process of integration."[11] In return for de Gaulle's support in the face of crude Soviet threats, Adenauer supported de Gaulle's controversial positions on the CAP and on Britain's membership application. More important, he also supported de Gaulle's plans for a new European security community.

At issue was de Gaulle's conception of the EC and his espousal of a "European Europe." In de Gaulle's view, European integration should be limited to the technical aspects of the Treaty of Rome. But these could succeed only in a broader framework of intergovernmental cooperation on political and security affairs. Such cooperation was an essential prerequisite for the emergence of an economically strong, politically assertive, and militarily independent Europe. Accordingly, de Gaulle sought to establish a "Union of States," both as a central plank of his European policy and as a prerequisite for subsequent efforts to challenge the United States and break down global bipolarity.

Having consulted Adenauer, de Gaulle launched his initiative for a new European security community in Paris in September 1960. Despite the small member states' misgivings, a committee under the chairmanship of Christian Fouchet, French ambassador to Denmark, eventually drafted a design for a confederation of European states. With the goal of a common foreign and defense policy, as well as cooperation on cultural, educational, and scientific matters, the Fouchet Plan outlined an institutional framework that included a ministerial council, a commission of senior foreign ministry officials, and a consultative assembly of delegated national parliamentarians.

The Fouchet Plan was clearly incompatible with European integration as envisioned by the EC's founders. Although Monnet and other leading Eurofederalists had commented favorably on de Gaulle's original idea, their opposition grew as the plan took shape. Fearing French or Franco-German hegemony in a putative European organization that lacked the safeguards of supranationalism, other member states followed the Netherlands' lead and fiercely resisted the idea. A series of acrimonious meetings in early 1962 caused the Fouchet Committee to collapse.

De Gaulle at least salvaged an institutionalized Franco-German alliance from the wreckage of the Fouchet Plan. By contrast with the indifference and hostility of the smaller European partners, Germany had resolutely backed de Gaulle's scheme. To be more precise, Adenauer had resolutely backed the Fouchet Plan. With Adenauer's political and temporal life obviously drawing to an end (the chancellor was then eighty-seven years old), de Gaulle borrowed the Fouchet Plan's infrastructure to cement Franco-German rapprochement. Thus de Gaulle proposed regular meetings of the French president and the German chancellor, with their relevant ministers, to discuss cultural, economic, educational, and international issues. In the ensuing Franco-German Treaty of Friendship and Reconciliation, signed at the Elysée Palace in January 1963, both sides pledged "to consult each other, prior to any decision, on all questions of foreign policy . . . with a view to reaching an analogous position."[12]

The Elysée Treaty was the pinnacle of Adenauer's diplomacy, symbolizing as it did Franco-German reconciliation and accord. But bitter political controversy in Germany came to a head during the ratification debate in May 1963, robbing the treaty of much of its value for de Gaulle. Alarmed by Adenauer's apparent acquiescence in de Gaulle's idiosyncratic European initiatives, a majority within the chancellor's own Christian

Democratic Party joined with the Social Democratic opposition to attach a codicil to the treaty asserting Germany's overriding commitment to existing NATO obligations. To make matters worse for de Gaulle, Adenauer resigned in April 1963. His successor, Ludwig Erhard, was a steadfast Atlanticist whose tenure as chancellor, from 1963 to 1966, saw a steady deterioration in Franco-German relations. "There is no point deceiving ourselves," de Gaulle remarked after a meeting with Erhard in July 1964, "the [Elysée] Treaty has not yet developed as we had hoped. . . . Europe will only be a reality when France and Germany are truly united."[13]

Ironically, the Elysée Treaty would achieve its potential and prove its worth as a cornerstone not of intergovernmentalism in the EC but of closer political and economic integration. Despite his dislike of Erhard, de Gaulle continued to attend regular bilateral meetings under the terms of the treaty. Subsequent French presidents and German chancellors, as well as a host of government ministers and officials, similarly stuck to a fixed schedule of bilateral meetings. With the rapid improvement of Franco-German relations in the early 1970s and a growing consensus in both countries about the utility of European integration, these frequent, institutionalized contacts became a major driving force of European integration.

CONSTRUCTING THE COMMUNITY

Franco-German rapprochement in the late 1950s, de Gaulle's benevolence toward certain provisions of the Treaty of Rome, and an extremely buoyant European economy helped get the EC off to a strong start. Robert Marjolin recalled the EC's first four years as "a honeymoon . . . a time of harmony between the governments of the member countries and between [EC] institutions."[14] Walter Hallstein, a former German state secretary for foreign affairs and an early collaborator of Jean Monnet's, presided over the first Commission. With nine members (two each from Germany, France, and Italy and one each from the other member states), the Commission spent the first few months of its existence settling into temporary quarters in Brussels, allocating responsibilities and portfolios among its members, and organizing the necessary staff and services. Commission officials came from the ECSC in Luxembourg, from the member states' civil services, or from academia and the private sector. Setting an important precedent, the first Commission recruited a bureaucracy that struck a national and regional balance "without becoming a slave to proportional representation."[15]

The Council, the EC's legislative body, began regular meetings in Brussels and located a small secretariat there. The Council also organized the Committee of Permanent Representatives (COREPER), consisting of ambassadors resident in Brussels and able to promote their countries' interests on a day-to-day basis. Despite some misgivings about dealing with ambassadors rather than ministers themselves, the Commission soon settled down to a harmonious relationship with COREPER. In Luxembourg the Court of Justice soon began to produce an impressive body of EC case law that would profoundly affect the course of European integration. The Assembly of the European Community, later to call itself the EP, met for the first time in Strasbourg in January 1958 and, initially at least, was the Cinderella of the new Community.

The first Commission's nine portfolios, one for each commissioner, are a useful indicator of the Community's early agenda. In addition to one covering administration, there were portfolios for external relations, economic and financial affairs, the internal market, competition, social affairs, agriculture, transport, and overseas countries and territories. In some of these areas the treaty dictated a specific timetable to implement certain measures; in others, it provided no more than general guidelines and statements of principle. The most immediate and tangible task was to establish the customs union. Thanks to French financial and economic reforms, the first intra-EC tariff reductions took place, on schedule, on January 1, 1959. As other rounds of tariff and quota cuts followed, member states put in place a common external tariff. The customs union came into being on July 1, 1968, eighteen months earlier than stipulated in the treaty.

The late 1950s and the early 1960s were years of extraordinarily high and sustained rates of economic growth in Western Europe, in large part because of an enormous escalation of international trade. Between 1958 and 1960 alone, trade among the Six grew by 50 percent. Mirrored by a similar development in the 1980s following the launch of the single market program, this dramatic rise was as much a result of "the increased activity of businessmen as [of] the actual reduction of tariffs. As soon as managers were convinced that the common market was going to be established, they started to behave in many ways as if it was already in existence."[16] High growth rates, a healthy balance of payments, and relatively stable prices provided incentives to coordinate member states' economic policies, a step the treaty merely hinted at but that the Commission eagerly pursued.

The EC's economic success facilitated the assertion and general acceptance of its international identity. With the exception of the Soviet Union and its satellites, third countries quickly acknowledged the Commission's responsibility for commercial policy and opened diplomatic missions in Brussels. The EC's early external initiatives pointed in two directions: multilateral trade negotiations and Third World development. Under the former, the Commission assumed responsibility for member state participation in the Dillon and Kennedy Rounds of the General Agreement on Tariffs and Trade (GATT). Under the latter, in 1964 the EC concluded the Yaoundé Convention with seventeen African states and Madagascar, a forerunner of the flagship Lomé Convention.

Successful first steps in commercial policy and external relations contrasted with the difficulty of fulfilling other treaty objectives. Whereas tariff barriers between member states could easily be identified and eliminated, policies in areas such as competition, social affairs, transport, and energy were far harder to formulate. Progress was impeded by a combination of sometimes vague treaty provisions, member state apathy or outright opposition, and philosophical and ideological differences between and within the Commission and Council—factors that are as cogent in the EU today as they were in the early years. The result was a mixed record of policy formulation and implementation. On transport policy, for instance, there was little progress. One of the first academic studies of European integration in the 1960s concluded that "transport . . . is primarily a dismal story of false starts, of politically inept Commission proposals, of persistent Council inaction, of divided government views, and of apparent drift in the direction of more nationally [oriented] policies."[17]

The EC faced its greatest challenge and enjoyed its first success in agriculture, although arguably at the cost of creating a monster. De Gaulle saw the vagueness of agricultural policy provisions as evidence of French weakness during the treaty negotiations. In his own words, he came to power resolved to "put up a literally desperate fight, sometimes going so far as to threaten to withdraw our membership [in the EC]" until ultimately "France and common sense prevailed."[18] Common sense or no, de Gaulle should have credited the Commission's help. His determination to negotiate a comprehensive agricultural policy made de Gaulle and the Commission unlikely but effective allies. At crucial times mediation by the Commission saved the talks from collapse, and the Commission's technical skill and expertise pushed the various proposals forward.

De Gaulle's refusal to acknowledge the Commission's contribution demonstrated his well-known hatred of the Brussels bureaucracy, a hatred fueled, paradoxically, by the Commission's invaluable assistance in formulating and implementing the CAP. The extent to which both sides used each other during the CAP negotiations led to a fatal miscalculation by the Commission, which sought to link a further surrender of sovereignty with a successful conclusion of pending negotiations on CAP financing. As it was, the Commission's growing prominence and political influence infuriated de Gaulle. By raising the political stakes, the Commission pushed de Gaulle too far and provoked a crisis that paralyzed the Community.

THE EMPTY CHAIR CRISIS

A dispute over the Commission's proposal to fund the CAP for the period between the expiration of the initial financial regulation in July 1965 and the end of the EC's transitional period in 1970 was the proximate cause of what became known as the empty chair crisis. Once fully operational, the CAP was to have been funded by levies on agricultural imports into the EC, supplemented by duties on industrial imports. Together, these would constitute the EC's "own resources." With the common markets due to be completed ahead of schedule in July 1967, the Commission proposed that the EC acquire its own resources at that time. Suggesting that member states give up their import duties early was itself controversial. But emboldened by the successful implementation to date of the treaty's commercial and agricultural provisions, and by de Gaulle's obvious interest in securing a new financial regulation for the CAP, the Commission rashly went too far: It proposed a complex budgetary system in which the Commission itself and the EP would greatly enhance their powers. The powers of the member states would correspondingly diminish through the substitution of majority voting for the unanimity requirement in certain cases.

This plan went far beyond what de Gaulle would ever accept and caused the inherently tense relationship between Paris and Brussels to explode into open antagonism in the spring of 1965. As it was, de Gaulle despised the Brussels bureaucracy, dismissing Commission officials as stateless and denationalized. He denounced the "tendentious impropriety" of the Commission in calling itself the EC's executive and protested its practice of accrediting third-country diplomats assigned to the Community.[19] De Gaulle especially detested Hallstein, who used every opportunity to push European integration along federal lines and enhance the Commission's power.

Marjolin warned his colleagues not to persist with the CAP proposals and violate the Commission's "golden rule" of not taking any action "likely to encounter an outright veto [by a member state] that would have left no room for negotiation."[20] Undeterred, Hallstein pressed ahead and took the additional inflammatory step of first announcing the proposals not to the Council in Brussels but to the EP in Strasbourg. Storm clouds immediately appeared, with the French foreign minister warning that "our partners are indulging in wishful thinking by putting forward proposals which they know France will not accept."[21]

Antagonized by de Gaulle's haughtiness and aware of his desire to complete the CAP, other member states prepared to call his bluff. A meeting between de Gaulle and Erhard on June 11, 1965, failed to avert the crisis. Nor did the Five act on a French proposal to continue funding the CAP by national contributions, thereby avoiding the contentious question of own resources. Few in the Five seemed alarmed by the looming deadline of June 30. Negotiations on the CAP, after all, had a reputation for running late.

The crucial Council meeting opened on June 28 with France in the chair. Taking a minimalist position, the French foreign minister pressed for a decision only on funding the CAP after July 1. With others insisting that the Commission's proposals would have to be considered as a whole, substantive discussions had not even begun by midnight on June 30. Two hours later, the meeting broke up. The French government promptly recalled its permanent representative and announced that French officials would no longer participate in the Council or its numerous committees.[22]

Faced with an empty French chair, the Community could do little more than conduct routine business. Far from backing down, however, de Gaulle raised the stakes by linking an additional, hitherto unrelated point to the original cause of the conflict. In a typically self-serving press conference on September 9, 1965, full of invective against the Commission and the EP, de Gaulle announced that France would not accept a provision of the treaty, due to be implemented on January 1, 1966, introducing qualified majority voting in the Council on a limited range of issues.[23]

De Gaulle's attack on qualified majority voting and insistence on unanimity (in which any nation could unilaterally veto legislation) greatly exacerbated the crisis. Other member states shared France's concern about being outvoted in the Council but argued that important national interests were unlikely ever to be ignored. At a Council meeting held without France on October 25–26, the Five reaffirmed their commitment to the treaty and refusal to renegotiate one of its few supranational provisions. At the same time, they expressed willingness to compromise on the Commission's earlier proposals and offered France every opportunity to return to the negotiating table.

The other member states' solidarity may have been a factor in de Gaulle's decision to resume talks. French public opinion was arguably a more important consideration. Farmers' organizations and business interests feared the consequences of a protracted crisis, and the presidential election of December 1965 gave them a timely opportunity to express their concern. Although other issues were involved, François Mitterrand, de Gaulle's main rival, called himself "the candidate of Europe."[24] Deprived of an absolute majority in the first round of balloting, de Gaulle and Mitterrand contested the second round alone. As expected, de Gaulle won, but by the surprisingly narrow margin of 11 percent.

The election result demonstrated the domestic limits on de Gaulle's European policy. Although notoriously insensitive to French public opinion, as the simmering student unrest of 1967 and 1968 would soon show, de Gaulle undoubtedly got the message. A week after the election, France announced its willingness to negotiate an end to the crisis, which was finally resolved at a foreign ministers' meeting on January 28–29, 1966. There, the Six agreed to adopt an interim financial regulation for the CAP, deferring the question of the EC's own resources and, by extension, the EP's budgetary power. Majority voting in the Council remained the outstanding issue. After restating their positions, both sides approved a short declaration, the Luxembourg Compromise, which amounted to an agreement to disagree:

1. When issues very important to one or more member countries are at stake, the members of the Council will try, within a reasonable time, to reach solutions which can be adopted by all members of the Council, while respecting their mutual interests, and those of the Community.
2. The French delegation considers that, when very important issues are at stake, discussions must be continued until unanimous agreement is reached.
3. The six delegations note that there is a divergence of views on what should be done in the event of a failure to reach complete agreement.
4. However, they consider that this divergence does not prevent the Community's work being resumed in accordance with the normal procedure.[25]

Ostensibly the outcome of the crisis was a draw, perhaps even a victory for the EC. The French presidential election had apparently clipped de Gaulle's wings, the Five had not reneged on majority voting, and the Council soon resumed full operation. In reality, the crisis ended in victory for de Gaulle. The Council approved temporary funding for the CAP in May 1966, and the Commission's ambitious proposals to revise budgetary procedures sank out of sight. Moreover, the crisis profoundly undermined both Hallstein's credibility and the Commission's confidence. Thereafter, the Commission refrained from asserting itself for over a decade.

Crucially, the Luxembourg Compromise impeded effective decisionmaking in the Council for a long time to come. De Gaulle's insistence on unanimity heightened the member states' awareness of each other's special interests and increased their reluctance to call a vote even when no vital interest was at stake. The Luxembourg Compromise did not disrupt established decisionmaking procedures because majority voting had never been the norm. Instead, as Joe Weiler has observed, "it symbolized a transformation from a 'Community' spirit to a more selfish and pragmatic 'cost-benefit' attitude of the member states. It was a change of ethos, at first rejected by the Five but later, especially after the first enlargement, eagerly seized upon by all. In this sense the danger to the Community, even if not always tangible, was significant."[26]

To some extent the crisis demonstrated that the Community depends on a political environment over which it has little control. But the crisis also helped shape the political climate in which the Community operated during the next decade. Six months of near paralysis in Brussels, a heavy blow to the Commission's morale, and a substantial setback to majority voting had an invidious effect. In the final analysis, "the Community and the Western European states moved closer to Gaullist confederal notions, while the European federalists lost ground."[27]

BRITAIN REBUFFED

The question of EC enlargement arose for the first time in 1961, when Britain applied to join. Prime Minister Harold Macmillan advocated British membership for negative rather than positive reasons. By the end of the 1950s it was readily apparent in London that the Commonwealth was an inadequate vehicle through which to promote British interests. By contrast, the EC flourished. Earlier attempts to dissolve the EC into a wider free trade area emphasized British fears of economic exclusion. The failure of the free trade initiative and the corresponding success of the fledgling customs union convinced Britain's political and business leaders that the country's interests lay in full EC membership.

Yet deep suspicion of European integration tempered British enthusiasm. The opposition Labour Party was deeply divided on the issue. A small group of passionate "pro-marketeers" balanced a corresponding clique of ardent "antimarketeers," with the bulk of the party either uncertain or moderately hostile to membership. The Conservatives generally favored joining, although Macmillan purged the cabinet of a few antimarketeers and appointed Edward Heath, who ultimately brought Britain into the EC in 1973, to lead the entry negotiations in Brussels.

In Macmillan's view, the decision to apply for EC membership complemented his foreign policy priority: restoring and maintaining the Anglo-American "special relationship." No sooner did Macmillan become prime minister in 1957 than he set off to meet President Eisenhower in Bermuda. The two had worked together in Algiers in 1943 trying to coordinate Anglo-American policy toward none other than de Gaulle, then fighting for his political life as leader of the Free French Movement. Memories of the war years helped to put the special relationship back on track. Coincidentally, while Eisenhower and Macmillan reminisced in Bermuda, leaders of the Six signed the Treaty of Rome, which Macmillan did not even mention in his diaries.[28]

President Kennedy's election caused Macmillan to fret again about Anglo-American relations. Kennedy's youth, charisma, and Irish ancestry convinced the older, staid Macmillan that the special relationship was imperiled. At their first meeting, in Key West, Florida, in March 1961, Kennedy put Macmillan's fears to rest. For the remainder of Kennedy's brief administration, a remarkably close personal friendship between the president and prime minister cemented Anglo-American ties.

Kennedy's unequivocal endorsement of British membership in the EC strengthened Macmillan's determination to join but aroused de Gaulle's suspicions. Kennedy's "Grand Design" for closer U.S.-EC relations and a stronger Atlantic Alliance, outlined in a famous Independence Day speech in 1962, seemed at variance with de Gaulle's conception of a "European Europe." In de Gaulle's view, an equitable transatlantic relationship was impossible as long as Western Europe was strategically subservient to the United States. By linking British accession and U.S. Atlantic Alliance strategy, Kennedy possibly sealed the fate of Macmillan's application.[29]

Macmillan tried to overcome these profound differences with de Gaulle by appealing to past friendship and pursuing a close personal relationship. Macmillan visited Paris soon after de Gaulle returned to power. As his biographer noted, "It was a momentous occasion for Macmillan, meeting again the man who had first come into his life in the dark days in Algiers fifteen years previously, and for whose cause he had fought so hard then. But for Macmillan's support for de Gaulle against Roosevelt and Churchill, almost certainly de Gaulle would not have been in Paris, at the helm, in 1958."[30]

Undoubtedly de Gaulle owed Macmillan a huge political debt, but the latter's efforts to overcome de Gaulle's opposition to Britain's EC membership were pitiful. Macmillan's diary entry for November 26, 1961, written after a private visit from de Gaulle, reveals the prime minister's extreme frustration with, and acute misunderstanding of, the French president's position: "De Gaulle was no more conciliatory over the Common Market. . . . The tragedy of it all is that we agree with de Gaulle on almost everything. We like the political Europe that de Gaulle likes. We are anti-federalists; so is he. . . . We agree; but his pride, his inherited hatred of England (since Joan of Arc) . . . above all, his intense 'vanity' for France—she must dominate—make him half welcome, half repel us, with a strange love-hate complex. Sometimes, when I am with him, I feel I have overcome it. But he goes back to his distrust and dislike, like a dog to vomit."[31]

The accession negotiations themselves quickly became mired in a mass of technical detail, mostly over the CAP, the Commonwealth, and EFTA. A British white paper outlined the problems in all three areas. In agriculture, Britain's twin policies of buying low-priced food on the world market and paying farmers direct price support were incompatible with the principles of the CAP. As for the Commonwealth, Britain feared the political and economic impact on its former possessions of a sudden disruption of traditional trade patterns. Finally, "given [Britain's] obligations to our EFTA partners, we should not be able to join the Community until [we agreed upon] . . . ways and means of meeting their legitimate interests."[32]

In the event, developments in Anglo-American relations soon overshadowed the enlargement negotiations. Matters came to a head in December 1962 at a meeting between Macmillan and Kennedy to negotiate a new Anglo-American missile accord. Under the terms of the Nassau agreement, Britain would use U.S. Polaris missiles as the delivery system for British nuclear warheads. Moreover, Britain's nuclear force would be integrated into NATO, except when the government "may decide that supreme national interests are at stake."[33]

For de Gaulle, then struggling to develop the French nuclear *force de frappe,* the Nassau agreement represented a damning surrender of sovereignty. Britain had relinquished to the United States technological and strategic responsibility for a supposedly independent nuclear deterrent. There could have been no more graphic demonstration of Britain's irreconcilability with de Gaulle's "European Europe." After a year of tough bargaining in Brussels, de Gaulle now had a cogent reason to break off the enlargement negotiations.

He did so dramatically in a press conference on January 14, 1963. In a long, wide-ranging response to a planted question, de Gaulle cataloged the history of Britain's relationship with the EC. Having attempted to submerge the EC in a broad free trade area, Britain now sought to join, "but on her own conditions." Thus far, the entry negotiations had given little assurance that "Britain can place herself . . . inside a tariff which is genuinely common . . . renounce all Commonwealth preferences . . . cease any pretense that her agriculture be privileged, and, more than that . . . treat her engagements with other countries of the Free Trade Area as null and void." More to the point, were Britain to join without fundamentally changing its international orientation, the EC "would not endure for long [but] instead would become a colossal Atlantic community under American domination and direction."[34] De Gaulle's statement amounted to a veto of Britain's EC application.

Paul-Henri Spaak, who had chaired the intergovernmental conference leading to the Treaty of Rome, wrote melodramatically that the date of de Gaulle's press conference was "fated to go down in history as the 'black Monday' of both European policy and Atlantic policy."[35] But as another observer remarked, the "crisis atmosphere" provoked by de Gaulle's statement "was not of long duration . . . because the concern of France's partners to push the Community forward was stronger than their irritation with French high-mindedness."[36] Though they regretted how the negotiations had come to an end, many national and EC officials agreed that Britain was not yet ready for accession. As Marjolin remarked in his memoirs, de Gaulle's decision to close the door on Britain "offended France's continental partners possibly more through its form than through its content."[37]

The suspension of Britain's application was a serious setback for Macmillan and contrasted starkly with his apparent success in concluding the Nassau agreement one month before. Nor can Macmillan have failed to notice that de Gaulle was far from isolated in his rejection of Britain's candidacy. There was nothing for Britain to do but await a favorable time to reapply for membership and review in the meantime why the negotiations had stalled. Dejected, Macmillan resigned in October 1963 because of a purportedly terminal illness—but he went on to enjoy twenty-three years of robust retirement.

BRITAIN REBUFFED . . . AGAIN

When Britain applied again for EC membership, on May 10, 1967, the Labour Party was in power. Prime Minister Harold Wilson was equivocal about joining but, like Macmillan before him, saw no feasible alternative. If anything, Britain's declining political and economic links with the Commonwealth and growing commercial contacts with the Continent increased the urgency of accession. Nevertheless the issue split the Labour Party, pitting a pro-Europe wing on the center and right against the antimarketeers (with powerful trade union support) on the left.

Also like Macmillan before him, Wilson hoped to overcome French opposition to British entry by cultivating de Gaulle. Symbolizing a break with the past, Wilson first met de Gaulle at Churchill's funeral in January 1965. In the following months Wilson fostered what he thought was a warm friendship, based in part on his ambivalence about the Anglo-American special relationship. Apart from strategic considerations, Wilson shared French concerns about the long-term implication for European industry of U.S. technological superiority.

While Wilson took various steps to bolster domestic support and allay Commonwealth concerns before formally resubmitting Britain's membership application, de Gaulle reserved judgment. Yet only four days after Britain resubmitted its application, de Gaulle condescendingly claimed that Britain had not yet achieved "the profound economic and political transformation which would allow (it) to join the Six."[38] A period of confusion followed, during which the Commission issued a favorable opinion and preparations went ahead for accession negotiations to resume. In December 1967, during his biannual press conference, de Gaulle announced that Britain's entry "would obviously mean the breaking up of a Community that has been built and that functions according to rules which would not bear such a monumental exception."[39] There was no longer any doubt about the issue. A week later the Foreign Office announced that Britain would shelve its application.

De Gaulle blocked Britain's second application for essentially the same reasons as before. Despite Wilson's difficulties with Washington, the Anglo-American special relationship remained fundamentally sound and, in de Gaulle's view, a barrier to British membership. In fact, Britain's inclusion in the EC would likely have had little impact on the Cold War and its underlying superpower system. Within the EC itself, de Gaulle sought to preserve France's leadership role by maintaining the status quo. Yet Germany, then "an economy in search of a political purpose,"[40] clearly had the potential to displace Paris as the center of gravity in the EC. British accession might therefore have bolstered French leadership by providing a bulwark against German economic and political resurgence.

DE GAULLE'S DEPARTURE

Domestic and international developments in 1968 abruptly ended the Gaullist illusion. At home, social unrest erupted in May 1968 in a series of riots and strikes that threatened to topple not only the government but also the regime. De Gaulle's focus on foreign policy had blinded him to the extent of growing domestic dissatisfaction. Significantly, he was on a visit to Romania when the crisis blew up. Protesting a rigid educational system and declining living standards, millions of students and workers poured onto French city streets. A brutal police response, relayed nightly on television news, exacerbated the problem. After a month of unrest, the Fifth Republic seemed on the brink of collapse. What saved it, perhaps, was the unwillingness or inability of the Communist Party to exploit the situation fully. The government also survived, but not because of de Gaulle, who fled Paris at the height of the crisis, leaving his prime minister, Georges Pompidou, to find a solution. Pompidou did so brilliantly, largely by gambling on time and capitalizing on the inevitable public reaction against incessant instability. Having dissolved parliament and called new elections in June 1968, the Gaullists and their allies won an overall majority.

It proved a pyrrhic victory. The events of May 1968 demolished de Gaulle's personal popularity and fatally compromised his credibility as president. Although his term of office was not due to expire for another four years, after the domestic and international upheavals of 1968 de Gaulle increasingly looked like a lame-duck president. Other member states awaited de Gaulle's departure before taking any new initiatives, and the EC gradually recovered from the disruption of the empty chair crisis. The Merger Treaty, a treaty to merge the institutions of the three communities (ECSC, EEC, and Euratom), signed in April 1965, came into effect on July 1, 1967. Also in 1967, the Kennedy Round of the GATT, in which the Commission negotiated for the member states, came to a successful conclusion.

Enlargement remained the outstanding internal and external issue for the EC, with de Gaulle seemingly the sole obstacle to British entry. That obstacle suddenly disappeared in April 1969 when de Gaulle resigned, having staked his presidency on the outcome of two referendums on minor administrative issues. De Gaulle's sudden departure raised concerns about the durability of the Fifth Republic. Could it survive without de Gaulle? When it easily did so, enlargement returned to the top of the EC's agenda.

Western European and North American leaders watched de Gaulle go with a mixture of relief and regret—relief because progress within the EC and harmony within the Atlantic Alliance finally seemed assured; regret because for all de Gaulle's foibles and illusions, few could doubt his eminence or achievements. De Gaulle had done more than restore French pride and self-esteem. He had saved his country's honor during the occupation and collaboration, ensured its stability during the liberation, and rescued its liberal democratic institutions during the Algerian crisis. In addition to leading France to prominence in the postwar world, de Gaulle gave Europe a greater sense of identity and purpose at a time of subordination to the superpowers. Even the Americans, who suffered most from de Gaulle's assertive foreign policy, readily acknowledged his sagacity and statesmanship. As Stanley Hoffmann observed, whatever one's point of view, "it is impossible not to be impressed by de Gaulle's life and works. . . . One does not often come so clearly in contact with greatness."[41]

NOTES

1. Stanley Hoffmann, review of *De Gaulle: The Rebel, 1890–1944*, by Jean Lacouture, *New Republic,* December 17, 1990, p. 34.
2. Quoted in Jean Monnet, *Memoirs* (Garden City, NY: Doubleday, 1978), p. 430.
3. Quoted in *Le Monde,* January 15, 1963.
4. Quoted in Edmond Jouve, *Le Général de Gaulle et la Construction de l'Europe (1940–1966)* (Paris: Librairie Générale de Droit et de Jurisprudence, R. Pichon et R. Durand-Auzias, 1967), p. 253.
5. David Calleo, *Europe's Future: The Grand Alternatives* (New York: Horizon Press, 1965), p. 54.
6. Harold Wilson, *Memoirs: The Making of a Prime Minister, 1916–1986* (London: Weidenfeld & Nicolson, 1986), p. 91.
7. Charles de Gaulle, *Memoirs of Hope: Renewal and Endeavor* (New York: Simon & Schuster, 1971), p. 143.
8. Ibid., pp. 165–166.
9. Ibid., p. 167.
10. Robert Marjolin, *Architect of European Unity: Memoirs, 1911–1986* (London: Weidenfeld & Nicolson, 1989), p. 318.
11. Hans von der Groeben, *The European Community: The Formative Years: The Struggle to Establish the Common Market and the Political Union (1958–66),* European Perspectives Series (Luxembourg: Office for Official Publications of the European Communities [OOP], 1985), p. 32.
12. Edward Kolodziej, *French International Policy Under de Gaulle and Pompidou: The Politics of Grandeur* (Ithaca: Cornell University Press, 1974), p. 316.
13. Quoted in *Le Monde,* July 7, 1964.
14. Marjolin, *Memoirs,* p. 310.
15. Von der Groeben, *Formative Years,* p. 45.
16. John Pinder, "Implications for the Operation of the Firm," *Journal of Common Market Studies* 1, no. 1 (1962): 41.
17. Leon Lindberg, *The Political Dynamics of European Economic Integration* (Stanford: Stanford University Press, 1963), p. 143.
18. De Gaulle, *Memoirs,* pp. 159, 186–187.
19. Charles de Gaulle, *Major Addresses, Statements and Press Conferences* (New York: French Embassy, Press and Information, 1964), p. 147.
20. Marjolin, *Memoirs,* p. 314.
21. Quoted in Françoise de la Serre, "The EEC and the 1965 Crisis," in F. Roy Willis, ed., *European Integration* (New York: New Viewpoints, 1975), p. 134.

22. See John Lambert, "The Constitutional Crisis, 1965–66," *Journal of Common Market Studies* 4, no. 3 (May 1966): 205–206.

23. *Le Monde,* September 10, 1965.

24. Lambert, "Constitutional Crisis," p. 220.

25. Reproduced in ibid., p. 226.

26. Joseph Weiler, "The Genscher-Colombo Draft European Act: The Politics of Indecision," *Journal of European Integration* 4, nos. 2 and 3 (1989): 134.

27. Kolodziej, *French Policy,* p. 337.

28. Alastair Horne, *Harold Macmillan,* vol. 2 (New York: Viking, 1989), p. 30.

29. See Alfred Grosser, *The Western Alliance: European-American Relations Since 1945* (New York: Vantage, 1982), pp. 199–208.

30. Horne, *Macmillan,* vol. 2, p. 312.

31. Quoted in 55ibid., p. 319.

32. The white paper is reproduced in Frances Nicholson and Roger East, *From the Six to the Twelve: The Enlargement of the European Communities* (Chicago: St. James Press, 1987), pp. 14–21.

33. Nicholson and East, *Enlargement,* pp. 25–26. On the Skybolt crisis that precipitated the Nassau agreement, see Richard Neustadt, *Alliance Politics* (New York: Columbia University Press, 1970), pp. 52–55.

34. Quoted in Nicholson and East, *Enlargement,* pp. 30–32.

35. Paul-Henri Spaak, "Hold Fast," in *Foreign Affairs* 41, no. 4 (1963): 611.

36. Lois Pattison de Menil, *Who Speaks for Europe? The Making of a Prime Minister, 1916–1986* (London: Weidenfeld & Nicolson, 1986), p. 136.

37. Marjolin, *Memoirs,* p. 338.

38. Nicholson and East, *Enlargement,* p. 49.

39. Ibid., pp. 52–53.

40. Henry Kissinger, *White House Years* (New York: Little, Brown, 1979), p. 97.

41. Hoffmann, review of *De Gaulle: The Rebel,* p. 29.

3

A Community in Flux, 1969–1979

The terms "Eurosclerosis" and "Europessimism" encapsulate the history of European integration in the mid-1970s. After the frustration of the 1960s, the EC seemed set at the start of the 1970s to shake off the shackles of Gaullism and begin an invigorating new phase of its development. "Completion, deepening, enlargement," a slogan popularized by French president Georges Pompidou and endorsed by the Six at the Hague summit of 1969, summed up the optimism of the post–de Gaulle era. But the accomplishments of the early 1970s—the accession of three member states, the adoption of a plan for Economic and Monetary Union (EMU), and the launch of a procedure for foreign policy coordination—soon gave way to severe economic and political strains as the EC absorbed the impact of enlargement and reeled under the shock of the oil embargo. For the remainder of the decade, the EC seemed to face a bleaker future than it had at the height of the Gaullist challenge.

The threat to the EC in the 1970s was of an altogether different kind than that of the 1960s. Whereas the Gaullist challenge originated in the determination of a single individual to defy and remold the existing international system, a profound transformation in the international system itself lay at the heart of the protracted crisis of the 1970s. Enfeebled by the Gaullist challenge, the EC struggled in the following decade with unforeseen circumstances such as fluctuating superpower relations, apparent U.S. decline, growing German assertiveness, oscillating exchange rates, and widely uneven economic performance among the member states. The history of the EC in the 1970s is the history of a Community in flux, attempting to cope with fundamental changes in the international system and fighting for survival in a radically altered political and economic environment.

The emergence of the European Council and the effectiveness of the Paris-Bonn axis, personified for much of the decade by the friendship between President Valéry Giscard d'Estaing and Chancellor Helmut Schmidt, explain to a great extent the EC's durability during that turbulent time. But

Table 3.1 Chronology, 1969–1979

1969	December	At a summit in The Hague, the heads of state and government decide to relaunch European integration
1970	April	Member states decide to finance the EU by a system of "own resources"
	June	Accession negotiations with Britain, Denmark, Ireland, and Norway resume
	October	Pierre Werner presents a plan for Economic and Monetary Union (EMU); foreign ministers adopt a plan by Etienne Davignon on European Political Cooperation (EPC)
	November	Foreign ministers meet for the first time "in EPC"
1971	August	The United States announces the suspension of dollar convertibility, thereby ending the Bretton Woods system
1972	April	Launch of the monetary "snake"
	October	The heads of state and government hold a summit in Paris and agree "to transform the whole complex of . . . relations [between member states] into a European Union" by the end of the decade
1973	January	Britain, Denmark, and Ireland join the EC
	July	The Conference on Security and Cooperation in Europe (CSCE) opens in Helsinki
	October	Following the Middle East war, Arab oil producers quadruple the price of oil and embargo the port of Rotterdam
	December	The heads of state and government discuss the oil crisis at a summit in Copenhagen
1974	April	The new Labour government asks for a renegotiation of Britain's membership terms
	September	The heads of state and government decide to form the European Council
	December	The heads of state and government hold their last informal summit in Paris
1975	February	The Lomé Convention is signed
	March	The European Council holds its inaugural meeting and concludes the renegotiation of Britain's membership terms
	June	In a constitutionally unprecedented British referendum, a large majority votes in favor of continued EC membership; Greece applies to join the EC
	July	Member states sign a treaty setting up the Court of Auditors and strengthening the budgetary powers of the European Parliament (EP)
	August	Thirty-five participating states sign the CSCE Final Act in Helsinki
	December	Leo Tindemans presents his report on European Union
1977	March	Portugal applies to join the EC
	July	Spain applies to join the EC
1978	July	Meeting in Bremen, the European Council approves the plan for the European Monetary System (EMS)
	December	Member states decide to launch the EMS in January 1978; eight of them decide to participate in the system's exchange rate mechanism (ERM)
1979	March	After a delay of three months, the EMS is launched
	May	Margaret Thatcher becomes prime minister of Britain
	September	Dirk Spierenburg presents his report on Commission reform
	November	The "Three Wise Men" present their report on EC reform

the formalization of summitry and the dynamism of the Franco-German alliance failed in the mid-1970s to invigorate the EC. For all their apparent commitment to European integration, Giscard and Schmidt made little effort to get the EC out of the abyss. Indeed, their highly personalized style accentuated and initially perpetuated one of the EC's gaping weaknesses at the time: the feebleness and impotence of the Commission. Only in the late 1970s, thanks in part to Commission president Roy Jenkins's role in launching the European Monetary System (EMS), did the Commission regain its confidence and sense of purpose.

The decade after de Gaulle's departure was dispiriting but nonetheless decisive in the EU's history. The oil price shocks, economic recession, bloated CAP, and recalcitrant British severely tested EC solidarity, especially in view of the optimism generated by the "Spirit of The Hague." Yet the EC survived and ultimately emerged in the early 1980s with a powerful European Council, a directly elected European Parliament (EP), a procedure for foreign policy cooperation, and a fledgling monetary system. More important, perhaps, the trials and tribulations of the 1970s convinced leaders in national governments, the Commission, and the EP of the urgent need for institutional reform and policy innovation. As a result, the years between 1969 and 1979 represent not only a transition in the postwar international system that tested the EC's resilience but also a critical bridge between the Community's early attainments and later triumphs.

THE SPIRIT OF THE HAGUE

Pompidou, de Gaulle's successor as president of France, held the key to the EC's development in the immediate aftermath of the general's resignation. Having served as prime minister for much of the 1960s, Pompidou was steeped in Gaullism. But de Gaulle had dismissed Pompidou in the immediate aftermath of the student unrest in 1968, and relations between them had quickly soured. Pompidou exacted sweet revenge by winning the presidential election in 1969. To what extent would personal bitterness color the new president's European policy?

Pompidou was intelligent, sophisticated, and highly educated. By nature cautious and conservative, he had finely honed political skills and instincts. Pompidou was too clever to let personal pique dictate his European policy. Instead, he sought to balance Gaullist hostility toward integration on the one hand with growing resentment throughout the EC against French obduracy on the other. This balancing act inevitably caused Pompidou domestic political difficulty. In order to appease the right, Pompidou had to emphasize his Gaullist lineage; in order to win support in the center of the French political spectrum, he had to encourage a departure from the past.

In one respect, Pompidou was unashamedly Gaullist. Like the general before him, Pompidou rejected supranationalism and espoused intergovernmentalism. Pompidou's election manifesto unequivocally advocated a confederalist rather than a federalist Europe. In other respects, Pompidou was far less dogmatic. Enlargement posed a particular dilemma. For Gaullist diehards, although not necessarily for de Gaulle himself, the veto of Britain's application had become sacrosanct. Yet for a growing portion of the French public and for France's EC partners, revoking the veto was the only means by which France could possibly retain influence and credibility in the EC.

Regardless of Pompidou's personal and political preferences, there was an obvious objective change in France's circumstances in the late 1960s that impelled the president toward accepting enlargement. The events of 1968 had enfeebled France economically. High inflation and a deteriorating balance of trade were a consequence of de Gaulle's generous wage settlement with the unions and his loose monetary policy to boost recovery and stimulate growth. The result was a run on the franc that culminated in Pompidou's decision to devalue in August 1969. These persistent economic and monetary problems lowered France's international standing and made continued French participation in the EC more important than ever before. Consequently, Pompidou was in a far weaker position than de Gaulle to veto British membership.

Just as France had declined economically in the late 1960s, Germany had surged ahead. Here was another objective consideration that affected Pompidou's range of EC policy options. Not only was Germany economically resurgent but under the new chancellor, Willy Brandt, the Federal Republic was also politically assertive. Gone were the days of Adenauer's subservience to de Gaulle. Germany's refusal to arrest the declining value of the franc by revaluing the mark emphasized Bonn's determination to assert itself internationally. In addition, the new German government was about to launch an ambitious initiative toward Eastern Europe and the Soviet Union. The combination of Germany's growing economic power and rising political confidence made enlargement a more appealing alternative for Pompidou. Together, Britain and France might counterbalance Germany's increasing weight and establish geopolitical symmetry in the EC.

As foreign minister in the Grand Coalition government of the mid-1960s, Brandt had taken the first tentative steps in the bold new direction of "normalizing" Germany's relations with the East. As chancellor of the Social Democratic–Free Democratic coalition that came to power in September 1969, Brandt elevated *Ostpolitik* to a central tenet of German foreign policy. The Christian Democrats, in opposition for the first time in the history of the Federal Republic, reacted predictably by denouncing *Ostpolitik* as a sellout of German interests in the East and a threat to Germany's ties in the West.[1]

Just as German unification in 1990 prompted speculation in the EC that Germany's foreign policy orientation would drift to the East, so too twenty years earlier did *Ostpolitik* raise the specter for Germany's allies of a rootless, neutralist Federal Republic loosening its moorings in the West. Allied and internal Christian Democratic concern about *Ostpolitik* obliged Brandt to emphasize his support for European integration, which in any event he genuinely espoused. Moreover, Brandt stressed the importance of British accession as a means of reassuring those member states who feared Germany's resurgence. In Britain, Prime Minister Harold Wilson used *Ostpolitik* to further his goal of EC entry by arguing that British accession would restrain German nationalist ambition. In France, Pompidou similarly cited *Ostpolitik* as a reason for enlargement. Whether or not Pompidou deliberately exploited *Ostpolitik* in order to undermine Gaullist opposition to British entry, undoubtedly he harbored genuine misgivings about the consequences for the EC of Germany's new foreign policy initiative.

Apprehensive about the possible impact of *Ostpolitik* and under pressure to launch an initiative of his own in the EC, Pompidou called for a special summit of the EC's heads of state and government in December 1969. The Hague summit—the Netherlands then held the rotating EC presidency—was the first meeting of EC leaders since the tenth-anniversary celebration of the Treaty of Rome in 1967. With de Gaulle gone and enlargement once again at center stage, most member states anticipated a decisive breakthrough. Frustration with the EC's poor political performance in the 1960s even caused an unusual demonstration at the summit of public support for European integration.[2]

The summit spawned the "Spirit of The Hague," a belief that the EC was once more on the move. Especially in view of what had happened in the mid-1960s and what would happen in the mid-1970s, the summit assumed a retrospective aura of harmony and unprecedented progress. Yet this atmosphere belied the reality of a tense encounter between Pompidou, trying to square the Gaullist circle, and the others, led by an assertive Brandt determined to force the issue of British entry. The summit's concluding sanction of Pompidou's catchphrase "completion, deepening, enlargement" disguised the continuing tension between France and the Five but met the disparate demands of the main protagonists—including Britain, hovering in the wings.

It was no accident that "enlargement" came after "completion" and "deepening." At the summit, Pompidou endorsed enlargement in principle but called first for a strengthening of existing Community competences. "Completion" meant finalizing the financing of the CAP, a cherished French objective put in abeyance since the 1965 crisis. Negotiating a financial regulation for the CAP and funding the EC by its own resources would inevitably involve reopening the debate about the EP's budgetary powers, a price Pompidou seemed willing to pay.

"Deepening" meant extending EC competences beyond existing policies and activities. Specifically, Pompidou advocated a system of foreign policy cooperation through regular meetings of foreign ministers and, possibly, the establishment of a secretariat in Paris. This smacked to the others of a revival of de Gaulle's Fouchet Plan, although they by no means rejected the idea of attempting to coordinate member states' foreign policies. Especially in the context of *Ostpolitik*, member states quickly grasped the importance of at least exchanging information on foreign policy issues of mutual interest. Accordingly, the heads of state and government appointed Etienne Davignon, a senior Belgian foreign ministry official, to prepare a report during Belgium's forthcoming Council presidency.

The devaluation of August 1969 and the consequent recognition that Germany's economy had become the driving force within the EC prompted Pompidou also to propose deepening the EC by coordinating the member states' monetary policies. Pompidou realized that further monetary instability would endanger the CAP by exposing farm prices to parity fluctuations. Brandt had little time for the CAP; during the Hague summit he repeatedly attacked the rapid accumulation of agricultural surpluses. Nevertheless he supported the idea of closer monetary policy coordination, not least as a means of demonstrating Germany's commitment to the EC in the face of Allied concern about *Ostpolitik*. But Brandt would not consider monetary cooperation in isolation. An ingrained fear of inflation led him also to urge greater economic convergence in the EC. Pierre Werner, prime minister of Luxembourg, agreed to draft a report on EMU by the middle of the new year.

As for enlargement, Pompidou refused to set a target date for the beginning, let alone the end, of accession negotiations. On the contrary, he insisted that a new system for financing the CAP would have to be agreed to before exploratory talks with the candidate countries could begin. The Dutch countered with the opposite argument—that a financial regulation for the CAP should be concluded only when the EC agreed upon a timetable for enlargement. A bilateral meeting between Pompidou and Brandt on the margins of the summit provided the basis for a breakthrough. It was a classic EC compromise: In return for a commitment from the Five to resolve the CAP's funding by the end of the year, France assured the others that enlargement negotiations would begin by June 1970. To save face for the French, the summit communiqué omitted any mention of a timetable for the accession talks, but the Dutch prime minister made no secret in his closing press conference of the French climbdown.[3]

The Spirit of The Hague soon bore fruit in an agreement to fund the CAP by granting the EC its own resources, consisting of all levies on agricultural products and duties on industrial goods imported into the EC, as well as a small portion (not to exceed 1 percent) of national revenues from value-added tax. By contrast with the original June 1965 proposals that sparked the empty chair crisis, the agreement granted the EP modest budgetary powers. Members of the EP would have an opportunity to modify the budget but could increase its overall amount only within certain narrow limits. Foreign ministers approved the new arrangement in an amendment to the Treaty of Rome on April 22, 1970, subject to ratification by the member states.[4] Even in France, ratification proceeded smoothly.

The 1970 budgetary agreement marks an important stage of the EC's development. Undoubtedly the acquisition "of clearly defined financial resources accruing directly to the Community and the expansion of the Parliament's budgetary authority were major steps on the path toward political integration."[5] Yet the 1970 agreement contained a serious flaw. Although it took place after the Hague summit had approved enlargement in principle, the applicant member states were not consulted. The consequence of this became apparent almost immediately after Britain's accession. Because it imported far more agricultural produce and industrial goods from outside the EC, Britain, like Germany, would become a net contributor to the budget. The Council recognized this anomaly but, largely at French insistence, went ahead and concluded the agreement anyway. In doing so, it sowed the seeds of the bitter British budgetary question that dominated the EC in the early 1980s.[6]

Progress on "deepening" the EC was less marked than on completing the financial regulation of the CAP. Efforts to coordinate foreign, economic, and monetary policies encountered not only inevitable differences of interpretation and enthusiasm among member states but also an increasingly complex and hostile international environment. The attempt to coordinate member states' foreign policies fared best. Davignon's report, submitted to the Council in May 1970 and adopted the following October, struck the lowest common denominator. Instead of advocating a permanent secretariat in Paris, as Pompidou had proposed, Davignon avoided altogether the issue of a secretariat and therefore of a location. He suggested that European Political Cooperation (EPC) consist of biannual meetings of foreign ministers and more frequent meetings of their political directors, with the country in the Council presidency presiding also over EPC and providing the necessary support.[7]

Germany immediately seized upon EPC as a means of building an EC-wide base for *Ostpolitik*. At the first meeting of the six foreign ministers "in EPC"—as distinct from a meeting of the Council of Ministers—in November 1970 during Germany's presidency, the German foreign minister stressed the importance of EPC as a potential contribution to détente in Europe. By that time *Ostpolitik* was well on track, but with only a narrow majority of seats in the German parliament, Brandt was especially vulnerable to continuing Christian Democratic criticism. EPC helped quell the domestic opposition's clamor by providing an additional forum in which Brandt could explain his Eastern initiative to Germany's Western neighbors.

Of those neighbors, France remained the most skeptical of Germany's new foreign policy orientation. A desire to appease France, and thereby indirectly to appease the domestic opposition, motivated Brandt's approach to EMU as well as to EPC. In October 1970 Werner presented an ambitious seven-stage plan to achieve EMU within ten years by means of institutional reform and closer political integration.[8] The plan glossed over the contending French and German emphases on monetary measures and economic policy coordination by proposing parallel progress in both spheres. A related difference between Paris and Bonn soon emerged over the scope and possible implementation of the plan. Although a firm supporter of monetary policy coordination, Pompidou was loath to take any measure likely to advance supranationalism. Brandt and other national leaders, by contrast, saw the plan as an ideal opportunity to achieve closer integration.

THE FIRST ENLARGEMENT

Franco-German friction over EMU and *Ostpolitik* was not unrelated to the enlargement negotiations then under way. Pompidou surely appreciated that once in the EC, Britain would support his gradualist position, whereas Brandt similarly sensed that agreement to quicken the pace of EMU would be harder to get after enlargement took place. As Brandt was willing to sacrifice a bolder position on EMU for the sake of *Ostpolitik* and supported British entry partly for the same reason, the question was moot from Germany's point of view. From the French point of view, Britain's well-known suspicion of supranationalism was a source of comfort. Although as a good Gaullist Pompidou had misgivings about the British, he could take some solace from Britain's record of Euroskepticism.

Ironically, Edward Heath, who replaced Wilson as prime minister in 1970, was the most Europhilic of British politicians. Heath enthusiastically championed his country's application and deeply regretted the lost opportunity of the early 1960s, when he had negotiated Britain's abortive entry effort. Few of Heath's fellow Conservatives shared the prime minister's ardor for European integration; they saw EC membership largely in negative terms—as Britain's only feasible option. On the other side of the political divide, the issue continued to split the Labour Party. Wilson, the Labour leader, who as prime minister in 1967 had led Britain's second entry effort, now equivocated. As the entry negotiations unfolded, Wilson moved from ambivalence toward open opposition of British accession, bringing the bulk of Labour with him. Jenkins, a future Commission president, led an increasingly isolated pro-EC group in the right wing of the party.[9]

The entry negotiations began on June 30, 1970, in Luxembourg and ended almost a year later in Brussels. Most of the work was done at the permanent representatives' level, although meetings at ministers' level took place regularly. Familiar issues from Britain's previous applications soon resurfaced. However, the talks were far less contentious and protracted than in the early 1960s. For one thing, Heath was so eager for membership that his approach seemed to be "to gain entry, and then to sort out any differences."[10] For another, Commonwealth and EFTA concerns about British membership in the EC had abated in the intervening decade. The impact on the Commonwealth of Britain's accession now focused exclusively on specific problems, such as imports of Caribbean sugar and New Zealand dairy products. Nevertheless, the negotiations occasionally stalled, particularly on the controversial questions of Britain's budgetary contribution during the transition phase and the related issue of the dubious benefit to Britain of the CAP.

A meeting between Heath and Pompidou in Paris on May 20–21, 1971, helped resolve the outstanding problems. According to the usually understated *Times* of London, relations between the two leaders reached a "dizzy pinnacle of mutual admiration" at the Paris tête-à-tête.[11] The surprisingly close rapport between Pompidou and Heath led some observers to speculate that France had finally jettisoned its lingering opposition to enlargement. Together with the contemporaneous deterioration in relations between Pompidou and Brandt, it also caused speculation that the Paris-London axis would replace the Paris-Bonn axis as the main bilateral motor of Community development, or at least that the Paris-Bonn axis might broaden into a trilateral axis that included Britain.[12]

A British government white paper published in July 1971 summarized the results of the accession negotiations and extolled the arguments in favor of entry. "Our country will be more secure," the document declared, "our ability to maintain peace and promote development in the world greater, our economy stronger, and our industries and people more prosperous, if we join the European Communities than if we remain outside them." On the sensitive question of sovereignty, the white paper blithely asserted that "there is no question of any erosion of essential national sovereignty; what is proposed is a sharing and an enlargement of individual national sovereignties in the general interest."[13] Such patent dissimulation infuriated opponents of entry and left a painful legacy for those in Britain today who advocate greater integration.

The government's proclivity for exaggeration and falsification kindled the highly flammable domestic debate on enlargement. To the government's undisguised joy, the Labour Party suffered most in the ensuing conflagration. Whether motivated by conviction or opportunism, Wilson denounced Heath's entry terms and declared that a Labour government would renegotiate Britain's membership terms. Nudged by growing anti-EC sentiment in his party, Wilson moved farther to the left, marooning Jenkins, the deputy leader, on the right. With ratification of British accession looming in 1972, strife within the Labour Party became more and more pronounced.

Pompidou's surprise announcement in March 1972 of a French referendum on enlargement, to be held on April 23, stunned the British government and boosted the antimarketeers. Despite British government fears of French backsliding on enlargement, domestic rather than international political calculations had inspired Pompidou's decision. A snap referendum provided a clever means of splitting the increasingly united opposition by driving a wedge between the Communists, who opposed the mere existence of the EC, and the Socialists, who favored British entry.[14] Referendums were a hallmark of Gaullist government; it seemed especially appropriate to use a widely recognized Gaullist instrument to undermine an equally well identifiable Gaullist position on the EC.

The great danger, as de Gaulle's last referendum clearly demonstrated and President Mitterrand's 1992 referendum on the Treaty on European Union (TEU) nearly demonstrated, was that Pompidou could lose. In the event, he easily won, but not as convincingly as expected. Only 60 percent of the French electorate bothered to vote. Of that number, an astonishingly high 7 percent spoiled their ballots, 32 percent voted against, and only 61 percent voted for. The result, like the reason for the referendum, should be seen in domestic political terms. The relatively low number of French voters who endorsed enlargement reflected Pompidou's popularity more than the merits of Britain's case.[15]

British opponents of enlargement exploited the French referendum to embarrass Heath's government into holding a referendum in Britain on EC membership. With the three other applicant countries—Denmark, Ireland, and Norway—all holding referendums on enlargement, British antimarketeers cited the French case as an additional reason to adopt such a procedure. Pompidou's decision to consult the electorate directly did nothing to change Heath's opposition to a referendum, but it helped push Wilson into the pro-referendum camp, prompting Jenkins's resignation from the Labour Party's front bench.[16]

The question of EC membership was even more contentious in Norway, where a narrow majority voted against accession in the referendum of September 24–25, 1972. Although the referendum result was not binding, the prime minister had already promised to resign in the event of a no vote. The government sought to reassure the electorate about the consequences of membership, especially for fishing and agriculture—even more protected in Norway than in the EC—and the fledgling oil industry. After a bitterly contested campaign that polarized Norwegian opinion, 53.5 percent voted against accession. True to his word, the prime minister resigned two weeks later. Only in the early 1990s, in response to the pull of the single market, did Norway reopen the domestic debate on EC membership. What followed, culminating in a negative referendum result in 1994, was an uncanny rerun of 1972.

Passions also ran high in Denmark, but the referendum there—held only one week after the Norwegian vote and binding on the government—resulted in an impressive endorsement of membership. Like the British, the Danes were, and remain, skeptical about European integration. Once Britain applied for membership, however, Denmark had little option but to follow suit. With the bulk of the country's exports going to Britain and Germany, it would have been economic suicide for Denmark to stay out of the enlarged EC. Despite familiar fears about the erosion of national sovereignty and the possible severance of traditional ties with the Nordic countries, 63 percent voted in favor of accession.

The Irish referendum, held on May 10, 1972, registered strong support for EC membership. Far more than Denmark's, Ireland's economic fortunes were tied to those of Britain. It would have been absurd economically for Ireland to stay outside the EC once Britain went in. Added to this sense of economic determinism were complementary elements of opportunism and political calculation. The former had to do with the expected windfall for Irish farmers of participation in the CAP, as well as a host of other benefits, mostly in the form of grants and loans, that would accrue to Ireland in the EC. The latter consisted of the anticipated impact of EC membership on Anglo-Irish relations. Despite becoming independent in 1922, Ireland remained relatively isolated from Europe, bound up instead in a suffocatingly close relationship with Britain. EC membership afforded Ireland the chance to place Anglo-Irish relations in a broader, more equitable, multilateral context. It was little wonder that a resounding 83 percent endorsed accession in the 1972 referendum.[17]

Therefore, of the four applicant states that had signed accession agreements, only three joined the EC on January 1, 1973. The ratification drama continued in Britain until almost the last minute. Having survived a series of procedural hurdles, the act of accession finally won parliamentary approval in October 1972. But that was not the end either of Labour Party posturing or of British misgivings about the EC. On the contrary, British—and Danish—aversion to European integration, the inevitable strains of absorbing three new member states, and a hostile international economic environment combined in the mid-1970s to put the newly enlarged EC sorely to the test.

FROM EUROSUMMIT TO EUROSLUMP

The Paris summit of October 19–20, 1972, which Pompidou convened to set the EC's agenda in the postenlargement period, marks the high point of Euro-optimism in the 1970s. The summit is famous—or infamous—for the last sentence of a "solemn declaration" that prefixed the concluding communiqué: "The member states of the Community, the driving force of European construction, affirm their intention before the end of the present decade to transform the whole complex of their relations into a European Union."[18] This was an extraordinary statement even by the standard of Eurorhetoric. Although nobody knew quite what "European Union" meant, the commitment to achieve it within eight years put an unnecessary and ultimately embarrassing onus on the member states. As the 1970s passed and nothing remotely resembling European union appeared on the horizon, the Paris Declaration served only to highlight the extent of the EC's disarray.

Yet at the time, the Paris Declaration played well politically in national capitals. The text was sufficiently warm and woolly to escape excessive criticism even in London and Copenhagen. The communiqué also struck a positive chord by expressing the EC's readiness to launch an impressive array of new initiatives. Apart from making inevitable references to EMU and EPC, the communiqué mentioned regional policy, industrial policy, energy, and the environment. Compared with the laundry list produced after the Hague summit, this was a striking catalog of Community "deepening."

Pompidou's apparent retreat from Gaullism should not be exaggerated, however. A close reading of the communiqué, supplemented by reports of the two-day meeting, suggests that the summit did not represent a radical departure from previous French policy. Pompidou advocated the European Regional Development Fund (ERDF) mostly in deference to Heath, who desperately needed to achieve something at the summit from which Britain might profit directly. Coming in the wake of the bitter accession debate, Heath saw the Paris summit largely in domestic political terms. A promise of financial assistance for depressed industrial and agricultural regions would offset criticism in Britain of the high cost of EC membership.

Pompidou's willingness to help Heath emphasized the rapport between the two leaders and fueled further speculation about a new Anglo-French axis. By contrast, the vaunted Franco-German axis seemed moribund. Personally, Pompidou had little time for Brandt ever since the chancellor stole the show at the Hague summit; politically, Brandt's repeated criticism of the CAP greatly angered the French president. In keeping with his complaints about unwarranted EC expenditure, voiced all the more loudly in the prelude to the approaching federal elections, Brandt distrusted the proposed Regional Fund, which looked too much like "an exercise in old-fashioned, pork-barrel politics rather than a political instrument for the unification of Europe."[19]

The vexing question of economic and monetary policy remained the greatest cause of friction between Paris and Bonn. In the eighteen months before the Paris summit, monetary matters had dominated European and wider international affairs. Apart from the inherently different French and German approaches to EMU, the collapse of the postwar system of fixed exchange rates had triggered markedly divergent reactions in both countries. In response to the May 1971 monetary crisis, caused by a reduction of interest rates in the United States and the consequent run on the dollar in favor of the more stable German mark, Brandt had advocated either that EC member states together float their currencies or that Germany alone do so. Immediate economic concerns, as well as a desire to appease Washington at a time of growing U.S. annoyance over both *Ostpolitik* and the cost of maintaining troops in Europe, motivated the chancellor. By contrast, Pompidou opposed a joint float because of its likely impact on the competitiveness of European products and because of lack of sympathy with the U.S. plight.

Although Pompidou's position softened in the summer of 1971, President Richard Nixon's announcement on August 15 that year of the suspension of dollar convertibility and the imposition of restrictive trade measures reopened a sensitive subject in Franco-German relations. At their meeting on August 20, EC finance ministers failed to agree on a joint response and instead issued a bland communiqué expressing concern about the U.S. action. A more harmonious finance ministers' meeting one month later led to pointed criticism of the United States and presaged a concerted Community approach to the Smithsonian talks of December 1971 that sought to repair the system.

The currency crises of 1971 had long-lasting effects and helped send European economies slipping into recession. Corrective measures in early 1972 had the unfortunate but predictable impact of fueling inflation. Circumstances were hardly propitious for the fledgling EMU, although the collapse of the international monetary system inevitably increased calls among the Six for closer coordination of economic and monetary policy. In April 1972 the Six hatched the "snake," a regimen to keep EC currency fluctuations within a 2.5 percent margin inside the "tunnel" established during the Smithsonian talks. Worried especially about the consequences of currency fluctuations for the CAP, Pompidou put EMU high on the agenda of the Paris summit. In response to Pompidou's call for exchange rate stability, Brandt stressed the importance of anti-inflationary measures. The result was a reaffirmation at the Paris summit of the need for parallel progress on economic and monetary measures. Recalling the member states' aspiration to European union by the end of the decade, the summit communiqué reiterated the heads of state and government's commitment to EMU "with a view to its completion not later than December 31, 1980."[20]

Continuing exchange rate fluctuations and divergences of member states' monetary and economic policies almost immediately made nonsense of the 1980 target date. Throughout 1973 soaring inflation, rising unemployment, yawning trade deficits, and a worsening oil crisis undermined the EC. The pernicious impact of those developments was blatantly obvious at the next summit, held in Copenhagen on December 14–15, 1973. Once again Pompidou called for the meeting, this time in a vain attempt to restore solidarity in the aftermath of the October 1973 Middle East war, the massive hike in oil prices, and the onset of the oil embargo.

The heads of state and government could not agree at the Copenhagen summit on how to respond to the impending oil shortage. Nor did the Commission provide much direction. To make matters worse, discussion of energy policy (or the lack thereof) became inauspiciously linked to other contentious issues, notably the fate of the ERDF and the far larger question of relations with the United States.

Differences in approaches to economic planning would have made it difficult in any case for member states to approve a common energy policy in the mid-1970s. The immediate impact of the October 1973 price hike and embargo—approximately 63 percent of the EC's energy needs were met by Middle East oil—shattered any prospect of a joint Community approach. With the port of Rotterdam targeted for total embargo, the Netherlands was worst hit at the beginning of the crisis. Germany supported the Netherlands' call at the Copenhagen summit for a concerted EC response. Britain and France, jealous to preserve what they considered their close relationships with the Arab oil-producing countries, strove to stifle discussion of a common energy policy. A declaration on energy policy attached to the summit communiqué included such platitudes as the need for an "orderly functioning of a common market for energy" and "concerted and equitable measures to limit energy consumption."[21]

The arrival of a group of Arab foreign ministers offering to ease the oil embargo in return for EC diplomatic support in the Middle East threw the summit into greater disarray. Policy toward the Middle East, as opposed to the possible development of a common energy policy, came under the rubric of EPC, a process already notorious for its propensity to promote fudging. Earlier, EC foreign ministers had produced a declaration that leaned toward the Arab position, a development pleasing to the oil producers.[22] At the summit itself, Germany and the Netherlands succeeded in toning down some of the more blatant pro-Arab points that Britain and France wanted to include in the communiqué's statement on the Middle East.

Member states' efforts to formulate a common position on the Middle East greatly exacerbated transatlantic tension. Apart from the substance of such a position, the fact that the Nine discussed sensitive international issues without consulting the United States bolstered Washington's negative perception of EPC. Incipient trade disputes, caused largely by the CAP, were a growing irritant in Euro-American relations. Additionally, in 1970 and 1971 the United States bitterly resented Europe's apparent unwillingness to relieve pressure on the dollar and to share more of the expense of keeping U.S. troops overseas. The August 1971 monetary crisis was due in part to Nixon's frustration with his European allies.

U.S. Secretary of State Henry Kissinger's response to the deteriorating U.S.-EC relationship was typically extravagant: a call for a "New Atlantic Charter" as part of the United States' "Year of Europe" in 1973.[23] This prompted the Nine to adopt their own "Document on the European Identity" at the end of the year.[24] A visit to Washington, D.C., by the Danish foreign minister in September 1973 to discuss transatlantic relations emphasized the point of Kissinger's legendary question: "Who speaks for Europe?" Denmark, then in the Council presidency, played the part that Kissinger thought should be reserved for a larger country.

Washington's brinkmanship during the Middle East war further strained Euro-American relations, as did Kissinger's call for a coordinated Western response to the subsequent oil crisis. The ensuing effort to formulate a joint consumers' approach exposed deep transatlantic tension, as well as considerable disarray in the EC. France opposed the initiative, fearing a U.S. attempt to monopolize the West's response and preferring both bilateral consumer-producer contacts on particular supply problems and multilateral negotiations in the UN on general political and economic differences. Germany, then in the Council presidency, angered France by supporting the U.S. position and criticizing bilateral consumer-producer deals.

Sharp differences between France and Germany reflected tension at the top between Pompidou and Brandt. Pompidou never overcame his distrust of *Ostpolitik*, which by 1973 had brought about treaties between the Federal Republic and Moscow, Warsaw, and Prague; a four-power (Britain, France, Soviet Union, and United States) agreement on Berlin; and an accord between the two Germanys. Thereafter the pace of Germany's diplomatic offensive in the East inevitably slowed down. But it was too late to restore harmonious relations between Pompidou and Brandt. Impaired by an illness that would soon prove fatal and fed regular doses of Germanophobia by his egregious foreign minister, Pompidou never raised his opinion of Brandt.

Nor were Brandt's relations with Heath much more cordial. British efforts to establish the ERDF in 1973 ran into repeated German opposition. With Britain's economy rapidly deteriorating and opposition to EC membership growing, Heath more than ever needed to negotiate generous EC regional funding. Secure in office after the 1972 federal elections and concerned about the nature and extent of EC expenditure, Brandt had no reason to budge. Conflict came to a head at the Copenhagen summit, when Heath blocked discussion on energy policy as long as Germany blocked a resolution on the ERDF. Given that EC energy policy was already in disarray, Heath did not have much leverage. The issue of regional funding was still unresolved when Heath left office, deeply disillusioned with Germany's policy in the EC.

The 1973 oil crisis had exacerbated deep divisions in the EC and inflamed relations between the leaders of its three most important member states. Within six months of the Copenhagen summit, however, the leadership of all three countries changed hands. In April 1974 Pompidou died, and on May 19 Giscard d'Estaing won the presidential election. Two weeks before Giscard's victory, Brandt resigned from office following the arrest of his personal assistant on charges of spying for East Germany; Helmut Schmidt, Brandt's finance minister, became the new chancellor. In Britain, Wilson returned to office after Labour's February 1974 election victory. The new constellation of leaders, and the domestic issues they faced, had an obvious impact on the EC. Wilson's indifference to EC membership and demand for a renegotiation of Heath's entry terms inevitably lessened Britain's importance and influence in Brussels. At the same time, Giscard and Schmidt grew increasingly close personally and politically, firmly reestablishing the primacy of the Franco-German axis in EC affairs. This was insufficient to pull the EC out of the doldrums, but undoubtedly the emergence of the Giscard-Schmidt duopoly helped the EC survive continuing economic crisis and portended its revival in the early 1980s.

BRITAIN'S RENEGOTIATION AND REFERENDUM

An Awkward Partner is the title of Stephen George's well-known book on Britain in the EU. The extent of British awkwardness became fully apparent in 1974, after Wilson's narrow general election victory. The French foreign minister scathingly contrasted Heath, "a man of the Rhine," with Wilson, "a man of the Scilly Isles" (a remote resort where Wilson had a holiday cottage).[25] For all his frustration over the ERDF, Heath was undoubtedly committed to European integration. Wilson, by contrast, personified Britain's ambivalence toward the EC and led a political party bitterly divided on the question of continued membership. The Labour Party manifesto for the February election promised a renegotiation of Britain's accession agreement. Having won the election, Wilson and James Callaghan, his foreign secretary, duly pursued the matter with their Community counterparts.

Giscard d'Estaing, the new French president, strongly opposed Britain's renegotiation of EC membership terms. Although conceding the validity of Britain's budgetary claim, Giscard was unconvinced that a successful renegotiation would end British dissatisfaction with the EC and unsatisfactoriness in the EC. German chancellor Helmut Schmidt was more sympathetic toward Wilson, a fellow socialist. Ultimately, Schmidt brokered the dispute between Giscard and Wilson.

Callaghan got the renegotiations off to a bad start at a Council meeting in April 1974, infuriating his fellow foreign ministers by reading them sections of the Labour Party manifesto. Apart from a recalculation of Britain's budgetary contribution, Callaghan's various demands included CAP reform, protection of Commonwealth interests, and retention of British parliamentary sovereignty. Other member states were able or willing to budge only on the budgetary and Commonwealth issues, although there was considerable resentment of the fact that the latter meant Wilson's personal preference for New Zealand dairy products.

What followed epitomized the EC's languor in the mid-1970s. The renegotiations lasted eleven months, dominated two summits, and drove Britain's partners to distraction. It is difficult to refute Jenkins's observation that the entire episode "produced the minimum results with the maximum ill-will."[26] At the expense of Britain's prestige in Europe, Wilson seemed to be engaged in a frantic effort to hold the Labour Party together. In the run-up to the October 1974 general election, the second in less than a year, Wilson pledged either another general election or a referendum to validate the renegotiation result. Labour's overall majority in the October 1974 election kept the question of continued EC membership at the top of the political agenda.

Jenkins credits Schmidt not only with successfully concluding the renegotiations but also with convincing a majority of Labour Party members to stay in the EC. Schmidt visited Britain in November 1974 and made a hugely successful speech at the Labour Party conference. At the same time he coached Wilson privately on the approach to take with Giscard. Schmidt's most valuable piece of advice was for the prime minister to signal clearly, before the Paris summit on December 9–10, 1974, his personal commitment to continued British membership in the event of a satisfactory renegotiation of the original entry terms. This Wilson did in a speech in London a week before the summit began. Schmidt also organized a private dinner between Giscard and Wilson on the eve of the summit, from which the British and French leaders emerged with a better understanding of each other's positions.[27]

Agreement at the Paris summit on the size of the ERDF undoubtedly appeased Wilson. Although Schmidt, like Brandt before him, desperately wanted to contain EC spending, he lacked Brandt's personal prejudice against granting Britain large-scale regional assistance. In the end, the fund was not as large as Heath had originally hoped, but Britain's share would be a sizable 28 percent. Italy, Ireland, and France would be the other main beneficiaries.[28]

A way to break the deadlock over Britain's budgetary contribution emerged at the end of the Paris summit after protracted Anglo-French wrangling: The Commission would design a "correcting mechanism" to prevent Britain, or any other member state, from paying too much into the EC. Based on the Commission's formula, the heads of state and government would decide at a summit in Dublin in March 1975 on the size of Britain's refund. As expected, Wilson announced that the government would hold a referendum on June 5 to decide whether Britain would stay in the EC, on the basis of the Dublin agreement.[29]

The Commission published its report—quaintly entitled *The Unacceptable Situation and the Correcting Mechanism*—on January 30, 1975.

Based on it, a committee of experts worked frantically through the first night of the Dublin summit to come up with an acceptable British rebate. A successful conclusion seemed to hinge on satisfying Wilson's demand for assurances about New Zealand dairy imports. Finally, out of tedium or despair, the other eight acceded to the New Zealand dairy request, and Wilson agreed that the correcting mechanism yielded a reasonable figure on which to base his referendum campaign for Britain to stay in the EC.

Regardless of its impact on public opinion, the result of Britain's lengthy renegotiation had failed to reunite the Labour Party. On the other side of the House, the Conservative Party had more than its fair share of Euroskeptics, yet the vast majority of its members favored staying in the EC. Margaret Thatcher's first major speech as the newly elected Conservative Party leader was on the referendum issue. Though deploring the constitutional precedent of a popular referendum, she strongly advocated a yes vote. With the leadership of the two main parties and the small Liberal Party urging a positive result, the outcome of the referendum was hardly in doubt. Of the 64 percent of the electorate who turned out, 67 percent voted for and 33 percent against staying in the EC.

Four days after the referendum, Wilson told the House of Commons that "the debate is now over . . . the historic decision has been made. . . . We look forward to continuing to work with [our partners] in promoting the Community's wider interests and in fostering a greater sense of purpose among the member states."[30] By then it was difficult to repair the damage of the renegotiation either inside or outside Britain. At home, according to Jenkins, "the handling of the European question by the leadership throughout the 1970s did more to cause the [Labour] Party's disasters of the 1980s than did any other issue."[31] Abroad, the renegotiation "added to the spirit of irritation and impatience with Britain that had been growing within the Community" since enlargement.[32] Even before Thatcher came to office in 1979 and promptly reopened the budgetary question, nothing about Britain's behavior after the referendum suggested a willingness to play a positive role in the Community. Callaghan's replacement of Wilson as prime minister in 1976 brought no appreciable change in Britain's approach. Britain's first presidency of the Community, from January to June 1977, was uninspiring, not least because some unreconstructed antimarketeers in the government had a golden opportunity to chair (and therefore stall) Council meetings.

GISCARD-SCHMIDT DUOPOLY

Although dominated by the British budgetary question and notable for the ERDF agreement, the Paris summit is now best remembered for two decisions that had a profound impact on the ECs' long-term development. The first was to hold direct elections to the EP by 1978 (later delayed until 1979); the second was to hold regular summits, henceforth known as European Councils. The move from ad hoc to institutionalized summitry reflected the need for routine meetings of the heads of state and government in order to maintain EC integrity at a time of increasing economic complexity and bureaucratic paralysis. Originally Giscard's idea, regular summits appealed also to Schmidt. With their unrivaled grasp of economic and monetary issues and their propensity to deal privately with fellow presidents and prime ministers, Giscard and Schmidt saw the European Council as an ideal forum in which to direct EC affairs. The simultaneous decision to hold direct elections to the EP was intended both to satisfy an obligation in the Treaty of Rome and to defuse criticism that the European Council would strengthen intergovernmentalism at the expense of supranationalism in the EC.

The European Council was a vehicle for the EC's most powerful politicians to thrash out thorny problems, but it did not guarantee that they would muster the political will either to find solutions or to launch new initiatives. The institutionalization of previously ad hoc summitry could not, in and of itself, revitalize the EC. On the contrary, for the next four years the EC remained in a rut because of its member states' inability or unwillingness to tackle unfavorable economic and political conditions on a Community-wide basis. The Commission was still ineffectual, and large member states failed to provide decisive leadership. Germany was strong economically but, for all Brandt's blandishments in the early 1970s, relatively unassertive politically; France was depressed economically and precarious politically, with Giscard under constant threat from left and right; Britain was feeble economically and volatile politically. Little wonder that few European Councils held in the mid-1970s are memorable today.

Nevertheless, European Councils provided a stage for the dazzling Schmidt-Giscard show that helped to maintain a modicum of integration during an otherwise inauspicious time. The affinity between the new French president and the new German chancellor was not immediate. Both had radically different characters and personalities—Giscard haughty, Olympian, condescending; Schmidt pretentiously unpretentious, moody, and temperamental, "a figure out of Wilhelm Busch, Elbe bargeman's cap and pipe."[33] But both were shrewd, incisive, and highly intelligent. Before reaching the highest office in their respective countries, both had also been unusually effective finance ministers. It was in that capacity, during the disputes over currency fluctuations in the early 1970s, that they got to know, respect, and ultimately like each other. Giscard and Schmidt spoke two common languages: economics and English.

The Privileged Partnership, the title of Haig Simonian's book on Franco-German relations in the 1970s, sums up the unique relationship between Giscard and Schmidt. They met for the first time as president and chancellor on May 31–June 1, 1974, and resolved from the outset to set Franco-German relations on a singular plane. Going well beyond the framework of the Elysée Treaty, Giscard and Schmidt got together often for dinner, spoke at least weekly on the telephone, and caucused regularly on the fringes of multilateral meetings. The frequency and diversity of their contacts set a pattern that François Mitterrand and Helmut Kohl followed a decade later. Despite the appearance of an easy Franco-German relationship based on a genuine friendship between the president and the chancellor, however, both sides worked hard to resolve occasional disputes and ease inevitable friction. As William Wallace observed, "The success of the Franco-German relationship [in the 1970s and 1980s] is a record of determination to accommodate divergent interests through positive political action, to explain and to tolerate differences and to minimize their impact; not a simple record of convergence in economic, industrial, political or security interests and outlooks."[34] This was an approach conspicuously absent from Britain's dealings with other Community member states during the same time.

The EC provided an ideal forum in which to exercise Franco-German initiative and especially to apply the personal rapport between Giscard and Schmidt. But it would be an exaggeration to say that Giscard and Schmidt single-handedly revived the EC. Given the circumstances of the mid-1970s, with the economic recession continuing unabated, it is more apt to speak of damage control than of rejuvenation. Growing economic divergence among member states undermined not only the surviving sense of political solidarity but also the prevailing extent of economic integration. Faced with soaring inflation and unemployment, member states applied an array of nontariff barriers and other protectionist measures that impeded the emergence of a single market. The prominence of issues such as budgetary contributions, monetary compensation to farmers for the impact of fluctuating exchange rates on the CAP, and Commission representation at the recently launched annual summits of major industrialized countries illustrated the extent of the malaise.

EMU was an early and inevitable victim of member state unilateralism. The Werner Plan, launched so audaciously in 1972 with a target date for full implementation of 1980, hardly got off the ground. Member state currencies wiggled in and out of the "snake." The mark, buoyed by Germany's low inflation and large trade surplus, pushed through the top; the pound, franc, and lire, weakened by their countries' high inflation and large trade deficits, fell through the bottom. By 1975 plans for EMU were quietly shelved.

Even in the best of times, Giscard and Schmidt's joint approach to EC affairs would not have facilitated the kind of all-around renaissance that the Community enjoyed in the mid-1980s. Schmidt's reported statement that

"Europe can only be brought forward by the will of a few statesmen, and not by thousands of regulations and hundreds of ministerial councils,"[35] was only half right. Schmidt and Giscard's impatience with the Commission and determination to avoid Brussels in favor of Paris and Bonn contributed to the EC's dysfunctionalism. The two leaders' infatuation with each other also alienated their fellow national leaders.

Regardless of relations among the heads of state and government, the inefficiency of the Brussels bureaucracy in the 1970s became a metaphor for the EC's decline. The Commission was dispirited and demoralized. As if to underscore its seeming unimportance, in 1972 the outgoing president, Franco Malfatti, left office early in order to stand for election to the Italian parliament. At the end of the decade Willy Haferkampf, a vice president, brought the Commission into disrepute over allegations about his extravagant traveling expenses.[36] This scandal was relatively trivial, but it reinforced the Commission's public image as being wasteful and mismanaged. Schmidt's intense dislike of the Commission reinforced Germany's reluctance to send top-rate people to Brussels as either commissioners or permanent representatives. For his part, Giscard inherited de Gaulle's antipathy toward the Commission and lost no opportunity to put its president in his place. More than the Commission's ineffectualness, however, the Council's indecisiveness lay at the root of Brussels' institutional immobility. By the early 1970s nearly 1,000 Commission proposals were said to be stuck in the decisionmaking pipeline because of the need for unanimity.

For all their supposed commitment to the Community, Giscard and Schmidt tinkered with various possible solutions but never injected into the process the political will so desperately lacking. The fate of the Tindemans Report was typical. Having been charged at the 1974 Paris summit with recommending ways to advance European integration, Belgian prime minister Leo Tindemans focused less on the lofty goal of a federal Europe than on the need for institutional reform and a modest extension of Community competence. The most controversial aspect of his report, published in January 1976, was its exploration of a possible "two-speed Europe," with differing rates of integration depending on the will and ability of each member state.[37]

Smaller member states recoiled against the prospect of first- and second-class EC membership; Britain and France fretted about a further loss of sovereignty. Giscard took the lead and stifled the report with the kind of bureaucratic asphyxiation that Tindemans had so bitterly complained about. The heads of state and government asked their foreign ministers to consider the report; the foreign ministers asked their senior officials to do so. The senior officials reported on the report to their foreign ministers; the foreign ministers reported on the report's report to the heads of state and government, who thanked Tindemans for his efforts and, as a consolation to him, called for an annual report from the Commission on progress toward European union.[38]

Another high-level report, that of the "Three Wise Men," suffered a similar fate. This had originated in a letter from Giscard to other EC leaders proposing a report on institutional reform, without requiring treaty revision, by three eminent Europeans. After the usual haggling over nationality and political orientation, the European Council settled on Barend Bushevel, a former Dutch prime minister; Edmund Dell, a former British government minister; and Robert Marjolin, a former vice president of the Commission. The wise men set about their task with enthusiasm. To the amazement of the heads of state and government, they presented their report on time, a month before the November 1979 Dublin summit.[39]

There, Giscard noted with pleasure the report's criticism of the Commission and its endorsement of the European Council. Beyond that, he did not delve too deep. After all, the report also criticized successive Council presidencies for lack of direction. France's presidency, in the first half of 1979, had been particularly poor, in part because of Giscard's anger with the outgoing EP for having passed its last budget in a form he thought illegal and in part because of his concern that the new, directly elected EP would be even more assertive. Nor did Giscard like the report's pointed observation that lack of political will was the main obstacle to the EC's revival. Thus after a perfunctory discussion of it at the Dublin summit, the report of the Three Wise Men joined the Tindemans Report in the EC's archive.

Commissioning high-level reports and then failing to act on them is a fitting comment on the European Council's activism in the late 1970s. As the decade drew to a close, the EC's fortunes looked bleak. Low economic growth, excessive unemployment, and high inflation—collectively called stagflation—plagued every member state. The political will to revive European integration was conspicuously lacking in national capitals. As the 1970s drew to a close, there were few economic, political, or institutional signs that the EC would ever turn the corner and transform itself dramatically within the next decade.

NOTES

1. See Wolfram Hanrieder, *Germany, America, Europe: Forty Years of German Foreign Policy* (New Haven: Yale University Press, 1989), p. 356.
2. See the *Times* (London), December 2, 1969, p. 1.
3. See *Le Monde*, December 3, 1969.
4. Commission, *1970 General Report*, points 515–518, 544–545.
5. Werner Feld, *West Germany and the European Community: Changing Interests and Competing Policy Objectives* (New York: Praeger, 1981), p. 13.
6. See Stephen George, *An Awkward Partner: Britain in the European Community* (Oxford: Oxford University Press, 1990), pp. 52–53.

7. "First Report of the Foreign Ministers to the Heads of State and Government of the Member States of the European Community (Luxembourg Report)," in Federal Republic of Germany, *European Political Cooperation (EPC),* 4th ed. (Wiesbaden: Press and Information Office of the Federal Government, 1982), pp. 28–35.

8. "The Werner Report on Economic and Monetary Union," Bull. EC S/11-1970.

9. See Roy Jenkins, *A Life at the Centre* (London: Macmillan, 1991), pp. 310–312.

10. George, *Awkward Partner,* p. 56.

11. *Times* (London), October 21, 1972, p. 6.

12. Haig Simonian, *The Privileged Partnership: Franco-German Relations in the European Community, 1969–1984* (Oxford: Clarendon Press, 1985), p. 114; Edward Kolodziej, *French International Policy Under de Gaulle and Pompidou: The Politics of Grandeur* (Ithaca: Cornell University Press, 1974), pp. 412–413.

13. *The UK and the European Communities,* Cmnd 4715, July 7, 1971.

14. D. Rudnick, "An Assessment of the Reasons for the Removal of the French Veto to UK Membership of the EEC," *International Relations* 14, no. 6: 658–672.

15. Kolodziej, *French Policy,* pp. 432–438.

16. Jenkins, *Centre,* pp. 327–348.

17. For an account of the 1972 referenda issues and results in Norway, Denmark, and Ireland, see Frances Nicholson and Roger East, *From the Six to the Twelve: The Enlargement of the European Communities* (Chicago: St. James Press, 1987), pp. 97–100, 113–115, 117–133.

18. Commission, *1972 General Report,* point 5.16.

19. Feld, *West Germany,* p. 67.

20. Commission, *1972 General Report,* point 5.1.

21. Commission, *1973 General Report,* Annex 1 to Chapter II, pp. 489–491.

22. "Statement of the Nine Foreign Ministers on the Situation in the Middle East," in Federal Republic of Germany, *European Political Cooperation,* pp. 55–56.

23. Henry Kissinger, *White House Years* (New York: Little, Brown, 1979), p. 1275.

24. "Document on the European Identity," in Federal Republic of Germany, *European Political Cooperation,* pp. 57–63.

25. Quoted in Roger Morgan, "The Historical Background, 1955–85," in Roger Morgan and Caroline Bray, eds., *Partners and Rivals in Western Europe: Britain, France, and Germany* (Brookfield, VT: Gower, 1986), p. 16.

26. Jenkins, *Centre,* p. 375.

27. Ibid., pp. 399–400.

28. Commission, *1974 General Report,* Annex to Chapter I, point 24.

29. Nicholson and East, *Enlargement,* pp. 165–180.

30. Quoted in ibid., p. 180.

31. Jenkins, *Centre,* p. 342.

32. George, *Awkward Partner,* p. 87.

33. James Goldsborough, "The Franco-German Entente," *Foreign Affairs* 54, no. 3 (April 1976): 499.

34. William Wallace, introduction to Morgan and Bray, *Partners,* p. 4.

35. Jonathan Storey, "The Franco-German Alliance Within the European Community," *World Today* (June 1980): 209.

36. The *Economist* broke the story on January 27, 1979, p. 43.

37. Bull. EC S/1-1976.

38. See A. N. Duff, "The Report of the Three Wise Men," *Journal of Common Market Studies* 19, no. 3: 238; and Bull. EC 11-1976, "Presidency Conclusions," point 2427.

39. Commission, *1979 General Report*, point 8; Bull. EC 11-1979, "Presidency Conclusions," points 1.5.1 to 1.5.2.

4

Turning the Corner, 1979–1984

At the beginning of the 1980s, there were few outward signs that the EC had survived the challenges of the 1970s. The twenty-fifth anniversary of the Treaty of Rome, observed in March 1982, was a dismal affair. Remarking on a report that the Council had canceled the official celebration, the president of the European Parliament (EP) compared the Community to "a feeble cardiac patient whose condition is so poor that he cannot even be disturbed by a birthday party."[1]

Academics were equally alarmed by the patient's precarious health. In *The European Community: Progress or Decline?* five prominent professors from five member states expressed their concern. Unusual in an academic publication, the opening paragraph got straight to the point: "This report is born out of a sense of alarm and urgency. The authors, with their different backgrounds as citizens of large or small member states . . . all share the conviction that Western Europe is drifting [and] that the existence of the European Community is under serious threat. . . . If nothing is done, we are faced with the disintegration of the most important European achievement since World War II."[2] As if to prove their point, the European Council at Athens in December 1983 ended in ignominy. For the first time in the history of EC summitry, the heads of state and government could not agree on a concluding communiqué.

The EC's problems were legion: a paralyzed decisionmaking process, a feeble Commission, a CAP apparently out of control, a new French president (François Mitterrand) pursuing a "dash for growth" that further strained Community solidarity, and a new British prime minister (Margaret Thatcher) incessantly demanding a budget rebate. Under the circumstances, Greenland's decision in February 1982 to become the first (and so far only) territory to leave the EC seemed entirely appropriate.

Yet a number of events and developments in the late 1970s and early 1980s presaged the Community's impending revival. A busy 1979 brought an accession treaty with Greece, the first direct elections to the EP, and the launch of the European Monetary System (EMS). Hopes that these events would cure the EC by prompting institutional reform, deeper integration, and renewed interest in Economic and Monetary Union (EMU) proved justified, but not right away. In the meantime, the EC became embroiled in the debilitating British budgetary question, which dominated the next five years and fifteen summits.

Only when the heads of state and government resolved the budgetary question in June 1984 did the EC suddenly revel in the impact of other, less perceptible but no less powerful developments that, over the past four years, had gradually generated momentum for greater integration. These included the trend toward deregulation and liberalization sweeping Europe from the United States; increasing cooperation between the Commission and leading industrialists to boost European competitiveness, especially in the high-technology sector; and growing business interest in the realization of a single market. These changes, combined with the EP's determination to revise the Treaty of Rome, member states' worries about Europe's apparent impotence during a sudden drop in Cold War temperatures, and consensus on the need to improve decisionmaking procedures in view of imminent enlargement, helped to set the EC on the road to "1992," that is, completion of the single market. As Christopher Tugendhat, a commissioner in the early 1980s, remarked at the time, "One has the feeling of ice breaking up and spring approaching."[3]

SECOND ENLARGEMENT, DIRECT ELECTIONS, AND THE EMS

The Commission's 1979 report on progress toward European union—an annual memento of the Tindemans Report—was unusually upbeat.[4] Three events that year held out the prospect of a modest improvement in the EC's fortunes: the Treaty of Accession with Greece, the first direct elections to the EP, and the inauguration of the EMS. The authors of the report could not have imagined how different the EC would be ten years later; the Single European Act (SEA) and Treaty on European Union (TEU) were beyond their wildest dreams. Little did they realize that Greece's accession—in the broader context of Mediterranean enlargement—direct elections, and the EMS would contribute, indirectly but importantly, to the EC's revival in the 1980s.

At the time, however, the report's guarded optimism seemed unfounded. Given the experience of British accession, further enlargement seemed dubious grounds for confidence. Nor did direct elections, delayed for many years and openly unwelcome to a number of member states opposed to a stronger EP, seem a likely source of resurgence. Even the EMS, an initiative launched with unusual speed to establish a degree of exchange rate stability, appeared to have little potential for the EC's long-term growth. Yet together these developments marked the beginning of the end of the EC's protracted malaise. Although major difficulties lay ahead, in 1979 the EC slowly began to turn the corner.

Much of the credit should go to Roy Jenkins, Commission president between 1977 and 1981. Having spent his entire career in British politics and with little experience in foreign affairs, Jenkins was a Brussels outsider. He would have preferred to stay in London, but his ardent Europeanism at the time of Britain's accession and during the subsequent renegotiation doomed Jenkins's career in the Labour Party. Most member states agreed that Britain, as a large recent arrival, should provide the next Commission president (small member states looked forward to a Commission president from a large member state other than France or Germany). Jenkins's seniority, pro-Community credentials, and underemployment at home made him the Labour government's obvious choice.

Especially because he succeeded the uninspiring François Ortoli, Jenkins's arrival in Brussels aroused inflated expectations. In fact, Jenkins got off to a slow and uncertain start, making it look by mid-1977 as if his presidency would be as forgettable as any in the years since Hallstein's resignation. Yet two of the three developments that later distinguished Jenkins's tenure were already in the works. The first was Greece's accession to the EC.

Greek Accession

Between 1967 and 1974, during the military regime in Athens, the EC had suspended its association agreement with Greece. Soon after the restoration of democracy Greece applied for full membership. Assessing the application on its economic merits, in January 1976 the Commission advised against accession. The Council, in contrast, saw the Greek case primarily from a political perspective. As German foreign minister Hans-Dietrich Genscher told the Bundestag, "Greece, only recently returned to the democratic fold, would march in future with the Community of European nations."[5] Exploiting such sentiments to the full, Greece began entry negotiations in Brussels in July 1976.

If the EC could have foreseen the problems that Greek membership would pose in the 1980s and early 1990s during the rule of Andreas Papandreou's anti-EC governments, the accession negotiations might not have concluded so swiftly, if at all. As it was, the Greek case coincided with the membership applications of Spain and Portugal, which similarly emerged from dictatorship in the mid-1970s. Faced with the prospect of a large southern enlargement, member states soon took the economic implications much more seriously. France especially feared the consequences of competition with another large, agricultural, Mediterranean member state.

Skillfully separating his country from the increasingly complex Iberian entry negotiations, Prime Minister Konstantinos Karamanlis successfully concluded an accession agreement in April 1979. Signed in Athens in May 1979 and duly ratified in Greece and the member states, the Treaty of Accession came into effect on January 1, 1981.[6]

Of the three Mediterranean applicants, Jenkins considered Greece "the least qualified for membership."[7] Yet he appreciated the political arguments in favor of enlargement and hoped that the accession first of Greece, then of Spain and Portugal, would help to propel the EC out of its institutional decline. If only to prevent greater sluggishness in EC decisionmaking once enlargement took place, Jenkins urged existing member states to introduce badly needed institutional reforms. Indeed, following Jenkins's departure, the impending accession of Spain and Portugal became an important impetus for change and was one of a number of factors that gave rise to the SEA. In the meantime, Jenkins had played a modest part in facilitating Greece's accession, launching the Spanish and Portuguese negotiations, and drawing attention to the institutional implications of further enlargement.

Direct Elections

The first direct elections to the EP had been planned well before the Jenkins presidency, and their contribution to the EC's revival became apparent only afterward. The Treaty of Rome provided for a directly elected assembly, but member state recalcitrance had so far prevented the switch from an appointed to an elected EP. As a gesture to counterbalance the creation of the European Council, the heads of state and government decided at the 1974 Paris summit to hold direct elections "as soon as possible."[8] Two years later the European Council was still haggling over the apportionment of seats in a directly elected EP, finally settling on 410 seats, over twice the number in the existing EP, distributed among member states approximately according to population size. Because of Britain's difficulty meeting the summer 1978 deadline for the elections, the European Council decided in December 1977 to postpone the first direct elections until June 1979.[9]

Britain and France openly disliked direct elections for fear that a powerful EP would undermine national supremacy in the EC's decisionmaking process. At the other end of the spectrum, Germany, the Netherlands, and Italy traditionally favored a stronger EP as a corollary to their support for supranationalism. Similarly, the Commission saw a stronger EP as a natural ally in its incessant struggle with the Council. Perhaps because of his years in the British political system, where the government is directly answerable to parliament, Jenkins especially encouraged direct elections and exaggerated their impact on the EP itself. Thus, he wrote at the time, the first direct elections "produced a potentially formidable new Parliament, twice the size of the old, which [the Commission] approached with a mixture of respect and apprehension."[10]

In the event, the direct elections of June 1979 did not cause a radical redistribution of power in the EC. Only a revision of the Treaty of Rome, as happened in the SEA and TEU, could enhance the EP's legislative role. However, direct elections brought a new breed of parliamentarian to Strasbourg and noticeably improved the EP's morale. The increasing amount of attention paid to the EP by the Commission and the Council also boosted the institution's assertiveness. Out of that higher morale, greater confidence, and soaring self-assurance came the "Draft Treaty Establishing the European Union," which played an important part in the EC's revival. In that sense, the Commission's 1979 report on European union was prophetic.

The European Monetary System

The third development in 1979 that helped get the Community out of the doldrums owed a great deal directly to Jenkins. This was the EMS, an initiative to establish a zone of relative monetary stability in a world of wildly fluctuating exchange rates. After a shaky start, the EMS helped participating member states to fight inflation and recover economic growth. According to the Dooge Report of 1985, the EMS "enabled the unity of the Common Market to be preserved, reasonable exchange rates to be maintained, and the foundations of the Community's monetary identity to be laid."[11] Unknown to the Dooge Committee at the time, the EMS would also provide a vital underpinning for the single market program.

Peter Ludlow chronicled the origins of the EMS in a masterly monograph that reads like a novel.[12] Jenkins's extensive *European Diaries* and his later political autobiography verify much of what Ludlow wrote. The story of the EMS has the ingredients of a political thriller: Jenkins's courage and prescience in proposing a monetary initiative after the failure of the Werner Plan and the currency "snake"; Ortoli's initial opposition in the Commission; German chancellor Helmut Schmidt's sudden espousal of a scheme for exchange rate stability and his determination to see it through despite strong domestic opposition; Giscard's less enthusiastic but nonetheless strong support, and his apparent U-turn at the last moment; the efficacy of the Franco-German alliance in ensuring adoption of the EMS; Britain's refusal yet again to take the plunge; and the value of the European Council for rapid decisionmaking at the highest level. Altogether, the EMS is an excellent case study of EC policy formulation and decisionmaking.

Despite the disappointment of his first few months in office, Jenkins yearned for an initiative that would boost the Commission's morale and reinvigorate the EC. Jenkins's knowledge of economics, experience as chancellor of the exchequer (finance minister) in Britain, and concern about the impact on the EC of oscillating international exchange rates led him inexorably toward action in the monetary field. Ortoli, he knew, would be skeptical. Renowned for his caution, enjoying considerable prestige as a former Commission president, and holding the senior portfolio of monetary affairs, Ortoli could have been a formidable potential adversary. Thus Jenkins proceeded gingerly in the Commission before broaching the subject publicly.

Jenkins used the occasion of a lecture at the EC-sponsored European University Institute in Florence in October 1977 to fly a trial balloon. Apart from making predictable points about advancing European integration and helping to realize the common market's full potential, Jenkins argued that monetary union would have the macroeconomic advantages of lowering inflation, increasing investment, and reducing unemployment. Nor, if properly implemented, would monetary union exacerbate regional economic disparities or intensify institutional centralization in Brussels.[13]

The tension between Jenkins's advocacy of what he called in Florence a bold "leap forward" and Ortoli's step-by-step approach resulted in a surprisingly cautious Commission communication to the Council on the subject of EMU.[14] Nor was there much discussion of EMU at the European Council in Brussels in December 1977, where Jenkins noted Schmidt's "benevolent skepticism" and detected "a fair if not tremendously enthusiastic wind behind our monetary union proposals."[15] Despite strong support from the Belgian presidency, which wanted an imaginative initiative in the spirit of the Tindemans Report, by the end of 1977 Jenkins's trial balloon seemed to have fallen flat. To compound Jenkins's disappointment, Germany was one of the least interested member states.

Jenkins's attempt to revive interest in EMU would have withered entirely but for Schmidt's sudden conversion to it, or at least to a modified version of what Jenkins wanted. Schmidt told Jenkins about his newfound enthusiasm for an effort to achieve EC-wide exchange rate stability during a meeting in Bonn on February 28, 1978, a date that marks the conception of the EMS. Jenkins was at a loss to explain the reason for Schmidt's sudden change of heart. Was it a function of the chancellor's mercurial personality? Was it an antidote to his domestic security problems? Was it anger with the United States over yet another drop in the dollar's value?[16] One or more of those reasons may explain the timing of Schmidt's espousal of a quasi-fixed exchange rate regime. The fundamental cause of his "conversion," however, went much deeper. Persistent depreciation of the dollar and a corresponding appreciation of the mark cut German industrial competitiveness and fed speculation that a U.S. economic recovery was happening at the expense of German prudence and prosperity.

Overnight, Schmidt replaced Jenkins as the principal proponent of a monetary policy initiative and championed what subsequently became the EMS. Yet Schmidt's crucial collaborator was not the president of the Commission but the president of France. Alone or with Jenkins's sole support,

Schmidt might not have been able to bring the monetary initiative rapidly to fruition. But with Giscard's backing the EMS proposal quickly gathered speed. Having survived the March 1978 parliamentary elections, Giscard and Raymond Barre, his prime minister and author of the Commission's first-ever plan for EMU, enthusiastically endorsed Schmidt's scheme. Giscard's support owed more to friendship with Schmidt than to a desire to reduce pressure on the mark. Regardless of Giscard's motivation, the birth of the EMS one year later "came from a clear convergence of French and German interests, confirming the two countries' leading roles in the Community."[17]

Regular meetings of the European Council provided Schmidt and Giscard with an opportunity to promote their monetary proposal and a forum in which to approve the EMS at the highest possible decisionmaking level. Giscard and Schmidt possessed enormous powers of political persuasion. When they unveiled their exchange rate idea in April 1978 at the European Council in Copenhagen, only British prime minister James Callaghan expressed serious concern. Resentment of close Franco-German collaboration and doubts about the scheme's validity soon convinced Callaghan not to allow British participation with France and Germany in subsequent planning for the EMS. Thus the blueprint put before the next European Council, convened in Bremen in July 1978, bore an exclusive Franco-German imprint.

The Bremen summit marked a decisive stage in the gestation of the EMS. Schmidt's forceful chairmanship contributed to a general acceptance of the Franco-German proposal for an Exchange Rate Mechanism (ERM) using a parity grid and a divergence indicator based on the European currency unit (ECU).[18] By contrast, Callaghan's sullenness presaged Britain's self-exclusion from the system. Britain's decision not to take part was of more than symbolic importance. As Helen Wallace has pointed out, "for many of those involved the EMS was viewed, rightly or wrongly, as a critical stage in the development of the EC as a whole."[19]

While Commission and member state officials worked in a number of specialized committees to thrash out details of the scheme, a last-minute political row erupted over compensation for poorer participating countries, with Ireland and Italy demanding an increase in regional development funding and subsidized loans for infrastructural development. The problem of resource redistribution ("concurrent measures" in Eurospeak) came to a boil when France and Britain insisted that their shares of a larger European regional development fund be equal to their shares of the existing fund and Germany balked at paying the bill. Nor would Giscard approve the amount of subsidized loans that Ireland and Italy requested. This did not augur well for the Brussels summit of December 1978, the final European Council before the EMS was to have been implemented in January 1979.

A last-minute compromise by Schmidt at the Brussels summit broke the "concurrent measures" deadlock. Yet fears of an aborted EMS grew when Giscard unexpectedly demanded abolition of monetary compensatory amounts (MCAs)—funds introduced in the early 1970s to cushion the CAP from exchange rate fluctuations—as part of the EMS package.[20] MCAs had benefited France little but were popular in Germany, where they helped prop up agricultural prices. Giscard's last-minute intransigence, due more to domestic politics than to international economics, delayed implementation of the EMS. In the event, Giscard's abandonment of the MCA issue was as swift as his embracing of it. Following agreement at a meeting of agriculture ministers in early March 1979 to abolish MCAs without specifying a timetable, Giscard announced his unconditional support for the EMS, which finally came into operation on March 13, 1979.

The EMS was substantially different from what Jenkins had originally envisioned. What emerged in 1979 was "a hybrid—not entirely Community, nor entirely outside it."[21] Only EC member states could participate in the EMS, although none was obliged to do so. The EMS was not based on the Treaty of Rome, although closer monetary coordination, and eventually EMU, were cherished EC objectives. Nor did it emerge from a Commission proposal, although EC institutions, notably the Council of Finance Ministers (ECOFIN), were central to its successful operation. Despite its peculiarities, the EMS represented an important breakthrough for Brussels. Regardless of its subsequent development, the fact of its existence and the relative speed with which it came into being marked an important milestone in the EC's history.

THE BRITISH BUDGETARY QUESTION

The launch of the EMS, the accession treaty with Greece, and the first direct elections to the EP ended an otherwise disappointing decade on a high note. Nevertheless, the long-term beneficial impact of these developments could not have been predicted in 1979. On the contrary, as the 1970s came to a close the EC seemed as desultory as ever. The French presidency during the first half of the year lacked imagination and direction. Giscard's petulance over MCAs set the tone for France's stewardship of the Council. An uneven struggle between the Council and Commission presidencies for power and prestige reopened with a vengeance. For Jenkins, the first six months of 1979 were "a test of nerves such as no other [national] Presidency has provided."[22] Little wonder that as the year progressed, Jenkins turned his thoughts more and more toward returning to British politics. The unedifying revival of the British budgetary question pushed Jenkins—for whom the initials BBQ came to mean Bloody British Question—irrevocably in that direction.[23]

The EC was no stranger to Thatcher, who came to power in May 1979. Four years earlier she had stoutly supported Britain's continued membership in the EC in her maiden speech as opposition leader in the House of

Commons. Yet according to one of her senior officials, "from the beginning [of her prime ministership] . . . she showed a deep-seated prejudice against the EC."[24] Thatcher also showed ignorance of the EC's institutions and policies and, according to one of her biographers, tended to see the EC as a branch of NATO.[25] But she grasped the potential for British trade of continued EC membership and later became one of the foremost proponents of the single market program. Although the EC was effectively moribund in 1979, she also grasped the Commission's aspiration to promote supranationalism and undermine the nation-state. These goals she strenuously rejected. In Thatcher's view, European integration should not go beyond the removal of barriers to trade and investment and the coordination of economic and foreign policies exclusively on an intergovernmental basis.

Thatcher grasped another thing about the EC even before she became prime minister: the obvious unfairness of Britain's budgetary contribution. Simply put, Britain paid too much and received too little in return. That should have been rectified in the mid-1970s at the time of Wilson's renegotiation of Britain's membership terms. The 1975 renegotiation, however, had been largely a cosmetic exercise to appease British public opinion and to try to keep the Labour Party together. Thereafter, special transitional arrangements for Britain cushioned the financial burden of membership. Only at the end of the 1970s did the extent of Britain's overpayment become fully apparent. The figures were striking: Britain's net payments to Brussels averaged 60 million pounds sterling between 1973 and 1976; they amounted to 369 million in 1977, 822 million in 1978, and 947 million in 1979.[26]

Here was a cause dear to Thatcher's heart. Britain's demand for reform was clear cut, easily comprehensible, fair, and assured of widespread domestic support. How could her EC colleagues possibly not concede the point? Even the Commission's own figures bolstered Britain's case. Thatcher surely had a natural ally in Schmidt, whose country also paid too much to the EC (although Germany could afford to do so and was unlikely to complain in any event because of lingering war guilt). Righting Britain's wrong would strengthen, not weaken, the EC. Thatcher correctly argued that without budgetary reform the British public, already equivocal about European integration, would turn solidly against the EC and might even insist on withdrawal. For Thatcher, the British budgetary question became not only a question of right and wrong but also a campaign to save the EC from itself.

Under these circumstances it seems surprising that the issue nearly wrecked the EC and filled a reservoir of ill feeling toward Britain in Brussels. Admittedly, Britain's partners were predisposed not to reopen the budgetary question. Wilson's handling of the original renegotiation had left a bitter taste in people's mouths. Yet such was the justice of Britain's case that even the most resentful of Eurocrats and member state officials conceded the fairness of further reform.

What turned a relatively straightforward case into one of the most complex and divisive issues in the EC's history was Thatcher's abrasive personality and truculent approach to the negotiations. Being the new kid on the block at European Council meetings, a woman in a hitherto exclusively male world, may have fired Thatcher's innate aggression. She also suspected the Commission and the other member states of uniformly opposing Britain's position. Thatcher soon discovered that an aggressive approach enhanced her reputation at home as a dogged defender of British interests and increased her political standing at a time of otherwise plummeting ratings.

Schmidt was the first EC leader to visit Thatcher as prime minister. She immediately informed him of her determination to get a better budgetary deal.[27] That set the stage for her first European Council, held in Strasbourg in June 1979. The Strasbourg summit turned into a skirmish, during which Thatcher fired a warning shot. According to Jenkins, who attended as Commission president, Thatcher "spoke shrilly and too frequently, and succeeded in embroiling not only Giscard (which maybe was unavoidable), but also in turn van Agt (the Netherlands), Jorgensen (Denmark) and Lynch (Ireland). Then, worst of all, she got into an altercation with Schmidt, whose support was crucial to her getting the outcome she wanted from the meeting."[28] That summer and fall Thatcher marshaled her forces and prepared for the first pitched battle: the Dublin summit in November 1979.

Jenkins tried before the Dublin summit to narrow the ground between Thatcher and everybody else. His main problem was that the ground had not yet been adequately prepared or defined. Although Thatcher demanded Britain's money back, neither she nor any of her interlocutors had mentioned a precise sum. Not surprisingly, the Dublin summit soon degenerated into open combat. Thatcher's tactics were to grind her enemies down by endlessly repeating her main arguments and keeping everyone up late after dinner. Infuriated, the Danish prime minister hurled insults; bored, the German chancellor feigned sleep; disdainful, the French president ignored her; embarrassed, the Irish prime minister wished it weren't happening.[29] The next summit, in Luxembourg in April 1980, saw a resumption of hand-to-hand fighting. This time precise figures were mentioned for an interim two-year period. Indeed, the difference between what Thatcher demanded and what the others offered (about 400 million ECUs a year) was relatively small. Nevertheless, Thatcher rejected what was on offer, departing the battlefield bloodied but unbowed. The other combatants left Luxembourg in despair.

Italy, then in the Council presidency, redoubled its efforts to resolve the problem. The decisive encounter took place at a Council meeting in May 1980, where the Eight refined their earlier offer of a truce. This the eminently reasonable Lord Peter Carrington, Thatcher's foreign secretary, accepted. The scene of hostilities then switched to the home front, where Carrington tried to convince Thatcher to endorse the Council's agreement. Thatcher eventually backed down when her usually compliant cabinet ministers stuck to their guns and recommended acceptance of the other member states' offer.

Why Thatcher wanted to reject the draft Council agreement is unclear. Her foreign secretary had brought back from Brussels the best deal possible. Rejecting it would have been tantamount to rejecting the EC, which Thatcher claimed not to want to do. Nor could she have gleaned much more political capital from saying no to Brussels. Already, public opinion in Britain was beginning to turn against her European histrionics, which robbed Britain of a potential leadership role in the EC. It is difficult to avoid the conclusion that Thatcher's fierce determination to settle only on her own terms was part of her political pathology.

The 1980 agreement was merely a temporary resolution of the British budgetary question. As expected, Thatcher returned to the charge when the interim agreement expired in 1983, the tenth anniversary of Britain's unhappy EC membership. This time she sought a permanent solution to the budgetary problem, not merely a series of annual remedies. The Stuttgart summit of June 1983 provided the first opportunity for a showdown. Yet the contrast with 1979 was striking. Then Thatcher had been a newcomer in the exclusive European Council club, long dominated by Giscard and Schmidt; now she was a veteran, flanked by François Mitterrand and Helmut Kohl, the relatively new leaders of France and Germany. Both were finding their feet domestically and internationally and had not yet struck up the firm friendship for which they would later become famous. Neither of them could match Thatcher's grasp of detail or passion for the budgetary question; Stuttgart was their baptism of fire.

Two other factors, one domestic and one European, further strengthened Thatcher's position. First, her popularity at home had soared in the aftermath of the Falklands/Malvinas War. Having taken on the Argentinians, Thatcher was set to take on the Continentals. This time the British public stood squarely behind her. Even the opposition Labour Party, at that time committed to pulling out of the EC if it ever got back into office, could hardly criticize her efforts to get a better budget deal for Britain. Second, the EC was financially strapped. In the early 1980s the CAP had run out of control with an obscene accumulation of surplus production for which farmers received guaranteed high prices. The EC would have to reform the CAP and/or increase its overall budget. Thatcher favored CAP reform, a politically unpalatable option for most other member states. But she was not about to approve a budget increase to cover unrestrained CAP spending unless Britain's contribution was once and for all resolved.

There was little progress on the budgetary dispute at the Stuttgart summit or during the remainder of 1983. The situation changed dramatically for the better when France took over the Council presidency in January 1984. Having jettisoned an initial effort to boost employment and economic growth through government intervention and high public spending, Mitterrand was in the process of switching to deregulation and market integration. He was eager to end the budgetary impasse and focus member states' attention instead on the need to complete the single market. A special European Council in Brussels in March 1984 afforded an opportunity to thrash out the various budgetary problems three months into the French presidency, but without success.

The French presidency was due to end in June with a European Council just outside Paris in the spectacular setting of the palace at Fontainebleau. Mitterrand and Roland Dumas, his European affairs minister, launched a concerted diplomatic offensive in the run-up to the summit. Despite these efforts, there was nothing to suggest that a breakthrough on the budget was imminent as the heads of state and government converged on Fontainebleau, covered by an army of 1,300 journalists. Talk in previous weeks of a possible "two-speed" Europe, with Britain in the slow lane, had not helped matters; nor had Thatcher's clever definition of what a two-speed Europe meant: "Those who pay most are in the top group and those who pay less are not."[30] Continued squabbling over Britain's budgetary contribution was a pitiful prelude not only to the Fontainebleau summit but especially to the second direct elections to the EP.

Mitterrand's strategy at Fontainebleau was to avoid the kind of friction that had marred the opening of the Brussels summit.[31] As the summit progressed, a surprising willingness to compromise gradually became apparent. Thatcher seemed eager to settle the long-standing dispute and move the EC in new directions; the others were equally war-weary and desperately wanted to reach a comprehensive budget agreement. That evening, the heads of state and government asked their foreign ministers to draft a resolution to the British dispute based not on previous proposals but on a rebate in the form of a fixed percentage each year of Britain's net contribution. Thatcher held out for 66 percent; Kohl demurred. Finally, after some concessions to Germany on the CAP, the chancellor lifted his objections at lunch on the second day of the summit. The British budgetary dispute was over.[32]

Had anything good come of it? Undoubtedly Thatcher's conduct antagonized other EC leaders and protracted the painful negotiations. Yet without her aggressive approach Britain might not have secured such a favorable result (the agreement saved Britain over 10 billion pounds sterling in the remainder of the 1980s). For all the aggravation and frustration of the previous two years, arguably Thatcher needed time to build her case, exhaust the opposition, and secure a satisfactory solution. It also may be argued that resolution of Britain's budgetary dispute helped the EC's long-term development, and not only in the obvious sense of removing a persistent irritant in relations among member states, for Thatcher brought home to the Community the folly of overexpenditure and the need to rein in the CAP. Indeed, the European Council resolved the British problem in the context of a wider budget reform, involving a decision to curtail CAP spending and increase the EC's own resources, effective in 1986, from 1.0 percent to 1.4 percent of the value-added tax collected in each member state.[33]

In a postsummit press conference Thatcher said she now looked forward to "pressing ahead with the development of the Community."[34] The other heads of state and government could not have agreed more. Mitterrand reveled in the success of "his" European Council not only in ending five years of friction over Britain's contribution to the EC's coffers but also in clearing the way for new initiatives. At Fontainebleau, Mitterrand had spoken eloquently about the need to revive the EC's policies and institutions and instill a new sense of European identity. Although France would no longer be in the presidency, the Fontainebleau summit created a favorable climate in which to push Mitterrand's pro-integration program.

One of the challenges for the EC that Thatcher identified in her report on the summit to the House of Commons was what she called "completion of the Common Market in goods and services."[35] Thatcher had not plucked that objective out of thin air. On the contrary, in the early 1980s the idea of implementing a single, EC-wide market had quietly gathered momentum in the shadow of the British budgetary question. More obtrusively, pressure for institutional reform and revision of the Treaty of Rome had also grown. At Fontainebleau, the European Council decided to convene a committee to consider the EC's future institutional structure and policy agenda. Little did it realize that the so-called Dooge Committee would suggest a means to fuse the twin goals of a single market and institutional reform and lay a political foundation for the 1992 program.

IDEOLOGY, HIGH TECHNOLOGY, AND THE SINGLE MARKET

A number of factors in the early 1980s fueled renewed interest in the EC's long-proclaimed goal of a single market. One was the ideological shift then sweeping Western Europe. Its most obvious manifestation was Thatcher's election victory in 1979. After five years of Labour Party rule, a powerful popular reaction against excessive government intervention in economic and social affairs swept Thatcher to power. The new government immediately launched a program of privatization and deregulation to unleash pent-up market forces and stimulate individual enterprise.

Across the Channel, by contrast, Mitterrand pushed a socialist agenda of state intervention and regulation after his election victory in 1981. The consequences were catastrophic: Inflation soared; investment slumped;

and the value of the franc plummeted, forcing devaluation within the EMS and prompting a tough domestic austerity program. In 1983 pragmatism overcame principle when Mitterrand, at the urging of Jacques Delors, his finance minister, abandoned a doctrinaire approach to economic recovery and began to bend with the prevailing economic wind blowing from the United States and Britain. Mitterrand's U-turn influenced other socialist leaders, notably Felipe González in Spain and Mário Soares in Portugal, two countries then on their way to joining the EC.

The success of Etienne Davignon, the commissioner responsible for industrial affairs between 1981 and 1985, in rallying European industry to the cause of cross-border collaboration also contributed to the momentum developing for a single, EC-wide market. Davignon's profound knowledge of international politics and economics, high social standing, and previous Brussels experience made him the most formidable member of Gaston Thorn's new Commission. During his second term in the Commission, Davignon made Western Europe's industrial performance and competitiveness a top priority.[36]

Davignon cultivated the CEOs of major European manufacturers in the high-technology sector. His so-called Round Table discussion group brought together leaders of the "Big 12" electronics companies in the EC, including Nixdorf and Siemens (Germany), Thomson and Bull (France), Olivetti (Italy), and Philips (the Netherlands).[37] Davignon gradually succeeded in getting these industrial giants to consider the advantages of intra-EC collaboration, something the persistent economic recession in any case predisposed them to do. Commission officials kept discreetly in the background; the last thing Davignon wanted was to scare off the Big 12 with a display of bureaucratic heavy-handedness.

Davignon's efforts bore fruit in ESPRIT (European Strategic Program for Research and Development in Information Technology), a basic research program involving major manufacturers, smaller firms, and universities throughout the EC. Technological collaboration, in turn, "created an important and vocal constituency . . . impatient for an end to such things as customs delays at borders, conflicting national standards in data processing or arcane rules on property ownership . . . and pressing for the completion of the internal market, for once these firms had lost their national champions status, it was imperative that they maximized the advantages to be gained from the single market."[38] Guy Gyllenhammer, the head of Volvo, catalyzed such thinking in the Community by organizing the European Round Table, a discussion group with a name and purpose similar to Davignon's, although his own firm was located in Sweden, a nonmember state.

As a corollary to its encouragement of technological collaboration in the EC, the Commission also championed the cause of market integration. The Commission's increasing agitation for completion of the single market is chronicled most clearly in the relevant sections of its own annual reports from the early 1980s. The 1980 report merely asserted "the need to continue building the common market" and outlined the advantages to be gained from doing so.[39] The report also noted that the Commission had followed up on a landmark decision of the Court of Justice that was to a have a profound effect on the interpenetration of member state markets. Based on the Court's rejection, in the *Cassis de Dijon (1979)* case, concerning a German prohibition on imports from other member states of alcoholic beverages that did not meet minimum alcohol content requirements, the Commission had spelled out the implications for free movement of goods in the Community: "Any product imported from another member state must in principle be admitted . . . if it has been lawfully produced, that is, conforms to rules and processes of manufacture that are customarily and traditionally accepted in the exporting country, and is marketed in the territory of the latter." Thus the Commission developed the principle of mutual recognition that would avoid the otherwise impossible process of harmonizing in detail the member states' diverse legal norms.

Based partly on that breakthrough, the Commission's 1981 report was far more assertive, opening with the claim that "during the year the Commission set out to restore confidence by stimulating the internal market and developing an industrial strategy for Europe."[40] The Commission's efforts included a communication to the European Council on the pitiful state of the internal market, which prompted the heads of state and government to declare in June 1981 that "a concerted effort must be made to strengthen and develop the free internal market which lies at the very basis of the European Community."[41] Moving from oratory to action, the Commission urged the Council later that year both to pass a number of proposals that impinged upon the internal market and to simplify intra-EC frontier formalities involving customs, taxation, and statistics.

In subsequent years the Commission sharpened its strategy of putting forward concrete proposals, notably on product standards, and politicizing the problem by prodding the European Council to act. Based in part on a Commission program to strengthen the internal market, in December 1982 the European Council reiterated the importance of removing existing barriers to intra-EC commerce.[42] The Commission's prodding bore fruit in 1983 when the Council defined a standardization policy for European industry. The next year the Commission prepared a detailed paper for the Fontainebleau summit on a number of internal market issues ranging from the abolition of customs barriers to the free movement of people, capital, and services.[43]

Thatcher, a leading proponent of market integration, came to Fontainebleau armed with a paper of her own. This contained the classic assertion that "if the problems of growth, outdated industrial structures and unemployment which affect us all are to be tackled effectively, we must create the genuine common market in goods and services which is envisaged in the Treaty of Rome and will be crucial to our ability to meet the U.S. and Japanese technological challenge."[44] In promoting the single market at Fontainebleau, Thatcher sought to advance deeply held convictions and establish beyond question her pro-EC credentials.

The Fontainebleau settlement of the British budgetary questions removed a major barrier to EC action on a wide range of issues and opened the door to achieving a genuinely single market. During the past few years a consensus had emerged in Brussels and among member states on the need for as much deregulation as possible at the national level coupled with as little reregulation as necessary at the Community level. Ideological, political, and economic transformations had brought about a reemphasis on the internal market and paved the way for an imminent breakthrough. Other developments, notably tension in the transatlantic relationship, the assertiveness of the first directly elected EP, and the impending accession of Spain and Portugal, caused attention to dwell also on institutional reform and constitutional change in the EC. These objectives—completion of the single market and a revision of the Treaty of Rome—were not unconnected. Each gave added impetus to the other, and both were to combine in the SEA of 1986.

TRANSATLANTIC TENSIONS

The EC's external relations were every bit as problematical as its internal development in the early 1980s. The onset of the "second Cold War"—the sudden heightening of East-West tension in the late 1970s after a decade of relatively benign relations—tested the Community's ability to act internationally. European Political Cooperation (EPC) proved an inadequate instrument for foreign policy coordination, especially in response to international crises such as the Soviet invasion of Afghanistan in December 1979 and the imposition of martial law in Poland two years later. At the same time, the unremitting hostility of the United States toward the Soviet Union severely tested EC solidarity and combined with other developments in U.S.-EC relations to put transatlantic ties under great strain. The new Reagan administration saw the Soviet Union as the root of all evil and pressured the United States' European allies to cease most economic and trade activities with the Soviet bloc. Washington cited Western Europe's more nuanced approach to the question of East-West relations as evidence of weakness and cowardice.

Matters came to a head in June 1982 when the United States announced sanctions against U.S. subsidiaries and license holders in Western Europe involved in the so-called Soviet gas pipeline, a massive infrastructural project to facilitate the export of Soviet gas to Western Europe through a pipeline thousands of miles long. Such arbitrary action galvanized latent anti-Americanism and alerted many Western European firms and governments to their excessive dependence on the United States.[45] It provided a powerful impetus for high-technology industries to accelerate collaboration in the EC, thereby asserting a European identity and declaring independence of the United States. To that extent, ESPRIT and other EC-sponsored high-technology research and development programs owe their development to strained U.S.-EC political relations, exacerbated by bitter transatlantic disputes over subsidized steel and agricultural exports from the EC.

At the same time, the United States and its European allies were mired in a political dispute over NATO's deployment in Western Europe of cruise and Pershing II missiles in response to the earlier Soviet deployment in Eastern Europe of SS-20 missiles. What had begun in the late 1970s as a show of Allied solidarity, with NATO adopting the "dual track" approach of missile deployment and arms control negotiations to counter the new Soviet threat, degenerated in the early 1980s into European accusations that the Reagan administration was interested only in deployment and U.S. accusations that the Europeans were giving in to Soviet pressure. The "Euromissile" crisis, played out publicly on the streets of many Western European cities as well as privately in the chancelleries of the Atlantic Alliance, cast a long shadow over Euro-American relations.

The United States and its allies in the EC also diverged over policy toward the Middle East, an especially sensitive issue for Washington. The United States viewed the Nine's declarations on the Arab-Israeli conflict, which tended to criticize Israel and support the Palestinians, as examples of the perniciousness of EPC. The so-called Venice Declaration of June 1980, in which the Nine recognized the special position of Palestine in the Arab-Israeli conflict, greatly irritated the United States, as did the resumption of the "Euro-Arab dialogue" shortly afterward. The United States disliked its European allies' taking an independent and relatively radical position on an issue that was both inherently explosive and part of the wider, all-encompassing Cold War conflict.

Those economic and political disputes with the United States emboldened the member states to assert themselves internationally. France, well known for its estrangement from Washington, took the lead. In May 1984, during France's Council presidency, Mitterrand made a famous speech to the EP calling for institutional reform and greater Community competence over internal and external affairs.[46] On external relations, Mitterrand advocated a permanent secretariat for the conduct of EPC and urged member states to make a common defense effort. An initiative by Hans-Dietrich Genscher, Germany's foreign minister, sought to assert the EC's international identity while reassuring the United States about Germany's and the EC's intentions. Officially launched in November 1981 and rapidly taken up by Emilio Colombo, Italy's foreign minister, the "Draft European

Act," popularly known as the Genscher-Colombo proposal, advocated more effective decisionmaking and greater Community competence in external relations.[47] Genscher-Colombo sought to change the existing situation whereby, as an unidentified German diplomat described it, "the Community operates in the world arena but acts as if it didn't belong there."[48]

Although Genscher-Colombo soft-pedaled the security implications of a more coherent EC foreign policy–making capacity, the United States nonetheless expressed concern. Thatcher shared Washington's anxiety. Moreover, for varying reasons a number of smaller Community countries disliked Genscher-Colombo's emphasis on closer security cooperation. Although a NATO member, Denmark opposed greater Community competence in the security domain. Under Andreas Papandreou's leadership Greece, also a NATO member, opposed deeper European integration in general and closer security cooperation in particular. Sensitive to public support for nonmembership in NATO and an ill-defined "neutrality," the otherwise indifferent Irish government objected to any EC initiative on security and defense.

Under the circumstances, Genscher-Colombo had little direct impact. It gave rise only to the "Solemn Declaration on European Union,"[49] a vague, insubstantial assertion of the Community's international identity. Indirectly, efforts to introduce a security dimension made an important contribution to the EC's revival in the 1980s. Mitterrand drew on Genscher-Colombo in his May 1984 speech to the EP, which in turn prepared the ground for the decision at Fontainebleau to establish a committee to consider the future of European integration. Member states' willingness to speculate about a possible security and defense community created a climate conducive to change.

THE DRAFT TREATY ESTABLISHING THE EUROPEAN UNION

At the same time, an initiative in the first directly elected EP complemented and reinforced the member states' openness to reform. For all the propaganda preceding the June 1979 direct elections, parliamentarians who convened in Strasbourg later that summer knew only too well that the EP lacked power or influence. They also appreciated the extent of the EC's difficulties and hoped to revive the process of European integration. Between April 1980 and February 1982, the EP passed no less than eight resolutions advocating institutional and policy reform in the EC.

Altiero Spinelli, the veteran Eurofederalist, was one of the best known and most influential members of the newly elected Parliament. In 1970 the Italian government had nominated Spinelli to the Commission, but he resigned unexpectedly in 1976 to take a seat in the EP. His decision to become a member of the relatively powerless Parliament surprised almost everyone. In fact, Spinelli was positioning himself to become a key figure in the first directly elected EP, due to convene at the end of the decade. He interpreted the results of the direct elections as nothing less than a mandate to overhaul of the Treaty of Rome.

In July 1980 Spinelli gathered together a small number of like-minded parliamentarians, representing a wide spectrum of political opinion, in the Crocodile Restaurant in Strasbourg. By the end of the year the "Crocodile Club," an otherwise heterogeneous collection of parliamentarians dedicated to reforming and reviving the EC, had grown from ten to seventy members. Their ideas ranged from a return to the EC's first principles—the need to complete the internal market—to drafting a constitution for Europe. Gradually a consensus emerged on the urgency of a new treaty to replace the original treaties and for a new European Union to replace the original European Community.

Grown too large to meet in its favorite Strasbourg restaurant, the Crocodile Club moved to a committee room at the EP. The group was relatively ineffectual as an unofficial caucus, so in July 1981 Spinelli convinced his colleagues to inaugurate a committee on institutional affairs. The committee met for the first time in January 1983, halfway through the EP's five-year term of office. Spinelli served not as chairman but in the crucial capacity of rapporteur.

Members of the Institutional Affairs Committee appreciated the potential pitfalls surrounding their work. Because the EP remained relatively powerless and its members were correspondingly unimportant, there was a predisposition in Brussels and in member state capitals to dismiss parliamentarians' agitation for reform as the ravings of reckless, overindulged, and underemployed politicians. Spinelli himself had a reputation for being idealistic, unrealistic, and excitable. Because of the EP's comparative weakness, national governments expected parliamentarians to demand a larger say for their institution in EC decisionmaking. The greatest danger facing the Institutional Affairs Committee was that its work would not be taken seriously.

Yet the crisis in the Community—prolonged economic recession, declining international competitiveness, institutional inertia, and decisionmaking paralysis—lent credence to the EP's efforts to revive European integration, as did the member states' own initiatives along the same lines. Fortunately for the EP, the Institutional Affairs Committee's first six months in operation coincided with Belgium's presidency of the Council. Eager to undertake major institutional reform, the Belgians set an important precedent in May 1982 by calling for a vote in the Council on that year's farm prices.[50] In and of itself, Belgium's assertiveness seemed unimportant, but its symbolism was not lost on the Commission and the member states, and certainly not on the EP.

Despite support from Belgium and from some other member states, the Institutional Affairs Committee proceeded cautiously, deliberately, responsibly, and successfully. By the middle of 1982 it had identified the main lines of a reform program and established subgroups to work on them. Issues included the legal personality of a possible new union, its institutional structure, competence, and relationship with the member states. The committee consulted experts throughout the Community in the fall of 1982. With the invaluable assistance of a group of noted jurists, the proposed reforms painstakingly wound their way procedurally through the committee and the Parliament in 1983, emerging at the end of the year as the "Draft Treaty Establishing the European Union."[51]

The draft treaty sought to substitute the existing treaties establishing the European communities with a single treaty establishing a European Union. The EU would maintain the basic institutional structure and legal competence of the three communities (the ECSC, EC, and Euratom) but revise their decisionmaking procedures and add to them new or expanded authority over certain aspects of economic, social, and political affairs. The purpose of decisionmaking reform was both to improve efficiency and to close a perceived "democratic deficit." Allowing for the member states' sensitivity to the centralization of power in Brussels, the draft treaty provided for something that received little attention at the time but suddenly became prominent a decade later during the TEU ratification debate: the principle of subsidiarity. In its preamble, the draft treaty stipulated that the EU would be responsible only for tasks that could be undertaken more effectively in common than by the member states acting independently.

In one of the most famous votes ever taken in the EP, in February 1984 the draft treaty passed by a resounding 237 to 31 with 43 abstentions.[52] Most of the preceding debate focused on the future: What impact would the draft treaty have on the course of European integration? The vast majority of parliamentarians, including the stalwart Crocodile Club members, knew that the draft treaty would never be ratified by the member states. Yet the EP decided to send it to national parliaments and governments anyway in an effort to increase the momentum for reform then gathering in the EC. Passage of the draft treaty was especially timely in the run-up to the second direct elections in June 1984: It demonstrated the EP's seriousness and commitment to European integration (although most of the electorate took little interest in Parliament's activities) and constituted a concrete legacy from the first directly elected Parliament to its successors. The timing of the vote on the draft treaty was also auspicious because France was in the Council presidency. The EP's overwhelming endorsement of the draft treaty provided President Mitterrand, by then an unquestioned champion of EC renewal, with additional political ammunition.

Synergy between collaborative ventures in high technology, renewed interest in the internal market, concern about international affairs, and paralysis in the decisionmaking process paved the way for serious consideration of the EC's potential contribution to Western Europe's political and economic development. Similarly, initiatives such as the Genscher-Colombo proposals, the Stuttgart solemn declaration, and the EP's draft treaty were essential precursors of the EC's revival following resolution of the British budgetary question. They provided a climate and a context in which the Dooge Committee, convened after the Fontainebleau summit, could operate successfully. The Dooge Committee, in turn, gave rise to the SEA and the single market program, which symbolized the EC's resurgence in the late 1980s.

NOTES

1. Quoted in Steven Lagerfeld, "Europhoria," *Wilson Quarterly* 14 (Winter 1990): 66.
2. Karl Kaiser et al. (eds.), *The European Community: Progress or Decline?* (London: Royal Institute of International Affairs [RIIA], 1983), p. 1.
3. Christopher Tugendhat, "How to Get Europe Moving Again," *International Affairs* 61 (winter 1990): 421.
4. Bull. EC S/1-1979, pp. 12–13.
5. Quoted in Werner Feld, *West Germany and the European Community: Changing Interests and Competing Policy Objectives* (New York: Praeger, 1981), p. 55
6. For details of the Greek application and negotiations, see Frances Nicholson and Roger East, *From the Six to the Twelve: The Enlargement of the European Community* (Chicago: St. James Press, 1987), pp. 181–206.
7. Roy Jenkins, *European Diary, 1977–1981* (London: Collins, 1989), p. 199.
8. Commission, *1974 General Report,* Annex to Chapter 1, point 18.
9. Bull. EC 12-1977, point 1.12.
10. Jenkins, *European Diary,* p. 375.
11. "Ad Hoc Committee for Institutional Affairs Report to the European Council (Dooge Report), March 1985," Bull. EC 3–1985, point 3.5.1.
12. Peter Ludlow, *The Making of the European Monetary System: A Case Study in the Politics of the European Community* (London: Butterworths Scientific, 1982).
13. Roy Jenkins, "Europe's Present Challenge and Future Opportunity," speech delivered at the European University Institute (Florence), October 27, 1977.
14. COM(77)620 final, November 16, 1977.
15. Jenkins, *European Diary,* p. 183.
16. Roy Jenkins, *Life at the Centre* (London: Macmillan, 1991), pp. 470–471.
17. Haig Simonian, *The Privileged Partnership: Franco-German Relations in the European Community, 1969–1984* (Oxford: Clarendon Press, 1985), p. 277.
18. Bull. EC 6-1978, "Presidency Conclusions," point 1.5.2.
19. Helen Wallace, "The Conduct of Bilateral Relations by Governments," in Roger Morgan and Caroline Brey, *Partners and Rivals in Western Europe: Britain, France and Germany* (Brookfield, VT: Gower, 1986), p. 154.
20. Bull. EC 12–1978, "Presidency Conclusions," point 1.14.
21. William Nicoll and Trevor Salmon, *Understanding the European Communities* (Savage, MD: Barnes & Noble, 1990), p. 197.
22. Jenkins, *European Diary,* p. 372.
23. Ibid., p. 545.

24. Sir Michael Butler, "Simply Wrong About Europe," *Times* (London), November 26, 1991, p. 3.

25. Hugo Young, *One of Us: A Biography of Margaret Thatcher* (London: Macmillan, 1989), p. 388. For Thatcher's own perspective on the EC and account of the ensuing budget dispute, see Margaret Thatcher, *The Downing Street Years* (New York: HarperCollins, 1993), pp. 34–35, 60–64, 78–88, 537–545.

26. *Financial Times,* June 28, 1989, p. 2.

27. Young, *One of Us,* p. 184.

28. Jenkins, *Centre,* p. 494.

29. Jenkins, *European Diary,* pp. 529–531. Granada Television, a private British television company, produced an entertaining and accurate reenactment of the Dublin summit called "Mrs. Thatcher's Billion."

30. Quoted in the *Daily Express* (London), June 4, 1984, p. 4.

31. For a lively account of the Fontainebleau summit, see John Newhouse, "One Against Nine," in *New Yorker,* October 22, 1984, pp. 64–92.

32. See Geoffrey Denton, "Restructuring the EEC Budget: Implications of the Fontainebleau Summit," *Journal of Common Market Studies* 23, no. 2 (December 1984): 117–140.

33. Bull. EC 6-1984, "Presidency Conclusions," point 1.1.1. et seq.

34. Quoted in *Financial Times,* June 28, 1984, p. 14.

35. Quoted in Young, *One of Us,* p. 388.

36. See Pierre-Henri Laurent, "Forging the European Technology Community," in Michael S. Steinberg, ed., *The Technological Challenges and Opportunities of a United Europe* (Savage, MD: Barnes & Noble, 1990), pp. 59–67.

37. See M. Sharp and C. Shearman, *European Technological Collaboration* (London: Routledge & Kegan Paul, 1987), p. 46.

38. Margaret Sharp, Christopher Freeman, and William Walker, *Technology and the Future of Europe: Global Competition and the Environment in the 1990s* (New York: Pinter, 1991), p. 73.

39. Commission, *1980 General Report,* point 120.

40. Commission, *1981 General Report,* point 129.

41. Bull. EC 6-1981, "Presidency Conclusions," point 1.10.

42. Bull. EC 12-1982, "Presidency Conclusions," point 1.12.

43. Commission, *1984 General Report*, point 133.

44. "Europe: The Future," reproduced in the *Journal of Common Market Studies* 23, no. 1 (September 1984): 74–81.

45. See Peter Marsh, "The European Community and East-West Economic Relations," *Journal of Common Market Studies* 23, no. 1 (September 1984): 9–10.

46. François Mitterrand, speech to the European Parliament, May 24, 1984, reprinted in *Vital Speeches of the Day,* August 1, 1984, p. 613.

47. The Genscher-Colombo proposals are reproduced in European Parliament, Committee on Institutional Affairs, *Selection of Texts Concerning Institutional Matters of the Community from 1950–1982* (Luxembourg: European Parliament, 1982), pp. 490–499.

48. Quoted in Newhouse, "One Against Nine," p. 68.

49. Bull. EC 6-1983, point 1.6.1.

50. Bull. EC 5-1982, points 2.1.73 to 2.1.97.

51. "Draft Treaty Establishing the European Union," Bull. EC 2–1984, point 1.1.2. For a comprehensive assessment of the draft treaty, see Roland Bieber, Jean-Paul Jacqué, and Joseph Weiler, eds., *An Ever Closer Union: A Critical Analysis of the Draft Treaty Establishing European Union,* European Perspectives Series (Luxembourg: Office for Official Publications of the European Community, 1985).

52. Bull. EC 2-1984, point 1.1.1.

5

The Transformation of the European Community, 1985–1988

In the mid-1980s the EC underwent an extraordinary transformation. After years of sluggish growth and institutional immobility, member states concluded the Single European Act (SEA), a major revision of the Treaty of Rome that underpinned the single market (1992) program. Jacques Delors, who became Commission president in January 1985, is generally credited with the Community's metamorphosis. "Delors is as important to the enterprise today," Stanley Hoffmann wrote at the height of the EC's transformation, "as Jean Monnet was in the 1950s."[1]

Yet Delors's importance should not be exaggerated. Undoubtedly he possessed an abundance of ambition, competence, and resourcefulness. The new president sought to infuse the Commission with a renewed sense of purpose and set the EC on the road to European union. But Delors could not possibly have realized those objectives had the economic, political, and international circumstances been unfavorable. It was his good fortune to have become Commission president at precisely the time when internal developments (resolution of the British budgetary question, agitation for institutional reform, and pressure to complete the internal market) and external factors (fundamental changes in the global system) made a dramatic improvement in the EC's fortunes almost inevitable. Without Delors, the single market program and the acceleration of European integration might not have happened exactly as they did, but that is not to say that they would not have happened at all.

One of the most remarkable aspects of the EC's transformation is that it coincided with the potentially disruptive Iberian enlargement. The accession of relatively impoverished Portugal and Spain threatened to throw European integration further off course. Without compensating mechanisms, completion of the internal market could have immensely aggravated the social and economic divide between the EC's rich and poor member states. Thus the SEA was more than a device to launch the single market program. It was a complex bargain to improve decisionmaking, increase efficiency, achieve market liberalization, and at the same time promote cohesion. The SEA made possible what French president Georges Pompidou had sought at an earlier stage of the EC's existence: "completion, deepening, enlargement." As Helen Wallace remarked, "The 1992 goal was clearly intended as completion, but new policies had been substantively embraced and institutions had been strengthened, thus deepening was in hand, and widening had occurred for a third time without momentum being lost."[2]

THE THIRD ENLARGEMENT

Formal negotiations to enlarge the EC a third time began with Portugal in October 1978 and Spain in February 1979. Having recently emerged from long periods of authoritarian rule, both countries desperately wanted to join the EC to end their relative international isolation, stabilize their newly established democratic regimes, and help develop their comparatively antiquated economies. As in the contemporaneous case of Greece, member states encouraged Iberian accession as a means of reinforcing reform there. As in the case of the newly independent Central and Eastern European countries more than a decade later, however, the likely political and economic challenges of Spanish and Portuguese membership drove a wedge between rhetoric and reality. Spain and Portugal were poor countries that between them had a population almost 20 percent of the existing EC's. Despite Brussels' genuine commitment to consolidating recent political changes on the Iberian Peninsula, the prospect of Spanish and Portuguese membership filled many member states with dread, not least because of the difficulties caused by the EC's first enlargement.

Realizing that the EC feared the economic and social consequences primarily of Spanish membership, Portugal tried to have its application considered separately and concluded swiftly. Portugal applied to join in March 1977, more than a year before Spain lodged its application. Portugal's accession negotiations also began before Spain's, but only four months earlier. Although the EC negotiated separately with each country, the short time between the opening of both sets of talks indicated the degree to which the EC considered them interrelated.

Portugal ascribed the protracted entry negotiations of the early 1980s to the lumping together of Lisbon's and Madrid's applications and the EC's preoccupation with internal budgetary and institutional issues. Undoubtedly these factors affected Lisbon's application, but a number of factors peculiar to Portugal—notably textiles (which represented over 40 percent of the country's industrial output and 33 percent of its exports), migrant workers, and agriculture—accounted as well for the talks' slow progress.[3] In its opinion of May 1978, the Commission had identified a host of economic, structural, and administrative issues that would have to be tackled before Portugal joined the Community.[4] As a result, the Commission refused to recommend a detailed timetable for accession, although Portugal pressed for a membership deadline of January 1, 1983. The fact that substantive negotiations did not get under way until 1980 finally convinced Portugal of the unlikelihood of its gaining entry only three years later.

Meanwhile, both sides signed a preaccession agreement revising existing bilateral agreements and providing for generous assistance to Portugal. The agreement, which entered into force on January 1, 1981, sought to facilitate Portugal's eventual integration into the EC by providing funds to help modernize the country's economy. In particular, the EC earmarked money for a plethora of projects in the industrial, agricultural, and fisheries sectors, as well as for infrastructural improvement and regional development.

The preaccession agreement was welcome evidence of the EC's commitment to eventual enlargement, especially after the political furor triggered by French president Valéry Giscard d'Estaing in June 1980. In a speech to French farmers' leaders in Paris, Giscard declared that especially in view of the British budgetary question, "the Community should give priority to completing the first enlargement" before undertaking another. The president's office later clarified his remarks to apply them to Spain and Portugal, not to Greece. Other member states distanced themselves from Giscard's statement, although German chancellor Helmut Schmidt supported his friend by declaring shortly afterward that "without the indispensable adjustments to its agricultural policy and without a more balanced distribution of burdens the Community cannot finance the tasks which face it in its expansion southwards."[5]

Spain and Portugal reacted with predictable outrage. But the key to Giscard's statement lay in its timing and its audience. With presidential elections less than a year away, Giscard pandered to French farmers, a powerful and vocal constituency. He may also have hoped to spite British prime minister Margaret Thatcher, who strongly supported Portuguese accession but who had exasperated her EC colleagues during the previous two years by aggressively pursuing Britain's budgetary claims. Thatcher supported Portuguese accession for traditional British foreign policy reasons: the tradition of alliance and friendship with Portugal and the tradition of wanting a wider and weaker Community. Thatcher delighted the Portuguese prime minister by declaring, during his visit to London in December 1981, that Spain and Portugal need not accede simultaneously and that Portugal could join by January 1984.[6]

As long as France opposed enlargement there was little hope of early Portuguese accession. Even when François Mitterrand succeeded Giscard in May 1981—and did not have to worry about another presidential election for the next seven years—France refused to endorse the EC's southern enlargement pending an acceptable arrangement for Mediterranean agriculture. In the meantime negotiations progressed on a wide range of thorny issues, including capital movements, regional policy, transport, services, and nuclear cooperation. Yet Commission president Gaston Thorn had to remind his hosts during a visit to Lisbon in April 1982 that apart from agriculture, such contentious questions as textiles, fisheries, and the free movement of labor remained unresolved between both sides.[7]

The formation of a relatively stable administration in Lisbon by the able and energetic Mário Soares in June 1983 increased EC goodwill toward Portugal, not least because the new government soon reached an agreement with the International Monetary Fund that included measures to reduce the country's substantial foreign debt and further restructure the economy. In the following months, Soares embarked on a frantic round of visits to EC capitals and cultivated a close relationship with Mitterrand, a fellow socialist. Soares impressed his interlocutors with Portugal's determination to become a model member state. Rapid agreement on a number of outstanding issues followed, although (much to Soares's annoyance) the fate of the Spanish and Portuguese negotiations became increasingly linked. Without a breakthrough in the EC's talks with Spain, especially concerning agriculture and fisheries, Portugal's prospects for immediate accession looked poor.

French misgivings about southern enlargement focused on Spain far more than on Portugal. Spain's accession would increase the EC's agricultural area by 30 percent and its farm workforce by 25 percent. Apart from the financial implications of such a development, especially at a time of budgetary crisis and attempted reform of the CAP, Spain and France would compete directly in the production and sale of fruit, vegetables, and olive oil. Nevertheless, France recognized the political imperative of Spanish membership, especially after an attempted military coup in Madrid in February 1981. The European Council, meeting in Maastricht the following month, expressed "great satisfaction at the reaction of the King, government and people of Spain in the face of the attacks recently made against the democratic system of their country." This reaction, the European Council concluded, "strengthens the political structures which will enable a democratic Spain to accede to the . . . European Communities."[8]

Doubtless the Spanish government appreciated the European Council's concern, but kind words could not compensate for lack of progress in entry negotiations. The fault did not lie entirely with the EC. Despite repeated Spanish rhetoric about the country's "European vocation," the government seemed unwilling to embrace all of the obligations of Community membership, especially the need to introduce a value-added tax, curtail subsidies, and end protectionism from the date of accession. Spain's recalcitrance prompted the European Council, meeting in London in November 1981, to chide Madrid by recalling the applicant countries' undertaking to "accede on the basis of the Community treaties and subordinate legislation in force on the date of accession, subject only to such transitional arrangements as may be agreed." Moreover, the European Council urged Spain to "make good use of the period until accession for careful preparations for . . . enlargement by introducing the necessary reforms so that the potential benefits for both sides can be realized."[9]

Thus apart from some technical arrangements, Spain's entry negotiations made little headway in 1982. Agreement on Spanish agriculture proved particularly elusive, becoming increasingly bound up with the EC's growing budgetary crisis. During a visit to Madrid in June 1982, Mitterrand stated bluntly that Spanish accession "under existing circumstances would mean an unfortunate state of anarchy, adding new pressures to those already facing the Communities."[10] For that reason, impending enlargement provided a catalyst for CAP reform, lest Iberian accession add wine and olive oil to the list of products in which the EC already had a huge surplus.

Earlier, at approximately the same time that Soares became prime minister in Lisbon, Felipe González formed a new government in Madrid. González was a passionate Europhile whose primary political objective was to bring Spain into the EC. Young, personable, and able, González emulated Soares by embarking on a series of visits to EC capitals, using personal charm, political savvy, and, where appropriate, ideological affinity to make the case for Spanish accession. An informal summit of the prime ministers—all socialists—of the EC's Mediterranean member states and the applicant countries on October 16–17, 1983, may have paved the way for the first breakthrough on agriculture in the enlargement negotiations. At a meeting in Luxembourg only two days later, agriculture ministers approved rules to organize the EC's fruit, vegetable, and olive oil markets.[11]

This was the first stage in the process of settling the contentious agricultural aspect of enlargement. By contrast, fisheries became increasingly disputatious between the EC on one side and Spain and Portugal on the other in 1984. On March 7, French patrol boats fired on two Spanish trawlers in the Bay of Biscay, about 100 miles off the southwest coast of France but well within the EC's 200-mile fisheries limit. At issue was the EC's effort under the Common Fisheries Policy to limit the access of Spain's fishing fleet, which was larger than the entire EC fleet. Spanish fishermen attacked foreign trucks in protest; French truckers, in turn, blockaded the Spanish border. Such incidents continued throughout the year—thirty-two Spanish trawlers were arrested off the Irish coast alone in 1984.[12]

The fisheries dispute eluded resolution until early 1985, by which time accession negotiations were well on track. The decisive breakthrough came not in the talks themselves but in the EC's internal affairs. Settlement of the British budgetary question at the Fontainebleau summit in June 1984 removed the biggest obstacle to enlargement: The summit communiqué set

January 1, 1986, as the date for Spanish and Portuguese accession.[13] As Spain had always suspected France of blocking enlargement, Mitterrand's pivotal role in securing a settlement at Fontainebleau greatly improved relations between both countries. In a move calculated to reassure González of French goodwill, Mitterrand flew to Madrid immediately after Fontainebleau to report personally on the summit's outcome.[14]

Yet the summit's call for an end to negotiations by September 30, 1984, proved too ambitious. Agriculture continued to dominate talks for the remainder of the year, and it was not until December 1984 that the European Council reached an agreement on fish, fruit, vegetables, and wine acceptable to the Spanish government.[15] When Delors became Commission president in January 1985, the agricultural agreement still had to be implemented, and a number of outstanding issues remained between Brussels and the applicant countries. Moreover, a new problem arose when Andreas Papandreou, the Greek prime minister, demanded that the EC finalize the Integrated Mediterranean Programs (IMPs) before concluding accession negotiations. Originating in a 1982 Commission proposal in response to a Greek government demand, IMPs sought to provide financial assistance primarily to Greece but also to Italy and southern France to help develop agriculture, tourism, and small business.[16]

Realizing that the final obstacles to accession had to be removed before the EC could advance on other fronts, Delors threw himself into the fray with characteristic energy and resolution, taking personal responsibility for the IMPs. At a meeting in Brussels in February 1985, EC agriculture ministers established an effective mechanism to implement the restrictions on wine production agreed to by the European Council the previous December. Two weeks later foreign ministers agreed on a five-year enlargement-linked program of structural aid to farmers. Foreign ministers resolved the remaining problems—fisheries, free movement of Spanish and Portuguese workers in the EC, and the applicant countries' budgetary contributions—at another marathon meeting at the end of March 1985.[17]

In order to draft and ratify the accession treaty in time for Spanish and Portuguese membership in January 1986, the EC still had to iron out the IMPs. Based on a new Commission proposal, the European Council agreed at a summit in Brussels at the end of March to a seven-year program of grants and loans to assist existing Mediterranean regions in the EC "to adjust under the best conditions possible to the new situation created by enlargement."[18] Despite Thatcher's initial opposition, member states finally accepted a figure of 6.6 billion ECUs (European currency units), of which Greece would receive approximately 30 percent. The Greek government had hoped for a larger allocation but obligingly went along with the majority, thus removing the final obstacle to the EC's third enlargement.

The outcome of the Brussels summit was a triumph for Delors, who had staked his political reputation on resolving the IMP dispute. Because he had taken personal responsibility for the IMPs, failure to clear the last hurdle on the road to Spanish and Portuguese accession would have seriously undermined the credibility of the new Commission president. After the Brussels summit, a relieved Delors declared that "all the family quarrels have been sorted out. The family is now going to grow and we can think of the future."[19] Indeed, for the first time in nearly twenty years the EC's future looked bright. Developments in the early 1980s had heralded a rapid acceleration in the pace of European integration. Imminent enlargement provided an additional psychological boost. Under Delors's leadership the new Commission made no secret of its determination to exploit this unique opportunity to improve the EC's fortunes. Following the protracted enlargement negotiations and short but sharp IMP dispute, the decks were cleared for the forthcoming European Council in Milan to consider, as Mitterrand put it, "what Europe will become."[20]

DEVISING A SINGLE MARKET STRATEGY

The Milan summit of June 1985 considered the EC's future on the basis of concrete proposals, not vague aspirations. The Commission's plan—the famous White Paper on completing the internal market by the end of 1992—was one of the most important documents prepared for the European Council's deliberations.[21] Lord Arthur Cockfield, the internal market commissioner, had drafted the White Paper in the spring of 1985. At the same time, Delors made the fateful decision to devote his first presidency principally to promoting the single market program. In retrospect, because of the success of the 1992 strategy, Delors's decision seems inevitable. Yet the Commission president thought carefully before putting most of his eggs in the single market basket. Although he readily grasped the economic importance of a fully functioning internal market, Delors was initially unsure that the single market program alone could generate the popular appeal and political impetus necessary to achieve his overriding objective: a thoroughly revitalized EC.

Apart from completing the internal market, Delors's means toward the greater end of a resurgent EC included an overhaul of decisionmaking procedures, a new monetary policy initiative, and an extension of Community competence in the field of foreign and defense policy. Delors stressed these themes in his first address as Commission president to the European Parliament (EP) in January 1985 and in a number of other speeches during the next few months.[22] As a former finance minister and a committed Eurofederalist, Delors's personal preference was to concentrate primarily on Economic and Monetary Union (EMU). Three of the incoming commissioners were also former finance ministers and shared their president's predilection for economic and monetary policy. The relative success of the

European Monetary System (EMS), then in its seventh year of operation, further encouraged Delors's thoughts in that direction.

Yet Delors's pragmatism caused him to be wary of the EMU option. Monetary policy lay too close to the core of national sovereignty for an initiative going beyond the EMS to prosper in the mid-1980s. Delors wanted to capitalize on the goodwill generated in the European Council by the successful Fontainebleau summit, not aggravate tension among national leaders by promoting a politically sensitive proposal. Similarly, an outright assault on unanimity in an effort to improve EC decisionmaking would only have raised member states' hackles. If he was to achieve the goal of a revitalized EC, Delors could not afford to risk alienating the heads of state and government.

By contrast, the advantages of choosing the internal market option were obvious. By going back to basics and emphasizing one of the original objectives of the Treaty of Rome, Delors could hardly be accused of overweening ambition. Regardless of their political preferences and personal opinions of each other, national leaders uniformly sang the praises of a single market. Thatcher was especially eloquent on the virtues of market liberalization. By championing a cause dear to her heart, Delors hoped to reconcile Thatcher to the Community and heal the wounds caused by the protracted British budgetary dispute.

In addition, Delors believed, a single market strategy would indirectly but inescapably result in an improvement in decisionmaking procedures and renewed interest in EMU. Political will to complete the internal market could never translate into action unless unanimity gave way to qualified majority voting in the Council. Without reform of the legislative process, single market proposals would ultimately bog down in disputes among member states. A successful single market strategy would most likely also fuel interest in EMU. How could the market be fully integrated without monetary union and a common macroeconomic policy? The political, if not the economic, logic of a large, vibrant internal market pointed inexorably, Delors thought, toward currency union.

The relationship between completing the internal market, decisionmaking reform, and a further monetary initiative intrigued Delors and underlay the entire single market strategy. Yet undue emphasis on the indirect objectives of the single market program threatened to undermine the whole project. Ever watchful for encroachments on national sovereignty, Thatcher would likely oppose Delors from the outset if he stressed the goal of EMU, let alone majority voting. Nor was Delors sure that Cockfield, Thatcher's senior appointee to the Commission and a former British trade and finance minister, supported more than mere completion of the single market. In the event, Cockfield "went native" in the Commission and became a staunch advocate of greater European integration. Predictably, Thatcher did not reappoint him in 1988 for a second term.[23]

Despite their strikingly different political and personal backgrounds, Delors and Cockfield became close colleagues, working tirelessly in early 1985 to fuel existing interest in the internal market and launch the White Paper. Both understood the importance of maintaining private-sector support. Thus Delors kept Etienne Davignon's door to European business leaders ajar and reiterated the Commission's commitment to an active industrial policy. To a great extent the Commission's subsequent proposals for collaborative research and development projects, and its involvement in Mitterrand's "Eureka" venture—a plan for closer European cooperation in the high-technology sector in response to President Reagan's Strategic Defense ("Star Wars") Initiative—sought to strengthen the Commission-industry alliance in anticipation of the single market program.

European business leaders needed little prompting on the virtues of a single market. In 1984 and 1985 alone, three major manufacturers published pamphlets on the need to complete the internal market as soon as possible.[24] The most striking and influential of these was a tract by Wisse Dekker, the head of Philips and a leading member of Davignon's European Round Table. Dekker's plan for a single market by 1990 bore a strong resemblance to the Commission's subsequent White Paper. It also reminded EC officials that the biggest challenge confronting them from the private sector was not to generate support for the single market but to allay doubts about the Commission's ability to deliver the goods.

The Commission's pivotal role in planning and implementing a single market strategy was a further reason for Delors's keen interest in the idea. Delors knew the EC's fortunes would never revive without a corresponding increase in the Commission's authority and morale. As incoming president, he wanted to give the Commission new direction and leadership. For its part, the Commission looked forward to acquiring a fresh sense of mission and importance after the drift of the previous two decades. A strategy to devise and put in place a fully functioning internal market ideally suited both Delors's and the Commission's aspirations. As a political priority involving most of the Commission's directorates-general, a comprehensive single market strategy would invigorate the Commission, returning it to center stage in the EC.

By early 1985, as Delors settled into the Commission presidency, there was widespread discussion in political, business, and academic circles about completing the internal market. In his January 1985 speech to the EP, Delors had proposed 1992—the end of two consecutive commissioners' terms of office—as a possible target date. The Commission's program for 1985 stressed the importance of the single market and urged the European Council "to pledge itself to completion of a fully unified internal market by 1992 and to approve the necessary program together with a realistic and binding timetable."[25] Delors pressed the point at the Brussels summit later that month. As "the necessary program" and "a realistic and binding timetable" did not yet exist, Delors convinced the heads of state and government to request the Commission to draw these up before the next European Council, due to take place in Milan at the end of June.

Having helped engineer the European Council's request, Delors accepted the challenge with alacrity. The Commission—fourteen of whose seventeen members were new to the job—threw itself into the task of preparing a detailed plan to complete the internal market with an enthusiasm not seen in Brussels since Walter Hallstein's day. Because a successful single market would affect almost every EC activity—from external relations to competition, from information to agriculture—few of the Commission's directorates-general were uninvolved in the ensuing round of meetings and consultations, drafting and redrafting. The result was a "rapid, bold and radical" proposal, presented publicly for the first time on June 15, 1985, two weeks before the Milan summit.[26]

The White Paper—a relatively short document—is often caricatured as a typical Commission product: unintelligible, obtuse, and tedious. Indeed, the highly technical nature of the internal market hardly lends itself to lively prose. Yet the White Paper is a surprisingly lucid piece, containing a ringing defense of market liberalization and a clear exposition of how and why the EC should achieve a single market. If anything, the Commission deliberately downplayed the White Paper's style in order to avoid unfavorable political comment. Only in the final paragraph did its authors put the White Paper in historical perspective, proclaim the venture's political significance, and allow free rein to their hortatory impulses:

> Just as the Customs Union had to precede Economic Integration, so Economic Integration has to precede European Unity. What this White paper proposes therefore is that the Community should now take a further step along the road so clearly delineated in the treaties. To do less would be to fall short of the ambitions of the founders of the Community, incorporated in the Treaties; it would be to betray the trust invested in us; it would be to offer the peoples of Europe a narrower, less rewarding, less secure, less prosperous future than they could otherwise enjoy. That is the measure of the challenge that faces us. Let it never be said that we were incapable of rising to it.[27]

The White Paper is best known for its appendix listing approximately 300 Commission proposals needing decisions by the Council of Ministers before the internal market could be implemented. Cockfield was able to put such an extensive compilation together in record time because most of the items on it already lay around in draft form, a legacy of the Commission's earlier internal market efforts. Nevertheless, Cockfield's job was much more than simply "one of trawling and of sieving."[28] The indispensable novelty of the White Paper's appendix was not the items listed in it but the way Cockfield organized them according to a timetable ending on

December 31, 1992. Thus the appendix constituted a detailed action plan against which Commission officials, politicians, and businesspeople could measure progress toward a single market.

Yet the White Paper's appendix represented only part of the large legislative agenda likely to be unleashed by the single market program. As mentioned but not spelled out elsewhere in the White Paper, completing the internal market would impinge directly on a wide range of policies and activities, notably in the fields of competition, research and development, the environment, consumer protection, social affairs, and EMU. Despite the simplicity of the "single market" slogan and the brevity of the Commission's action plan, the White Paper represented a huge leap forward for the EC. It was up to the heads of state and government, meeting in Milan only two weeks after the White Paper's publication, to decide whether the single market program would get off the ground.

THE SINGLE EUROPEAN ACT

The momentum to complete the internal market that had built up in the early 1980s ensured that the European Council endorsed the White Paper at the Milan summit. Although each member state had reservations about specific Commission proposals, the European Council had long since committed itself in principle to completing the internal market. But as Delors pointed out in a series of speeches before the Milan summit, the European Council's acceptance of the White Paper would not suffice to ensure the single market program's success. As long as serious procedural problems remained unresolved, the White Paper's detailed proposals likely would languish in the Council. The challenge for the Milan summit, therefore, was to tackle the politically charged question of legislative reform in the EC, a process that resulted in the convening of an intergovernmental conference (IGC) in September 1985 and the conclusion of the SEA in February 1986.

The Dooge Report

The issue of institutional reform was already on the Milan agenda, not only indirectly in the form of the White Paper but also directly in the form of a report presented by the Ad Hoc Committee on Institutional Reform, set up after the Fontainebleau summit and chaired by James Dooge, a former Irish foreign minister. The so-called Dooge Committee's political significance was evident from the outset. Its composition reflected the importance that each member state placed on closer European integration and the approach each would probably take in any future negotiation to revise the Treaty of Rome. As a mark of his determination to revive the EC's fortunes, Mitterrand nominated Maurice Faure, a close associate, a lifelong champion of European union, and a signatory of the Treaty of Rome. As a mark of her determination to restrict institutional reform, Thatcher nominated Malcolm Rifkind, a junior foreign and Commonwealth minister, a vigorous advocate of deregulation and market liberalization, and a staunch defender of national sovereignty.

Incessant interest in the EC's revival following the Genscher-Colombo initiative of 1981—fueled by the EP's draft treaty, the inevitability of a third enlargement, and resolution of the British budgetary dispute—ensured that the Dooge Report would avoid the fate of the Tindemans Report a decade earlier. "Spaak II," the Dooge Committee's other informal name, heightened expectations about its deliberations by drawing a parallel between the heady days of European integration in the mid-1950s and the Community's possible resurgence in the mid-1980s. Just as the 1955 Messina Conference had given birth to the Spaak Committee, which in turn gave birth to the Treaty of Rome, so EC enthusiasts hoped that the 1984 Spaak II Committee would similarly stimulate deeper European integration.

Predictably, the committee devoted considerable attention to internal market issues. Rifkind identified a "solid consensus" in the committee and in the Community as a whole about completing the single market by 1990, or 1992 at the latest.[29] Partly for that reason, but also because of mounting pressure for institutional reform, the committee examined a host of options for improving the legislative process, strengthening the commission and EP, and ending decisionmaking deadlock in the Council. In addition, the Committee considered formally extending EC competence, notably in areas such as competition, research and development, consumer affairs, and monetary policy. The committee also discussed intensifying European Political Cooperation (EPC) and extending it to include security and defense discussions.

In view of the scope of its deliberations, the committee presented a surprisingly short final report to the Brussels summit in March 1985.[30] The report outlined a number of "priority objectives" deemed necessary to deepen integration. As expected, they included a "homogeneous internal economic area," restrictions on the use of unanimity in the Council, an enhanced legislative role for the EP, greater executive power for the Commission, and new initiatives in selected policy areas. Because of the nature of the committee's mandate and recognition by committee members of wide differences over the future of European integration, the report was replete with reservations and minority opinions. For instance, as the personal representative of the prime minister of neutral Ireland, Dooge felt obliged to dissociate himself from the report's recommendation that member states attempt to coordinate security as well as foreign policy, although both he and Garret FitzGerald, the Irish prime minister, privately endorsed the idea. Much more important, three committee members—the representatives of

Britain, Denmark, and Greece—disagreed with the report's central suggestion that the heads of state and government convene an IGC to negotiate a treaty on European union based on existing EC law, the Stuttgart Declaration, and the Dooge Report and "guided by the spirit and method of the [EP's] Draft Treaty."

The Milan Summit

Preoccupied with critical enlargement negotiations in March 1985, the European Council deferred discussion of the Dooge Report until its Milan meeting. Agreement on enlargement, the vague but far-reaching Spaak II Report, and the Commission's recently completed White Paper gave the Milan summit an air of expectation not seen in the EC since the Hague summit of 1969. As at The Hague sixteen years previously, a pro-integration demonstration heightened public awareness of an imminent breakthrough. Moreover, as a vigorous proponent of European union, Italy wanted to end its six-month Council presidency with a historic decision at the Milan summit to launch an IGC to negotiate a new treaty, or at least major reform of the existing treaties.

Quick endorsement of the White Paper apparently presaged a smooth summit, but the meeting soon became mired in a difficult procedural discussion. Arguing against a treaty revision, Thatcher instead advocated informal arrangements to quicken decisionmaking in the Council. Taking a coordinated position, Mitterrand and German chancellor Helmut Kohl urged major institutional reform but disagreed about the EP's possible new powers. With Delors's strong support, Italian prime minister Bettino Craxi finally forced the issue by proposing an IGC to negotiate a treaty on foreign policy and security cooperation, as well as a revision of the Treaty of Rome to improve decisionmaking and extend EC competence. Jealous of their national sovereignty, Britain and Denmark objected to holding an IGC, and obstructionist Greece followed suit. Italy again forced the issue by calling for a vote under Article 236 (now Article 48 TEU), which permits an IGC to be convened if a majority of member states approve. It was unprecedented for the heads of state and government to vote on anything at a European Council. In the ensuing ballot seven voted in favor of an IGC and three—the British, Danish, and Greek prime ministers—voted against.

It was nothing new for Thatcher, the lone crusader for reform of the EC budget, to be isolated at a European Council. But she found herself in a novel situation at the end of the Milan summit. In the past, Thatcher's intransigence had thwarted the EC's development. Now she was powerless to prevent the EC from holding an IGC that could change its character completely. Thatcher felt especially offended because the single market program, at the root of the Community's metamorphosis, owed much to her initiative. She also recognized that excessive use of the veto posed a roadblock to efficient decisionmaking and supported closer foreign policy cooperation. Indeed, only days before the Milan summit, Britain had circulated a paper proposing new EPC procedures.

The prospect of an IGC elicited a mixed response from the "progressive" member states. On the one hand, it was gratifying that the Ten, plus the two candidate members, would move forward together into the next stage of the EC's development. On the other hand, smarting from their isolation at Milan and renowned for their "minimalist" positions on European integration, Britain, Denmark, and Greece might attempt to sabotage the IGC from within. Under Papandreou's vindictive leadership, Greece was capable of such an approach, but there was too much for Britain and Denmark to lose in terms of market integration by pursuing blatantly negative tactics. In the event, the minority member states defended their interests tenaciously at the IGC in a creditable and constructive manner.

The IGC

The IGC that brought about the SEA took place formally at the foreign minister level, although the heads of state and government devoted themselves exclusively to the subject at the Luxembourg summit in December. The foreign ministers opened the IGC in Luxembourg in early September 1985 and met for a further six sessions before concluding the conference, again in Luxembourg, in late January 1986. In between foreign ministers' meetings, two "working parties" of high-ranking officials thrashed out most of the details. The first, consisting largely of permanent representatives, dealt with treaty revisions. The second, made up of the political directors of the foreign ministries (the "political committee"), tackled EPC and also drafted the act's preamble. In addition to member state ministers and officials, commissioners or Commission officials participated at each level of the conference.[31]

The procedural problem of parliamentary involvement in the negotiations proved almost as contentious as the substantive issue of increasing the EP's political power. Citing the supposedly pivotal role of the 1984 draft treaty in accelerating European integration and their status as directly elected representatives, Europarliamentarians claimed a moral right to sit at the conference table. Although Article 236 did not provide for parliamentary participation in the IGC, it required the consent of the EC's institutions before such a conference could take place. The Commission and Council approved without difficulty or delay, but the EP seized the opportunity to complain about its likely exclusion from the negotiations. Although vainly demanding "full and equal participation in drafting the new treaty," the EP provided the necessary assent in a resolution on July 9, 1985.[32] This was the first in a series of parliamentary resolutions in 1985 and early 1986 expressing dissatisfaction with the IGC and its outcome.

At their opening conference session, the member states and the Commission tried to appease the EP by agreeing to "take account" of the draft treaty and any other parliamentary proposals and to "submit" to the EP the results of their deliberations. The EP pounced on this offer and proposed a mechanism to consider the results of the conference, suggest amendments, and, if necessary, settle differences by a conciliation procedure. Needless to say, the other parties had no intention of adopting such an elaborate system and, after much discussion, explained to the EP that "submit" meant no more than "inform." The EP was welcome to express opinions on whatever the conference submitted to it, but the conference was under no obligation to consider those opinions in turn.

Written submissions from member states and the Commission provided fodder for the IGC. One of the Commission's earliest contributions urged the conference to draft a single concluding document rather than a treaty on foreign and security cooperation and a separate compilation of Rome Treaty revisions. Member states were skeptical, but soon they saw the political advantage of having a single document emerge from the IGC. Yet it was only at a late stage of the negotiations that foreign ministers endorsed the idea of *unicité* and named the eventual outcome of their deliberations the *Single* European Act.

Other contributions to the conference covered foreign and security policy, the internal market, the environment, research and development, economic and monetary policy, cohesion between rich and poor regions in the EC, culture and education, and institutional affairs. The political committee considered foreign and security policy in a separate working party. Current trends in East-West relations—intensified Cold War rivalry gradually giving way to possible direct U.S.-Soviet bargaining without European involvement—convinced most member states of the need to assert the EC's international political identity. At the same time, they were eager not to risk alienating a sensitive United States by appearing to undermine NATO. In the end, the conference agreed that member states would "coordinate their positions more closely on the political and economic aspects of security" and "endeavor jointly to formulate and implement a European foreign policy." As a sop to the United States and to those member states—notably Britain and the Netherlands—most sensitive about U.S. opinion, the conference declared that greater foreign policy coordination would not "impede closer cooperation in the field of security" among relevant member states "in the framework of the Western European Union or the Atlantic Alliance."

Despite divergent national positions on the conduct and scope of EPC, the political committee's deliberations were far less contentious than those of the working group charged with proposing treaty revisions. The conference had little difficulty endorsing the goal of an internal market, defined as "an area without internal frontiers in which the free movement of goods, persons, services and capital is ensured." But discussion of the procedural steps necessary to implement the internal market was predictably pugnacious. In the end, the conference revised Article 94 (formerly Article 100) to allow majority voting on harmonization, but only for approximately two-thirds of the measures outlined in the White Paper. The remainder—the least tractable ones—still were subject to unanimity. The IGC also conceded a number of national derogations for aspects of the single market program. As a result, a despondent Delors wondered whether the SEA would suffice to bring about the internal market by 1992.

The IGC did not confront head-on the Luxembourg Compromise. In the SEA's commitment to qualified majority voting for most of the single market program, some member states saw the beginning of a concerted effort to undermine the national veto. Others reached the opposite conclusion by citing the use of unanimity for the White Paper's most controversial proposals. Undoubtedly member states would remain sensitive to each other's concerns, thus perpetuating "the very strong inclination of the Council to seek consensus irrespective of the voting rules."[33] Only time would tell, however, how the formal changes brought about by the SEA in the Council's decisionmaking process would affect ministers' behavior in legislative areas where unanimity had become the norm.

The role of the EP in the decisionmaking process was an equally sensitive procedural issue. To push the EC more in a federal direction and to increase its democratic legitimacy, Germany and Italy urged greater power for the EP; for ideological reasons Britain took the opposite tack, and for a combination of political and practical purposes France also opposed strengthening Parliament's legislative role. The issue dominated a number of negotiating sessions, including the December 1985 European Council. Eventually the IGC agreed to extend "compulsory" consultation between the Council and the EP to new policy issues and, more important, to establish a "cooperation procedure" to involve the EP fully in the legislative process, notably for most of the single market directives. The conference also gave the EP the right to approve future accession and association agreements. As these concessions were limited by comparison with those in the draft treaty, the EP, supported by the Italian government, expressed serious dissatisfaction.

During the IGC, Delors returned repeatedly to his pet project of including "a certain monetary capacity" in the SEA. This would bring about "an alignment of economic policies" in the EC, "and outside it would enable Europe to make its voice heard more strongly in the world of economic, financial and monetary matters."[34] EC finance ministers considered the question at an informal meeting in Luxembourg on September 21, 1985—the only sectoral council to discuss IGC issues—after which Delors submitted a formal proposal, as did the Belgian government. Britain strongly opposed any move toward EMU, France was broadly in favor, and Germany remained equivocal. Without strong support from a large member state, Delors succeeded only in including a new chapter in the treaty that recognized the need to converge economic and monetary policies "for the further development of the Community" and also mentioned the EMS and the ECU.

Meeting in Luxembourg on December 2–3, 1985, the European Council failed to resolve outstanding issues and conclude the SEA even after two full days of discussion. A foreign ministers' session in mid-December brought agreement closer, but lingering Danish and Italian reservations (the Danes complained that the SEA's institutional provisions went too far, and the Italians complained that they did not go far enough) carried over into the Dutch presidency. The wording of an article on working conditions, buried in a subsection on social policy, also caused last-minute delays. The ultimate ministerial session of the IGC took place in Luxembourg on January 27, 1986, to approve final compromises reached in the working party and the political committee and to sanction the draft SEA put together by the Dutch presidency, the Commission's legal service, and the Council secretariat.

Only nine member states signed the SEA in Luxembourg on February 17, 1986, the date stipulated by the IGC. Denmark, Italy, and Greece were the three recalcitrant countries. The Danish government awaited the outcome of a referendum on ratification called for February 27, following the Danish parliament's vote against the SEA on January 21; the Italian government needed more time to discuss the SEA in the Italian parliament; and the Greek government decided to delay signing the SEA until the remaining two states were ready to do so. After the successful outcome of the Danish referendum and the Italian parliamentary debate, the three remaining member states signed the SEA in The Hague on February 28, 1986.

Ratification of the SEA in 1986 was by no means as difficult as ratification of the TEU would be six years later. Despite official British and Danish protestations before and during the IGC, there was little popular concern throughout the EC about an excessive loss of national sovereignty or an exorbitant accumulation of power by the Commission. Most national parliaments held lively debates on the SEA, and almost all voted in favor of ratification. Denmark's parliament was the exception, but the positive outcome of the subsequent referendum ensured Danish ratification. (The reverse happened in 1992, when a majority of Danes rejected the TEU following the Danish parliament's acceptance of it.)

One of the SEA's procedural provisions stipulated that the SEA would come into force one month after the last country ratified it. Member states and the Commission hoped that the SEA would be ratified by December 1986, allowing it to come into effect in January 1987. In the event, a last-minute upset in Ireland delayed everything. First, the Irish government postponed ratification in the national parliament until the year's end. Then a private citizen, concerned about the compatibility of the SEA's political cooperation provisions with Ireland's foreign policy, challenged the act's constitutionality. The case went all the way to the Supreme Court and ran into early 1987. When the Supreme Court ruled that the SEA was indeed unconstitutional, an embarrassed Irish government had no option but to call a referendum to change the constitution. Held in May 1987, for practical purposes the referendum became a vote on whether Ireland should stay in the EC. The result—70 percent in favor, 30 percent against with an exceptionally low turnout of less than 45 percent—was far from an overwhelming endorsement of EC membership, but at least it permitted ratification of the SEA. Thus after an unexpected holdup, the SEA came into effect on July 1, 1987.

Revision of the Treaty of Rome in 1985 and 1986 had proved a messy and protracted affair. For that reason Delors especially disliked the stipulation in the act's "monetary capacity" subsection that further steps toward EMU involving institutional change could be taken only in an IGC. Yet his confidence in the likely revival of member states' interest in EMU led Delors to talk presciently at the end of the SEA negotiations about the possibility of a new IGC in a relatively short time.[35] In other respects, too, the SEA disappointed Delors. He felt that member states had been unwilling to take bold initiatives, thus reducing progress to the level of the lowest common denominator. In that sense, Franco-German leadership had not been decisive. Far from pushing a radical reform agenda, Mitterrand and Kohl had apparently succumbed to Thatcher's minimalist position.

Thatcher's delight and Delors's disappointment with the SEA aptly indicate its apparent significance in 1986. As the *Common Market Law Review* editorialized at the time, "Measured against Parliament's Draft Treaty, the results [of the IGC] are disappointingly meager. They also fall short of the expectations . . . of the Commission and some of the member states. . . . But they reflect the limits of what was possible at the turn of the year [1985–1986]."[36] Yet the SEA had real potential for the EC's rapid development. First, provision for qualified majority voting could not only expedite the internal market but also encourage the Council to be more flexible in areas where unanimity remained the norm. Second, a successful single market program might advance European integration in related economic and social sectors. Third, the SEA's endorsement of the White Paper and formal extension of EC competence could strengthen the Commission's position. Fourth, the introduction of a legislative cooperation procedure could help close the EC's supposed "democratic deficit" and boost the EP's institutional importance. Finally, the SEA's incorporation of EPC into the treaty (while keeping it on an intergovernmental basis) and agreement on new foreign policy coordination procedures might enhance the EC's international standing. Within a short time, proponents and opponents of greater integration would know whether and how the SEA's potential would be realized.

MAKING A SUCCESS OF THE SINGLE ACT

In the late 1980s, at a time when the historical inevitability of communism was shown to be false, the word "irreversible" crept into the lexicon of the EC. It came to mean the point at which completing the single market program, both legislatively and economically, had become unstoppable. A profile of Cockfield in the *Times* of London in November 1987 claimed that the internal market commissioner aimed to create "a feeling of irreversibility" about the 1992 program in case governments failed to agree on vital parts of it.[37] At approximately the same time Lord Michael Young, the British trade and industry secretary, detected "a realization that . . . the internal market is now inevitable. . . . It's going to happen."[38] Young's judgment may have been premature: The following January, in an address to the EP, Delors reported that "progress made to date has lent credibility to the large [single] market but it is not yet irreversible." In the months ahead, Delors declared, "the Commission will concentrate on making the process irreversible."[39]

Regardless of when, if ever, completion of the single market program became irreversible, undoubtedly it got off to a slow start. In retrospect, the years 1986 and 1987 resemble the eye of the storm, preceded by agitation for reform and succeeded by a rapid acceleration of European integration. In the meantime, the Council of Ministers began the legislative task of completing the single market. Britain made the internal market one of its presidency's priorities during the last half of 1986. With the SEA still unratified, member states were not obliged to use qualified majority voting, but the political momentum generated by the single market program encouraged rapid decisionmaking in the Council. Yet progress was pitifully slow. By the end of the year, the Council had adopted 31 of the White Paper's 300 measures. By March 1987 the Council's record was 56 proposals adopted out of 170 submitted by the Commission. Six months later, the Council had adopted only an additional 8 proposals.

Legislative delay did not prevent the single market program from taking off in the real world of business and commerce. "Italian businessmen talk about it, the French have visionary dreams about it, the West Germans plan quietly for it." "It," the *Economist* informed the unenlightened in February 1988, "is December 31, 1992, the date by which the European Community is supposed to become a true common market."[40] Entrepreneurs and businesspeople were already enthralled by the single market program. For over two years they had been bombarded by conferences, newsletters, and advertisements organized and disseminated by the Commission, national governments, and the private sector on how to exploit a frontier-free EC. Large enterprises were best able to do so. In 1987 and 1988 "merger mania," part of "a veritable stampede toward big business in Western Europe," swept the EC as companies attempted to realize economies of scale and improve their transnational distribution networks. Sixty-eight major mergers and acquisitions took place in the Community in 1986; by contrast, 300 happened the following year.[41]

The Commission based its most extravagant claims about the likely economic benefits of a single market on a report by Paolo Cecchini, a retired Commission official, who in 1986 and 1987 led a group of researchers in a huge, Commission-funded project on the "costs of non-Europe." The purpose of the project was to quantify the cost to the Community of maintaining a fragmented market. Based on data from the four largest member states, Cecchini's team of independent consultants assessed the costs and benefits of maintaining the status quo by analyzing the impact of market barriers and comparing the EC with North America. Cecchini looked at the financial costs to firms of the administrative procedures and delays associated with customs formalities, the opportunity costs of lost trade, and the costs to national governments of customs controls. In early 1988 Cecchini's team produced its optimistic findings in a massive, sixteen-volume publication.[42]

Based in part on the Cecchini Report, the private sector's love affair with 1992 disguised the program's slow legislative progress. The problem lay not only with the complexity and sensitivity of many of the White Paper's proposals—the Council dealt swiftly and easily with the least controversial measures—but also with a looming dispute over a Commission plan for the EC's finances over the next five years. The Commission plan bore Delors's personal imprint and later became known as Delors I to distinguish it from the similar Delors II post-TEU budgetary proposals for the period 1993–1999. The purpose of the Delors I package was implicit in its official title: *Making a Success of the Single Act*.[43] The SEA had committed the EC to achieve a single market by 1992 and to implement a number of related "flanking" policies without which a single market could not come into existence. Cohesion—closing the economic gap between the EC's rich and poor member states and between rich and poor regions within the member states—was one of those policies.

Cohesion became the largest obstacle blocking implementation of the single market program in 1987, as the poorer member states (Ireland, Greece, Portugal, and Spain) demanded greater spending on regional and social policy in return for market liberalization. During that time, while the private sector embraced the single market program, the Commission and member states became embroiled in a sharp dispute over how much money to spend on cohesion as part of Delors I. Delors himself characterized the package as a "marriage contract between the Twelve" and struggled throughout 1987 to bring Thatcher to the altar.[44] The British prime minister had an instinctive aversion to increasing the size of the EC's coffers and let it be known that regardless of any budgetary alteration, Britain would retain its current rebate, for which she had fought so hard in the early 1980s. Otherwise, Thatcher applauded Delors's determination to limit spending on agriculture and impose overall budget discipline, two key elements of his financial package.

Thatcher's general dislike of Delors I brought her into conflict with the Commission and the poorer member states The first shots in the new budgetary battle were fired at a foreign ministers meeting in May 1987. Deadlock there set the stage for a series of frustrating encounters in two succeeding European Councils. At the first of these, in Brussels the following June, the European Council made surprising headway toward agreement on Delors I. In an effort to out-Thatcher Thatcher, the other summiteers approved a communiqué that stressed budgetary discipline and CAP reform but did not adequately tackle the cohesion question.[45] Thatcher remained obdurate, objecting to two points in the long document, one about switching the basis of member state contributions and the other about selecting a base year against which to measure changes in farm spending. For old-timers at the European Council, this was vintage Thatcher; for newcomers such as Jacques Chirac, the Gaullist prime minister of France who attended the summit alongside the socialist president, it was unbearable.

In the months before the December 1987 Copenhagen summit, attitudes hardened on all sides. The poorer member states, apparently acquiescent at the Brussels summit, grew more assertive in demanding a greater distribution of EC resources. Unofficially led by Felipe González, the Spanish prime minister, they pressed hard for acceptance of the original Delors package. A series of preparatory meetings in Brussels in late November failed to find common ground between the northern and southern countries and between Thatcher and the rest. At Copenhagen itself, the expected disaster promptly occurred. With Thatcher reverting to her early 1980s negativism, Kohl and Mitterrand reluctant for domestic political reasons to cut the CAP, and González agitating for additional resources, the Copenhagen summit ended in disarray.[46] The European Council's immobility could not have contrasted more sharply with either the vibrancy of the EC's economy in the entrepreneurial climate of the single market program or the superpowers' ability at their simultaneous Washington summit to make decisions about Western Europe's security over the heads of Western Europe's leaders and people.

Delors was despondent about the failure of the Copenhagen summit. Member states had tossed his budgetary package around for nearly a year without reaching agreement. In the meantime, the single market program had fallen seriously behind schedule. Delors had hoped that Germany, coming into the Council presidency in January 1988, would have been able to devote itself exclusively to pushing the single market program. Instead, it looked as if the German presidency, like the immediately preceding Danish and Belgian presidencies, would remain preoccupied with the budgetary question.

The same concern motivated Kohl to call a special summit in Brussels in February 1998 to try to resolve the impasse over Delors I. Hoping to turn his presidency to domestic political advantage, Kohl wanted credit for breaking the EC's latest deadlock. As a result he was more willing than he might otherwise have been to pay the cohesion bill. Yet there was no certainty that the Brussels summit would be successful. A month before the event, a concerned Delors warned the EP that "the consequences of failure will be extremely serious. It would mean that we could not put our minds to attaining the objectives of the Single Act."[47]

Even more than Kohl's statesmanship, Thatcher's surprising tractability saved the Brussels summit from becoming yet another flop. Although the summit began badly with Kohl indecisive, Thatcher strident, and Chirac caustic, the heads of state and government eventually got down to the kind of detailed negotiations that should properly have been left to subordinates. After intense bargaining, they agreed to double the structural funds by 1992, to introduce a new method of budgetary assessment, and to reform the CAP. Thatcher's willingness to increase the EC's budget seemed a remarkable climbdown, especially in light of previous budgetary battles. The prime minister may have been grateful for her colleagues' continuing acceptance of Britain's rebate, but most likely a desire to end the dissipating Delors I struggle and proceed with the single market program—of particular importance to Britain—convinced her to compromise. Whatever the reason, her decision removed a huge obstacle on the road to 1992.

NOTES

1. Stanley Hoffmann, "The European Community and 1992," *Foreign Affairs* 68, no. 4 (fall 1989): 32.
2. Helen Wallace, "Widening and Deepening: The EC and the New European Agenda," Royal Institute of International Affairs (RIIA) discussion paper no. 23, 1989, p. 6.
3. Frances Nicholson and Roger East, *From the Six to the Twelve: The Enlargement of the European Community* (Chicago: St. James Press, 1987), pp. 246–248.
4. Bull. EC S/5-1978.
5. *Le Monde,* June 7, 1980, p. 1; *Financial Times,* June 10, 1980, p. 42.
6. Nicholson and East, *Enlargement,* p. 246.
7. Bull. EC 4-1982, point 2.1.5.
8. Bull. EC 3-1981, "Presidency Conclusions," point 1.1.5.
9. Bull. EC 11-1981, "Presidency Conclusions," point 1.1.5.
10. Quoted in Nicholson and East, *Enlargement,* p. 222.
11. Bull. EC 10-1983, points 1.1.1 to 1.1.20.
12. Nicholson and East, *Enlargement,* pp. 225–226.
13. Bull. EC 6-1984, "Presidency Conclusions," point 1.1.5.
14. *Le Monde*, June 30, 1984, p. 2.
15. Bull. EC 12-1984, "Presidency Conclusions," point 1.2.15.

16. For the original Commission proposal, see Bull. EC 2-1982, point 1.2.4.

17. See Bull. EC 2-1985, point 1.1.2; Bull. EC 3–1985, points 1.1.1 to 1.1.4 and 1.2.2.

18. Bull. EC 2-1985, point 1.2.1.

19. *Le Monde,* April 2, 1986.

20. Quoted in Nicholson and East, *Enlargement,* p. 229.

21. Commission, *Completing the Internal Market: White Paper from the Commission to the European Council,* June 14, 1985, COM(85)210 final.

22. See Jacques Delors, address to the European Parliament, January 14, 1985, Bull. EC S/1-1985; and Jacques Delors et al., *La France par l'Europe* (Paris: Bernard Grasset, 1988), pp. 50–51.

23. See Lord Arthur Cockfield, *The European Union: Creating the Single Market* (Chichester: John Wiley, 1994). For Thatcher's perspective on the single market and the SEA, see Margaret Thatcher, *The Downing Street Years* (New York: HarperCollins, 1993), pp. 551–554.

24. Wisse Dekker, *Europe 1990: An Agenda for Action* (Eindhoven, The Netherlands: Philips, 1984); Fiat, *La Communauté Européenne et l'Industrie* (Turin: Fiat, 1985); and Ford of Europe, *Building a More Competitive Europe* (London: Ford of Europe, 1985).

25. Bull. EC S/4-1985.

26. Helmut Schmitt von Sydow, "The Basic Strategies of the Commission's White Paper," in Roland Bieber, Renaud Dehousse, John Pinder, and Joseph Weiler, eds., *1992: One European Market?* (Baden-Baden: Nomos, 1988), p. 88.

27. Commission, *White Paper,* p. 55.

28. Nicholas Colchester and David Buchan, *Europower: The Essential Guide to Europe's Economic Transformation in 1992* (New York: Times Books, 1990), pp. 30–31.

29. Quoted in *Agence Europe,* February 1, 1985, p. 1.

30. "Ad Hoc Committee for Institutional Affairs Report to the European Council," Bull. EC 3-1985, point 3.5.1.

31. For descriptions and analyses of the IGC and the SEA, see Jean de Ruyt, *L'Acte Unique Européen: Commentaire* (Brussels: Editions de l'Université de Bruxelles, 1987); Richard Corbett, "The 1985 Intergovernmental Conference and the Single European Act," in Roy Pryce, ed., *The Dynamics of European Union* (London: Croom Helm, 1987), pp. 238–272; Andrew Moravcsik, "Negotiating the SEA: National Interest and Conventional Statecraft in the European Community," *International Organization* 45 (winter 1991): 19–56; and David Cameron, "The 1992 Initiative: Causes and Consequences," in Alberta Sbragia, ed., *Europolitics: Institutions and Policymaking in the "New" European Community* (Washington, DC: Brookings Institution, 1992), pp. 23–74. For the SEA itself see Bull. EC S/2-1986.

32. *Official Journal of the European Communites* [*OJ*] C–229, September 9, 1985, p. 29.

33. Roland Bieber, Jean-Paul Jacqué, and Joseph Weiler, eds., *An Ever Closer Union: A Critical Analysis of the Draft Treaty Establishing the European Union* (Luxembourg: Office for the Official Publications of the European Communities [OOP], 1985), pp. 372–373.

34. Quoted in Marina Gazzo, ed., *Toward European Union,* 2 vols. (Brussels: Agence Europe, 1985 and 1986), vol. 2, p. 24.

35. See Gazzo, *European Union,* vol. 2, p. 9.

36. *Common Market Law Review* 23 (1986): 251.

37. *Times* (London), November 16, 1987, p. 15.

38. Quoted in the *Times* (London), November 20, 1987, p. 12.
39. Bull. EC S/1-1988, pp. 8, 26.
40. *Economist,* February 13, 1988, p. 11.
41. *Economist,* February 13, 1988, pp. 46–47, and July 9, 1988, p. 30.
42. Commission, *Research on the "Cost of Non-Europe": Basic Findings*, 16 vols. (Luxembourg: OOP, 1988). For a condensed version of the Cecchini Report, see Paolo Cecchini, *The European Challenge: 1992* (Aldershot: Wildwood House, 1988).
43. Bull. EC S/1-1987.
44. Bull. EC S/1-1988, p. 14.
45. Bull. EC 6-1987, "Presidency Conclusions," point 1.1.5.
46. Bull. EC 12-1987, "Presidency Conclusions," point 1.2.4.
47. Bull. EC S/1-1988, p. 7.

6

From European Community to European Union, 1989–1993

Nineteen-eighty-nine was an *annus mirabilis,* a "miracle year" that ushered in the "New Europe" of the post–Cold War era. It was a year of peaceful revolution that hastened the collapse of communism and led directly to the unification of Germany in 1990 and the disappearance of the Soviet Union in 1991. It was a year in which Europe's future looked bright, with Western Europe fully immersed in the single market program and about to embark on the road to Economic and Monetary Union (EMU) and Central and Eastern Europe embracing liberal democracy. More than any other event, the unexpected breach of the Berlin Wall on the night of November 9, 1989, symbolized a renunciation of the Cold War division and an affirmation of Europe's common destiny.

Yet within a short time the high hopes of 1989 had given way to cynicism and disillusionment. By 1992, when the single market was to have been completed and the Treaty on European Union (TEU) was to have been implemented, economic recession had spread throughout Western Europe while the former Soviet bloc countries struggled to implement market reforms and consolidate newly established democratic institutions. In Central Europe, Germany grappled with the startlingly high social and financial costs of unification. To the southeast, Europe's first post–Cold War conflict engulfed Yugoslavia and threatened to ignite a wider Balkan conflagration.

The TEU ratification crisis symbolized the unexpected reversal of the EC's fortunes. At issue were public alienation from an increasingly complex and intrusive policymaking process, poor democratic accountability in Brussels, and doubts about the EU's ability to cope with profound change in the international political system. Worries about the long-term impact of German unification and eventual EU enlargement to the East contributed to a climate of uncertainty in which the ratification drama unfolded. Implementation of the TEU in November 1993 did not end popular dissatisfaction with the EU but at least paved the way for European integration to progress beyond the single market program toward monetary union and the single currency.

THE ACCELERATION OF HISTORY

What Jacques Delors called "the acceleration of History"—the quickening tempo of developments in Central and Eastern Europe that culminated in the revolution of 1989—began the previous summer with a series of leadership changes, strikes, and demonstrations in Hungary, Czechoslovakia, and Poland.[1] The pace of change picked up in May 1989 with the opening of the border between Hungary and Austria, through which thousands of East Germans fled to the West. Events reached a climax in November 1989, when thousands of West Germans tore down the Berlin Wall without resistance from East German guards. In a fitting finale to a remarkable year, on December 29 Václav Havel, the internationally known writer and anti-Communist dissident, became president of newly independent Czechoslovakia.

The acceleration of history coincided with a huge boost in the EC's fortunes. Germany's presidency in the earlier part of the year had been unusually productive, notably in resolving the contentious Delors I budgetary dispute and in advancing the single market program. Interest in the internal market, both inside and outside the EC, increased daily. Capitalizing on the single market's success, Delors focused attention on his primary goal—EMU. Primed by Delors, pressed by French president François Mitterrand, and with German chancellor Helmut Kohl's lukewarm support, the European Council decided in June 1988 to instruct a group of experts, chaired by Delors and including member state central bankers, to "study and propose concrete changes" that could result in EMU.[2]

The so-called Delors Committee completed its report in April 1989.[3] At the next European Council, in Madrid the following June, the heads of state and government endorsed the committee's three-stage approach to EMU and decided that Stage I, involving greater coordination of member states' macroeconomic policies, the establishment of free capital movement, and membership of all EC currencies in the EMS, should begin on July 1, 1990. They also agreed that an intergovernmental conference (IGC) to determine the treaty changes needed to launch the subsequent stages of EMU would meet "once the first stage had begun."[4]

France was the most powerful proponent of the Delors Report. Edouard Balladur, finance minister during the period of right-wing "cohabitation" with Mitterrand's socialist presidency in 1987 and 1988, had lobbied for a European central bank as a means of ending the Bundesbank's (German central bank's) dominance of Western European monetary policy.[5] Mitterrand fully endorsed the view that only if monetary policy decisions were taken on an EC-wide basis could France hope to regain some of the influence it had lost to Germany in the EMS because of the mark's predominance in the exchange rate mechanism (ERM).[6]

For precisely that reason, Kohl was indifferent about EMU, although the Bundesbank seemed surprisingly open to the idea. Karl-Otto Pöhl, the Bundesbank president, had played an active part on the Delors Committee. As the EC set out once again on the road to EMU, Pöhl resolved that a future European central bank should have as its main goal the Bundesbank's overriding objective of price stability. Better to influence the development of EMU from the outset and from the inside, Pöhl thought, than to disregard the idea and subsequently face an unacceptable fait accompli.

Alone among EC leaders, British prime minister Margaret Thatcher unequivocally opposed EMU, seeing it as an unacceptable abrogation of national sovereignty and an effort to aggrandize power in Brussels. Opposition to EMU had led in part to Thatcher's famous speech at the College of Europe in Bruges, a citadel of Eurofederalism, in September 1988. Thatcher's speech, peppered with barbed attacks against the Commission and against Eurofederalism, was a brilliant articulation of her conception of the EC and of Britain's role in it. The best-remembered part of her peroration was music to the ears of British Euroskeptics: "We have not successfully rolled back the frontiers of the state in Britain only to see them reimposed at a European level with a European superstate exercising a new dominance from Brussels."[7]

Yet Thatcher's hostility toward Brussels in general and EMU in particular lacked widespread support within both the Conservative Party and the British cabinet. Nigel Lawson, her chancellor of the exchequer, advocated early ERM participation and pursued a policy of "shadowing" the mark by maintaining an unofficial parity. Geoffrey Howe, the foreign secretary, feared the impact on Britain of a wholly negative policy toward the EC. Under intense pressure from Lawson and Howe, at the Madrid summit Thatcher committed Britain to participate eventually in the ERM and reluctantly went along with the decision to launch Stage I of EMU in July 1990. In the words of a senior British official, this was a rare case for the prime minister "of reason triumphing over prejudice."[8]

Reaction to events in Central and Eastern Europe also distinguished Thatcher from her EC colleagues, although initially not to such an extent as EMU. The European Council first discussed the rapidly changing Central and Eastern European situation in December 1988, after which it issued a bland statement about the need to overcome "the division of our continent."[9] Six months later, although the pace of reform in Central and Eastern Europe had quickened appreciably, the European Council was too preoccupied with the Delors Report to have more than a brief discussion at the Madrid summit of the "profound changes" sweeping the Soviet bloc.[10] That proved to be the last time the heads of state and government could distinguish rigidly between events in both parts of Europe. Such was the inexorable rate of reform in the Soviet bloc and the consequent transformation of the international system that several of the assumptions underlying European integration, as well as many of the EC's policies, programs, and procedures, were quickly called into question.

The most immediate issue was the sudden prospect of German unification, which throughout the EC's existence had remained a remote aspiration. It is impossible to exaggerate the shock that probable unification caused the EC and its member states (including Germany). The challenge for the EC was both procedural (how to absorb the underdeveloped German Democratic Republic [GDR]) and political (how to prevent a resurgent, united Germany from tipping the institutional balance and subverting the EC system). The challenge for Germany was to reassure EC partners of its commitment to European integration; the challenge for other member states was to overcome latent fear of Germany's size in the EC (a united Germany would account for 27 percent of the EC's GDP and, with 77 million people, 25 percent of its population). The solution to these problems seemed to lie in deeper European integration.

From the fall of the Berlin Wall until the first free general elections in East Germany in mid-March 1990, unification suddenly seemed probable but not necessarily near at hand. After the East German elections, in which the surprising victory of Kohl's Christian Democratic Party signaled an overwhelming urge for immediate unification, the GDR's incorporation into the Federal Republic appeared inevitable before the end of the year. The pace of political change had already quickened when the East German elections were brought forward by two months. It picked up further when German monetary union, initially scheduled for January 1, 1991, took place instead on July 1, 1990. In a final burst of irredentism, full unification came into effect on October 3.[11]

The months immediately after the fall of the Berlin Wall were especially testing for the EC and its member states. This was when Kohl seized the initiative, dealt directly with Soviet president Mikhail Gorbachev, and forced the pace of unification. It was also the time when Mitterrand, Council president until the end of 1989, expressed serious reservations about Kohl's haste and unilateralism, thus straining the much-vaunted Franco-German relationship; when Thatcher displayed deep distrust of German motives, thus alienating herself further from the EC; and when Delors enthusiastically endorsed unification and deeper European integration, thus ensuring the EC's centrality in the events that unfolded and cementing his close personal and political connection with Kohl.

Links between German unification and deeper political integration and between EMU and European Political Union (EPU) were forged in the closing months of 1989. First, a speech by Delors at the College of Europe in Bruges, where Thatcher had issued her infamous antifederalist manifesto the previous year, pointed the EC squarely in the direction of EPU. In response to events in Central and Eastern Europe, Delors called for a huge "leap forward" in the EC to meet the challenge of a new international system. Delors specifically advocated greater EC competence, improved decisionmaking, and less centralization of authority in Brussels.[12] Second, intensifying street demonstrations in East German cities culminating in the collapse of the Berlin Wall gave added impetus to Delors's remarks by accelerating the process of political change. Third, the European Council discussed Delors's ideas and the situation in Germany at an extraordinary summit in Paris on November 18. What Dutch prime minister Ruud Lubbers called the "gastronomic summit"—a short meeting over dinner—afforded participants an opportunity to express informally their initial reactions to the previous week's dramatic developments in Berlin.[13] Delors was delighted, Kohl euphoric, Mitterrand cautious, and Thatcher troubled.

Kohl's speech to the German parliament on November 28, 1989, in which he outlined a ten-point program for German and European unification, further quickened the political tempo. The speech was a political masterpiece that deflected criticism of Kohl's supposed lack of vision and rallied support behind an inherently popular cause. Sometimes caricatured for his atheoretical approach, Kohl gleefully conceded that "abstract models are of no assistance" in ending the East German drama. While acknowledging that "no one today knows . . . how a united Germany will finally look," Kohl declared his willingness "to develop confederative structures between the two States in Germany, with the object of then creating a federation, that is, a national federal system in Germany." Based on his own conviction and on a need to assuage restive neighboring states, Kohl proclaimed that "the future architecture of Germany must be fitted into the future architecture of Europe as a whole." In particular, the EC and the Conference on Security and Cooperation in Europe (CSCE) would provide the two essential pillars for a united Germany in post–Cold War Europe.[14]

The relationship between German unification and European integration was a constant theme in subsequent official pronouncements. Thomas Mann's famous call in 1953 "not for a German Europe, but for a European Germany" became the leitmotif of Bonn's unification policy. Yet Kohl's earliest articulation of it failed to reassure all of his EC colleagues. Thatcher was the most obvious opponent of German unification, and Mitterrand initially followed her lead. Thus Kohl's unequivocal call for unification, Thatcher's and Mitterrand's frosty responses, and Delors's earlier appeal for deeper European integration set the scene for the Strasbourg summit of December 8–9, 1989.

Detailed discussion in Strasbourg of probable German unification allowed Kohl to amplify his idea of a "European Germany." Mitterrand, torn between an instinctive antipathy toward German unification and an equally instinctive affinity for European integration, forged a link between both. Above all, Mitterrand wanted in his second term as president of France to promote "the construction of Europe."[15] Obstructing German unification at the Strasbourg summit, the highlight of France's Council presidency, would have impaired European integration and destroyed the latest initiative for EMU. A key passage in the summit's conclusions outlined the Franco-German bargain, to which other member states subscribed: German unity through free self-determination "should take place peacefully and democratically, in full respect of the relevant agreements and treaties and of all the principles defined by the Helsinki Final Act [of the CSCE], in a context of dialogue and East-West cooperation [and] in the perspective of European integration."[16]

TOWARD THE INTERGOVERNMENTAL CONFERENCES

In concrete terms, the Franco-German bargain manifested itself immediately in a decision in Strasbourg to hold an IGC to work out the changes necessary to move on to Stages II and III of EMU. As Mitterrand announced after the summit, the decision to hold an IGC on EMU represented "the sole objective link" in the European Council's deliberations between German and European integration.[17] Unlike at the Milan summit in June 1985, where the European Council president called for a vote to convene the IGC, in Strasbourg the president merely announced that a majority existed to hold a new IGC. Thatcher made no secret of her minority opinion but saw no point in being formally outvoted.

Thatcher's opposition to German unification and EMU persisted. The prime minister's vociferous support for EC enlargement into Central and Eastern Europe barely disguised her determination to prevent deepening at all costs. Far from weakening the other member states' resolve to deepen European integration, Thatcher's negativism merely emphasized her isolation in the EC and contributed to her ouster as prime minister less than a year later. An infamous outburst by Nicholas Ridley, her close confidante and a government minister, probably reflected Thatcher's private utterances on Germany and Europe. In an interview published in July 1990, Ridley not only decried the emergence of an "uppity" Germany but also denounced deeper EMU as "a German racket."[18] Ridley's prompt resignation failed to dispel a widespread feeling that Thatcher fully agreed with his remarks.

The rapid pace of events in East Germany continued to discomfit Mitterrand. During a previously scheduled visit to East Germany at the end of December 1989, Mitterrand warned against rapid unification. Mitterrand's prevarication undermined the success of the Strasbourg summit, exasperated Kohl, and weakened Franco-German leadership in the EC. Four days before the crucial East German elections of March 18, Mitterrand ostentatiously received the leader of the Social Democratic Party in East Germany and a proponent of long-term rather than immediate unification. Only with the Social Democrats' resounding electoral defeat did Mitterrand make a virtue of necessity and throw himself fully behind imminent German unification.

Efforts to launch European Political Union were already well under way. In a speech to the European Parliament (EP) in January 1990, outlining the Commission's program for the year, Delors called for a stronger executive, a more powerful EP, a more effective procedure for foreign policy cooperation, and implementation of the principle of subsidiarity.[19] On March 20 Belgium became the first member state to submit a formal proposal for EPU, emphasizing the need for institutional reform, reducing the democratic deficit, and developing a common foreign policy.[20] In keeping with earlier efforts to revise the treaties, the EP played a prominent part in the renewed initiative to deepen integration. The second directly elected EP, which met for the first time in July 1989, was fully aware of the recently deceased Altiero Spinelli's contribution to the EC's revival and determined to follow Spinelli's lead by playing an equally constructive part in future negotiations for European union.

Gianni de Michelis, Italy's flamboyant and energetic foreign minister, played a key role in pushing the EC toward EPU even before Italy's presidency in the last half of 1990. The cause of EC reform combined de Michelis's love of the political limelight with his country's genuine enthusiasm for a federal Europe. Although typically extravagant, de Michelis's remark in early 1990 that "never before have [the member states] been more in tune" revealed a growing consensus in the EC about the need for another IGC to negotiate EPU.[21] Only Britain and Denmark remained unconvinced. France was in favor, but Mitterrand's lingering opposition to German unification and the consequent stress in Franco-German relations prevented a clear lead coming from that direction.

The outcome of the East German elections finally swung Mitterrand fully behind imminent German unification and cleared the way for a decisive Franco-German initiative on EPU. That initiative, representing also an act of Franco-German reconciliation, came in the form of a short letter on April 19, 1990, from Kohl and Mitterrand to the president of the European Council. Kohl and Mitterrand linked the need "to accelerate the political construction" of the EC to recent developments in Central and Eastern Europe, as well as to moves already under way to achieve EMU. The letter also anchored the proposed political changes in the SEA's commitment "to transform relations as a whole among the member states into a European Union."[22]

The Kohl-Mitterrand letter is a landmark in the history of EPU and is rightly credited with getting the negotiations going. It was further testimony to the decisiveness of the Franco-German axis in the EC's development, not least because of Britain's marginalization. Yet the Kohl-Mitterrand letter needs to be understood in the context of a growing momentum for a revision of the treaties: It gave added impetus to, but did not initiate, the thrust in late 1989 and early 1990 for EPU.

More immediately, the Kohl-Mitterrand letter set the agenda for a previously scheduled meeting of the European Council in Dublin in April 1990. Instead of discussing German unification and relations with Central and Eastern European countries, the European Council focused on preparations for the IGC on EMU (due to open before the end of the year) and the possibility of a parallel IGC on EPU. Kohl and Mitterrand did not define EPU but instead identified four essential elements of it: stronger democratic legitimacy; more efficient institutions; unity and coherence of economic, monetary, and political action; and a common foreign and security policy. Only Thatcher adamantly opposed a parallel IGC, telling her bemused colleagues that the British monarchy and parliament would survive the EC's efforts to force the pace of European integration. In deference to Thatcher, the European Council postponed a formal decision but left no doubt about its determination to proceed sooner rather than later with negotiations on political union.[23]

Charles Haughey, the Irish prime minister, did not want his end-of-presidency summit (Dublin II) in June 1990 marred by a row with Thatcher. Although Haughey and Thatcher reputedly loathed each other, in his presummit diplomacy the Irish prime minister urged restraint on the pro- and anti-EPU sides. The Irish presidency prepared a deliberately nonprovocative paper that included almost all the suggestions so far made by others on treaty reform. In the event, the summit was surprisingly uncontentious. Thatcher went along with the decision to convene an IGC "to transform the Community from an entity mainly based on economic integration and political cooperation into a union of a political nature, including a common foreign and security policy." The European Council agreed that both IGCs (on EMU and EPU) would begin at the Rome summit in December 1990.[24]

By mid-1990 the EC was well on its way to absorbing the GDR. Even during the Cold War, East Germany had enjoyed a unique relationship with the EC involving an exemption from the common external tariff (CET). Yet German unification presented enormous administrative challenges for the EC. A special group of commissioners chaired by Martin Bangemann (Germany's senior commissioner) met weekly to provide overall direction. A temporary committee of the EP produced a comprehensive and generally positive report (the Donnelly Report) in June 1990 on the implications of German unification.[25] Both the Commission and the EP took care to involve East German officials in their deliberations. The European Council followed suit, inviting East Germany's last prime minister to attend lunch at the Dublin II summit, the first outsider ever accorded such an honor.

The run-up to the launch of the IGCs, which covered most of Italy's presidency, saw the member states' understanding of EMU come into sharper focus and their understanding of EPU become more blurred. This disparity reflected the concrete nature of EMU, especially after publication of the Delors Report, and the inherently imprecise nature of EPU. The ultimate goal of EMU was obvious, whereas the definitive objective of EPU was far from certain. Most member states agreed on what EPU could or should include—closing the democratic deficit, strengthening subsidiarity, improving decisionmaking, extending Community competence, and devising a Common Foreign and Security Policy (CFSP)—but disagreed on the extent of those changes and how to bring them about.

Moves toward EMU received a further boost at an extraordinary European Council in Rome on October 27–28, 1990, when eleven member states agreed to launch Stage II on January 1, 1994. The summit's conclusions identified Britain as the odd one out in discussions of both EMU and EPU.[26] Thatcher's recalcitrance had an unexpected side effect: It precipitated her ouster as Conservative Party leader and prime minister. Ever since their poor performance in the June 1989 EP elections, British Conservatives had seen Thatcher's implacable opposition to European integration as a serious liability. By itself, Thatcher's Europhobia would not have lost a general election; combined with a hugely unpopular tax reform, it threatened to tip the scales in favor of the opposition Labour Party. Thatcher's strident remarks on her return from Rome sparked a leadership struggle the following month, which John Major, her finance minister, surprisingly won. This was the first time in the EC's history that "Community affairs" had impinged so dramatically and so directly on domestic politics.

While Britain's domestic political drama unfolded, the Gulf crisis, hurtling toward a climax in January 1991, cast a shadow over the impending IGCs. Whereas in the summer of 1990 Europhoria apparently knew no bounds, less than six months later attitudes were changing perceptibly. Exhilaration over the revolution in Central and Eastern Europe and its apparent spread to the Soviet Union gradually gave way to concern about economic, political, and military instability in the East. Guarded optimism about German unification conflicted with latent fear of the country's resurgence and more realistic anxiety about the unexpectedly high cost of assimilating East Germany into the Federal Republic. At the same time, U.S.-EC relations were on a collision course in the Uruguay Round of the General Agreement on Tariffs and Trade (GATT).

Accordingly, the European Council inaugurated the IGCs in December 1990 with trepidation rather than elation. John Major's presence alleviated some of the unease. Although, as the *Economist* facetiously remarked, Thatcher's departure had robbed the Community of "the grit around which the other eleven formed their Euro-pearl,"[27] her erstwhile colleagues were glad to see her go. It was impossible at that stage to judge whether Major's ascendancy represented more than a welcome stylistic change in Britain's dealings with Brussels. Other heads of state and government happily gave Major the benefit of the doubt.

Apart from the neophyte British prime minister, Kohl was one of the few heads of government in a buoyant mood at the summit. Having easily won the first all-German general elections only the previous week, Kohl was understandably elated. Otherwise, despite the inevitable excitement surrounding the IGCs' launch, few in the European Council seemed to share the Italian prime minister's conviction that "we are moving toward a progressive and irreversible growth of the supranational momentum, from which will emerge European union."[28]

THE TREATY ON EUROPEAN UNION

The two IGCs that opened in Rome in December 1990 began in earnest in Brussels early in the new year. Some member states hoped that the IGCs might conclude as early as the Luxembourg summit in June 1991, but negotiations continued until December 1991, culminating in an intensive bargaining session at the Netherlands' regular end-of-presidency summit, held in the southern city of Maastricht. The Maastricht summit crowned a yearlong series of negotiations among member states with the Commission as a formal participant, the Council secretariat playing a crucial behind-the-scenes role, and the EP effectively marginalized. Although the lowest common denominator often prevailed, the IGCs and the ensuing TEU nonetheless marked a watershed in the history of European integration.

Procedure

At its October 1990 summit in Rome, the European Council charged the General Affairs Council (foreign ministers) with maintaining "parallelism" between both IGCs. Regular contacts between the presidents of the Commission and the Council of Ministers would also help to ensure consistency, as would summit meetings. In addition to the regular end-of-presidency European Councils, there was one extraordinary summit in 1991. It took place in Luxembourg on April 8 but concentrated almost exclusively on the political aftermath of the Gulf War and touched only briefly on the IGCs.

What did parallelism really mean? After all, the precise objectives of the conferences were not closely related. Despite rhetoric to the contrary, member states could have devised EMU without EPU and vice versa. Indeed, they had already decided to launch a new monetary initiative before events in Central and Eastern Europe and the prospect of German unification impelled them also toward EPU. If the purpose of EPU was to establish a single government to which a European central bank, responsible for monetary policy, would be answerable, then the negotiations would indeed have had to be congruent. But a single government was far from what the member states had in mind in the IGC on political union.

Because the conferences on EMU and EPU would contribute to the ultimate attainment of European union and because the Commission wanted to maximize its involvement in all aspects of European integration, the Brussels bureaucracy had a keen interest in linking the two sets of negotiations as closely as possible. But few member states did. Only Germany advocated a close link between EMU and EPU, to the point of threatening to veto EMU without a far-reaching agreement on EPU. The reason, quite simply, was that Germany had the most to lose from EMU and the most to gain from EPU. By agreeing to a single currency, Germany would be giving up the mark and surrendering control over European monetary policy, which it currently enjoyed in the EMS. In return, Germany wanted an EU with a familiar federal system of government in which controversial domestic issues (such as asylum policy and defense) might be resolved and in which a more powerful EP (with a large German contingent) would play a greater legislative role.

Negotiations took place at heads of state and government level (during European Councils), at ministerial level (during monthly meetings of finance ministers to discuss EMU and foreign ministers to discuss EPU), and at official level (during bimonthly meetings of finance ministry and central bank officials to discuss EMU and weekly meetings of the foreign ministers' personal representatives—mostly the permanent representatives in Brussels—to discuss EPU). Although the negotiations were intergovernmental, the Commission participated at all levels, but it lacked the authority to veto a final agreement.

Member State Perspectives

Each delegation brought to the table a particular set of expectations and objectives.[29] Of the larger member states, Germany was most committed to EMU and EPU. On EMU the Bundesbank, rather than the government, seemed to determine Germany's position. Even before the IGC opened, Pöhl, the Bundesbank president, outlined Germany's objectives in a number of forceful speeches and lectures. His main point was the indivisibility of monetary policy. Responsibility for it at the European level would have to reside in a single, independent institution with the unambiguous, statutory mandate of maintaining price stability. In other words, the proposed European Central Bank (ECB) should replicate the Bundesbank. Pöhl also urged a gradual approach to EMU, stressing the need for economic convergence between potential participants. Because of the disparity in economic performance among member states, Pöhl raised the unpopular prospect of a two- or multispeed move to EMU.

Pöhl's blunt statements about EMU and about the excessive cost of German economic and monetary union did not endear him to Kohl. Nevertheless, Pöhl's resignation in mid-1991, four years before the end of his second term as Bundesbank president, was unexpected. Far from letting up on the government, however, Pöhl's successor continued the offensive, focusing especially on the danger of establishing an ECB at the beginning of Stage II, before the EC was ready to launch a single currency. The Bundesbank's stridency caused a rift in the German government, with Theo Waigel, the finance minister, echoing Frankfurt's position and Kohl and Hans-Dietrich Genscher, the foreign minister, taking a more flexible line.

France wanted EMU at almost any cost and did not have an independent central bank counseling caution. Mitterrand was not eager to have an independent ECB but conceded the point early in the negotiations. However, France strongly urged the inauguration of an ECB at the beginning of Stage II rather than Stage III. According to the French, a functioning ECB and a strict timetable for a single currency would spur member states to prepare their economies for EMU. Although overeager for EMU, France had reservations about many aspects of EPU. While advocating EPU as a means of tying united Germany closer to its EC partners, France pursued traditional institutional objectives at the IGC. In particular, France opposed giving the EP any more power and sought a stronger European Council at the expense of both the EP and the Commission.

In a series of speeches in early 1991, Major had promised to put Britain "at the very heart of the Community." The new prime minister's message sounded strikingly similar to Thatcher's statement in November 1990 that "Britain's future lies in the EC: not on the fringes of it, but in the mainstream."[30] Such was the aversion toward Thatcher in the EC, however, that Major's declaration seemed a radical reversal of British policy. In fact, an arcane attachment to national sovereignty, in an age of increasing economic and political interdependence, continued to fuel British opposition to a single currency and to an EU organized on federal lines. Britain's performance in both IGCs demonstrated the philosophical and ideological distance between London and other EC capitals. On a range of issues—from EMU to legislative reform to CFSP decisionmaking—Britain took a minimalist position.

A prolonged controversy over the "F-word" demonstrated the difference between Britain and its EC partners. A revised draft treaty presented by the Luxembourg presidency in June 1991 described European integration as "a process leading to a Union with a federal goal." Douglas Hurd, the British foreign secretary, immediately announced that his country did "not intend to be committed to the implications which, in the English language, the phrase 'federal goal' carries."[31] The issue was not simply linguistic. After all, Americans understood "federalism" to mean something positive and worthwhile. A British Europarliamentarian explained the problem differently: "On the Continent, [federalism] is a harmless label, neither exciting nor controversial. In Britain, it carries connotations of unspeakable disloyalty and unmentionable perversity."[32]

To be more specific: In certain sections of the Conservative Party federalism had extremely negative connotations. Conservative Euroskeptics equated federalism with the excessive centralization of power in Brussels. Thatcher, the leading Conservative back-bench Euroskeptic after her ouster as party leader, warned shortly after leaving office that "coming together in Europe" must not mean "more centralization. That would be a most undesirable constraint on liberty. Much of the rest of the world is finding liberty in devolution of power away from the center; it would be ironic if the Community were to move in the opposite direction."[33] Thatcher later developed the "liberty" theme before sympathetic U.S. audiences, contrasting the EC's supposed centralization with the Soviet bloc's disintegration.

Thatcher was right to caution against an unreasonable concentration of power in Brussels. But by 1991 the Commission was fully committed to subsidiarity—a federal principle—thanks partly to Thatcher's earlier warnings. Indeed, a desire to enshrine subsidiarity in the new treaty was one of the few issues in the political union negotiations on which every delegation agreed. The irony was not that the EC was going the way of the former Soviet bloc but that Thatcher subscribed to a federal remedy (subsidiarity) for a supposed federal affliction (centralization) and that during her eleven years as Britain's prime minister she had further centralized power in her own already overcentralized state.

With Thatcher hovering in the wings and a general election looming, it was not surprising that the British government protested about the F-word. It was an easy battle to fight because there was nothing of substance at stake. At the Luxembourg summit in June 1991, Major denounced the draft treaty's reference to a "federal goal." To his annoyance, the new Dutch presidency merely changed this phrase to "federal vocation." As the IGCs gathered speed, Major escalated his campaign to excise the F-word. Eventually his colleagues gave in. "What does the word matter, as long as we have the actual thing?" asked Delors.[34] The word mattered, of course, because Major needed to claim a political victory at home.

By contrast with Britain, Italy was a wholehearted champion of supranationalism. As a weak and highly decentralized state with strong regional rather than national allegiances, Italy welcomed the emergence of a federal Europe. There were few proposals on political union to which Italy objected. However, because of its excessive budget deficit, Italy feared being relegated to the second division of EMU. Spain shared Italy's concern about a two-speed EMU and advocated a lengthy transition from Stages II to III. Inevitably, as part of an EMU package Spain demanded compensatory finance for poorer member states. Prime Minister Felipe González's threat to block agreement at Maastricht unless his colleagues approved a "cohesion fund" nearly undid the IGCs.

Smaller member states shared many of the larger member states' objectives but lacked the political clout to influence the negotiations' outcome. Ireland and Portugal contributed creditably to the debate on economic and social cohesion, whereas Greece, hitherto kept out of the Western European Union (WEU) because of its feud with fellow NATO member Turkey, spent most of its time at the IGC trying to win WEU membership. Luxembourg—the smallest member state—had unusual leverage by virtue of being in the presidency during the first half of 1991. But as in the pre-SEA negotiations, which coincidentally it also chaired, Luxembourg scrupulously played the role of honest broker.

Bargaining and Coalition Building

No two countries had identical positions on EMU and EPU, and no single country—not even Britain—was completely isolated. Regardless of the reason for a country's position—whether principle, pragmatism, tradition, or size—there was considerable scope for ad hoc coalition building, which took place at a series of formal and informal meetings. For instance, in late November 1991 leaders of the six member states with Christian Democratic governments—Germany, Italy, Belgium, the Netherlands, Luxembourg, and Greece—met to preview the Maastricht summit. Despite differences over many details of EMU and EPU, Christian Democratic leaders shared a commitment to deeper European integration, especially along federal lines.

Major's visit to Dublin less than a week before the Maastricht summit is an example of the kind of coalition building that took place as the IGCs came to an end. Major was a right-winger, Haughey a centrist. Britain generally opposed EMU and EPU; Ireland generally favored deeper integration. Yet neither country wanted a stronger EP (Britain wanted to protect national sovereignty; Ireland felt underrepresented in Strasbourg) or a greater EC responsibility for social policy (Britain on principle; Ireland for financial reasons). Both favored unanimity in CFSP decisionmaking (Britain wanted to protect national sovereignty; Ireland was sensitive about neutrality) and opposed an EC-WEU merger (Britain because of its Atlanticism; Ireland again because of its neutrality).

Occasionally bilateral contacts resulted in formal initiatives at the IGCs. For instance, a joint declaration reconciling Britain's Atlanticist and Italy's Europeanist positions contributed to the IGC debate on a European defense identity and dispelled the impression that the negotiations pitted Britain against the other eleven on every issue.[35] Franco-German initiatives were more common, although the EC's two leading member states disagreed sharply on many points. France took a less rigorous approach than Germany on the convergence criteria for EMU and on the independence of the ECB, which it wanted established at the beginning of Stage II. Unlike Germany, France wanted a stronger European Council and a weaker EP and pushed hard for an aggressive EC industrial policy.

Major's assiduous cultivation of Kohl in early 1991 fueled predictable speculation about an emerging Anglo-German or Anglo-Franco-German alliance to rival the Franco-German axis. The British media made much of the warm relationship between the young prime minister and the avuncular elder statesman. Yet a marked improvement in Britain's relations with Germany could hardly diminish, let alone supplant, the Franco-German axis that lay at the heart of the EC's development. Moreover, it became obvious in the run-up to the Maastricht summit that Major was as unyielding in his defense of British interests as Thatcher had ever been. Nevertheless, Major's friendship with Kohl may have paid dividends during the summit itself, especially when Kohl helped Lubbers and Major to reach a last-minute agreement on social policy.

Institutional Input

Despite the explicitly intergovernmental nature of the IGCs, the Commission participated fully in both sets of negotiations. Given his long-standing interest in the subject and the impact of his committee's report, Delors took a particularly keen interest in EMU. The Commission lost the battle to establish the ECB at the beginning of Stage II rather than at the beginning of Stage III, with the launch of the single currency, but won the more important arguments—in favor of a timetable for the final stages of EMU and against a formal "two-tier" structure. Yet Delors had been one of the first to raise the possibility of an informal two-tier system when he proposed, in November 1990, letting Stage III begin with less than a full complement of Community member states. Based on a suggestion by Commission vice president Leon Brittan, Delors also proposed an "opt-out" for any member state not wishing to join the currency union until a later date.[36] Thus the Commission generally favored the treaty's final provisions on EMU.

Preoccupied with EMU and with a host of other issues in 1991—notably CAP reform, the Uruguay Round of the GATT, and relations with Central and Eastern Europe and the disintegrating Soviet Union—the Commission fared poorly in the IGC on EPU. Early in the negotiations the Commission suggested several treaty reforms with which a majority of member states strongly disagreed. These included a radical increase in the Commission's responsibility for international trade relations and greater powers of policy implementation for Brussels. In addition, Delors made a famous speech in London in March 1991 on security and defense. Only weeks after the end of the Gulf War and in the midst of a contentious debate between member states on a possible CFSP, Delors called for the new

EU to subsume the WEU and advocated greater independence from the United States.[37]

Delors's speech and some of the Commission's proposals caused a backlash in certain member states. Thereafter, the Commission was on the defensive in the IGC, fighting a rear-guard action to defend its existing prerogatives. In particular, Delors had to fend off a strong attack on the Commission's exclusive right to initiate legislation and a move to permit the Council to amend Commission proposals by qualified majority voting instead of unanimity. Had the latter happened, Delors told the EP, the Commission would have been reduced to "a sort of Secretariat General" for the Council.[38]

Delors blamed the Luxembourg presidency and the close cooperation between it and the Council secretariat for many of the Commission's difficulties in the EPU negotiations. Delors took exception to the apparent ascendancy in the IGC of Neils Ersbøll, the Council's pragmatic and highly political secretary-general. Even before the IGC began, Ersbøll had helped draft the discussion document on EPU for the December 1990 Rome summit, a document that eventually became the basis for the negotiations themselves. Subsequently, Ersbøll contributed extensively to Luxembourg's lengthy draft treaty of April 1991. Ersbøll had no intention of upsetting the EC's delicate institutional balance, but he had little sympathy for Delors's desire for a stronger Commission and even less for the Commission's efforts to strengthen the EP.

From Delors's perspective, the structure of the Luxembourg draft treaty was its most egregious aspect and the most obvious example of Ersbøll's influence. Delors wanted a unitary structure, in which every policy area came under the Rome Treaty, rather than a structure consisting of three "pillars": an EC pillar (including EMU) and two intergovernmental pillars (for cooperation on foreign and security policy and on Justice and Home Affairs [JHA]). Despite an apparent consensus at the Luxembourg summit in June 1991 to accept a treaty with pillars, Delors fully supported the Dutch presidency's presentation of a draft treaty with a single structure. The humiliating rejection of the Dutch draft treaty by almost every other member state was as much of a setback for Delors as for the Dutch presidency. With typical sullenness, Delors later described the pillar approach as "organized schizophrenia" and threatened to denounce the final version.[39]

Unlike the Commission, the EP was not a participant in the IGCs. Instead, the European Council decided in October 1990 to involve the EP in the forthcoming negotiations by establishing regular contacts between the presidents of the Council, the Commission, and the Parliament and by allowing the president of the Parliament to address ministerial sessions of the conference. The EP considered those measures inadequate. Its president visited all twelve EC capitals during the IGCs, a more productive procedure than interinstitutional meetings. The EP itself could not veto the

IGCs, but two countries, Belgium and Italy, threatened not to ratify the final treaty unless the EP approved it.[40]

The EP had outlined its objectives for the IGCs in a series of reports named after David Martin, rapporteur of the Committee on Institutional Affairs, calling for a radical extension of Community competence, more supranational decisionmaking, and, not surprisingly, greater power for the EP (including legislative codecision with the Council and a right to initiate legislation).[41] As the negotiations proceeded and the EP's exorbitant demands came nowhere near being met, a torrent of speeches and resolutions condemning the IGCs flowed out of Strasbourg. Speaking in Athens on the 2,500th anniversary of democracy, the president of the EP could not forgo an opportunity to deplore the IGCs' stinginess toward his institution.[42] Although a number of member states—notably Germany, Italy, and Belgium—sought greater parliamentary power, it was obvious in the run-up to Maastricht that legislative codecision would, at most, give the EP the ability to block decisions in the Council.

Despite its disappointment with the outcome of the IGCs, the EP was markedly less upset than it had been six years previously at the end of the SEA negotiations. It had learned in the meantime that seemingly small gains could be turned to large political advantage. In 1986, after all, the newly agreed-upon cooperation procedure seemed to be a paltry advance, yet within a short time it had immeasurably enhanced the EP's previously limited legislative power.

Drafting the Treaty

Based on extensive bilateral meetings and on shrewd observations made during negotiating sessions, in mid-April 1991 Luxembourg produced a lengthy draft TEU. Its most striking feature was architectural: The putative EU would consist of three pillars capped with the European Council. By keeping the Common Foreign and Security Policy and cooperation on Justice and Home Affairs on an intergovernmental basis outside the Rome Treaty, Luxembourg hoped to reconcile the two extremes of federalism (supported mainly by Germany, Italy, and the Netherlands) and antifederalism (epitomized by Britain and Denmark).

Predictable federalist criticism of the Luxembourg draft treaty led to a revised version on June 18. Belgium argued forcefully for a "tree with branches" rather than a "temple with pillars"; in other words, for a unitary treaty structure.[43] The new Luxembourg draft did not abandon the three-pillars approach but stressed the institutional links among the pillars and, in a concession to the "maximalist" member states, included a reference to the Union's federal goal.

The Luxembourg presidency also tabled draft treaty provisions for EMU, negotiation of which had made little progress in early 1991 because government officials stuck to rigid positions at the IGC. The length and purpose of Stage II were especially controversial. For practical and symbolic reasons, France and the Commission wanted to establish the ECB at the beginning of a relatively short Stage II. Although a single currency would not be introduced until Stage III, the prior existence of the ECB, together with a deadline for the end of Stage II, would encourage member states to expedite preparations for a single currency. In the meantime, the ECB would reinforce monetary cooperation among national central banks. Germany (specifically, the Bundesbank) saw great danger in establishing the ECB prematurely during Stage II, largely because an underemployed ECB would lack credibility and possibly lose sight of its primary objective: price stability.

The Luxembourg presidency proposed a relatively insubstantial Stage II in which a committee of central bank governors, established toward the end of Stage II, would try to coordinate national monetary positions. The Luxembourg proposals also sparked the first serious discussion of convergence criteria and of possible opt-outs from a single currency. Toward the end of the Luxembourg presidency, a consensus emerged that no member state should be allowed for political or economic reasons to prevent others from moving to Stage III. Nor would any member state (i.e., Britain) be forced to adopt a single currency. That informal understanding proved decisive for the IGC's success. As Luxembourg's finance minister remarked, "The prospect of a two-speed monetary union was raised, and no one was shocked."[44]

Luxembourg's chairmanship of the IGCs culminated in a summit on June 25–26, 1991. Although the European Council was not yet ready to conclude the IGCs, the agreement eventually reached at Maastricht bore a striking resemblance to the draft treaty discussed at the Luxembourg summit. On his return to London, Major described the summit as "a stocktaking exercise" with each delegation explaining its positions on EMU and EPU.[45] The summit was overshadowed in any case with the outbreak of war in Yugoslavia, with the troika of foreign ministers flying to Belgrade on the first day of the summit and returning to Luxembourg the following morning. Like the Gulf War six months earlier, the outbreak of war in Yugoslavia emphasized the importance of a comprehensive CFSP. Yet also like the Gulf War, the protracted and—for the EC—much more serious Yugoslav war would make an effective CFSP far harder to achieve.[46]

The Netherlands' presidency of the Council and chairmanship of the IGCs in the second half of 1991 was controversial and, at the outset, ineffectual. For one thing, the government was deeply divided and became embroiled in late 1991 in a domestic political dispute over social welfare payments. For another, it took on too many international responsibilities. The foreign minister spent most of his time trying to mediate the war in Yugoslavia and the prime minister (Lubbers) was preoccupied with the proposed Energy Charter, an initiative to help the Soviet Union by developing its oil and natural gas industries. Other pressing international issues included the final stages of the negotiations to establish a European Economic Area and the ubiquitous Uruguay Round.

As a result Piet Dankert, the junior foreign minister and a former president of the EP, had unusual latitude to formulate policy toward the IGCs. A committed Eurofederalist, Dankert sought to replace Luxembourg's draft treaty with a new draft that included a unitary structure. As word of Dankert's intentions spread, other member states warned the Netherlands to stick to the agreed-upon pillars approach. By that time the Dutch had drafted a new treaty to which, according to a government spokesman, "we are ready to make some changes in specific areas, but there is no question of us throwing our draft away and going back to the proposals of the Luxembourg presidency earlier this year."[47] Predictably, the Dutch draft triggered an angry reaction when presented at a foreign ministers meeting on "Black Monday," September 30, 1991. Only Belgium supported the text, which Lubbers had earlier proclaimed "acceptable to all our partners."[48] A combination of characteristic haughtiness and uncharacteristic political miscalculation—based largely on supposed German support—accounted for the Dutch blunder. In any event, the near-unanimous rejection of the Dutch draft inadvertently put the Luxembourg draft on a pedestal, thereby ensuring that the TEU would have a three-pillars structure (see Figure 6.1).

Earlier in September, Wim Kok, the Dutch finance minister, had suffered a similar rebuke in the negotiations on EMU when he proposed an explicit two-speed system. According to the Dutch proposals, any six member states that met specific economic criteria concerning inflation rates, low budgetary deficits, stable interest rates, and stable exchange rates by 1996 could establish their own central bank and single currency. The laggardly member states would be excluded not only from the single currency but also from decisionmaking about Stage III. Although the proposals did not mention any country by name, there was a general feeling that France, Germany, the Netherlands, Belgium, and Luxembourg were among the top six.

Member states had already discussed and effectively endorsed an implicit two-speed EMU, but only Germany supported the Dutch draft for an explicit two-speed system. Other member states, regardless of economic performance, resented a proposal that would have created a permanent underclass of EU member states. Faced with such opposition, Kok backed down, disavowing responsibility for the proposals. A consensus soon emerged that the EU should decide collectively when to move to Stage III and establish a single currency, although not every member state would be economically able or politically willing to participate in the currency union at the outset.[49]

Despite the Netherlands' poor presidential performance, the success of the Maastricht summit owed much to Lubbers's negotiating skills. Late in

Figure 6.1 The Temple Structure of the European Union

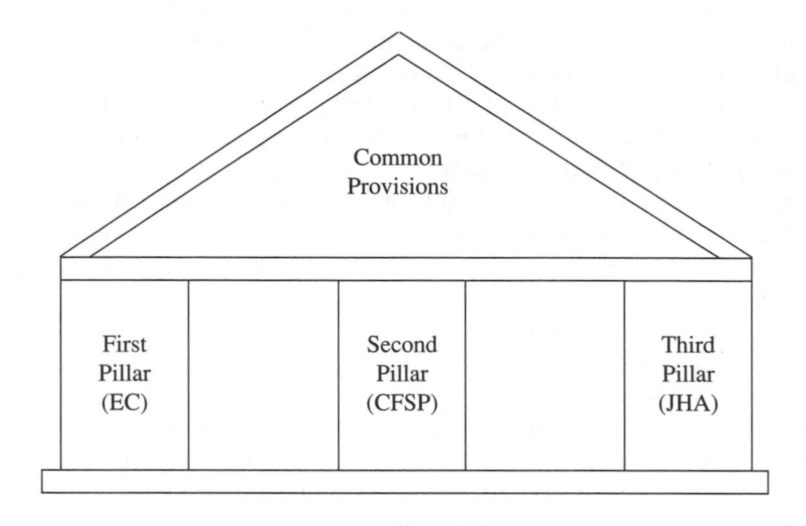

the evening of the second day it seemed that the IGCs were about to collapse because of Britain's rejection of greater EU involvement in social policy. Lubbers first proposed weakening the provisions on social policy. When Major refused to budge, at Delors's prompting Lubbers proposed removing the chapter of new social policy provisions entirely from the treaty and including them in a separate protocol to which the other member states would subscribe. This set a dangerous precedent for European integration and reinforced the emergence of a "multispeed" Europe already inherent in the provisions for EMU. In a prophetic comment on British opposition to the social chapter, Helen Wallace had written in 1989 that a decision by the other member states to go ahead without Britain "would be an example of deepening and narrowing."[50] Such a development was hardly in the EU's interest, but creating the social protocol may have prevented a British walkout and thereby saved the TEU.

Under the terms of the new treaty, the third stage of EMU, involving the introduction of a common currency, would take place by 1999 at the latest. On EPU, member states approved new cooperative arrangements for foreign and security policy and for judicial and home affairs. The EP acquired greater political and institutional oversight—including a right of inquiry, a more formal right of petition, and the appointment of an ombudsman—and greater legislative power through the codecision procedure. The TEU redefined or extended Community competence in a number of areas, notably education, training, cohesion, research and development, environment, infrastructure, industry, health, culture, consumer protection, and development cooperation, although with only a limited extension of qualified majority voting.

Some member states had scored more negotiating points than others during the IGCs and at the Maastricht summit, but none was an absolute winner or loser. For the EU's institutions the outcome of the IGCs was more clear cut: The Council and the EP gained most; the Commission gained least. As well as being an intensive bargaining session, the Maastricht summit was an opportunity to permit each participant, including the Commission, to claim victory on a variety of issues. Clearly, there was something in the final agreement for everyone. Even Major was able to claim "game, set, and match" for Britain.[51]

Public and Parliamentary Interest

Despite the difficult and highly publicized TEU ratification process, there was little public or national parliamentary interest in the negotiations themselves. Britain was a notable exception. There, an opportunist opposition, a large minority of Euroskeptic MPs on the government's back benches, and a general election due to take place by mid-1992 ensured that the IGCs became a contentious political issue. Many commentators thought Major would hold the election before December in an effort to win an undisputed mandate for the Maastricht summit. Instead he called a two-day parliamentary debate on the IGCs in late November in which he delineated for the country and the Community the limits of Britain's tolerance on EMU and EPU. By postponing the election until 1992 and emphasizing the unreliability of a new Labour government, Major hoped to strengthen his position at Maastricht.

The Bundestag, the lower house of Germany's parliament, took little interest in the IGCs. By contrast, the Bundesrat, the upper house, pressed the case for subsidiarity from the outset. As the representative of the federal states, the Bundesrat opposed excessive centralization of power in either Brussels or Bonn. The Bundesrat retained a keen interest in subsidiarity after the Maastricht summit, threatening in 1992 to block ratification of the treaty unless the government gave it a greater say in EU affairs.

Only on the eve of Maastricht did the IGCs become a lively public issue in Germany, and then not because of subsidiarity but because of the single currency. Before and during the negotiations themselves, the Bundesbank tried to alert public opinion to the dangers, as it saw them, of EMU: Germany would lose the mark, the Bundesbank would no longer formulate monetary policy but instead would become a regional member of a federal central banking system, the rest of Europe lacked Germany's historical fear of inflation, and the ECB might not be rigorously independent of political control. These harangues stiffened the government's resolve in the IGC on EMU but otherwise fell on deaf ears until, days before the Maastricht summit, a series of articles in the mass-circulation *Bild* newspaper struck a popular chord. On the second day of the summit, a banner headline proclaimed "The End of the D-Mark." Widespread concern in Germany about the implications of EMU, fueled by the rising costs of unification, came too late to affect the IGCs themselves but became a powerful element in the treaty ratification crisis.

The IGCs sparked little public discussion or political controversy in France. Most major parties supported the government's objective of a strong franc and, eventually, a single European currency. In any event, opposition parties could hardly challenge the president's powerful position in the foreign policy realm. Undoubtedly the socialist government's popularity declined during the IGCs, but not because of the negotiations themselves. Conversely, a change of leadership in June 1991, when Edith Cresson became prime minister, emphasized the government's commitment to an interventionist industrial policy at national and European levels but hardly affected the negotiations in Brussels.

Surprisingly in view of what happened in 1992, there was little public discussion of the IGCs in Denmark. The Danish parliament's EC committee monitored the negotiations and insisted on Denmark's right to decide by referendum in due course whether to participate in Stage III of EMU. Despite Denmark's traditional distrust of deeper European integration, the government played a constructive part in the negotiations on EPU. Nothing in Denmark's performance at the IGCs or in the public's reaction to the Maastricht summit presaged the protracted ratification crisis of 1992 and 1993.

THE RATIFICATION CRISIS

In 1986 a majority of Danes endorsed the SEA after the Danish parliament's rejection of it. At the end of 1986 the Irish Supreme Court judged the SEA unconstitutional, thereby obliging the government to hold a referendum. The Supreme Court's ruling and the subsequent referendum delayed implementation of the SEA until July 1987. Yet at no time after the Danish parliament's rejection of the SEA or the Irish Supreme Court's ruling on it did anyone talk about a crisis in the Community. In June 1992, by contrast, the Danish electorate's narrow rejection of the TEU jeopardized the future of European integration and shook the EC to its core.

The impact of the Danish result was all the more striking because ratification was proceeding smoothly in every other member state. As early as April 1992 the EP, despite its disappointment with the TEU, called by a resounding vote of 226 to 62 (with 31 abstentions) for member states to ratify it as quickly as possible. Even after the Danish referendum, ratification continued relatively smoothly except in France, where Mitterrand called for a referendum, and in Britain, where a combination of bad luck and poor judgment impeded the government's efforts. Indeed, with the exception of Denmark, Britain, and Germany, where a challenge to the treaty's constitutionality held up proceedings, every member state ratified the treaty by the target date of December 1992.

The Danish Referendum

Like the SEA, the TEU had to be ratified by each member state in order to come into force. Ratification procedures differed from country to country. In Denmark's case, it was up to the electorate to decide, in a referendum, whether to approve the treaty. Consequently, the negative result of the June 2 referendum—by a narrow margin of 50.7 percent against to 49.3 percent in favor—tied the government's hands and thwarted implementation of the treaty.

Danish opinion seemed evenly divided immediately before the referendum. Yet the result came as a complete shock to the Commission and to national governments. Denmark was known for its ambivalence toward European integration, but the positive results of the 1972 accession referendum and the 1986 SEA referendum suggested that on polling day, a majority would support the treaty. The Commission, the Danish government, and other governments were extraordinarily complacent. Having spent a year negotiating the treaty, they never considered that a majority of Danes, or of any other nationality, would vote against it.

Although oblivious to the possibility of a no vote, EC leaders immediately grasped the seriousness of the Danish result. There was no question of renegotiating the treaty. Member states had already rejected an Irish request to change a protocol dealing exclusively with a clause in the country's constitution. Most governments feared that renegotiation of any treaty provision or protocol, however specific or technical, would open a Pandora's box. Clearly groping for a solution, foreign ministers announced on June 4 that other member states would press ahead with ratification in the hope that Denmark would reconsider before the end of 1992.[52]

Fewer than 30,000 votes had determined the outcome of the Danish referendum. Exhaustive analyses indicated a host of reasons for the result. Some were peculiarly Danish, others were common to the EC; some were reasonable, others irrational; some were consistent, others contradictory. They included concerns about EMU, about losing national identity, about the role of small states in the EC, about the Commission's overweening ambition, about the EP's increasing power, about the Common Fisheries Policy, about the economic and political impact of German unification, about the possible emergence of a European army, about Germans' ability to buy Danish holiday homes, and about a diminution of environmental and social welfare standards.

Whatever the reasons, the result showed how oblivious the Danish and other governments were to growing public resentment toward the EC. The Council seemed secretive and self-serving, the Commission remote and technocratic, and the EP expensive and irrelevant. There had been little public interest in the IGCs themselves, but Maastricht soon became a topic of popular discourse. Without even having read the treaty, people fretted about its contents. Worries ranged from the desirability of EMU to the rigors of convergence to voting rights for nonnationals to the prospect of mass migration to the likelihood of bureaucratic intrusion from Brussels. In most cases a perusal of the treaty's unintelligible text merely reinforced popular antipathy toward it.

Table 6.1 TEU Ratification Referendums

Country	Date	% Turnout	% Yes	% No
Denmark	June 2, 1992	82.9	49.3	50.7
Denmark	May 18, 1993	71.4	56.7	43.3
Ireland	June 18, 1992	57.0	69.0	31.0
France	Sept. 20, 1992	70.0	51.05	48.95

The Irish and French Referendums

Ireland was the only other member state constitutionally obliged to ratify the treaty by referendum. Coming two weeks after the Danish result, the Irish referendum assumed special significance. Given Ireland's traditional support for European integration, a positive result seemed inevitable and would do little to revive the EC's fortunes. A negative result, however, would have worsened the EC's predicament. The government's referendum campaign concentrated on crude calculations of economic self-interest. Without any basis in fact, the government warned the electorate that Ireland would lose ECU 10 billion in assistance in the event of a no vote. Despite the government's threats, the result was by no means an unequivocal endorsement of the TEU. Of the 57 percent who voted (low by Irish standards), 69 percent were in favor and 31 percent against. Undaunted, the prime minister called the outcome "a tribute to the maturity of the Irish people" and proclaimed that "Eurosceptics do not have much of a following here."[53]

A much more important test for the treaty came on September 20, when the French electorate went to the polls. Although France could have ratified the treaty by an easily obtainable three-fifths majority of both houses of parliament meeting in joint session, Mitterrand announced immediately after the Danish result that France would also ratify by referendum. The timing and manner of Mitterrand's announcement suggest that he acted impetuously and unwisely. Mitterrand was a master politician, yet risking so much on a highly unpredictable referendum result seemed out of character. Then in the middle of his second seven-year term, Mitterrand was deeply committed to European integration. By winning a resounding referendum victory, he hoped both to breathe new life into the TEU and to give his presidency an indelible "European" imprint. Clearly Mitterrand believed that France's historical contribution to the EC and the electorate's appreciation of the treaty's importance for the future of European integration would produce a comfortable majority and dispel the gloom caused by the Danish result.[54]

Yet developments in France and elsewhere favored the treaty's opponents. In June 1992 Mitterrand reluctantly replaced Edith Cresson, his hugely unpopular prime minister. The president's own popularity continued to slump as the economic situation worsened and unemployment rose. The deteriorating situation in Bosnia reflected poorly on Mitterrand, who had shown his solidarity with the besieged citizens of Sarajevo by flying there in June 1992, and especially on the EC, whose peace efforts did nothing to stop the fighting. Opinion polls in late August showed that the treaty's opponents were inching ahead and that frustration over the EC's inability to broker a Bosnian cease-fire was a powerful impetus to vote no.

The concurrent EMS crisis—Britain and Italy dropped out of the ERM in September 1992 and the franc came under heavy pressure—further eroded public confidence. The high cost of unification and the Bundesbank's correspondingly high interest rates exacerbated the EC's economic situation and fueled resentment of Germany. There was an understandable public reaction against what looked like a German-designed EMU. In fact, EMU offered the best chance to curb German unilateralism and end currency instability.

The French government went on the offensive late in the campaign, cajoling the electorate to vote yes. Mitterrand assigned Jack Lang, his former culture minister, to coordinate the government's efforts and appointed the photogenic Elizabeth Guigou, minister for European affairs, as leading spokesperson. In keeping with the earlier Danish and Irish campaigns, Lang used an unlikely array of arguments to bolster support for the TEU. "A 'no' vote would be unimaginable," he declared. "It would destroy the collective work of Charles de Gaulle, Georges Pompidou, Valéry Giscard d'Estaing, and François Mitterrand. . . . It would mean that Washington and Tokyo would rub their hands, that the yen and the dollar would triumph, and that the mark would become Europe's definitive currency. . . . [It would cause] a bourse crisis, a crisis of confidence, a depression that would hit the whole of Europe."[55] The normally unexcitable *Le Monde* editorialized on the eve of the referendum that "a 'no' vote would be for France and for Europe the greatest catastrophe since Hitler's coming to power."[56]

Lang's histrionics may have alienated as many people as they attracted. In the event, Mitterrand's gamble narrowly paid off. In a 70 percent turnout, 51.05 percent voted in favor and 48.95 percent voted against. The result was too close to justify the political and emotional effort invested. Far from boosting Mitterrand or Maastricht, it accelerated the president's political decline—his socialist government lost heavily in the March 1993 general election—and further shook the EC establishment.

The EC's Response: Subsidiarity, Openness, and Opt-Outs

Delors was quick to respond to the Danish referendum result. Alert to the extent of popular alienation from EU policies and institutions, Delors resolved to break the bureaucratic barrier surrounding Brussels, make the legislative process more transparent, and emphasize subsidiarity as the best way to ensure the EU's compatibility with the political aspirations of its citizens. In search of a doctrine that would allow the EU to become involved in certain "high political" issues traditionally at the core of national sovereignty without encroaching on policy areas that ought to remain in the national or regional domain, Delors had begun to explore subsidiarity from the time that he became Commission president in 1985.[57] As he told *Le Figaro* in June 1992, subsidiarity was the essence of federalism because "the federal approach is to define clearly who does what."[58] Thus, subsidiarity would provide guidelines as to where Brussels could or could not act just as similar constitutional provisions determine the proper functioning of U.S. or German federalism.

Unlike the Tenth Amendment to the U.S. Constitution, which reserves for the states all powers not delegated to the federal government, or Germany's Basic Law, which vests all powers in the Länder (states) except those prescribed in Article 30, subsidiarity was notoriously difficult to define. According to commissioner Leon Brittan, "subsidiarity must be treated as a guiding political principle as well as a legal restraint." Brittan claimed that Article 5 EC (formerly Article 3b), which formalized the principle of subsidiarity, "places a legally-binding limitation on the scope of action of the Community; it applies without caveat, limitation or exception. . . . Once the Treaty has come into effect, every single new legislative act of the Community can be held up and judged under this standard."[59] Yet Article 5 was imprecise and open to many interpretations. In the prevailing climate of resentment against Brussels, the EU would need a far firmer definition of subsidiarity and explanation of its possible use.

Even before the ratification crisis erupted, the Commission had started to drop proposed legislation that seemingly belonged at the national level. After the Danish result, the Commission redoubled its efforts to concentrate on key policy areas and divest itself of issues best dealt with at lower levels of government. Member states eagerly exploited subsidiarity, advocating it as a means of allaying popular concern about excessive centralization in Brussels and possibly hoping to use it to roll back intrusive but generally beneficial policies such as the aggressive enforcement of competition law. In Britain, subsidiarity became a political panacea for the EC's manifest ills. Inevitably, the British government and the Commission understood the term to mean completely different things. For London, subsidiarity was a vital safeguard of national sovereignty and a way to prevent the EC from involving itself unduly in member states' affairs; for Brussels, subsidiarity was a central tenet of Eurofederalism.

A summit in Lisbon at the end of June 1992 gave the European Council its first opportunity to assess the Danish debacle. Predictably but unrealistically, the heads of state and government reaffirmed their determination to press ahead with the treaty's ratification "with no renegotiation and no modification, to ensure [its] entry into force on January 1, 1993." As if to emphasize "business as usual," the European Council extended Delors's term as Commission president. After hearing a report on subsidiarity from Delors and discussing the issue in depth, the European Council "stressed the need for this principle to be strictly applied, both in existing and in future legislation, and called on the Commission and the Council to look at the procedural and practical steps needed to implement it and to report back to the [December 1992] European Council in Edinburgh."[60]

After a special summit in Birmingham in October 1992, the European Council issued a folksy explanation of subsidiarity: "We reaffirm that decisions must be taken as closely as possible to the citizen. Greater unity can be achieved without excessive centralization. It is for each Member State to decide how its powers should be exercised domestically. The Community can only act where Member States have given it the power to do so in the treaties. Action at the Community level should happen only when proper and necessary. . . . 'Subsidiarity' or 'nearness' is essential if the Community is to develop with the support of its citizens."[61]

Less than two weeks later the Commission submitted to the Council and the EP a lengthy political, technical, and legal analysis of subsidiarity. The Commission developed the "two dimensions" of subsidiarity—the need for action and the intensity (proportionality) of action—and asserted that the burden of proof in both cases lay with the EU's institutions. Because of its exclusive right of initiative, the Commission accepted special responsibility in that regard. But the Commission also argued that subsidiarity could not become an excuse for member states either to blame Brussels for unpopular actions or to curb the Commission's legitimate legislative and executive authority.[62]

The Commission's communication, together with a foreign ministers' report, set the stage for the Edinburgh summit's discussions on subsidiarity. The summit conclusions included a lengthy section outlining the basic principles of subsidiarity, guidelines for their application, and institutional procedures and practices, as well as concrete examples of pending proposals and existing legislation in light of the "need for action" and "proportionality" criteria. The European Council also called for an interinstitutional agreement on the effective application of subsidiarity.[63]

The development of subsidiarity in late 1992 went hand in hand with efforts to make the EC's legislative process more transparent. The European Council acknowledged the need for greater openness and fleshed out some ideas at the Birmingham summit. These included wider use of prelegislative consultation documents (green papers), greater public access to the work of the Council and the Commission, and clearer and simpler legislation. The European Council adopted a number of specific measures to promote transparency at the subsequent Edinburgh summit. Foremost among them was a decision to televise the opening sessions of some Council meetings and to publish the record of formal votes taken in the Council. Given the Council's history of secretiveness, these were truly remarkable measures. Even more so than the debate on subsidiarity, the European Council's frenzied efforts at the Birmingham and Edinburgh summits to make the EU more comprehensible to its citizens demonstrated the profound impact on national governments of the TEU ratification crisis.

The European Council promoted subsidiarity, transparency, and openness to placate irate citizens throughout the EC but especially in Denmark. Indeed, the response so far to the ratification crisis was primarily intended to make the treaty more palatable to Danish voters. Despite earlier statements that the treaty would not be modified, the Commission and national governments realized that unless Denmark won opt-outs from specific provisions and protocols, the electorate was unlikely to ratify the treaty in a second referendum. Opt-outs would appease the Danish electorate without undermining the treaty's validity or salience for the EC as a whole.

In early October the Danish government produced a lengthy white paper outlining eight options for a solution to the EC dilemma. Two of these involved negotiating special concessions that would free Denmark from certain treaty obligations. At the end of the month Denmark submitted a memorandum identifying a number of sticking points, including the treaty's defense policy provision, the third stage of EMU, EU citizenship, and cooperation on Justice and Home Affairs. The European Council hammered out an agreement at the Edinburgh summit that included Danish opt-outs from Stage III of EMU (the single currency) and from CFSP discussions, decisions, or actions having defense implications. Based on the Edinburgh opt-outs, a comfortable 56.7 percent voted in favor of ratification in the second Danish referendum in May 1993.

The European Council was careful to explain that the Edinburgh optouts were "fully compatible with the Treaty, . . . designed to meet Danish concerns, and therefore apply exclusively to Denmark and not to other existing or acceding Member States." Nevertheless the opt-outs reinforced the tendency toward an à la carte EU in which, depending on their leverage and negotiating power, member states could pick and choose whatever policies suited them. The combined effect of the treaty's provisions on EMU, the social chapter, and the Edinburgh agreement was to emphasize the emergence of variable geometry in an increasingly diverse EU.

Final Hurdles: Britain and Germany

A combination of weak political leadership, unfortunate timing, and arcane parliamentary procedures produced a potentially disastrous ratification debacle in Britain. Given Major's supposed triumph in Maastricht and his election victory in April 1992, Britain should have ratified the treaty without undue delay. Although about thirty government members of parliament (MPs)—the diehard Euroskeptics—vehemently opposed the TEU, a majority of opposition MPs supported it. As a result, in a free vote (unencumbered by the obligations of party allegiance), around two-thirds of Britain's 650 MPs would have supported the treaty.

The first hint of trouble came immediately after the first Danish referendum, when the government announced a postponement of the parliamentary debate pending legal clarification. Major insisted that Britain would ratify the treaty as planned, before the end of 1992, and nothing seemed seriously amiss when Britain took over the Council presidency in July 1992. Within a short time, however, the ERM crisis turned Britain's presidency into one of the worst in the Community's history, a point ruthlessly exploited by the opposition Labour Party. It was difficult for Major to put Britain "at the heart of Europe" after his country left the ERM so suddenly and disastrously in September. Recrimination over the currency crisis exacerbated tension between London and Bonn, and Major lost political support in the EC capital that mattered most.

By mid-1992 the prime minister was a hostage of the Euroskeptics in his own party, who capitalized on the treaty's growing unpopularity and on the opposition's determination to discomfit the government. Major looked for salvation to the specially convened European Council in Birmingham. Unfortunately for him, a government announcement two days before the summit of plans to close more than thirty coal mines provoked a popular outcry that completely overshadowed the event. The other heads of state and government left Birmingham despairing of the British government's ability to focus on the EC at a critical time in the ratification process. Their despondency seemed justified when the treaty barely survived a Commons vote on November 4, and Major promptly announced that Britain would delay ratification until after the second Danish referendum in May 1993.

The British government redeemed its otherwise uninspiring presidential performance by successfully chairing the Edinburgh summit. Moreover,

Major grew increasingly assertive in early 1993 when the Labour Party tried to link British acceptance of the social chapter with ratification of the treaty. Considering his rejection of the social chapter at the Maastricht summit, Major was not about to embrace it during the ratification debate because of domestic political difficulties. Although peculiar parliamentary procedures gave opponents of the treaty great scope to filibuster, even the staunchest Euroskeptics admitted the unlikelihood of being able to prevent ratification. Yet only after narrowly surviving another vote of confidence did the government finally win ratification of the TEU, in August 1993.

Only in Germany was the treaty still not ratified. There the problem was not parliamentary—in December 1992 large majorities had voted in favor of ratification in both the Bundestag and Bundesrat—but legal: Opponents of the treaty challenged its constitutionality on a variety of grounds. In a landmark ruling in October 1993, the Federal Constitutional Court upheld the treaty's constitutionality, but not without criticizing the EU's democratic credentials.[64] Despite its long-term implications for Germany's role in the EU, the Constitutional Court's judgment removed the last obstacle to ratification of the TEU, allowing it finally to come into effect on November 1, 1993.

NOTES

1. Jacques Delors, speech at the College of Europe, Bruges, September 20, 1989.

2. Bull. EC 6-1988, point 1.1.14. For an examination of the origins and development of EMU in the 1980s, see David Andrews, "The Global Origins of the Maastricht Treaty on EMU: Closing the Window of Opportunity," in Alan Cafruny and Glenda Rosenthal, eds., *The State of the European Community, Volume 2: The Maastricht Debates and Beyond* (Boulder: Lynne Rienner, 1993), pp. 107–123.

3. *Report of the Committee for the Study of Economic and Monetary Union* (Luxembourg: Office of Official Publications of the European Communities [OOP], 1989).

4. Bull. EC 6-1989, "Presidency Conclusions," point 1.1.11.

5. See *Le Monde,* January 8 and January 15, 1988.

6. Ronald Tiersky, "Mitterrand, France and Europe," *French Politics and Society* 9, no. 1 (winter 1991): 16.

7. Margaret Thatcher, *Britain in the European Community* (London: Conservative Political Centre, 1988). For her own account of events in the late 1980s, see Margaret Thatcher, *The Downing Street Years* (New York: HarperCollins, 1993).

8. Sir Michael Butler, "Simply Wrong About Europe," *Times* (London), November 26, 1991, p. 10.

9. Bull. EC 12–1988, "Presidency Conclusions," point 1.1.10.

10. Bull. EC 6–1989, "Presidency Conclusions," point 1.1.16.

11. See Adam Daniel Rothfeld and Walther Stutzle, eds., *Germany and Europe in Transition* (Oxford: Oxford University Press, 1991); and Renata Fritsch-Bournazel, *Europe and German Unification* (New York: Berg, 1992).

12. Jacques Delors, speech at the College of Europe, Bruges, September 20, 1989.

13. Quoted in Jan Werts, *The European Council* (Amsterdam: North-Holland, 1992), p. 288.

14. Chancellor's press release, 134/1989, pp. 1141 ff.

15. See Franz-Olivier Giesbert, *Le Président* (Paris: Seuil, 1990), p. 363.

16. Bull. EC 12-1989, "Presidency Conclusions," point 1.1.20.

17. Quoted in *Le Monde,* December 9, 1989. p. 1.

18. Nicholas Ridley, interview in *Spectator,* July 14, 1990.

19. Bull. EC S/1-90, *Commission's Program for 1990.*

20. The Belgian proposal is reproduced in Finn Laursen and Sophie Vanhoonacker, eds., *The Intergovernmental Conference on Political Union* (Maastricht: European Institute of Public Administration [EIPA], 1992), pp. 269–275.

21. Quoted in *Financial Times*, March 30, 1990, p. 2.

22. Reproduced in Laursen and Vanhoonacker, *Intergovernmental Conference,* p. 276.

23. Bull. EC 4-1990, "Presidency Conclusions," points 1.1 to 1.12; *Agence Europe,* April 30 and May 1, 1990.

24. Bull. EC 6-1990, "Presidency Conclusions," points 1.1 to 1.8.

25. European Parliament Session Documents A3-183/90, July 9, 1990. See also Lily Gardner Feldman, "The EC and German Unification," in Leon Hurwitz and Christian Lequesne, *The State of the European Community: Policies, Institutions and Debates in the Transition Years* (Boulder: Lynne Rienner, 1991), pp. 310–329.

26. Bull. EC 10-1990, "Presidency Conclusions," points 1.2 to 1.6.

27. *Economist,* March 23, 1991, p. 15.

28. Giulio Andreotti, speech to the European Parliament, November 21, 1990, Debates of the European Parliament, *Official Journal of the European Communites* [*OJ*] 3–396, November 1990, p. 138.

29. On the negotiations and their outcome, see Michael Baun, *An Imperfect Union: The Maastricht Treaty and the New Politics of European Integration* (Boulder: Westview Press, 1996); Kenneth Dyson and Kevin Featherstone, *The Road to Maastricht: Negotiating Economic and Monetary Union* (Oxford: Oxford University Press, 1998); Colette Mazzuchelli, *France and Germany at Maastricht: Politics and Negotiations to Create the European Union* (New York: Garland, 1997); and Wayne Sandholtz, "Monetary Bargains: The Treaty on EMU," in Cafruny and Rosenthal, *Maastricht and Beyond*, pp. 125–141.

30. Margaret Thatcher, "My Vision," *Financial Times,* November 19, 1990, p. 10.

31. Quoted in *Financial Times,* June 18, 1991, p. 1.

32. Lord O'Hagan, "Federalism," *Manchester Guardian Weekly,* July 7, 1991, p. 12.

33. Thatcher, "My Vision."

34. Quoted in *Agence Europe,* December 6, 1991, p. 4.

35. *Agence Europe* Documents 1735, October 7–8, 1991.

36. *Agence Europe,* November 10, 1990.

37. Jacques Delors, speech at the Royal Institute for International Affairs, London, March 20, 1991.

38. *Agence Europe,* April 18, 1991.

39. Jacques Delors, speech to the European Parliament, November 20, 1991, Debates of the European Parliament, *OJ* 3–411, November 1991, p. 126.

40. See Sophie Vanhoonacker, "The Role of Parliament," in Laursen and Vanhoonacker, *Intergovernmental Conference,* p. 219.

41. Martin I, PE A3-47/90; Martin II, Europe Parliament (PE) A3-166/90.

42. *Agence Europe,* September 27, 1991, p. 3.
43. *Agence Europe,* June 4, 1991, p. 1.
44. Quoted in *Financial Times*, May 13, 1991, p. 3.
45. Quoted in Reuters, July 1, 1991.
46. See Pia Christina Wood, "EPC: Lessons from the Gulf War and Yugoslavia," in Cafruny and Rosenthal, *Maastricht and Beyond,* pp. 227–244.
47. Quoted in the *Guardian,* September 28, 1991, p. 2.
48. Quoted in *Financial Times,* September 21–22, 1991, p. 3.
49. *Agence Europe,* September 15, 1991.
50. Helen Wallace, "Widening and Deepening: The EC and the New European Agenda," Royal Institute of International Affairs (RIIA) discussion paper no. 23, 1989, p. 8.
51. Quoted in *Financial Times,* December 12, 1991, p. 3.
52. Bull. EC 6-1992, point 1.1.3.
53. Quoted in the *Cork Examiner,* June 20, 1992, p. 1.
54. For a discussion of the French referendum's importance for the EC, see Andrew Moravcsik, "Idealism and Interest in the European Community: The Case of the French Referendum," *French Politics and Society* 11, no. 1 (winter 1993): 45–56, and Sophie Meunier-Aitsahalia and George Ross, "Democratic Deficit or Democratic Surplus: A Reply to Andrew Moravcsik's Comments on the French Referendum," *French Politics and Society* 11, no. 1 (winter 1993): 57–69.
55. See *Le Monde,* special supplement, *L'Europe de Maastricht* (August-September 1992): 2.
56. *Le Monde,* September 20–21, 1992, p. 1.
57. See Jacques Delors, *Le Nouveau Concert Européen* (Paris: Editions Odile Jacob, 1992), and his speech to the European Parliament in January 1985, Bull. EC S/1-1985.
58. *Le Figaro,* June 8, 1992, p. 1.
59. Leon Brittan, speech delivered at the European University Institute, June 11, 1992, IP/92 1477, 92/06/11.
60. Bull. EC 6-1992, "Presidency Conclusions," points 1.1 to 1.6.
61. Bull. EC 10-1992, "Presidency Conclusions," point 1.8.
62. Commission, "The Principle of Subsidiarity," SEC(92)1990 final, October 27, 1992.
63. Bull. EC 12-1992, "Presidency Conclusions," point 1.4.
64. See Karl M. Meessen, "Hedging European Integration: The Maastricht Judgment of the Federal Constitutional Court of Germany," in *Fordham International Law Journal* 17: 511–530.

7

The Emerging European Union, 1993–1999

Implementation of the Treaty on European Union (TEU) seems an obvious turning point in the history of European integration. Yet there was more continuity than change after the launch of the EU in November 1993. The greatest challenges confronting the EU in the late 1990s—enlargement, Economic and Monetary Union (EMU), and popular dissatisfaction with "Brussels"—had emerged a decade earlier and had helped shape the TEU and fuel the ensuing ratification crisis.

Plans to implement EMU were already in train when the TEU came into effect, although the criteria and timetable for participation in Stage III preoccupied member states for the remainder of the 1990s (the road to EMU is examined in detail in Chapter 16). The domestic impact of EMU demonstrated the inextricable relationship between Europolitics and national politics. EMU provided the impetus and pretext for governments to rein in public spending and undertake long-overdue reforms. Prospects for EMU looked slim in the mid-1990s until Europe's economic recovery made it possible for most member states to meet the key reference point for budget deficits (3 percent of GDP). The anticipated benefits of EMU, both positive (improving the EU's global competitiveness) and negative (averting a major political crisis if the venture failed), focused governments' attention and made it necessary for them to stay the course.

A public backlash, driven in part by the perception that EMU exacerbated unemployment, increased the EU's unpopularity. Member states' determination to proceed with EMU regardless was one of the most striking aspects of European integration in the 1990s. Much of the credit belongs to Helmut Kohl, who doggedly advocated EMU despite major misgivings in Germany and weak political leadership elsewhere in the EU. Ironically, having been voted out of office in September 1998 because of widespread dissatisfaction with his domestic economic record, Kohl did not preside over completion of his cherished goal of monetary union.

Kohl's departure after sixteen years as chancellor was the most dramatic change in EU leadership at the end of a decade that saw the departure of nearly every key player in the transformation of the EC and the launch of the EU. François Mitterrand left politics in May 1995 when his second presidential term came to an end (he died shortly afterward). Jacques Delors had stepped down from the Commission presidency in January 1995 after an unprecedented ten years in office. In January 1996 Felipe González lost the Spanish general election.

Europe's new leaders included some familiar faces, notably Commission president Jacques Santer and French president Jacques Chirac. But the development of European integration would depend also on the contributions of national leaders relatively unknown domestically and/or internationally. Chief among these, Prime Minister Tony Blair personified a more positive British approach toward the EU, and German chancellor Gerhard Schröder personified the ascendancy of domestic German interests. Personal, political, and ideological differences between Chirac and Schröder would put the Franco-German axis to a new test.

The triumph of the center-left in much of Europe (Chirac and Spanish prime minister José Aznar were the main exceptions) resulted in a greater emphasis on domestic social policies and the fight against unemployment, although within the EMU-imposed straitjacket of reduced public expenditure. At a time when the collapse of Asian and emerging markets threatened Europe's economic recovery, governments sought to reconcile the apparently conflicting objectives of more spending on social policies and more deficit and debt reduction. These domestic and international circumstances raised doubts about the feasibility of EMU, despite the successful launch of the euro in January 1999.

Apart from EMU, enlargement was the biggest item on the EU's agenda for most of the 1990s. The collapse of the Soviet empire in the late 1980s, and of the Soviet Union in 1991, gave rise to a hitherto unimaginable enlargement scenario. First the European neutrals, no longer constrained by the Cold War, applied for EU membership. Later the newly independent countries of Central and Eastern Europe, plus Cyprus and Malta, followed suit. Austria, Finland, and Sweden joined the EU in 1995; three years later, the EU opened accession negotiations with five Central and Eastern European states plus Cyprus. The eventual accession of ten or more mostly small and poor Central and Eastern European states was bound to change the EU profoundly. Although the 1996–1997 intergovernmental conference (IGC) provided an opportunity to reform the EU's founding treaties in anticipation of enlargement, member states ducked the most difficult institutional issues. Nevertheless, the unrelenting pressure of imminent enlargement presaged both a major institutional overhaul and a wide-ranging reform of key policies and programs.

THE EEA AND EFTAN ENLARGEMENT

On January 1, 1995, the new European Union enlarged for the first time when Austria, Finland, and Sweden joined. Called the Eftan enlargement because the three new entrants had been members of the European Free Trade Association (EFTA), the 1995 enlargement promised to change the EU in a variety of ways. Most striking, the membership of two Nordic states would extend the EU into the far north of Europe and increase its size by 33 percent, although its population by only 6.2 percent. Economically, Eftan enlargement would bring into the EU three affluent member states, all potential net contributors to the budget. Politically, as one EU official wrote during the enlargement negotiations, Finland's and Sweden's accession would strengthen within the EU "traditions of democracy, participation and openness of government"—a welcome development at a time of widespread public concern about accountability and legitimacy in Brussels.[1] Another EU official opined that "northern Protestant uprightness will serve as a useful counterbalance to the more passionate political traditions of the (Catholic) Mediterranean countries."[2] In terms of public policy, the new member states would bring greater concern for environmental issues; a new perspective on regional development and investment; a strong commitment to free trade and Third World development; progressive social policies; and a unique perspective on relations with Russia (Finland's immediate neighbor to the east), the Baltic states (across the sea from Finland), and Slovenia (across the mountains from Austria).

The comparative swiftness of the Eftan accession negotiations belied their complexity and disguised their sobering impact on the EU's consideration of further enlargement into Central and Eastern Europe. Negotiations opened with Austria, Finland, and Sweden on February 1, 1993, and on April 5 with Norway (another EFTA member); negotiations ended with all four countries on March 30, 1994.[3] This fifteen-month span contrasted favorably with previous accession negotiations that had ranged from almost three years (in the case of Greece) to more than ten years (in the case of Britain). Superficially it is not surprising that the Eftan negotiations were relatively rapid. After all, the candidate countries were economically better off than many existing member states, had administrative structures capable of understanding and implementing EU legislation, and, despite varying degrees of public opposition, had governments eager to bring them into the EU.

The most important reason the negotiations proceeded relatively quickly, however, was that the candidate countries had already adopted much of the EU's complicated and voluminous *acquis communautaire*. They had begun to do so in the mid-1980s in an effort to minimize the possible negative consequences for outsiders of the EC's soon-to-be-completed single market program. Dissatisfied with a passive reaction to developments in the EC, the Eftans soon insisted on a role in formulating single market and related policies. This pressure provoked a strong response from Brussels. In May 1987, Willy de Clercq, the external affairs commissioner, asserted the EC's sole decisionmaking authority and stressed the primacy of internal integration over EC-EFTA cooperation.[4]

A number of EFTA countries reached the obvious conclusion and considered applying for EC membership. Until it digested the recent Iberian enlargement and fully implemented the single market program, however, the EC was uninterested in acquiring new members. Hoping to fend off applications from the Eftans, in a speech to the European Parliament (EP) on January 17, 1989, Commission president Jacques Delors recalled an earlier EC-EFTA initiative and proposed "a new form of association, with common decisionmaking and administrative institutions."[5]

The European Economic Area

This was the genesis of the European Economic Area (EEA)—initially called the European Economic Space—a huge integrated market intended to encompass the twelve EU and seven EFTA members (Austria, Finland, Iceland, Liechtenstein, Norway, Sweden, and Switzerland). With nineteen countries and 380 million people accounting for 40 percent of global trade, the proposed EEA would become the world's largest and most lucrative commercial bloc. Although meant largely to forestall EU enlargement, the EEA instead became, for three of its leading Eftan members (Austria, Finland, and Sweden), a brief waiting room for EU accession. Thus, although unknown at the time, the EEA negotiations constituted a first, unofficial step in the Eftan enlargement process. By that reckoning, the Eftan enlargement negotiations lasted a total of almost five years.

EFTA's enthusiastic response to Delors's January 1989 proposal presaged intensive preparatory work to shape the putative EEA. A joint EC-EFTA steering group with responsibility for working groups covering the single market program, flanking policies (environment, transport, social policy, etc.), and legal and institutional issues began work immediately. By October 1989 the steering group had established a basis for preliminary negotiations and identified the EC's willingness to concede only "decision-shaping" and EFTA's demand for full participation in "decision-making" as one of the most contentious questions. After various procedural steps, both sides announced that negotiations to establish the EEA would begin in mid-1990.[6]

Much to the Commission's dismay, the acceleration of EC-EFTA talks did not deter Austria from opting for EC membership. As recently as 1988 the Soviet Union had repeated long-standing reservations about Austria's accession but changed its position when reform swept Central and Eastern

Europe. Not wanting to miss a "historical opportunity," Austria applied to join the EC on July 1, 1989. Although Soviet opposition was no longer an issue, neutrality itself, to which Austrians were still attached, remained a potential stumbling block. In its application, Austria pledged to accept the responsibilities of membership but clung to its international status of "permanent neutrality."[7] Although Brussels ruled out further enlargement until after completion of the single market, Austria's application immediately raised difficult questions about the compatibility of neutrality with the EC's efforts to strengthen foreign policy and security cooperation.

The EC's preoccupation with treaty reform in 1991 contributed to the complexity of the EEA negotiations. Even without that distraction, the Commission's chief negotiator described the talks as "the most complex negotiations . . . ever conducted on behalf of the EC."[8] On the internal market alone, the EFTA countries had to adopt approximately 1,400 existing EC acts covering over 10,000 pages of legislation. Although the EFTA countries scaled back various demands in an effort to expedite an agreement, talks soon stalled over institutional arrangements and picked up only after the EC agreed in May 1991 to canvass EFTA opinion on draft legislation and to establish a panel of EC and EFTA judges to adjudicate EEA-related disputes.

By the fall of 1991 negotiations were again bogged down. Fishing rights, alpine trucking, and financial support for the EC's poorer member states posed almost insuperable obstacles to a final agreement. Spain and Portugal demanded generous access to Norwegian and Icelandic fishing grounds, Switzerland and Austria wanted to limit heavy-truck transit from EC member states, and Spain wanted a substantial increase in EFTA's initial offer to the EC's cohesion coffers. When the negotiations missed their third deadline, in September 1991, an exasperated Dutch presidency announced that an EEA agreement could prove impossible to reach and was in any case not an EC priority.

Clearly, the EFTA countries had more to lose from a complete breakdown of negotiations. Yet Switzerland and Iceland held out until the last moment before accepting final offers on trucking and fishing, paving the way for the agreement to be signed on October 22, 1991. No sooner was the ink dry than the European Court of Justice (ECJ) ruled that a proposed EC-EFTA court would contravene EC law.[9] Renewed negotiations ended in February 1992 with a compromise over the legal mechanism to resolve EEA disputes. Both sides eventually signed the definitive agreement on May 2, 1992, after a last-minute revision of the Austrian truck-transit deal.[10]

From the EEA to EU Accession

At the beginning of negotiations in 1989, the EFTA countries—with the exception of EC applicant Austria—saw an EEA agreement as a way to enjoy the benefits of the single market without necessarily joining the EC. Two years later, at the end of the negotiations, most of the EFTA countries saw the EEA as a staging post to full membership. What had happened in the meantime? First, although EFTA countries generally had outperformed their EC counterparts in the past, most of them stagnated economically in the early 1990s and saw better prospects for improvement inside the EC than outside it. Second, most EFTA countries were dissatisfied with the limited "decision-shaping" offered by Brussels and decided that full EC membership was the only way to acquire decisionmaking power. Third, EFTA countries feared exclusion from EMU and accordingly from EMU-related economic growth (were there to be any). Fourth, few of the Eftans wanted to be left outside the EC once their fellow Eftans joined. Thus Sweden applied for membership in June 1991, Finland in March 1992, and Switzerland in May 1992. Haunted by the specter of the 1972 referendum campaign, the Norwegian government delayed its application until November 1992. Iceland decided not to apply, largely because of concerns about the EC's Common Fisheries Policy.

With the end of the Cold War, neutrality virtually disappeared as an obstacle to EC membership. Some European neutrals were willing to abandon neutrality entirely; others clung to the label but conceded that it meant little in practice. In its opinions on Austria's, Sweden's, and Finland's applications, the Commission stressed the security and possible defense obligations of EU accession. At the Maastricht summit in December 1991, the European Council asked the Commission to examine the implications of enlargement in the context of the TEU. The Commission's report, presented at the Lisbon summit in June 1992, took a tough line on neutrality: Applicants would have to give "specific and binding assurances . . . with regard to their political commitment and legal capacity to fulfill their Common Foreign and Security Policy (CFSP) obligations."[11]

The Commission declared categorically that "widening must not be at the expense of deepening." Accordingly, the European Council decided in Lisbon not to begin new entry negotiations until the member states had ratified the TEU and settled the Delors II budgetary package.[12] Britain appeared eager to jump the gun on enlargement by beginning preliminary negotiations during its presidency in late 1992, prompting suspicion among other member states that Britain favored widening over deepening. Although formal enlargement negotiations were supposed to await ratification of the TEU, the European Council decided at the Edinburgh summit in December 1992 to begin negotiations with Austria, Sweden, and Finland in early 1993 and with Norway as soon as the Commission published its opinion on that country's application.[13]

Completion of the EEA gave the EU accession negotiations a huge head start. Eleven of the twenty-nine "chapters," or issue areas that made up the negotiations, had already been almost fully covered by the EEA (notably the single market, transport policy, competition policy, and research and information technologies); five chapters (social policy, energy, the environment, agriculture, and fisheries) were partly covered by the EEA; six chapters were covered by the EC but not the EEA (the customs union, external economic relations, structural policy, regional policy, industrial policy, and taxation); four chapters were new "Maastricht issues" (notably EMU, the CFSP, and cooperation on Justice and Home Affairs [JHA]); and the final three chapters dealt with general issues such as the budget and institutions.[14]

In the event, the most contentious issues were not the EU's intergovernmental policies—the neutral applicants were willing to square their neutrality with the CFSP and had few serious problems with JHA—but the chapters only partly covered by the EEA. Indeed, the difficulty of tackling parts of these chapters in the earlier EEA negotiations presaged the even greater difficulty of tackling more far-reaching aspects of them in the enlargement negotiations. Some of the fiercest battles were fought over environmental policy (standards were generally higher in the applicant states), agricultural policy (price supports and subsidies were higher in three of the applicant states), energy policy (Norway was unwilling to relinquish control over its vast oil and natural gas reserves), and fisheries policy (again, Norway was unwilling to relinquish control over its lucrative territorial waters). Other difficult dossiers included financial support for remote and sparsely populated areas of the Nordic applicant states, the right of other EU citizens to buy second homes in Austria, alpine transit, the EC's ban on the sale of snuff (to which a large and vocal minority of Sweden's population is addicted), and state monopolies on alcohol sales in the Nordic applicant states.

Member states and the Commission adamantly opposed granting the applicant states long-term derogations from the *acquis communautaire*, let alone permanent opt-outs. Understandably, the TEU opt-outs won by Denmark at the Edinburgh summit tempted the applicant states to seek similar concessions. But the EC was not inclined to give in to the applicant countries, which in any case lacked the leverage that Denmark had enjoyed during the TEU ratification crisis. Under the circumstances, it is ironic that Denmark, in the Council presidency during the first half of 1993, presided over the opening round of the enlargement negotiations. It is also ironic that the Nordic applicants seemed more enthusiastic than Denmark about European integration, given Denmark's tendency to object to controversial aspects of the TEU on the dubious grounds of "Nordic solidarity."

Meeting in Copenhagen in June 1993, the European Council called for enlargement to take place by January 1995 so that the new member states would be able to participate fully in preparations for the 1996 IGC.[15] Under the terms of Article O of the TEU, enlargement was contingent on "the assent of the European Parliament, which shall act by absolute majority of component members." Because direct elections were due to take place in June 1994, the EP would have to consider the accession agreements by May 1994 at the latest (if it waited until after the elections, when committees would first have to be formed, there would not be sufficient time left to take the other ratification measures necessary to implement the agreements by January 1995). Accordingly, in December 1993 the European Council called for the accession negotiations to end by March 1, 1994.[16]

This schedule put the negotiators under great pressure to resolve a variety of issues on which wide disagreement remained. Eventual compromises included transitional arrangements for difficult regulatory matters; a decision to create a new category of structural funds (Objective 6) for Arctic areas; various measures to maintain farmers' incomes following the realignment of agricultural prices in the new member states to lower EU levels; and a promise to review EU environmental directives within four years of enlargement, during which time the new member states could maintain their higher standards. Inevitably the negotiations went beyond the stipulated deadline, but only by four weeks and only on a small number of highly contentious issues, including truck transit through the Austrian Alps and Norwegian fisheries.

The most memorable and politically significant dispute at the end of the negotiations erupted not between the EU and the candidate countries but among member states themselves. This was on the question of the threshold for a blocking minority in the reweighted system of qualified majority voting (QMV). Under the terms of the accession agreements, the number of weighted votes in the Council was due to increase from 76 to 90 (in the event, Norway did not join, and the total number of votes was reduced to 87). The blocking minority was currently 23; most member states agreed that after enlargement the blocking minority should be raised proportionately to 27 (or 26 following Norway's decision not to join). Britain and Spain strongly objected and attempted to keep the blocking minority at 23 even in the enlarged EU. Although both countries were genuinely concerned about the diminution of power inherent in a blocking minority of 26 votes (more member states would be needed to form a larger coalition of countries to block undesirable legislation), the British government was responding also—and arguably primarily—to strong anti-EU sentiment on its own back benches in parliament.[17]

The dispute threatened to delay ratification of the accession agreements and therefore push enlargement well beyond the January 1995 target date. True to EU form, agreement was reached at the last minute. At the specially convened General Affairs Council in Ioannina, Greece, on March 29, 1994, member states worked out a compromise: "If members of the Council representing a total of 23 to 25 votes indicate their intention to oppose the adoption by the Council of a decision by a qualified majority, the Council will do all within its power to reach, within a reasonable time . . . a satisfactory solution that can be adopted by at least 65 votes" (Britain's preferred qualified majority).[18]

The "Ioannina Compromise" showed how institutional disputes could overshadow and possibly derail future enlargement negotiations. Apart from the weighting of Council votes, increasingly troublesome institutional questions included the number of commissioners per member state and the size of national delegations in the EP. In an influential report adopted in January 1993, the EP had urged member states to undertake major institutional reform before proceeding with the Eftan enlargement.[19] The unseemly dispute over QMV strengthened the EP's conviction that large-scale institutional reform was pressing, and the newly conferred (by the TEU) right to grant its assent to enlargement gave the EP a valuable opportunity to make the point. Although the EP delivered a resounding endorsement of the accession treaties in a series of votes in May 1994, parliamentarians made clear during the preceding debate their dissatisfaction with the Ioannina Compromise and with the institutional situation in general.[20]

Following the EP's assent and the Council's subsequent approval of the accession agreements, ratification proceeded quickly in the applicant states. Apart from the terms of the agreements themselves, the lingering TEU ratification crisis had negatively affected opinion in the applicant countries, where support for EU membership was already fragile. In addition to general concerns about loss of sovereignty and neutrality, each country had particular reasons to be wary of joining the EU. All complained that the CAP would ruin their heavily subsidized agricultural sectors, Austrians feared an additional influx of foreigners and worried about the anonymity of their bank accounts, the Nordics fretted about the integrity of their environmental laws, and Swedish snuff-takers abhorred the EU's efforts to put a stop to their bad habit. The prominence of EU-related issues during general elections in the early 1990s demonstrated the high level of public interest in accession in the candidate countries.

Hoping to generate a momentum for victory in all four countries, the applicants tacitly agreed to schedule their accession referendums in the summer and fall of 1994 so that the more Euro-enthusiastic of them would go to the polls first. Thus Austria held the inaugural referendum, on June 12; the result was a resounding 66.4 percent in favor. Finland voted next, on October 16; the result was a respectable 56.9 percent in favor. The Swedish referendum took place on November 13; the result was a narrow 52 percent in favor. That set the stage for the final referendum, in Norway on November 28. There, the fault lines of the bitter 1972 campaign had eerily reopened. Indeed, the 1994 and 1972 campaigns were remarkably similar except that in 1994 the prime minister had the good sense not to threaten to resign in the event of defeat. After a bruising contest, only 47.5 percent voted in favor.

Norway's referendum result consigned the country to an unusual position in Europe: Together with Switzerland, it became one of only two Continental countries neither in nor actively seeking to join the EU. Like Norway, Switzerland had applied for EC membership (in May 1992). Also like Norway, a narrow majority rejected membership in a referendum in December 1992, albeit a referendum on participation in the EEA. Norway and Switzerland have other similarities and some striking differences: Both are highly nationalistic and wealthy (although not for the same reasons) but differ markedly in their security policies, with Norway in NATO and Switzerland doggedly neutral. Both are obviously Euroskeptical, yet a near majority of their populations and the vast majority of their governing and business elites want them to join the EU. Given the seemingly inexorable trend toward regional integration in Europe and elsewhere, nonmembership of the EU may ultimately prove economically disadvantageous, if not disastrous, for Norway and Switzerland. For domestic political reasons, however, their accession to the EU seems highly unlikely in the foreseeable future.

The Implications of Eftan Enlargement

A majority of Sweden's electorate soon regretted having joined the EU (the results of the country's first direct elections to the EP in September 1995 revealed widespread dissatisfaction). Swedish civil servants dealing with the EU are extremely critical of the Commission and the Council, and in deference to public opinion the Swedish government decided not to participate in Stage III of EMU.[21] Deep economic recession and few tangible benefits of membership exacerbated Swedish Euroskepticism. Although it became commonplace to say after enlargement that a majority in Sweden would vote to leave the EU, however, such an outcome is by no means certain. The EU is unloved in Sweden, as it is in other member states; but EU membership seems essential for Sweden's long-term economic well-being, as is the case with other member states.

By contrast, Austria and especially Finland are satisfied, if not overjoyed, with the EU. Apart from a positive perspective on economic integration—both are enthusiastic EMU participants—Austria and Finland see the EU primarily as a security community. Long dominated by its neighbors and now deeply concerned about Russia's future, neutral Finland appreciates the enhanced security that comes with EU accession. While geographically less vulnerable than Finland and also less committed to neutrality, Austria has a similar appreciation of the security benefits of belonging to the EU.

As expected, the new member states have helped the EU to become more open, transparent, and accountable and have contributed to the development of EU social, environmental, and trade policies. Also as expected, they have helped shape EU policy toward neighboring Central and Eastern European states and Russia, with Finland advocating a "Northern Dimension" for the EU. Without Austrian, Finnish, and Swedish support, Estonia and Slovenia would most likely not be in the first rank of Central and Eastern European candidates for EU membership.

Yet the experience of negotiating Eftan enlargement dampened enthusiasm in the EU (if there had been any to begin with) for Central and Eastern European enlargement. First, the EU's experience of arduous accession negotiations in 1993 and 1994 showed how difficult the negotiations with the Central and Eastern European applicants were likely to be. Second, a last-minute dispute in the Eftan negotiations reverberated loudly for the subsequent Central and Eastern European negotiations. In December 1994, after the accession agreements had been ratified by virtually all relevant parties, the Spanish government threatened not to ratify—and therefore to scuttle enlargement—unless the EU agreed to give Spain a fishing deal similar to Norway's. The crisis was resolved at a meeting of the Fisheries Council on December 22, when ministers promised to integrate Spain into the Common Fisheries Policy by January 1, 1996, six years earlier than the date stipulated in Spain's own accession agreement. Spain's tactics caused an obvious foreboding: During the next round of enlargement some member states (not least Spain) would surely claim that enlargement threatened their national interests. Would they provoke a dramatic confrontation to win concessions? If so, would other member states be able or willing to buy them off?

Finally, the row over Council voting in 1994 raised the specter of further enlargement being held up by a bitter dispute among member states over institutional restructuring. Fortuitously for the EU, a prearranged IGC provided an ideal opportunity to negotiate wide-ranging reform before beginning the next round of enlargement negotiations. Due partly to the legacy of Eftan enlargement and largely to impending Central and Eastern European enlargement, institutional reform took center stage at the 1996–1997 IGC.

FROM MAASTRICHT TO AMSTERDAM

The origin of the 1996–1997 IGC that resulted in the Amsterdam Treaty was unique. Whereas previous IGCs originated in a strong impetus for deeper integration, the 1996–1997 IGC took place only because it was mandated under the terms of the TEU (Article N). Provision for another IGC so soon after 1991 reflected both unfinished business at Maastricht and a conviction that the TEU's new decisionmaking procedures would need adjustment after a relatively brief shakedown period.

Subsequently, the institutional implications of enlargement came to dominate discussions about the impending IGC. Apart from the Eftan applicants, by the early 1990s as many as ten Central and Eastern European countries, plus Cyprus and Malta, were knocking on the EU's door. Even before Austria, Finland, and Sweden joined, the European Council had conceded the inevitability of further enlargement, although without specifying a timetable. Clearly, a future EU of twenty-five or more member states seemed unworkable without major institutional change. Asked in October 1995 why an IGC was necessary the following year, Carlos Westendorp, chairman of the preparatory Reflection Group, answered that an IGC "is indispensable to carry out reforms that will allow us to admit new members without risk to them or to us."[22]

Although there may have been good reasons for treaty reform based on some of the TEU's flawed procedures and on the implications of enlargement, it is unlikely that member states would have convened an IGC in 1996 unless they had been obliged to do so. On the one hand, the TEU had come into operation only in November 1993; it was still too soon to make an authoritative judgment about how badly or well it worked. On the other hand, the institutional consequences of Eftan enlargement seemed manageable, and the much more disruptive Central and Eastern European enlargement was by no means imminent. It was not surprising, therefore, that the Amsterdam Treaty failed to include major institutional changes. Instead, the treaty's significance lay in two aspects of it barely discussed when the IGC was planned: the institutionalization of "flexibility" and the progressive establishment of an area of "freedom, security, and justice."

Preparation

Thanks to the lessons of the TEU, if anything the 1996 IGC was overprepared. Poor planning for the 1991 negotiations on political union, together with the TEU ratification debacle, convinced member states that they would have to prepare the next IGC early and thoroughly. Mindful of the 1992 Danish referendum result, member states also undertook to plan and conduct the IGC as openly as possible. Such transparency was alien to most national governments with the notable exception of Denmark, the Netherlands, Sweden, and Finland.

In the event, most Europeans remained unaware of the IGC, and those aware of it were mostly bored by it. Regardless of its importance, a protracted conference of government officials discussing such arcane issues as flexibility, codecision, QMV, and subsidiarity could hardly appeal to a mass audience. Commission president Santer was right to say in March 1995 that "public opinion has come into play, which we must welcome," but wrong to claim that "there will be a real public debate this time before the end of the IGC."[23]

The Reflection Group

There had been various calls as early as 1993 for the establishment of a high-level committee to prepare the IGC. Member states agreed on the desirability of such a step, but not on the proposed committee's name, terms of reference, or composition. The most difficult issue was the role of the EP, which, understandably, wanted to be included in the preparatory group. Reflecting the usual division between member states, Belgium, Germany, Italy, and the Netherlands strongly supported involving the EP directly in the committee's work; France and Britain opposed. The question was thrashed out at the Corfu summit in June 1994, in the EP's favor. As well as formally approving the establishment of the Reflection Group to prepare the ground for the IGC, the European Council agreed that it would consist not only of national representatives and a commissioner but also of *two* MEPs (members of the European Parliament).[24]

Almost a year elapsed between the decision to establish the Reflection Group and the launch of the group itself. In the meantime, member states, the Commission, and the EP made their own preparations for the IGC. The first step was to choose the membership of the Reflection Group; the second was to draft three reports on the functioning of the TEU—one each from the Council, Commission, and EP—to serve as a basis for the group's deliberations. As its representatives, the EP selected two highly experienced and influential members, one French Socialist (Elizabeth Guigou) and one German Christian Democrat (Elmar Brok). Marcelino Oreja, commissioner with responsibility for interinstitutional affairs, represented the Commission in the Reflection Group and later in the IGC itself. Member states appointed one representative each. The three largest—France, Germany, and Britain—chose serving government ministers.

The institutions' preparatory reports, drawn up in early 1995, developed common themes: the need for greater openness, legitimacy, simplification of procedures, and effectiveness in the EU's operations, especially with respect to the two intergovernmental pillars. The EP eschewed its usual propensity to make excessive demands for greater power, having earlier decided not to adopt a Spinelli-like approach to the challenge of EU reform. Predictably, the EP's main demands were a revision of the TEU architecture and an extension of the codecision and assent procedures. By contrast, the Council criticized the EP for occasionally overstepping its legislative prerogatives, and especially for linking codecision and comitology (decisionmaking and implementation). In its report, the Commission emphasized the ineffectiveness of intergovernmental cooperation and regretted the failure of the treaty to bring the EU closer to its citizens. Although rectifying these deficiencies would be a priority at the IGC, the Commission was at pains to point out that it sought extra powers neither for itself nor for the EU.[25]

Together the reports provided a useful snapshot of the TEU's functioning in mid-1995. Beyond that, they conspicuously lacked "any explicit theory or conceptual framework linking the different approaches (to institutional improvement and greater legitimacy) together into a simple vision of a wider and stronger Union which might help the citizens understand the rationale of the whole endeavor."[26] The reports' limited approach was symptomatic of a lack of leadership and audacity within the EU (with the marked exception of Kohl's fixation on EMU) that generally characterized the entire IGC experience.

Member states launched the Reflection Group at a special meeting of foreign ministers in Messina, Sicily, on June 2 and 3, 1995, to celebrate the fortieth anniversary of the conference that had taken place there at a critical stage of the EC's history. The fact that the original Messina Conference had given rise to the Treaty of Rome seemed auspicious for the Reflection Group's deliberations, but the contemporary cloud of war in not-too-distant Bosnia was a more realistic omen. The ongoing siege of Sarajevo and the EU's continuing failure to broker a cease-fire sapped morale in the member states and proved the woeful inadequacy of the EU's foreign and security policy. The situation in Bosnia deteriorated further in August and September 1995, resulting in the Dayton Peace Accords and U.S. military intervention. These events deflected public attention from the Reflection Group's work just as the renegotiation of the U.S. troop presence in Bosnia dominated the news in late 1996 during an important stage of the IGC itself.

Much more so than Bosnia, EMU overshadowed every phase of the IGC. Throughout 1994, with Europe still in recession, member states' economies were diverging, not converging. Unofficial Italian calls for a relaxation of the EMU convergence criteria elicited a frosty German response. Paradoxically, Germany itself seemed incapable of bringing its budget deficit below 3 percent of GDP, a figure that became an article of faith for the EMU-obsessed. Because renegotiation of the criteria would have unraveled the entire project, there was a tacit agreement to keep EMU out of the IGC.

Nevertheless EMU was never far from member states' minds. It haunted them by threatening, if it collapsed, to derail the IGC and throw the EU into crisis. Although circumstances had changed markedly by the end of the IGC in mid-1997, through 1995 and most of 1996 EMU's prospects looked bleak. Violent protests in France in December 1995 against proposed cuts in public spending brought home the fragile nature of the EMU project. The Socialist Party's victory in the French parliamentary elections of May 1997 briefly shook confidence in EMU, as the new prime minister, Lionel Jospin, had campaigned vigorously against the excesses of EMU-driven austerity. Indeed, much of the IGC's work in 1996 and 1997 coincided with Franco-German bargaining over the terms of the stability pact to ensure the sustainability of EMU after its launch in 1999. A Franco-German row over the stability pact even overshadowed the opening of the Amsterdam summit itself.

It was in these inauspicious circumstances that the Reflection Group got down to work in June 1995, under the strict chairmanship of Carlos Westendorp, Spain's state secretary for foreign affairs. Altogether it met fifteen times before presenting a final report to the European Council in Madrid in December 1995. The group's remit was not to negotiate on the member states' behalf but to prepare the IGC by drawing up a manageable agenda and identifying areas of likely agreement. Member states' different approaches and ambitions were evident from the outset with the more integration-minded countries (notably Belgium, Germany, Italy, Luxembourg, and the Netherlands) ranged against those less inclined toward supranationalism, especially Britain.

The extreme Euroskepticism of Britain's Conservative government hobbled the Reflection Group's work just as it would hobble all but the final stage of the IGC itself. The Reflection Group's conclusions were split along recognizable national lines (although countries were not identified by name). Thus on a wide range of issues, the report noted a divergence between "a large majority" or "a majority" on the one hand and "one member" (invariably Britain) or "some members" (invariably including Britain) on the other. Without making precise or dramatic recommendations, the Reflection Group report identified three main areas for reform: making the EU more relevant to its citizens (i.e., human rights, internal security, employment, and the environment); improving the EU's efficiency and accountability (i.e., closing the democratic deficit); and improving the EU's ability to act internationally (i.e., strengthening the CFSP).[27]

The Flexibility Debate

The possibility of institutionalizing differentiated integration as a basic principle rather than an ad hoc arrangement emerged during the preparatory stage as one of the most important and contentious issues likely to dominate the IGC. Three main factors accounted for the timing and intensity of the debate over flexibility. The first was British obstructionism. Having given John Major the benefit of the doubt when he succeeded Margaret Thatcher as prime minister in 1990, Britain's partners grew bitterly disappointed with Major's growing Europhobia. Matters came to a head in 1994 when Major provoked the row over QMV that resulted in the Ioannina Compromise and later vetoed Belgian prime minister Jean-Luc Dehaene's nomination for the Commission presidency. The debate about flexibility, with its subtext of possible British exclusion, served as a warning to Britain that other member states were reaching the limits of their patience.

EMU was the second factor driving the flexibility debate. From the perspective of the early 1990s, it looked as if the euro zone would consist of a minority of only five or six member states, centered on France and Germany. Such a small group would need to act together in a number of economic policy areas using mechanisms not specifically provided for in the existing treaties. The anticipated small group of countries about to embark on Stage III of EMU would therefore need flexible treaty provisions to allow them to integrate further.

The prospect of EU enlargement to include up to ten mostly small, poor Central and Eastern European states, plus Cyprus and Malta, was the third factor propelling the flexibility debate. With the exception of Britain, existing member states feared that enlargement would seriously hinder further integration. Given that institutional reform in the context of enlargement had become the IGC's main rationale, an innovation such as flexibility seemed an essential option to explore.

The budding flexibility debate burst into the open in September 1994 when the parliamentary groups of the conservative parties in Germany's coalition government published their "Reflections on European Policy."[28] Popularly known by the names of its two authors, the Lamers/Schäuble paper was important because of its provenance (although not an official German government paper, clearly it reflected official German ideas about the EU's future) and especially because of its bold assertion that "the existing hard core of countries oriented to greater integration and closer cooperation must be further strengthened" and that "the further development of the EU's institutions must combine coherence and consistency with elasticity and flexibility." Not only did the authors use contested terms like "hard core" and "flexibility" but they went on to identify the core group as Germany, France, Belgium, Luxembourg, and the Netherlands. In other words, the original EC member states *minus Italy*. As for recalcitrant Britain, the authors argued that "determined efforts to spur on the further development of Europe are the best means of exerting a positive influence on the clarification of Britain's relationship to Europe and on its willingness to participate in further steps toward integration."

Already sensitive to criticism of its seeming inability to meet the TEU convergence criteria and embroiled in post–Cold War political upheavals, Italy was deeply offended by the German paper. Indelicate remarks by Theo Waigel, Germany's finance minister, about the parlous state of Italy's public finances further exacerbated German-Italian relations. Smaller member states, even the three Benelux countries included in the putative hard core, shared Italy's fear that the Lamers/Schäuble paper presaged a Franco-German scheme to pursue closer political integration outside the EU system.

Nor was one of the main thrusts of the paper lost on the British government. For some time Major had been talking cavalierly about flexibility, by which he meant an à la carte, pick-and-choose EU. He developed this theme in response to the Lamers/Schäuble paper, rejecting the idea of an EU "in which some (member states) would be more equal than others." By arguing against a hard core and implicitly two-tier EU and advocating instead a system in which member states could opt in and out of certain policies, Major drew one of the most important battle lines of the IGC.[29]

Although not specifically addressed to the Reflection Group, the Lamers/Schäuble paper was one of the most important IGC preparatory documents. Some months later, the Commission, Council, and EP reports provided an official point of departure for the Reflection Group's work, as did shorter, more focused reports from the Court of Justice and the Court of Auditors. Hundreds of other reports, think-pieces, and position papers on all aspects of European integration were presented for the IGC's consideration. These came from international organizations, national and regional governments, political parties, EP party groups, public and private interest groups, and research institutes.

Buried under more preparatory documents than had been generated by all previous treaty reforms, member states launched the IGC at a special summit in Turin on March 29, 1996. There was no prearranged date to end the IGC, although negotiations were expected to continue into the new year. The performance of Britain's representative in the Reflection Group convinced most other participants that the IGC would make little progress until after the next British election, due by May 1997 at the latest, which the Conservatives were widely expected to lose. In the event, the IGC ran until the Amsterdam summit of June 1997.

Negotiation

Process and Players

As in past IGCs, the 1996–1997 conference was negotiated by junior ministers or senior diplomats during regular working sessions (three or four times a month), by foreign ministers during regular monthly sessions of the General Affairs Council and specially convened meetings, and by the heads of state and government during regularly scheduled European Councils and extraordinary summits. The extent to which the European Council participated in detailed negotiations, already evident in previous IGCs, became even more marked in 1996 and 1997. Indeed, the European Council negotiated far into the night in Amsterdam, well beyond the summit's scheduled end, in an effort to reach agreement on institutional reform, the conference's most contentious issue.

As in past IGCs, the Commission had a seat at the table, although unlike national delegations it did not have the authority to veto agreement. In 1996, at the outset of the conference, the Commission was still coming to terms with its reduced influence in the aftermath of the TEU, under Santer's unassertive presidency. Accordingly, the Commission approached the IGC cautiously, emphasizing its wish to promote the EU's rather than the Commission's interests (although the two are surely inseparable).

Having participated fully in the Reflection Group, the EP pressed also for a seat at the IGC table. Predictably, France and Britain opposed EP participation in the conference itself; Italy (in the presidency when the conference began) and Germany supported the EP. The European Council eventually decided that the EP would not participate fully in the IGC but would be briefed regularly by the negotiators and could give its views on issues under discussion.[30]

Also as in past IGCs, France and Germany took a number of joint initiatives, notably on flexibility and the CFSP. But Franco-German leadership was noticeably weak in 1996 and 1997, as each country struggled with domestic and European problems. On the German side, Kohl's attention was focused almost exclusively on EMU. Just as he did not want EMU to intrude on the IGC, neither did he want the IGC to intrude on EMU. Hence Kohl's relatively unambitious IGC agenda and expectations, especially in view of growing domestic opposition to EMU and the government's slim parliamentary majority.

On the French side, changes in political leadership in 1995 and 1997 were not conducive to close Franco-German cooperation in the conduct of EU affairs. Chirac, who replaced Mitterrand as president in May 1995, had been evasive during the election campaign about both EMU and deeper European integration. Efforts to meet the magical 3 percent budget deficit criterion proved unpopular and politically costly in France, causing the defeat of the conservative government in May 1997 in an election that Chirac had hoped would consolidate his hold on power. Instead, Chirac found himself having to share power ("cohabit") with a left-wing government whose head, Jospin, had also equivocated about EMU during the election campaign. Like Chirac, Jospin had little choice once in office but to endorse EMU, although plans to combat France's high unemployment by legislating a thirty-five-hour working week seemed incompatible with the kinds of reforms needed to meet the convergence criteria.

Aware of the potentially damaging impact of some of his pronouncements and policies on Franco-German relations, Chirac made reassuring remarks during a speech in March 1995, when he was a leading candidate for the presidency. "One point must be quite clear," Chirac stated. "The Franco-German couple will remain at the heart of the [EU] mechanism." He went on to stress that he would "give priority to tackling with Chancellor Kohl the need for a common Franco-German approach to the 1996 IGC."[31] Indeed, on the day after his inauguration as president of France, Chirac met Kohl in Strasbourg to cement Franco-German ties.

Chirac and Kohl were seasoned politicians who understood the vagaries of the ballot box and accepted its outcome. It was not up to each to choose the leader of the other's country. History, geography, and economics are the driving forces behind the Franco-German tandem. Nevertheless, the rapport between a French president and German chancellor can determine the effectiveness of Franco-German leadership in the EU, especially in the highly personal environment of the European Council. Kohl had little rapport with Chirac. Moreover, following the parliamentary elections of 1997 Kohl had to work closely as well with Jospin. Given Jospin's dislike of EMU, inevitably this proved difficult. The few Franco-German initiatives taken during the IGC barely concealed these personal strains or disguised the fact that neither government seemed particularly interested in the proceedings.

As for the other large member states, Britain had marginalized itself and lost all influence in EU affairs until the election of May 1997, when Labour swept the Conservatives from office, as other member states hoped would happen. The change of government was fortuitous for the IGC, allowing a breakthrough on a number of important issues, notably free movement of people and the circumstances under which flexibility could be used. Italy's influence in the EU was minimal throughout, as the government focused its attention almost exclusively on the economic reforms necessary to participate in Stage III of EMU. By contrast, Spain was surprisingly assertive in the IGC despite a change of government in January 1996, when the inexperienced Aznar replaced González, one of the EU's most experienced statesmen.

Smaller member states invested proportionately more effort in the IGC than their large counterparts, although inevitably their influence was limited. By chance, two small member states (Ireland and the Netherlands) were in the presidency during the IGC's substantive stages. For much of Ireland's presidency the IGC proceeded in a desultory fashion. Sensitive to German and French criticism that political momentum was flagging, the Irish convened a special summit in October 1996 in Dublin, where the European Council reaffirmed its request, first made at the Florence summit four months earlier, for the Irish to prepare for the next summit in December "a general outline for a draft revision of the treaties." Based on "successive approximations" of member state positions on the less contentious IGC issues—in effect, the same procedure used by the Reflection Group—the Irish produced an incomplete draft treaty,[32] leaving the most difficult parts of the final version for the incoming Dutch presidency to work out.

The Dutch were haunted in 1997 by their mishandling of the 1991 IGC. Nevertheless, having inherited from the Irish the most difficult issues on the IGC's agenda—notably flexibility, institutional reform, and the free movement of people—the Dutch steadfastly set about narrowing member state differences and drafting the final text. They did so by circulating various "nonpapers" and by convening the European Council for a special summit in Noordwijk in May 1997. The IGC finally reached full speed between Noordwijk and Amsterdam, with the new British government fully on board. Failure to agree on institutional reform in the waning hours of the Amsterdam summit was less a reflection on the Dutch presidency than on the overloaded agenda of EU summits and the exhaustion of the summiteers.

Issues and Outcomes

In the run-up to the IGC, governments and EU institutions had put a large number and variety of issues on the table. Although dealt with separately in the IGC, inevitably these became linked in the give-and-take of the negotiations, especially toward the end of the conference as member states brokered agreements and constructed package deals. The IGC was not a zero-sum game; there were no absolute winners and losers. On the key issues of flexibility, institutional change, CFSP reform, and the free movement of people, all parties in the process, whether member states or institutions, could fairly claim satisfaction with the outcome. Whether the outcome was worth the effort, and whether it greatly benefited the EU, are another matter.

Flexibility. The three factors that drove the initial debate on flexibility—British recalcitrance, the supposed size of the euro zone, and concerns about enlargement—changed significantly during the course of the IGC. By the end of the conference the British Conservatives were out of power; Stage III of EMU seemed set to start in January 1999 with a large majority of member states, and enlargement looked likely to be staggered over a lengthy period. Whereas in 1994 there was a sense of urgency about the need for flexibility, in mid-1997 flexibility aroused more academic interest than political passion.

Nevertheless, flexibility remained a salient and contentious issue during much of the IGC. In its pre-IGC report, the Reflection Group had cautioned that whatever form it took, flexibility should be used only when all other possible solutions had been exhausted and only as a temporary solution to meet specific challenges. While emphasizing the importance of flexibility in an enlarging and diversifying EU, Kohl and Chirac also stressed, in a joint initiative in December 1995, that flexibility should develop inside rather than outside the EU, if possible using the EU's institutions, procedures, and mechanisms.[33] Although some member states remained wary, a consensus began to emerge that the principle of flexibility should be included in the treaty as long as the practice of flexibility was limited to precisely defined conditions that would not endanger the *acquis communautaire*.

Discussion of what these conditions might be proceeded cautiously during the Irish presidency. The Irish draft treaty contained a section that reviewed the debate on flexibility to date but did not propose treaty language. It was left to the Dutch presidency to craft an agreement on flexibility that included both general "enabling" clauses applicable to the EU as a whole for member states wishing to cooperate more closely and particular clauses applicable to specific policy areas. One of these, a provision allowing member states to block the use of flexibility on the grounds of "national interest," harked back to the days of Charles de Gaulle and the Luxembourg Compromise. It also showed that Britain's Conservative government need not have been too concerned about the applicability of flexibility. However, Britain's change of government facilitated rapid progress on flexibility in the closing weeks of the IGC, so much so that the European Council spent little time discussing it at the Amsterdam summit.

Common Foreign and Security Policy. There was general agreement before the IGC on the need to improve the CFSP's effectiveness, but considerable disagreement about how that should be done. A consensus emerged early in the negotiations on the desirability of establishing a CFSP unit for analysis and planning inside the Council secretariat, with Commission involvement. France pushed hard for the creation of a new position, a "Mr. or Mrs. CFSP," to give CFSP greater visibility and continuity. Other member states acquiesced in the French proposal but, not wanting to have a new political office in the EU's already cumbersome institutional architecture, insisted that the Council secretary-general be designated the new "High Representative" for the CFSP.

Member states had more difficulty deciding how to simplify and improve CFSP decisionmaking procedures. The more integrationist of them, such as Germany, Italy, and the Benelux countries, failed to curtail unanimity but succeeded in introducing constructive abstentionism, whereby member states not wishing to take CFSP-related decisions could at least allow the others to do so, subject to an "emergency brake" (again, the invocation of a "national interest").

In order to give greater substance and effectiveness to the EU's security and defense identity and strengthen the European pillar of the Atlantic Alliance, a majority of member states wanted the EU and WEU to merge. Faced with strong opposition from Britain and Denmark, which opposed the militarization of the EU, and the neutral member states, which remained opposed to participation in a military alliance, the IGC agreed only to "the possibility of the integration of the WEU into the EU, should the European Council so decide." The conference nevertheless agreed to an important step with military implications: inclusion in the treaty of so-called Petersberg tasks (peacekeeping and related operations).

Institutional representation and decisionmaking. Most member states favored extending QMV to a number of policy areas in the first pillar subject to unanimity. Once again, the defeat of Britain's Conservative government removed a major obstacle to achieving that goal. Yet one of the greatest surprises of the Amsterdam summit was that for reasons of domestic politics, Kohl gave in to pressure from the German Länder (states) and blocked the extension of QMV to two new policy areas. Still, QMV was extended to areas over which the Länder were unable to exert influence, notably research and development policy.

The question of greater use of QMV inevitably became bound up in the highly political but seemingly technical question of the mechanics of QMV, that is, the possible reweighting of votes in the Council. Larger member states favored either an increase in the number of their votes or the introduction of a double majority combining the traditional requirement of a qualified majority with a new demographic criterion. They argued that without such a change, following successive rounds of enlargement, a qualified majority could be formed by a group of member states that together did not represent a majority of the EU's population. As French prime minister Edouard Balladur had pointed out well before the IGC, QMV in an enlarged EU could mean that "the five big states representing four-fifths of the [EU's] population and wealth could be put in a minority."[34]

Negotiations about the reweighting of votes inevitably became bound up with another controversial institutional issue: the size of the Commission. Intellectually, every member state conceded that the Commission was too large; politically, few would countenance a Commission smaller in size than the total number of EU member states. Not least because large member states wanted to increase their relative weight in Council voting, small member states adamantly opposed the possible loss of "their" commissioner. With varying degrees of enthusiasm, large member states expressed willingness to give up at least their second commissioner, but only in return for a reweighting of votes in the Council. France alone favored a radical reduction in the Commission's size—to ten or twelve commissioners. That was because France also wanted to reduce the Commission's authority, for instance, by abolishing its exclusive right of legislative initiative.

Negotiations over the Commission's size and the reweighting of Council votes dominated the closing hours of the Amsterdam summit. Having failed to reach agreement, the European Council settled on a temporary solution: A protocol attached to the treaty stipulated that the Commission would comprise one representative per member state as soon as the next EU accession took place, provided that Council votes were reweighted in order to compensate large member states for the loss of a second commissioner. The protocol also stated that at least one year before the EU enlarged to twenty-one member states (thereby bringing the Commission's size to more than twenty) an IGC would have to be convened "to carry out a comprehensive review of the provisions of the treaties on the composition and functioning of the institutions" (in order to decide, specifically, how to apportion twenty commissioners among more than twenty member states).

EP-related issues—Parliament's size, location, and legislative powers—proved relatively painless at the IGC. The conference accepted the EP's own proposal to limit the EP to 700 members and agreed to enshrine in the treaty an earlier agreement (reached at the Edinburgh summit in December 1992) to hold the bulk of the EP's plenary session in Strasbourg. Following the change of government in Britain, the conference acceded to the EP's request that the number of legislative procedures be reduced to three: consultation, a simplified form of codecision, and assent. The extension and simplification of the codecision procedure further enhanced the EP's legislative power and political influence.

Free movement of people. The thirteen EU member states that had signed the Schengen agreement on the free movement of people (Britain and Ireland being the odd ones out) wanted to bring Schengen into the EU framework. The change of government in Britain made it possible to do so, although Britain and Ireland secured opt-outs (Britain because of its insistence on controlling its own borders, Ireland because of its wish to retain a common travel area with Britain). The issue was further complicated by the size and complexity of the so-called Schengen *acquis* (laws and regulations that had accrued since the launch of the Schengen process in 1985) and by the fact that Iceland and Norway, two non–EU member states, also participated in Schengen.

Immigration and asylum policy, already subject to intergovernmental cooperation in the EU's third pillar, were integral to the success of Schengen. Concerned about the weakness of the third pillar, member states agreed to move its provisions on immigration and asylum to the supranational first pillar and pledged themselves to establish an area of freedom, security, and justice. Largely in deference to Germany, which absorbs the bulk of refugees and asylum seekers in the EU and where the Länder share responsibility for the matter, the new first-pillar provisions on immigration and asylum were hedged with intergovernmental and other qualifications.

Other issues. Other important issues negotiated in the IGC ranged from the role of national parliaments in EU decisionmaking to subsidiarity to social policy to transparency and openness. Important outcomes included

- a protocol on the role of national parliaments, giving the Conference of European Affairs Committees of national parliaments the right to send comments on EU legislative proposals to the Commission, Council, and EP

- incorporation of the Edinburgh summit's subsidiarity protocol into the treaty
- incorporation of the TEU's social protocol into the treaty proper, thereby extending its applicability to all fifteen member states
- a new transparency clause in the treaty stipulating that any natural or legal person residing in the EU has a right of access to EU documents

The Amsterdam Treaty

Judged by the main reason given by politicians in 1996 for embarking on another IGC—the need to adapt the EU to meet the challenge of enlargement—the Amsterdam Treaty is a failure. Having ducked institutional reform at the time of the Eftan enlargement, member states were unlikely to have agreed soon afterward to major institutional changes in anticipation of another enlargement that lay several years in the future. Elizabeth Guigou, one of the EP's representatives in the Reflection Group, remarked in September 1995 that she did not see "any political will on the part of the governments to make a substantial reform."[35] Her observation was still valid almost two years later, at the time of the Amsterdam summit.

The treaty's institutional provisions are therefore disappointing but not surprising. Greater power for the EP and greater recourse to QMV are welcome improvements but are unlikely greatly to enhance the EU's efficiency, credibility, or legitimacy. Changes in CFSP decisionmaking are modest and will probably be ineffective. Equally important, by deferring the hard institutional questions about the Commission's size and member states' weighted votes until another IGC, the EU sent a negative signal to its own citizens and to the applicant states.

The treaty's main innovation is that it includes "the first institutionalization of the concept of flexibility as a *basic principle* in the Treaties."[36] Yet surrounded as they are by qualifications and safeguards, the treaty's flexibility clauses will be difficult to apply. What emerged in the Amsterdam Treaty is a far cry from what some self-described hard core countries advocated and what some of the implicitly peripheral countries feared shortly before the IGC opened. Nevertheless, most member states expressed satisfaction with the flexibility provisions. For the presumed hard core, having the principle of flexibility written into the treaty was an important political victory; for the others, what mattered most was having a seat at the table if and when flexibility was ever invoked.

The treaty will be known for its flexibility clauses and also for its establishment of an area of freedom, security, and justice. External border control and visas, asylum and immigration policy, and judicial cooperation are close to the core of national sovereignty but are also issues on which most Europeans want to see more effective transnational cooperation.

Because of a five-year transition period before the use of QMV in these areas, changes will not come immediately. Similarly, the thirteen Continental member states are committed to opening their internal borders only by 2004. As soon as people move freely throughout the EU, however, and once the EU has greater external border protection, the Amsterdam Treaty will be seen in a more favorable light.

In the meantime, other provisions of the treaty promise more immediate benefits for EU citizens. For instance, the treaty extends EU competence in areas of obvious popular concern, such as public health and consumer protection. More controversially, the treaty includes a chapter on employment allowing the Council to draw up guidelines for member states, encourage new initiatives and pilot projects, and establish an advisory employment committee to promote coordination among member states. Europeans are rightly worried about high unemployment, but the measures in this chapter are unlikely to alleviate the problem. EU meetings and committees cannot create jobs; only through its single market can the EU hope to bring about the economic conditions conducive to economic growth, and only through labor market and other reforms will such growth lead to a substantial increase in employment. The chapter on employment is largely cosmetic, intended to demonstrate the EU's sensitivity to mass unemployment.

Regardless of its substance, the treaty's length and language are by no means citizen-friendly. With more than fifty pages of text, including numerous references to existing treaty provisions, the document is not an easy read. Ironically, a treaty intended to make the EU more intelligible to its citizens is almost unintelligible even to experts. In that sense, the treaty is a fitting testimonial to the impossibility of reconciling the complexity of EU governance with citizens' demands for greater lucidity and comprehensibility of EU policies and procedures.

Ratification

Understandably in view of what had happened after Maastricht, the specter of a post-IGC ratification crisis loomed over the 1996–1997 negotiations. Governments handled ratification carefully, dragging the process out until well into 1999. Ratification procedures in most member states did not include holding a referendum. This time, the president of France did not take the unnecessary risk of putting the proposed treaty to a vote of the people.

Nevertheless, ratification of the Amsterdam Treaty was neither as controversial nor as problematic as ratification of the TEU had been. Given the difference between the two treaties and the fact that member states had already gone through the TEU ratification crisis, there was much less at stake in 1997 and 1998. A no vote in Denmark in 1998 would not have had the same impact as it had in 1992, not least because the negotiation of special Danish opt-outs after the 1992 referendum showed that Danish rejection of the Amsterdam Treaty could be similarly finessed. Undoubtedly a negative result in Denmark would have unsettled the EU, but it would hardly have derailed either EMU or enlargement. Still, member state and EU officials breathed a huge sigh of relief in May 1998 when the result of the Danish referendum became known: 55.1 percent in favor, 44.9 percent against.

A week before the Danish referendum, Irish voters had endorsed the treaty by a vote of 61.7 percent to 38.3 percent. Although a majority of nearly 24 percent was comfortable by any standard, the size of the no vote—substantially larger than the no votes in previous EU-related referendums—demonstrated both the treaty's unpopularity and growing disillusionment in Ireland with the EU as a whole. Many of those who voted against the treaty complained that they did not know enough about it. Undoubtedly the treaty is difficult to understand, but there was a surfeit of creditable and comprehensible information on the treaty's nature and content available to interested voters. The perception of an information deficit at a time of information overload confirms the public relations problem facing the EU in the lingering post-Maastricht climate of skepticism and distrust.

TOWARD A PAN-EUROPEAN EU

In 1988, as the EC embarked on the single market program, there seemed little prospect of enlargement in the foreseeable future. Only Turkey had an application on the table, which the Commission put on hold when it issued a negative opinion in December 1989.[37] Otherwise, with Europe still divided by the Cold War, the countries of Central and Eastern Europe could only dream of one day joining the EC; strategic considerations prevented the Western European neutrals (Austria, Finland, Switzerland, and Sweden) from submitting membership applications. Ten years later, not only had three of the neutrals (Austria, Finland, and Sweden) joined the EU but five of the Central and Eastern European States (CEES) had started accession negotiations and five more had their applications under active consideration. The EU had also begun accession negotiations with Cyprus, despite the opposition of Turkey, whose application still languished in Brussels.

The enlargement of the EU to encompass the CEES is qualitatively and quantitatively unprecedented. Enlargement of the original six–member state EC to the fifteen–member state EU took place piecemeal, over a period of twenty-two years. Five later arrivals (Austria, Britain, Denmark, Finland, and Sweden) had long histories of liberal democracy and had levels of economic development greater or equal to the prevailing EU average. Three later arrivals (Greece, Portugal, and Spain), had fledgling democratic systems but were significantly poorer than the EU average. Ireland, the remaining later arrival, was also poorer than the EU average but had a solid democratic tradition.

By contrast, all ten Central and Eastern European applicants are economically far worse off than even the poorest EU member state, and all are fledgling democracies. All had been cut off from Western Europe either by incorporation into the Soviet Union (i.e., Estonia, Latvia, and Lithuania) or by Soviet occupation and domination. The end of the Cold War and disintegration of the Soviet Union therefore presented a historic opportunity to reintegrate Europe culturally, politically, and economically. EU enlargement into Central and Eastern Europe is an important part of that process.

Following the end of the Cold War, the CEES looked to the EU not only for financial support, market access, and technical assistance but also for recognition of their "Europeanness." As democratic countries, the newly independent CEES had every right to apply for EU membership. For its part, the EU had an opportunity and a responsibility to help neighboring countries develop economically and democratically while promoting stability and security throughout the continent and fostering a genuinely pan-European integration. In order to succeed, the EU would have to see the potential and not just the pitfalls of eastward enlargement; to look outward at a time of post-TEU introspection; to overcome vested interests threatened by Central and Eastern European imports in sensitive sectors like agriculture, steel, and textiles; to restructure its institutions and policies in order to accommodate a diverse group of new member states; and to rethink Europe's future in a radical, post–Cold War environment. These were immense challenges. Given its own political and economic constraints, inevitably the EU could not meet all of them in a timely, effective, and generous fashion.

Initial Response

Rapidly unfolding events in the Soviet bloc in the late 1980s forced the EC to confront for the first time its glaring lack of an *Ostpolitik*. For nearly three decades the EC had prospered in a divided Europe, appropriating the name of the entire continent. Early intimations of change in the East had prompted the Dooge Committee to preface its 1985 report on institutional reform with the lofty claim that the EC "has not lost sight of the fact that it represents only a part of Europe" and that " any progress in building the Community is in keeping with the interests of Europe as a whole."[38]

Yet the EC *had* lost sight of the fact that it represented only a part of Europe. For the EC's founding fathers, European integration was synonymous with *Western* European integration, centered on the Rhine. As a result of the Cold War, to which the EC owed much of its early development, Eastern Europe seemed irrevocably cut off from the West. Thus the emergence of the Central and Eastern European reform movement in the mid-1980s, leading rapidly to the end of the Cold War, challenged the EC's assumptions about the meaning and definition of "Europe" and the potential scope of "European" integration.

Given the rapid pace of change in Central and Eastern Europe in the late 1980s and the consequent shock of the Cold War's end, it is remarkable that the EC initially reacted so quickly and so well. The European Council first discussed a concerted EC response at the Rhodes summit in December 1988.[39] Seven months later, at the G7 (Group of Seven Most Industrialized Countries) summit in Paris, the Commission agreed to take responsibility for coordinating Western aid to Poland and Hungary, the politically most advanced countries in the region.[40] In December 1989 the EC launched the Poland-Hungary: Actions for Economic Reconstruction (PHARE) program "to support the process of reform in Poland and Hungary, in particular by financing or participating in the financing of projects aimed at economic restructuring . . . in particular in the areas of agriculture, industry, investment, energy, training, environmental protection, trade and services."[41] Although an EC initiative, PHARE soon became synonymous with assistance to Central and Eastern Europe from the "G24": the EC Twelve, the EFTA countries, the United States, Canada, Turkey, Australia, New Zealand, and Japan.

In July 1990 the EC decided to extend PHARE to Bulgaria, Czechoslovakia, East Germany, and Yugoslavia. Because of the brutal suppression of student demonstrations in Bucharest the previous month, Romania was not included. East Germany dropped out in October 1990, when it united with West Germany and thereby joined the EC, but in October 1991 the Community included the Baltic states in PHARE. In 1990 Brussels allocated ECU 500 million for PHARE; this amount increased to ECU 785 million in 1991 and ECU 1 billion in 1992.[42]

While developing the PHARE program, the EC concluded trade and cooperation agreements with virtually all of the CEES. Other EC assistance included emergency food aid and balance-of-payments loans. In addition, the EC played a prominent part in the French-sponsored European Bank for Reconstruction and Development (EBRD), which Mitterrand proposed at the extraordinary European Council in Paris in November 1989. The other G24 countries soon endorsed the idea of using public money from the West to help develop the private sector in the East. Representatives of numerous governments and public institutions from East and West approved the EBRD's statute at a ceremony in Paris in May 1990. Of the bank's ECU 10 billion capital, the EC Twelve, the Commission, and the European Investment Bank contributed 51 percent; the United States, 10 percent; Japan, 8.5 percent; and the USSR, 6 percent. After a political wrangle about the bank's location and president, the EBRD began operating in London in April 1991.[43]

Coping with the Central and Eastern European challenge and coordinating the concerted G24 aid effort had a profound institutional, operational, and procedural impact on the EC. The Commission had to open delegations (embassies) throughout the region, establish a PHARE office in Brussels, and reorganize internally. Directorate-General I (DG I—external relations) took the lead in dealing with Central and Eastern Europe, but few of the other directorates-general were unaffected. In particular, the Commission drew heavily on DG II (economic and financial affairs) and DG VIII (development assistance). Chairing G24 meetings imposed a heavy administrative burden on the Commission.

The EP experienced a similar upheaval. Central and Eastern European parliamentarians regularly visited Strasbourg, and members of the European Parliament journeyed to Central and Eastern Europe. Moreover, the EP had the budgetary authority to allocate funds for PHARE and other EC assistance. Parliament's ability to block association agreements increased its political leverage when the EC began to negotiate such arrangements with Czechoslovakia, Hungary, and Poland. A reorganization of the EP's staff and services reflected its enhanced involvement in international affairs as a result of the EC's emerging *Ostpolitik*.

Impressive though it was, the EC's initial response to developments in Central and Eastern Europe had been improvised and understandably ad hoc. The rapid pace of events made it difficult for the EC, already coping with the impact of German unification, to devise a coherent strategy. The EC sought to promote stability, democracy, and economic reform in the region but was unable to respond positively to calls for immediate enlargement. The EC was in an invidious position. For thirty years it had decried the division of Europe and called for pan-European integration. It was hardly surprising that with the sudden end of the Cold War, Central and Eastern European countries used the EC's own rhetoric to demand entry. Nor was it surprising that they cited the examples of Greece, Portugal, and Spain, countries that had also sought EC membership to help consolidate economic and political reform and realize a "European" vocation. When Václav Havel, president of Czechoslovakia (later of the Czech Republic), called in June 1990 for the two countries to "return to Europe," clearly he meant accession to the EC.[44]

The model as well as the rhetoric of postwar integration strengthened the CEES' case for membership. Commenting on the fate of the former Soviet bloc, Czechoslovakia's foreign minister remarked in January 1992 that "we will be secure only if the relations among all European countries are, let's say, like the relations between Belgium and the Netherlands."[45] The strength and persistence of Central and Eastern European aspirations for accession were strikingly apparent at a meeting in Prague in June 1991 to discuss Mitterrand's proposal for a "European Confederation." In his opening remarks, Havel stressed that "the Confederation should view [the

EC] as its driving force and the model of its future. . . . The nascent Confederation should . . . make way for [the democracies of Central and Eastern Europe] to join the EC, prepare them and be a mediator."[46]

The EC had no choice but to endorse Central and Eastern European appeals for accession while arguing the impossibility of immediate enlargement. The obstacles to early entry were formidable. Forty years of Communist rule had left an appalling personal, political, and economic legacy. In order to make a successful transition from command to free market economies, and therefore meet a basic requirement for EC membership, the CEES faced a daunting array of legal and business reforms, including the introduction of property rights and a code of business law, the development of banking and financial services, the privatization of most state-owned companies, and the launch of a stock market. In order to lay a foundation for economic growth they needed to overhaul outmoded infrastructure, begin large-scale agricultural and industrial modernization, attract foreign investment, and find new markets. Additional problems requiring expensive solutions included massive environmental degradation and unsafe nuclear reactors. While coping with the social dislocation of wrenching economic reform, Central and Eastern Europeans had to learn the kinds of basic skills and attitudes taken for granted in the West, such as enterprise and intellectual curiosity. Politicians had to learn how to run a government or an opposition along liberal-democratic lines. Government officials at local and national levels had to learn how to provide modern administrative services.

As the high cost and full extent of the reform process became apparent, even enthusiasts of early Central and Eastern European accession realized that further EU enlargement was improbable before the end of the decade. Eleven years had elapsed before Portugal and Spain joined the EC after the restoration of democracy in 1975. It seemed highly unlikely that any of the CEES would be ready to join the EU—an EU far more economically and politically integrated than the EC of 1986—within eleven years of the fall of the Berlin Wall. The economic disparity between the two halves of Europe was too great for the EU to expand eastward in the foreseeable future. Going beyond the emergency aid it applied in the immediate aftermath of the Cold War, the EC therefore set about preparing the CEES for the long road to eventual accession by adapting the PHARE program and by offering comprehensive political and economic packages in the form of special association agreements.

From Europe Agreements to Accession Partnerships

In August 1990 the Commission proposed that the EC conclude "second generation" agreements with the Visegrad Three (Czechoslovakia, Hungary, and Poland) to broaden and deepen the scope of the "first generation" trade and cooperation agreements concluded in 1988 and 1989. Called Europe agreements to distinguish them from the EC's existing association agreements, the new accords aimed to strengthen political and economic reform in the Visegrad Three, paving the way for their eventual membership.[47] Subsequently available to all CEES, Europe agreements would have similar structures but different content according to the needs of each associated state.

Negotiations between the Commission and the Visegrad Three took a full year to complete and pitted the member states' protectionist proclivities against their political rhetoric. When it came to granting the Visegrad Three liberal market access, a number of member states succumbed to domestic protectionist pressure—especially for steel, agriculture, and textiles—and blocked generous terms. "You cannot shed tears of joy for the people of Eastern Europe one day and the next tell them that you will not buy their products," an exasperated Delors remarked after a demonstration by French farmers protesting plans for greater access to EC markets for Central and Eastern European produce.[48]

Only when Hungary and Poland embarrassed the EC by threatening to walk out of the talks and Havel warned that "right-wing authoritarian and nationalist forces" would exploit a failure to reach agreement did the recalcitrant member states—notably France, Spain, and Portugal—come to their senses.[49] Accordingly, Europe agreements were signed with Czechoslovakia, Hungary, and Poland in December 1991 (the agreement with Czechoslovakia was nullified by the breakup of the country in December 1992 and was replaced by separate agreements with the Czech Republic and Slovakia in October 1993). Europe agreements went far beyond existing accords by providing for the eventual establishment of free trade areas, the gradual adoption by the Visegrad Three of EC legislation on the single market and related areas, and the launch of a political dialogue. Most important for the new associates was an acknowledgment that their "final objective" was to join the EC.[50]

Because the Europe agreements were "mixed"—covering areas of EU and member state competence—they required ratification at both the EU and national levels. In order to facilitate closer economic cooperation during the lengthy ratification process, the Commission concluded "interim" agreements with the Visegrad Three covering those areas of the Europe agreements within Community competence. The EU concluded Europe and interim agreements with the other CEES over the course of the next four years.

The first Europe agreement negotiations coincided with the 1991 IGCs and formally ended only six days after the Maastricht summit.[51] There was considerable relief among the CEES that the IGCs had not resulted in insurmountable obstacles to EU membership. If anything, the new treaty's provisions for EMU and for closer political cooperation intensified the

CEES' eagerness to join lest they be further marginalized outside a more integrated EU. Nor did any of the newly independent CEES seem unduly concerned about the loss of sovereignty inherent in EU membership. Speaking just before the Maastricht summit, a Polish official remarked that his people were "now beginning to enjoy [their] freedom and independence" while simultaneously seeking EU membership.[52] The CEES appreciated the economic and political advantages of joining the EU, a voluntary, rule-based organization. Only Euroskeptics within some of the existing member states compared the EU to the old Soviet empire.

Just as the EEA initiative had failed to deter EC membership applications from the Eftan countries, the Europe agreements similarly failed to delay EU membership applications from the CEES, if that was partly their purpose. Instead, criticism within and outside the EU—notably from the CEES and from the United States—of the Europe agreements' limited trade concessions and of the EU's tardy response to the CEES' aspirations for accession prompted the member states to spell out the conditions for eastward enlargement sooner rather than later. Also, the ongoing TEU ratification crisis was advantageous to the CEES because it forced the EC to counter criticism of its introspection by appearing to be outward-looking and inclusive.

Yet the prospect of eastward enlargement was highly controversial among the member states. Whereas Britain hoped that early accession would weaken European integration, most member states feared that an ill-prepared enlargement could turn the EU into a glorified free trade area. There were different points of view about the ideal speed and extent of enlargement even among the more enthusiastic member states. Eager to fill a new strategic void on its eastern border, Germany wanted to bring the Czech Republic and Poland into the EU as soon as possible and supported Hungary's accession largely as a reward for that country's contribution to the fall of the Berlin Wall in 1989. Beyond that, Germany was lukewarm about enlargement. For its part, France fretted about the economic implications of enlargement, and also about the political implications of a German sphere of influence in the eastern part of an enlarged EU. The cohesion countries—Spain, Portugal, Greece, and Ireland—worried about the consequences for them of having to compete for structural funds with new, more deserving member states.

The Copenhagen Criteria

Although member states continued to ponder the practical implications of enlargement, mounting moral and political pressure in 1992 and 1993 for an early commitment to CEES accession led the EU formally to acknowledge its inevitability and to describe the preconditions for its occurrence. In June 1992 the Commission itemized the factors that would influence the EU's consideration of each country's application. These included geographical location (although the Commission conceded that it was impossible to define precisely where Europe ended); a democratic political system; a commitment to human rights; a functioning and competitive free market economy; an adequate legal and institutional framework; acceptance of the *acquis communautaire;* and a willingness to participate in the CFSP and, possibly, a common defense policy.[53] The European Council, meeting in Edinburgh in December 1992, welcomed the Commission's report but was too preoccupied with the TEU ratification crisis to deal with it then. Accordingly, it was not until the Copenhagen summit in June 1993 that the European Council turned its attention fully to the EU's prospective eastward enlargement.

Having declared unequivocally that "the associated countries in Central and Eastern Europe which so desire shall become members of the European Union," the European Council spelled out the so-called Copenhagen criteria, by which candidate countries would be judged for accession:

- stability of institutions guaranteeing democracy, the rule of law, human rights, and respect for and protection of minorities
- existence of a functioning market economy, as well as the capacity to cope with competitive pressure and market forces within the EU
- ability to take on the obligations of membership, including adherence to the aims of political, economic, and monetary union

Recognizing the likely impact of enlargement on the EU itself, the European Council also stipulated that "the Union's capacity to absorb new members, while maintaining the momentum of European integration," would be "an important consideration" in the accession process.[54] Critics saw this statement as a potential excuse for the EU to postpone enlargement indefinitely. In the shorter term, the European Council's emphasis on the internal implications of enlargement focused member states' attention on the upcoming IGC, which presented an opportunity to facilitate enlargement by making necessary institutional adjustments.

Also in Copenhagen, the European Council invited the Commission "to submit proposals for developing the existing trade agreements with the Baltic states into free trade agreements" and declared that "it remains the objective of the Community to conclude free trade agreements with the Baltic states as soon as the necessary conditions have been met." Thus the net for potential new member states was cast wider than the Visegrad Four (Hungary, Poland, the Czech Republic, and Slovakia) plus Bulgaria and Romania to cover northeastern Europe as well. Later it would cover more of southeastern Europe when a Europe agreement was concluded with Slovenia, the first of the former Yugoslav republics to declare independence, following resolution of a long-standing dispute over property rights between that country and Italy.

The Structured Dialogue and White Paper on Participation in the Single Market

Germany placed special emphasis on eastward enlargement during its otherwise lackluster Council presidency in the second half of 1994. As a result, the European Council decided in Essen in December 1994, on the eve of the accession of Austria, Finland, and Sweden, to accelerate the process of eastward enlargement by launching a "structured dialogue" between the soon-to-be EU Fifteen and the CEES collectively.[55] Covering a wide range of EU policy areas, including CFSP and JHA, the structured dialogue involved regular ministerial-level meetings as well as annual meetings of the heads of state and government of the EU and of the CEES on the margins on the European Council. Impatient to begin entry negotiations as soon as possible, most of the CEES dismissed the structured dialogue as a necessary but nonsubstantive public relations exercise.

From a practical point of view, another decision taken in Essen proved more significant than the launch of the structured dialogue. That was a request by the European Council for the Commission to draft a white paper on preparations by the CEES for participation in the single market, one of the EU's most complex and far-reaching policy areas. Published in May 1995, the white paper included detailed guidelines for the CEES to map their own route to participation in the single market, sector by sector, and therefore to membership in the EU.[56] The conditions set out in the white paper were daunting for countries with low levels of economic development, little experience of free market economics, and inadequate administrative structures. Precisely because the challenges were so great, the white paper also became an invaluable guide for directing financial, legal, and technical assistance from the EU and its member states to the CEES. As a result, the Commission reformed the PHARE program in order to devote more resources to such mundane but essential objectives as competent regulatory and bureaucratic structures in the recipient CEES.

Guided generally by the Copenhagen criteria and specifically by the Europe agreements, white paper, and other Commission documents, the CEES set about trying to meet the high political and economic standards for EU membership. In 1996 and 1997 most of the applicant states adopted detailed preaccession plans as part of an overall accession strategy, including quantifiable measurements of progress toward the approximation of national and EU legislation in the area of market integration.

Agenda 2000

While the applicant states adopted detailed accession strategies, EU member states embarked on the pre-Amsterdam IGC. Ostensibly intended to prepare the EU for enlargement, the IGC and its outcome had little bearing directly on the applicant states' preparations for accession except to provide a yardstick for the beginning of negotiations (no sooner than six months after the end of the IGC). Much more important for the CEES was the Commission's intensive preparation during 1996 and early 1997 of opinions on all the membership applications and of a comprehensive report on the impact of enlargement on the EU. Collectively, the opinions and report composed *Agenda 2000,* released by the Commission in July 1997.[57]

The Commission based its opinions on a wealth of information collected from a variety of sources, including responses to a lengthy questionnaire that it sent to the applicants in April 1996 and demanded back only three months later. The Commission reached the following conclusions about the applicants' suitability for EU membership:

- *Democracy and the rule of law:* All applicants had adequate constitutional and institutional arrangements, and all except Slovakia had put these arrangements successfully into practice.
- *Functioning market economy, competitive pressures, and market forces:* All applicants had made good progress, but structural reforms were far from complete, especially in the banking and financial sectors and in social security.
- *The* acquis communautaire: All applicants had begun to embody the voluminous *acquis* into national law, but all still had a long way to go. The difficulty partly lay in the limited administrative and judicial capacities of the CEES.

Accordingly, the Commission recommended that the EU begin accession negotiations in early 1998 with the five most advanced CEES—the Czech Republic, Hungary, Poland, Estonia, and Slovenia—plus Cyprus. The Commission's selection of the Czech Republic, Hungary, and Poland was not surprising, but why also Estonia and Slovenia? In part because only a week before the Commission released *Agenda 2000*, NATO had announced that the Czech Republic, Hungary, and Poland would be invited to join the Atlantic Alliance in 1999. Although not wanting to be seen to offer EU accession as a consolation prize for some of the countries rejected for early NATO membership, the Commission also did not want to be seen as endorsing the same three countries tapped to join NATO. The Commission's main concern was the possible perception by Russia and the other CEES that the EU and NATO were drawing a new dividing line in Central Europe around the Czech Republic, Hungary, and Poland.

How many and which countries other than the Czech Republic, Hungary, and Poland should the Commission recommend for accession negotiations? Objectively, there was a marked difference in economic performance between Estonia and Slovenia, on the one hand, and Latvia, Lithuania, Romania, Bulgaria, and Slovakia, on the other. Subjectively, member states had particular preferences. France wanted Romania included in the first round of EU enlargement, but even France had to admit that Romania was economically unprepared for early EU membership. Denmark, Finland, and Sweden championed the Baltic states' early accession, but the three Baltic states were at different levels of economic development, making it unlikely that all would be invited to start accession negotiations at the same time. As the most economically advanced of them, and having lobbied assiduously for early membership, Estonia was the obvious candidate for preferential treatment. In southeastern Europe, Austria championed the case of Slovenia, an economically advanced and politically stable country. Accordingly, the Commission added Estonia and Slovenia to the list of applicants with which it recommended the EU begin accession negotiations.

Accession Partnerships

The European Council endorsed the Commission's recommendation without any dissent at the Luxembourg summit in December 1997.[58] The European Council also endorsed a related recommendation for individual accession partnerships between the EU and the five "fast-track" CEES to plan, assist, and assess each applicant's path to accession. These involve

- precise commitments by the applicants to democracy, stable macroeconomic policies, and nuclear safety
- a national program in each applicant country to adopt the *acquis* within a particular time according to priorities identified in the Commission's opinion; the EU would base its financial assistance to the applicant countries on progress in this area
- a reorganization of EU resources needed to support the applicants' membership preparations
- annual EU reports on the applicants' progress toward accession

Bilateral accession partnerships, constituting a detailed map for each of the fast-track applicants to follow on the road to EU accession, replaced the multilateral structured dialogue.

Cyprus

The EC had concluded an association agreement with Cyprus as long ago as 1973, but it was not until July 1990 that Cyprus applied to join. Cyprus had a good political and economic case for membership, and the Commission issued a favorable opinion in June 1993.[59] Inevitably the Cypriot application was overshadowed by the concurrent Central and Eastern European applications. More troubling for Cyprus and the EU was the division of the island into the Greek Cypriot south and the self-styled Turkish Republic of Northern Cyprus (TRNC). Backed by Turkey, whose own EU membership application was in limbo, the TRNC hotly disputed the right of the (Greek) Cypriot government to seek EU membership on behalf of the entire island. Thus the contentious cases of Turkish and Cypriot membership in the EU became inextricably bound up with each other and with the bitter rivalry between Greece and Turkey. In March 1995 the EU linked conclusion of a customs union with Turkey (something Turkey saw as a stepping-stone to membership and therefore something Greece wanted to thwart) to a commitment to begin accession negotiations with Cyprus at the same time as the opening of negotiations with the CEES (something Greece very much wanted).

Turkey

Although never fully implemented because of Greek opposition, and despite Turkey's brinkmanship in a dispute with Greece over a tiny Aegean island in early 1996, the EU-Turkey customs union led to a gradual improvement in the EU's relations with Turkey. Having applied for EU membership far earlier that any of the CEES and with compelling strategic arguments in its favor, Turkey pressed for participation in the accession negotiations slated to begin early in 1998. This pressure put the EU in a quandary. How could it admit a country so dissimilar from other European countries, a country that, with 61 million people, would become the EU's second-largest member state; a country with a deplorable human rights record; a country engaged in a war against Kurdish guerrillas in northern Iraq; and a country where, as recently as mid-1997, the army had helped oust a democratically elected government (admittedly in order to restore a government more acceptable to the West)? Yet Turkey's European orientation and vocation were undeniable; Turkey was a big emerging market; Turkey needed positive signals and support from the EU to help counter the rise of Muslim fundamentalism; and Turkey had assumed great strategic importance after the Cold War in the Balkans, the Middle East, and parts of the former Soviet Union.

Well aware of the EU's dilemma and discomfiture, Turkey knew exactly what buttons to press. "Will the future of the Europe Union be limited by religious and ethnic considerations, or will it be one that reaches out and boldly contributes to diversity and unity?" asked Ismail Cem, Turkey's foreign minister, in an article in the *International Herald Tribune* only days before the decisive Luxembourg summit.[60] Apart from seizing the moral high ground, Turkey had a more pragmatic card to play: its ability to influence the Cypriot accession negotiations through its control over the self-styled TRNC.

Given the sensitivity of the Turkish case, the European Council had to tread warily in Luxembourg. Although deciding to open accession negotiations with five of the CEES and with Cyprus, the European Council sought to reassure Turkey that the EU's door was open. Perhaps preoccupied with yet another row over EMU and with the complexity of the enlargement issue, the European Council badly mishandled the Turkish situation. While acknowledging that Turkey would eventually join the EU, the European Council put Turkey's application on hold, placing it behind all the other applications in the accession queue. As a consolation, the EU invited Turkey to attend the inaugural meeting of the European Conference. Devised by the Commission to show that enlargement was a long-term process affecting the whole of Europe, the European Conference would bring together the heads of state and government of all EU and applicant states to consult on a broad range of CFSP and JHA issues.

Turkey's reaction to the Luxembourg decision convinced many EU leaders that they were right to keep Turkey at arm's length. Deeply affronted because the EU had deemed it less worthy of accession than countries like Bulgaria and Romania, Turkey retaliated by freezing its official ties with the EU. More ominously, Turkey threatened to block progress on the reunification of Cyprus unless the EU reconsidered Turkey's candidacy and to integrate the TRNC into Turkey if the EU opened accession negotiations with only the (southern) Cypriot government. Intended as a celebration of European unity on the eve of new enlargement negotiations, the inaugural European Conference, held in London in March 1998, was marred by Turkey's absence.

Prospects for Enlargement

Accession negotiations with the "5+1" (the Czech Republic, Estonia, Hungary, Poland, and Slovenia, plus Cyprus) began ceremoniously in Brussels on March 31, 1998, when the foreign ministers of the applicant states held separate opening talks with their EU counterparts. It was a momentous occasion: the culmination of nearly ten years of hard work on both sides and the beginning of the end of the long accession process. Despite optimistic statements about the negotiations' eventual outcome, however, there were no illusions about the difficulties that lay ahead and few realistic hopes that the talks might end before 2002.

The first stage of the negotiations consisted of an analytical review of the *acquis communautaire* in multilateral sessions conducted by officials of the Commission's Task Force for the Accession Negotiations (TFAN) and officials of the candidate countries. The purpose of this so-called screening process, which was to last from March 1998 until July 1999, was to examine in minute detail the extent to which each of the candidates met the rules and obligations of membership, and to identify difficult or contentious issues likely to arise in later stages of the negotiations. The screening process, Europe agreements, and accession partnerships constitute a continuous program of intensive preparation for membership, conducted alongside the substantive, bilateral negotiations themselves. These began in November 1998, on seven of the thirty-one specific chapters or issue areas covered by the negotiations that had already been screened. Negotiations take place at the ministerial and deputy-ministerial level. The TFAN prepares draft positions for the Council presidency, which conducts the negotiations themselves, and liaises with the candidates' accession negotiating teams on a day-to-day basis.

The bilateral nature of the substantive negotiations and differences among the applicants themselves mean that the applicant states might not all join at the same time. Moreover, the other five CEES, apparently condemned to a slow track to EU accession, may accelerate their economic or, in the case of Slovakia, political reforms and catch up with the fast-track five. Fears in some member states that differentiation among the CEES would demoralize the slow-track applicants and cause their reform movements to lag proved unfounded.

Just as none of the Central and Eastern European applicants will be held up by political or economic setbacks in one of the other Central and Eastern European applicant states, neither will they be held back by difficulties in the EU's negotiations with Cyprus. Although well positioned economically for EU membership, Cyprus's prospects suffer from the seemingly insurmountable political obstacle of partition. The (Greek) Cypriot government thinks that the fact of negotiations itself will convince the Turks and the Turkish Cypriots to agree to reunification of the island. Yet the Turkish Cypriots have refused to join the government's negotiating team in Brussels; Turkey warned the EU on the opening day of accession negotiations not to start talks with Cyprus; and tension in Cyprus has been mounting, not falling, since the negotiations began. Turkey is likely to change its attitude, and therefore also the attitude of the Turkish Cypriots, only if the EU agrees to move on Turkey's own application. France and Germany have clearly stated their unwillingness to bring a divided country into the EU, but Greece may veto the entire enlargement package unless Cyprus is included, in whole or in part. It is unclear how the EU can resolve this dilemma—a dilemma partly of its own making. Had the EU thought more carefully about the Cypriot problem and handled Turkey with greater sensitivity, the Greek-Turkey-Cyprus situation would hardly be as perplexing as it seems today.

Internal EU Reform

Apart from political problems in Cyprus and economic problems in the CEES, institutional and policy problems in the EU pose a major challenge to enlargement.[61] Shortly before the end of the IGC in June 1997, the EU began the politically painful process of internal policy reform to prepare itself for enlargement. The Commission set the ball rolling with *Agenda 2000,* which, apart from its opinions on the ten Central and Eastern European applications, contained a lengthy analysis of the likely costs of enlargement and proposals for reform of the EU's most expensive and contentious policies: agriculture and cohesion. Given the size and relative poverty of most of the CEES' farming sectors—enlargement would eventually mean a 50 percent increase in EU agricultural land and a doubling of the agricultural labor force—the EU could not extend an unreformed Common Agricultural Policy (CAP) to prospective new member states without risking bankruptcy. Similarly, promoting economic and social cohesion in an EU that included new member states so much poorer than the EU average would be prohibitively expensive without a major overhaul of existing mechanisms.

Intellectually, most member states agreed that such reforms were necessary for their own sake, let alone for the sake of enlargement. Politically, however, few were willing to incur the wrath of farmers and other constituents likely to suffer from a reduction of agricultural and cohesion spending. Inevitably, the opening rounds of the reform process were acrimonious; member states that would benefit most from EU spending on agriculture and cohesion denounced the Commission's proposals. (The proposed CAP and cohesion reforms are examined in Chapters 12 and 15, respectively.)

Overall, the Commission estimated that enlargement would cost the EU up to ECU 75 billion, spread out over several years. Yet the Commission concluded that enlargement would not require an increase in the EU's current level of "own resources" (1.27 percent of GDP), assuming an average growth rate of 2.5 percent in the EU and 4 percent in the applicant countries during the period of enlargement. These optimistic assumptions exposed the Commission to criticism that it deliberately underestimated the likely costs of enlargement in order to assuage member state sensitivities and avert a bruising battle during the negotiations in 1999 on the EU's next financial perspective.

As well as policy reform in order to make enlargement affordable, the EU needed to undertake institutional reform to make enlargement workable. The institutional issues ducked in the Amsterdam Treaty—a reweighting of Council votes, a reduction of the number of commissioners, and an extension of QMV—grew more pressing as the enlargement negotiations gained momentum. Thus pressure of looming enlargement may help member states make the kind of concessions that eluded them in the 1996–1997 IGC. Moreover, without adequate institutional reform the EP could block enlargement, as it threatened to do in 1994 at the close of the Eftan accession negotiations.

The unpopularity of policy reform in some member states, together with disputes among member states over institutional reform and budgetary contributions, could rebound on the accession negotiations, which proceeded slowly in 1999. Closely related negotiations in 1999 and 2000—on institutional reform, CAP and structural policy reform, a new financial perspective, and enlargement—will be complex and contentious. Even without additional complications, the later stages of the accession negotiations will not be easy. Although the five CEES earmarked for early membership have made great advances economically and administratively since the early 1990s, much restructuring remains to be done, especially with respect to deregulation, privatization, and macroeconomic policymaking. As the talks progress, applicant countries will fight tenaciously for concessions and derogations in problematic areas such as agriculture, environmental policy, and services. The EU will drive a hard bargain, and the CEES seemingly have little leverage. As it is, some applicants complain that the EU treats them like supplicants and that the accession partnerships are not partnerships at all but an opportunity for the EU to bully the CEES. For its part, the EU tends to see the CEES as excessively demanding and grasping. Typically, EU officials complain that Polish negotiators behave as if the EU wants to join Poland rather than Poland wanting to join the EU.

Although the applicant states appear to have a much weaker hand than their EU interlocutors, they have an ace up their sleeve: The EU cannot afford to let the accession negotiations languish or fail. As the EU often points out, promoting democracy and prosperity in Central and Eastern Europe is the EU's primary foreign policy goal, and enlargement is the primary means of achieving that goal. If enlargement is unduly delayed by an impasse in the negotiations or by the EU's failure to make internal policy and institutional reform, the damage to the EU's already fragile political image and international credibility would be incalculable.

NOTES

1. David Spence, "Towards Enlargement of the European Union," unpublished paper, p. 24.
2. Francisco Granell, "The European Union's Enlargement Negotiations with Austria, Finland, Norway, and Sweden," *Journal of Common Market Studies* 33, no. 1 (September 1995): 134.
3. On the negotiations and their aftermath, see John Redmond, ed., *The 1995 Enlargement of the European Union* (Aldershot: Ashgate, 1997); and Lee Miles, ed., *The European Union and the Nordic Countries* (New York: Routledge, 1996).
4. Bull. EC 5-1987, point 2.2.12.
5. Bull. EC S/1-1989, p. 17.
6. See Finn Laursen, "The Community's Policy Toward EFTA: Regime Formation in the European Economic Space," *Journal of Common Market Studies* 28, no. 4 (June 1990): 320–325; and Clive Church, "The Politics of Change: EFTA and the Nordic Countries' Response to the EC in the Early 1990s," *Journal of Common Market Studies* 28, no. 4 (June 1990): 408–410.
7. T. Wieser and E. Kitzmantell, "Austria and the European Community," *Journal of Common Market Studies* 28, no. 4 (June 1990): 431–449.
8. Quoted in the *International Herald Tribune*, February 15–16, 1992, p. 1.

9. See Trevor C. Hartley, "The European Court and the EEA," *International and Comparative Law Quarterly* 41 (October 1992): 84–88.

10. Bull. EC 5-1992, point 2.2.1.

11. Commission, *Report on Enlargement,* Bull. EC S/3-1992, p. 13.

12. Lisbon European Council, "Presidency Conclusions," Bull. EC 6-1992, points 1.3 to 1.4.

13. Edinburgh European Council, "Presidency Conclusions," Bull. EC 12-1992, points 1.1 to 1.3.

14. Granell, "Enlargement Negotiations," p. 122.

15. Copenhagen European Council, "Presidency Conclusions," Bull. EC 6-1993, point 1.4.

16. Brussels European Council, "Presidency Conclusions," Bull. EC 12-1993, points 1.3 to 1.4.

17. See *Agence Europe,* March 30, 1994, pp. 1–2.

18. Bull. EC 3-1994, point 1.3.27.

19. Klaus Hansch, *Report of the Committee on Institutional Affairs on the Structure and Strategy for the European Union with Regard to Its Enlargement and the Creation of a Europe-Wide Order.* European Parliament Session Documents PE 152.242 final, May 21, 1992.

20. Debates of the European Parliament, 1994/1995 Session, Report of Proceedings from May 2–6, 1994, *Official Journal of the European Communities* [OJ] 3–448, pp. 123–144, 157–166, 167–177.

21. For the perspective of Swedish officials, see "Views and Experiences of Swedish Civil Servants Regarding the Structure and Working Methods of the EU," in *Statskontoret*, 1996/6.

22. Quoted in the *International Herald Tribune*, October 21–22, 1995.

23. Quoted in *Agence Europe*, March 17, 1995, p. 2.

24. Corfu European Council, "Presidency Conclusions," Bull. EC 6-1994, point 1.6.

25. The EU institutions' reports to the Reflection Group are published together in European Parliament, *White Paper on the 1996 IGC,* vol. 1, *Official Texts of the EU Institutions* (Luxembourg: European Parliament, 1996).

26. Finn Laursen, "The Lessons of Maastricht," in Geoffrey Edwards and Alfred Pijpers, eds., *The Politics of European Treaty Reform: The 1996 Intergovernmental Conference and Beyond* (London: Pinter, 1997), p. 62.

27. The Reflection Group report is published in European Parliament, *Official Texts,* pp. 149–212.

28. Christian Democratic Union/Christian Social Union Group in the German Lower House, "Reflections on European Policy," Bonn, September 1, 1994.

29. John Major, "Europe: A Future That Works," William and Mary Lecture, Leiden University, September 7, 1994.

30. Madrid European Council, "Presidency Conclusions," Bull. EC 12-1995, points 1.3 to 1.4.

31. Quoted in *Agence Europe*, March 17, 1995, p. 3.

32. "The EU Today and Tomorrow: Adapting the EU for the Benefit of Its Peoples and Preparing It for the Future: A General Outline for a Draft Revision of the Treaties," Council Secretariat, Brussels, December 5, 1995.

33. Letter from President Chirac and Chancellor Kohl to President-in-Office González, December 10, 1995, reproduced in *Agence Europe,* December 13, 1995, p. 1.

34. Quoted in *Le Monde,* November 30, 1994, p. 1.

35. Quoted in *Agence Europe,* September 13, 1995, p. 3b.

36. Alexander C-G. Stubb, "The Amsterdam Treaty and Flexible Integration," *ECSA Review* 11, no. 2 (spring 1998): 1–5 (emphasis in original).

37. "Commission Opinion on Turkey's Request for EC Accession," Europe Documents, 1589, December 20, 1989.

38. "Ad Hoc Committee for Institutional Affairs Report to the European Council," March 1985, Bull. EC 3-1985, point. 3.5.1.

39. Rhodes European Council, "Presidency Conclusions," Bull. EC 12-1988, point 1.1.10.

40. Bull. EC 7/8-1989, points 1.1.1 to 1.1.6.

41. Council Regulation (EEC) 3906/89, December 18, 1989.

42. See Commission of the European Communities, *PHARE: Assistance for Economic Restructuring in the Countries of Central and Eastern Europe, an Operational Guide* (Luxembourg: Office for Official Publications of the European Communities [OOP], 1992).

43. See John Pinder, *The European Community and Eastern Europe* (London: Royal Institute of International Affairs [RIIA], 1991), pp. 87–88.

44. Quoted in William Wallace, *The Transformation of Western Europe* (London: RIIA, 1990), p. 29.

45. Quoted in the *New York Times,* January 26, 1992, p. 10.

46. Quoted in the *European,* June 14, 1991, p. 6.

47. COM(90)398 final, August 2, 1990.

48. Quoted in the *Washington Post,* October 10, 1990, p. B1.

49. Quoted in the *Guardian,* July 15, 1991, p. 4.

50. Bull. EC 12-1992, points 1.3.2 to 1.3.4.

51. Bull. EC 12-1991, point 1.3.2.

52. Quoted in the *Financial Times,* December 9, 1991, p. 3.

53. *Commission Report on Enlargement,* Bull. EC S/3-1992, pp. 11–12.

54. Copenhagen European Council, "Presidency Conclusions," Bull. EC 6-1993, point 1.4.

55. Essen European Council, "Presidency Conclusions," Bull. EC, 12-1994, point 1.1.10.

56. COM(95)163 final.

57. Commission, *Agenda 2000: For a Stronger and Wider Europe,* Brussels, July 16, 1997, COM(97)2000 final.

58. Luxembourg European Council, "Presidency Conclusions," Bull. EC 12-1993, points 1.3 to 1.4.

59. Bull. EC S/5–1993.

60. "Isn't Europe Ambitious Enough to Admit Turkey?" *International Herald Tribune,* December 10, 1997, p. 10.

61. See Graham Avery and Fraser Cameron, *The Enlargement of the European Union* (Sheffield: Sheffield Academic Press, 1998).

Part 2

Institutions

8

The Commission

The European Union has a singular governmental structure. Superficially, it resembles that of a familiar national system: The EU has a council, a parliament, and a court of justice that apparently replicate a national government's executive, legislature, and judiciary. Yet the similarity is misleading. The Council, made up of member states' government ministers, shares legislative authority with the directly elected Parliament. Only the Court of Justice, consisting of judges appointed by the member states, approximates its national counterpart.

In addition, the EU has a number of unusual ancillary institutions and bodies. The Court of Justice includes a lower court, the Court of First Instance. The Court of Auditors examines the EU's financial affairs and officially has the same status of the Council, Parliament, and Court of Justice. The Economic and Social Committee formally represents vocational interests in the policymaking process, and the Committee of the Regions similarly represents subnational interests. The European Investment Bank is an independent financial body within the EU. Hundreds of committees, ranging from the powerful Committee of Permanent Representatives (member states' ambassadors to the EU) to obscure committees on arcane aspects of Community legislation, buttress the EU's institutional structure.

Last but by no means least, the EU has another institution—the European Commission—with no analogue in national governmental systems. With its members appointed by national governments but pledged to act in the EU's interests, its multinational civil service, its exclusive right to initiate legislation in the first pillar, and its quasi-executive authority, the Commission epitomizes supranationalism and lies at the center of the EU system. Not surprisingly, the Commission and the Berlaymont, its headquarters building in Brussels, are synonymous with the EU itself.

Yet the Berlaymont—a large, star-shaped glass and concrete structure—has become a potent symbol of the Commission's unpopularity. Like the name "Commission," the building seems remote, technocratic, and uninviting. The Berlaymont's fate also symbolized the institution's apparent decline: In 1991 the Commission evacuated it "on the grounds that health and safety conditions had become altogether unsatisfactory."[1] During a decade-long renovation, the Berlaymont stood empty, directly across the street from the Council's huge new office complex. Nothing could illustrate more graphically the Commission's institutional retreat in the face of a more assertive Council.

Paradoxically, the Berlaymont's emptiness and the Commission's relative weakness conflict with a widespread misunderstanding, throughout the EU and abroad, that the Commission is greedy for power and eager to acquire as many of the prerogatives of a national government as possible. The Commission's efforts over the years to harmonize product standards were undoubtedly heavy-handed and occasionally intrusive, and its poor press increased dramatically during the Treaty on European Union (TEU) ratification crisis in 1992 and 1993. Ironically, the Commission neither played a prominent role in negotiating the TEU nor benefited greatly from its provisions, yet politicians and the press generally blamed the Commission for the treaty's defects.

The Commission's fortunes plummeted in March 1999, when the college resigned en masse in the face of withering charges of corruption and mismanagement. The Commission had fallen from the height of its influence ten years previously under the presidency of Jacques Delors. For those who disliked the Commission, Delors personified all that is wrong: He was overambitious, aloof, and arrogant. For those who admired the Commission despite its faults, Delors was a hero without whom the EC's transformation might never have happened, or would certainly not have happened as it did. In the words of Stanley Hoffmann, one of Delors's greatest admirers: "While the Community's progress . . . depended on a series of bargains among its main members, Delors . . . skillfully prodded them and enlarged the opportunities for further integration."[2] As Hoffmann and others point out, Delors's leadership was atypical. But the extent to which that leadership altered the nature of the Commission and its presidency is a difficult question to answer.

THE POTENTIALLY POWERFUL PRESIDENCY

The Commission—in the sense of the commissioners themselves—is supposed to be collegiate. As "first among equals," the Commission president sets the tone for the Commission's term in office. Not surprisingly, Commissions are generally known by the president's name. In the late 1990s, people routinely spoke of "the Santer Commission."

Apart from personifying the Commission, the president's roles and responsibilities include

- mediating disputes and forging agreement within the Commission
- announcing to the European Parliament (EP) the Commission's annual work program
- launching major EU policy initiatives
- representing the Commission in meetings of the General Affairs Council (of foreign ministers)
- representing the Commission in meetings of the European Council
- representing the Commission in key international forums, notably annual G7 meetings and biannual U.S.-EU summits

A president's performance of these duties depends on a variety of personal, political, and economic circumstances such as individual experience, expertise, and acumen; relations with other commissioners and with national government leaders; prevailing political support for further integration; and current economic conditions. Presidential performance has varied widely over the years, and presidents have generally been judged by the perceived strength or weakness of their political leadership.

Table 8.1 Commission Presidents

Name (Years Served)	Member State	Highest Prior Position in National Government	Type of Leadership
Walter Hallstein (1958–1967)	Germany	State Secretary, German Foreign Ministry	strong
Jean Rey (1967–1970)	Belgium	Minister of Economic Affairs	weak
Franco Malfatti (1970–1972)	Italy	Minister for Posts and Telecommunications	weak
Sicco Mansholt (1972)	The Netherlands	Minister of Agriculture	weak
François-Xavier Ortoli (1973–1977)	France	Minister of Finance	weak
Roy Jenkins (1977–1981)	United Kingdom	Chancellor of the Exchequer (Minister of Finance)	strong
Gaston Thorn (1981–1985)	Luxembourg	Prime Minister	weak
Jacques Delors (1985–1995)	France	Minister for the Economy, Finance and Budget	strong
Jacques Santer (1995–1999)	Luxembourg	Prime Minister	weak

Profile and Selection

When he became Commission president, Santer fit the profile of previous incumbents: All were male, late middle-aged, and thoroughly immersed in their own country's political processes. Although unique in two respects—

the degree of political controversy it generated and the need for EP approval—Santer's appointment serves as a useful guide to the abstruse politics of choosing a Commission president. According to the unofficial rota, it was the turn of a Christian Democratic candidate from a small member state to succeed Delors, a French socialist. Ruud Lubbers, the Dutch prime minister, seemed the obvious choice, especially as the Netherlands had not previously held the presidency, apart from Sicco Mansholt's temporary tenure more than twenty years earlier.

Two months before the European Council was due to nominate Delors's successor at the Corfu summit in June 1994, it was clear that Lubbers's candidacy was running into difficulty. Miffed by Lubbers's seeming lack of support for him at the time of German unification and during the 1991 intergovernmental conference (IGC), German chancellor Helmut Kohl cast about for another candidate. With French president François Mitterrand's support, Kohl settled on Jean-Luc Dehaene, like Lubbers a Christian Democrat and prime minister of a small country (Belgium). Irritated by Kohl's and Mitterrand's high-handedness but aware of the two leaders' inordinate influence in the European Council, the other heads of government reluctantly went along with the Dehaene nomination.

Thus far the procedure resembled previous presidential selections. Indeed, Delors had also been a compromise candidate after Germany, whose "turn" it was to produce a president, failed to nominate anyone. What distinguished the choice of Delors's successor was not that France and Germany had ditched the early front-runner but that Britain unexpectedly blocked the Franco-German candidate. The reason was not principled opposition to Franco-German dominion but domestic political opportunism: Faced with a shrinking parliamentary majority and growing Euroskepticism on his own back benches, Prime Minister John Major attempted to score political points by caricaturing Dehaene as a rabid Eurofederalist and vetoing his nomination.

The incoming German presidency convened a special summit in Brussels two weeks later to try to resolve the problem. Almost at the last moment, Santer emerged as an ideal compromise candidate: Not only was he Christian Democratic but, because he came from Luxembourg, his nomination could be construed as a consolation to Belgium and the Netherlands, the other Benelux countries. Ironically Santer was as Eurofederalist as Dehaene, but British Euroskeptics were satisfied for the time being with Dehaene's head.

The highly politicized nature of the compromise distinguished Santer's nomination. Britain's humiliating veto of Dehaene and the attempted Franco-German stranglehold on the appointment procedure reflected badly not only on the European Council but also, indirectly, on Santer himself. This veto in turn had a negative impact on the second novel aspect of his selection: the vote of approval in the EP, held under the terms of the recently implemented TEU.

Opinion in the EP in July 1994 differed on Santer's qualifications and suitability for the job, and also on the appropriateness of endorsing a candidate selected, according to the leader of the socialist group, in such "a squalid, shabby, and ill-judged way."[3] Many members of the European Parliament (MEPs) thought that the EP should reject Santer in order to force the European Council to choose another candidate more on the basis of merit than expediency, although there was no guarantee that the European Council would have acted any differently next time around. The MEPs especially resented national governments' warnings that the EP would be held responsible for the consequences of Santer's rejection, and national governments' pressure on MEPs to vote in Santer's favor. In the event, Santer's narrow endorsement averted a public relations disaster and political crisis but further weakened the president-designate's stature.[4]

Despite criticism in the EP and elsewhere of the manner of Santer's selection, the Amsterdam Treaty did not substantially alter the selection procedure. The "governments of the member states" (in effect the heads of state and government) retain the right to "nominate by common accord the person they intend to appoint as President of the Commission" (Article 214.2 TEC). Domestic political circumstances may not again intrude so blatantly into the nomination of a Commission president, but the extremely contentious selection in May 1998 of the European Central Bank's first president demonstrates the high political stakes in appointments to top EU positions. Similarly, the EP's increasing assertiveness together with growing public unease about the Commission's apparent unaccountability suggests that a major change in the presidential appointment system may be imminent, probably as part of an overall institutional reform.

Performance

During the parliamentary debate on his nomination, Santer expressed a wish "to become a strong President at the head of a strong, coherent, determined Commission." Santer was quick to point out that coming from the EU's smallest member state would not prevent him from becoming a strong president.[5] Yet being a Luxembourger put definite limits on Santer's leadership. Moreover, in the wake of the TEU ratification crisis, the European Council did not want a Commission president in the mold of Delors. Nevertheless Santer was an experienced prime minister with the potential to become a reasonably forceful president. During his visits to member state capitals before assigning portfolios, Santer made the statements expected of a president-designate about imperviousness to national lobbying.

A comparison between Santer's and Delors's backgrounds and experiences helps to demonstrate the limits and the potential of the Commission presidency. Delors had a profound impact on the office that he held longer than any other Commission president and for almost a quarter of the EU's history. He brought unique attributes and skills to the job. Delors was an experienced and able administrator, had shrewd political judgment and a firm grasp of economics, and was an inspiring speaker. Moreover, Delors had a vision to communicate: a strong, politically and economically united EU that was organized on federal lines, constituted a cohesive "social space," and asserted itself internationally vis-à-vis the superpowers. When the Cold War came to a sudden end, Delors's vision soared: The EU would anchor the New Europe and form the inner of a series of concentric circles radiating outward geographically, economically, and strategically. Delors believed strongly in his and the EU's destiny and their collective place in history.

Delors had other advantages that he exploited to the full, notably a formidable reputation as a powerful politician with a future in French national politics and close friendships with a number of key EU leaders, especially Kohl. The prospect of an important career in national politics distinguished Delors from other Commission presidents. With the exception of Franco Malfatti, who resigned from the Commission in order to contest Italian parliamentary elections, previous Commission presidents were political has-beens, which weakened their credibility when dealing with forceful, egomaniacal leaders in the member states. Whereas Malfatti—an inconsequential president in any case—returned to political life in Italy, Delors had the prospect of returning to political life in France, one of the two most important EU member states. Moreover, Delors was tipped to return either as prime minister or as a candidate for the French presidency, which he seemed to have had a good chance of winning until the TEU setback. The perception of Delors as a potential president of France, not merely as president of the Commission, enhanced his stature immeasurably.

Building on such a solid foundation, Delors contributed greatly to the Commission's and the Community's transformation in the late 1980s. Delors viewed the Commission as the indispensable "engineer of European integration"; without a revitalized Commission, the EC would remain moribund.[6] Thus the EC's achievements at that time—the breakthrough on Iberian enlargement, negotiation of the Single European Act (SEA), agreement on the Delors I cohesion package, success of the single market program, and the launch of Economic and Monetary Union (EMU)—owed much to Delors's personal and the Commission's political leadership.

Delors's prominence and forcefulness in the late 1980s became particularly apparent at meetings of the European Council. Roy Jenkins had won for the Commission a right to participate fully in these summits. Gaston Thorn, Commission president between Jenkins and Delors, dutifully attended European Councils but never made much of an impression. Delors, by contrast, reveled in the limelight. Some of his and the Commission's greatest triumphs came at European Council meetings.

Similarly, Delors capitalized on his reputation as architect of the single market program and his unrivaled grasp of complex economic questions to assert the Commission's identity on the broader international stage. Once again, Jenkins had fought hard to win Commission participation at the annual economic summits of the seven most industrialized countries (G7). It was appropriate that the Commission received its greatest international recognition at the Paris economic summit in July 1989, when U.S. president George Bush requested it to lead the Western aid effort for Hungary and Poland. The Transatlantic Declaration of November 1990, which institutionalized meetings among the U.S. president, the president of the Council, and the Commission president, was a further tribute to Delors's and the Commission's growing international stature.

Delors's achievements prove the point that a Commission president's performance depends not as much on the attributes of the office itself as on his personality, country of origin, national political experience and prospects, the economic and political circumstances in the EU, and the caliber of his closest advisers. The experiences of Walter Hallstein and Roy Jenkins are similarly revealing. Hallstein, a forceful character from a large member state (although Germany was then economically underdeveloped and politically meek), had considerable political experience as a senior government official but not much prospect of a future career in politics. Like Delors, Hallstein served as Commission president during a period of sustained economic growth. Also like Delors, he pushed hard to increase the Commission's power and promote supranationalism. But unlike Delors, Hallstein had to contend with the leader of the EC's most important country (Charles de Gaulle in France), who abhorred political integration. (Because of Britain's relative weakness within the EC, Delors's confrontation with Prime Minister Margaret Thatcher cannot fairly be compared to Hallstein's confrontation with de Gaulle.) Jenkins was the only other incumbent on a par with Hallstein and Delors, although he presided over the Commission at a time of economic recession and political gloom in the EC. Moreover, Jenkins tried too hard to appease both his Commission colleagues and the powerful partnership of French president Giscard d'Estaing and German chancellor Helmut Schmidt.

The Presidency

When Santer became Commission president, he faced a number of challenges: absorbing the first post-TEU enlargement (Austria, Finland, and Sweden became members in January 1995, the same month that Santer became president); developing a preaccession strategy for the countries of Central and Eastern Europe; devising a new EU-Mediterranean partnership, preparing for EMU; and preparing for and participating in the

1996–1997 IGC. In general, Santer's goal as president was to substitute the Commission's current image of ambition and intrusiveness, personified by Delors, with that of discretion and pragmatism. The key to Santer's success, both symbolically and substantively, was to make subsidiarity meaningful; consult and inform as widely as possible; encourage deregulation and competitiveness; complete the single market; promote EMU; fight fraud in the EU; and put the Commission's house in order.

Santer enjoyed only mixed success. In the run-up to EMU member states shared his interest in consolidating the single market and boosting European competitiveness, although few were willing to undertake major structural economic reforms. Santer became best known for the fight against fraud in the Commission, not because he had initiated it upon becoming Commission president, but because in January 1999 the EP voted to oust the entire Commission amid allegations of corruption and mismanagement. Although unsuccessful, the EP's vote of censure triggered a series of events that resulted in the Commission's resignation in March 1999.

Santer will forever be associated with the ignominious collapse of his Commission. Nevertheless, his presidency was not entirely uninspiring. For instance, in January 1996, Santer proposed the Confidence Pact on Employment among employers, trade unions, and governments to boost jobs in the EU not only by completing the single market but also by curbing state aid, strengthening education and training, and promoting small businesses. During the next three months, Santer toured EU capitals, talking to employers and trade unions to win their support, and held a round-table conference in Brussels in April with more than seventy-five representatives of employers' and trade union organizations. Santer also tried to persuade member states to allow surplus EU funds to be diverted into the proposed Trans-European Networks (TENs), multibillion euro road, rail, and telecommunication projects that would become a symbol of EU public investment as well as a means of strengthening communications links inside the single market. But national governments, led by Britain and Germany, refused to back Santer's expensive TENs initiative at the June 1996 Florence summit.

Santer's employment initiative sought not simply to alleviate a major EU-wide social and economic problem but also to assert the Commission's role as an agenda setter and policy entrepreneur and to enhance the Commission's credibility and legitimacy. In that sense the Confidence Pact was analogous to Delors's promotion of cohesion policy in 1988. The different outcomes of these admittedly dissimilar initiatives reveal much about the differences between Santer's and Delors's leadership of the Commission. In 1988 the political and economic climate was ripe for a bold Commission initiative. Despite member state resistance to the expense of the proposed structural funds and to the possible political implications of involving regions more directly in EC decisionmaking, Delors pushed through his ambitious cohesion package. In so doing, he boosted his own and the Commission's fortunes. Eight years later, by contrast, with Europe slowly emerging from recession and member states struggling to meet the EMU convergence criteria, Santer's proposal received only rhetorical support from the heads of state and government. The failure of the employment initiative showed the limits of Commission influence and activism in the unpropitious circumstances of the mid-1990s.

The lessons of the contrasting Delors and Santer presidencies are clear: An activist with a sound political past, and ideally with a powerful political future in a leading member state, is best suited to advance the Commission's interests and "engineer" deeper European integration. In the rough-and-tumble world of intra-EU bargaining, a Commission president needs to be forceful, authoritative, and direct. It is difficult for a Commission president to act decisively in the European Council and on the broader international stage without being equally decisive in the Commission itself.

Partly in acknowledgment of that fact, member states agreed in the Amsterdam Treaty to strengthen the Commission president's political authority (Article 219 TEC) and to allow the Commission president greater discretion in allocating and reshuffling commissioners' portfolios (Article 214.2 TEC). Yet as currently constituted the Commission is unable to sustain the achievements of a dynamic president. Even with the changes in the Amsterdam Treaty, commissioners will still be appointed arbitrarily, the civil service will remain understaffed, and the Commission's ability to execute policy will not improve substantially. A strong president may exacerbate those problems by sometimes riding roughshod over his fellow commissioners and over the civil service, occasionally engendering deep resentment throughout the bureaucracy. Without doing so, however, a president cannot expect the Commission to realize its full political potential "at the heart of the Union."[7]

THE UNCOLLEGIATE COMMISSION

Platitudes about the Commission's collegiality notwithstanding, in reality commissioners are far from equal. The way commissioners are popularly known emphasizes the point. Rather than using names, commentators frequently refer to nationality: the "Portuguese commissioner," the "Dutch commissioner," the "senior German commissioner," and so on. Because Germany is a far more powerful country than either Portugal or the Netherlands, the senior German commissioner generally has more influence than his Portuguese and Dutch counterparts. Yet hailing from a large country is not a precondition for success in the Commission. Conversely, commissioners from small member states often fare well.

"By common accord with the nominee for (Commission) President" (Article 214.2 TEC), the heads of state and government decide the Commission's composition. In reality, the European Council rubber stamps national governments' nominations of a commissioner or commissioners (France, Germany, Britain, Italy, and Spain have two each; the other countries have one each).

Member states generally announce their choice of commissioner(s) three or four months before the current Commission's term expires. Governments have complete discretion in choosing commissioners "on the grounds of their general competence" (Article 213.1 TEC). Personal and political considerations, rather than ability or merit, determine who gets the prestigious and powerful Commission appointments. In countries that appoint two commissioners, there is generally an understanding that one commissioner will come from the governing party and one from the opposition, or that each commissioner will come from a particular party or group of parties in a coalition government. In countries that appoint a single commissioner, nominees rarely come from outside the governing party or coalition. By contrast with early commissioners, most are now career politicians whose standing at home enhances their status and performance

Table 8.2 Commissioners per Member State

Dates	Number of Member States	Member States (Number of Commissioners)	Total Number of Commissioners
1967[a]–1972	6	France, Germany, and Italy (2 each); Belgium, the Netherlands, and Luxembourg (1 each)	9
1973–1980	9	France, Germany, Italy, and **Britain** (2 each); Belgium, the Netherlands, Luxembourg, **Denmark**, and **Ireland** (1 each)	13
1981–1985	10	France, Germany, Italy, and Britain (2 each); Belgium, the Netherlands, Luxembourg, Denmark, Ireland, and **Greece** (1 each)	14
1986–1994	12	France, Germany, Italy, Britain, and **Spain** (2 each); Belgium, the Netherlands, Luxembourg, Denmark, Ireland, Greece, and **Portugal** (1 each)	17
1995–	15	France, Germany, Italy, Britain, and Spain (2 each); Belgium, the Netherlands, Luxembourg, Denmark, Ireland, Greece, Portugal, **Austria**, **Finland**, and **Sweden** (1 each)	20

Note: a. Under the terms of the Merger Treaty, which came into effect on July 1, 1967, the ECSC High Authority combined with the Commissions of the EEC and Euratom to form the Commission of the European Communities. Subsequent changes were the result of the accession of new member states, which in the table appear in **boldface**.

in the Commission. Indeed, having held senior elected office has become an unofficial criterion for appointment to the Commission in order to enhance vicariously the Commission's democratic legitimacy.

Commissioners may be reappointed any number of times. Hans von der Groeben, a German commissioner, served for fourteen years. It is not unusual for commissioners to serve two full terms (ten years). Commissioners may resign from office but cannot be recalled by their member states. Nor must they step down if their political patrons at home resign from government or lose an election. When a commissioner resigns, the government that nominated him simply nominates a substitute, who usually receives the same portfolio.

Commissioner's responsibilities include

- heading the Commission's directorates-general (departments) and services
- representing the Commission at meetings of the Council
- accounting for the Commission's activities before the EP
- publicizing the Commission's work
- exchanging information and ideas between the Commission and the highest levels of national government

Accountability

The Commission is accountable to the EP. By a two-thirds majority the EP may sack the entire Commission but may not dismiss individual commissioners. Parliament has never voted the Commission out of office, but its increasing willingness to threaten the Commission with censure testifies to a growing assertiveness and to the seriousness with which it wants to hold the Commission accountable. In 1997, for instance, the EP threatened to censure the Commission based on a damning report of the Commission's handling of the bovine spongiform encephalopathy (BSE) crisis by a (parliamentary) temporary committee of inquiry. At a stormy plenary session of the EP in March 1998, parliamentarians again threatened the Commission with censure, this time over the Commission's alleged mishandling of the EU budget. Parliamentary criticism of the Commission's poor budgetary performance, coupled with allegations of mismanagement and cronyism on the part of individual commissioners, came to a head in a censure effort in January 1999. Although the EP failed to muster the necessary votes to kick out the Commission, the episode clearly signaled the EP's determination to hold the Commission more accountable than ever before.

Under the terms of the TEU, the Commission's term of office increased from four to five years beginning in January 1995, bringing it more closely into line with the EP's five-year term. The TEU also stipulated that a new Commission "shall be subject as a body to a vote of approval" by the EP, after which the commissioners "shall be appointed by common accord of the governments of the member states" (Article 214.2 TEC). That provision, intended to bolster the Commission's weak legitimacy, formalized a practice begun by Delors whereby his Commissions (1985–1989, 1989–1993, and 1993–1995) received votes of confidence from the EP before taking their oaths of office at the European Court of Justice (ECJ).

The EP's post-TEU investiture procedure was applied for the first time in 1994–1995. To the dismay of the Commission and some member states, the EP successfully interpreted the procedure to include not only a vote on the Commission-designate (as a college) but also hearings on commissioners-designate. Held in early January 1995, the hearings were well publicized but hardly insightful. Each commissioner-designate was interviewed by the relevant parliamentary committee or committees for his or her portfolio. After the hearings, the EP questioned the suitability of five of them, although the EP could vote only on the Commission as a whole. The three Nordic commissioners-designate felt that they had been singled out for being too honest and for not telling parliamentarians what they wanted to hear (MEPs were especially annoyed by Ritt Bjerregaard's alleged comment that the EP "was not a real parliament").[8]

The EP's approval of the Commission-designate by a large majority (416 votes to 103 with 56 abstentions) may have enhanced the Commission's legitimacy, but both institutions have a long way to go before winning widespread public support. Moreover, the entire appointments procedure took too long (beginning with the debate on Santer's nomination in July 1994 and ending with Parliament's vote on the commissioners-designate in January 1995, the process lasted nearly seven months). It also contributed to the changing dynamics of Commission-EP relations, which, as the increasing recourse to censure motions show, are becoming less complementary and more conflictual.

Allocation of Portfolios

The EP has no authority to decide which commissioner gets what portfolio. Those important decisions remain with the Commission president and the heads of state and government. The fierceness with which governments fight for important portfolios, regardless of the Amsterdam Treaty's granting of responsibility to the Commission president for the allocation of portfolios, suggests that commissioners are not "completely independent in the performance of their duties," as the TEC claims that they should be and as commissioners swear in their oath of office that they will be (Article 213.2).

The spectacle of too many commissioners chasing too few important portfolios feeds the related allegation that commissioners are in their national governments' pockets. As early as 1977, only four years after the EC's first enlargement, British prime minister Harold Wilson remarked on "the excessive number of Commissioners" and their "continuing search for work."[9] The 1979 Spierenburg Report recommended that member states appoint only one commissioner each, but to no avail. Thus as Roy Jenkins, who authorized the report, bitterly remarked, "the position of too many Commissioners chasing too few jobs, with which I was confronted [as Commission president] in 1977, was exacerbated by the Greek entry of 1981 and the Spanish and Portuguese entry of 1986."[10] The Dooge Report also recommended only one commissioner per member state, but neither the SEA nor the TEU addressed the issue.

The impact of the Eftan enlargement and the anticipated impact of the Central and Eastern European enlargement made it impossible to avoid the question of the Commission's size at the 1996–1997 IGC. However, the refusal of most member states to reduce the Commission's size below a number that would make it impossible for each of them in future to appoint at least one commissioner emphasized the political importance attached to having a commissioner in Brussels. Although controversy over the Commission's size consumed a lot of time and energy at the IGC, radical reform was not necessarily in the Commission's interest. Arguably, it is more important for member states, their citizens, and the Commission to have direct, high-level channels of communication via "national" commissioners than to go through the politically painful and essentially unrewarding exercise of drastically reducing the Commission's size. As Niels Ersbøll, former secretary-general of the Council secretariat observed, the fact that each member state has at least one of its senior officials or politicians on the Commission "undoubtedly contributes to . . . general confidence in the Commission and the acceptance of its wide powers."[11]

In any event, there is an important distinction between recognizing and upholding a national interest and taking instructions from a national government. The commission functions best when commissioners thrash out proposals from their own ideological, political, and national perspectives as well as on the abstract basis of what is best for the EU. It is not to the EU's discredit or disadvantage that "Commissioners . . . are national champions who defend their national positions in the Commission."[12]

Walter Hallstein denied "most emphatically that the relative strengths or weaknesses of the individual Commissioners brought the slightest advantage or disadvantage to the member countries whose nationals they were."[13] That may have been the case during the EC's first decade, when Hallstein was Commission president. But the scramble for portfolios at the beginning of each new Commission since the late 1970s suggests a widespread perception by national governments that commissioners generally serve the national interest.

Internal Organization

Commissioners often use their *cabinets* to absorb excessive national pressure and conduct a public relations campaign for domestic consumption. The *cabinet* system reflects a strong French influence on the EU's administrative apparatus. Over the years, *cabinets* have grown larger and more powerful. Most commissioners have a seven-member *cabinet* that includes career Eurocrats and appointees who came to Brussels with the commissioner. A good *cabinet* can boost the standing of an otherwise poor commissioner, and a poor *cabinet* can pull down an otherwise good commissioner. It is no coincidence that the most effective commissioners in any Commission have the best-staffed and best-organized *cabinets*.

Until implementation of the TEU, the Commission had six vice presidents, five more than it needed. Governments generally distributed vice presidencies among the five largest member states, excluding any one of them that happened to have had the presidency; the remaining one or two positions went to smaller countries. Under the terms of the TEU, the Commission itself may appoint one or two vice presidents. A vice president occasionally stands in for the Commission president and accompanies the president to meetings of the European Council.

Commissioners meet every Wednesday in Brussels, or in Strasbourg if the EP is in plenary session there, to discuss and resolve various initiatives and proposals to go before the Council. Usually the president gets his way, although Commission meetings sometimes become bruising battles that the president does not always win. The most notable struggles have been over competition policy and agriculture. A simple majority vote finally decides an issue. The increasing uncollegiality of the Commission does not always work to the president's advantage. Just as a strong president has a lot of discretionary power, a strong commissioner may also act independently. Commissioners frequently make speeches or release statements that are intended to annoy the president or score domestic political points rather than elucidate Commission policy.

THE UNLOVED CIVIL SERVICE

The Commission's civil service is surprisingly small. Despite the picture that Euroskeptics paint of a vast bureaucracy extending its reach throughout the EU, the Commission has a staff of less than 17,000, including 3,200 personnel at the Joint Research Center (a legacy of Euratom) and 3,000 interpreters and translators (the EU works in eleven official languages). Apart from the research institutes and specialized services, the bureaucracy is organized into twenty-four directorates-general (DGs) corresponding to the Commission's activities and responsibilities.

Table 8.3 Commission Directorates-General and Services, 1995–2000

DG I	External relations: commercial policy and relations with North America, the Far East, Australia, and New Zealand
DG IA	External relations: Europe and new independent states, external missions, and common security
DG IB	External relations: southern Mediterranean, Middle and Near East, Latin America, South and Southeast Asia, and North-South cooperation
DG II	Economic and social affairs
DG III	Industry
DG IV	Competition
DG V	Employment, industrial relations, and social affairs
DG VI	Agriculture
DG VII	Transport
DG VIII	Development
DG IX	Personnel and administration
DG X	Information, communication, culture, and audiovisual
DG XI	Environment, nuclear safety, and civil protection
DG XII	Science, research, and development—Joint Research Center
DG XIII	Telecommunications, information market, and exploitation of research
DG XIV	Fisheries
DG XV	Internal market and financial services
DG XVI	Regional policies and cohesion
DG XVII	Energy
DG XVIII	Credit and investments
DG XIX	Budgets
DG XX	Financial control
DG XXI	Customs union and indirect taxation
DG XXII	Education, training, and youth
DG XXIII	Enterprise policy, distributive trades, tourism, and cooperatives
DG XXIV	Consumer policy and consumer health protection

Neither the number nor the responsibilities of the DGs correspond to the number or the portfolios of the commissioners. Thus a commissioner may have more than one DG in his portfolio, and the responsibilities of a DG may be spread over the portfolios of more than one commissioner. Conversely, a commissioner may not have a directorate-general at all. The Commission includes a number of other services alongside the DGs, such as the legal service and spokesman's service, and various task forces, such as the one on enlargement.

The Commission's secretariat-general is a separate unit. It is, first and foremost, the commissioners' own secretariat. For that reason, the secretary-general is one of a handful of noncommissioners allowed to participate in the Commission's formal meetings (apart from a *chef de cabinet* standing in for a commissioner). The secretary-general also presides over the regular Monday morning meeting of *chefs de cabinet* and the regular Thursday morning meeting of directors-general and attends European Councils with the Commission president.

The Commission has had only three secretaries-general in its history: Emile Noël (1958–1987), David Williamson (1987–1997), and Carlo Trojan (since 1997). Noël, a seasoned French public servant, was a brilliant administrator and confidant of several Commission presidents. Williamson, from the British civil service, grew politically close to Delors and helped to provide "the administrative base of the Presidential regime."[14] Based on his experience in the British cabinet office, Williamson set up better lines of communication not only between the Commission's notoriously territorial directorates-general but also between the Commission and the EP and between the Commission and the Council secretariat. Williamson resigned at the end of the 1996–1997 IGC and was replaced by Trojan, a Dutch civil servant and longtime Commission insider.

Physically, the Commission is surprisingly spread out. A majority of its officials work in Brussels, but some are based in Luxembourg. In Brussels itself, the Commission is dispersed in scores of buildings rented from or through the Belgian government. Pending renovation of the Berlaymont, the commissioners, their *cabinets*, and the secretariat-general are lodged in the Breydel building, a short walk from the larger and more imposing Council and EP buildings.

Recruitment and Promotion

The Commission recruits civil servants for its administrative grades through a highly competitive, EU-wide selection process (the *concours*) for university graduates. The small number of successful candidates who pass the aptitude tests, written examinations, interviews, and language proficiency tests begin work mostly at the A7 level. Some may already have gained experience in the Commission as *stagiaires* (paid student interns). Based on previous experience or personal predilection, a new recruit may ask to work in a particular DG or service but is unlikely to get the assignment of his or her choice.

From the beginning of their careers, Commission civil servants enter a world of unstated but finely balanced national quotas. Because the Eurocracy needs to reflect the population distribution and size of the EU's member states, the intake of new recruits and their promotion through the ranks is subject to an unofficial allocation of positions among each member state's nationals at each rung of the ladder. Enlargement causes these quotas to be recalculated, as nationals of new member states need to be accommodated at all levels of the correspondingly expanded civil service.

Women are poorly represented in the Commission's administrative category, especially at the senior levels. As a result, the Commission introduced a policy of positive discrimination in favor of women in 1995. This policy aims to achieve parity among officials at the top A2/A3 levels from the three newest member states (Austria, Finland, and Sweden) and a quota of 25 percent of women at the same level among the other member states. Progress has been slow. As Erkki Liikanen, the commissioner responsible for human resources, commented in 1998, "The initial [gender] gap was so great that a few good years are not sufficient to redress the imbalance inherited from the past."[15]

It is difficult to say precisely what motivates people to join the Commission. Money is probably the deciding factor. Commission civil servants are extremely well paid and enjoy many fringe benefits unavailable to their national counterparts. Idealism may also play a part, although rampant cynicism in parts of the Commission would soon cause even the most idealistic new arrivals to rethink their commitment to European integration. A desire to live and work abroad may prompt some candidates (excluding Belgians) to take the *concours*, although Brussels is by no means Europe's most interesting or appealing city. High regard for public service could also point toward a Commission career. Yet there are greater opportunities for advancement and for assorted assignments in national bureaucracies, and some countries with strong bureaucratic traditions, such as Britain and France, encourage their brightest people to eschew the Commission in favor of the national civil service.

Promotion through the junior and midcareer grades is generally predictable and uncontroversial and is based largely on seniority. However, entry into the senior grades—A3 and above—is highly politicized and extremely difficult. Not only is there a smaller number of jobs available than at lower levels but national civil servants and others who "parachute" into the senior ranks of the Commission—for instance, as part of a commissioner's *cabinet*—reduce the availability of senior jobs for career Eurocrats. Despite an ECJ ruling in March 1993 that the Commission was breaking EC rules by using national quotas rather than merit to recruit high-ranking officials, an unofficial national quota system still applies at the higher levels. Thus promotion to grades A3 and above tends to be granted as part of a package involving a number of people and negotiated by the commissioners, their *chefs de cabinet*, and the directors-general (heads of the directorates-general).

The difficulty of progressing beyond A4 engenders a lot of frustration and resentment in the midcareer level of the Commission. The politicized nature of promotion and an obsession with national quotas at the senior level mean that competence and merit become less relevant at the top. In an infamous address to the Commission's directors-general in March 1991, Delors reportedly warned that some were doing a bad job, that he knew who they were, and that he would, if he could, fire them.[16] But the president's inability to get rid of poor performers and the stranglehold that national governments have on certain senior positions expose some of the Commission's serious administrative weaknesses. The Spierenburg Report pointed those problems out as early as 1979, but most of its recommendations were never implemented.

Although the Commission is generally portrayed as a unitary actor, inevitably its officials have various outlooks, ideological orientations, and polity preferences. Based on numerous interviews and questionnaires, one scholar described senior Commission officials as constituting "a special microcosm of the European public space: less nationalist than most citizens, but divided on the mix of intergovernmental and supranational architectural principles; center-left of the average political actor, but disagreeing on the desirable mix of market and state, opportunity and equity."[17] Orientations and preferences vary from directorate-general to directorate-general. Another scholar, investigating administrative culture in the Commission, identified in the competition directorate-general "a distinctive set of beliefs linked to a commitment to neo-liberal values and a legalistic way of working," and in the environment directorate-general "a very specific world view based on the relationship between trade and ecological concerns."[18]

Internal Organization

The preoccupation with national prerogatives that stymies promotion also prevents mobility in the Commission. Commissioners and directors-general clung to existing staff levels even as the Commission's priorities shifted dramatically in the 1990s. Thus the Commission itself is far from overstaffed, but certain parts of it have become bloated while others, notably the external relations directorates-general and DG IV (competition) have remained seriously understaffed. Nor will the member states sanction a sizable increase in the civil service, especially at a time of public hostility toward European institutions.

Delors's success as president in the late 1980s raised the Commission's morale, yet by the end of the decade Eurocrats identified Delors himself as part of the Commission's problem. Delors's disregard for fellow commissioners, disdain for many directors-general, and aggrandizement of power in his *cabinet* fueled so much resentment and backbiting that, according to a retired A1, "internally the Commission [had] come to resemble Tammany Hall with a French accent."[19] With the unexpected rise in the Commission's responsibilities in the early 1990s and no commensurate increase in its size or efficiency, many officials felt the institution would soon self-destruct. During the TEU crisis, when the Commission unfairly came under widespread attack, the Eurocracy's morale reached rock bottom.

Although Delors made a belated effort in the early 1990s to streamline the Commission, Santer made internal Commission reform a priority of his presidency. Yet the Commission's structural and managerial problems are rooted in the member states' determination to retain as much control as possible over the Commission and have been compounded by successive enlargements, the proliferation of portfolios, and the excessive power of the *cabinets*. Spierenburg identified these problems as long ago as 1979, but they have never been seriously challenged. Staff policy remains underused as an instrument of internal reform, new management techniques have rarely been introduced, and a decentralization process introduced in the 1990s has had only mixed results.

It is impossible for even the most zealous president (which Santer was not) to suddenly and successfully reform the Commission, not lease because of inertia or even outright opposition to reform within parts of the bureaucracy itself. But Santer's apparent seriousness about correcting the most egregious cases of Commission maladministration and beginning a process that could ultimately result in far-reaching reform are both symbolically and substantively important. Hypercritical public and Europarliamentary opinion may be unsympathetic to Santer and may judge him solely by the results that he does or does not achieve. Nevertheless, Santer has done the EU a service by launching a serious reform effort and especially by pointing out that member states, which keep a stranglehold on key aspects of the Commission's structure and staff policy, deserve most of the blame.

THE COMMISSION'S ROLE AND RESPONSIBILITIES

The Commission is often described as the EU's executive body, yet it has only limited authority and ability to execute EU policy. The Commission is more accurately and informally called the "motor" of European integration, not only because of its almost exclusive right to initiate policy in the first pillar but also because of its history, composition, culture, and European rather than national outlook. Moreover, the Commission protects treaties from infringement or violation and traditionally defends the interests of small member states. As stipulated in the treaties and developed over time, the Commission's primary responsibilities include

- proposing and shaping legislation
- administering and implementing Community policy
- managing the budget
- conducting external relations
- policing Community law
- pointing the way forward

Legislative Power

It is an old axiom that "the Commission proposes and the Council disposes," but this view omits the EP's role as colegislator with the Council. Article 211 TEC authorizes the Commission to flesh out the treaty's skeletal framework by formulating recommendations, delivering opinions, and proposing legislation. Most of the Commission's legislative proposals have a clear legal base in the founding treaties (the TEC and the TEU) or in amendments to the treaties. Others may flow from legislation already adopted under the treaties or from a judgment of the Court. Member states sometimes dispute the legal base of a Commission proposal either because of a genuine difference of interpretation or for political reasons: They may not want the EU to involve itself in certain matters or may not want a legal base that involves qualified majority voting in the Council.

The volume of Commission proposals diminished in the post-TEU climate of suspicion toward the EU's legislative agenda and in the aftermath of the single market program's heavy legislative schedule. Member states may invoke subsidiarity to prevent the enactment of legislation at the European level and the implementation of European legislation at the national level, on the basis of Article 5 of the TEC: "In areas which do not fall within its exclusive competence, the Community shall take action, in accordance with the principle of subsidiarity, only if and insofar as the objectives of the proposed action cannot be sufficiently achieved by the Member States and can therefore, by reason of the scale or effects of the proposed action, be better achieved by the Community," and on the basis of a protocol (Number 30) on the application of the principles of subsidiarity and proportionality attached to the TEC by the Amsterdam Treaty.

Proposing Legislation

Regardless of the legal and political limits that subsidiarity imposes, the Commission jealously guards its right to propose legislation, based on the principle that the Commission alone can best articulate and defend the EU's collective interest. Since the introduction of direct elections, the increasingly assertive EP has occasionally attempted to win for itself a similar right of initiative. Although the Commission has successfully resisted these efforts, the TEU gave the EP the right to request the Commission to submit a proposal just as the Council has the right to do so under Article 208 TEC. Also under the TEU, the Commission won a shared right of initiative in the Common Foreign and Security Policy (CFSP) (Article 22.1 TEC), which is an intergovernmental rather than a supranational undertaking.

Apart from the formal right of the Council and Parliament to ask the Commission to initiate legislation, proposals may originate in any number of ways. A zealous Commission president, commissioner, director-general, or section director might ask his subordinates to prepare legislation, or an ambitious and energetic midlevel Commission official could send his superiors suggestions for draft proposals. Similarly, a proposal could come as a result of a widely perceived need to develop EU policy in a certain area as a response to the suggestion of a member state or an interest group.

After the launch of the single market program and implementation of the SEA, the Commission sought to develop an annual legislative program with the EP. The Commission's purpose was to identify priority objectives and help ensure the success of the new cooperation procedure for legislative decisionmaking introduced in the SEA. In 1991 a representative of the Council presidency participated for the first time in the Commission-Parliament dialogue. The three institutions now firmly contend that legislative programming is indispensable if the EU's decisionmaking procedure is to operate effectively.

However they originate and whether or not they are part of the legislative program, proposals must work their way through the Commission bureaucracy. A network of internal and external committees assists the Commission's work. Internal committees are mostly ad hoc and are convened to ensure coordination between various parts of the Commission if a proposal cuts across departmental boundaries. The secretariat-general plays a key coordinating role, as do the commissioners' *cabinets*. Of course, there is frequent informal coordination between commissioners, members of their *cabinets*, and other senior Commission officials, which may take place casually in a corridor, at lunch, or over coffee.

External committees, most of which are chaired and serviced by the Commission, are of two kinds: expert committees and consultative committees. Expert committees consist of specialists from inside and outside the government appointed by the member states. These committees are especially important not only because they provide useful technical advice but also because some of the national civil servants who sit on them may also sit on the Council working groups that will evaluate the proposal when the Commission formally submits it. The consultative committees are larger and more diverse and consist entirely of Commission nominees drawn mostly from interest groups and professional associations. Consultative committees are also valued for their technical advice and help the Commission keep in tune with the real world of business and commerce.

The proposal-drafting stage in the Commission is an opportune time for interest groups to try to modify the shape and content of the contemplated legislation. The Commission is a relatively open organization; its officials are easily contacted and are generally susceptible to outside influence. This is also the stage when small member states, whose power in the Council is relatively limited, make a sustained lobbying effort—outside the external committee structure—often including contacts between government ministers and "national" commissioners.

Ideally, the college of the Commission would discuss and approve proposals before formally submitting them to the Council and the EP. But the volume of proposals prepared annually makes that impossible. To expedite the process and cut down on the commissioners' workloads, draft proposals that seem uncomplicated and uncontroversial are circulated among the commissioners and, if not objected to within one week, are adopted by default. Alternatively, a subgroup of commissioners may agree to deal with routine proposals on behalf of their colleagues. Either way, the commissioners' *cabinets* play a decisive role.

The advisory committees' input, as well as the political astuteness of most of the commissioners and their *cabinets*, usually assures that the Commission never submits a proposal that the Council would be likely to reject outright. The Commission does not want to alienate the Council and risk paralyzing the legislative process. But the Commission is not servile or afraid to introduce controversial proposals. It rarely wants to isolate or embarrass member states, yet it knows that certain member states are likely to oppose particular proposals.

Shaping Legislation

Once the Commission's proposal is sent "out of the house," the Commission becomes the Council's main interlocutor throughout the entire legislative process. This relationship is symbolized by the Commission's presence at the other end of the rectangular table from the Council presidency during the various decisionmaking stages, beginning with the Council working groups, continuing through the Committee of Permanent Representatives, and ending with the meeting of the Council itself. As a result of its intensive participation in all stages of the legislative process, the Commission learns the member states' positions and the possibilities for maneuver and compromise. Supposedly the Commission acts as a mediator and honest broker. By changing or threatening to withdraw its proposal, however, the Commission can facilitate coalition building in the Council to win enough votes to form a qualified majority or to engineer a consensus where unanimity is required.

The fact that the Council can request the Commission to change its proposal only by unanimity (something always difficult to muster) and that only the Commission can withdraw a proposal strengthens the Commission's legislation-shaping capability. Not surprisingly, the Commission has objected strenuously to suggestions, such as those made during the 1991 IGC, that the Council be allowed to change Commission proposals by qualified majority voting (QMV) instead of unanimity. As Delors told the EP in April 1991, such a reform would turn the Commission into an organ of the Council and the Parliament for the preparation of their legislative work.[20]

Despite an inherent tension in the Commission-Council relationship, close cooperation between both institutions is vital for efficient and timely EU decisionmaking. At the beginning of each Council presidency, virtually the entire college of the Commission and the entire cabinet of the presidency country meet for a full day's discussion. The purpose of the meeting is to try to reconcile each side's legislative agenda so that the forthcoming presidency can be as productive as possible. During the presidency itself, officials from the Commission and the presidency meet regularly to iron out policymaking problems, and the presidency's foreign minister usually meets the Commission president and/or relevant commissioners before each meeting of the General Affairs Council. Given the Commission's importance in the decisionmaking process, it is little wonder that "efficient presidencies, as a general rule, are those that have maintained a close and confident working relationship with the Commission."[21]

Administrative and Implementation Powers

The Commission is generally described as the EU's executive body. However, the Commission's executive powers are constrained in two important respects. First, the Commission conspicuously lacks the ability to implement EU policy "on the ground." There is no EU customs service, immigration service, veterinary service, or most of the myriad other services that are necessary to give real effect to Community legislation. Instead, the Commission depends heavily on the member states' civil services. Without assistance from the member states' agriculture departments, for instance, the Commission could not possibly make the Common Agricultural Policy (CAP) work. Thus at the level where Community legislation should matter most—on farms, in factories, at airports and docks—the Commission depends entirely on national officials. Yet national officials can be notoriously recalcitrant when it comes to implementing EU legislation, either because they do not want to lose their jobs (as in the case of customs services), because they resent interference from Brussels, or because they genuinely misunderstand the latest Commission regulation.

The Commission's executive powers therefore refer not to ground-level implementation but to the enactment of numerous rules and regulations necessary to give EU legislation (as enacted by the Council and EP) practical application. Thus the Commission issues approximately 5,000 directives, regulations, and decisions annually (although these are qualitatively different from Council acts bearing the same name), dealing mostly with highly technical aspects of common policies. The increasing encroachment of Commission regulations, directives, and decisions into everyday life in the EU is a major reason for growing public hostility toward the Brussels bureaucracy. The Commission is too easily caricatured and reviled for its real or supposed rules on such arcane issues as the length of a British sausage, the local environmental impact of a public works project, or the size and shape of potted plants. Most people do not realize that the Commission lacks a free hand in implementing EU policy.

Comitology

Jealous of their national prerogatives, and generally reluctant to concede too much lest the Commission attempt to alter the Council's acts with its implementing legislation, member states from the outset devised a complicated procedure known as "comitology" to constrain the Commission's executive powers. The cumbersome comitology procedure includes three types of committees—advisory, management, and regulatory—all chaired by Commission officials but made up of national civil servants. As the name suggests, advisory committees merely counsel the Commission on rule making. Management and regulatory committees, by contrast, are able to send proposed legislative measures to the Council for review. Management committees were first set up in 1962 to help implement the CAP, whereas regulatory committees came about to help manage the common external tariff and are now concerned with a wide range of harmonization issues.

As a concession to the Commission, the SEA amended Article 145 TEC (now Article 202), making it a general rule that powers of implementation be conferred on the Commission, but member states could not agree during the 1985 IGC on a set of principles and rules to define the exercise of those powers. In March 1986 the Commission proposed to the Council that the three "tried and tested procedures" (the advisory committee, the management committee, and the regulatory committee) remain in use but urged the Council to give the advisory committee predominance in matters concerning the single market.[22] The EP delivered a nonbinding opinion in October 1986 expressing concern that comitology might tie the Commission's hands and make implementation of certain single market directives impossible.

It took the Council until July 1987 to decide on new procedures.[23] The Council stipulated that the Commission would exercise powers of implementation either alone or by one of the three committee procedures. However, the Council added two variants on the regulatory committee and inserted a safeguard clause, to which the Commission strongly objected. In a speech to the EP on January 20, 1988, Delors complained that "the Council has not hesitated to resort to institutional guerrilla tactics . . . to impose [procedural changes] which are incompatible with efficient administration and fly in the face of the SEA."[24] Delors was particularly put out by the Council's reluctance to allow the Commission to use the advisory committees to implement harmonization legislation in the single market program.

Since 1987 the Council and Commission have sparred over the appropriate procedure for each legislative act. Yet the Council-Commission dispute became more ritualistic than real. In effect, the Commission enjoys a considerable degree of autonomy, the culture of the Commission in any case stresses the importance of legislative initiation rather than implementation, and the efficiency of the various procedures was never an issue (although the variety of procedures available often leads to protracted and theoretical discussions about which one to use, thereby slowing down the legislative process). Thus the Commission reached the logical but politically surprising conclusion in its report for the pre-IGC Reflection Group that with one exception, "the implementing procedures operate satisfactorily and present no major obstacles to actual implementation." The Commission also provided compelling statistics: Of the more than 200 comitology committees in existence, only thirty were of the kind that could block decisions; and of the thousands of decisions taken by comitology committees since 1992, only six were referred back to the Council, which then made a decision in each case.[25]

If comitology were still restricted to Council-Commission relations, controversy about it would erupt only in the lifeless pages of the *Official Journal* and the Commission's *General Report*. But by giving the EP real legislative powers (codecision), the TEU added a new twist to an already complicated issue. Because it championed the Commission's implementing powers and wished, in turn, to control the executive, the EP had always taken a keen interest in comitology. Until implementation of the TEU, however, the EP lacked a reason to become directly involved in the procedure. Thereafter the EP could argue that it should have equal rights with the Council to control implementation by the Commission of legislation enacted jointly with the Council (through codecision). Most member states were aghast at the idea of parliamentary involvement in comitology and claimed that the Council's and Parliament's roles were not comparable in that respect.

In his inaugural speech in July 1994, EP president Klaus Hänsch warned the Council "not to try to use comitology to deprive Parliament of co-decision rights [to which] it is entitled . . . under the Maastricht Treaty."[26] The intensity of parliamentary feeling became clear shortly afterward when the EP caused the conciliation phase of the new codecision procedure to fail for the first time (in legislation on voice telephony) because of the Council's refusal to make concessions on comitology. The EP's concerns about comitology therefore threatened to paralyze codecision and poison relations between the EP and the Council.

An interinstitutional agreement in December 1994 resulted in a truce but committed the parties to settle the matter definitively at the forthcoming IGC. A possible extension of the scope of codecision, also to have been discussed at the IGC, would have a bearing on the comitology question. Although favoring more codecision in order to enhance the EP's legislative role, the Commission did not advocate parliamentary involvement in comitology but sought instead to devise the simplest procedures with the minimum amount of interference either from the Council or Parliament. In the event, the IGC agreed on an extension of the codecision procedure but deferred further discussion about comitology.

Budgetary Responsibilities

Submitting Proposals

Each year, the Commission submits a preliminary draft budget to the two arms of the EU's budgetary authority: the Council and the EP. The Commission's preliminary draft is the first step needed to translate into material terms the EU's political, economic, and social objectives. However, the Commission's preliminary draft is not a proposal in the legislative sense; therefore it is not subject to the rule that the Council can amend it only by unanimity. Since the "Delors I" package of 1988, the Commission submits its annual draft budget in the context of a multiannual framework or perspective (Delors I covered a five-year period). The negotiation of budgetary perspectives has become a major political event in the life of the EU. Although essentially an intergovernmental process, the fact that the outcome unofficially bears the Commission president's name attests to the centrality of the Commission's role in it.

Overseeing Expenditure

The Commission has some obligations on the revenue side—namely, overseeing the collection of the EU's own resources—but its responsibilities lie primarily on the expenditure side. These include administering appropriations for

- the Guarantee Section of the European Agricultural Guidance and Guarantee Fund (the main mechanism for financing the CAP), which still accounts for approximately 50 percent of total expenditure
- structural funds—made up of the European Social Fund, the Guidance Section of the European Agricultural Guidance and Guarantee Fund, and the European Regional Development Fund—which account for approximately 25 percent of total expenditure
- the EU's external relations, including development and humanitarian assistance

Fighting Fraud

The Commission has devoted a lot of effort in recent years to fighting fraud, which is reputedly rampant in many policy areas. Given that payments are made by national authorities on the EU's behalf, most fraud probably takes place at the national level. Nevertheless, a number of Commission officials have been implicated. The Commission also faces growing criticism for its alleged poor financial management of various EU policies and programs, and for its spendthrift habits. The Court of Auditors' frequent censure of the Commission has triggered lively debates in the

EP—including an unprecedented debate and vote in January 1999 on whether to remove the entire Commission from office—and fuels predictably unfavorable media coverage. Well before the censure vote in January 1999, under Santer's leadership the Commission put a far greater emphasis on financial responsibility. Liikanen, the budget and personnel commissioner, and Anita Gradin, commissioner for financial control and fraud prevention, jointly spearheaded the reform effort. Significantly, both commissioners came from the new Nordic member states, which have a reputation for openness and bureaucratic integrity.

External Relations Responsibilities

The Commission is an international actor whose stature increased dramatically during the 1990s. In July 1989, following the collapse of communism, the Commission assumed responsibility for coordinating Western aid to newly independent Hungary and Poland. Soon afterward, the Commission became the main interlocutor for the EU in its dealings with the new democracies in Central and Eastern Europe and with the former Soviet republics. The launch of the Common Foreign and Security Policy (CFSP) in November 1993 added a new dimension to the Commission's international involvement. The Transatlantic Declaration of November 1990 and the New Transatlantic Agenda (NTA) of December 1995 strengthened the Commission's role in U.S.-EU relations; the conclusion of the Uruguay Round of the General Agreement on Tariffs and Trade and the launch of the World Trade Organization (WTO) highlighted the Commission's importance as an international trade negotiator. Also, the Commission is in charge of the EU's development policy, including the Lomé Convention for assistance to over seventy African, Caribbean, and Pacific (ACP) countries. As a result of these responsibilities, most third countries and international organizations have diplomatic relations with the EU, and the Commission maintains nearly 100 delegations and offices throughout the world.

Despite its burgeoning responsibilities in the area of external affairs, however, the Commission has yet to organize its international relations portfolios and directorates-general satisfactorily. In 1993 Delors established a new directorate-general—DG IA—for external *political* relations, thereby restricting DG I (the long-standing external relations DG) to *economic* affairs—apart from development policy, which remained the responsibility of DG VIII. Two years later Santer reorganized external economic relations along geographical lines. Thus DG I, previously responsible for all trade relations, kept responsibility only for the WTO and for EU trade relations with North America, the Far East, Australia, and New Zealand; DG IA took over relations with Central and Eastern Europe and the former Soviet Union; and a new directorate-general—DG IB—acquired relations with the southern Mediterranean countries, the Middle East,

Latin America, and South and Southeast Asia. DG IA remained responsible for the Commission's limited involvement in the CFSP, although subject to coordination with the Commission president. A special Commission service and two other commissioners are also responsible for major aspects of EU external relations: DG VIII for development policy, and the European Community Humanitarian Office for international humanitarian assistance.

The proliferation and reorganization of external relations portfolios under Santer has not enhanced the Commission's international image or effectiveness (Santer was motivated in part by the need to redistribute the Commission's responsibilities among twenty commissioners, three more than in the Delors Commission following the 1995 enlargement). Santer's external relations commissioners include some of the college's most ambitious and assertive individuals. Turf wars and rows over resources inevitably abound. Under the circumstances, it is surprising that the Commission manages its external relations responsibilities as well as it does. Proposed reforms include merging the various external relations DGs into a "super DG" under a powerful Commission vice president. However, the situation is likely to change radically only when the Commission is radically reduced in size, a politically charged issue contingent on the equally politically charged question of the reweighting of votes in the Council.

Most of the EU's external economic relations are based on Articles 133 and 300 TEC. These authorize the Commission to conduct the EU's international trade negotiations but keep the Council closely involved in the process. The Council approves the Commission's negotiating mandate and endorses the final agreement, officially by qualified majority vote but in practice by unanimity. As well as setting negotiating directives and endorsing the final agreement, member states exert considerable influence over the Commission's conduct of international trade negotiations themselves. Named after the relevant treaty article (before being renumbered in the Amsterdam Treaty), the so-called 133 Committee (formerly the 113 Committee) of member state civil servants meets regularly with Commission officials to approve the Commission's negotiating strategy and proposals. Although members of the committee do not participate directly in most negotiations, their presence behind the scenes ensures that Commission negotiators stick to the agreed-upon Council position. Commission negotiators often turn such oversight to the EU's advantage by pointing out to their interlocutors the impossibility of accepting a proposal without first getting the member states' approval.

The Commission's competence to negotiate and conclude international trade agreements does not extend to trade in services or trade-related aspects of intellectual property rights. The Commission overstepped its competence when it attempted to conclude the agreements in these areas in the Uruguay Round. The Commission sought to extend the scope of what was then Article 113 as part of the treaty revisions negotiated in the 1996–1997 IGC, but member states could not agree among themselves to make the necessary changes. As a result, with the new international trade agenda dominated by disputes over services and intellectual property rights, the Commission's influence in the realm of external economic relations has been considerably curtailed.

In addition to negotiating trade accords, managing development policy, and liaising internationally for the EU, the Commission negotiates association agreements with third countries and plays an important part in the process of EU enlargement. The Commission's role in the enlargement process involves delivering opinions on applicant countries' membership requests and negotiating the terms of accession. These became particularly onerous responsibilities following the end of the Cold War when Austria, Finland, Norway, and Sweden submitted membership applications, followed by the Central and Eastern European states, Cyprus, and Malta. Coming on top of preparations for EMU and negotiation of the Amsterdam Treaty, the Commission's compilation in 1997 of *Agenda 2000,* a voluminous report on the likely impact of Central and Eastern European enlargement that also included opinions on the candidate countries' applications, strained Commission resources to the limit.

Policing Community Law

The Commission is sometimes grandiloquently called the "guardian" of the treaties. This means that under Article 226 (formerly Article 169) TEC, the Commission may bring a member state before the ECJ for alleged nonfulfillment of treaty obligations. Member states frequently fail to live up to their commitments, and the Commission occasionally institutes judicial proceedings. But member states generally respect the treaties; otherwise the EU would collapse. Most member state violations result from genuine misunderstandings or misinterpretations or from delays in transposing Community legislation into national law. Deliberate noncompliance nonetheless exists, notably in the area of competition policy and the internal market. For political and public relations reasons, member states and the Commission are reluctant to pursue cases all the way to the ECJ, and most disputes are resolved at an early stage.

The Commission may become aware of a possible infringement for any number of reasons. An individual, an enterprise, or another member state may complain, or an investigation by Commission officials could uncover possible violations. If the Commission decides to take action, it first sends a "letter of formal notice" asking the member state concerned to explain the alleged breach. The member state then has about two months to reply. If it fails to reply or does not provide a satisfactory explanation, the Commission issues a "reasoned opinion" outlining why it considers the member state to be in violation of the treaty. Again, the Commission usually gives the member state two months to comply. Most cases end with a letter of formal notice or a reasoned opinion. The Commission generates approximately 1,000 letters of formal notice annually.

Compliance with Community law is a sensitive political issue both for member states and for the Commission. Member states resent being taken to court, and the Commission is reluctant to risk alienating them. Although the Commission realizes that noncompliance by one member state is unfair to the others and that the EU's credibility may be at stake, examples of political deals between the Commission and the member states abound. As a rule, the Commission acts in infringement cases neither swiftly nor impulsively.

With the launch of the single market program the Commission won some important new powers with which to enforce Community law, notably in the area of competition policy. A vigorous competition policy was a logical corollary of the single market program. Peter Sutherland and Leon Brittan, his successor as competition commissioner, fought tenaciously to win for the Commission sole authority to approve or block large EC mergers and acquisitions. Under the terms of the December 1989 Community regulation on merger control, the Commission has one month after notification to begin an inquiry into a proposed merger and another four months to issue a legal decision.

The Commission now has a large merger task force, predictably called the trustbusters. The task force's relatively expeditious handling of many complicated and sensitive cases has generally won the respect of European companies and national competition watchdogs, although some member states have expressed annoyance with the task force's methods and recommendations. The task force sends its recommendations to the full Commission, which despite political pressure from national governments in particular cases, invariably supports the task force. The Commission's responsibility for competition policy did not become an issue during the 1996–1997 IGC despite threats by some member states to take merger control at the EU level away from the Commission and give it instead to an independent agency.

Pointing the Way Forward

During a celebration in Rome in March 1987 to mark the EC's thirtieth anniversary, Delors described the Commission as a "strategic authority" established by the founding fathers to "guarantee the continuity of the [integration] project despite the political or geopolitical hazards." Acting as a "custodian of European interests [and] as a repository of past achievements," Delors declared that the Commission has a unique obligation to point "the way to the goal ahead."[27] Speaking to the EP the following

January, Delors explained that "the Commission itself cannot achieve much but it can generate ideas. Its main weapon is its conviction."[28]

The history of the EU is replete with examples of the Commission pointing the way ahead, notably during the Hallstein, Jenkins, and Delors presidencies. The single market program and EMU are good case studies. Capitalizing on the member states' eagerness to complete the internal market, the Commission put the necessary package of proposals together and mapped out a strategy to succeed. The Commission provided the encouragement, explication, and enthusiasm to push the program forward from its inception in 1985 until its completion in 1993. Similarly, the Commission took the initiative in the late 1980s to draft a plan for EMU and contributed decisively to the outcome of the 1991 IGC on monetary union. By contrast, the EU tends to stagnate when the Commission is either unable or unwilling to lead.

The TEU ratification crisis fueled speculation that "the motor [of European integration] has all but stalled."[29] Undoubtedly developments in the early 1990s shattered the Commission's self-confidence. At a time of serious economic recession and political uncertainty it was difficult for the Commission to regain the initiative and forge ahead. Invidious comparisons were made between the setback to the Commission's fortunes caused by the empty chair crisis in 1965 and the TEU ratification crisis in 1992–1993. The unexpected resignation of the Commission in 1999 dealt a further blow to the institution's image and influence. In the prevailing Euroskeptical climate, the Commission faced a difficult challenge to restore to itself and to the EU a strong commitment to greater European unity. Only by successfully meeting that challenge, however, can the Commission hope to reaffirm and ultimately achieve the EU's fundamental strategic objective of deeper economic and political integration.

NOTES

1. Commission, *1991 General Report,* point 1196.

2. Stanley Hoffmann, "The Case for Leadership," *Foreign Policy* 81 (winter 1990–1991): 24.

3. Debates of the European Parliament, *Official Journal of the European Communities* [*OJ*] 4–449, July 19–22, 1994, p. 79.

4. See Simon Hix and Christopher Lord, "The Making of a President: The European Parliament and the Confirmation of Jacques Santer as President of the Commission," *Government and Opposition* 31: 62–76.

5. Debates of the European Parliament, *OJ* 4–449, July 19–22, 1994, p. 75.

6. Jacques Delors, address to the European Parliament, January 20, 1988, Bull. EC S/1-1988, p. 8; Delors, *Le Nouveau Concert Européen* (Paris: Editions Odile Jacob, 1992).

7. Neill Nugent, ed., *At the Heart of the Union: Studies of the European Commission* (Basingstoke: Macmillan, 1997).

8. See *Agence Europe,* January 6, 1995, p. 3.
9. Quoted in the *Times* (London), June 28, 1977, p. 16.
10. Roy Jenkins, *A Life at the Centre* (London: Macmillan, 1991), p. 376.
11. Neils Ersbøll, "The European Union: The Immediate Priorities," *International Affairs* 70, no. 3: 413.
12. Peter Ludlow, "The European Commission," in Robert Keohane and Stanley Hoffmann, eds., *The European Community: Decisionmaking and Institutional Change* (Boulder: Westview Press, 1991), p. 91.
13. Walter Hallstein, *Europe in the Making* (London: Allen & Unwin, 1972), pp. 60–61.
14. Ludlow, "Commission," p. 120.
15. European Information Service, *Monthly Report on Europe,* April 1998, p. III.5.
16. See George Ross, *Jacques Delors and European Integration* (Oxford: Oxford University Press, 1995), p. 154.
17. Liesbet Hooghe, "Serving Europe: Political Orientations of Senior Commission Officials," paper presented at the Fifth Biennial Conference of the European Community Studies Association, Seattle, May 29–June 1, 1997, p. 1.
18. Michelle Cini, "Administrative Culture in the European Commission: The Case of Competition and Environment," paper presented at the Fourth Biennial Conference of the European Community Studies Association, Charleston, South Carolina, May 11–14, 1995, p. 1.
19. Roy Denman, letter to the editor, *Times* (London), January 27, 1992, p. 10.
20. Debates of the European Parliament, *OJ* 3–404, April 17, 1991, pp. 113–114.
21. Guy de Bassompierre, *Changing the Guard in Brussels: An Insider's View of the EC Presidency* (New York: Praeger, 1988), p. 25.
22. *OJ* C 70, March 25, 1986; Bull. EC 2-1986, point 2.4.14.
23. *OJ* L 197, July 18, 1987.
24. Jacques Delors, address to the European Parliament, Bull. EC S/1-88, p. 10.
25. Commission, *Report on the Operation of the Treaty on European Union,* SEC(95)731 final, p. 22.
26. Debates of the European Parliament, *OJ* 4–449, July 19–22, 1994, p. 13.
27. Jacques Delors, speech on the occasion of the thirtieth anniversary of the signing of the Treaty of Rome, March 25, 1987, Bull. EC S/2-1987, p. 10.
28. Delors, address to the European Parliament, January 20, 1988, Bull. EC S/1-1988, p. 9.
29. *Economist,* October 10, 1992, p. 66.

9

The European Council and the Council of Ministers

The European Council and the Council of Ministers (officially called the Council of the European Union and generally known as the Council) are related but separate entities. Strictly speaking, only the Council is an EU institution. It consists of government ministers and a European commissioner who meet frequently to reconcile national interests and enact EU legislation. By contrast, the European Council consists of each country's top political leaders (heads of state and/or government) and the Commission president, assisted by their foreign ministers and a Commission vice president. Members of the European Council may also constitute the Council of Ministers, but invariably they meet not to adopt formal legal texts but to resolve otherwise intractable problems and to lead the EU at the highest political level.

Many meetings of the European Council (summits) stand out as turning points in the EU's history, such as Milan in 1985 (go-ahead for the intergovernmental conference that led to the Single European Act); Maastricht in 1991 (agreement on the TEU); Amsterdam in 1997 (conclusion of the Amsterdam Treaty); and Brussels in 1998 (selection of eleven member states to participate in Stage III of EMU). Some of the most prominent and portentous meetings of the heads of state and government took place even before the European Council formally came into existence in 1975: the 1969 Hague summit that endorsed "completion, deepening, enlargement" and the 1972 Paris summit that called for EMU by the end of the decade.

That partial list of historical landmarks indicates the political importance of EU summitry. Without regular working sessions of government leaders, the EC might not have survived Eurosclerosis in the 1970s or successfully launched the single market program in the mid-1980s. Nor could the EU have adjusted, however hesitatingly and inadequately, to a radically altered international environment in the 1990s. Thus the European Council is far more than a glorified meeting of the Council, although it sometimes runs the risk of doing the Council's job.

The Council combines elements of intergovernmentalism and supranationalism (it consists of member states' representatives, who agree under certain circumstances to be outvoted in the decisionmaking process). By contrast, the European Council is "the epitome of intergovernmentalism in institutionalized Europe."[1] Ardent Eurofederalists therefore lament the European Council's ascendancy. Yet the European Council's emergence in the 1970s coincided with a gradual strengthening, rather than weakening, of supranationalism in the EU. Aware of the threat to supranationalism that regular summitry could pose, when launching the European Council in 1974 the heads of state and government deliberately called for direct elections to the European Parliament (EP) as a counterweight to more intergovernmentalism in the EC. Member states took other steps to strengthen supranationalism—modest expansion of the EP's powers and increasing use of majority voting in the Council—at subsequent EU summits. Thus the European Council's appearance in the 1970s generated a dynamic interrelationship between intergovernmentalism and supranationalism that contributed to the EC's transformation in the mid-1980s.

THE ROTATING PRESIDENCY

The rotating presidency of the European Council and the Council of Ministers is one of the EU's most distinctive features. Every six months, on the first of January and the first of July, a different country assumes the presidency of both bodies. The six-monthly rotation used to be based on the alphabetical listing of the name of each country in its own official language. It has since been reconfigured a number of times to ensure a sequence of big and small, old and new, member states and to ensure that the presidency's workload is distributed evenly among member states. Because EU governance virtually ceases during the holidays in August and accelerates rapidly at other times of the year according to a fixed legislative calendar in key areas, it would be unfair for the same countries always to be in the presidency either in the first or the second half of the year.

Accommodating the presidential rota to the vagaries of the EU's legislative calendar suggests that the presidency's work is preordained, and to a certain extent it is. Particular EU business must be transacted at definite times of the year—for instance, farm price negotiations (each spring) and a budget agreement (each fall). Also, specific EU programs (such as completing the single market in the late 1980s and the three-stage EMU process in the 1990s) have relatively rigid timetables regardless of the country in the Council presidency.

Nevertheless, for three main reasons it can matter a great deal which country holds the presidency at any particular time. First, each country's approach to even the most routine and uncontroversial EU business is

Table 9.1 The Council Presidency Rota, 1993–2003

Denmark	January–June 1993
Belgium	July–December 1993
Greece	January–June 1994
Germany	July–December 1994
France	January–June 1995
Spain	July–December 1995
Italy	January–June 1996
Ireland	July–December 1996
Netherlands	January–June 1997
Luxembourg	July–December 1997
United Kingdom	January–June 1998
Austria	July–December 1998
Germany	January–June 1999
Finland	July–December 1999
Portugal	January–June 2000
France	July–December 2000
Sweden	January–June 2001
Belgium	July–December 2001
Spain	January–June 2002
Denmark	July–December 2002
Greece	January–June 2003

bound to be slightly idiosyncratic. Second, countries inevitably have preferences for certain EU policies, programs, or activities. Third, changing circumstances inside and outside the EU sometimes confront a presidency with unexpected challenges that call for quick responses. Accordingly, the variables most likely to determine a country's presidential performance are size and resources, diplomatic experience and tradition, familiarity with the EU system, degree of commitment to European integration, and domestic political circumstances.

The presidency's importance has grown steadily throughout the EU's history because of a number of related developments: the progressive deepening of European integration; the Council's enhanced political importance; the profusion of technical or sectoral councils; the corresponding expansion of the influence and authority of the Committee of Permanent Representatives (made up of member states' ambassadors to the EU); the proliferation of Council working groups; the emergence and growing prominence of the European Council; and the impact of intergovernmental cooperation in the fields of foreign and security policy on the one hand and justice and home affairs on the other. As a result, the presidency's functions and responsibilities have expanded over the years and now include

- arranging and chairing meetings of the European Council (summits)
- preparing and chairing meetings of the Council and its subcommittees—the Committee of Permanent Representatives (COREPER),

various special committees, and a large number of standing or ad hoc working groups
- brokering deals in the Council in order to reach agreement on a particular legislative proposal or on a package of legislative proposals
- launching strategic policy initiatives
- coordinating member states' positions at international conferences and negotiations in which the EU participates
- representing the EU internationally
- acting as an EU spokesperson
- leading the EU side in enlargement negotiations
- chairing intergovernmental conferences

In the Chair

In Eurospeak, the terms "presidency" and "chair" are often synonymous because the foremost responsibility of a country in the presidency is to chair the European Council, the Council, and the Council's numerous subcommittees. The Council's rules of procedure for the presidency include such routine functions as planning the Council's six-month calendar, convening meetings, preparing the agenda and minutes, and drafting conclusions. Member states judge presidential performance primarily by how a country manages European Council and Council meetings during its six months in the chair.

Running a good meeting is not purely procedural but also involves crafting compromise agreements and steering participants toward a decision. A country may organize meetings well, but unless it knows the issues thoroughly, understands other countries' points of view, appreciates how a discussion is developing, and judges properly when to call for breaks, adjournments, or decisions, the best-prepared meetings can end inconclusively or disastrously. Brokering not just a single agreement but a whole package of agreements is an indispensable task of the presidency.

Countries in the presidency play a dual role in Council meetings and have a split personality. They seek both to advance their own positions and to act as impartial arbiters; they are biased and neutral at the same time. That dichotomy is formally recognized in the seating arrangements for Council meetings, where the country in the presidency not only sits at the head of the table but also maintains a separate national representation immediately perpendicular to it, on the right-hand side of the table.

Yet the difference between a country's national and presidential roles should not be exaggerated. Of the two representatives present, the most senior minister or official always wears the presidency hat, and countries generally see presidential service as being in their national interest. As part of their preparations for holding the presidency, countries coordinate interministerially in order to reconcile national and presidential interests, and if necessary subsume national under presidential interests. Thus it is rare for countries in the presidency to vote in their own national interest in order to produce the required majority. As a longtime senior adviser to two British prime ministers observed, "The accepted wisdom is that holding the presidency makes it harder, not easier, to pursue specific national aims."[2]

Responsibility for organizing, chairing, and running hundreds of meetings during a Council presidency puts enormous pressure materially and politically on the member state in question. Large countries have an obvious advantage: Their big bureaucracies provide solid infrastructural support. By contrast, it is sometimes difficult for small countries to find enough qualified people to chair all the meetings that take place during a six-month period, especially when unforeseen circumstances increase the presidency's workload. Most small countries—Ireland in late 1996, Austria in late 1998, Finland in late 1999—radically reorganize their bureaucracies in order to absorb the shock of the presidency, often at the cost of diminishing domestic government service.

Without compromising its neutrality or credibility, the presidency can influence the conduct of EU business in a number of ways. Organizing the Council's agenda and chairing Council meetings afford the presidency considerable control over the pace of EU legislation. If the presidency wants progress on a certain issue, "it will secure determined support from the Commission, as well as from some other member states. And it will put into place an active and capable working group chairman."[3]

Relations with Other Institutions

The presidency is also responsible for maintaining good relations with other EU institutions. Because of inherent political tension between the Council and the Commission and the latter's political decline since the early 1990s, Council-Commission relations are potentially awkward. Yet harmonious relations between the institutions are essential for effective decisionmaking. Clearly, a successful presidency involves continuous contact with officials at all levels in the Commission and requires especially close cooperation between the Council secretariat and the Commission's secretariat-general. For symbolic and substantive reasons, virtually the entire cabinet of the country in the presidency meets the entire college of the Commission in the opening days of each new presidential rota.

It is especially important for the Council to work closely with the EP, the Council's colegislator in a growing number of policy areas and an institution with considerable political clout. However, the Council-EP relationship is far touchier than the Council-Commission relationship. The EP tends to see the Council as a jealous guardian of intergovernmentalism, and the Council tends to see the EP as greedy in its demands for greater power and ineffectual in its exercise of existing power. The country in the presidency therefore has the politically sensitive task of liaising with parliamentary committees and political groups, heading the Council delegation in contentious meetings of the conciliation committee, reporting to the EP after each summit and at the beginning and end of each presidential rota, and answering a series of written and oral questions from parliamentarians.

Agenda, Initiatives, and Representation

Foreign ministers outline their countries' presidential agendas during an inaugural address to the EP. These speeches contain predictable rhetoric about European integration and emphasize what a country hopes to achieve during its six months in office. Of course, there is no guarantee that the presidency's legislative objectives will ever be realized. Much depends on the prevailing political and economic climate and on the prestige, popularity, and skill of the country in the presidency.

Whether in speeches to the EP or elsewhere, the Council president may also launch strategic policy initiatives, a prerogative shared with the Commission president. Just as some Commission presidents are more active than others, some countries are more likely to launch strategic initiatives than others, and prominent politicians in a particular country inevitably differ in their degrees of Euro-activism. The coincidence of a dynamic Commission president, a country in the Council presidency with a reputation for promoting European integration, and imaginative leaders in that country can benefit the EU greatly. The 1990s have been conspicuously bereft of such occasions.

Along with the Commission president, the Council president speaks on behalf of the EU. Each president supposedly deals only with specific subjects, depending on whether they come under exclusive EU competence or mixed (member state and EU) competence. The Commission and Council presidents customarily give a joint press conference at the end of each summit, often presenting noticeably different accounts and interpretations of the same negotiations from their respective institutional perspectives.

External Affairs

Dual representation is particularly prominent and perplexing in the EU's external relations. Nowhere is it more evident than in dealings with the United States. Under the terms of the 1990 Transatlantic Declaration, the president of the United States meets every six months with the presidents of the Commission and the Council. Similarly, the Council and Commission presidents represent the EU at the annual G7 economic summits. As long as one of the four EU countries in the G7—Britain, France, Germany, and Italy—happens to be in the Council presidency, such dual representation hardly matters. But when one of the smaller EU member states is in the presidency during a G7 summit, the EU's dual representation seems especially anomalous.

In the Common Foreign and Security Policy (CFSP), the Council president is unencumbered by joint Commission representation. As long ago as 1974, the heads of state and government stipulated that "the President-in-office will be the spokesman for the [member states] and will set out their views in international diplomacy. He will insure that the necessary consultations always take place in good time."[4] The Single European Act (SEA) established a legal basis for the presidency's role in European Political Cooperation (EPC), the forerunner of the CFSP, and codified existing practices whereby the Council president managed the process of political cooperation. Furthermore, the SEA established a small EPC secretariat, housed in the Council building, and put it under the authority of the presidency. The TEU, which replaced EPC with the CFSP, strengthened the presidency's role in EU foreign and security policy representation (Article 18, formerly Article J.8 TEU).

The presidency's prominence in the CFSP is burdensome for small countries and highlights some disadvantages of the rotational system. The large number of CFSP working groups (nearly thirty altogether) calls for a sizable pool of competent chairpersons, which small member states have difficulty providing. In addition, the presidency's responsibility to represent the EU internationally can be detrimental to the EU's status and influence when a small country is in the chair. For instance, having Luxembourg in the presidency in 1991 during the Gulf War and the early stages of the fragmentation of the former Yugoslavia reinforced the international image of a weak and indecisive EC response to both conflicts.

The Council Secretariat

Small countries in the presidency depend heavily for logistical support on the Council secretariat. With a staff of approximately 2,000 people, including about 300 A-grade officials, the Council secretariat assists the Council by helping to draft the six-month legislative program, providing legal advice, briefing government ministers on current EU issues, preparing the agenda for Council meetings, and drafting the meetings' minutes. Nearly two-thirds of the Council staff are translators and interpreters. Like the Commission secretariat, the Council secretariat is divided into directorates-general, although along different lines.

The legal service represents the Council before the Court of Justice, ensures that all texts adopted are compatible, and advises the Council at all levels. Indeed, a representative of the legal service sits to the right of the president during Council meetings and often intervenes, especially during discussions on intergovernmental policy areas. Given the presidency's importance in the process of treaty reform, the Council's legal service plays

Table 9.2 Council Secretariat Directorates-General

Directorate-General A	Personnel and administration; protocol, organization, security, and infrastructure; translation and document production
Directorate-General B	Agriculture; fisheries
Directorate-General C	Internal market: customs union; industrial policy, approximation of laws; right of establishment and freedom to provide services; company law; intellectual property
Directorate-General D	Research; energy; transport; environment; consumer protection
Directorate-General E	External economic relations; common foreign and security policy
Directorate-General F	Relations with the European Parliament and the ESC; institutional affairs; budget and staff regulations
Directorate-General G	Economic, monetary, and social affairs

a critical role on such momentous occasions. For instance, the Council's legal service drafted the opt-outs granted to Denmark at the December 1992 Edinburgh summit, which paved the way for ratification of the TEU, and also drafted the key article on flexibility in the Amsterdam Treaty.

The Council secretariat describes itself as "entirely at the service of the Presidency, supporting it in its efforts to find compromise solutions, coordinate work or arrive at an overall view."[5] Indeed, the presidency is the presidency plus the Council secretariat. What is involved is much more than close cooperation; it is a form of common action or symbiosis in regard to preparing and carrying out the presidency program. A member of the secretariat always accompanies the presidency unless a particular bilateral issue is being discussed.

The Council secretariat has acquired a higher public and political profile under successive secretaries-general beginning with Neils Ersbøll's appointment in 1980. The Council secretariat successfully took on new tasks during the 1985, 1991, and 1996–1997 IGCs, acting in support of successive presidencies. Insofar as heads of state and government and foreign ministers treat the secretary-general as a preferred adviser, the Commission president and his colleagues often charge that he is exercising undue influence, not least when the European Council and the Council decide not to follow the Commission's advice. The Commission also resents the Council secretariat's higher institutional profile in the 1990s: The TEU revised the EC treaty to include a reference to the Council secretariat for the first time in one of the founding treaties (Article 207.2, formerly Article 151.2 TEC).

The Amsterdam Treaty changed the role of the Council secretary-general in a potentially important respect. Previously, the secretary-general simply ran the Council secretariat. After Amsterdam, the secretary-general became the "High Representative" for the CFSP, and a deputy secretary-general assumed responsibility for running the General Secretariat (Article

207.2 TEC). Depending on how the CFSP develops, the secretary-general could assume a representational and possibly a political role distinct from that of previous secretaries-general.

The Politics of the Presidency

Despite the onerous responsibilities of the Council presidency (even with the Council secretariat's expert assistance), member states jealously guard their right to take a turn at the EU's helm. Small countries especially welcome the opportunity to play a more prominent part in shaping the EU's agenda and understandably enjoy being in the international limelight. The presidency can easily be turned to domestic political advantage either by distracting attention from pressing problems or by enhancing the government's prestige and popularity. The presidency hosts numerous events during a six-month term, ranging from at least one European Council to informal meetings of EU ministers to cultural and academic conferences. By distributing these spoils throughout the country, the government can score valuable political points. Presidencies also have an important educational function, especially in Euroskeptical countries. Thus the new Labour government attempted to use Britain's presidency in early 1998 to enlighten the British public about the potential benefits of EU membership.

Politically, the presidency can hold a crumbling coalition together. The Dutch coalition government survived a political crisis in August 1991 over social welfare partly because all parties agreed that the cabinet's collapse would have damaged the country's presidency. The Danish government was not so lucky in January 1992, when holding the Council presidency did not prevent it from falling as a result of a domestic political scandal. National elections sometimes coincide with a country's turn in the presidency, generally to the presidency's detriment. Such was the case during Germany's presidency in late 1994 (federal elections took place in October) and during France's presidency in early 1995 (presidential elections took place in May). On each occasion, the German or French leaderships were preoccupied with electoral politics at the expense of Europolitics.

In their eagerness to trumpet presidential achievements, member states take credit for agreements reached during their term in office even if the necessary preparatory work took place during a previous presidency. Countries about to assume the presidency may be tempted to obstruct decisionmaking during the dying days of their predecessors' presidencies in order to delay agreement until they themselves are sitting in the Council chair. However, the risks are great that such behavior would rebound on the incoming presidency. As a result, member states almost always play by the rules.

Also for domestic political reasons, the country in office is more likely than other member states to make concessions, especially during a meeting of the European Council, in order to increase its presidency's productivity and prestige. Such was the case in Cannes in May 1995, when Jacques Chirac, the newly elected French president, dropped his earlier opposition to increasing France's contribution to the European Development Fund, thereby resolving an issue that threatened to overshadow the summit.

The rotating presidency is a powerful symbol of equality between member states. It also brings home to each government "the full responsibilities of Community membership."[6] Yet the system is inherently inefficient: Some small countries have great difficulty managing a successful presidency; six months is arguably too short a term to pursue a particular legislative program; and frequent rotation impedes the continuity of some EU activities, notably in the intergovernmental pillars. Member states tackled the problem of continuity by establishing the "troika," a system whereby officials from the foreign ministries of the current, immediately preceding, and immediately succeeding presidencies cooperate closely and continuously.

The EU has frequently addressed but never resolved the fundamental problems of the rotating presidency. The 1975 Tindemans Report advocated extending the presidency to twelve months, but to no avail.[7] A twelve-month presidency would mean that countries would have to wait twice as long for their turn in the limelight (a wait of twenty years in a twenty–member state EU), a prospect uncongenial to politicians and national civil servants alike. Alternative proposals have included allowing only the larger countries to assume the presidency alone with other member states sharing the office on a regional basis. Suggestions to that effect by Commission president Jacques Delors in early 1992 triggered a strong reaction in Denmark and may have caused some voters there to reject the TEU in the fateful June referendum.

Roy Jenkins, Commission president in the late 1970s, observed in his *European Diary* that "the authority of Council presidencies varies substantially. A new member country can be overawed, a small country overstrained and even a big old member country like Germany can suffer from a lack of coordination within its government. France was neither new nor small and its government, whatever else could be said about it, did not suffer from a lack of coordination. The tradition and the expectations therefore were that France provided the most authoritative Presidency."[8] Jenkins experienced a particularly bumpy French presidency in early 1979, when Giscard d'Estaing was at his most ambivalent about European integration. Two of the three subsequent French presidencies proved extremely productive: Under François Mitterrand's strong pro-EC guidance, France provided excellent leadership in early 1984 during the final stages of the British budgetary question and in late 1989 during the revolution in Central and Eastern Europe.

Portugal held its first-ever presidency in early 1992. Despite intense preparation in Lisbon, few other member states believed that Portugal had either the experience or the resources to do an adequate job. Partly for that reason, member states resolved to wrap up the IGCs at Maastricht in December 1991 and not, as happened during the 1985 IGC, delay important decisions until the new year. In the event, the Portuguese presidency conducted routine EU business competently and skillfully, made impressive progress on the single market program, and negotiated the final stage of Common Agricultural Policy (CAP) reform. It was unfortunate for Portugal that the Danish referendum and the outbreak of war in Bosnia took place during its watch.

Britain has a mixed record as Council president but has a well-deserved reputation at least for running good meetings. Britain's presidency in early 1998 was especially significant because of the new Labour government's self-proclaimed support for European integration despite a continuing reservation on the question of a single currency. The Labour Party's long period in opposition (between 1979 and 1997) put the new government at a disadvantage in the Council: Few ministers had any experience of Council meetings or much acquaintance with ministers from other member states. Nevertheless, Britain's noted organizational and negotiating skills helped the government make progress in one of it's priority areas: completion of the single market (despite the 1992 deadline, a number of proposed directives had not been enacted and many directives had not been implemented). Britain was able to bask in the glory of two ceremonial events: the launch of enlargement negotiations and the selection of eleven member states (excluding Britain itself) for participation in Stage III of EMU. In other respects Britain's presidential record is mixed, mostly because of circumstances beyond the country's control. For instance, Britain was unfairly criticized for not having brokered an agreement between France and Germany over the selection of the first president of the European Central Bank at the Brussels summit in May 1998. Usually in such circumstances, it is incumbent upon the presidency to come up with a compromise and head off a crisis. Britain failed to do so not because of indifference or neglect, however, but because of the entrenched and highly publicized positions of France and Germany.

The EU's impending enlargement to twenty or twenty-one member states, and ultimately perhaps to twenty-six member states, highlights the impracticability of a rotating presidency. Yet new member states appreciate the symbolism of occasionally representing the EU, and all member states value the potential political advantages of being in the presidency. As a result, it is unlikely that the rotating presidency will ever be reformed fundamentally; instead it will remain one of the EU's most distinctive governmental features.

EUROPE'S MOST EXCLUSIVE CLUB

In a press conference at the end of the December 1974 Paris summit, French president Giscard d'Estaing declared with a rhetorical flourish that "the European Summit is dead, long live the European Council."[9] The EC's leaders had just decided to replace their ad hoc meetings with regular triannual get-togethers. The Paris summit communiqué can therefore be called "the constitution of the European Council";[10] but the European Council never became a formal institution. In the three sets of treaty amendments since 1974—the SEA, the TEU, and the Amsterdam Treaty—the European Council never received the status of an official institution (the official institutions are listed in Article 7.1, formerly Article 4.1). The SEA merely recognized the European Council's existence and importance, whereas the TEU codified its composition and number of annual meetings. The TEU nevertheless specified that "the European Council shall provide the Union with the necessary impetus for its development and shall define the general guidelines thereof" (Article 4, formerly Article D TEU).

It seems paradoxical that the TEU enhanced the European Council's political importance but failed to formalize its institutional status. From the outset, however, informality and spontaneity have characterized the European Council and ensured its effectiveness. Undoubtedly, meetings of the European Council have become more methodical, structured, and stylized over the years; yet their relative freedom from legal rules and regulations remains a key ingredient of their success. Nor do the member states want to tip the EU's constitutional balance in favor of intergovernmentalism by formally institutionalizing the European Council. Although the emergence of the European Council did not weaken supranationalism, by elevating it to the status of an institution the member states would implicitly reinforce intergovernmentalism in the EU system.

Origin and Development

Giscard d'Estaing was primarily responsible for the European Council's emergence, but most of his EC colleagues agreed by 1974 that top-level meetings would have to take place more often. The decisive contribution of the 1969 Hague summit and the 1972 Paris summit to the EC's revitalization after the "decade of de Gaulle" convinced most government leaders of the need for regular meetings. Giscard, who had a penchant for intimate gatherings of powerful people, invited his fellow national leaders to meet without foreign ministers or civil servants at the Elysée Palace in September 1974 to discuss the EC's future. British prime minister Harold Wilson, who had replaced Heath earlier that year, recalled sitting uncomfortably "in high-backed chairs [without tables] in a horse-shoe formation" while Giscard proposed holding regular summit meetings.[11] Wilson and

Chancellor Schmidt suggested that foreign ministers attend also, and all agreed to defer a decision until later in the year.

Fundamental changes in the international system, rather than simply de Gaulle's departure, had made regular summit meetings more important than ever before. The early 1970s were years of rapid political, economic, and monetary transformation. The zenith of détente, the launch of *Ostpolitik,* the unveiling of EPC, international currency turmoil, and the onset of Eurosclerosis broke down barriers among domestic and foreign policy and called for closer coordination among member states. The EC's institutional framework was ill-equipped to provide the kind of direction and leadership needed in a distinct new phase of the postwar period. Only the heads of state and government had the authority and perspective required to steer the EC through the shoals ahead.

In his final contribution to European integration, Jean Monnet, then in his nineties but still intellectually alert, advocated a "provisional European government" to cope with the changing circumstances of the early 1970s.[12] Giscard and others never saw the European Council in that light, but their desire for regular summitry squared with Monnet's call for stronger political leadership in the EC. Monnet's valedictory blessing enhanced the European Council's Eurocredentials and helped protect it from charges that it unduly strengthened intergovernmentalism in the EU system.

The first European Council took place in Dublin in March 1975 and brought the renegotiation of Britain's EC membership to a successful conclusion. However, for the remainder of the 1970s the European Council dealt less with emergency matters than with prevailing economic and political problems. With decisionmaking in the Council thrown into low gear by the Luxembourg Compromise and member states reeling from the impact of the oil crisis and the ensuing recession, the European Council played a pivotal role in keeping the EC together. These were the years of undisguised Franco-German predominance, personified by the Giscard-Schmidt duopoly of EC leadership. The French and German leaders dominated European Council proceedings with masterful, impromptu presentations on international affairs. They barely tolerated the Commission president's attendance, although Roy Jenkins eventually won their respect.

In his diary, Jenkins recalls a summit at which Schmidt took Jenkins aside while Giscard was speaking: "Giscard allowed this to go by without comment or sign of umbrage. If one is so foolish as to believe in the equality of the [European] Council," Jenkins remarked, "one has only to think how differently he would have reacted if it had been, say, [Irish prime minister] Lynch or [Luxembourg prime minister] Thorn who had come round the table and taken me away."[13] More than twenty years later, the inequality inherent in such an ostensibly egalitarian body was obvious when Chirac and Kohl ignored their colleagues for several hours at the Brussels summit in May 1998 in order to argue privately over the selection of the president of the European Central Bank. The French and German leaders' behavior led Jean-Luc Dehaene, prime minister of Belgium and host of the summit, to quip that the other participants should abandon Chirac and Kohl and go downtown for lunch.[14]

In the early 1980s, the European Council's composition, rationale, and internal dynamics changed dramatically. Over a three-year period Mitterrand and Kohl replaced Giscard and Schmidt. The Franco-German alliance continued to predominate, but Mitterrand and Kohl lacked their predecessors' intellectual sharpness and, initially at least, their personal closeness. For five years, while the European Council was bogged down in the British budgetary question, the heads of state and government found themselves debating the minutiae of agricultural prices and member states' financial contributions. Resolution of the budgetary dispute at Fontainebleau in June 1984 finally allowed the European Council to revert to its original role as a forum for discussion of the EC's long-term political and economic direction. Nevertheless, the European Council remained directly involved in the EC's immediate development and became "the decisive actor, the final arbiter, in the development of the internal market."[15] The heads of state and government immersed themselves in detailed bargaining during the IGC that led to the SEA, spending twenty hours at the December 1985 Luxembourg summit locked in technical negotiations.

Undoubtedly the European Council had proved its usefulness, but three meetings annually seemed unnecessary. Accordingly, the SEA stipulated that the European Council "shall meet at least twice a year" (now Article 4 TEU). Thereafter the European Council settled into a routine of meeting at the end of each presidency, although additional, "extraordinary" summits tend to take place at least once a year, if not once a presidency.

If the European Council appeared to be lapsing into lethargy after the decisive deliberations leading up to the SEA, developments in the late 1980s and early 1990s—the success of the single market program, the situation in Central and Eastern Europe, and the TEU ratification crisis—emphasized the significance of summitry for the EU's future. The European Council found itself convening extraordinary meetings to resolve such fundamental issues and discuss such critical questions as the Delors I budgetary package (Brussels, February 1988), the fall of the Berlin Wall (Paris, November 1989), imminent German unification (Dublin, April 1990), and the impending IGCs (Rome, October 1990).

Just as changes in the international system had precipitated the European Council's inauguration in the mid-1970s, a sudden transformation to an entirely new international system in the late 1980s, prompting widespread treaty reform, enhanced the European Council's importance. The high political stakes and intergovernmental nature of treaty change ensured a key role for the European Council in the 1991 and 1996–1997 IGCs. National leaders were as involved in negotiating treaty reform at the Maastricht summit in December 1991 and the Amsterdam summit in June 1997 as they had been at the Luxembourg summit in December 1985. Moreover, specific policy or procedural provisions of the TEU and Amsterdam Treaty, such as for EMU and the CFSP (in the TEU) and flexibility (in the Amsterdam Treaty) specified key decisionmaking roles for the European Council.

The European Council operates almost exclusively on the basis of consensus. Although participants may disagree strongly on many issues, regular voting would sour the atmosphere and alter the dynamics of the cozy Euroclub. Only rarely has the presidency ever called for a vote in the European Council. The most notable occasion was in June 1985, when the European Council voted by 7 to 3 (there were then ten member states) to hold the IGC that resulted in the SEA.

Roles and Responsibilities

Apart from a few specific decisionmaking functions, the European Council's primary purpose is to provide strategic direction by considering the EU's and the member states' policies and priorities as an organic whole rather than as separate and competing ingredients. Other functions that have either existed from the outset or developed during the past two decades include acquainting the heads of state and government with each other and with each other's views on economic, social, and political issues; discussing recent international developments and issuing important foreign policy statements and declarations; reconciling differences between the EU's external economic relations and the member states' foreign policies; resolving extraordinary budgetary disputes and deciding the multi-annual budgetary framework; setting the agenda for further integration; negotiating key treaty revisions during intergovernmental conferences; and appointing the Commission president and the president of the European Central Bank.

Because of their political sensitivity, these roles and responsibilities are peculiar to the European Council and could not be performed by another EU body. But the European Council serves another purpose that possibly weakens the EU system. By acting as a "court of appeal" for the Council of Ministers, the European Council undermines its own and the Council's efficiency. Although the European Council must take ultimate responsibility, too often it becomes involved in deciding issues that should have been settled at a lower level.

The "Three Wise Men" (Barend Bushevel, Edmund Dell, Robert Marjolin) advised in 1979 that the European Council should not allow regular decisionmaking to dominate its agenda lest it become merely "an extension of the Council of Ministers."[16] Six years later, the Dooge Report warned emphatically that "the trend toward the European Council becoming simply another body dealing with the day-to-day business of the Community must be reversed."[17] The increasing use of qualified majority voting (QMV) since the early 1980s has reduced some of the pressure on the European Council to replicate the Council's work, but a continuing need for unanimity on certain issues ensures that to some extent, the European Council will always be the final decisionmaking authority.

Procedures

Under the direction of the Council presidency, member state civil servants, Commission officials, and officials of the Council secretariat prepare the European Council agenda. An informal agenda and a draft summit communiqué begin to take shape at meetings of COREPER and of CFSP and Justice and Home Affairs (JHA) supporting committees, and are discussed at length at a foreign ministers meeting held about two weeks before each summit. Traditionally, a few days before the European Council the prime minister or president of the host country sends a letter to the other summit participants outlining the principal themes and agenda for the meeting. In keeping with the European Council's supposed informality, however, participants decide the final agenda themselves at the opening session. Apart from good preparatory work and a competent presidency, material considerations such as the summit's location can affect the outcome.

Regardless of its functions, the European Council's format has not changed much over time. Most summits are two-day affairs, usually beginning with lunch on day one and ending on the afternoon of day two. Extraordinary summits, convened by the presidency to discuss specific issues or developments, tend to be shorter, lasting no more than a day or even a single evening. The heads of state and government, their foreign ministers, the Commission president, and a Commission vice president participate in almost all of the sessions, and the Council and Commission secretary-generals are present throughout. The president of the EP makes a statement before the opening session of each European Council (but does not attend the summit proper), setting forth Parliament's views on the various agenda items. Because unemployment is one of the most important items on the EU agenda, the troika of heads of state and government meets representatives of the social partners on the evening before the summit begins.

Although the principals meet in a relatively small group, an army of advisers and handlers is never far away. Permanent representatives, members of the CFSP and JHA supporting committees, and other high-level officials cluster in groups in adjoining rooms, furiously drafting bits of the communiqué that, piece by piece, comes before the heads of state and government for adoption. The Danish presidency set a precedent at the Copenhagen summit in April 1978 by asking the Council secretariat to provide note-takers at the main sessions. However, the note-takers' main function is unofficial: After their twenty-minute spells with the heads of state and government, they immediately tell accompanying officials what transpired in the meeting. Including interpreters, a relatively small number of people—usually about forty-five—are privy to the European Council's deliberations.

Dinner at the end of day one is restricted to the heads of state and government and the Commission president. Depending on the length of the preceding session, dinner can begin late and end in the early hours of the morning. Dinner is usually followed by the traditional "fireside chat," when EU leaders are supposedly at their most relaxed and informal. The halcyon days of the fireside chat were in the 1970s, during the Giscard-Schmidt duopoly. Since then, EU leaders have often canceled the European Council's most intimate session in order to continue ordinary business.

Most summits officially end with the Council and Commission presidents' press conference after the morning session on day two. Since the Essen summit of December 1994, at least one European Council each year ends with lunch attended by the heads of state and government of all the EU's applicant and member states. Occasionally summits run late into the afternoon or evening of day two. Such was the case at Maastricht in December 1991, where agreement on the social chapter proved elusive. In addition to making various political and intellectual arguments, Ruud Lubbers, the Dutch prime minister, used hunger, fatigue, and exasperation to coax a settlement and save the TEU. The relatively youthful Lubbers and Major had considerably more stamina than their older colleagues, notably the septuagenarian Mitterrand. A similar situation happened at Amsterdam in June 1997, although there the heads of state and government failed to reach agreement on institutional reform and decided to conclude the IGC without it.

Personalities, Politics, and Publicity

The heads of state and government meet often in the European Council and get to know each other well. Few leaders have ever missed a Eurosummit. EU leaders also participate in a dense network of bilateral and plurilateral meetings. Some are institutionalized; others are not. Examples include the annual European Conference; bilateral meetings between the Council president and the other heads of state and government before each European Council; summits of European political party leaders, also held regularly before each European Council; and six-monthly Franco-German summits held under the auspices of the 1963 Elysée Treaty. In addition, many heads of state and government meet at other international events, such as NATO summits, Organization for Security and Cooperation in Europe (OSCE) summits, and Asia-Europe meetings.

Despite personal and political differences, the heads of state and government have a powerful common denominator: All were elected to their country's highest office. Well aware of the perils and pitfalls of political life, knowing each other extremely well, and enjoying membership in Europe's most exclusive club, they are careful never to do or say anything that could weaken their colleagues' domestic positions. Even Margaret Thatcher and John Major, who infuriated their fellow EU leaders, enjoyed the respect of their political peers. Only Greek prime minister Andreas Papandreou, a vituperative critic of the EU, was despised in the European Council to the point that other leaders longed for his political downfall.

Being astute politicians, EU leaders appreciate the European Council's publicity value. As one observer noted early in the history of the European Council, "all summit meetings are to a greater or lesser degree public relations exercises."[18] Indeed, recent European Councils have turned into huge media events with over 1,500 journalists covering important summits. Although intimate and supposedly private, summit deliberations are far from confidential. Even as discussions continue, the note-takers' reports to officials quickly make their way to waiting journalists and into news bulletins. During session breaks and immediately after the summit, ministers and officials brief journalists—especially journalists from their own countries—on what transpired.

Responding during the TEU ratification crisis to public criticism of the EU's opaque decisionmaking process, John Major proposed televising a one-hour opening session of the special Birmingham summit in October 1992. His colleagues were horrified. Allowing television cameras into the summit, even for a short session, would encourage posturing and grandstanding and wreck the European Council's intimacy. In any event, summits are relatively transparent. An observation made by Roy Jenkins in 1989 is as valid today as it was then: The European Council is "a restricted meeting with full subsequent publicity, which is perhaps not a bad formula."[19]

THE COUNCIL OF MINISTERS

By contrast with the European Council, the Council of Ministers' deliberations were rarely disclosed to the public before the upheaval caused by the TEU ratification crisis. Indeed, due to excessive secretiveness, a leading scholar noted in 1991 that "[political] behavior inside the Council of Ministers is the least well studied or understood part of the activities of the European Community."[20] The Council's opaqueness was a major cause of the democratic deficit and inflamed the TEU ratification crisis. As Neils Ersbøll later commented, only one country, the Netherlands, was aware during the 1991 IGC that there could be a transparency problem. Not only that, but "all the other countries tried to strangle the Dutch attempt" at openness.[21] In a bid to regain public confidence after the Danish rejection of the TEU, the heads of state and government pledged themselves at the

Birmingham summit to open up the work of EU institutions, "including the possibility of some open Council discussions."[22]

Government ministers were never shy about publicizing their achievements in the Council, but they usually did so in a way that increased the perception of democratic unaccountability and heightened institutional tension. In the run-up to Birmingham, an unidentified Commission spokesman deplored the way that ministers manipulated the media and vilified the Commission after Council meetings. "Ministers who hold their own press conferences for journalists from their countries in rooms reserved for national representatives at the top of the Council building," the Commission official complained, "have a disgraceful habit of presenting the outcome as a victory of their national delegation against the Commission. That's not the best attitude to adopt if you want to create a European spirit."[23]

Pressure from the Dutch, from the public, and from other institutions (notably the EP) for transparency in EU decisionmaking appalled COREPER, the Council secretariat, and most of the ministers themselves. As far as most national and Council civil servants were (and still are) concerned, public involvement would distract decisionmakers and impair the Council's efficiency. As for the ministers themselves, the confidentiality of Council deliberations was a welcome corrective to the intrusiveness that generally pervades domestic political decisionmaking. Given that neither body wanted to open its doors, it is ironic that the Council charged COREPER with finding ways to implement the Birmingham summit's promise of greater transparency. By the same token, it is not surprising that COREPER's recommendations and the Council's actions were so timid.

In its defense, the Council could legitimately claim that it is not only the EU's colegislator but also an intergovernmental negotiating forum. Critics point out that the Council is the only legislature in the Western world that severely curtails public access to its deliberations; the Council contends that its diplomatic persona precludes full disclosure of its activities. The Council and its critics have attempted to tackle the transparency problem by providing access to Council documents and meetings, although the Council is unenthusiastic about doing either. Access to meetings is severely restricted. Media representatives and members of the public may not attend meetings themselves but may view a small number of "public ministerial debates," televised live in an auditorium in Brussels (or in Luxembourg if the Council meets there), only if they have received permission in advance to enter the auditorium (some of the debates are also broadcast live or later by the Commission's audiovisual "Europe by Satellite" information service).

Inevitably these broadcasts have a small audience (few people can afford to go to Brussels or Luxembourg to watch them, and Europe by Satellite is not widely available). Few people might watch them even if they were widely broadcast, although the popularity of C SPAN in the United

States shows that even the most arcane political discussions have a peculiar fascination. Yet the limited openness of Council meetings reveals little of how the Council really works because ministers restrict themselves while on television to bland, predictable statements. John Palmer, doyen of the Brussels press corps and a persistent critic of the Council, claimed that "the decision to open certain sessions of the Council of Ministers is in danger of becoming an irrelevant circus where ministers read from texts and do not engage in any debate or exchange whatsoever. This is actually making a mockery of the openness principle."[24]

What some ministers see as an assault on their privacy has led them to seek refuge in a sacred Brussels institution: the working lunch. Not only are ministers free of cameras at lunchtime but they are also free of the hordes of officials who attend them in meetings. This dual freedom allows ministers to be unusually frank with each other and to make concessions that they might not otherwise make. Sometimes even the most senior officials are absent from the detailed and substantive discussions that take place in that way. Apart from complicating the officials' work (minutes of the lunchtime discussions need to be constructed from the ministers' often unreliable memories), the ministers' lunchtime seclusion means that officials cannot brief reporters on the course of the discussions (an indirect way of broadcasting Council meetings).

Whereas access to Council meetings remains extremely limited, public access to Council documents has improved greatly since the early 1990s. By a declaration annexed to the TEU and by a decision of December 1993 on public access to its documents, the Council established a right of access to information and a procedure for those wanting to exercise that right (an earlier interinstitutional agreement, of October 1993, dealt with the same matter). Angered by the Council's refusal to grant access to documents requested by it, Britain's *Guardian* newspaper took the Council to the Court of Justice in 1994 with the support of the EP, the Netherlands, and Denmark. The *Guardian*'s victory (the Court ruled in October 1995 that the Council had failed to strike a balance between the public's need for access and the Council's need for confidentiality) led the Council to revise and relax its policy toward transparency.

Nevertheless, the quality of Council documents released to the public remains poor, as they do not include substantive accounts of bargaining and negotiating. Writing in 1996, a scholar of EU decisionmaking noted that "with its notorious and contested secrecy, there is very little knowledge about what really happens in Council meetings."[25] Under further public pressure, and under internal pressure not only from the Netherlands but also (since 1995) from Finland and especially Sweden, member states agreed during the 1996–1997 IGC to include a "transparency clause" in the Amsterdam Treaty (Article 255 TEC). This stipulates that "any citizen of the Union . . . shall have a right of access to European Parliament,

Council or Commission documents" subject to certain principles and conditions. A separate treaty article clarified this clause with reference to the Council's dual nature as a legislative and a diplomatic body: "The Council shall define the cases in which it is to be regarded as acting in its legislative capacity, with a view to allowing greater access to documents in those cases, while at the same time preserving the effectiveness of its decision-making process. . . . When the Council acts in its legislative capacity, the results of votes and explanations of votes as well as statements in the minutes shall be made public" (Article 207.3 TEC).

Composition and Subcommittees

In the original EC treaty, Article 146 stipulated that "each government shall delegate to [the Council] one of its members." This stipulation was changed in the TEU, which described the Council as consisting of "representatives of each member state at ministerial level authorized to commit the government of that member state" (now Article 203 TEC). The reason for this change was to accommodate federal member states, such as Germany and Belgium, where members of regional governments had insisted on representation in the Council when the Council discussed issues that, in their own countries, were the responsibility of regional rather than federal government. Thus members of subnational as well as national governments occasionally sit around the Council table.

Although legally there is only one Council, in practice there are several councils organized along horizontal (e.g., foreign affairs, finance) and sectoral (e.g., agriculture, internal market, transport) lines. All are technically equal, but some are more equal than others. Because of the EU's expanding competence, the number of these councils has grown steadily over the years to more than twenty. The multiplication of councils supposedly increases efficiency by allowing government ministers to decide issues in their particular areas of expertise and also distributes responsibility for EU decisionmaking among a wider circle of cabinet colleagues.

The number of council meetings held annually depends on the scope and intensity of EU legislation and on the political momentum behind a particular issue. Some councils meet monthly; others meet every six months. Regardless of which sector it represents, a council has supreme decisionmaking authority. It is also empowered to make decisions relating to issues beyond its particular area of expertise. A council automatically approves any "A" points on its agenda whether or not those points pertain to that council's area of responsibility ("A" points are items already agreed or at a lower level that COREPER places on the Council's agenda for formal approval).

Despite the official pretense of equality, there is a strict hierarchy of councils based on political and economic importance. The Council of Foreign

Ministers—the so-called General Affairs Council (GAC)—was traditionally at the top. This placement harks back to the early days of European integration, when countries saw EC membership as a fundamental foreign policy concern. As integration intruded into "every nook and cranny of daily life,"[26] however, it became impossible to distinguish between the foreign and domestic implications of EU membership. Accordingly, finance and economics ministers, who make up the so-called ECOFIN Council, demanded a greater say in EU affairs and, in many member states, challenged their foreign affairs colleagues for preeminence in domestic interministerial coordination. National bureaucratic rivalry over policymaking toward Brussels, and over decisionmaking in Brussels itself, remains endemic. EMU has greatly enhanced ECOFIN's prominence in Brussels and finance ministers' influence in the coordination of national policy toward the EU. As a result, foreign ministers are struggling to retain their predominant bureaucratic positions.

The GAC has two main responsibilities: decisionmaking in the field of EU foreign policy (mostly trade and development policy) and horizontal coordination of other policy areas (on the ground that foreign ministers possess a broad political and economic perspective on European integration that other ministers lack). The development of EPC and subsequently of the CFSP further enhanced the status and increased the workload of the GAC and its members. Originally, foreign ministers had to distinguish rigidly between EC business and foreign policy cooperation. But as member states grew less sensitive about EPC and more concerned about reconciling the EC's external economic relations with their own foreign policies, the distinction became blurred. Finally, member states agreed in Title III of the SEA that as well as meeting specifically to discuss international issues, foreign ministers could "discuss foreign policy matters within the framework of Political Cooperation on the occasion of meetings of the Council of the European Communities."

The sheer volume of CFSP, trade policy, and development policy issues that come up for discussion at the GAC leaves foreign ministers with little time to devote to coordination of other policy areas. The agenda of the monthly GAC meetings includes "high political issues" that cut across sectoral lines as well as issues that the sectoral councils could not decide. Here the GAC runs the same risk as the European Council: Issues that should be settled at a lower level are pushed up to a higher level. The GAC's tendency to become a glorified sectoral council or even a glorified COREPER diminishes the foreign ministers' effectiveness and tends to increase absenteeism.

Foreign ministers' extraordinary travel schedules also explain why they sometimes miss regular GACs. In addition to attending numerous bilateral and multilateral meetings under the EU's auspices, foreign ministers participate in a host of other meetings—for instance, meetings of the United Nations, the OSCE, the Western European Union, and NATO.

At these gatherings, they have additional opportunities to conduct EU business and to get to know each other better (personal considerations and political empathy are as important in the GAC as in the European Council). Although they see each other often, however, foreign ministers have far less intimate meetings in the GAC than their bosses have in the European Council. Whereas attendance at the European Council is strictly limited, General Affairs Councils include large numbers of officials. Offended by the "football pitch atmosphere," British foreign secretary David Owen tried to reduce the attendance at General Affairs Councils during Britain's presidency in 1977.[27] Using the same metaphor, Roy Jenkins described the General Affairs Council as having "up to 300 people present in a huge room, talking from one end of the table to the other as though across an empty football pitch."[28]

In fact, each delegation has three seats at the General Affairs Council table and six seats behind, although sometimes as many as ten additional advisers accompany each delegation's top three (the foreign ministers, the most senior foreign ministry adviser, and the Brussels-based permanent representative). The Council president can cut down on the number present by calling for a restricted session—usually "inner table only," occasionally ministers and Commissioner only. As already noted, lunch affords an opportunity for an intimate gathering of the meeting's principals.

Once during each presidency, the foreign ministers and the Commission president or vice president escape with a few aides for an informal discussion of foreign and security policy. The first such event was at Schloss Gymnich, during Germany's presidency in early 1974. These biannual retreats are now known as "Gymnich-type" meetings and always take place in lavish settings and surroundings. Most are memorable for their cuisine and conviviality rather than for serious work.

ECOFIN is on a par with, or is still perhaps one rung immediately below its foreign ministers counterpart, followed by the Agriculture Council. Despite the steady decline in EU spending on agriculture, it would be wrong to think that the Agriculture Council's importance is decreasing. Protracted debate in the early 1990s about CAP reform, especially in the context of the Uruguay Round negotiations, maintained the Agriculture Council's political prominence, as did debate in the late 1990s about further CAP reform in the context of enlargement. Of the other councils, the Internal Market Council is especially important. Founded in 1983 to help remove nontariff barriers (NTBs) to intra-EC trade, the Internal Market Council was instrumental in launching and sustaining the single market program.

The Committee of Permanent Representatives

COREPER plays a vital part in preparing council meetings. Article 4 of the 1965 Merger Treaty recognized COREPER's existence and responsibilities. A separate development early the following year further enhanced

COREPER's standing: The Luxembourg Compromise of January 1966 boosted the institutional position of the Council vis-à-vis the Commission and in the process strengthened COREPER's role. At the Paris summit in December 1974, the heads of government decided to give COREPER additional power "so that only the most important problems need to be discussed in the Council."[29]

The Commission has always looked askance at COREPER, a highly influential committee of the member states' most senior civil servants. As the Commission's own position strengthened under Delors, however, relations with COREPER improved. Indeed, the harmonious COREPER-Commission relationship—specifically, the relationship between COREPER and the Commission's secretariat-general—was a key ingredient of the Community's transformation in the late 1980s and early 1990s.

The member states' permanent representations (embassies) to the EU include national bureaucrats from a range of government departments on assignment in Brussels. Member states rank the permanent representation among their most important diplomatic missions. The caliber and effectiveness of permanent representative officials determines to a great extent how countries fare in the EU. As for the officials themselves, it may be more prestigious to serve in Washington, D.C., or in the capital of another member state (notably London, Paris, or Bonn), but a posting to the permanent representation in Brussels is a sound career move.

The heads of the permanent representations sit on COREPER, although the committee's huge workload has resulted in COREPER I, consisting of the deputy permanent representatives, and COREPER II, consisting of the permanent representatives themselves. COREPER I has an especially heavy workload, covering agriculture, fisheries, the internal market, industry, the budget, research, transport, the environment, social affairs, energy, education, cultural affairs, health, and consumer protection. COREPER II deals with "high policy issues" that come before the General Affairs Council (notably external economic relations, CFSP, JHA, treaty reform, and enlargement) and ECOFIN (notably non-EMU–related issues). Once a subject is given to COREPER I, COREPER II has nothing more to do with it. The division between one list of subjects and another is strict.

COREPER's job is to prepare the councils' agendas, to decide which issues go to which council, and to set up and monitor legislative working groups of permanent representatives or other national officials (at least ten such groups meet on a given workday in Brussels). Each part of COREPER meets at least once a week. The permanent representatives also brief visiting ministers and other dignitaries and report regularly to their national capitals on developments in the EU. Like their ministerial bosses, permanent representatives become well acquainted with each other. Also like their senior ministers, they enjoy biannual retreats at the expense of the Council presidency.

A special agriculture committee substitutes for COREPER by preparing meetings of the Agriculture Council, although COREPER continues to deal with the political implications of agricultural issues (such as CAP reform or international trade agreements) on behalf of the GAC. ECOFIN also has a committee that sidesteps COREPER on certain matters. Whereas COREPER prepares a number of ECOFIN agenda items, a separate monetary committee (renamed the Economic and Finance Committee in January 1999) made up of officials from national finance ministries (plus representatives of national central banks after 1999) advises ECOFIN on EMU issues without reference to COREPER.

COREPER escaped criticism during and after the TEU ratification crisis because its existence and functions were little known outside Brussels. Yet COREPER is extremely powerful and even more secretive than the Council. COREPER's ability to shape the Council's agenda and influence decisionmaking by categorizing items as either ready for automatic approval (A items) or for discussion and decision (B items) illustrates its importance and suggests that, in certain cases, COREPER is the EU's real legislature. COREPER's unaccountability to the electorate and inaccessibility to the public are key contributors to the EU's democratic deficit. Yet COREPER's obscurity continues to shield it from public criticism, and its professionalism ensures generally favorable media coverage.

DECISIONMAKING

Speaking at the opening session of the intergovernmental conference that preceded the SEA, Delors denounced "the ball and chain of unanimity that bedevils the whole Community system."[30] Under the terms of the TEC, a number of issues became subject to qualified majority voting (QMV) in the Council on January 1, 1966. However, the Luxembourg Compromise at the end of the month meant that in practice the Council did not adopt QMV. In consequence, decisionmaking slowed to a snail's pace as member states refrained from calling for a vote in deference to each other's real or supposed "vital national interests." Legislative paralysis became chronic in the mid-1970s following the first enlargement (Britain and Denmark strongly opposed majority voting) and during a period of prolonged recession when most countries sought national rather than EC solutions to Eurosclerosis.

The legislative situation improved gradually in the early 1980s as political pressure mounted to complete the single market and revive European integration. A plethora of reports and proposals—from Tindemans (1975) to the Three Wise Men (1979) to Genscher-Colombo (1981)—called on member states to expedite decisionmaking by voting rather than vetoing in the Council. In a famous speech to the EP in May 1984, Mitterrand renounced the Luxembourg Compromise, which de Gaulle had been instrumental in bringing about, and advocated a "return to the Treaty" through "the more frequent practice of voting on important issues."[31]

The EC's imminent enlargement and the member states' increasing interest in completing the single market focused attention in the mid-1980s squarely on reform of the Council's decisionmaking procedure. In the SEA, national governments not only committed themselves to achieving a single market by the end of 1992 but also agreed to do so largely through QMV in the Council. By implication, this was the end of the Luxembourg Compromise. Subsequent practice confirmed that countries were indeed willing to play by new rules and risk being outvoted on a wide range of issues. Also, subsequent treaty changes (especially in the TEU) extended the applicability of QMV in EU decisionmaking.

The specter of the Luxembourg Compromise rose briefly in 1996 when the British government embarked upon a policy of "noncooperation" in the Council in order to protest the EU's ban on exports of British beef during the bovine spongiform encephalopathy (BSE) crisis. For two months (May and June), the British blocked agreement on a number of items in the Council that required unanimity. The policy was a failure, both tactically and strategically, and served largely to isolate Britain in the EU. It also demonstrated the limited usefulness of a national veto in an EU that encompasses so many interconnected policy areas. Thus the British applied their noncooperation policy selectively and often against their immediate policy interests.[32]

Ironically in view of the demise of the Luxembourg Compromise, a Luxembourg Compromise–like decisionmaking procedure found its way into the Amsterdam Treaty with respect to the possible use of flexibility (closer cooperation among member states). Article 11.2 TEC states that "for important and stated reasons of national policy," a member state may prevent a vote being taken in the Council on whether to allow flexibility. In such circumstances, the Council could decide by QMV to send the matter to the heads of state and government for a decision by unanimity. However, the inclusion of a quasi-national veto in the Amsterdam Treaty with respect to flexibility and, elsewhere in the treaty, with respect to "constructive abstention" in CFSP decisionmaking reflects the extreme political sensitivity of these policy areas rather than a reassertion of intergovernmentalism in the EU system.

The Vagaries of QMV

Paradoxically, the general post-SEA demise of the Luxembourg Compromise has not necessarily resulted in many more items literally being put to a vote. In other words, since the late 1980s there has been greater use of QMV in *principle* rather than in *practice*. Member states agree to abide by majority decisions, but because of deference to national sensitivities and a deep-rooted culture of consensus issues rarely come to a vote in the Council. The presidency may call for a vote, but voting does not always follow. Instead, the country or countries in the minority may simply accept the inevitable and acquiesce in the passage of legislation.

Another paradox of majority voting, whether in principle or in practice, is that it can deepen the democratic deficit. Although majority voting in the Council is inherently democratic, it weakens the already tenuous ties between governments and national parliaments on EU issues. By renouncing the national veto, governments reduce their parliaments' already weak leverage over EU legislation. After all, a national parliament could try to punish its government for not vetoing controversial legislation if the government were able to impose a veto. But a national parliament can hardly hold its government accountable for being outvoted.

Depending on its legal base in the treaty and its stage in the legislative process, a proposal before the Council may be subject to a simple majority vote, a qualified majority vote, or unanimity. In QMV, votes are weighted crudely according to each country's size. Article 205.2 (formerly Article 148.2 TEC), amended by successive accession agreements but not by successive treaty reforms, stipulates the member states' votes.

The arithmetic of QMV means that no single country can block legislation, and even two of the largest countries acting together lack enough votes to constitute a blocking minority. Thus on any particular proposal, both sides (for and against) need to muster coalitions in order to prevail. The composition of such coalitions varies considerably according to the item under discussion.

Concerned about the greater difficulty that it would have mustering a blocking minority in an enlarged EU (and under intense pressure from Euroskeptical Conservative back-benchers), in 1994 the British government attempted to keep the blocking minority at its existing threshold (23 votes) even after the Eftan accessions, when, based on the experience of previous

Table 9.3 Weighted Votes in the Council

Country	Votes
Britain, France, Germany, Italy	10
Spain	8
Belgium, Greece, the Netherlands, Portugal	5
Austria, Sweden	4
Denmark, Finland, Ireland	3
Luxembourg	2
Total	87
Qualified majority	62
Blocking minority	26

enlargements, it should have been increased to 27 votes (or 26 votes following Norway's decision not to join). After a bitter dispute, the other member states agreed to the so-called Ioannina Compromise, whereby "if members of the Council representing a total of 23 to 25 votes indicate their intention to oppose the adoption by the Council of a decision by a qualified majority, the Council will do all within its power to reach, within a reasonable time . . . a satisfactory solution that can be adopted by at least 65 votes" (Britain's preferred qualified majority).

The Ioannina Compromise was largely a face-saving device for Britain and had little practical effect on EU decisionmaking. Its real significance lay in what it portended for future EU enlargements. Britain's government at that time was obstructionist and Euroskeptical; other large member states also grew concerned about the impact on their relative voting weight of the likely accession, well after the Eftan enlargement, of five small member states (ranging in size from Cyprus to Hungary) and only one big member state (Poland). This concern led to efforts at the 1996–1997 IGC to overhaul QMV either by substantially increasing the number of votes for each large country, or by introducing a double majority system that would combine the traditional requirements of a qualified majority with a new demographic criterion. Large member states based their call for a demographic criterion on their understandable concern that without it, a qualified majority could be formed in the future by a group of member states that together did not represent a majority of the EU's population. In the event, the Amsterdam Treaty did not include major decisionmaking reform but stipulated instead that Council votes would have to be reweighted to compensate large member states for the loss of their second commissioner, which is due to happen at the time of the next enlargement.

A country's block of votes is indivisible, although Flemish politicians once proposed that Belgium's five votes be split between Flanders (3) and Wallonia (2) when the Council voted on issues that, in Belgium, were the responsibility of regional government (the Flemish politicians apparently forgot that Belgium has a third regional government: the Brussels capital region). Needless to say, neither the Belgian government nor the other member states supported the proposal.[33]

As well as automatically approving A points on the agenda, the Council may also approve without a vote (although usually after considerable discussion) some of the B points—items thoroughly discussed at a lower level but on which COREPER was unable to reach agreement—or may send some of them back to COREPER for further deliberation. Occasionally the president will call for an "indicative vote" on contentious B points to see where each country stands. Depending on the outcome, he may resume discussion and try to reach consensus, call for a definitive vote, or postpone the issue until another meeting.

Contentious items often become part of a package deal that accumulates during a number of Council meetings. Shortly after becoming Commission president in 1985, Delors deplored what he called "linkage diplomacy": the member states' tendency to link issues in an effort to negotiate the best deal possible.[34] Despite Delors's denunciation of it, linkage diplomacy flourished during the single market program. Indeed, the inherent give-and-take of legislative package dealing made it possible to make rapid progress toward the 1992 target date.

After each meeting, the Council issues a press release that lists the legislation just enacted (if any). Since the TEU ratification crisis, the Council has also revealed how member states voted (if a formal vote took place). Journalists reconstruct what happened by piecing together information from the national delegations, the Commission's spokesperson, and the Council press office. The Council president and the relevant commissioner usually give a press conference. Based on such evidence, it seems that voting is relatively infrequent and that consensus remains the preferred path for the enactment of legislation in the Council.

NOTES

1. Joseph Weiler, "The Genscher-Colombo Draft European Act: The Politics of Indecision," *Journal of European Integration* 4, nos. 2 and 3 (1983): 140. David Cameron called the European Council "an extra-treaty manifestation of institutionalized intergovernmentalism" in his chapter "The 1992 Initiative: Causes and Consequences," in Alberta Sbragia, ed., *Euro-Politics: Institutions and Policymaking in the "New" European Community* (Washington, DC: Brookings Institution, 1992), p. 63 (emphasis in the original).

2. Sir Charles Powell, "Few Chances for Heroics," *Financial Times,* January 5, 1998, p. 15.

3. Guy de Bassompierre, *Changing the Guard in Brussels: An Insider's View of the EC Presidency* (New York: Praeger, 1988), p. 12.

4. Paris summit communiqué; Commission, *1974 General Report,* p. 297.

5. Council of the European Communities General Secretariat, *The Council of the European Community: An Introduction to Its Services and Activities* (Luxembourg: Office for Official Publications of the European Communities [OOP], 1991), p. 29.

6. Helen Wallace and Geoffrey Edwards, *The Council of Ministers of the European Community and the President-in-Office* (London: Federal Trust, 1977), p. 550.

7. "Tindemans Report," Bull. EC S/1-1976, p. 31.

8. Roy Jenkins, *European Diary, 1977–1981* (London: Collins, 1989), p. 371.

9. Quoted in *Agence Europe,* December 17, 1974, p. 4.

10. Council of the European Communities, *Report on European Institutions Presented by the Committee of Three to the European Council (Report of the Three Wise Men)* (Luxembourg: OOP, 1981).

11. Quoted in the *Times* (London), June 28, 1977, p. 10.

12. Jean Monnet, *Memoirs* (Garden City, NY: Doubleday, 1978), pp. 598–599.

13. Jenkins, *European Diary,* pp. 248–249.

14. Quoted in *Agence Europe,* May 4, 1998, p. 4.

15. Cameron, "The 1992 Initiative," p. 63.

16. *Report of the Three Wise Men,* pp. 16–17.

17. "Ad Hoc Committee for Institutional Affairs Report to the European Council (Dooge Report)," March 1985, Bull. EC 3-1985, point 3.5.1.

18. Annette Morgan, *From Summit to Council: Evolution in the EEC* (London: Chatham House, 1976), p. 56.

19. Jenkins, *European Diary,* p. 75.

20. Helen Wallace, "The Council and the Commission After the Single European Act," in Leon Hurwitz and Christian Lequesne, eds., *The State of the European Community: Policies, Institutions, and Debates in the Transition Years* (Boulder: Lynne Rienner, 1991), p. 20. For subsequent analysis of Council decisionmaking, see Fiona Hayes-Renshaw and Helen Wallace, *The Council of Ministers* (New York: St. Martin's Press, 1996), and Martin Westlake, *The Council of the European Union* (London: Catermill, 1995).

21. European Commission, *Openness and Transparency in the EU Institutions,* proceedings of a seminar in Brussels, November 22, 1995, p. 22.

22. Birmingham European Council, "Presidency Conclusions," Bull. EC 10-1992, point 1.8.

23. Quoted in *Le Monde,* October 13, 1992, p. 2.

24. Commission, *Openness and Transparency,* p. 14.

25. M.P.C.M. Van Schendelen, "'The Council Decides': Does the Council Decide?" *Journal of Common Market Studies* 34, no. 4 (December 1996): 531.

26. This is how British foreign secretary Douglas Hurd famously described the EC's pervasiveness. Quoted in the *Financial Times,* January 10, 1992, p. 1.

27. Quoted in the *Times* (London), June 28, 1977, p. 16.

28. Jenkins, *European Diary,* p. 74.

29. Commission, *1974 General Report,* Annex to Chapter 1, point 8.

30. Quoted in Marina Gazzo, ed., *Towards European Union,* vol. 1 (Brussels: Agence Europe, 1985), p. 26.

31. François Mitterrand, speech to the European Parliament, May 24, 1984, reprinted in *Vital Speeches of the Day,* August 1, 1984, p. 613.

32. See Martin Westlake, "'Mad Cows and Englishmen': The Institutional Consequences of the BSE Crisis," *Journal of Common Market Studies* 35, *Annual Review* (1996): 11–36.

33. See *De Standaard,* March 19, 1996, p. 1.

34. Jacques Delors, speech to the European Parliament, March 12, 1985, Bull. EC S/4-1985, p. 6.

10

The European Parliament

Just as the Commission has no analogue in national political systems, the European Parliament (EP) could easily be misconstrued as the EU equivalent of a national parliament. Most members of the EP (MEPs) think that the EP *should* have all the powers and prerogatives of a national parliament instead of having to share legislative power with the Council. They argue that the EP's limited legislative authority undermines the EU's democratic legitimacy and have long found it "unacceptable that a union of democratic states should not itself be democratic."[1] Directly elected every five years in EU-wide elections, MEPs are understandably aggrieved that their institution lacks the political clout of the Council and even, to some extent, of the Commission.

The history of the EP is a history of relentless efforts by MEPs to increase their institution's power. Using the argument of democratic unaccountability in the EU—the so-called democratic deficit—as a potent weapon, MEPs have sought, especially since the advent of direct elections in 1979, to redress the institutional imbalance among the Commission, Council, and Parliament. With the indispensable assistance of genuinely sympathetic or guilt-ridden governments, the EP has succeeded since the mid-1980s in obtaining substantially greater legislative and supervisory authority during successive waves of treaty reform.

By introducing a "cooperation" procedure (the right to a second reading for certain legislation, notably concerning the single market), the Single European Act (SEA) proved a turning point in the EP's procurement of legislative power. The TEU extended cooperation to other important areas and gave the EP a limited form of legislative codecision with the Council. Finally, the Amsterdam Treaty virtually abolished the cooperation procedure in favor of a simplified codecision procedure. Earlier, in the 1970s, national governments gave the EP significant budgetary authority. The combination of budgetary and legislative power, an assent procedure for ratification of association and accession agreements, and an ability to scrutinize the

Commission's activities make the EP a formidable player in the EU political system.

MEPs claim the high moral ground in the ubiquitous interinstitutional struggle over the EP's powers. Yet MEPs' management of parliamentary affairs weakens their moral authority. The monthly trek between Brussels and Strasbourg, four hours apart by road or rail, is an obvious but important example. MEPs spend three weeks each month in Brussels attending committee and political group meetings and the other week in Strasbourg attending plenary sessions. A large part of the Parliament's secretariat is located in Luxembourg, approximately halfway between Brussels and Strasbourg. The cost and inconvenience of constantly transporting MEPs, officials, and innumerable boxes of papers in a 600-mile circuit every month and of maintaining three separate office sites have seriously and possibly irreparably eroded public confidence in the EP.[2]

In their defense, MEPs point out that the EP would like to move entirely to Brussels and that it already took the initiative to hold committee meetings, political group meetings, and occasional plenary sessions there, but national governments are responsible for the practice of holding regular plenary sessions in Strasbourg and for keeping the secretariat in Luxembourg. Over the years the governments of France and Luxembourg have gone to great lengths, including taking legal action and blocking decisions about where to locate new EU institutions and agencies, in order to prevent the EP's plenary sessions and secretariat from moving permanently to Brussels. For its part, the Belgian government built a lavish facility in Brussels in an effort to lure all of the EP's activities there. Not to be outdone, the French government built an equally lavish facility in Strasbourg, where the EP had previously shared a more-than-adequate building with the Council of Europe. Both were inaugurated in 1998.

In the meantime, at the December 1992 Edinburgh summit, the heads of state and government decided that the EP's secretariat would forever stay in Luxembourg and that the EP would always hold its regular monthly plenaries in Strasbourg, but additional plenaries could take place in Brussels.[3] A protocol of the Amsterdam Treaty settled the matter definitively: "The European Parliament shall have its seat in Strasbourg where the twelve periods of monthly plenary sessions, including the budget session, shall be held. The periods of additional plenary sessions shall be held in Brussels. The committees of the European Parliament shall meet in Brussels. The General Secretariat of the European Parliament and its departments shall remain in Luxembourg."

Although MEPs can legitimately claim that the decision to stay in Strasbourg was beyond their control, they continue to bear the political brunt of Parliament's monthly migration. MEPs' generous allowances and seemingly lavish lifestyles, as well as the EP's peculiar procedures, linguistic muddle (the EU's eleven official languages are constantly used), and poorly attended plenaries contribute to the EP's low public esteem. They also generate an endless supply of silly stories, even in the sympathetic press, causing the institution grave political damage. Undoubtedly a majority of MEPs are hardworking, dedicated, and sensitive to popular cynicism about parliamentarians in general and Europarliamentarians in particular. But until the EP ends its monthly road show, simplifies its procedures, and makes it easier for the public to attend committee meetings in Brussels and plenaries in Strasbourg (one of Western Europe's least accessible cities), redressing the institutional imbalance by giving the EP more legislative power will not resolve the EU's democratic deficit. After all, the democratic deficit is based on popular perception as well as political reality, and most Europeans tend to see the EP as part of the problem rather than part of the solution.

SIZE

The size of the EP grew with successive enlargements as seats were allocated to each new member state. With an EP of 626 seats after the Eftan enlargement, and in anticipation of the accession of numerous Central and Eastern European states, member states agreed in the Amsterdam Treaty to limit the number of MEPs to a maximum of 700 (Article 198 TEC).

The distribution of seats among member states, resulting in great differences in the ratio of MEPs to population from one member state to another, is one of the most striking anomalies in the Europarliamentary system. For instance, before unification Germany had an MEP to population ratio of 1:984,000. In the wake of unification, when Germany's population increased by 17 million, Germany asked for extra representation in the EP. After a major political struggle the European Council agreed to redistribute and increase the total number of seats in the EP (even governments that liked the EP least and resisted supranationalism most fought tenaciously for larger national representation, suggesting that the size of a parliamentary delegation is a matter of both national pride and political advantage). As a result, Germany's MEP to population ratio improved to 1:805,000. This compares ludicrously to Luxembourg's ratio of 1:66,000.

DIRECT ELECTIONS

The adjective "direct" distinguishes the current system for MEP selection from the "indirect" system in operation before 1979. Originally, national parliaments nominated a number of members to sit also as MEPs in Strasbourg.

The size of each national delegation was vaguely proportional to a country's population, and the composition of each delegation depended on the distribution of seats between political parties in the national parliaments.

Article 138.3 of the original TEC (now Article 190.4 TEC) called on the EP to draw up a proposal "for elections by direct universal suffrage in accordance with a uniform procedure in all Member States." The EP did so in 1961 and again in 1963 and 1969, but the Council never acted "to lay down [unanimously] the appropriate provisions, which it shall recommend to Member States for adoption in accordance with their respective constitutional requirements." Efforts to move from "indirect" to "direct" elections fell victim to the pervasive struggle between supranationalism and intergovernmentalism. Supranationalists hoped, and intergovernmentalists feared, that direct elections would strengthen the EP's legitimacy and power and thereby weaken the Council's authority. French president Charles de Gaulle's guardianship of intergovernmentalism and disdain for the Strasbourg Assembly ensured that direct elections did not come about in the 1960s.

The relaunch of European integration after de Gaulle's departure revived the question of direct elections. A decision at the 1974 Paris summit to offset the nascent European Council (an institutionalization of intergovernmentalism) with direct elections to the EP (a sop to supranationalism) prompted the EP once again to revise its electoral proposals. Parliament adopted new ones in January 1975 and the European Council approved a modified version in Brussels in July 1976.[4] Apart from the lingering reluctance of some old (notably France) and new (notably Britain) member states to give the EP additional authority by moving from indirect to direct elections, governments differed widely on a myriad of organizational and procedural points. As a result, in September 1976 the Council finally authorized direct elections to be held every five years, but not with a uniform electoral system.[5]

Procedural differences among member states regarding the conduct of direct elections include the way that candidates are nominated, the order of names on voting papers, campaign rules, the validation of election results, the filling of vacant seats, and the choice of election day (within a three- or four-day period in mid-June). However, until the 1999 elections the most important differences concerned the electoral system, eligibility to vote and stand for elections, and the demarcation of constituency boundaries:

• *The electoral system:* Fourteen member states used various systems of proportional representation, and one (Britain) used a "first-past-the-post system" (except in Northern Ireland). The British system, used also in domestic elections, was notorious for causing overrepresentation or underrepresentation of political parties in the national parliament and to a lesser extent in the EP. In theory, a small swing in electoral support for a British political party could have resulted in a large gain or loss of seats for that party in Strasbourg and could have determined which political group (coalition of national political parties) formed a majority in the EP. Thanks to the cooperation of the Labour government that came to power in May 1997, member states agreed in the Amsterdam Treaty to allow the EP to draw up a proposal for elections by direct universal suffrage in accordance with "principles common to all Member States" (Article 190.4 TEC), thereby paving the way for a common, EU-wide electoral system involving some form of proportional representation (the new government also agreed to introduce a form of proportional representation in Britain in the 1999 elections). The EP lost little time drafting an electoral act for approval by the Council, to govern the direct elections in 2004. Reflecting the difficulty of harmonization among member states, however, the EP's draft act left plenty of room for national variations in a supposedly common electoral system.[6]

• *Eligibility to vote and stand for elections:* Apart from the same minimum voting age (eighteen) in all member states, voting rights still differ markedly throughout the EU. Some member states allow absentee voting without restrictions; others extend it only to their nationals resident elsewhere in the EU. The minimum age to stand as a candidate varies throughout the EU. More significantly, for a long time nationality and residency requirements differed from member state to member state, with some restricting the right to vote to their own nationals and others extending it to residents from elsewhere in the EU. Accordingly, the TEU stipulated that the Council had to arrange, by December 31, 1993, to allow "Union citizens" to vote and stand as candidates in EP elections regardless of where they resided in the EU. Aware of the sensitivity of voting rights in some member states and acknowledging the unlikelihood of uniform voting rights by the end of 1993, the treaty permitted derogations "where warranted by problems specific to a Member State." Inevitably, such derogations meant that many EU citizens resident in a member state other than their own could not vote in the 1994 elections to the EP (the first ones after implementation of the TEU).

• *Constituencies:* In some member states the whole country forms a single constituency; in others the country is divided into a number of regional constituencies that do not correspond to the constituencies used in national elections. A drawback of large, national constituencies is the difficulty of developing close constituent-MEP relations in a majority of member states. The EP wants to make regional constituencies obligatory in large and medium-sized member states. (The Eurofriendly Labour government obliged by organizing ten regional constituencies for EP elections in mainland Britain.)

Although the EP's profile and political power have increased greatly since the first direct election in 1979, the experience of direct elections themselves—in terms of political party behavior and voter turnout—has been disappointing. The EU-wide turnout in direct elections declined steadily during the first four direct elections from 62.5 percent in 1979 to 56.4 percent in 1994.[7]

Whereas most candidates campaign to some extent on EU issues and proclaim their EP party group affiliation, inevitably national political parties and issues predominate during EP elections. In some countries general elections coincided with and completely overshadowed European elections; in others, European elections invariably became referendums on the performance of governments. Just as they dominated the election campaigns, national political parties also dominated the selection of candidates.

Eurocandidates (and consequently MEPs) tend to fall into one of the following categories:

- aspiring politicians who failed to win selection as candidates for national elections
- aspiring politicians who won selection as candidates for national elections but subsequently lost the election
- established politicians who are either temporarily out of national office because of resignation or a government reshuffle or have retired from national politics (this category includes a number of former government ministers and even a former president of France)
- successful regional or local politicians who want to be MEPs either as an end in itself or as a stepping-stone to national political office
- prominent trade unionists and farmers' leaders
- former officials of EU institutions and, in a few cases, former commissioners
- politicians with or without a background in local, regional, or national politics who choose to make a career as an MEP

Regardless of why they stand for election to the EP, an increasing number of MEPs (although arguably still a minority of them) take their work seriously. Fortunately for the EP, only committed and competent MEPs make their way into leadership positions. The high caliber of leadership has contributed to the EP's success in acquiring and executing new political powers since the advent of direct elections.

A few MEPs still hold the "dual mandate," that is, they are members of both their national parliaments and the EP. The dual mandate has the advantage of personifying a close relationship between national parliaments and the EP, but the demands of being an MP and MEP make it difficult for someone to hold both positions simultaneously. Because holders of the dual mandate tend to devote more time to national politics, they unwittingly reinforce a negative stereotype of the EP as a publicly supported leisure center. Accordingly, the EP disapproves of the dual mandate and a number of countries and political parties have prohibited it.

POLITICAL GROUPS

The EP's rules of procedure and allocation of resources strongly encourage MEPs to join transnational political groups in the EP. MEPs from the same member state may form a political group, but they need to have at least twenty-nine seats to do so. The threshold required to form a political group declines as the number of member states involved increases. Thus at least twenty-three MEPs from two member states may form a political group; eighteen MEPs from three member states; and fourteen MEPs from four or more member states. MEPs join a particular group for reasons of ideological affinity, shared interest, or convenience.

The number of political groups has varied over time (in 1999 there were eight groups in the EP embracing members of nearly 100 national political parties, plus a small number of independents).[8] From the beginning of the party group system in the mid-1950s three generic groupings

Table 10.1 Political Groups in the European Parliament (before the 1999 elections)

Group	Composition	Size
Party of the European Socialists (PES)	Members from Social Democratic Parties in all member states	214
European People's Party (EPP)	Members from Christian Democratic Parties in all member states	200
European Liberal, Democratic, and Reformist Group (ELDR)	A large number of Dutch Liberals, and Liberals from a few other member states	41
Union for Europe (UFE)	A heterogeneous group made up mostly of Gaullists and members of Ireland's Fianna Fáil	36
Confederal Group of the European United Left/ Nordic Green Left	Members from fringe environmental and ex-Communist parties from a variety of member states	33
Greens	Members of Green parties from nine member states	28
European Radical Alliance (ERA)	A heterogeneous group of French and some other radicals and regionalists	20
Independent Europe of the Nations Group	Nationalists from France and a few other member states, some of whom oppose their countries' membership in the EU	17
Independents	Nonaffiliated members from various member states	37
Total		626

(or families, as they like to call themselves) have eclipsed all others in the EP. These are the Socialists, Christian Democrats, and Liberals. Since the third direct election in 1989, the Socialists and Christian Democrats have predominated: Both are the only groups to include political parties or individual politicians from each member state, and both have provided the bulk of EP presidents.

The Socialist and Christian Democratic Groups

The Socialist group benefited more than the Christian Democratic group from successive enlargements, although the sizable British Labour contingent took its seats in the EP only after the successful outcome of the 1975 referendum on whether or not Britain should stay in the EC. Since then the Socialists have been the largest group in the EP, dominated by large contingents of British Labour Party and German Social Democratic Party MEPs. The Socialists also benefited most from Spanish and Portuguese accession in 1986 and from the accession of Finland and Sweden—two countries with strong social-democratic traditions—in 1995. In a postscript to the end of the Cold War, in January 1993 twenty Communists (mostly Italians) crossed over and joined the Socialist group.

Following the EC's first enlargement in 1973 the Christian Democrats did not enjoy an influx of British and Danish Conservatives, who instead set up their own group, the European Conservatives, which later changed its name to the European Democratic Group. With the EP becoming more important after the SEA, the European Democratic Group requested membership in the Christian Democratic group immediately after the 1989 direct elections. However, concern among Christian Democrats about British and Danish Euroskepticism delayed its incorporation into the Christian Democratic group until 1992.

The Socialists and Christian Democrats are not simply coalitions of MEPs from separate Socialist and Christian Democratic parties in the EU but are the EP branches of united, transnational Socialist and Christian Democratic parties, called the Party of European Socialists (PES) and the European People's Party (EPP). Accordingly, the Socialists in the EP are officially called the Group of the Party of European Socialists, and the Christian Democrats in the EP are officially called the Group of the European People's Party. The Christian Democrats were the first EP group to form a transnational party, the EPP, in 1976. Yet it was not until the early 1990s, when the scope of European integration had greatly increased as a result of the SEA and the TEU, that national parties constituting the EPP (including their members in the EP) made a serious effort to turn the EPP into more than a mere umbrella organization.

The TEU itself recognized that "political parties at the European level are important as a factor for integration within the Union. They contribute to forming a European awareness and to expressing the political will of the citizens of the Union" (Article 191, formerly Article 138a, TEC) This view reflected the thinking of some member states that Europe-wide party organizations would bolster the federal structure of the emerging EU. Moreover, the treaty's implicit encouragement of transnational political parties was linked to its concept of Union citizenship and extension of voting rights in local and European elections to Union citizens resident in a member state other than their own. Party activity at the European level would make it easier for citizens throughout the EU, regardless of their national origin, to participate in European elections.

The newly energized EPP group had little impact on popular participation in European elections but quickly became more cohesive and effective in the EP than the preceding loose association of Christian Democratic MEPs. At the same time, constituent national parties and the EPP group started working closely together in the transnational party to try to influence EU policymaking in a variety of ways, notably by organizing summits of Christian Democratic party leaders in the run-up to European Councils. The EPP group also sought to influence the outcome of the 1996–1997 IGC by submitting position papers and lobbying national actors.

The PES developed into an equally well organized transnational party, using similar methods to influence European integration in a social-democratic direction. Not only does the PES have the largest group in the EP but its constituent parties also form a majority of member state governments. Despite the attenuation of ideological differences in European politics since the late 1980s, the EPP and PES differ in their approach to key European issues such as the single market and EMU. Both support deeper economic integration but part company on social policy. Similarly, both are concerned about high unemployment in the EU, but the PSE advocates a more interventionist policy response than does the EPP.

Other Groups

The Liberals—officially the European Liberal, Democratic, and Reformist Party (ELDR)—experienced a relative decline as a result of successive enlargements. Well before the first enlargement the Gaullists broke away (in 1965) to form the European Democratic Union (EDU). After the first enlargement (in 1973), Ireland's Fianna Fáil MEPs joined the Gaullists, who first renamed their group the European Progressive Democrats, later the European Democratic Alliance (EDA). In 1995 the EDA merged with Forza Europa, a group made up exclusively of members of the new Italian party (Forza Italia) of media tycoon Silvio Berlusconi, and renamed itself the Union for Europe (UFE) group. In the process, it briefly surpassed the Liberals in size until a number of the Forza Italia members broke away in 1998 and joined the EPP as individual members.

Other political developments since the 1970s spawned new political groups and caused others to disappear. The Euro-Communist movement (based in part on the acceptance by Western European Communists of the EC's existence) led in 1973 to the establishment of the Communist Group. Fissiparous tendencies on the far left, especially after the collapse of communism in Central and Eastern Europe, caused the Communists to split after the 1989 direct election into two separate groups, the United European Left and Left Unity. Despite the declaration of solidarity implicit in each group's title, United European Left consisted mostly of Italian and Spanish Communists, whereas the small, more doctrinaire Left Unity consisted mostly of French, Greek, and Portuguese Communists. The decision by twenty Italian Communists to join the Socialist group in January 1993 brought the United European Left's existence to an end: the small Left Unity group disappeared after the 1994 election. The remaining Communists in the EP joined some far-left Scandinavian environmentalists to form a new group: the Confederal Group of the European United Left/Nordic Green Left.

The reemergence of the extreme right in Europe in the mid-1980s manifested itself in the appearance in the EP of the Technical Group of the European Right. The prefix "Technical Group" indicated a marriage of convenience: The French National Front had too few seats to form its own group and coalesced uneasily with the German Republican Party, with which it at least agreed on the supposed evils of immigration. The handful of Italian Social Movement MEPs in the EP in the late 1980s would ordinarily have joined the European Right group, but the Italian and German rightists fell out over a historical dispute over the South Tyrol; accordingly, the Italian Social Movement MEPs sat as independents. The German Republicans disappeared after the 1994 election, thus ending the representation of the far right as a separate group in the EP.

In 1984, newly elected Green and alternative MEPs joined with a few independents to form the Rainbow group. Five years later, after the 1989 election, a larger Green contingent formed its own group (the Green group), and the Rainbow group became a heterogeneous collection of regional parties, disaffected members of other parties, and a few Danes dedicated to taking their country out of the EC. The Rainbow group disappeared after the 1994 election; some of its members joined a new group of advocates of regional autonomy in the context of European integration: the Group of the European Radical Alliance. Finally, another new group emerged out of the anti-TEU movement after the 1994 election. Called the Independent Europe of the Nations Group, it consisted of French and Danish MEPs avowedly opposed to further integration.

MEPs cover the spectrum of European politics—a much broader spectrum than exists in the United States—from the far left to the far right. It is easy to place the Confederal Group of the European United Left/Nordic Green Left and the independent neo-Fascists at opposite extremes. The

Socialist group is left of center; the Liberals and the Christian Democrats are right of center; and the Union for Europe (mostly Gaullists and Berlusconi-ites) and anti-TEU Europe of Nations group are squarely on the right. Because these are catchall groups, some include political parties that could be placed elsewhere, although not far away, on the political spectrum. It is difficult to place the European Radical Alliance and the Greens on the political spectrum. Whereas some of the Greens' constituent parties are definitely on the left, most are not; and almost all of the parties that later joined the European Radical Alliance are organized on regional lines and lack a particular ideological orientation.

With six political groups spanning the political spectrum and two organized along regional and ecological lines, the party group system in the EP resembles the political party system in national parliaments. Two of the EP's political groups (the Socialists and Christian Democrats) are substantially larger than the others and are on opposite sides of the left-right divide. Nevertheless, ideological rivalry is far from intense and the party group system is by no means rigidly bipolar. Moreover, unlike their national counterparts, EP party groups do not form or support a government. This intensifies the Socialists' and Christian Democrats' mutual interest in working closely with each other to promote the EP's institutional agenda and to secure the necessary majorities in order to have an impact on the legislative process.

The role of "intergroups" illustrates the difference between the party group system in the EP and the political party system in national parties. As the name implies, intergroups consist of MEPs from a variety of party groups who share a common interest. Intergroups range in subject matter from specific issues (such as animal welfare) to broad themes (such as disarmament). Intergroups—there are about fifty altogether—serve a useful social and political purpose. By linking members of different political groups they help to build broad support for important initiatives and proposals. Yet their existence, or at least the existence of the overtly political intergroups, highlights a relative lack of party group discipline and emphasizes the difference between the national parliamentary and the Europarliamentary systems.

THE EP'S ROLE AND RESPONSIBILITIES

Whatever else may be said of it, the EP cannot be dismissed as a "windy debating chamber." MEPs spend only one week—in effect, three days—each month in full plenary sessions. Plenary sessions include agenda setting, voting, question time with or without debate, speeches by commissioners or the Council presidency, discussions of emergency issues, and debates on general topics. Speaking time is carefully parceled out to political groups and independent MEPs and strictly controlled—usually by the simple stratagem of turning off the microphone. MEPs rarely have an opportunity to prattle on. Moreover, some Continental political cultures discourage intense parliamentary exchanges. British MEPs, whose domestic political system thrives on fierce debate, find Europarliamentary discussions disappointingly tame.

Apart from procedural problems and cultural differences, language is another obstacle to purposeful debate. Not all MEPs are fluent in a second EU language. Thus the EU's eleven official languages are always in use. An anthropologist who observed the EP in action was struck most by "the amputation that political speech undergoes during interpretation. . . . To make oneself understood through the interpreter, one must be brief and simplify one's language to the maximum—there is room neither for rhetoric, nor for wit. And despite all this, the message sometimes doesn't get through." The costs of interpreting and translating are exorbitant, accounting for nearly one-third of Parliament's total staff and about 30 percent of its annual budget. In the anthropologist's opinion, "the inability to choose a single headquarters for the European Parliament is echoed by the impossibility of finding a common language."[9]

Despite those constraints, debates are an important part of the legislative process in the EP and an opportunity for it to try to raise awareness and consciousness throughout the EU of certain important issues. For instance, the EP prides itself on its advocacy of human rights, always an area selected each month for urgent debate in plenary. The EP's influential Committee on Foreign Affairs, Security, and Defense Policy monitors human rights in third countries with the assistance of a special human rights unit. The committee's annual report on human rights forms the basis of a major parliamentary debate.

Apart from raising awareness of important political, economic, and humanitarian issues, the EP has a number of well-defined roles and responsibilities in the EU system covering the budget, the legislative process, scrutiny and oversight, and external relations.

Budgetary Powers

Parliaments have the "power of the purse" in liberal democratic regimes. Inspired by that analogy but reluctant to cede too much authority, in the early 1970s member states gave the EP some budgetary power when the EC acquired its own resources (funds that originate in the member states but belong to the Community) and became independent of national financial contributions. As a result of amendments to the Treaty of Rome in April 1970 (implemented in 1975), Parliament and the Council became the EC's joint "budgetary authority," sharing responsibility for EC spending but not for raising revenue, which is fixed annually by the Council acting alone. Inevitably, the relationship between the two branches of the budgetary authority was far from harmonious: The EP rejected the budget in 1979 and 1984 and continually tried to increase the size of "noncompulsory expenditure" (spending on policies and programs that are not specifically mentioned in the treaties), for which Parliament has the power to make budgetary amendments. The EP may only propose modifications to compulsory expenditure, a category that covers over 70 percent of the budget and includes agricultural spending, the single biggest budgetary item.

Because of the likelihood of budgetary disputes between them, the EP and the Council established a conciliation procedure as early as 1971. This involves biannual Council-Parliament meetings, first when the Council prepares to adopt the draft budget (on the basis of a Commission proposal) and later when the Council is about to decide on the EP's proposed amendments. In addition, the Council president, the budget committee chair, and the budget commissioner hold "budgetary cooperation meetings" in December, during the plenary session at which the EP adopts the budget. Failure to reach agreement triggers a complicated procedure for month-by-month expenditure (using a system called "provisional twelfths") until the EP and Council settle their differences.

The budgetary conciliation and cooperation procedure did not prevent the EP and Council from clashing repeatedly in the 1970s and 1980s. Parliament's main concerns were to curb agricultural expenditure and increase spending on policy areas in the noncompulsory category. Only as a result of the Delors I budgetary package agreement of February 1988 and ensuing interinstitutional agreement of June 1988 did the situation improve. The Delors I package curbed spending on agriculture and substantially increased spending on cohesion through the structural funds. More important for the budgetary process, it also contained a framework for a five-year financial perspective (1988–1992) that included an annual ceiling for expenditure (expressed in terms of Community GNP).[10]

The new financial framework removed much of the rancor from the annual budgetary procedure. Significantly, the EP and the Council completed the 1989 budget on time without a major dispute. The Community never ran over budget during the lifetime of the 1988 interinstitutional agreement despite the financial consequences of the upheaval in Central and Eastern Europe and the Gulf War. The positive impact of Delors I generated momentum for a Delors II package to cover the years 1993–1999, although recession in the early 1990s strengthened opposition in the EU's northern member states to a large Cohesion Fund for the southern member states. In the event, acceptance of the Delors II package at the Edinburgh summit in December 1992 (followed by a new interinstitutional agreement in October 1993) owed as much to the success of the 1988 budgetary reform as to the inherent importance of the additional expenditures needed to move "from the Single Act to Maastricht and beyond."[11]

Because they continued to squabble over the distinction between compulsory and noncompulsory expenditure—a squabble that led the European Court of Justice (ECJ) to declare the 1995 budget illegal because the

EP had changed some of the classifications—Parliament and the Council agreed to raise the budget procedure at the 1996–1997 IGC. In the event, apart from CFSP financing, budget issues were almost wholly absent from the IGC and the ensuing Amsterdam Treaty, and the distinction between compulsory and noncompulsory expenditure remained a source of Council-EP friction.

Based on a 1975 agreement that became operational in 1977, Parliament has exclusive authority to grant a "discharge" of the general budget. This is the only budgetary power vested solely in the EP. The purpose of granting a discharge is to verify the accuracy of the Commission's budgetary management and to determine precise revenue and expenditure for a given year. The discharge procedure is arduous and time consuming and involves close cooperation with the Court of Auditors. The EP usually votes on whether to grant a discharge two years after the budget in question.

The EP's exclusive power to grant a discharge has considerable political implications. Parliament has sometimes used that power to attempt to censure the Commission, although arguably to the detriment of the budgetary and accounting aspects of the discharge function. At a plenary session in July 1979, the budget commissioner opined that refusal to grant a discharge would be "a political sanction . . . an event of exceptional seriousness [that] would have to lead to the dismissal of the existing [Commission] team. I venture to think that we shall never reach that point."[12] Yet five years later, in November 1984, the EP refused a discharge of the 1982 budget as a means of censuring the Commission. A political crisis was averted only by the expiration of the Commission's term in office (the EP finally granted a discharge for the 1982 budget in March 1985). In 1998 the EP delayed discharge of the 1996 budget to protest the Commission's poor management of successive budgets, based on highly critical reports by the Court of Auditors. This action triggered the events that culminated in the EP's unsuccessful but highly publicized effort to vote the Commission out of office in January 1999 and the Commission's resignation two months later.[13]

Since the early 1970s and especially since the first direct elections in 1979, the EP has attempted to use its overall budgetary authority to raise its political profile and enhance its institutional standing. Yet the EP's ability to leverage its budgetary authority is constrained by the relatively small size of the EU's budget. Devoid of responsibility for such big-ticket items as health, social security, defense, and education, the EU's public finances are puny in comparison with those of a nation-state. It may be argued that this is a major factor preventing the emergence of a stronger EP. The EP may have acquired considerable budgetary authority, but as long as the budget remains relatively insignificant and the EP cannot raise any revenue, its power will remain correspondingly weak. As David Coombes has observed, "the history of representative government in Europe and elsewhere suggests that the Community's weakness in public finance" is an important reason for "its failure to develop [strong] parliamentary institutions."[14]

Legislative Powers

In the legislative field even more than in the budgetary field, the EP has acquired greater powers over the years. Initially, the EP's legislative powers were limited and were exercised solely through the consultation procedure (so-called because of the original treaty's stipulation in a number of articles that the Council could enact legislation in such cases only "after consulting the Assembly"). The SEA enhanced the EP's legislative powers by introducing the cooperation procedure (Article 189c, now Article 252 TEC) and requiring parliamentary assent in a small number of cases. The TEU went a step further and introduced the codecision procedure (Article 251, formerly Article 189b, TEC) whereby the EP and the Council could adopt legislation jointly in a large number of policy areas. The Amsterdam Treaty simplified and extended the scope of the codecision procedure.

Parliament does not have the right to initiate legislation, although the TEU formally gave it the same authority as the Council to request that the Commission submit legislative proposals (Article 192, formerly Article 138b, TEC). Such requests (the EP has made only a few of them) do not oblige the Commission to put forward a proposal; however, under a code of conduct concluded with the EP in 1995, the Commission agreed to take the greatest possible account of them.

Consultation Procedure

The consultation procedure gives the EP the right to submit a nonbinding opinion before the Council adopts a Commission proposal. The original TEC designated twenty-two articles under which the Council could enact legislation only after consulting the EP. With the introduction subsequently of new, more far-reaching procedures, the scope of the consultation procedure was correspondingly reduced. Following the Amsterdam Treaty—the latest round of treaty change that resulted in an extension of the EP's legislative powers—the consultation procedure remains in use but is applicable to only a small number of policy areas over which national governments are reluctant to cede control.

The consultation procedure works as follows:

- *Step 1:* The Commission submits a proposal to the Council, which asks the EP for its opinion.
- *Step 2:* The EP gives its opinion (no time limit).
- *Step 3:* The Commission may amend its proposal on the basis of the EP's opinion but is not obliged to do so.
- *Step 4:* On the basis of unanimity or qualified majority voting (depending on the relevant treaty provisions for each applicable policy area), the Council may adopt the proposal (in its original or EP-amended form); alternatively, the Council may itself amend the proposal (in its original or EP-amended form) before adopting it,

> but only on the basis of unanimity. If the Council fails to reach agreement, the proposal stays on the table, sometimes indefinitely.

Initially the consultation procedure appeared to give the EP no more of a legislative role than that of an advisory body such as the Economic and Social Committee. The EP sought to maximize its potential under the procedure by exploiting the fact that "as long as the Council has not acted, the Commission may alter its proposal at any time [before] the adoption of a Community act" (Article 250, formerly Article 189a, TEC). In other words, leverage of the consultation procedure depended on the EP's ability to convince the Commission to adopt parliamentary amendments to draft legislation. In addition, the TEC did not place a time limit on the EP's right to submit an opinion. In a landmark decision in 1980 (in the so-called *Isoglucose* case), the ECJ annulled a legislative act because the EP had not yet given its opinion in an area covered by the consultation procedure. The Council argued in the *Isoglucose* case that it had waited for a parliamentary opinion but that the EP had procrastinated; the EP counter-argued that the Council had proceeded peremptorily. Regardless of what happened, the Court's ruling gave the EP de facto delaying power over legislation subject to the consultation procedure.

The first directly elected EP quickly changed its rules to make the most of the Court's decision. Since then, the EP's strategy has been to vote on amendments to a proposal but, before preparing a formal parliamentary opinion by voting on the resolution as a whole, to try to get the Commission to accept the amendments. Even if the Commission agrees, there is no guarantee that the Council will approve the amended proposal, although the unanimity requirement makes it difficult for the Council to change the EP's amendments if approved by the Commission. Clearly, the degree of parliamentary leverage over the Council depends on how badly the Council wants a particular piece of legislation. For its part, the EP does not want to delay legislation indefinitely, both because it wants the EU to produce legislation and because it does not want to be seen to be responsible for the EU's failure to do so.

Cooperation Procedure

The SEA sought to increase the EP's legislative power and to improve the efficiency of EC decisionmaking. It did so by giving Parliament the right to have a second reading of certain draft legislation and by extending the use of qualified majority voting in the Council. The new cooperation procedure incorporated both measures and formed "the institutional core of the SEA."[15] Originally the new procedure applied to ten EC treaty articles, most dealing with the single market program. The TEU extended the cooperation procedure to fourteen policy areas, but the Amsterdam Treaty virtually abolished it in favor of a revised codecision procedure that gives the EP far greater legislative power. Because the cooperation procedure is hardly applicable anymore, its workings are not explained here. Nevertheless, the profound impact of the cooperation procedure on the EP's development in the late 1980s and early 1990s needs to be understood, not least because elements of the cooperation procedure were incorporated into the later codecision procedure.

The cooperation procedure revolutionized the EP's legislative role and introduced a new dimension into EU decisionmaking. Although unhappy with the new procedure's limited applicability, the EP resolved from the outset to realize the SEA's political and institutional potential. In December 1986 the EP radically revised its rules to make the most of the cooperation procedure. It especially appreciated the importance of the first reading, using it to shape the final legislative outcome by apprising the Council of its intentions and by building the coalition of party groups required to amend, or possibly reject, a "common position" (the Council's decision at the end of the first reading, which formed the basis for deliberations in the second stage). For its part, the Council sought to avoid major parliamentary amendments and, especially, the EP's outright rejection of its common position, which it could counter only by an often unobtainable unanimous vote. Finally, the cooperation procedure cast the Commission in the role of arbitrator between the Council and Parliament.

The cooperation procedure had a profound impact on political group behavior in the EP. Parliament could only amend or reject a common position by the vote of an absolute majority of MEPs, and only political groups could organize MEPs and muster the required number of votes. On ideological issues, either the Socialists or the Christian Democrats form the core of a parliamentary majority, vying for the support of groups in the center. Whereas the Socialists can usually depend on support from the far left, the Christian Democrats dislike having to depend on support from the far right. When issues are not contested along ideological lines, the two major political groups often collaborate to amend or reject a common position in order to enhance the EP's institutional authority.

The increasing importance of majority voting instilled in political groups a greater sense of identity and cohesion and enhanced consensus and coalition building among them. Nevertheless, political group discipline is extremely lax by the standards of national parliaments, where a government's survival may depend on fierce party loyalty. In addition, the heterogeneity and cultural diversity of political groups militates against strict control of members' behavior. Most important, "one must never underestimate the fact that [MEPs] always consider themselves as representatives of national interests."[16] Consequently, when pressed, MEPs tend to vote along regional or national rather than ideological or political group lines.

The cooperation procedure also resulted in a profusion of lobbying directed at EP committee meetings in Brussels and plenary sessions in Strasbourg. Before the SEA, lobbyists had little reason to cultivate MEPs.

Afterward, when Parliament acquired more power and MEPs became proficient at using the cooperation procedure, lobbyists seized the opportunity to shape legislation through amendments. In many cases lobbyists alerted MEPs to the cooperation procedure's potential and provided them with information about impending legislation that their small staffs were often otherwise unable to obtain. Given the strength of MEPs' commitments to their own countries, industries and interest groups frequently organize lobbies along national lines, at least for the larger delegations.

The EP and the Commission were generally pleased with the cooperation procedure's impact on policymaking and on the political process. According to the influential Prag Report, this procedure "transformed the role of Parliament in . . . limited though vital fields, and introduced a degree of democratic control over the establishment of a single market by the end of 1992." Nevertheless, the report identified three major defects in the procedure: its limited scope (despite changes in the TEU), the Council's ability to "kill legislation by default," and the Council's "right to adopt legislation in face of Parliament's rejection of all or parts of it."[17] According to an earlier assessment by the commissioner responsible for relations with the EP, the cooperation procedure "had worked during a period of intense legislative activity," proving that "democracy and efficiency are compatible."[18]

By contrast, some member states were less enamored of the cooperation procedure, seeing it as an opportunity for the EP to promote its institutional agenda at the expense of effective decisionmaking. Although the procedure required close interinstitutional collaboration to work properly, the Council sometimes stood aloof. For instance, the EP persistently complained that the Council refused to explain fully its reasons for rejecting parliamentary amendments. This prompted the EP to call on the Council to reveal "the results of the votes [on common positions] in the Council and the views of each Member State, enabling the peoples and parliaments of the Community to form a view of their governments' position."[19]

Disputes between the Council and the EP over the cooperation procedure focused mostly on the choice of "legal base": the relevant treaty article on which the EU should base its legislative action. If the legal base was ambiguous, the EP would invariably opt for an article that stipulated the cooperation procedure, whereas the Council would choose the consultation procedure in order to avoid a second reading. Until the TEU, environmental issues lent themselves to such ambiguity because the SEA extended EC competence to environmental policy subject to the consultation procedure (Article 130s TEC) but also introduced a new article for the harmonization of national standards subject to the cooperation procedure (Article 100a). Thus for certain environmental legislation, the Council favored Article 130s as a legal base, whereas the EP preferred Article 100a. Although the TEU extended the cooperation procedure to environmental policy and the Amsterdam Treaty in turn extended codecision to environmental policy, plenty of scope remained for disagreement between the Council and EP over the choice of legal base in other areas, not least because of the introduction by the TEU of the new codecision procedure.

As well as introducing codecision, the TEU incorporated the cooperation procedure into a new article (Article 252, formerly Article 189c, TEC), unchanged from its SEA formulation. Although the TEU switched some policy areas from cooperation to codecision, it also switched a number of others from consultation to cooperation. As a result, the cooperation procedure covered fourteen policy areas, making it the most important procedure used in the enactment of EU legislation until implementation of the Amsterdam Treaty.

Codecision Procedure

According to the Prag Report, the EP regarded the cooperation procedure as "part of a preparatory stage in the introduction of genuine co-decision." "Genuine co-decision" meant endowing the EP with legislative power equal to that of the Council. However, the form of codecision introduced by the TEU disappointed the EP, which received only a limited right of rejection rather than a positive right of approval. The new procedure was extremely complicated. Its major innovations were to give the EP a right to a third reading and, failing agreement at that stage, to establish a Council-EP conciliation committee. A compromise reached in the conciliation committee required ratification by both the EP and the Council.

The experience of codecision since implementation of the TEU in November 1993 belied those critics (especially in the Council secretariat) who claimed that the procedure was too complex to work efficiently and expeditiously. The EP's experience with the cooperation procedure should have shown that the EP would also master codecision, which it did. The conciliation committee was codecision's most serious potential pitfall. After the 1995 enlargement the committee consisted of fifteen representatives each of the Council and the EP. Initially the EP had wanted the Council to be represented on the conciliation committee only by government ministers, but not unreasonably, the Council pointed out that ministers were too busy to come to Brussels for relatively frequent but irregular conciliation committee meetings. The practice soon developed whereby, apart from the presidency (which sends a junior minister), national governments sent their permanent representatives to conciliation committee meetings. On the other side of the table a vice president leads the EP delegation. Although denied a key role in the conciliation committee, the Commission is represented by the commissioner responsible for the legislation in question.

The EP adopted the vast majority of legislation proposed under the TEU version of the codecision procedure (i.e., before implementation of the Amsterdam Treaty revisions) without convening the conciliation committee.

The EP rejected only a handful of proposals either at the third reading stage or after agreement in the conciliation committee, often in order to make a political point. More often than not the point at issue had to do with the appropriate implementing committee for a particular measure (i.e., the arcane dispute between the Council and the EP over "comitology").

Despite a "revisionist" academic critique of the EP's role in the codecision procedure, most participants and observers agree that codecision greatly enhanced the EP's legislative powers.[20] The EP generally succeeded in having its legislative amendments accepted by the Commission and the Council. Moreover, successful efforts by the EP at the 1996–1997 IGC to extend the scope of codecision, and unsuccessful efforts by the British government (before it changed in May 1997) to thwart the extension of codecision, suggest that codecision was indeed politically advantageous to the EP.

Not only did the Amsterdam Treaty greatly increase the scope of codecision by extending its coverage to most of what had hitherto been covered by the cooperation procedure but also it revised the third reading stage so that should the Council and Parliament fail to agree on a joint text in the conciliation committee, the Council may no longer (as it could under the original version of codecision) act unilaterally by going back to the common position it had agreed upon before the conciliation procedure and adopt the act by qualified majority. Apart from tidying up the procedure, altering the one-sided third reading put the EP on an equal legislative footing with the Council. The post-Amsterdam version of codecision works as follows:

Step 1: The Commission submits a proposal to the Council and the EP.
Step 2: EP first reading. The EP gives its opinion.
Step 3: Council first reading. Acting by a qualified majority the Council may *either*

a. adopt the proposal with all the amendments contained in the EP's opinion *or*
b. adopt the proposal without amendments if the EP has not proposed any *or*
c. adopt a common position and send it to the EP, informing the EP fully of the reasons for its common position.

Step 4: EP second reading. In the case of option (c) above, within three months the EP may *either*

a. approve the common position (if the EP fails to act, the proposal is adopted by default in accordance with the common position) *or*
b. reject the common position by an absolute majority of its members (if so, by default the proposal is not adopted) *or*
c. propose amendments to the common position by an absolute majority of its members and forward them to the Commission and the Council (*second reading*).

Step 5: In the case of option (c) above, the Commission delivers an opinion on the EP's amendments.
Step 6: Council second reading. Within three months the Council may *either*

a. approve all the EP's amendments by a qualified majority, except those amendments on which the Commission has delivered a negative opinion (these the Council must approve by unanimity; however approved, the proposal is then deemed to have been adopted in the form of the common position thus amended) *or*
b. if it does not approve all amendments, the Council must within six weeks convene a meeting of the conciliation committee (in agreement with the president of the EP).

Step 7: In the case of option (b) above, working with the common position on the basis of amendments proposed by the EP and within six weeks of being convened, the conciliation committee *either*

a. fails to agree on a joint text (in which case the proposal is deemed not to have been adopted) *or*
b. agrees to a joint text by a qualified majority of the Council representatives and by a majority of the EP representatives.

Step 8: In the case of option (b) above

a. EP third reading. The EP, acting by an absolute majority of the votes cast (not an absolute majority of its members), has six weeks from the date of that approval to adopt the joint text, *and*
b. Council third reading. The Council, acting by a qualified majority, has six weeks from the date of that approval to adopt the joint text.

Step 9: If either the EP or the Council fails to approve the joint text, the proposal is deemed not to have been adopted.

The TEU version of codecision also had time constraints, but legislation enacted under it took nearly a year to work its way through the system. This delay led the member states to attach a protocol to the Amsterdam Treaty adjuring the Council, Commission, and EP to use the codecision procedure as expeditiously as possible.

Assent Procedure

The SEA introduced an "assent" procedure covering a small number of legislative items. Under this procedure, the EP may neither delay nor amend proposals but has the power either to accept or reject them. The TEU extended the assent procedure to certain policy areas, notably citizenship, specific tasks of the European Central Bank and amendments to its stature, and the structural funds and the Cohesion Fund. The EP is unhappy with the assent procedure in the legislative field because of the procedure's blunt nature. By contrast, the EP is pleased with the assent procedure in nonlegislative fields such as EU enlargement and association with third countries (examined further on). In another area of EU activity the EP attempted unsuccessfully in the 1996–1997 IGC to win the right of assent, that is, the amendment of the treaties (Article 48, formerly Article N, TEU).

Scrutiny and Supervision

The EP has a variety of powers and responsibilities to scrutinize the work of the Commission and the Council and to approve the appointment of the Commission president and the college of commissioners. MEPs may submit written and oral questions as a limited means of parliamentary supervision over the Council and Commission. Additional supervisory powers range from the innocuous (discussion of the Commission's annual *General Report*) to the vigorous (ability to force the Commission to resign as a body by a two-thirds majority). The EP uses these powers of scrutiny and supervision not only to improve the quality of EU administration and governance but especially to maneuver itself into the classic role of a legislature holding the executive to account.

Fearful of provoking a major political crisis that could escalate beyond its control, the EP has generally been reticent about tabling, let alone adopting, motions of censure against the Commission. For example, the EP's response to the bovine spongiform encephalopathy (BSE) crisis in 1996 demonstrated Parliament's increasing assertiveness vis-à-vis the Commission, tempered by its lingering reluctance to adopt a vote of censure. Although the EP had enough votes to table a motion of censure, the EP's leadership decided instead to adopt a resolution of "conditional censure" to pressure the Commission to implement the EP's recommendations for administrative improvements in the wake of the BSE crisis.[21] In January 1999, however, following protracted criticism of the Commission's financial mismanagement and allegations of impropriety by individual commissioners, the EP voted on whether to oust the entire Commission. Although highly controversial within the EP itself and ultimately unsuccessful, the vote nonetheless showed the EP's willingness to raise the political stakes especially in the run-up to the 1999 direct elections.

Although the EC treaty did not give Parliament a role in appointing the Commission, since 1981 the EP has voted on the investiture of the newly appointed Commission. This practice was formalized in the TEU (Article 214.2, formerly Article 158.2, TEC), which stated that the newly nominated president and other members of the Commission "shall be subject as a body to a vote of approval by the European Parliament." In its usual thrusting way, the EP interpreted this as meaning that it could vote separately on the presidential nomination (which it did for the first time in July 1994) and collectively on the nominations of the other commissioners following individual "investiture" hearings (which it held for the first time in January 1995). The conduct of the 1994 vote on Jacques Santer's nomination (fearing that the vote would go against Santer, some national governments pressured MEPs to vote in his favor) and of the 1995 investiture hearings (MEPs quizzed some commissioners-designate aggressively) graphically illustrated the EP's determination to make the Commission accountable to Parliament.[22]

The TEU confirmed another supervisory practice that the EP had already developed: convening temporary committees of inquiry. At the request of one-quarter of its members, the EP can appoint a temporary committee of inquiry to investigate "alleged contraventions or maladministration in the implementation of Community law" (Article 193, formerly Article 138c, TEC). This gave the EP another weapon with which to extend its supervision of the Commission. Indeed, it was a highly critical report of a temporary committee of inquiry that led to the EP's resolution of conditional censure of the Commission in the BSE case.

Other tools in the EP's supervisory arsenal are intended to assist EU citizens suffering from alleged maladministration of Community law. Two were also established in the TEU. One is an EU citizen's right to petition the EP "on a matter which comes within the Community's fields of activity and which affects him directly" (Article 194, formerly Article 138d, TEC). Another is the office of the ombudsman, appointed by the EP and "empowered to receive complaints from any citizen . . . concerning instances of maladministration in the activities of the Community's institution's or bodies" (Article 195, formerly Article 138e, TEC). Upon receiving a complaint, the ombudsman investigates and makes a report to the EP and the institution concerned.

The office of the ombudsman got off to a bad start because of quarrels among political groups over the selection of the first incumbent. After an unseemly delay of nearly two years, in July 1995 the EP eventually elected Jacob Soederman to the job. The ombudsman receives an increasing number of complaints annually (currently well over 1,000), although not all of them are admissible. The ombudsman's two biggest problems have been a lack of resources and the difficulty of defining "maladministration." Put positively, the ombudsman's job is to improve the quality of EU administration from the citizen's point of view. To help do so, in his 1997 annual report Soederman urged EU institutions to adopt a "code of good administrative behavior."[23]

External Relations Responsibilities

The prominence of the EP's Committee on Foreign Affairs, Security, and Defense Policy indicates the EU's increasing competence in external relations and the EP's determination to become fully involved in that field. Parliament's role in the CFSP built on its limited involvement in European Political Cooperation (EPC): The old Political Affairs Committee (forerunner of the Committee on Foreign Affairs, Security, and Defense Policy) regularly discussed foreign policy issues, held a special colloquy four times a year with the Council presidency, and organized meetings between its leadership and the political directors of national foreign ministries. In addition, plenary sessions included a short period for EPC-related questions to the Council presidency and member state foreign ministers. In reality, these forays into the foreign policy sphere were peripheral to the EP's main activities, and EPC itself was extremely restricted in its scope and effectiveness.

The EP hoped that the TEU would give the EU a greater capacity in foreign and security policy, and with it give the EP a policymaking role. The EP was disappointed on both counts: The CFSP was procedurally and substantively weak, and as a strictly intergovernmental affair, the EP's involvement in it was limited to being consulted by the presidency "on the main aspects and the basic choices" of the CFSP, being kept regularly informed by the presidency and the Commission "on the development of the Union's foreign and security policy," being allowed to ask questions of the Council and make recommendations to it, and being obliged to hold an annual debate on progress on implementing the CFSP (Article 21, formerly Article J.11, TEU). The EP's role in this regard was unchanged in the Amsterdam Treaty.

Governments are generally averse to parliamentary involvement in foreign affairs, and EU governments are particularly averse to involving the EP in the CFSP in any meaningful way. Limited EP involvement is only one of the shortcomings of the CFSP, but it highlights a major problem: the dearth of "an EU-wide debate on a common foreign and security policy; the Union still lacks a sufficiently broad and informed political public of a European dimension; too many debates about important interests remain in the national arena and/or are restricted to a ministerial and diplomatic elite."[24]

Surprisingly, given that it lies squarely within the first pillar, the EP's role in the common commercial policy is virtually nonexistent. Article 133 (formerly Article 113) TEC states that "the Commission shall submit proposals to the Council for implementing the common commercial policy" and that the Council "shall act by a qualified majority." The original Article 113 was unchanged in the SEA and TEU and changed in the Amsterdam Treaty only to allow the Council to extend the scope of the article to cover international negotiations and agreements on services and intellectual property (a touchy issue between the Commission and the Council during the closing stages of the Uruguay Round of the GATT), acting unanimously on a proposal from the Commission "and after consulting the European Parliament."

By contrast, the EP is coequal with the Council in another important foreign policy sphere: EU enlargement and association with third countries. Under the assent procedure introduced by the SEA, an absolute majority of MEPs must approve accession and association agreements. Initially this provision seemed a small concession to the EP: In 1986, after the third enlargement, the EU's boundaries looked set for several years to come. Nor did a new series of association agreements appear imminent. Yet the success of the single market and the sudden end of the Cold War soon gave rise to a new round of accession negotiations and association agreements. Moreover, the assent procedure covers revisions or additions to existing association agreements, such as financial protocols. The EP has repeatedly used the assent procedure to leverage respect for human rights in countries having or wanting to have association agreements with the EU, notably Turkey, Israel, Morocco, and Syria. The TEU extended the assent procedure to all international agreements that set up institutions, have major financial implications, or require legislation under codecision.

INTERNAL ORGANIZATION

Parliament carries out its budgetary, legislative, supervisory, and other responsibilities through an elaborate leadership structure, a strong committee system, and frenzied plenary sessions.

Leadership Structure

The EP's leadership structure and responsibilities are as follows:

- The *president of the Parliament* presides over plenary sessions, chairs meetings of the Bureau and the Conference of Presidents, represents the EP at interinstitutional meetings, and signs the budget into law.
- The fourteen *vice presidents* preside over plenary sessions when the president is absent and represent the EP in the conciliation committee.
- The *Bureau* (the EP president and vice presidents) makes key budgetary and personnel decisions.
- The *Conference of Presidents* (the EP president and the presidents of the political groups) decides the agenda for plenary sessions; discusses the annual legislative program, interinstitutional relations, and relations with non-EU institutions; and manages the committee system.
- The five *quaestors* (ordinary MEPs) make important day-to-day administrative decisions.

The Bureau, Conference of Presidents, and quaestors meet approximately twice a month—in Strasbourg during plenary sessions and in Brussels during committee or political group meetings.

All are elected positions; elections take place every two and a half years, at the beginning and in the middle of the EP's five-year term. Because of a pact between the Socialists and Christian Democrats, who together command an absolute majority, the presidency alternates between them. Members of other groups have rightly denounced this "more or less automatic [presidential] election system," although their claim that it "harms the credibility of the EP in the eyes of the elector" exaggerates the extent of public awareness of the EP's internal opeations.[25] However unfairly selected, recent presidents have at least taken the institution seriously and worked hard to raise its political profile both inside and outside the EU. The president's presentation of the EP's position at the beginning of each European Council testifies to the EP's growing influence throughout the EU system and to the need for the EP to have a politically weighty president.

The outcome of the presidential election determines the outcome of the elections for other leadership positions (except for political group leaders, who are elected by political group members). Although other leadership elections are supposedly open, the party groups decide among themselves who gets what. The leadership's composition generally reflects the distribution of EP seats by political group and nationality.

Committee System

The EP could not manage its burgeoning budgetary, legislative, and nonlegislative agenda without an adequate committee system. The EP's committee system evolved along with the EU, changing over the years to reflect the EU's increasing competence and the EP's growing assertiveness and responsibility. For instance, in response to the TEU the EP revamped and renamed its Political Affairs Committee (it became the Committee on Foreign Affairs, Security, and Defense Policy) and established a new Committee on Civil Liberties and Internal Affairs. The EP now has twenty permanent committees covering every facet of EU activity.

Clearly, some committees are more important than others. For instance, the Environment Committee and the Committee on Budgetary Control are influential because the EP exercises considerable power in those areas. The importance of the Budgets Committee (as distinct from the Committee on Budgetary Control) is undiminished despite the new interinstitutional arrangement for medium-term financial planning. Other committees, such as the Committee on Transport and Tourism, have always been relatively unimportant, although much sought after by MEPs who like to travel.

Table 10.2 European Parliament Committees and Subcommittees

C1	Committee on Foreign Affairs, Security, and Defense Policy
SC1A	Subcommittee on Security and Disarmament
SC1B	Subcommittee on Human Rights
C2	Committee on Agriculture and Rural Development
C3	Committee on Budgets
C4	Committee on Economic, Monetary Affairs, and Industrial Policy
SC4	Subcommittee on Monetary Affairs
C5	Committee on Research, Technological Development, and Energy
C6	Committee on External Economic Relations
C7	Committee on Legal Affairs and Citizens' Rights
C8	Committee on Social Affairs and Employment
C9	Committee on Regional Policy
C10	Committee on Transport and Tourism
C11	Committee on the Environment, Public Health, and Consumer Protection
C12	Committee on Culture, Youth, Education, and the Media
C13	Committee on Development and Cooperation
C14	Committee on Civil Liberties and Internal Affairs
C15	Committee on Institutional Affairs
C16	Committee on Budgetary Control
C17	Committee on Fisheries
C18	Committee on the Rules of Procedure, the Verification of Credentials, and Immunities
C19	Committee on Women's Rights
C20	Committee on Petitions
TC	Temporary Committee on Employment

Thus a committee's popularity among MEPs is not necessarily related to its inherent importance, although popularity can enhance a committee's influence. The Environment Committee, one of the largest in the EP, is popular with MEPs not only because of the EP's legislative authority in that area but also because environmental issues have growing political and economic salience throughout the EU (and beyond). By contrast, the Committee on Budgetary Control, one of the most powerful in the EP, deals with a complicated and colorless issue (discharge of the budget) and has a correspondingly small membership. Foreign and security policy are as fashionable as environmental policy. Accordingly, the Committee on Foreign Affairs, Security, and Defense Policy is as large as the Environment Committee and has an equally powerful chairman but only limited power. The Committee on Institutional Affairs has no real power either, yet it attracts prominent MEPs because of its reputation as a driving force in the process of European integration (a legacy of Altiero Spinelli, the committee's founder).

The EP leadership divides committee seats among party groups according to their strength in Parliament; the groups in turn allocate seats to their members based on seniority, personal preference, and nationality. Certain party groups and nationalities have strong preferences for particular committee assignments. Obvious examples are the Greens (environment, energy) and the Irish (agriculture, regional policy). Committee assignments are reallocated every two and a half years; there is no time limit on an MEP's committee service.

Parliament designates two weeks of each month for committee meetings. The frequency of each committee's meetings depends on the business before it; most meet at least monthly. Committee meetings take place in the EP's labyrinthine Brussels building, a complex of offices and conference rooms near Schuman Circle. Most meetings last the equivalent of one full day. MEPs' attendance is often sporadic. Meetings may also be attended by officials of the EP, Council, and Commission and occasionally by commissioners and government ministers (especially from the country in the presidency).

Given their smaller size and less formal nature, committee meetings are less beset by language problems than are plenary sessions. Nevertheless, interpreters not only provide the essential service of making people mutually intelligible but also, because of the costs involved, ensure that meetings do not run over the allotted time. Apart from paying for simultaneous interpretation, committees run up extra costs by producing documents in eleven languages (each step of the legislative process necessitates translation into each official language). The most striking sight on entering a committee meeting, regardless of the committee's size, is a mountain of documents immediately inside the door. The committee leadership structure replicates the EP's leadership structure: Each committee has a chair and three vice chairs, who form the committee's bureau. Each committee also has a coordinator, who marshals its members for key votes, and a rapporteur, who drafts its reports (EP reports are commonly known by the names of their rapporteurs).

In the case of legislative proposals, committees do the preliminary work on which the EP as a whole bases its decisions during plenary sessions. Before examining proposals in detail, committees verify the legal base in consultation with the Legal Affairs Committee. For proposals subject to the codecision procedure, rapporteurs follow the draft legislation's progress through the Council's working groups, through COREPER, and though the Council itself. Committee preparation of draft amendments gives interested parties an opportunity to influence legislation. Predictably, certain committees are a target of intense lobbying. As well as its twenty standing committees and occasional committees of inquiry, the EP regularly establishes temporary committees to work on important but transient issues.

Plenary Sessions

Plenaries are the most visible and least flattering part of the EP's existence. For a week each month (in reality, from Monday afternoon until the following Friday morning, although most members leave on Thursday evening), MEPs participate in a full session of the entire body. Plenaries include debates, speeches by commissioners and the Council presidency, question time, and, most important, votes on legislative amendments and other resolutions. A legislative resolution constitutes the EP's opinion on draft legislation, indicating whether the EP approves, rejects, or amends the relevant proposal. Outside the chamber itself (in Eurospeak, the "hemicycle") but within the cavernous building where plenaries take place (in Brussels or Strasbourg), MEPs hold political group, intergroup, and occasional committee meetings; entertain constituents; and parry lobbyists (a corner of the concourse near the entrance to the Strasbourg hemicycle is appropriately called the "lobbyists' bench").

Too much happens during plenaries in too short a time. Voting alone can occupy several hours despite a change of rules reducing the number of amendments (previously about 1,000 per session) that reach the hemicycle. Such is the pressure of voting and the difficulty of knowing what each vote means that many MEPs simply stay away. Because amendments require at least a majority of the whole house to pass, rampant absenteeism frequently causes important amendments to fail. Presidents constantly urge MEPs to deal with technicalities in committee and keep the plenaries for debating big issues.

Staff

MEPs have an allowance to hire staff, who often include their own spouses. MEPs rely for policy and legislative assistance on their political group's staff. Staff size depends on the number of MEPs in each group (the Socialist group has a staff of more than fifty A-grade officials and 100 assistants). Committees have small staffs of their own (drawn from the EP's civil service) to help rapporteurs draft and write reports; large national delegations also have separate staffs funded by constituent national parties of the transnational political parties of which their groups are members. Finally, the EP has a secretariat (civil service), similar to the Council secretariat and Commission civil service, to provide the institution with support ranging from research to public relations to translation and interpretation. As in other branches of the EU's civil service, promotion in the upper echelons of the EP's secretariat is highly political and depends on ideological affinity as well as nationality.

THE DEMOCRATIC DEFICIT AND RELATIONS WITH NATIONAL PARLIAMENTS

A democratic deficit always existed in the EU but became increasingly prominent after the SEA in the mid-1980s. In a narrow sense, the democratic deficit is the gap between the powers of the Commission and Council, on the one hand, and those of national parliaments and the EP, on the other. It was accentuated by the SEA and subsequent treaty changes that transferred responsibility for a wide range of policy areas from the national to the EU level of government. Before such large-scale transfers, national parliaments had the legislative authority to enact laws in the policy areas concerned. At the EU level, the EP shares legislative authority with the Commission and, primarily, the Council.[26]

National parliaments lost legislative authority not only because the EU acquired new competencies but also because, beginning in the 1980s, the Council moved steadily away from unanimity toward qualified majority voting. The decline of unanimity may have improved the EU's legislative record, but it meant also the decline of national parliaments' control over their governments. As long as a government could veto EU legislation, its national parliament could hold it accountable for exercising (or not exercising) that veto. Once governments subscribed to qualified majority voting, however, national parliaments could not reasonably hold them accountable for being outvoted and abiding by a majority decision.

Before the increasing use of qualified majority voting, few national parliaments paid much attention to EU decisionmaking. Denmark's was an exception: The Folketing's powerful Committee for Relations with the Common Market held government ministers strictly accountable for their behavior in the Council and European Council. Paradoxically, Denmark's parliament disliked the antidemocratic implications of qualified majority voting and voted down the SEA in 1986 (the SEA was rescued in an ensuing Danish referendum). It was cold comfort for the Danish and other national parliaments that the EP, which had always enjoyed limited legislative authority (the consultation procedure), gained additional power (the cooperation procedure) under the SEA to offset the extension of qualified majority voting.

The EP itself was unhappy with the cooperation procedure's relatively narrow scope, especially with the existence after the SEA of a number of policy areas subject to qualified majority voting but not subject to the cooperation procedure. As the Council successfully implemented the single market program in the late 1980s using (or at least threatening to use) qualified majority voting to great effect, national parliaments and the EP became increasingly alarmed by the widening democratic deficit but differed in their suggested solutions to it.

Predictably, MEPs consistently proposed giving the EP more legislative, budgetary, and supervisory powers. The member states' extension of the cooperation procedure and introduction of the codecision procedure under the TEU went some way to meet MEPs' demands, but not far enough. At the same time, the TEU's expansion of the EP's legislative authority increased national parliaments' estrangement from the EU's decisionmaking apparatus.

Before direct elections, MEPs were also members of their national parliaments (i.e., they held the dual mandate). Subsequently, the vast majority of MEPs had little formal involvement with their national parliaments and the vast majority of national parliamentarians had little formal involvement with the EPs. National MPs generally resented their European counterparts' lifestyles and posturing, and MEPs resented not being taken seriously by their national counterparts. Clearly, closer contacts between MPs and MEPs was needed not only to improve each institution's perception of the other but also to involve national parliaments more in EU-level government.

Accordingly, a number of forums for formal contact between the EP and national parliaments emerged in the late 1980s:

- Conference of Presidents and Speakers of the Parliaments of the EU (meeting every six months)
- Conference of European Affairs Committees of the National Parliaments and the European Parliament (meeting every six months)
- Conference of the Parliaments—the so-called assizes of several hundred MEPs and national parliamentarians (no fixed schedule)
- bilateral and multilateral meetings between specialized committees to discuss planned and proposed EU legislation (no fixed schedule)

Concerned about the democratic deficit and about national parliaments' estrangement from the EU decisionmaking process, member states attached two declarations to the TEU on the role of national parliaments. The first promised that national governments would send to their own parliaments "proposals for (EU) legislation in good time for information or possible examination" and generally encouraged contact between MEPs and national parliamentarians. The second encouraged further assizes and promised to "consult" the Conference of the Parliaments "on the main features of the European Union." These anodyne declarations had little practical effect. Some national governments were more assiduous than others about informing their parliaments of impending EU legislation (and some national parliaments were more assiduous than others about insisting on such information). Moreover, the Conference of the Parliaments was too large and unwieldy to play anything other than a symbolic role.

National parliamentary pressure for greater involvement in EU affairs intensified after the TEU. In particular, Germany's parliament pressed the government successfully during the TEU ratification crisis for the right to evaluate draft EU legislation. In 1995, enlargement brought into the EU two Nordic countries whose parliaments were unwilling to cede control of EU legislation entirely to the Council and the EP. At the same time, the Euroskeptical British and Danish parliaments continued to press for more involvement in the EU legislative process.

Under the circumstances it was not surprising that the issue emerged during the 1996–1997 IGC. There, governments agreed on the need to keep national parliaments better informed but could not agree on the feasibility or desirability of a new body to represent national parliaments at the European level. Finally, member states attached a protocol to the Amsterdam Treaty outlining practical ways in which national parliaments would receive information on developments in the EU and encouraging the Conference of European Affairs Committees (CEAC) of the National Parliaments and the European Parliament to "make any contribution it deems appropriate for the attention of the institutions of the EU."

Despite the difficulty of institutionalizing a role for national parliaments at the European level, national parliamentarians and MEPs are gradually overcoming their mutual suspicion and resentment. The most encouraging sign of this is close collaboration between national parliamentarians and MEPs in transnational political parties such as the PES and EPP. It is also through the work of these parties that national parliamentarians and MEPs, outside their respective institutions, have most success shaping EU policy.

In a celebrated Euroskeptical speech in September 1994, British prime minister John Major declared that "the EP sees itself as the future democratic focus for the Union. But that is a flawed ambition, because the EU is an association of States, deriving its basic democratic legitimacy through *national* parliaments. . . . It is national parliamentary democracy that confers legitimacy on the EU."[27] The EU is much more than an association of states, and Major was wrong to denigrate the EP's contribution to its democratic legitimization. But he had a point about the EP's flawed ambition. The democratic deficit will not be solved simply by giving the EP more power. Indeed, few people outside the EP consider the EP capable of providing a solution to the EU's crisis of democratic legitimacy. MEPs are marginal figures at the national level, regardless of their political power at the European level, and the public is not clamoring to transfer more sovereignty to Strasbourg.

Will the democratic deficit ever be rectified? Certainly not simply by giving more power to the EP. The EU is not a state, and its institutional framework and political system will never correspond to that of a classic liberal democracy. Similarly, the Commission will never acquire the characteristics of a national executive. The EU is a unique system with unique institutions; the solution to the democratic deficit will be equally novel and unconventional. Conventional views of the democratic deficit and conventional proposals for its resolution are unconvincing. Undoubtedly the EP will remain an essential ingredient of political accountability in the EU, but in an evolving EU of traditional or transformed nation-states the democratic deficit will have to be resolved by an imaginative blend of public representation and involvement at the regional, national, and European levels, involving parliamentary bodies from all three spheres.

NOTES

1. "Prag Report on the Cooperation Procedure," as reproduced in *Agence Europe* Documents, 1820/21, January 30, 1993, pp. 10–12.

2. See Shirley Williams, "Sovereignty and Accountability in the European Community," in Robert O. Keohane and Stanley Hoffmann, *The New European Community: Decision-making and Institutional Change* (Boulder: Westview Press, 1991), p. 172.

3. Edinburgh European Council, "Presidency Conclusions," Bull. EC 12-1992, point 1.14.

4. Bull. EC 7/8-1976, points 1101–1109.

5. Bull. EC 9-1976, points 5201–5207.

6. European Parliament Session DOC PE 271.049, pp. 10–11, July 15, 1998.

7. See Francis Jacobs, Richard Corbett, and M. Shackleton, *The European Parliament,* 3d ed. (London: Catermill, 1995), pp. 25–30.

8. On the composition and role of political groups, see Simon Hix and Christopher Lord, *Political Parties in the European Union* (Basingstoke: Macmillan, 1997).

9. Marc Abelès, "Political Anthropology of a Transnational Institution: The European Parliament," *French Politics and Society* 11, no. 1 (winter 1993): 16–17.

10. Commission, *1988 General Report,* points 80–84.

11. See Commission of the European Communities, *From the Single Act to Maastricht and Beyond: The Means to Match Our Ambitions*, COM(92)2000 final, Brussels, February 11, 1992; Edinburgh European Council, "Presidency Conclusions" Bull. EC 12-1992, point 1.14.

12. Quoted in Daniel Strasser, *The Finances of Europe*, 7th ed. (Luxembourg: Office for Official Publications of the European Communities [OOP], 1992), p. 290.

13. See *Agence Europe,* January 11–15, 1999, and March 16–18, 1999.

14. David Coombes, "Public Provision in an Economic and Monetary Union: New Functions for the Budget of the European Community," paper presented at the Second Biennial Conference of the European Community Studies Association, George Mason University, May 1991, p. 1.

15. John Fitzmaurice, "An Analysis of the European Community's Cooperation Procedure," *Journal of Common Market Studies* 26, no. 4 (June 1988): 390.

16. Abelès, "Political Anthropology," p. 12.

17. See "Prag Report," pp. 10–12.

18. Quoted in *Agence Europe,* January 22, 1992, p. 1.

19. "Prag Report," p. 12.

20. For the revisionist perspective, see George Tsbelis, "The Power of the European Parliament as a Conditional Agenda Setter," *American Political Science Review* 88: 128–142; George Tsbelis, "Decisionmaking Inside the European Parliament," in B. Eichengreen, J. Frieden, and J. von Hagen, *Politics and Institutions in an Integrated Europe* (Heidelberg: Springer, 1995), pp. 42–64; and George Tsbelis and Geoffrey Garrett, "Agenda Setting, Vetoes, and the European Union's Co-Decision Procedure," *Journal of Legislative Studies* 3, no. 3. For a convincing rebuttal, see Roger Scully, "The European Parliament and the Co-Decision Procedure," *Journal of Legislative Studies* 3, no. 3.

21. See Martin Westlake, "'Mad Cows and Englishmen': The Institutional Consequences of the BSE Crisis," *Journal of Common Market Studies* 35, *Annual Review* (1996): 11–36.

22. See Simon Hix and Christopher Lord, "The Making of a President: The European Parliament and the Confirmation of Jacques Santer as President of the Commission," *Government and Opposition* 31: 62–76.

23. Jacob Soederman, *1997 Ombudsman Report* (Luxembourg: OOP, 1998), p. 16.

24. Wolfgang Wessels, "The EU as an Actor in the International System: The CFSP After Amsterdam," paper presented at the conference "The External Dimension of the EU," The Hague, December 1997, p. 5.

25. Statement by Gijs de Vries and Yves Galland, MEPs, quoted in *Agence Europe*, July 18–19, 1994, p. 4.

26. See Dimitris N. Chryssochoou, Stelios Stavridis, and Michael J. Tsinisizelis, "European Democracy, Parliamentary Decline and the 'Democratic Deficit' of the European Union," *Journal of Legislative Studies* 4, no. 3 (1998).

27. John Major, "Europe: A Future That Works," William and Mary Lecture, Leiden University, September 7, 1994.

11

Other Institutions and Bodies

Article 7 (formerly Article 4) of the Treaty Establishing the European Community (TEC) identifies five EU institutions—the European Parliament (EP), the Council, the Commission, the Court of Justice, and the Court of Auditors—and two advisory bodies, the Economic and Social Committee and the Committee of the Regions. This chapter examines the Court of Justice, the Court of Auditors, the Economic and Social Committee, and the Committee of the Regions, together with the Court of First Instance (attached to the Court of Justice), the European Investment Bank (an autonomous lending institution), and a growing and diverse group of "Community agencies." The remaining parts of the EU system—the European System of Central Banks (ESCB) and the European Central Bank (ECB)—are examined in Chapter 16.

THE COURT OF JUSTICE

For much of its existence the European Court of Justice (ECJ) was the EU's least-known institution. Located in Luxembourg, far from the political fray in Brussels and Strasbourg, the Court initially received little outside attention as it waded through a growing number of seemingly arcane and unimportant cases. Only gradually did the significance of the Court's rulings become apparent to the nonlegal world. In the dark days of the late 1960s and the 1970s, while the EC languished politically, economically, and institutionally, the ECJ persevered and produced an impressive amount of case law that maintained the momentum for deeper integration. In so doing, the Court not only defined and shaped a new legal order but also contributed to the EC's revival and transformation in the 1980s. Critics accuse the Court of judicial activism, testimony to its enormous impact on the EU's political development.[1] Despite a few instances of apparent activism in the late 1980s and early 1990s, the Court grew less adventurous later in the 1990s, partly because most of the principles of EC law had been established and partly because of its sensitivity to criticism in a number of member states—not only the Euroskeptical ones.

The Court's principal purpose is "to ensure that in the interpretation and application of [the treaties] the law is observed" (Article 220 TEC). The original treaties, the treaties of accession, and the various treaty amendments constitute the EU's "primary legislation," whereas laws made in accordance with the treaties constitute the EU's "secondary legislation." Primary and secondary legislation are the main sources of Community law, a "self-sufficient body of law that is binding on [the member states] and on their subjects."[2]

From the outset the ECJ has seen the original treaties not simply as narrow international agreements but, because of the member states' unique decision to share sovereignty, as the basis of a constitutional framework for the EU. "If one were asked to synthesize the direction in which the case law produced in Luxembourg has moved since 1957," Federico Mancini, a member of the Court, wrote in 1991, "one would have to say that it coincides with the making of a constitution for Europe."[3] In a compelling series of cases the ECJ showed that the EU's "constitution" is based on custom and on shared values as well as on treaties and secondary legislation.

Fundamental human rights—an essential ingredient of any constitutional democracy—underpin EC law. Although the original treaties made no mention of human rights, the preamble of the SEA acknowledged the Court's repeated emphasis on the issue by declaring the member states' determination "to work together to promote democracy on the basis of the fundamental rights recognized in the constitutions and laws of the Member States, in the Convention for the Protection of Human Rights and Fundamental Freedoms and the European Social Charter, notably freedom, equality and social justice." The Treaty on European Union (TEU) did not institute a charter of fundamental rights and freedoms, as the EP had wanted it to,[4] but it did include a new article explicitly stating that "the Union shall respect fundamental rights, as guaranteed by the European Convention for the Protection of Human Rights and Fundamental Freedoms signed in Rome on November 4, 1950, and as they result from the constitutional traditions common to the Member States, as general principles of Community law" (Article 6.2, formerly Article F.2, TEU).

Despite its use of the European Convention for the Protection of Human Rights and Fundamental Freedoms (ECHR) as a source for upholding the fundamental rights of individuals under EC law, the Court ruled in March 1996 that the EC could not, without a treaty amendment, accede to the ECHR.[5] Moreover, the Court expressed concerns about incorporating a separate international legal order into the EU legal system. Based partly on the Court's misgivings, member states decided during the 1996–1997 intergovernmental conference (IGC) that the EC should not accede to the ECHR, although the member states themselves are all signatories to the convention. The solution adopted was to confirm that Community law is subject to the European Convention, but as applied by the Court in Luxembourg.

As it did with human rights, the ECJ developed the concept of European citizenship before the member states gave substance to it in TEU (now Article 17 TEC).[6]

Basic Rules of EC Law

Apart from identifying the sources of Community law and endowing the treaties with the attributes of a constitution, the Court also developed two essential rules on which the new legal order rests: direct effect and supremacy. These twin pillars emerged in a series of cases early in the EU's history and clarified the working relationship between the national and Community legal orders.

Direct Effect

The Court first ruled on the direct effect of primary legislation in a case that, though technical and tedious, raised a fundamental principle of Community law. In *Van Gend en Loos* (1963), a Dutch transport firm brought a complaint against Dutch customs for increasing the duty on a product imported from Germany. The firm argued that the Dutch authorities had breached Article 12 (now Article 25) TEC, which prohibits member states from introducing new duties or increasing existing duties in the common market. Thus the Dutch firm claimed protection, citing the "direct effect" of Community law.

The Court agreed. In a landmark judgment it ruled that the article in question had direct effect because it contained a "clear and unconditional prohibition." Seizing the opportunity to make its mark, the Court declared that any unconditionally worded treaty provision, being "self-sufficient and legally complete," did not require further intervention at the national or Community levels and therefore applied directly to individuals. Not mincing its words, the Court stated that "the Community constitutes a new legal order . . . the subjects of which comprise not only the member states but also their nationals. Independently of the legislation of member states, Community law not only imposes obligations on individuals but . . . also confers rights upon them. These rights arise not only where they are expressly granted by the Treaty, but also by reason of obligations which the Treaty of Rome imposes in a clearly defined way upon individuals as well as upon member states and upon the institutions of the Community."

The Court continued to push the principle of direct effect in cases involving directives (addressed to member states) as well as regulations (addressed to individuals) and treaty provisions. The Court delivered a landmark judgment in *Grad v. Finanzamt Traunstein* (1970) when it ruled that a directive had direct effect if it contained a clear and unconditional obligation on a member state and had not been implemented by that state within the period prescribed in the directive. The reasoning was that "a Member State should not be able to take advantage of the fact that it had infringed the Treaties by failing to implement the directive or by failing to implement it properly. The individual citizen must be able to rely on his legal position under Community law before the national courts."

Supremacy of Community Law

The principle of direct effect would have had little impact if Community law did not supersede national law. Otherwise member states would simply ignore EU rules that conflicted with national rules. Although the TEC is equivocal on the issue, the ECJ had no hesitation in asserting the supremacy of Community law over national law. The Court's first chance to do so came in *Costa v. ENEL* (1964), only a year after *Van Gend en Loos*, when the Court pointed out that member states had definitively transferred sovereign rights to the Community and that Community law could not be overridden by domestic legal provisions without the legal basis of the Community itself being called into question. The Court expanded on the primacy of Community law in *Simmenthal v. Commission* (1978) when it ruled that "every national court must . . . apply Community law in its entirety . . . and must accordingly set aside any provisions of national law which may conflict with it."

The *Costa*, *Van Gend en Loos*, and *Simmenthal* cases established the twin principles of direct effect and primacy of Community law, taking the national courts by surprise. Some national courts reacted strongly against what they saw as the encroachment of a new legal order. A major challenge came in the late 1960s when the constitutional courts of Italy and Germany hinted that because Community law apparently guaranteed a lower standard of fundamental rights than national law, the validity of Community law could be called into question at the national level. In a move that not only developed the Community's human rights case law but also warded off a potentially serious threat from national courts, the ECJ held in *Nold v. Commission* (1974) that "fundamental rights form an integral part of the general principles of [Community] law."

Types of Cases

Cases before the ECJ originate in one of three ways:

1. requests from national courts for "preliminary ruling" on points of EC law

2. actions brought directly to the Court by other institutions, member states, or natural and legal persons
3. appeals against judgments of the Court of First Instance, the ECJ's "lower court"

The bulk of ECJ cases, and the most important ones in terms of developing a body of EC law, arise out of requests for preliminary rulings and direct actions.

Requests for Preliminary Rulings

Under Article 234 (formerly Article 177) TEC, if an individual argues before a national court that a national law or policy conflicts with EC law, and if the court is unable or unwilling to resolve the dispute itself based on previous EC case law, the court may seek "authoritative guidance" from the ECJ by making a preliminary ruling reference (request). The parties involved, as well as EU institutions and national governments, may submit legal arguments to the ECJ. Based on its assessment of the arguments, relevant case law, and relevant treaty provisions, the ECJ issues a ruling, which the national court then applies to the case in question. Requests for preliminary rulings came slowly at first but accelerated in the 1970s and 1980s. In the 1990s, there were approximately 200 requests for preliminary rulings annually.

Clearly, the success of Community law depends to a great extent on the willingness of national courts to seek preliminary rulings and abide by them (under Article 234, lower national courts *may* seek guidance from the ECJ in cases involving Community law, but the highest national courts *must* do so). The general complicity of national courts in consolidating EC law is all the more striking because, in most cases, landmark ECJ judgments have come in response to requests from national courts for preliminary rulings. The original intent of Article 234 was to ensure uniform interpretation and application of Community law in each member state. Almost immediately, however, Article 234 became a powerful tool with which the ECJ could strengthen Community law and the Court's own role within the EU system. It also became a device that citizens could use to ascertain the compatibility of national and Community law. As a result, "the preliminary rulings procedure is of fundamental importance to the proper functioning of the legal and economic system established by the EEC Treaty. It is in the framework of that procedure that basic principles of the Community legal order, such as direct effect and primacy, have been developed."[7]

The increasing rate of preliminary ruling requests from lower courts has enhanced the stature of the ECJ, effectively giving it the power to review national law and thereby turning it into a supreme court. Increasingly, the ECJ has reformulated national courts' questions in order to elucidate what it considers to be the most important points at issue. This allows the ECJ to address important points of law that otherwise might not come before it. In so doing, Article 234 has gradually undermined the authority of the highest national courts. Why do so many lower national court judges apply for preliminary rulings "given that such judges must attend to their career prospects within hierarchically organized national judicial systems?"[8] According to a former member of the Court of First Instance, the answer may be simply that "the concept of a Community governed by law is naturally attractive to all Judges." Whatever the reason, Article 234 has brought about a special relationship, indeed a close partnership, between national courts and the ECJ. As a result, "the National Judge . . . in his capacity as Community Judge, becomes the upholder of Community Law in his own member state."[9]

Direct Actions

References for preliminary rulings constitute one branch of ECJ case law; direct actions make up the other. Direct actions usually take one of the following forms:

- *Cases brought by the Commission against a member state or, rarely, by a member state against another member state for failing to fulfill a legal obligation (Articles 226 and 227):* If the Court agrees that the case is well founded, it declares that an obligation has not been fulfilled. The number of such so-called infringement cases has increased steadily over the years and now averages about 100 annually.
- *Cases against the Commission, Council, EP, or ECB concerning the legality of a particular regulation (Article 241):* These are called "proceedings for annulment" because the Court may annul a particular act. Grounds for annulment include lack of competence, infringement of an essential procedural requirement, infringement of the treaties or of any rules relating to their application, and misuse of powers. The Court's famous *Isoglucose* (1980) ruling—in which it annulled a regulation because the Council acted before the EP had delivered its opinion, thereby infringing one of the essential treaty provisions concerning allocation of powers—falls into this category.
- *Cases brought by member states or other institutions against the Commission, Council, or EP for failure to act (Article 232):* The most famous case of that kind was *Parliament v. Council* (1985), in which the EP brought the Council to court for failing to lay the foundation of a common transport policy. The EP was only partially successful.

- *Cases for damages against the EU for the wrongful act of an EU institution or an EU servant (Articles 235 and 288):* These are known as actions to establish liability.
- *Staff cases (Article 236):* These are brought by EU civil servants for unfair dismissal, unlawful failure to promote, etc.

Organization and Procedure

Articles 220–245 (formerly Articles 164–188) of the TEC stipulate the role, composition, location, procedure, jurisdiction, and powers of the Court. The Court's size has increased over time to reflect the EU's enlargement. It now has fifteen judges and nine advocates-general. Although the treaty does not declare that each member state should appoint a judge, in practice that is what happens (formally judges are appointed by common accord of the governments of the member states). The unwritten principle of one judge per member state is an important factor in the evolution of Community law and in the acceptance of the Court's rulings by the member states.

The treaty stipulates that judges must act independently, and generally they do. The president—elected by the members of the Court for a period of three years—never asks a judge to be rapporteur for a case involving that judge's member state (the rapporteur is responsible for writing the "report for the hearing"—a summary setting out the facts, procedural history, and arguments of the case—for use by the Court as a whole). As the Court's impact on the EU's development became more conspicuous with the Court occasionally adjudicating politically charged cases under media scrutiny, there were suggestions that the judges' independence would need to be safeguarded. A government's most obvious means to pressure or influence "its" judge is to threaten not to renew the judge's six-year term. A solution could be to lengthen the judges' terms to twelve years, a suggestion made by the president of the Court as long ago as 1977 on the grounds that judges need a long time to familiarize themselves with Community law and build essential camaraderie and rapport.[10] The EP has also proposed having a say in judicial appointments, supposedly as a way of strengthening the judiciary's independence.

Judges come from the upper levels of national judiciaries, from the legal profession, and from academia. Nine advocates-general, who have similar backgrounds as the judges and are appointed according to an unofficial national rota, complete the Court's membership. Advocates-general consider cases and give opinions for the Court's guidance at the end of the oral procedure. Judges are free to reject an advocate-general's opinion but in most cases they accept them.

By majority vote, after consulting the advocates-general the judges select a registrar (*greffier*) for a renewable six-year term. The registrar is responsible for conducting proceedings before the Court, maintaining records, publishing the Court's judgments, and administering the Court. The registrar meets regularly with members of the Court to schedule cases and decide procedural aspects. The Court has a relatively small staff of about 750 to provide research, language, and administrative support.

The Court meets either in plenary session (with a quorum of seven members) or in chambers. There are six chambers ranging in size from three to seven judges each. The Court's rules of procedure determine where cases are heard (for instance, cases brought by member states or institutions must be heard before the full Court), although the TEU made greater allowance for cases to be dealt with by chambers of judges. The Court hears cases two days a week and has an administrative session every two weeks.

The ECJ gives requests for preliminary rulings a higher priority than direct action cases because national courts must await a result before proceeding with the case in question. Direct action cases involve written proceedings, an investigation or preparatory inquiry, oral proceedings, and the judgment. Requests for preliminary rulings are not contentious and have a less cumbersome procedure than direct actions, although the original parties may submit written observations to the Court and may attend the oral hearing. Cases are heard in the EU's official languages, but French is the Court's working language.

Each judge has a small *cabinet* of legal secretaries, although most judges draft opinions without assistance after internal deliberations limited exclusively to the judiciary. Judges neither prepare nor issue minority opinions: nor do they indicate how many of them supported a decision, which the Court always announces as unanimous. Understandably, legal scholars complain that this makes it difficult to track the influence of individual judges' preferences and philosophies on the Court's judgments, although judges occasionally make speeches, publish articles, and give interviews.

Impact of EC Case Law

Apart from establishing the principles of direct effect and supremacy, EC case law has profoundly advanced the objectives of the treaties. Indeed, some of the landmark rulings in the elaboration of direct effect and supremacy have also proved decisive in helping to achieve the EU's economic and social goals. Examples include

- *Freedom of establishment:* In the *Reyners* (1974) case, the Court upheld an individual's right to take up employment in another member state under the same conditions as a national of that state.
- *Free movement of goods:* In the famous *Cassis de Dijon* (1979) case, the Court gave the Commission an opportunity to develop the

principle of mutual recognition, which underpinned the single market program.

- *Freedom to provide services:* The Court's ruling in *Vereniging Bond van Adverteerders v. The Netherlands State* (1988), a case involving cross-border telecommunications services, opened the way to the removal of barriers against the provision of services throughout the EU.
- *Competition policy:* A number of Court rulings have furthered the EU's competition policy, notably by confirming the Commission's powers to order repayment of illegal government aid to industry and by interpreting the treaty's provisions on public enterprises and enterprises granted special or exclusive rights.
- *Social policy:* The Court's activism in this area is especially marked in the realm of equal pay for men and women. In the *Defrenne* (1971) case, the Court ruled that the treaty's provision for equal pay was directly applicable and that it was the duty of national courts to ensure that all citizens enjoyed the benefit of that principle. This ruling emboldened the Commission to implement a series of directives on women's issues that forced member states to end systematic and blatant discrimination. A subsequent stream of cases dealt with pensions, training, promotions, part-time work, and so forth.
- *External economic relations:* In its judgment in the *ERTA* (1971) case, the Court held that member states were no longer entitled to enter into obligations with third countries affecting common rules, thus establishing the important principle that in the field of external relations the EU's powers are evolving.

Despite the profound impact of EC case law, few ECJ rulings attract much public attention, especially throughout the EU as a whole. *Union Royale belge des sociétés de football association ASBL v. Bosman* (1995), a case that radically affected nationality and transfer rules in European soccer clubs, was an obvious exception. In a case involving a Belgian soccer player unable to transfer to a French club because his former club set an exorbitant transfer fee, the Court threw out the soccer association's transfer rules because they constituted an obstacle to the free movement of workers (Article 39 TEC). Also based on Article 39, the Court rejected rules requiring soccer clubs to field teams with only a limited number of professional players who were nationals of other member states (except for international matches).

Enforcement

Although national courts and member state governments accept the principles of direct effect and supremacy of Community law, the problem of enforcement remains acute. The worst areas of noncompliance are environmental policy, the single market, and agriculture; the worst offenders are Italy, Greece, Spain, and Portugal.

The Court is well aware that inability or refusal to implement EU rules and regulations uniformly in each member state will erode public confidence in Community law. In *Johnson v. RUC* (1984), the Court declared that the right to a judicial remedy is a general principle of EC law and continued its assault on the enforcement problem in a series of cases in the early 1990s. The most important of these was *Francovich and Bonifaci v. Italy* (1991), in which the Court held that in certain circumstances, individuals are entitled to sue governments for damages sustained as a result of the government's failure to implement a directive within the prescribed period. In a series of subsequent cases, the Court spelled out what these circumstances were: where the rule of law infringed is intended to confer rights on individuals, where there has been a sufficiently serious breach of that rule of law, and where there is a direct causal link between the breach of the obligation resting on the member state and the damage sustained by the injured party.[11]

Aware of the growing problem of enforcement, member states agreed during the 1991 IGC on political union to give the Court some enforcement power. One of the TEU's least-publicized provisions allows the Court to impose fines on member states for refusing to act on a Court ruling that "it failed to fulfill its obligations under the Treaty" (Article 228 TEC). Given the political sensitivity of this provision, the ECJ has been extremely reluctant to make use of it.

The ECJ's Relations with Other Institutions and with Member States

Because of the far-reaching nature of its rulings, the ECJ has a unique relationship with the Council, Commission, the EP, and member states, all of whom are frequent litigants in ECJ cases. Although the Court has often ruled against the Commission (especially in cases where the Commission has attempted to extend its competence in the field of external economic relations), the Commission is nonetheless an obvious ally; after all, as "guardian of the treaties" the Commission prosecutes many Court cases. The Commission and the Court work closely together to promote economic integration, particularly through the use of infringement proceedings and competition policy instruments.

Similarly, the Court and the EP share a common integrationist and supranationalist outlook. Indeed, the Court has generally promoted the EP's institutional interests, most notably in the *Isoglucose* case. The Court also corrected the anomaly whereby, under the original Article 173 TEC, the EP could not bring proceedings for judicial review of Community acts, a provision that seemed especially incongruous following the enhancement of the EP's legislative power under the SEA. In the *Chernobyl* case (1990), the Court ruled that in order to ensure institutional equilibrium in the post-SEA period, the EP should have the right to take action against Council and Commission acts in cases involving parliamentary prerogatives. Despite some member states' criticism of the Court's assertiveness, negotiators in the 1991 IGC incorporated almost verbatim the operative part of the *Chernobyl* judgment into a revised version of Article 173 (now Article 230).

As criticism of the *Chernobyl* judgment showed, the Court's relationship with the Council, and especially with certain member states, can be strained. Institutionally, the Council upholds national interests in the EU system, whereas the Court upholds supranationalism. The Court's sometimes liberal interpretation of the treaties in order to deepen economic and political integration has occasionally angered the Council. By the same token, specific Court rulings have frequently angered particular member states, including those member states generally in favor of further integration. For instance, in the early 1990s the ECJ came under sharp criticism from the German government for some preliminary rulings protecting the rights of Italian and non-EU migrants. The Germans' criticism focused on the right of lower national courts to ask the ECJ for preliminary rulings (a fundamental principle of EC law) and on the ECJ itself for giving preliminary rulings supposedly hostile to national governments' interests.

Not surprisingly, Britain's conservative government was especially sensitive to the Court's behavior. Indeed, there was a national furor in Britain in 1991, when the ECJ for the first time overruled a British act of parliament. In *The Queen v. Secretary of State for Transport, ex parte Factortame* (1991), the Court ruled that the 1988 Merchant Shipping Act, which states that 75 percent of directors and shareholders in companies operating fishing vessels in UK waters must be British, contravened EC law. Basing its ruling on the freedom of establishment and freedom to provide services, the Court declared that the UK could not demand strict residence and nationality requirements from owners and crews before granting their vessels British registration.

The ECJ and the Amsterdam Treaty

The *Factortame* and a number of later judgments led the British government to propose at the 1996–1997 IGC a number of measures to curb the ECJ's effectiveness and to establish a right of appeal against the Court's decisions. Combined with other countries' criticism of the Court, this proposal fueled speculation that the ECJ's prerogatives would be seriously curtailed in the ensuing Amsterdam Treaty, and even that Article 234 (preliminary ruling) might be annulled. For its part, the ECJ recommended in its submission to the pre-IGC Reflection Group a number of changes in the

Court's composition and operations and an extension of judicial review to the EU's two intergovernmental pillars.

In the event, most member states were too appreciative of the ECJ's overall importance to reduce its role in the EU system, and there were no fundamental challenges to the basic tenets of EC law. Moreover, the Labour government that came to power in Britain toward the end of the IGC lacked its predecessor's reforming zeal. If anything, the ECJ emerged from the Amsterdam Treaty slightly better off than before: The treaty brought much of the old third pillar into the first pillar (where the Court is fully involved) and extended judicial review to what remains of the third pillar (subject to certain conditions). However, the treaty did not extend judicial review to the second pillar (the Common Foreign and Security Policy). Also, because of several delegations' distrust of the Court, the treaty's new nondiscrimination clause (Article 13 TEC) does not have direct effect and allows only for secondary legislation.

THE COURT OF FIRST INSTANCE

For more than thirty-five years the EU had only one court, responsible for hearing cases involving everything from important issues of Community law to trivial matters of staff promotion and dismissal. Apart from its wide jurisdiction, the ECJ's rapidly increasing caseload threatened to become unmanageable. The ECJ and the Commission appreciated the problem by the early 1970s and asked the Council to help, suggesting it establish a tribunal to hear staff cases. In 1978 the Court formally complained to the Council about its excessive workload, but to no avail. Only in 1985, when member states convened an IGC in order to make treaty changes to spur market integration, did the Court successfully rekindle the issue of judicial reform. By that time the Court's problems were pressing: As the caseload increased, the time taken to hear cases also increased. The Court's caseload had jumped from 79 in 1970 to 433 in 1985; the average length of proceedings for a preliminary ruling rose from six months in 1975 to fourteen months in 1985; and the average length of a direct action increased from nine months in 1975 to twenty months in 1985. As a result, the Court's accumulated backlog went from 100 cases in 1970 to 527 cases in 1985.[12]

In October 1985, shortly after the IGC began, the ECJ's president raised the prospect of a subsidiary court in a letter to the Council presidency. Member states responded by delegating the issue to a group of experts, who proposed amending Article 168 of the treaty "to attach to the Court of Justice a court with jurisdiction to hear [certain cases] and determine [them] at first instance." The SEA duly empowered the Council, acting unanimously on a proposal from the Court and after consulting the Commission and the EP, to set up a Court of First Instance (Article 225, formerly Article 168a, TEC). In so doing, the SEA gave rise to "a hierarchy of judicial institutions at the Community level."[13]

After implementation of the SEA, the ECJ duly presented a proposal to establish the Court of First Instance (CFI). Following lengthy deliberations by an ad hoc committee drawn from the permanent representations, the Council decided in October 1988 on the CFI's composition and jurisdiction.[14] The new court began operating in October 1989, delivered its first judgment in January 1990, and adopted its own rules of procedure in May 1991.

Jurisdiction

The CFI's initially narrow jurisdiction reflected the member states' difficulty in deciding what to hive off from the ECJ's caseload. Member states were unsure what to entrust to the CFI, apart from staff cases. Their uncertainty was already evident in Article 225, which denied the CFI any jurisdiction over cases brought by member states or Community institutions or over questions referred for preliminary ruling under Article 234. Thus the CFI could hear only "certain classes of action or proceedings brought by natural or legal persons." In the event, the Council's October 1988 decision gave the CFI even narrower jurisdiction than that contemplated in the SEA. It encompassed

- *Competition cases:* These are generally actions by firms contesting fines imposed by the Commission under the EU's competition policy.
- *ECSC cases:* Most stem from the system of production quotas imposed on the steel industry in an effort to deal with recession and overcapacity.
- *Staff cases.*
- *Claims for damages:* These are brought by natural or legal persons where the damage allegedly arises from an action or failure to act that falls into one of the three categories just outlined.

Shortly after its establishment, the CFI published a paper urging an increase in its jurisdiction.[15] Under renewed pressure from the ECJ, at the 1991 IGC on political union member states rewrote Article 225 to permit an extension of the CFI's jurisdiction, although the TEU reiterated the prohibition against the CFI's hearing requests for preliminary rulings. Accordingly, in June 1993 the Council agreed to expand the CFI's competence by transferring to it all proceedings brought by individuals and companies with the exception of proceedings against EU trade defense measures (such as antidumping).[16]

According to the original Council decision setting up the CFI, the court's purpose is to hear cases that require "an examination of complex facts." For instance, ECSC and competition cases usually involve intricate technical legislation and detailed questions of fact. Thus a useful way to understand the distinction between the ECJ and the CFI is that "the Court of First Instance is the judge of factual matters, while the Court of Justice is in principle the judge of points of law."[17]

Composition and Procedure

Like the ECJ, the CFI consists of fifteen judges (one per member state) appointed for renewable six-year terms. It has no advocates-general, but any judge may be asked to perform the task of advocate-general for a particular case. As with their counterparts on the ECJ, judges on the CFI must be independent of national governments. In view of the highly technical work they sometimes perform, CFI judges need not come from the legal profession, although in practice almost all of them do. To maintain continuity between the new and the existing courts, a number of the CFI's first judges were closely connected with the ECJ. For instance, the CFI's first president was a former ECJ advocate-general. The CFI meets in four chambers of three or five judges each, although chambers can also meet in an extended composition of seven members. The judges elect one of their members to serve as president for a renewable three-year term and appoint a registrar, who serves in a capacity similar to that of the ECJ's registrar.

In providing for the CFI, the SEA included a right of appeal to the ECJ. However, litigants may appeal to the ECJ on a point of law only, such as the CFI's lack of competence to hear the original case, breach of procedure, or infringement of Community law. An appeal must be lodged within two months of notification of the decision.

Assessment

Despite the CFI's existence, the ECJ continues to bear a heavy workload. Of course, if the CFI did not exist, the ECJ would have the additional burden of hearing all the cases that currently come before the CFI (as it is, the ECJ hears about 20 percent of them on appeal). However, the CFI itself is even more overburdened than the ECJ, or at least its productivity seems much lower than that of the ECJ. In 1997 the CFI disposed of only 173 cases (compared to 456 cases disposed of by the ECJ), many of which were staff cases. Apart from staff cases, on average the CFI took nearly thirty months to deal with cases, leaving the court with 624 cases in hand at the end of 1997 (up from 220 at the end of 1996). By contrast, the ECJ took an average of twenty-one months to deal with preliminary rulings—the most complicated category of its cases—and had 683 cases in hand at the end of 1997 (not an unusually high amount of work in hand for the ECJ).[18]

The CFI's difficulties may be transient rather than systematic (newspapers occasionally report on rivalries among the CFI judges and between them and the ECJ judges).[19] The court itself believes, however, that its workload is becoming unmanageable. Accordingly the CFI requested, in a submission to the pre 1996–1997 IGC Reflection Group, that the Council appoint more judges to it and that certain cases be heard by one judge sitting alone.[20] But many national governments (and many lawyers who appear before the court) dislike the idea of single-judge rulings, and no national government relished the prospect of fighting with other governments over the nationalities of a handful of new CFI judges. As a result, the Amsterdam Treaty did not incorporate the CFI's recommendations.

The CFI's first president remarked at the court's official launch in September 1989 that "this moment does not mark the end of an era in European judicial history, but rather a stage along the road towards the ultimate maturity of the judicial system of the Communities."[21] Since then there have been two major rounds of treaty reform, neither of which radically revised the EU judicial system. Instead, the Council tinkered with the CFI's jurisdiction in an effort to alleviate the ECJ's workload. Now that the CFI is itself swamped, it is up to it to improve its procedures and productivity rather than wait for a solution based on further reform of the treaties.

THE COURT OF AUDITORS

The TEU elevated the Court of Auditors to the institutional status of the Council, Commission, EP, and ECJ. Moreover, a declaration attached to the treaty emphasized the Court of Auditors' "special importance" and called on "other Community institutions to consider . . . ways of enhancing the effectiveness of its work." The Court of Auditors' greater stature and significance reflect not only a substantial increase in the EU's revenue and expenditure since the late 1980s but also growing public and political concern about fraud, waste, and mismanagement of EU resources. The Court of Auditors is not a judicial court; its responsibility lies solely in examining the EU's financial affairs. By exposing financial irregularities in the Community, however, it can exert considerable pressure for reform.

Indeed, the court's scrutiny of EU spending has provided telling evidence to substantiate anecdotal accounts of financial squandering and incompetence. By boosting the court's status, member states tacitly warned the Commission, which is legally responsible for EU spending, to put its financial house in order. Paradoxically, because management of EU spending is highly decentralized, member states themselves are responsible on a day-to-day basis for most EU expenditure.

The problem of inadequate control over Community resources is as old as the Community itself. In an effort to rectify the situation, and as a corollary to the granting of budgetary authority to the EP, the 1975 budget treaty replaced the old Auditor Board with the new Court of Auditors, which began functioning in October 1977. The 1975 treaty extended the court's authority to cover all bodies created by the Community and all payments made before the year's accounts are closed. In a financial regulation of December 1977, revised in March 1990, member states (through the Council) gave the court complete administrative and budgetary autonomy.

The court consists of fifteen members, appointed for six-year renewable terms, having experience with the financial control of public funds in their own countries. In practice, each member state nominates a member of the court. The Council then appoints the members unanimously, after consulting the EP. Here, as elsewhere, the EP has attempted to extend its authority by insisting on a right of approval. Parliament's objection to two court appointees in 1989 caused a political furor, and as a result one member state changed its nominee. The Council ignored the EP's recommendation against two appointees to the court in 1994.

The court elects one of its members as president to serve a renewable three-year term. A change of president is followed by a general change of portfolios; each member of the court is responsible for a sector or audit work corresponding to a specific area of the EU budget. The court is located in Luxembourg and has a staff of about 500. The Court of Auditors is supposed to be completely independent of national governments.

The court publishes an annual report on each year's budget in November of the following year and also publishes special reports and opinions. All are adopted by a majority vote of the court's members. The annual report consists mostly of a financial management assessment, which involves comparing the general goals and specific targets of EU policies and programs with the results obtained. Special reports allow the court more flexibility than do annual reports, and their highly critical assessments of EU policies and programs often attract media attention. The court's opinions are fewer than its special reports but are not necessarily less spirited.

Before adopting its annual and other reports, the court and the Commission engage in what is called the *procedure contradictoire,* whereby the Commission tries to tone down the court's criticisms. Every court publication includes the Commission's reply to the court's findings, which are often politically sensitive. Indeed, the Commission generally objects to what it sees as the court's tendency to make critical political judgments. On a day-to-day basis, the court deals mostly with the Commission's financial controller and with the directorate-general for budgets; on special occasions the president of the court and the budget commissioner engage in the *procedure contradictoire*.

Another innovation in the TEU was its requirement for the court to provide the Council and the EP "with a statement of assurance as to the reliability of the accounts and the legality and regularity of the underlying transactions" (Article 248.1 TEC). Beginning in November 1995, the court included such a statement in its annual report. To date, the court's statements of assurance have been far from reassuring, with the court noting too many errors with respect to EU payments to give a positive assurance as to their legality or regularity. Although, as the budget commissioner pointed out in the Commission's defense, the court blamed the member states for 90 percent of the substantial errors in payments transactions, the EP nonetheless took the Commission to task for the court's findings, threatening in 1998 to censure the Commission by not granting discharge of the 1996 budget. Thus notwithstanding occasional problems involving appointees to the court, it would seem that the court and the EP are allies in the battle to improve financial management in the EU. The court has helped indirectly to increase the EP's budgetary authority, especially in the area of discharge, and the EP has helped to boost the court's institutional status.

Other EU institutions, any bodies managing revenue or expenditure on behalf of the EU, and national audit bodies or government departments must provide the court with documents on request. If necessary, the court may examine these "on the spot in the other institutions . . . and in the Member States" or "on the premises of any body which manages revenue or expenditure on behalf of the Community [and] any natural or legal person in receipt of payments from the budget" (Article 248.3 TEC). The court works closely with its national counterparts when carrying out investigations in member states. Special liaison officers ensure that the court and the national audit bodies collaborate as successfully as possible. The liaison officers meet in Luxembourg at least once a year, and the presidents of the court and the respective national bodies meet annually either in Luxembourg or in a national capital. In response to sensitivity in some member states about the court's perceived intrusiveness, the Amsterdam Treaty included an amendment to Article 248.3 stating that "the Court of Auditors and the national audit bodies of the Member States shall cooperate in a spirit of trust while maintaining their independence."

THE ECONOMIC AND SOCIAL COMMITTEE

The Economic and Social Committee (ESC) consists of 222 representatives of workers, employers, professional, and consumer organizations, appointed for four years by the Council on the recommendation of national governments, who meet in plenary session about ten times a year, more frequently in smaller sections. The ESC's purpose is to advise the Commission and the Council on social and economic issues, but neither institution is obligated to heed the committee's advice. More often than not the committee's reports sit, unread, in Council meetings; in that way the Council fulfills its legal responsibility to solicit the committee's views on certain kinds of legislative proposals.

The ESC is modeled on national systems for institutionalizing interest group participation in policy formulation and implementation. The committee's raison d'être is to increase democratic accountability, make EU decisionmaking more transparent, and familiarize the economic and social sectors with the Council's legislative output. Originally the ESC had almost the same political stature as the EP, but as soon as the EP acquired budgetary authority in the early 1970s, and especially after the introduction of direct elections, the EP became far more powerful and prominent.

Members represent a wide variety of social and economic interests in the EU and form three distinct groups of approximately equal size:

- *Group I:* employers (from industry and the service sector)
- *Group II:* workers (mostly from national trade unions)
- *Group III:* various interests (farmers, environmentalists, consumers, professionals, etc.)

Committee members are unpaid but are reimbursed for expenses. Although the committee has little clout, its members enjoy occasional trips to Brussels and the prestige of being involved in EU affairs. National governments look upon the committee as a means of dispensing patronage. The committee has its own permanent staff (about 500 strong).

Despite its relative insignificance, the ESC generally produces readable and relevant reports, either in response to a Commission request or on its own initiative. Article 262 TEC specifies that the Council and Commission must consult the ESC on issues specified elsewhere in the treaty (notably on agriculture, transport, and social policy). The SEA extended the area of mandatory consultations to areas such as the environment, the single market, cohesion, and research and technology. The TEU changed Article 262 so as to make the committee more independent of the Council, in particular with regard to adopting its rules of procedure, and gave

Table 11.1 Membership in the Economic and Social Committee and the Committee of the Regions

Country	Number of Members
Britain, Germany, France, Italy	24
Spain	21
Austria, Belgium, Greece, the Netherlands, Portugal, Sweden	12
Denmark, Finland, Ireland	9
Luxembourg	6
Total	222

the ESC authority to meet on its own initiative. The Amsterdam Treaty extended the ESC's policy scope to include the new TEC title on employment and gave the committee the right to be consulted by the EP. However, the Amsterdam Treaty disappointed the ESC by not granting it the status of an EU institution.

The ESC elects a president to represent it in relations with EU institutions, member states, nonmember states, and interest groups and with national economic and social councils and similar national bodies. In 1998—its fortieth anniversary—the ESC elected its first female president. The president and the thirty-member elected bureau (committee leadership) assign members to one of nine sections, each comprising a mix of nationalities and groups. Sections cover

- agriculture and fisheries
- industry and commerce, crafts, and services
- economic, financial, and monetary questions
- social, family, educational, and cultural affairs
- transport and communications
- external relations, trade and development policy
- energy, nuclear questions, and research
- regional development and town and country planning
- protection of the environment, public health, and consumer affairs

Sections draft opinions and reports on their respective policy areas and may solicit expert advice on technical matters. Opinions are adopted by a simple majority in the plenary sessions. Needless to say, consensus is almost impossible to achieve in such a diverse body, and opinions often include dissenting points of view.

The ESC looks to the Commission for political support. Relations between the ESC and the Commission grew especially close in the late 1980s and early 1990s because of Commission president Jacques Delors's strong interest in social policy. Delors briefly brought the committee to prominence in 1988 when he asked for its advice on the proposed Social Charter, a list of fundamental workers' rights. Delors presented the Commission's annual program at an ESC plenary session early each year and insisted that commissioners with relevant portfolios attend at least one ESC plenary session annually, which they still do. The Council politely ignores the ESC, although a representative of the Council presidency—usually a junior minister—outlines the presidency's six-month program at an ESC plenary. For its part, the EP no longer sees the ESC as any kind of threat.

Despite its marginal role, the committee serves some useful functions. It brings to Brussels representatives of influential social and economic interests and provides a forum for them to hold regular and systematic exchanges of views on important issues. The ESC also acts as a conduit for information from Brussels to the member states and alerts special interests to the implications of social and economic policy. Although it aspires to a greater role in EU policymaking, the combination of a stronger, more effective EP and a highly organized lobby of interest groups in Brussels leaves little room for the ESC to assert itself.

Even after the establishment of the ESC in 1958, the Consultative Committee of the European Coal and Steel Community (ECSC)—a body analogous to the EC's Economic and Social Committee—continued to function. The ECSC Consultative Committee has ninety-six members divided into equal groups of producers, workers, consumers, and retailers. The ECSC Consultative Committee meets about six times annually and produces reports on such issues as the application of state-aid rules to the steel industry.

THE COMMITTEE OF THE REGIONS

"Europe of the Regions" is a popular catchphrase. It describes an EU more inclusive and democratically accountable because of the involvement in its policymaking process of local and regional representatives. In 1985, on the eve of the EC's transformation, individual regions came together on their own initiative and formed the Assembly of European Regions (AER), a pan-European body that sought a formal role in EC affairs. Partly for reasons of democratic legitimacy and partly because it sees regionalism as integral to federalism, the Commission supported the AER's efforts to give regions and localities a greater sense of involvement in the Community system. But the AER itself was too large and unwieldy to play such a role, and some of its constituent regions were not even in the EC. Accordingly, in October 1991 the Commission submitted a paper to the IGC on political union proposing the establishment of a Committee of the Regions (COR) to advise the Council and Commission on relevant policy issues, notably cohesion policy.[22] National governments concurred and included in the TEU a provision to that effect (Articles 263–265 TEC).

The Commission clearly stated in its submission to the IGC that the new committee's members should hold *elective* office, but the TEU merely stipulated that the COR should consist of "representatives of regional and local bodies." The Council decided in June 1992 that it was up to each government, using its own criteria, to nominate people to represent regional and local communities (formally, the Council appoints COR members "acting unanimously on proposals from the prospective member states"). Most governments duly nominated elected representatives, but the question of the COR's composition became a vexing issue in Britain, then under Conservative rule. The British government had instinctively opposed the Commission's proposal to establish the committee but reluctantly went along with the idea in the TEU. Moreover, because Britain was a highly centralized state, there were no elected representatives to designate from mainland Britain's three constituent nations (England, Scotland, and Wales). Understandably perhaps, the government used the opportunity to try to buy off Scottish and Welsh nationalists by overrepresenting Scotland and Wales in Britain's COR delegation.

The Labour government, elected in May 1997, launched a constitutional revolution that included holding successful referendums to establish separate parliaments in Scotland and Wales, thereby bringing Britain more into line with the internal origination of large EU member states (France remains an exception). Nevertheless, a fundamental problem with the COR continues to be the great disparity between the size and political power of regions in the EU and the fact that smaller member states themselves constitute a single region. Thus a relatively small, unitary state like the Netherlands has little or no interest in the COR. By contrast, regions in the EU's three federal member states (Austria, Belgium, and Germany), and especially in member states where there is a strong movement in favor of federalism (such as Italy and Spain), see the COR as a vehicle to assert their independence vis-à-vis the central government—much to the discomfiture of the member states concerned.

Many members of the committee therefore have a double agenda: to carry out their functions as stipulated in the treaties and to advance regionalism in their own countries and throughout the EU. Either way, they are eager to raise the committee's institutional profile. In that regard, most members resented a protocol attached to the TEU stating that the ESC and the COR "shall have a common organizational structure" (both have 222 members drawn in the same numbers from all member states). They also resented the fact that at the beginning of its operations, the COR shared facilities and administrative support with the ESC.

Within two years of the committee's establishment, relations between the COR and the ESC were so strained that ESC staff staged a strike against the COR and the COR moved out of the ESC's premises into a building recently vacated by the EP. Nor, apart from its size, did the COR replicate the ESC's organization. Like the ESC, the COR elects a president for a two-year term, but unlike the ESC it has a "first" vice president and fourteen other vice presidents (one from each of the other member states). The COR also has a slightly larger bureau (thirty-six members) than has the ESC. More important, unlike the ESC the COR is organized into eight specialized commissions and four subcommissions and holds only about five plenary sessions a year.

The TEU tasked the COR with providing advice to the Commission and the Council in five policy areas that have a direct bearing on local and regional government: cohesion, transport, public health, education and youth, and culture. The Amsterdam Treaty extended the committee's consultative role to other policy areas, notably employment and the environment, and in general to issues involving cross-border cooperation. The TEU gave the COR authority to issue opinions on its own initiative, which it frequently does. Indeed, in its report to the Reflection Group that preceded the 1996–1997 IGC, the Commission criticized the COR for "running the risk of casting its net too wide" by straying outside the bounds of its mandate in issuing own initiative opinions.[23] Like the ESC's opinions, the COR's opinions are useful and informative. As expected, they always reflect regional and local perspectives and emphasize especially the importance of the subsidiarity principle. Also like the ESC's opinions, they go mostly unread in the Council.

Raising the committee's profile is a means for some members to promote regionalism in their own countries and in the EU as a whole. Potentially, the committee provides a platform for propagating regional autonomy or even independence in the context of market integration and security cooperation at the European level of government. Thus regionalism and supranationalism complement rather than conflict with each other. Indeed, supranational institutions and regional authorities share a mutual suspicion of national governments, their natural political adversaries.

The COR pushed hard during the 1996–1997 IGC to enhance its political agenda. Among other things, the committee requested in its submission to the Reflection Group that the principle of subsidiarity be redefined in order to refer explicitly to subnational levels of government, that the committee be allowed to bring subsidiarity cases before the ECJ, and that the committee be designated an EU institution in Article 7 TEC.[24] The Amsterdam Treaty enhanced the COR's position, but not nearly as much as the COR hoped, or at least had requested. Apart from extending the committee's consultative role to new areas, the treaty strengthened the independence of the committee by allowing it to adopt its own rules without reference to the Council and by repealing the protocol in the TEU that called for a common organizational structure in the COR and ESC.

In a series of written questions in 1992 and early 1993 on the eve of the COR's establishment, members of the EP expressed concern about the committee's relationship with their own institution. In reply, the Council reassured them that the COR "will have no direct dealings with the EP" and will not duplicate Parliament's role in any way.[25] Fears that the COR might undermine the EP indeed proved unfounded, although members of the EP have a reasonable point when they complain that the COR is redundant because parliamentarians are elected to represent local, regional, and national interests (the same is true for the ESC because parliamentarians also represent employers, workers, and other interests). Nevertheless, the EP and the COR have had a relatively harmonious relationship, and the Amsterdam Treaty also gave the COR the right to be consulted by the EP. However, the treaty also included a stipulation that "no member of the committee may also be a Member of the European Parliament" (Article 263 TEC).

THE EUROPEAN INVESTMENT BANK

The European Investment Bank (EIB) is an autonomous public financial body within the EU. Established in 1958 under Articles 129 and 130 TEC (now Articles 266 and 267), the EIB seeks to promote economic development in the EU. It does so by offering loans to the public and private sectors, guaranteeing loans from other financial institutions, and putting financial packages together. The Commission and the recipient country's government must confirm that an EIB loan will help to meet national and EU objectives. A sizable number of EIB loans are also directed outside the EU in pursuit of the EU's external relations objectives.

EU member states are the EIB's shareholders with the size of their subscriptions depending on their economic weight. Thus Britain, France, Germany, and Italy each subscribe 17 percent of the EIB's capital, whereas Luxembourg subscribes only 0.1 percent. EU finance ministers decided in 1998 to increase the EIB's capital base to €100 billion (100 billion euros) (this is guarantee capital; only 7.5 percent is actually paid in). The bank's statute stipulates that aggregate loans and guarantees may not exceed 250 percent of subscribed capital. Accordingly, the EIB may lend and borrow up to €250 billion.

The EIB raises almost all funds necessary to finance its lending operations by borrowing on capital markets, mainly through public bond issues quoted on the world's major stock exchanges. The bank's enviable record and reputable shareholders give it a top (AAA) credit rating. This rating allows it to mobilize extensive resources without burdening the budgets of the member states and to channel resources in an economically efficient way to regions and sectors in need of support. The EIB borrows more than any other international financing institution, including the World Bank. It borrows and lends in about fifteen currencies, the most important of which is the euro.

The EIB makes long- and medium-term loans in keeping with strict banking management. But the EIB is not a normal bank: It waits for projects to be brought to it and expects them to be largely financed commercially first. The bank can contribute up to 50 percent of a project's cost but typically lends only about 25 percent. Also, the bank's lending rates are highly competitive because of its excellent credit rating and nonprofit status. As well as offering loans, the bank finds cofinanciers and increasingly issues guarantees to commercial banks to encourage them to lend rather than lending directly itself.

The bank is located in Luxembourg and has a staff of about 750. It has its own legal personality and a unique administrative structure:

- *Board of governors:* Fifteen government ministers (usually finance ministers); chairmanship rotates in the same order as in the Council but for a full year (June–June). Lays down general directives on credit policy; approves the balance sheet and annual report; decides on capital increases; appoints members of the board of directors, management committee, and audit committee.
- *Board of directors:* Twenty-two members (twenty-one nominated by the board of governors and one by the Commission); five-year terms. Decides on loans and guarantees, fund-raising, and lending rates; decisions may be taken by majority, but majority must represent at least 45 percent of subscribed capital; meets on average ten times a year with the bank's president as chair.
- *Management committee:* Eight members (the bank's president and seven vice presidents); six-year terms. Controls all current operations; recommends decisions to the directors and then carries them out.
- *Audit committee:* Three members; three-year terms. Verifies that the bank has carried out its operations and kept its books in order.

A number of developments in the late 1980s and early 1990s greatly enhanced the EIB's stature and importance. First, the single market program increased demand for EIB loans to improve the EU's infrastructure and increase industrial competitiveness. Second, the SEA's emphasis on economic and social cohesion, and the subsequent reform of the EU's structural funds, led to massive EIB financing for projects located in regional development areas. Third, German unification further fueled demand for EIB financing, especially for environmental programs. Fourth, the Commission's leadership of the Central and Eastern European assistance effort extended the bank's financing activities in that direction.

The TEU confirmed the EIB's centrality in the EU system and essential role in financing European integration. As with the articles concerning the Court of Auditors, the articles concerning the EIB were moved to the section on institutions (although the EIB was not designated an EU institution). The treaty reaffirmed that the bank's main task is to provide funding for investment in underdeveloped regions and included a new paragraph instructing the bank to "facilitate the financing of investment programs in conjunction with assistance from the structural funds and other Community financial instruments" (Article 267 TEC). The TEU also called for greater EU involvement in areas in which the bank was already heavily committed: trans-European transport, telecommunications, and energy supply networks; industrial competitiveness; environmental protection; and development cooperation with third countries. Regional development remains the EIB's top priority and accounts for most EIB lending, notably to projects in the EU's less well-off rural regions (in Ireland, Portugal, Greece,

Spain, and Italy) and in declining industrial areas (in Britain, France, and the Netherlands).

The EIB's activities within the EU can be broken down into the following major categories:

- *Improving the transport and telecommunications infrastructure, including highways, airports, railways (for instance, the TGV high-speed train), and communications networks:* For instance, the Channel tunnel was the EIB's largest-ever single project. As the EIB's president pointed out during the project itself, "financing the tunnel fits the EIB's task of furthering the development and integration of the EC. It forms a key element in the development of the transport infrastructure necessary to meet the challenges of the single market."[26] Infrastructural projects account for about 45 percent of the bank's lending activity in the EU.
- *Protecting the environment:* Even before the TEU emphasized the need for environmental protection, the bank had identified this as a priority area. The EIB assesses the environmental impact of all projects under consideration.
- *Strengthening the international competitive position of EU industry and promoting cross-border collaboration:* The bank assists industry's adjustment to structural change and promotes the growth of enterprise and innovation.
- *Supporting the activities of small and medium-sized enterprises (SMEs):* The bank channels money to SMEs mostly through "global loans" concluded with intermediary institutions.

The vast majority of the EIB's lending activity takes place inside the EU (including the EU's overseas countries and territories). Outside the EU, the bank provides assistance under various financial agreements, mainly with three groups of countries:

1. *Mediterranean countries:* The Mediterranean Environmental Technical Assistance Program, the bank's showcase activity in the Mediterranean region, is a collaborative venture involving the World Bank and the UN Development Programme.
2. *African, Caribbean, and Pacific (ACP) countries:* Under the Lomé Convention, the EIB offers subsidized loans and risk capital assistance to African, Caribbean, and Pacific countries for industrial, agricultural, tourism, telecommunications, and transportation programs.
3. *Central and Eastern European countries:* The EIB has assisted large-scale economic development in the region since 1990, sometimes through cofinancing projects with the European Bank for Reconstruction and Development.

As well as helping these three groups of countries, in the 1990s the EIB extended its lending activities on a smaller scale to those Latin American and Asian countries with which the EU has cooperation agreements.

While upholding its existing obligations inside and outside the EU, the EIB took on yet more responsibilities in the early 1990s. As part of an emergency growth package to try to stimulate economic recovery, the European Council asked the EIB in December 1992 to manage a new, temporary lending facility to help fill the huge, recession-induced gap in EU investment and accelerate the financing of capital infrastructure projects.[27] Accordingly, the EIB and the Commission worked with other financial institutions to establish a European Investment Fund (EIF). The EIB subscribed 40 percent of the capital; the Commission and other institutions 30 percent each. The EIF was launched in 1995 with the president of the EIB acting as chair of the EIF's supervisory board.

AGENCIES AND OTHER BODIES

At the national level of governance, the transition from the interventionist to the regulatory state has brought with it a proliferation of independent agencies to regulate economic and social policy.[28] In many cases these are statutory bodies, that is, they are established by statute to regulate former state monopolies, such as telecommunications and electricity. In addition, deregulation at the national level in Europe has resulted in (and been facilitated by) a degree of reregulation at the transnational level. Thus the EU has also acquired a plethora of regulatory agencies, although with limited powers. The relative powerlessness of EU agencies reflects their ambiguous legal position (the founding treaties refer only to specific institutions and bodies), member state reluctance to confer extensive rule-making and enforcement authority on them, and the lack of an "agency culture" in Europe (in contrast to the United States, for instance).[29] Nevertheless, some EU agencies play an important role in the formulation and implementation of key economic and social policies, specifically because of their expertise and credibility. The most significant of these agencies are as follows:

- the European Environment Agency (EEA)
- the European Agency for the Evaluation of Medicinal Products (EMEA)
- the Office for Harmonization in the Internal Market (Trademark Office)

(The role of the EEA is discussed in the section on environmental policy in Chapter 15; the EMEA and Trademark Office are discussed in Chapter 13.)

Table 11.2 Agencies and Bodies of the European Community

Title	Location	Date of Foundation	Task
European Center for the Development of Vocational Training (CEDEFOP)	Berlin (1975–95); Thessaloniki, Greece (1995–)	1975	Contributes to European vocational training
European Foundation for the Improvement of Living and Working Conditions	Dublin	1975	Disseminates information to improve living and working conditions
European Environmental Agency (EEA)	Copenhagen	1994	Provides environmental data
European Monitoring Center for Drugs and Drug Addiction (EMCDDA)	Lisbon	1994	Provides information at a European level on drugs, drug addiction, and their consequences
Office for Harmonization in the Internal Market	Alicante, Spain	1994	Registers and administers Community trademarks
Translation Center for Bodies in the European Union	Luxembourg	1994	Translates for the other agencies (except CEDEFOP and the European Foundation)
European Agency for the Evaluation of Medicinal Products (EMEA)	London	1995	Ensures equal application of pharmaceutical product usage and evaluation
European Training Foundation	Turin	1995	Coordinates and supports EU activities in post-compulsory education
Community Plant Variety Rights Office	Brussels (temporary)	1995	Implements Community plant variety rights regime
European Agency for Safety and Health at Work	Bilbao, Spain (temporary)	1995	Provides information on health and safety at work

The EU's other agencies and bodies range from think tanks (such as the European Center for the Development of Vocational Training) to a public health information provider (the European Monitoring Center for Drugs and Drug Addiction) to a functional service provider (the Translation Center for Bodies in the European Union).

Inevitably in an entity like the EU, the location of agencies and other bodies is a controversial and politically charged issue. Largely for reasons of prestige, each member state wants a piece of the agency action. This competition resulted in a major row in the early 1990s that held up a decision about the location of the European Central Bank (ECB) and that was resolved only at the highest political level: a meeting of the European Council in Brussels in October 1993. As part of a package that centered on an agreement to locate the ECB in Frankfurt (an almost nonnegotiable German demand), the European Council decided to move the European

Center for the Development of Vocational Training from Berlin (where it had resided since 1975) to Thessaloniki, Greece. The package also allowed the EEA to open its doors in Copenhagen (the aggressively green Danish government coveted this agency) and removed a final obstacle to the functioning of the Trademark Office in Alicante, Spain.

NOTES

1. See, for instance, Patrick Neill, *The European Court of Justice: A Case Study in Judicial Activism* (London: European Policy Forum, 1995).
2. Klaus-Dieter Borchardt, *ABC of Community Law*, 3d ed. (Luxembourg: Office for Official Publications of the European Communities [OOP], 1991), p. 38.
3. G. Federico Mancini, "The Making of a Constitution for Europe," in Robert O. Keohane and Stanley Hoffmann, eds., *The New European Community: Decision-Making and Institutional Change* (Boulder: Westview Press, 1991), p. 177.
4. See the EP's resolution of April 12, 1989, in *Official Journal of the European Communities* [*OJ*] C120, May 16, 1989, p. 51, and the Martin Report on the results of the IGC, European Parliament Session Documents A3-123/92, March 26, 1992 (PE 155.444 final).
5. Opinion 2/94, *Accession by the EC to the ECHR*, ECR I-1759.
6. See especially Case 186/87, *Cowan v. Tresor Public*.
7. Anthony Arnull, "Reference to the European Court," in *European Law Review* 15 (October 1990): 391.
8. Martin Shapiro, "The European Court of Justice," in Alberta Sbragia, *Euro-Politics: Institutions and Policymaking in the "New" European Community* (Washington, DC: Brookings Institution, 1992), p. 127.
9. Donal Barrington, "Progress Toward European Union: EC Institutional Perspectives on the Inter-Governmental Conferences," paper presented at the Second International Conference of the European Community Studies Association, George Mason University, May 23, 1991, pp. 7–8.
10. Lord Mackenzie Stuart, "The European Communities and the Court of Law," *Hamlyn Lectures, 29th Series* (London: Stevens, 1977).
11. See Jo Shaw, "Legal Developments," in *Journal of Common Market Studies* 35, *Annual Review* (1996): 105.
12. See Tom Kennedy, "The Essential Minimum: The Establishment of the Court of First Instance," *European Law Review* 14 (1989): 7–12; and Spiros A. Pappas, *The Court of First Instance of the European Communities,* European Institute for Public Administration (EIPA) professional papers (Maastricht: EIPA, 1990).
13. Phil Fennell, "The Court of First Instance," *European Access* 1 (February 1990): 11.
14. Council Decision 88/591, *OJ* L 319, November 25, 1988, p. 1.
15. CFI, "Reflections on the Future Development of the Community Judicial System," December 3, 1990, reproduced in *European Law Review* 16, no. 3 (June 1991): 175–189.
16. *OJ* L 144, June 16, 1993.
17. Pappas, *Court of First Instance,* p. xii.
18. European Court of Justice, *1997 Annual Report* (Luxembourg: OOP, 1998), pp. 130–131.

19. See, for instance, "European Paper Mountain," *Financial Times,* May 5, 1998, p. 10.

20.The CFI's submission to the Reflection Group is published in European Parliament, *White Paper on the 1996 IGC*, vol. 1, *Official Texts of the EU Institutions* (Luxembourg: European Parliament, 1996), pp. 373–382.

21. José Luis da Cruz Vilaca, speech at the official launch of the CFI, September 25, 1989, reproduced in Pappas, *Court of First Instance,* p. 10.

22. Bull. EC S/2-1991, pp. 178–179.

23. Commission, *Report on the Operation of the Treaty on European Union*, SEC(95)731 final, Brussels, p. 15.

24. The COR's submission to the Reflection Group is published in European Parliament, *Official Texts,* pp. 415–428.

25. Written question #1250/92, *OJ* C 247, Vol. 35, September 24, 1992, p. 53, and written question #1206/92, *OJ* C 6, Vol. 36, January 11, 1993, pp. 10–11.

26. Hans-Gunther Bröder (EIB president), interview in *Europe Magazine,* November 1991: 20.

27. Edinburgh European Council, Presidency Conclusions, Bull. EC 12-1992, point 1.30.

28. See Giandomenico Majone, *Regulating Europe* (London: Routledge, 1996).

29. Giandomenico Majone, "The Agency Model: The Growth of Regulation and Regulatory Institutions in the European Union," *Eipascope* 3 (1997): 9–14.

Part 3

Policies

12

The Common Agricultural Policy

The Common Agricultural Policy (CAP) is one of the oldest and most controversial policies of the European Union. The CAP covers almost every aspect of farming life in an EU that, with successive enlargements, has acquired an ever more diverse agriculture sector, incorporating small family farms and large factory farms, farms in the flatlands of Holland and in the mountains of Austria, farms in the frozen north of Finland and the sweltering south of Italy. The range of agricultural products covered by the CAP is as diverse as EU farm size and type, ranging from cereals, beef, milk, olive oil, fruit, and vegetables to tobacco and reindeer meat. Agriculture in the EU employs 8 million people (5.3 percent of the working population), and agricultural exports account for 8 percent of total EU exports.

The CAP is controversial because it is expensive, wasteful, and environmentally unfriendly. It accounts for approximately €50 billion (50 billion euros) a year of EU expenditure, causes huge food surpluses that are warehoused throughout the EU, and encourages land and river pollution through farmers' excessive use of fertilizers. Given its complexity and munificence, the CAP is poorly managed and prey to large-scale fraud. The CAP is also a source of friction in the EU's external economic relations by virtue if its import restrictions and export subsidies. Finally, the eruption of the bovine spongiform encephalopathy (BSE) crisis in 1996 sparked widespread public criticism of the CAP. For these reasons alone, the CAP is in urgent need of radical reform.

Yet an additional factor is at the root of the current CAP reform effort: the impending accession to the EU of several Central and Eastern European states, which, taken together, have a large and impoverished agricultural sector. Further CAP reform may therefore be imminent but will not necessarily be radical. The EU is moving away from a system of price supports to one of direct income supports but is not about to abandon large-scale subsidization of agriculture. At French prompting, the EU rationalizes such subsidization on the grounds that agriculture in the EU is different from agriculture anywhere else in the world, that the "European Agriculture Model" with its mixture of social, environmental, and economic elements requires a high degree of government intervention and support.[1] Undoubtedly agriculture is a unique sector: Food is a basic need, agriculture has a primeval aura, and farms have a romanticism about them that factories and offices do not. Perhaps for those reasons, the 94.7 percent of European workers not in agriculture—many of whom have to survive in the real world of global competition, restructuring, and job losses—are surprisingly indulgent of their fellow workers on the land.

ORIGIN AND DEVELOPMENT

Even before the EC came into existence in 1958, agriculture was a sensitive issue for most European governments. Near-famine conditions in much of postwar Europe made food security a national priority. The centrality of peasant proprietorship in European political culture, the romantic lure of the land, and the emergence of a highly influential farmers' lobby gave agriculture added political salience. A decline in the relative economic weight of the primary sector and a corresponding drop in farmers' incomes raised the political stakes. Not surprisingly, by the mid-1950s agriculture had become a heavily protected and subsidized sector.

Notwithstanding their general support for market integration, governments were loath to give up the traditional interventionist measures widely used to protect agricultural price levels and buttress farmers' earnings. Some governments, such as the German and the Dutch, would have been happy to exclude agriculture entirely from the new EC, continuing instead to subsidize agriculture at the national level. The French government, by contrast, wanted to include agriculture in the EC in order to shift the cost of subsidizing France's large and unproductive agricultural sector from the national to the European level. As France made this a condition of accepting a common market in manufactured goods, France's partners had little choice but to commit themselves in the treaty to establishing an EC-level agricultural policy.

There was no disagreement among member states on the general objectives of that policy (Article 33, formerly Article 39, TEC) to

- increase agricultural productivity
- ensure a fair standard of living for farmers
- stabilize agricultural markets
- guarantee regular supplies of food
- ensure reasonable prices for consumers

Nor did member states think that agricultural production and trade should be subject to the mechanisms for market liberalization laid down for industrial products. Hence Article 36 (formerly Article 42) excluded agriculture from the scope of the treaty's general provisions on competition (Articles 81–89, formerly Articles 85–94). Instead, member states agreed to replace various "national organizations" of agricultural markets with one "common organization" that would have at its disposal such interventionist measures as "regulation of prices . . . and common machinery for stabilizing imports or exports" (Article 34, formerly Article 40). The treaty charged member states with establishing the new European agricultural regime by developing a Common Agricultural Policy before the end of the transition to the customs union and charged the Commission with taking the first step: convening a conference of member states "with a view to making a comparison of their agricultural policies, in particular by producing a statement of their resources and needs" (Article 37, formerly Article 43).

Given the sensitivity of agricultural policy and the nature of the treaty's provisions for agriculture, it is hardly surprising that, according to a key participant, "during the [Community's] first five years the question that dominated all others, by far, was the progressive construction of the CAP."[2] The process began in July 1958 when Sicco Mansholt, vice president of the Commission with responsibility for agriculture, convened the obligatory conference of Commission, government, and farmers' representatives in Stresa, Italy, to devise the CAP's following guiding principles:

- *A single market:* Agricultural produce should be able to move freely throughout the EC.
- *Community preference:* Priority should be given to EC produce over that of other countries.
- *Financial solidarity:* The cost of the policy should be borne by the EC rather than by individual member states.

Although officially unstated, another principle subsequently emerged: Farmers should receive an income "equivalent" to that received by other sectors of society.[3]

Throughout most of the EU's history these principles were sacrosanct. However, in October 1998 the Commission questioned the feasibility of financial solidarity in a controversial paper on budgetary reform (see further on).

Following the Stresa Conference, the Commission formulated proposals to replace individual member states' systems of customs duties, import quotas, and minimum prices with a harmonized Community-wide market, free intra-Community trade in agricultural products, and common protection vis-à-vis third countries. Detailed discussions to launch the CAP culminated in a series of legendary marathon meetings of the Council in December 1961 and January 1962. By the simple stratagem of "stopping the clock" at midnight on December 31, the ministers ostensibly reached agreement by the statutory deadline, although talks continued until January 14.[4] The result was a package that included a common system of price supports covering 85 percent of total EC production, a framework to raise levies on imports into the EC, and the establishment of the European Agricultural Guarantee and Guidance Fund (EAGGF) to underwrite the entire operation. The guarantee section (accounting for the bulk of the fund) would cover the costs of market intervention; the guidance section would pay for structural improvements. The Council agreed to finance the EAGGF by member state contributions only for the first three years, after which a new arrangement would have to apply. Commission proposals to fund the EAGGF from July 1965 using the EC's own resources sparked the infamous empty chair crisis; it was only in 1970, as part of a wide-ranging budgetary agreement, that member states finally switched to Community funding of the CAP.

The basic elements of the CAP are

- *Target price:* the EC-wide guaranteed minimum price for a particular agricultural commodity or product
- *Intervention price:* the price at which specially designated intervention agencies in the member states buy surplus produce in unlimited quantities (guaranteed withdrawal from the market)
- *Entry price:* the minimum price at which produce may be imported into the EU
- *Levy:* a duty imposed on agricultural imports to raise their prices to the level of the entry price (levies are part of the EU's "own resources")
- *Refund:* a rebate paid to EU exporters to bridge the gap between lower world prices and higher EU prices

The target price ensures that farmers have adequate incomes, the intervention system guarantees the sale of their products regardless of market demand, the entry price protects the EU market from being inundated with cheap imports, and the refund is an export subsidy that enables farmers to sell their products on the world market even though the EU's guaranteed minimum price is generally higher than prevailing world prices.

Because the target price and intervention price are the same throughout the EU, the CAP has been susceptible since the late 1960s to exchange rate fluctuation among member state currencies. Distortions in cross-border pricing because of exchange rate changes led to the introduction of "green money" for the CAP: a complicated agrimonetary system involving payments to farmers of monetary compensatory amounts (border taxes and subsidies to compensate for price differences within the EC caused by fluctuating exchange rates). The introduction of an artificial currency gave farmers in border areas ample opportunity to cheat the system and allowed certain member states to manipulate exchange rates in order to keep support prices higher than they would otherwise have been. Following numerous efforts to reform the agrimonetary system, often linked to major currency fluctuations in the real world and linked as well to implementation of the single market program, the EU decided in 1996 to freeze green exchange rates until January 1999, when the introduction of the euro obviated the need for a contrived agrimonetary system in the eleven member states participating in the euro zone.

Apart from the peculiarities of the agrimonetary system, annual farm price negotiations in the Agriculture Council (the council of agriculture ministers) remain one of the most important and distinctive features of the CAP. Price packages sometimes contain fifty or sixty regulations that may include not only monetary amounts but also complex changes to already complex market mechanisms.[5] Farm price negotiations proceed as follows:

1. The Commission sends the Council a detailed package of proposals early in the year, usually in January.
2. The Special Committee for Agriculture, rather than the Committee of Permanent Representatives (COREPER) as in most other EU policy areas, considers the proposals during the next two or three months in close consultation with the Commission.
3. The European Parliament (EP) also considers the Commission's proposals and delivers an opinion. The EP's input is based on the consultation procedure, not codecision. Nevertheless, given the EP's political stature, the Council and the Commission pay close attention to the EP's proposed amendments.
4. The European farmers' lobby—notably the powerful Committee of Professional Agricultural Organizations of the European Community (COPA)—is active throughout these early stages, contacting Commissioners and their officials, Europarliamentarians and their officials, and agriculture ministers and their officials (especially the senior officials on the Special Committee for Agriculture).
5. The Special Committee and the agriculture ministers try to reach agreement on the price package during the Council's monthly meeting in April or May, but negotiations sometimes continue into June or even into the beginning of a new Council presidency in July.

This brief, dry description belies the monumental effort involved in concluding the annual package of farm prices. Indeed, the effort is so great that the presidential rota is deliberately constructed so that a member state in the presidency for the first half of the year (and therefore responsible for managing the agriculture negotiations) assumes the presidency for the second half when its turn next comes round. In the latter stages of the price-fixing process, negotiations can last several days, taxing the patience and stamina of the negotiators themselves. Ministers and officials are acutely aware that farmers' livelihoods depend on the outcome—not least because farmers often gather outside the Council building to press their case for higher prices. Although many key product prices are now negotiated in the context of CAP reform and international pressure to bring EU prices into line with world prices, price-fixing negotiations retain their familiar ritual and sense of drama.

CAP REFORM: FROM MANSHOLT TO MACSHARRY

The CAP's market-regulating mechanisms—target prices, intervention, levies, and export subsidies—ensured that the CAP soon met most of its objectives: Agricultural production increased greatly, farmers enjoyed a fair standard of living (although some benefited more than others from the CAP's largesse), agricultural markets were stabilized, and food security was assured. However, consumers clearly lost out as high prices in shops and supermarkets reflected high target prices for farm products and high levies on imported foodstuffs.

Although the CAP could therefore be judged a success on the basis of its stated objectives, the policy's market-regulating mechanisms caused serious economic, environmental, and political problems:

- Guaranteed prices bore no relation to demand and encouraged massive overproduction.
- Surplus produce had to be stored in "intervention" in warehouses throughout the EC at considerable cost to taxpayers (these were the infamous butter mountains, wine lakes, etc.).
- Big farmers (farmers with large farms) produced more and thereby earned more money, whereas small farmers, who most needed assistance, earned less.
- In order to increase output from their already overworked fields, farmers used excessive amounts of herbicides, pesticides, and artificial fertilizers, thus accentuating the EC's acute environmental problems.
- The maintenance of quotas, levies, and tariffs in agricultural trade angered exporters to the EC and contrasted unfavorably with the EC's efforts to promote global market liberalization in other sectors.
- Export price supports distorted world prices and undercut non-EC exporters, leading to trade disputes.

All of these problems or potential problems became apparent early in the CAP's existence. At the end of the 1960s Sicco Mansholt, father of the CAP, tried to rectify some of the CAP's most obvious excesses. The -

so-called Mansholt Plan was the first, ill-fated effort to avoid surpluses yet still provide an adequate income to those who stayed on the land.[6]

The EC's first enlargement made matters worse by bringing into the EC a small country (Ireland) with a large agricultural sector and a large country (Britain) with a small agricultural sector but many big farmers. Britain's accession introduced a new political twist because Britain had traditionally pursued an agricultural policy that was the antithesis of the CAP (it was even called the "cheap food" policy). Not since the beginning of the industrial revolution had Britain attempted to be self-sufficient in food production. Britain's population was too large and its amount of arable land too small to feed everyone on the island solely from home-grown stocks. Accordingly, Britain imported cheap food from the empire and, as the empire shrank, from Commonwealth countries and other inexpensive suppliers—hence Commonwealth concerns about Britain's entry into the EC; hence also Britain's instinctive antipathy to the CAP. Britain's accession therefore brought into the EC a persistent critic of the CAP and, in the person of Margaret Thatcher in the 1980s, a powerful advocate of CAP reform.

By that time, however, vested agribusiness and rural interests had a firm grip on the CAP and could successfully resist major reform. Farmers maximized political support for the CAP by lobbying effectively and by portraying themselves as a disadvantaged and beleaguered group providing a vital service to society. Despite paying high prices over the counter, the nonfarming sector had relatively little information about or interest in the CAP and failed to appreciate the program's pernicious economic impact. Thus politicians could win farmers' votes without alienating the support of other social groups and political constituencies. As a result, not just agriculture ministers but also foreign ministers and even heads of state and government aggressively advocated farmers' interests, often invoking the national veto to do so.

The idiosyncratic nature of the Agriculture Council compounded the problem. Apart from convening more often than most other councils, being served by the Special Committee on Agriculture rather than by COREPER, and engaging in the annual price-fixing ritual, the Agriculture Council consists mostly of ministers with strong ties in the rural community and a strong personal and political awareness of the CAP's importance. Harold Wilson, Britain's prime minister in the mid-1970s, often "heard the most powerful heads of government aver that the agricultural cabal in the EEC—their own ministers—have so powerful a leverage that they have become a power center transcending the authority of national cabinets and prime ministers."[7]

Obscene levels of overproduction in the late 1970s triggered a renewed discussion of CAP reform. In 1979 the Council introduced a modest change in the system of price guarantees and imposed a "coresponsibility" levy on dairy farmers to help meet the cost of intervention storage and subsidized sales of surplus produce. When the coresponsibility levy failed to curb excess output, the Commission proposed a production quota.[8] To the surprise of his colleagues on the Agriculture Council, Ignaz Kiechle, the powerful German agriculture minister, supported the Commission's proposal. (Despite the popular notion that France, the EC's agricultural powerhouse, was the CAP's most tenacious defender, Germany proved more obdurate than other member states in perpetuating price-driven support and blocking meaningful reform, thanks largely to the Bavarian farm lobby's immense influence over the smaller faction of the governing Christian Democratic Party.) Although a former Bavarian dairy farmer, Kiechle saw milk quotas as the only alternative to price cuts. After an intensive series of negotiations at the highest level, which at one point saw Garrett FitzGerald, the Irish prime minister, walk out of a summit meeting, the EC agreed in March 1984 on a quota system for milk production.[9]

The milk quota was an inadequate response to the problem of overproduction and did little to reduce spending on the CAP (by 1984 the CAP accounted for over 70 percent of EC expenditure). The possibility of bankruptcy, impending Mediterranean enlargement, and Thatcher's insistence on budgetary reform intensified pressure for radical action. Indeed, as part of the budgetary package agreed to at the June 1984 Fontainebleau summit, the heads of state and government resolved to curtail the growth of CAP expenditure.[10] At the same time, however, they agreed to increase the EC's own resources, thereby eliminating the most compelling reason for far-reaching CAP reform: the threat of running out of money.

Budgetary pressure again brought the question of CAP reform to the top of the EC agenda in 1987 and 1988. As part of the Delors I budgetary package, introduced in 1987 in the wake of the Single European Act, the Commission proposed a mix of measures to prevent overproduction, limit expenditure, diversify support for farmers, and promote rural development.[11] Far from wanting to curb the CAP, German chancellor Helmut Kohl would happily have sanctioned a rise in agricultural expenditure. For most of 1987, during contentious negotiation of the Delors I package, Kohl's fragile coalition government faced crucial local elections. Curtailing the CAP was unpopular with Germany's small but influential farm sector and could have cost the government valuable votes. The Delors I negotiations therefore made little progress until after the German elections and culminated at an extraordinary summit in Brussels in February 1988 held under Germany's presidency of the Council. From the point of view of agriculture the most important feature of the Delors I package was an agreement to control spending within a strict budgetary discipline whereby the agricultural guidelines of the EAGGF would not be increased beyond 74 percent of the rate of increase in the EC's GNP as of 1988.

Like previous reform efforts, the 1988 package proved only moderately successful. Pressure for effective reform continued to build not only because of the CAP's exorbitant cost but also because of two new developments. First, the CAP encouraged unfavorable international comment on the recently launched single market program. Although the single market program was popular within the EC itself, it raised fears abroad about the possible emergence of a fortress Europe. Undoubtedly, the CAP's abominable international image fueled concern in third countries about the single market's consequences. If the protectionist and trade-distorting CAP was an example of a common policy in action, the single market would hardly help the rest of the world. Thus the EC's vigorous efforts to combat pessimistic prognoses about the single market's external impact intensified internal pressure for CAP reform.

Second, and much more important, poor progress in the Uruguay Round negotiations of the General Agreement on Tariffs and Trade (GATT), due largely to disagreements over agricultural export subsidies, heightened international pressure on the EC to reform the CAP. The inclusion of agriculture in the Uruguay Round had put the EC on the defensive even before the negotiations opened in September 1986, with the Council insisting that "the fundamental objectives and mechanisms both internal and external of the CAP shall not be placed in question."[12] Nevertheless, the EC soon came under fierce pressure from the United States and the Cairns Group (an informal association of agricultural free-traders led by Australia) to curtail subsidies for agricultural production and exports. Third World countries insisted on progress on agricultural trade liberalization in return for concessions in other sectors.

In 1987 the United States set the scene for a protracted quarrel with the EC by demanding the complete elimination of all trade-distorting measures within ten years. The irreconcilable positions of the United States and the Cairns Group, on the one hand, and the EC, on the other, caused the midterm review of the Uruguay Round in December 1988 to end in acrimony. The row over agriculture affected other areas; India blocked agreement on intellectual property rights and a number of South American countries threatened to reopen negotiations on tentatively agreed-upon issues unless the EC conceded more on farm trade.[13]

The Uruguay Round made little progress after the midterm review; all parties to the GATT avoided commitments or concessions until the run-up to the final ministerial meeting scheduled for December 1990, where the round was to have been wrapped up. After several battles in the Commission and in the Council—each institution was divided internally on the merits of further CAP reform, especially if made under international duress—the EC eventually tabled an offer to reduce farm subsidies by 30 percent over ten years from 1986, a far cry from its trading partners' moderated demand for cuts of 90 percent in export subsidies and 75 percent in other farm support over ten years from 1991/1992. Moreover, the EC insisted that any agreement to reduce farm subsidies and other supports would have to permit "rebalancing"—that is, allowing the EC partially to offset cuts in some areas with increases in others, provided the overall trend in supports was downward.

As expected, the Brussels talks broke down largely because of the EC's refusal to make a more substantial offer on agriculture. Negotiations resumed in early 1991 and continued fitfully thereafter.[14] Although the EC rejected a compromise proposal by the secretary-general of the GATT in late 1991 because it "called into question the very principles of the Community's agricultural policy,"[15] mounting pressure from international trading partners to cut agricultural price supports provided a powerful impetus to undertake serious CAP reform both to save the Uruguay Round and to rein in a system plagued by overproduction and spiraling costs. In addition, unrelated international developments in 1990 and 1991—notably in Central and Eastern Europe and in the Persian Gulf—caused a sharp drop in export prices and aggravated the CAP's imbalances.

This was the context in which the Commission reopened the reform debate in February 1991 with its "Reflection Paper on the Development and Future of the CAP."[16] As well as offering the usual mix of corrective mechanisms, the Commission for the first time recommended a proposal to break the automatic link between price support and volume of food production. To balance the deepest price cuts ever contemplated by the Community, the Commission proposed full compensation for small farmers and scaled compensation for big farmers, subject to big farmers' removal of large tracts of land from production (so-called set-asides).

Agriculture commissioner Ray MacSharry was the plan's architect and prime political mover. As Ireland's first-ever agriculture commissioner, MacSharry seemed more suited to maintaining the status quo, but the extent of the CAP's inefficiency genuinely appalled him. MacSharry pleaded with the EP in July 1991 "to look at the background of these proposals and the situation that exists in European agriculture today. . . . We have 20 million tonnes of cereals in intervention [that] is going to rise to 30 million tonnes. . . . There are almost 1 million tonnes of dairy produce in intervention and that cannot be given away throughout the world. . . . There are 750,000 tonnes of beef in intervention and rising at the rate of 15,000 to 20,000 *per week*."[17]

MacSharry was just as passionate about the inequitable distribution of price supports between big and small farmers, not least because his political roots lay in the poor west of Ireland. The most effective method of CAP reform would have been to replace the system of guaranteed payments entirely with a fair program of income support for farmers. But the visible cost of such a program was politically unacceptable. Farmers like to pretend that they operate in a free market system; direct aid would have exposed the truth. Nor would it have been easy to target assistance to those farmers who needed it most. Accordingly, although the MacSharry Plan included some direct income support, it did not propose to abolish guaranteed prices.

Predictably, agriculture ministers and farmers' organizations almost uniformly opposed the MacSharry Plan. The leader of the Irish Farmers Association compared MacSharry to Oliver Cromwell, the seventeenth-century English general who destroyed Irish towns and slaughtered their inhabitants, and accused the agriculture commissioner of attempting "to destroy the CAP."[18] Representatives of other farmers' organizations were less excitable but equally irresponsible, claiming that the plan would bankrupt small farmers and unfairly penalize big, efficient producers.

Given the unfavorable reaction engendered by the reflection paper, it seems remarkable that the Agriculture Council approved the plan, albeit in a modified form, over a year later. At first MacSharry appeared to lack even the Commission's support. Fearful of alienating French political opinion, Commission president Jacques Delors never backed MacSharry completely. Because of the proposed reform's likely beneficial impact on the Uruguay Round, external relations commissioner Frans Andriessen should have supported MacSharry enthusiastically. But as a former Dutch agriculture minister and a former agriculture commissioner, Andriessen equivocated. Only after intensive discussion did the Commission eventually approve the plan in July 1991 and forward it to the Council.[19]

Discussion of the MacSharry Plan in the Council proved far more contentious than in the Commission. British, Dutch, and Danish ministers complained that the plan discriminated against large producers; Spanish, Greek, Portuguese, and Irish ministers complained that it did not compensate small farmers adequately; and the French government opposed reform of any kind. Unusually, Ignaz Kiechle, Germany's veteran agriculture minister, stood up to the farmers' union (there were no elections in Germany at the time) and rallied to the MacSharry Plan. Hoping to reach a GATT agreement before the G7 economic summit in Munich in July 1992 (which proved impossible) and apprehensive about the impact of German unification on farm policy, the German government abandoned its unconditional defense of the CAP.

The agreement finally reached by the Agriculture Council on May 21, 1992, after a classic fifty-hour meeting, was a triumph for the Commission and for the Portuguese presidency, which got the package through by qualified majority vote.[20] Although smaller than the cuts in MacSharry's original proposal, the price reductions approved by the Council were nonetheless substantial and included a 29 percent drop in cereals prices over four years. Most important, the package began the process of shifting the basis of agricultural assistance from price supports to direct income supplements (in this case paid to big farmers in return for land set-asides of 15 percent). As a concession to the French and British governments, the compensation offered to big farmers was substantially higher than MacSharry's original offer.

Paradoxically, the generous compensation package agreed to by the Agriculture Council made the reformed CAP more expensive than the unreformed CAP. But by cutting guaranteed prices and taking land out of production, the reform helped reduce the EU's ruinous agricultural surpluses. At the same time, farmers did not experience the drops in income predicted by their leaders; on the contrary, farm incomes across the board rose steadily in the following years. Because price cuts would translate into lower (if any) export subsidies within four or five years (depending on world price levels), the MacSharry reforms gave an urgently needed boost to the moribund Uruguay Round, which finally came to an end in December 1993.

CAP REFORM: FOOD SAFETY, THE WTO, ENLARGEMENT, AND THE BUDGET

Far from being the end of a sporadic reform effort that began a decade earlier, the MacSharry Plan represented the beginning of a reform process that is accelerating in the face of important internal and external developments. Internally, consumers are finally waking up to the CAP's inequities not because of high prices but because of concerns about food safety. Whereas food security (i.e., self-sufficiency in food production) was one of the CAP's main objectives, for most of the CAP's history farmers and agricultural officials paid little or no attention to food safety (i.e., the quality and healthiness of food). By contrast, consumers gradually grew more concerned about food safety in the 1980s and 1990s, largely as a spin-off of the environmental and ecological movements. European farmers and agricultural officials happily jumped on the bandwagon when it involved issues such as hormones in beef and genetically modified organisms (GMOs), despite a lack of scientific evidence that the use of artificial growth hormones in cattle and the genetic modification of cereals compromised food safety. As such practices were prevalent in the United States rather than in Europe, opposing them was a useful way primarily to oppose beef and cereals imports into the EU.

Food Safety

However, consumer concerns about hormones in beef and GMOs paled in comparison with concerns about BSE, a disease affecting cattle that appeared in Britain in the 1980s. BSE hit the headlines and caused widespread panic in March 1996 when the British government announced a possible link between BSE and Creutzfeld-Jacob disease (CJD), a human brain condition that affects mostly young people and can be fatal. Here was an indigenous food safety crisis; no one could blame the Americans (the United States is BSE-free). Moreover, European officials had been aware for the previous decade of BSE's existence but had done little or nothing to control or eradicate the disease. Suddenly, in March 1996, the Commission leapt into action, banning exports of beef from Britain to other EU member states or anywhere else in the world. A major political crisis followed with the Commission being blamed by Britain for punishing it unfairly and by the EP for mishandling the whole affair.[21]

Regardless of its political implications, the British announcement caused an immediate public health scare throughout the EU and depressed the European beef market overnight. Consumers questioned not only the safety of beef generally but also the safety of other products of a system (the CAP) that emphasizes mass production and pays little attention to product quality. Although farmers in other member states fell over themselves to present their products as unquestionably safe for human consumption, it was too late to put the genie of consumer criticism back into the bottle. The CAP itself became a target for consumer complaints, forcing farmers and officials to recast the CAP in an environmentally friendly and health-conscious light.

The BSE crisis shook farmers' and agricultural officials' complacency about the CAP and introduced a new dynamic for reform, a dynamic with its roots in the environmental movement, which has been a feature of European politics for nearly two decades. The first mention of environmental policy in the EC treaties—Article 25 of the SEA (now Articles 174–176 TEC)—had no direct impact on the CAP but served notice of the increasing importance of environmental issues in the EU. The TEU went considerably further by including respect for the environment as a basic objective of the EC (then as now Article 2 TEC), and the Amsterdam Treaty went further again by specifying that such respect meant "a high level of protection and improvement of the quality of the environment" and that "environmental protection requirements must be integrated into the definition and implementation of the Community policies and activities . . . with a view to promoting sustainable development" (Article 6, formerly Article 3c, TEC).

The WTO

Apart from new consumerism and a more assertive environmentalism, renewed pressure for CAP reform in the late 1990s emanated more directly and compellingly in circumstances similar to those that had given rise to the MacSharry Plan: a desire to reach a global trade agreement under the auspices of the World Trade Organization (WTO) and concerns about the

CAP's unaffordability, this time in the context of the EU's impending enlargement into Central and Eastern Europe.

The GATT agreement on agriculture (converted, when the GATT changed itself into the WTO, into the WTO agreement on agriculture) set the framework in which global trade in agriculture could take place after the Uruguay Round. The agreement has three elements:

- *Domestic support:* establishes three categories of temporarily permissible price supports in domestic markets
- *Export subsidies:* limits export subsidies in terms of base quantities and budget expenditures
- *Market access:* ensures minimum levels of imports and contains a commitment to convert all nontariff barriers to tariffs on an equivalent basis

The agreement also set up the WTO Committee on Agriculture to monitor compliance and stipulates that new negotiations to continue the process of liberalizing the agricultural sector should start by the end of 1999. At a ministerial meeting in Singapore in December 1996, the WTO decided to launch the preparatory stage of the 1999 negotiations with a process of analysis and an exchange of information. The EU is active in this and in the other work of the Committee on Agriculture.

As in the preparatory stage of the Uruguay Round over ten years ago, however, the EU is on the defensive while preparing for the WTO agricultural negotiations. The Cairns Group has put the EU on notice that it will press for the abolition of farm subsidies and other trade distortions. Together with the United States, the Cairns Group used the occasion of the WTO meeting in Geneva in May 1998, on the fiftieth anniversary of the postwar global trading system, to blast EU protectionism and call for opening up the EU agricultural marketplace.

The EU awaits the WTO negotiations with some trepidation and would prefer to subsume agriculture into a broader round of trade talks—the so-called Millennium Round—similar to the Uruguay Round. Negotiations on such a wide range of issues would give the EU some leverage to extract concessions for market opening in agriculture in areas such as services and procurement. After the experience of the Uruguay Round, which lasted nearly eight years and whose results are still being digested, other WTO members, including the United States, are reluctant to commit themselves to a mammoth Millennium Round.

Enlargement

While preparing for the WTO talks, the EU faces the far more challenging task of launching a new round of enlargement. Whereas previous EU enlargement had necessitated readjustments of the CAP regime, for the first time in the EU's history the prospect of enlargement has prompted proposals for major CAP reform. That is because, in agriculture as in other areas, Central and Eastern European enlargement is qualitatively different from previous enlargements. Specifically, whereas only 5.3 percent of the EU's workforce is engaged in agriculture, over 22 percent of the workforce in the applicant states is so engaged. The accession of all ten Central and Eastern European applicant states would result in a doubling of the EU's farm labor force and a doubling of EU agricultural land. Moreover, agricultural prices in Central and Eastern Europe are much lower than in Western Europe. Thus extending the CAP to the new member states in Central and Eastern Europe necessitates either a big increase in its budget—a political impossibility—or major cuts in price supports.

The impetus of enlargement and, to a lesser extent, of upcoming WTO negotiations and of growing environmental and consumer concerns underlay the following proposals for CAP reform in *Agenda 2000*, the Commission's strategy "for strengthening and widening the Union in the early years of the 21st century," released in July 1997:[22]

- Improve the EU's global competitiveness through lower prices.
- Guarantee the safety and quality of food to consumers.
- Ensure stable incomes and a fair standard of living for the agricultural community.
- Make agricultural production methods environmentally friendly and respectful of animal welfare.
- Integrate environmental goals into the CAP's instruments.
- Seek and create alternative income and employment opportunities for farmers and their families.

The Commission's revised policy objectives for the CAP revealed the influence on agricultural policy of new social movements and economic trends and showed how far the EU had changed in the four decades since the Stresa Conference of 1958.

In essence, *Agenda 2000* proposed that the EU continue the MacSharry reforms by shifting agricultural subsidies from price supports to direct payments. The Commission suggested cutting the cereals intervention price by 20 percent in the year 2000, cutting guaranteed prices for beef by 30 percent between 2000 and 2002, and cutting milk support prices by 10 percent by 2006. Farmers in all sectors would be compensated with direct payments of one kind or another. Indeed, the Commission estimated that the cost of the compensatory direct payments would exceed the savings from reduced price supports by €6 billion annually. However, anticipated increases in EU revenue (linked to projected annual economic growth) would mean that CAP spending remained within existing guidelines and continued to shrink as a percentage of overall EU spending.

Following up on the final declaration of a Commission-sponsored conference in Cork, Ireland, in November 1996, *Agenda 2000* paid particular attention to rural development, stressing the "obligations and opportunities for agriculture" presented by growing environmental awareness and the increasing use of the countryside for recreation. Accordingly, *Agenda 2000* proposed a more prominent role for agri-environmentalism and organic farming.

Improving CAP management was another major thrust of *Agenda 2000,* which particularly emphasized the desirability of giving member states and regions more responsibility for implementation of EU agricultural policy. However, the Commission sought to balance the vogue for decentralization and subsidiarity against the risk of renationalizing the CAP.

The European Council endorsed the general thrust of *Agenda 2000* in Luxembourg in December 1997 with a statement that "the process of reform begun in 1992 should be continued, deepened, adapted, and completed."[23] As for the Commission's specific proposals, farmers' reactions were predictably negative. Most national governments also reacted negatively, but not necessarily for the same reason. For countries critical of the CAP, such as Britain, the proposals did not go far enough to cut price supports; for others, such as France, they went too far. As on so many occasions in the past, Germany's reaction was moderated by the Bavarian government's unequivocal rejection of *Agenda 2000.* With a weak Chancellor Kohl facing federal elections in September 1998, the German government was not willing to risk alienating the conservative farmers' vote by endorsing *Agenda 2000.*

The Commission followed up the broad outlines of *Agenda 2000* with precise legislative proposals in March 1998. These included proposals for Council regulations for the common organization of markets in cereals, beef, milk, and olive oil. The Commission had earlier submitted such a proposal for tobacco and would later submit a proposal for wine. The legislative proposals mostly adhered to the guidelines in *Agenda 2000*, although the proposal for milk included a cut in intervention prices by 15 rather than 10 percent, partly offset by a 2 percent increase in the milk quota. Sensitive to the general perception that many farmers were bilking the system, the Commission proposed a ceiling on the amount of direct aid that a farm could receive under various support schemes. Finally, the Commission also submitted a legislative proposal for a new regulation on rural development.

The Budget

The financial impact of enlargement has triggered widespread debate not only about reform of agricultural and cohesion policies but also about reform of the entire EU budget. The EU's biggest net contributors (those member states that pay more into the EU than they receive back through various forms of financial transfers, notably Germany and the Netherlands) began agitating in 1998 for a more equitable budgetary system in the run-up to the negotiation of the post–Delors II multiyear financial perspective. The Commission surprised everyone in October 1998 when it suggested as an option in a position paper on budgetary reform that 25 percent of CAP expenditure (covering direct income supports) be switched back to member states, thereby removing some of the transnational subsidization that is a major source of the budgetary imbalance. The option was politically appealing because it could be implemented by a qualified majority vote in the Council (proposals to reform the budget on the revenue side require unanimity in the Council and ratification by national parliaments). At the same time, the proposal was politically risky because it raised an EU taboo: the possibility of renationalizing, however partially, one of the EU's few truly "common" policies. Sensitive to that charge, the Commission claimed that a system of partial reimbursement would not amount to renationalization because "neither the degree of integration, nor the level of decisionmaking or the overall amount of financial resources available to pursue [the CAP's] objectives would be modified."[24]

PROSPECTS FOR REFORM

As is the case with all proposals for agricultural legislation, the Commission's reform proposals were chewed over by the Agriculture Council and its Special Committee. Early in the process, agriculture ministers signaled their concerns about the extent of the proposed cuts and complained that the various compensatory schemes were inadequate. However, given the overall political importance of *Agenda 2000*, the General Affairs Council (foreign affairs ministers) staked a claim to oversee the legislative program for CAP reform. Despite deep differences among a number of governments on specific parts of the proposals, foreign ministers were more likely than their agricultural counterparts to take a broader view of things. Moreover, the change of government in Germany in October 1998 augured well for a CAP reform. With the farmer-friendly Bavarian conservatives out of the coalition government and the environmentally conscious Greens in, Germany was more inclined to overhaul the CAP's budget and priorities. Ultimately, the European Council would have to resolve the most intractable disputes.

In the event, CAP negotiations proceed in a relatively desultory fashion later in 1998 before picking up speed in the run up to the European Council's self-imposed deadline of March 1999 for completion of the entire *Agenda 2000* package. Farm ministers reached agreement on the CAP component of the package in early March 1999, although the cost of offsetting their proposed cuts in price supports with direct payments would have increased the cost of the CAP, at least in the medium term. Far from demanding further reform and reining in agricultural spending, however, the European Council diluted the farm ministers' agreement and decided to delay key cuts in guaranteed prices at its decisive summit in Berlin on March 24–25. This surprising outcome was due to the tenacity of French president Jacques Chirac, an unabashed defender of French farmers; the inability of German chancellor Gerhard Schröder to assert himself at the summit and push through a radical reform package; and the unwillingness of other leaders to stand up to the farmers' lobby. In the end, enlargement seemed too remote a prospect—the first Central and Eastern European applicants are not expected to join the EU until near the end of the new financial perspective in 2006—to convince the European Council of the urgency of major reform. Nor, apparently, is the EU seriously concerned about the impact of an unreconstructed CAP on global trade talks.

Thus the *Agenda 2000* CAP reform was extremely modest, involving as it did neither a radical shift from a price support system nor a major diminution of farmers' incomes. The agreed-upon price cuts do not go far enough to ensure the manageability of agricultural policy in the postenlargement period, let alone appease critics in the WTO of EU agricultural protectionism. Regardless of prices and protectionism, at least environmental standards in European agriculture are going up and the EU is paying greater attention to food safety. But consumers can be certain of one thing: in defiance of basic economic principles, food prices will remain high in the EU even though supply far exceeds demand.

NOTES

1. See Luxembourg European Council, "Presidency Conclusions," Bull. EC 12-1997, point 1.5.11.
2. Robert Marjolin, *Architect of European Unity: Memoirs, 1911–1986* (London: Weidenfeld & Nicolson, 1989), p. 312.
3. See Graham Avery, "New Options for Agricultural Policy," *European Affairs* 1 (1987): 64.
4. For an account of the CAP's origin and development, see Hans von der Groeben, *The European Community: The Formative Years: The Struggle to Establish the Common Market and the Political Union (1958–66)* (Luxembourg: Office for Official Publications of the European Communities [OOP], 1987), pp. 70–78. See also Leon Lindberg, *The Political Dynamics of Economic Integration* (Stanford: Stanford University Press, 1963), pp. 145–151.
5. See Martin Westlake, *The Council of the European Union* (London: Catermill, 1995), pp. 204–207.
6. COM(68)1000, December 21, 1968.
7. Quoted in the *Times* (London), June 28, 1977, p. 16.
8. Bull. EC S/4-1983, point 4.14.

9. See Michael Petit et al., *Agricultural Policy Formation in the European Community* (Amsterdam: Elsevier, 1987).

10. Bull. EC 6-1984, point 1.1.7.

11. COM(87)100.

12. Bull. EC 3-1985, point 2.2.12.

13. See Finn Laursen, "The EC, GATT, and the Uruguay Round," in Leon Hurwitz and Christian Lequesne, eds., *The State of the European Community: Policies, Institutions, and Debates in the Transition Years* (Boulder: Lynne Rienner, 1991), pp. 378–381; Anna Murphy and Peter Ludlow, "The Community's External Relations," in Peter Ludlow, ed., *The Annual Review of European Community Affairs 1990* (Brussels: Center for European Policy Studies [CEPS], 1992), pp. 176–179.

14. For an account of the GATT negotiations in 1991 and 1992, see Finn Laursen, "The EC, the U.S., and the Uruguay Round," in Alan Cafruny and Glenda Rosenthal, eds., *The State of the European Community: The Maastricht Debates and Beyond* (Boulder: Lynne Rienner, 1993), pp. 245–264.

15. Bull. EC 12-1991, point 1.3.93.

16. COM(91)100, February 1, 1991.

17. Debates of the European Parliament, *Official Journal of the European Communities* [*OJ*] 3–407, July 11, 1991, p. 282.

18. Quoted in the *Irish Times*, July 10, 1991, p. 1.

19. COM(91)258, July 22, 1991.

20. Council press release 6539/92, May 18–21, 1992, 1579th Council Meeting (Agriculture).

21. See Martin Westlake, "'Mad Cows and Englishmen': The Institutional Consequences of the BSE Crisis," *Journal of Common Market Studies* 35, *Annual Review* (1996): 11–36.

22. Commission, *Agenda 2000: For a Stronger and Wider Europe*, Brussels, July 16, 1997, COM(97)2000 final.

23. Luxembourg European Council, "Presidency Conclusions," Bull. EC 12-1997, point 1.5.11.

24. Commission, *Financing the European Union: Commission Report on the Operation of the Own Resources System*, Brussels, October 7, 1998, COM(98)560 final, p. 35.

13

The Single Market

Short of a monetary union, a single market is the most advanced form of economic integration between sovereign states. Indeed, in order to reach the stage of economic integration inherent in a single market, states need to exercise jointly a great degree of authority that previously rested at the national level. The original version of the Treaty Establishing the European Community (TEC) contained the basic building blocks for a single market; in the mid-1980s a majority of member states thought it necessary to revise the treaty and extend the scope of qualified majority voting in order to generate sufficient decisionmaking momentum to complete the project. They did so in the Single European Act (SEA).

The origins, development, and political salience of the SEA and of the single market program were examined in Chapter 5. This chapter looks at the implementation of the single market itself, beginning with the Commission's famous White Paper of June 1985, which contained the detailed legislative blueprint—and set a deadline of December 31, 1992—for completion of the single market.[1] Nevertheless, it is important to bear in mind that many directives enacted in the years before the launch of the White Paper laid a legislative foundation for the single market program and that many non–White Paper directives also helped consolidate the single market. Additional directives were tabled in some cases in an effort to tidy up previously enacted parts of the program; in other cases they were enacted in response to changing technology (such as the advent of the Internet), or changing social and environmental priorities. Also, completion of the single market required measures to remove quotas and other trade restrictions imposed by member states in order to protect their markets from third-country imports and prompted member states to liberalize fully energy and telecommunications, two sectors initially excluded from the single market program. As well as examining the White Paper, this chapter looks at supplementary measures since 1992 and at the continuing problems of transposition and enforcement of single market legislation.

THE 1992 PROGRAM

By identifying the steps necessary to complete the single market, the Commission's 1985 White Paper underpinned the 1992 program. Despite its comprehensiveness and seemingly microscopic specificity the White Paper represented an educated estimate of the measures needed to bring about a single market rather than a revealed truth. It also served to give new momentum to old proposals by repackaging them as part of an exciting new initiative. Moreover, the White Paper was far from sacrosanct: The number of proposals to complete the single market hovered around 282, but they were not always the same 282. Some were discreetly deemed unnecessary when they failed to win support; others spawned additional measures. Given the complexity of the EC market, it is not surprising that the lines between the Commission's three categories of barriers to integration—physical, technical, and fiscal—were neither neat nor self-evident.

Physical Barriers

Physical barriers—customs and immigration posts at border crossings between member states—were the most tangible obstacles to a single market. Accordingly, the Commission sought unequivocally "to eliminate in their entirety . . . internal frontier barriers and controls . . . by 1992." Physical barriers included impediments to the movement of people (covering passport controls and residence restrictions) and goods. The latter proved far easier to remove than the former.

Movement of Goods

Ending onerous and costly delays at internal borders proved politically uncontentious. The Commission took a lengthy, phased approach to the abolition of customs formalities and inspections by the end of 1992. Measures included the consolidation and eventual abolition of all the paperwork needed at frontier crossings as well as miscellaneous provisions such as duty-free admission for the fuel in the tanks of goods lorries, an end to routine checks of passenger car documentation, and a new statistical system for tracking trade among member states once border posts disappeared. By the end of 1991 the Council had adopted all the necessary measures. In October 1992 the Commission published the Common Customs Code, supplementing it with a long-overdue digest of customs practices.[2]

The removal of physical barriers had a direct bearing on agriculture, as border checks ensured compliance with a wide array of plant and animal health and food safety requirements. Under byzantine CAP rules, farmers were compensated at internal borders, and border inspections enforced quota arrangements granted to Spain and Portugal at the time of their accession. Sixty-three of the White Paper's proposals covered disease control and livestock trade generally, as well as trade in meat, poultry, fish, and similar food products. Another eighteen covered phytosanitary (plant health) measures, the control of pests common to plants, pesticide-residue limits, and the gene pool of ornamental plants. Of the eighty-one measures in these two categories, only three remained outstanding at the end of 1992.

Movement of People

Barriers to the movement of people proved the most intractable part of the 1992 program. Key elements, such as passport and visa requirements, remained the exclusive province of member states, some of which agreed to eliminate all border formalities under the auspices of the so-called Schengen regime, outside the treaty framework. Although signed in 1985 by France, Germany, and the Benelux countries, the Schengen agreement was still not operational in 1992. Aware that it was running out of time, in May 1992 the Commission issued a communication describing lack of progress on the free movement of people as "worrying at all political levels" and reminded member states of their commitment under Article 8a of the SEA (now Article 14 TEC) to abolish all controls at frontiers, without exception, by the end of the year.[3]

The legally complicated and politically contentious question of free movement of people became bound up with the provisions of the Treaty on European Union (TEU) for intergovernmental cooperation on Justice and Home Affairs (JHA). At the 1996–1997 intergovernmental conference (IGC), the thirteen member states that eventually signed the Schengen agreement (Britain and Ireland being the odd ones out) wanted to bring Schengen into the treaty framework. The change of government in Britain in May 1997 made it possible to do so in the Amsterdam Treaty (although Britain and Ireland secured opt-outs). Schengen therefore became an integral part of the EU's putative area of "freedom, security, and justice." Free movement of people, Schengen, JHA, and the corresponding provisions of the Amsterdam Treaty are examined in Chapter 15.

Technical Barriers

The White Paper used the term "technical barriers" almost as a catchall: Proposals under this heading covered product standards, testing and certification, movement of capital, public procurement, free movement of labor and the professions, free movement of services, transport, new technologies, company law, intellectual property, and company taxation. Not surprisingly, it was by far the largest category of White Paper measures.

Standards, Testing, and Certification

The use of different product standards, testing, and certification in each member state—and the need for multiple approvals in some product areas—traditionally posed major barriers to intra-European trade. Despite a general prohibition on technical barriers in Article 28 (formerly Article 30) TEC, member states frequently abused the escape clause in Article 30 (formerly Article 36), which allowed them to impose their own product standards for reasons of health and safety. Article 94 (formerly Article 100) allows the council to try to develop harmonized standards in cases where member state standards differ. However, the arduous and politically sensitive process of harmonization led to a huge backlog of cases before the Council by the mid-1980s.

To end the backlog and remove a major obstacle to the free movement of goods, the Commission developed the principle of mutual recognition of national regulations and standards. Instead of trying to harmonize a potentially limitless number of product standards throughout the EC, member states would recognize and accept each other's standards as long as those standards satisfied certain health and safety concerns. Mutual recognition rests squarely on the outcome of the famous *Cassis de Dijon* (1979) case, in which the European Court of Justice (ECJ) overruled a ban imposed by German authorities on the importation of cassis, a French liqueur, because it failed to meet Germany's alcohol-content standards.[4]

Building on the *Cassis de Dijon* judgment, the White Paper proclaimed that "subject to certain important constraints . . . if a product is lawfully manufactured and marketed in one member state, there is no reason why it should not be sold freely throughout the Community." By emphasizing mutual recognition on the basis of treaty obligations and EC case law, the Commission expected to trigger "the withdrawal of numerous harmonization proposals pending before the Council and . . . the abandonment of even more drafts envisaged by the Commission's staff."[5] The Commission hoped that a combination of self-interest, common sense, goodwill, and peer pressure would reduce member states' recourse to Article 30. Yet there could be no question of member states' forsaking legitimate health and safety concerns about specific products manufactured elsewhere in the EC. The White Paper sought to maximize mutual recognition, not to abolish harmonization. Where harmonization remained essential, the White Paper proposed a two-track strategy. The first involved a pathbreaking "new approach," approved by the Council in May 1985, while the White Paper was still being drafted; the second followed the old approach of sectoral harmonization.[6]

The new approach. The first part of the new approach limited legislative harmonization by means of Article 94 to the establishment of essential health and safety requirements with which products had to conform. Member states would transpose those fundamental requirements into national regulations but could not impose further regulatory requirements on the products in question.[7] The White Paper included "new approach" directives on a wide range of products such as toys, machinery, and implantable medical devices.

Because manufacturers would have some problems proving that their products met fundamental requirements without the aid of further technical specification, the second part of the new approach required the Commission to contract with European standards organizations—CEN (European Standardization Committee), CENELEC (European Electrotechnical Standardization Committee), and ETSI (European Telecom Standards Institute)—to develop voluntary European standards (European Norms, or ENs). Manufacturers adhering to those standards would be presumed to comply with the essential requirements set in the directive and their products would therefore be assured free circulation throughout the EC. Manufacturers would also have the option of complying with national standards or, perhaps with less promise of success, of trying to demonstrate compliance with the essential requirements without the assistance of any standard.

In order to make the system work, member states had to reach agreement not only on the essential requirements themselves but also on the level of proof needed to demonstrate compliance (i.e., reach a consensus on testing and certification requirements). The Council filled the gap in December 1989 by adopting a "global approach" that described a set of standard "modules" for testing and certification of products, in most cases offering manufacturers some degree of choice.[8] The options ranged from the least burdensome—in which a manufacturer could simply declare that a product met essential requirements—to the most burdensome, where, for instance, a third party (such as a nationally approved laboratory) would test and evaluate the product.

Another option involved a "quality systems" approach, in which a manufacturer's consistent application of quality-control measures from design through production would be certified by an outside body. The rigor of the requirements specified in the "new approach" directives—the module(s) that manufacturers are required to follow—varies according to the perceived risk attached to the product. Thus a manufacturer of stuffed animals may simply declare his products in compliance with the relevant directive, whereas a maker of cardiac pacemakers would need to seek third-party certification of the product or of his quality systems. Where required, "notified bodies"—laboratories or other institutions nominated by national governments—would perform third-party tests or certification. In a further application of the principle of mutual recognition, member states are required to allow free circulation of goods certified by the notified bodies of other member states.

The European conformity (CE) mark, applied either by the manufacturer or by the notified body certifying the product, plays a key part. CE marks are intended primarily to show customs and regulatory authorities that products comply with essential requirements; they should not be confused with quality marks, such as those awarded by other national bodies.

Although new-approach directives covering a wide range of products were largely completed by the end of 1992, application of the system ran into trouble. European standards bodies, bureaucratic and slow, soon lagged behind in developing the ENs necessary to allow manufacturers to comply with the directives. Some requirements for use of the CE mark turned out to be inconsistent and in some cases incompatible (e.g., products subject to more than one directive were not able to comply with each set of marking requirements). A directive on the CE mark retroactively harmonizing existing directives and laying down a single set of rules was eventually agreed on in April 1993.

The continuing lag in the development of ENs was a more serious problem. A 1989 Commission green paper suggesting ways to remove bottlenecks met with a frosty response from the leadership of CEN and CENELEC and raised concerns outside the EC that hasty setting of standards could lead to divergences between European and international standards. In the end there were few fundamental changes, but at least the standards bodies agreed to streamline procedures as much as possible. The slow pace at which member states notified testing bodies created another bottleneck in the system, especially because the bodies so notified faced an initial surge in demand as manufacturers rushed to certify their existing product lines.

The old approach. Recognizing that the new approach could not be applied to all sectors, the Commission took the old approach of working toward total sectoral harmonization—developing a single, detailed set of technical specifications for a given product that all member states would have to accept—in a number of key areas traditionally subject to intensive member state regulation because of safety risks and/or public concern. In the White Paper, the Commission advocated the old approach for motor vehicles, food, pharmaceuticals, chemicals, construction, and a number of other items.

In the case of pharmaceuticals, where the European market was highly fragmented, the White Paper included fifteen directives addressing such questions as common testing rules, price transparency, patient information, advertising, and, above all, centralized approval of new drugs. The Commission envisioned a European-level agency that would eventually take responsibility for all new drug approvals, backed by a host of new harmonizing directives. On the basis of the catchall Article 308 (formerly Article 235) TEC, member states finally decided in 1992 to establish the European Agency for the Evaluation of Medicinal Products (EMEA), which has responsibility for approving all medicines based on biotechnology and all veterinary medicines likely to improve the productivity of farm animals (this peculiar list resulted from a previous debate over the safety of biotechnology generally and over the possible approval of bovine somatotropin [BST], a controversial new drug that improved milk yields of dairy cows).

Movement of Capital

Since the 1960s, the EC had achieved considerable liberalization of the initially tight postwar restrictions on capital flows. As member states became richer and more confident of their own stability, many lifted restrictions unilaterally. Three White Paper directives aimed to complete the process with a sequence of measures intended to phase out controls. The first two liberalized rules governing cross-border securities transactions, long-term commercial loans, and admission of corporate securities to capital markets in other member states (e.g., stock exchanges); the third superseded these and obliged member states to lift all restrictions on capital movements except measures intended to ensure the continuing liquidity of local banks or temporary restrictions in response to major disruptions in foreign exchange markets. The Commission saw enactment of these measures as a final step on the road to "an effective and stable Community financial system"—a prerequisite for Economic and Monetary Union (EMU).

Public Procurement

Member states made initial moves toward opening procurement in the 1970s with two directives intended to increase transparency in Europe's traditionally protected public markets, which accounted for as much as 15 percent of Community GDP. However, transparency alone did little to improve the success of cross-border bids on public tenders. For a variety of reasons ranging from active obstruction by local authorities to the inadequacy of the directives themselves, public procurement remained overwhelmingly the preserve of national suppliers. In 1992, the Commission estimated that only 2 percent of the ECU 600 billion public market had been won by firms from outside the home country.

The Commission correctly characterized such a distortion of competition as "anachronistic" and contrary to the spirit of a free market. Moreover, the Commission had a particular concern about the telecommunications sector, fearing that closed public markets and a cozy relationship between public authorities and cosseted but internationally weak "national champions" would hinder the development of a European telecommunications industry capable of competing in the harsher world market. The need to open public procurement and encourage competition generally became a recurring theme of the Commission's developing industrial policy.

The White Paper proposed seven directives to eliminate distortions caused by local procurement bias. Proposals covered essential elements of an open bidding system, such as transparency (effective public notice), review procedures to penalize violations, use of common standards (national or European), and procedures for award of public contracts. The directives also extended the scope of those rules to cover nearly all public procurement above certain thresholds (which vary by sector and by type of contract—i.e., supply, work, or service contracts).

The most important of these directives was the so-called utilities, or excluded-sectors, directive, extending EC public procurement rules to enterprises (not necessarily publicly owned) offering public services in the water, energy, transport, and telecommunications sectors. As well as setting out minimum thresholds for application of its rules and procedures to ensure transparency, the directive also required public authorities to evaluate bids on objective and nondiscriminatory criteria—for example, lowest price or most economically advantageous package (an exception to this rule allowing member states to discard bids with less than 50 percent EC content and providing a 3 percent price preference for EC bids later caused trouble with the United States). Other procurement directives applied similar principles to the supply of services and public works (i.e., construction and similar projects) and developed legal remedies for violations. All but one were adopted by the end of 1992; the remaining proposal, on procurement of services in the excluded sectors, was adopted in the spring of 1993.

Free Movement of Labor and the Professions

The White Paper included proposals for putting into practice the right, enshrined in the treaty, of EC citizens to live and work in other member states. Directives extending residency rights throughout the EC to students, retired persons, and other members of the nonworking population came into force on June 30, 1992. Those relating to workers and their families built on a 1968 directive guaranteeing nondiscrimination in employment and a right of establishment. White Paper proposals sought to extend nondiscrimination to various employment-related subsidies and social benefits, as well as granting residence and social and educational rights to non-EC nationals in the extended family of EC national workers.

In order to facilitate the movement of workers among countries, the Commission also took on the task of establishing equivalencies among the various types of professional and vocational training available in each member state and of removing traditional restrictions that prevented members of regulated professions (e.g., doctors and lawyers) from freely offering their services in other member states. The Council adopted two directives on the recognition of diplomas (one on training of less than three years, the other on training of three years or more). In addition, the Commission undertook extensive studies and published comparative lists of member state qualifications and credentials covering over 200 vocations, enabling employers to evaluate qualifications in nonregulated areas.

Freedom of Movement of Financial Services

The Commission followed three basic principles to permit free movement for financial services: harmonization of essential standards; mutual recognition among supervisory authorities; and home-country control (i.e., making a financial institution's branches the responsibility of the member state in which the institution's head office is located).

The White Paper proposed eight directives intended to allow *banks* incorporated in one member state to operate across national borders without having to seek authorization from national regulatory authorities in each member state. Clearly, member states would have to agree to common rules and criteria for judging the soundness of banks in order to develop the necessary mutual confidence to allow the home-country control system to work.

The second banking directive, which entered into force January 1, 1993, established a single banking license, valid throughout the EU, allowing banks to open branches anywhere without additional authorizations. Overall supervision of a bank with multiple branches is a cooperative venture: The home country monitors solvency, and the country in which a branch is located may monitor the liquidity of the branch and impose other local conduct rules. The directive also contains provisions on foreign banks designed to give the Commission leverage in negotiating conditions for EU banks in foreign markets.

The Commission based its approach to creating a single market for *insurance* services on the principles used in the banking sector. Nine White Paper directives built on an existing body of EC legislation in the insurance area, beginning with a 1973 directive harmonizing criteria for the formation and activities of non–life insurance firms.

Similarly, in *investment services,* the investment-services directive set out the system for a single authorizing procedure, reciprocity with third countries, common prudential rules, cooperation among supervisory authorities, and other necessary elements. Neither the investment-services directive nor a supplementary directive harmonizing member state capital requirements (capital adequacy) were formally adopted when the single market supposedly became operational on January 1, 1993.

Transport

Opening up the EC's highly regulated transport markets required twelve directives covering six discrete and dissimilar sectors including air, road haulage (goods), and maritime transport.

Most *international air transport* markets are regulated by government agreements that usually inhibit competition. The situation in Europe was a particularly egregious example, combining a number of relatively small markets with "national champions" (frequently government-owned) protected through market-sharing arrangements, fixed fares, and occasional massive subsidies—all governed by 200 bilateral agreements covering twenty-two countries. Not surprisingly, the result was high consumer costs. The Commission tackled the ensuing morass in three stages with the Council adopting aviation packages in 1987, 1990, and 1992 that gradually liberalized the market in areas such as competition on fares, sharing of passenger capacity, access to routes for all operators, application of EC competition rules, and a right to carry passengers between two cities inside another member state (the right of cabotage) for European airlines (starting in January 1997).

Before the 1985 White Paper, *road haulage* between member states was generally subject to quotas that restricted rights to carry cargo on the return leg of any journey. As a result, large numbers of empty trucks trundled through the EC, adding to congestion and pollution and raising transport costs. Truckers were also prohibited from engaging in cabotage. In addition, trucks were subject to different and often incompatible work rules or technical specifications (e.g., weight and size limits). The Commission approached the problem with three initiatives: harmonization to the extent possible of technical specifications and work rules, abolition of all quotas on road haulage between member states, and the gradual introduction of cabotage. Full cabotage rights—the final step in establishing a single transport market—were finally granted in June 1993, when member states agreed on a fair way to assess road taxes on foreign operators.

New Technologies

The 1985 White Paper included five directives on "new technologies," focusing on opening markets in areas such as cable and satellite broadcasting. The most important follow.

- A directive on mutual recognition of member state approvals for telecommunications terminal equipment (telephones, faxes, modems, etc.).
- A framework directive on Open Network Provision (ONP) in the telecommunications area to ensure open access for equipment and service providers to the public telecommunications infrastructure. The directive prohibits public telecommunications networks from restricting access except on grounds of security, data protection, or the need to preserve interoperability. It also provides for a gradual development of mutual recognition of authorizations for service providers.

- A follow-up directive on open competition in the market for non-voice telecommunications services.
- The television-without-frontiers directive, which liberalized member state television markets by prohibiting discrimination against works from other member states (with the exception of some remaining language quotas). The directive also harmonized advertising standards (e.g., prohibited advertising of tobacco) and obliged broadcasters to encourage local talent by showing a majority of EC-origin programming where practicable (a requirement that sparked fierce opposition from the United States).

Other related directives covered mobile telephones, a European code of conduct for electronic payments systems, radio frequencies, data protection, and high-definition television standards. Also included was a Council decision calling on the Commission to develop an action plan to develop a European market for information services.

Company Law

Article 48 (formerly Article 58) TEC empowers the EC to take action in the field of company law "to coordinate . . . safeguards . . . required by member states of companies or firms . . . with a view to making such safeguards equivalent throughout the Community." In 1968 the Council adopted the first in a long and often arcane series of directives in this area; as with those that initially followed, its purpose was to approximate member state law to allow maximum freedom of movement for enterprises. The White Paper directives went beyond that goal by aiming to create an EC framework regulating cross-border corporate activity. As in the case of the procurement directives, one of the Commission's objectives was to increase the competitiveness of European firms by allowing them to become larger and more efficient.

The White Paper proposed a number of directives in this area, including the European Company Statute, which had already languished for some time in the Council, and a regulation defining the European Economic Interest Grouping (EEIG), a legal entity created to accommodate firms or other entities wanting to pool their resources for a common goal, but not wanting to merge. Perhaps the best-known example was Airbus Industrie, before it became a limited company in 1999. Some trade associations also applied for recognition as an EEIG.

The EEIG measure was adopted by the end of 1992, as were the eleventh company law directive (disclosure requirements for branch operations), the twelfth directive (single-member companies), and a directive covering transparency in major holdings in company capital. The Commission had far less success with the remainder of the program. After years of blockage, it eventually made a virtue of necessity and declared the fifth, tenth, and thirteenth directives (dealing, respectively, with corporate structure and voting rights, cross-border mergers, and harmonization of rules on takeover bids) "nonpriority" for the creation of the single market. In a triumph of hope over experience, the Commission declared that the European Company Statute remained a top priority for the 1992 program.

Intellectual Property

Also under the general heading of removing technical barriers, the Commission proposed nine directives dealing with various aspects of intellectual property rights, only four of which were adopted by the end of 1992. The major disappointment in this area was the legislation establishing the Community Trademark Office, which was thoroughly derailed by nonsubstantive but intractable disputes over the location of the office itself and the working languages to be used.

Company Taxation

To address the question of differing rates of tax on corporations in different member states, the Council finally adopted three proposals in 1990 that had been on the table for nearly twenty years. One covered taxes on capital gains resulting from mergers, share exchanges, and other forms of company restructuring; the other two concerned the problem of double taxation on intracompany dividend transfers and on profits of affiliated companies. A number of other draft directives remained on the table at the end of 1992 (tax proposals were particularly difficult to adopt because they required unanimity in the Council).

Fiscal Barriers

The White Paper included an ambitious set of initiatives for harmonizing taxation—a prerequisite not only for eliminating borders (where many taxes were assessed) but also for reducing distortion and segmentation of the EC market through disparate tax practices. To take one of the more extreme examples, consumer groups calculated that the cost of a car varied as much as 100 percent across Europe because of excise, value-added, and other tax differentials.

Value-Added Tax

Of the wide variety of indirect taxes assessed on European goods, value-added tax (VAT) is the most visible and probably the most important. Before 1992, standard VAT rates varied up to 11 percent among member states. Some states charged luxury rates on certain categories of goods or charged no VAT at all on others. The White Paper called on member states to harmonize VAT rates and to develop a system for charging VAT on cross-border sales once border posts had been eliminated.

The road to VAT harmonization proved especially arduous. Because VAT revenues were in many cases the mainstay of member state social welfare systems, high-VAT countries could be relied on to resist harmonization downward, even into the broad bands proposed by the Commission. Governments feared having to explain to voters why they were cutting back on prized social security regimes for the sake of the single market. There was speculation in 1992 that popular anxiety in that regard contributed to Denmark's narrow rejection of the TEU. Elimination of such local exceptions to VAT as food or children's clothing was equally certain to create political fallout. The alternative, proposed by some member states such as Britain, was to leave VAT unharmonized and let the market force member states to align their VAT rates with those of their neighbors, if need be. This was a prospect only an island nation could face with equanimity; others feared that hordes of consumers, streaming across borders to get the best tax deal, would bankrupt local retailers and cut into the revenues of high-tax states.

Member states eventually adopted a general framework for harmonization, stipulating a standard rate of 15 percent or above in each country as of January 1993. Luxury rates were to be abolished, but member states could apply lower rates, or zero rates, to an agreed list of items during a transition period. Itself a result of political horse trading, the list yielded a few anomalies: In deference to Britain, for example, member states could apply lower rates to food but had to apply the standard rate to "snacks" (needless to say, consumers were not allowed to make the distinction between food and snacks).

As well as harmonizing rates, member states agreed on rules for who should pay VAT and where. In 1987 the Commission proposed a straightforward system: VAT was to be paid in the country of sale. However, member states insisted on adopting an ungainly "transitional" system in which VAT on cross-border trade must be paid in the country of destination. To make the system work, sellers and buyers are required to declare their cross-border transactions regularly to tax authorities, including such information as the VAT registration number of the buyer, and pay the VAT applicable in their own country on imports from other member states (firms whose cross-border transactions fall below a threshold are exempt from regular reporting). Private consumers shopping in other member states, by contrast, pay VAT in the country of sale—except on mail-order purchases and on cars, for which VAT is payable at registration.

Excise Tax

The second aspect of the indirect taxation dossier concerned excise taxes—internal taxes levied mainly on fuels, liquor, and tobacco. Member states adopted a harmonized structure and rates for excise duties in October 1992. Earlier, in March 1991, the Council had decided to eliminate restrictions on cross-border purchases of those items by ordinary consumers. When harmonizing rates, the Council set "indicative levels" to help enforcement officers distinguish between ordinary citizens and commercial traders. As a result, citizens could carry up to 800 cigarettes, 90 liters of wine, 110 liters of beer, 20 liters of aperitif, and 10 liters of spirits across borders for their own use.

The logical consequence of removing fiscal frontiers should have been an end to duty-free shops in airports and on ferries. However, politics overcame logic in this case: Many airports and ferry operators gathered a large chunk of their operating revenues from highly profitable duty-free operations. Accordingly, the Council decided to put off the demise of duty-free shopping until 1999.

RELATED MEASURES

In order to eliminate internal borders, the Commission also had to address the problem of quotas and other restraints imposed by individual member states under Article 134 (formerly Article 115) TEC. Nearly 1,000 such measures, including over 100 restrictive quotas, were in place at the beginning of the single market program. Using its power to deny quotas under Article 134, the Commission managed to phase out all but six of them by July 1992. This led the Commission to proclaim that its track record "dispels in concrete terms the too widespread notion that a Fortress Europe is being constructed."[9]

For exporters to the EC of certain products—notably textiles, bananas, and Japanese cars—the Commission's exultation was premature. For instance, member state quotas on textiles phased out by the Commission had been codified under the long-standing Multifiber Arrangement (MFA), a web of import quotas imposed mainly on developing countries by developed ones. Although the EC continued to negotiate in the GATT for an eventual phaseout of the MFA, elimination of those quotas was not politically feasible. As a result, they were replaced by a set of bilateral quotas negotiated by the Commission on behalf of the EC as a whole, effective January 1, 1993, but subsequently phased out under the Uruguay Round agreement establishing the World Trade Organization (WTO). To assuage lingering member state discomfort, particularly in Spain and Portugal, over the possibility of market disruption resulting from the elimination of country-specific quotas, the Commission appropriated a substantial chunk of new EC funding to restructure the textile industry.

Nor were Japanese car manufacturers fated to enjoy the immediate benefits of an open EU market. Responding to French and Italian consternation at the prospect of losing their harsh import restrictions and at the potentially disastrous consequences for their sluggish national champions, the Commission negotiated a voluntary-restraint agreement with Japan. Coyly entitled "Elements of Consensus," the agreement allowed Japanese car imports a steadily increasing market share, reaching a ceiling of 15.2 percent of the European auto market by 1999, after which the EU was expected to lift all restrictions. Import ceilings would also apply to markets that had previously had quotas or other restrictive arrangements (mainly France, Italy, Spain, and Portugal). At least in theory, production of Japanese-brand cars in Europe, so-called transplants, were not to be counted as part of the overall ceiling. Nevertheless, the agreement effectively protected European producers for most of the decade.

One of the bitterest and more risible rows to emerge from the internal market program erupted over banana quotas. Seeking to protect the market position of high-cost bananas from Caribbean countries with which the EC has a development assistance program (as well as some even more inefficient growers in the Canary Islands), France, Britain, Spain, and Portugal imposed on an indignant Germany and the Netherlands a restrictive tariff quota limiting imports of so-called dollar bananas from Latin America. Outvoted in the Council, Germany, whose per capita banana consumption had hitherto been the highest in Europe, threatened to bring the decision to the ECJ, and the Latin Americans initiated a GATT challenge to the EC's banana regime. The WTO subsequently concluded that the European system violates world trade rules. Efforts by the Commission to devise a system that preserves protection for Caribbean producers while technically falling within the WTO ruling have elicited both internal and external criticism.

Other member state practices also had the potential to block the full abolition of borders. The most difficult to resolve were those in which member states were suspicious of the ability or will of other member states to enforce existing obligations or where the disappearance of border controls required member states to develop a framework to carry out each other's decisions. These included controls on trade in endangered species under the Convention on Trade in Endangered Species (CITES), controls on the movement of waste, and controls on the export of cultural treasures. Because of lack of Community competence over export of dual-use goods (those with military as well as civilian applications), the Commission was confined to proposing procedural measures for carrying out controls at external borders.

Finally, a seemingly minor but politically explosive issue remained far from resolved: "accompanying animals." A directive on that innocent-sounding subject would require Britain and Ireland to lift their rabies quarantine requirements in the case of animals with proof of vaccination. Although justifiable on both veterinary and internal market grounds, such a measure would undoubtedly have provoked a visceral public reaction in rabies-free Britain and Ireland. Originally scheduled for release just before the June 1992 referendum in Ireland on the TEU, the draft directive inexplicably failed to appear and has not been seen since.

BEYOND 1992

The official unveiling of the single market on January 1, 1993, happened at an inauspicious time. The EC was in the doldrums with parts of it, such as Britain, in a deep recession. The brisk economic growth of the late 1980s, which lent credence to extravagant claims for the single market, had suddenly dissipated. It seemed unlikely that merely announcing the official existence of the single market would get the EC economy going again.

Sensing public skepticism and even hostility during the TEU ratification crisis, the Commission kept the celebrations low key. Aside from sponsoring a chain of bonfires across Europe and a fireworks display in Brussels, the Commission's main response was to issue reams of information keyed to perceived citizen concerns about such issues as conditions for transporting horses or the fate of unemployed customs agents. Thus the long-awaited advent of the single market came almost as an anticlimax. As the bonfires smoldered, the griping began. Businessmen complained vociferously about the computerized VAT reporting system, with smaller firms threatening to stop shipping across European borders. Members of the EP were irate when asked for their passports in the Strasbourg airport, and journalists tried to provoke border guards by walking through border posts carrying armloads of bananas. The only conspicuously happy constituency was the horde of Britons reboarding ferries at Calais with vans full of cheap French wine.

Amid all the bluster, there were some real grounds for criticism: Transition periods and derogations stretching toward the end of the century meant that the single market program was far from being entirely in place on January 1, 1993. The highly visible failure to abolish border checks on people was bound to tarnish the image of the single market, already under fire from environmental and social groups characterizing it as a heartless sellout to business interests. Important ancillary measures, such as rules on export of dual-use goods or trade in endangered species, were unfinished. Manufacturers of products covered by new-approach directives faced uncertainty and disruption over the pace at which European standards could be developed and introduced. Taxation policies and exemptions from competition rules that prevent cross-border price shopping meant that customers would benefit little from lowered manufacturers' costs brought about by harmonization. Consumer banking charges, especially in the foreign exchange area, remained opaque and disparate. The double-barreled VAT system became a fertile source of confusion.

Beyond the expiration of the 1992 deadline, the success of the single market depended on three things:

- the legislative enactment of those proposals still on the table and new proposals necessitated by changing social, economic, and technical circumstances
- the complete liberalization of the energy and telecommunications sectors, hitherto largely excluded from the single market program
- the level and quality of member state transposition of directives into national law and the Commission's ability to resist the proliferation of new trade barriers

Completing the Legislative Framework

In the mid- and late 1990s the EU had enacted most of the remaining 1985 White Paper and related proposals, although a few key items continued to elude agreement. There was a considerable reduction in the number of new legislative proposals either because most areas had already been covered or because of the vogue for subsidiarity. The most important legislative developments after 1992 involving preexisting and new proposals included the following:

- In the area of *product standards,* the "novel food" regulation, governing the marketing and labeling of novel food and food ingredients (including genetically modified organisms) took effect in May 1997. This represented a major step toward completing the single market for foodstuffs.
- With respect to the *free movement of financial services,* a directive adopted in March 1997 providing minimum protection for small investors across the EU in the event that an investment firm defaults substanially reinforced the single market for securities transactions; complementing existing single market legislation in the insurance sector, the Commission proposed a directive in November 1997 tightening supervision of EU insurance groups.
- Concerning *new technologies,* the Commission revived the ONP directive in February 1995 after the EP had rejected the original proposal in July 1994 because of a procedural dispute with the Council. The new proposal included some EP amendments in the area of consumer protection. The Council adopted the long-delayed directive in December 1995.
- In the field of *company law,* in February 1996 the Commission proposed a new streamlined directive on public takeover bids in the EU, replacing the moribund proposal for a thirteenth company law directive, one of the original White Paper proposals.

- Concerning *intellectual property rights,* in December 1995 the Commission presented a new proposal for a directive on the legal protection of biotechnological inventions after the EP had rejected the original proposal in March 1995 because of ethical concerns related to animal welfare. It was adopted in 1998. In March 1996 the Council adopted a directive on the legal protection of databases, providing copyright protection to computerized and manual databases for the first time, thereby affording legal protection for database creators and investors throughout the EU. Legislation establishing the Community Trademark Office (CTMO) was finally unblocked following a political package deal in October 1993 on the location of EU institutions and agencies. The CTMO opened in Alicante, Spain, in January 1996, allowing companies to file for a single Community trademark for products and services marketed in the EU.
- With respect to *company taxation,* in October 1997 the Commission revived a White Paper proposal to eliminate the double taxation of interest and royalty payments made between parent companies and their subsidiaries in different member states (the Commission had dropped the proposal three years previously due to insufficient political support). Reflecting a changed political climate due to the momentum generated by the impending launch of the single currency, the Council approved the proposal only two months later in December 1997.

Regardless of these successes, a small number of single market proposals remained doggedly beyond reach of agreement. One of the oldest and most intractable of these was the proposal for a European Company Statute, intended to allow enterprises to declare themselves "European companies" subject primarily to EC law rather than nationals of a member state subject to member state law. Originally proposed in 1970, the statute was inserted into the 1992 program in the hope that the post-SEA euphoria would carry it through. In the event, it foundered once again on fundamental conflicts among member states over the issues of worker rights and provision for a European works council of union representatives in multinational firms operating under the statute.

By the end of 1992, after years of unavailing discussion (including sixteen separate Council debates), some member states began again to question the necessity for such a statute. The proposal was put on hold but sprang back to life when the Commission launched its single market action plan in June 1997. Hoping to implement as many outstanding single market proposals as possible during their Council presidency, the British almost secured agreement on the stature in early 1998, only to see it founder once more on the rock of member state opposition to accompanying measures on worker participation (opposition the former British Conservative government had spearheaded in the 1980s and early 1990s).

Value-added tax was another area impervious to agreement with some national governments refusing to go beyond the interim regime established in 1993 for payment of the tax. Thus a definitive VAT system based on payment in the country of origin rather than the country of destination remains elusive because of concerns about the possible loss of VAT revenue.

Energy and Telecommunications

While continuing to work on the single market program, the EU also attempted in the mid- and late 1990s to liberalize energy and telecommunications, two important sectors excluded from the 1992 program except with respect to procurement and, in the case of telecommunications, with respect to measures relating to new technologies.

Energy

Traditionally, national energy markets were monopolized by state-owned suppliers because of national governments' concerns about security of supply and the related public service obligation of universal, uninterrupted provision. Efforts to establish a single energy market in the EU, limited to electricity and natural gas, therefore required a fundamental change in attitude based on growing trust between member states and on growing acceptance of the economic philosophy of liberalization and competition. The Commission sought to establish a competitive regime, accompanied by the necessary regulation imposing certain indispensable constraints, in order to satisfy the requirement for safe, uninterrupted supply to all parts of the EU.

As an opening gambit, the Commission decided in 1991 that an agreement concluded among a number of electricity companies constituted an infringement of Article 81.1 (formerly Article 85.1) TEC insofar as it had the effect of impeding imports and exports by private industrial consumers. Beyond that, the Commission initially took a flexible and gradual approach to energy market liberalization, hoping to some extent that the 1992 momentum would push the electricity and gas monopolies into a more competitive environment.

Practical steps necessary to achieve a single energy market included the removal of numerous obstacles and trade barriers, the approximation of tax and pricing policies, the establishment of common norms and standards (mostly through CEN and CENELEC), and the setting of environmental and safety regulations. When work on the further opening of electricity and gas networks bogged down politically, the Commission made completion of a single energy market a top priority in the mid-1990s. Based on extensive investigation and consultation, and preceded by a green paper, in 1995 the Commission published a long-awaited White Paper, *An Energy Policy for the European Community*. Following an examination of the general political context and market trends, the White Paper proposed a work program and timetable for liberalizing energy markets.[10]

Politically, more market-oriented countries like Britain and Germany criticized the Commission for not going far enough with its proposals, whereas more protectionist countries such as France criticized the Commission for going too far. These differences were compounded by the existence of two separate systems of electricity market organization in the EU, one of which was peculiar to France. Partly by threatening to use its power under Article 86 (formerly Article 90) TEC to break up national monopolies, but largely because of the pressure from influential industrial consumers of electricity, national resistance to market liberalization began to ease. A breakthrough came in June 1996 when the Council agreed on a common position on the gradual creation of a single market for electricity that would allow industrial users to shop around for the lowest-cost EU provider. The EP approved the common position without change, permitting the Council to adopt the directive in December 1996.

Efforts to open national gas markets were equally contentious but followed the same political and economic logic as the liberalization of electricity markets. In February 1998 the Council adopted a common position on a directive to open up the natural gas market, dealing with issues such as transmission, supply, storage, and distribution.

Telecommunications

Like the energy sector, the telecommunications sector in Europe was traditionally the preserve of national monopolies and resulted in such anomalies as calls between member states often costing twice as much as calls of equivalent distance within member states. Unlike in the energy sector, however, the impetus to liberalize telecommunications received an additional boost from rapid technological changes having huge commercial implications, such as the development of the Internet. In October 1994, the Commission issued the first part of a green paper on telecommunications policy, recommending full liberalization for voice-telephone services by January 1, 1998 (countries with less developed networks would have until 2003 to adjust). In June 1994, the Council endorsed the Commission's proposed timetable but could not agree on early liberalization of "alternative networks," such as those owned by railways and utilities.

The second part of the green paper, issued in January 1995, dealt with the regulatory framework for key issues such as interconnection and interoperability; licensing of telecommunications infrastructures, networks, and services; and the provision of universal service (access to a minimum defined service of specified quality to all users at an affordable price); and third-country reciprocity. The Commission suggested that responsibility for regulation should remain primarily at the national level. Accordingly, EU regulation would provide a framework in which national regulators would operate in accordance with national and EU law and the principles of the single market.[11]

Building on widespread support among interest groups, telecommunications providers, and national governments, the Commission adopted much of the necessary legislation under Article 86 TEC, including directives to liberalize the mobile telephone sector (the fastest growing in the EU) by January 1, 1996; lift restrictions on the use of alternative infrastructures for telecommunications services; and implement full competition in the EU telecommunications market by January 1, 1998.

In November 1997 the Commission brought legal proceedings against seven member states for not abiding by one or more of its market-opening directives. Nevertheless, the single telecommunications market began as planned on January 1, 1998, although Greece, Ireland, and Portugal had derogations from it. Thus in principle, any telephone company can offer callers in most member states a local or long-distance service. Like the success of the single market program, the success of the single telecommunications market depends on Commission vigilance and member state compliance. Uniquely, however, it also depends on the ability of new national regulatory authorities to enforce directives in an area still overshadowed by powerful former monopolies.

Problems of Transposition and Enforcement

Enactment of directives at the EU level was only the first step in establishing the single market. The second step involved transposing those directives into law at the national level within the time prescribed in the directive. Without transposition into national law, the single market could not possibly work on a day-to-day basis. Transposition rates varied from member state to member state and from sector to sector. In some cases governments deliberately delayed transposition in order to gain a temporary competitive advantage or for fear of aggravating domestic constituencies; in most cases delays were the result of the technical complexity of legislation and procedural problems due to decisionmaking processes in the member states themselves.

In the immediate aftermath of the 1992 deadline, the Commission publicly adopted a circumspect tone on member state transposition with the internal market commissioner even suggesting that gentle encouragement was the best means of moving forward. In private the Commission took a tougher line, backed up with the threat of legal action. As "guardian of the treaties," the Commission could begin infringement proceedings against member states for nonimplementation of single market measures (or other EU obligations, for that matter).

The third step necessary to make a success of the single market was for member states to enforce the national law into which they had transposed EU directives. Just as transposition at the national level depended in large part on the quality and clarity of the relevant directive, enforcement at the national level depended on the quality and clarity of implementing legislation (claims that transposed directives were vague or unreasonable sometimes gave member states a good excuse to avoid enforcement on the ground).

In April 1992, the Commission charged an ad hoc committee, chaired by former commissioner Peter Sutherland, with developing a strategy to ensure the proper functioning of the single market after January 1, 1993. Released in October 1992, the Sutherland Report advocated a number of broad initiatives that could apply not only to the internal market but also to general EC legislation and stressed two areas in pressing need of improvement: transparency and enforcement.[12] The report urged the Commission to develop a "communication strategy" to inform consumers and firms of their rights, and to publicize draft legislation, or intent to draft legislation, at a much earlier stage. The report also called for codification of EC law to help people wade through long strings of directives intended to amend other directives and suggested that all directives be systematically succeeded by regulations on the same topic to ensure consistent interpretation.

On enforcement, the report called for a greater role for national courts, possibly including efforts to train lawyers and judges in EC law. In addition, the report suggested developing enforcement networks among member states to compare notes on the transposition of EC directives into national law. Under the system suggested, prime responsibility for enforcing product regulations would lie with the "home authority" in the place where the product was made or imported, subject to Commission oversight.

In December 1992, the Commission responded with a communication promising to follow many of the report's guidelines and adjuring member states to improve their administrative infrastructures in order to transpose single market legislation more quickly and effectively.[13] This was the first of a seemingly interminable number of communications, papers, and reports on implementation of the single market issued by the Commission over the years. Ritualistic statements at successive European Councils about the need for greater member state compliance with directives and regulations were another staple feature of EU efforts to complete the single market.

The Commission's annual reports on the single market, promised in response to the Sutherland Report, contain useful information about the enactment of directives and their transposition (or nontransposition) at the national level. The annual reports show a steady increase in both the enactment of single market legislation and the overall transposition rate in the member states. Transposition was consistently poor in the insurance, intellectual property, and procurement sectors; and Germany and France were often among the worst offenders. Indeed, league tables regularly ranked member states on their level of implementation of directives in force, and the press mulled over the occasional dramatic leaps registered by Italy or the irony that politically recalcitrant Denmark consistently topped the charts.

The Commission began to take a tougher line on implementation in the mid-1990s, as reflected in a steady increase in infringement proceedings in order to correct what internal market commissioner Mario Monti called the "enforcement deficit."[14] Infringement proceedings were begun in response not only to tardy transposition of legislation but also to complaints from businesses and individuals about poor national application of single market measures. Yet implementation and infringement statistics yielded little real information on the state of the single market, as they failed to reflect the quality of implementing legislation or the likelihood that national authorities would take enforcement measures.

In June 1997, the Commission launched the single market action plan, a concerted effort finally to complete the single market by January 1, 1999, in parallel with the launch of the euro.[15] The action plan contained four strategic objectives: making the rules more effective, dealing with key market distortions, removing obstacles to market integration, and making the single market relevant to EU citizens. Specific actions (nineteen in all) were of three kinds:

- taking measures that did not require new legislation (e.g., transposition of directives)
- enacting technically complicated but not necessarily politically contentious proposals still in the EU decisionmaking process (perhaps awaiting approval in the Council or a vote in the EP)
- enacting politically contentious (and perhaps also technically complicated) proposals that in some cases had been languishing for years (e.g., the European Company Statute)

The European Council endorsed the action plan at the Amsterdam summit in June 1997. At the Luxembourg summit six months later, the European Council asked the Council to pursue the action plan vigorously. What gave weight to the European Council's usual hortatory references to the single market, however, was the special emphasis on the action plan in the incoming British presidency's work program. The British were not averse to "naming and shaming" in order to improve their partners' compliance with

EU obligations. In the Internal Market Council, the British presidency focused especially on better implementation, for instance, prodding other member states on mutual recognition and public procurement issues as well as enforcement. The British also sought to broaden the single market "scoreboard" instrument to include market integration indices, such as price-level differentials and volumes of intra-EU trade, alongside the more legalistic yardstick published at the time.

CONCLUSION

Despite all the effort put into its completion initially by 1992 and subsequently by 1999, the single market is still unfinished, although its patchwork of derogations and transitions is steadily disappearing.[16] Nevertheless, the EU marketplace is far more integrated than many people thought possible at the outset of the single market program. Moreover, market integration is a continuing process requiring enforcement of existing rules and the occasional enactment of new ones. Threats to market integration come from a variety of sources, such as poor implementation of directives, the slow pace of standards development, and lack of mutual recognition. New trade barriers that could render market integration irrelevant or ineffective are an additional concern. High on the list are certain types of environmental measures that hinder the free circulation of goods and are extremely difficult to challenge. Member states resist limiting their own freedom to enact environmental restrictions affecting products; environmental activists are especially resistant to arguments favoring trade benefits over environmental ones.

Despite the single market's shortcomings and the threats to its fulfillment, the original White Paper stands up well to the test of time. Notwithstanding a lack of perfection and logic—inevitable in any political process—the White Paper functioned largely as intended. By tying so many elements to a coherent and attractive vision, the Commission managed over the years to push the Council into adopting proposals that would not otherwise have engendered much political enthusiasm. There was also a risk that the Commission would become a victim of its own publicity success, that failure to "complete" the single market precisely on time would deal a crushing political blow to the Commission's credibility. In the event, public reaction was measured, and the Council continued to adopt the remaining proposals at a respectable pace.

The main achievement of the 1992 initiative may well have been psychological. It created a climate in which individuals as well as firms could begin to identify themselves as European and look for opportunities beyond their own borders. It also created an atmosphere in which national governments could contemplate surrendering further sovereignty. Despite the political setback of the TEU ratification crisis, and lingering citizen anxieties about cultural identity and economic competition, those attitudinal and psychological changes have persisted. The single market program, and the drive and energy displayed by the Commission in pushing it through, restored the image of the EU as a vital and modern entity and paved the way for the successful launch of the single European currency.

NOTES

1. COM(85)310 final, June 14, 1985.
2. Council Regulation 2913/92, Bull. EC 10-1992, point 1.3.18.
3. Bull. EC 5-1992, point 1.1.7.
4. For an assessment of the wider implications of the case, see Karen Alter and Sophie Meunier-Aitsahalia, "Judicial Politics in the European Community: European Integration and the Pathbreaking *Cassis de Dijon* Decision," *Comparative Political Studies* 24, no. 4 (1996): 535–561.
5. Helmut Schmitt Von Sydow, "The Basic Strategies of the Commission's White Paper," in Roland Bieber, Renaud Dehousse, John Pinder, and Joseph Weiler, eds., *1992: One European Market? A Critical Analysis of the Community's Internal Market Strategy* (Baden-Baden: Nomos Verlagsgesellschaft, 1988), p. 93.
6. Council Resolution, May 7, 1985, *Official Journal of the European Communities* [*OJ*] C 136, p. 1. See also Lord Cockfield, *The European Union: Creating the Single Market* (Chichester: John Wiley, 1994), pp. 37–60.
7. See Jacques Pelkmans, "The New Approach to Technical Harmonization and Standardization," *Journal of Common Market Studies* 25, no. 3 (March 1987): 32–55.
8. Council Resolution, *OJ* C 10, January 16, 1990.
9. Commission press release IP(92)546, July 3, 1992.
10. Commission, *An Energy Policy for the European Community,* COM(95)682.
11. *Liberalization of Telecommunications Infrastructure and Cable Television Networks,* COM(94)440 and COM(94)682.
12. Commission, *The Internal Market After 1992: Meeting the Challenge. Report to the EEC Commission by the High-Level Group on the Operation of the Internal Market,* Brussels, 1992.
13. SEC(92)2277, December 2, 1992.
14. Quoted in *Eurecom* 9, no. 5 (May 1997): 3.
15. Commission, *Action Plan for the Single Market,* CSE(97)1, June 4, 1997.
16. See Michael Calingaert, *European Integration Revisited: Progress, Prospects, and U.S. Interests* (Boulder: Westview Press, 1996), pp. 19–38.

14

Making the Most of the Single Market

The Treaty Establishing the European Community (TEC) identified competition policy as an area in which the EC would have to become involved in order to buttress the projected common market and create a level playing field: Without rigorous antitrust rules, control of state subsidies, and liberalization of restricted industries, the common market would be seriously undermined. As the EC's fortunes fluctuated in the 1960s and 1970s, there was little progress in completing the internal market, let alone in developing a rigorous competition policy. Only when efforts to complete the single market gained momentum in the early 1980s did attention focus also on the closely related issue of competition policy. Making the most of the single market means going beyond merely policing it, however; it also involves maximizing economic opportunity through industrial policy, research and technology policy, the development of Trans-European Networks (TENs), and employment policy. Combined with the single market program itself, these ancillary activities seek to boost Europe's competitiveness in the global economy.

COMPETITION POLICY

Competition policy comprises two main branches, one dealing with the activities of private enterprise, the other with the activities of member states and state-sponsored bodies. The first covers what is generally referred to in the United States as "antitrust," that is, the prevention of practices by private entities that could inhibit competition and distort the marketplace, such as restrictive agreements or abuse of dominant position. The second pertains to the control of "state aids" (all forms of public subsidies to firms) and the liberalization of "regulated industries" (companies either owned by or having a special relationship with national governments).

The EU's antitrust efforts draw heavily on the U.S. experience. U.S. secretary of state Dean Acheson's first reaction to the Schuman Plan—that it might bring into being "a gigantic European cartel"—strengthened Jean Monnet's determination to include robust antitrust measures in the treaty establishing the European Coal and Steel Community (ECSC).[1] U.S. lawyers helped Monnet set up the ECSC; later, U.S. antitrust doctrine exerted considerable influence over officials in the EC Commission's competition directorate-general (DG IV), many of whom studied U.S. competition law.

Unlike competition policy in the United States, however, competition policy in the EU deals not only with private-sector abuses in the marketplace but also with massive government financial assistance to national enterprises and with utility services—such as electricity, water, and telecommunications—which European governments have traditionally controlled. By including efforts to curb state subsidies to industry and confront government monopolies, EU competition policy involves much more than antitrust.

In addition, competition policy has a political purpose in the EU that goes far beyond its economic objective in the United States. As well as policing the marketplace, EU competition policy seeks to break down barriers between national markets, thereby promoting European integration. Speaking at the University of Chicago—famous for its scholarship on antitrust law and economics—Sir Leon Brittan, a former competition commissioner, jocosely described the "Brussels School" of competition policy: "It includes rules on state aids and on firms granted special or exclusive rights, and has special concerns to promote market [and European] integration."[2]

Competition policy's relevance for market integration became readily apparent in the mid-1980s with the launch of the 1992 program. Enforcement of competition law was an obvious corollary to the development of a single market. Without the vigorous application of competition rules, the benefits of market liberalization could easily have been nullified by price fixing and market sharing between firms as well as by rampant government intervention.

EU competition law has an important dimension beyond the EU itself. The European Economic Area, which went into effect on January 1, 1994, provides for extensive cooperation on competition matters between the Commission and the European Free Trade Association's Surveillance Authority. Europe agreements between the EU and the Central and Eastern European applicant states also contain competition provisions based on EC law. Moreover, EU competition rules affect the activities of all companies operating in the EU or having an impact on the EU marketplace (subject to business turnover thresholds) regardless of where those firms are based. This can cause considerable friction in the EU's external relations, especially with the United States.

Private Enterprise

Restrictive Practices and Abuse of Dominant Position

Articles 81 and 82 (formerly Articles 85 and 86) TEC form the legal basis of EU antitrust policy. Article 81 prohibits agreements and concerted practices between undertakings that prevent, restrict, or distort competition and that affect trade between member states. This article generally refers to collusion between companies to fix prices or control production. Individual or block exemptions may be granted under certain circumstances. A *de minimus* rule means that agreements of minor importance do not fall under Article 81. Article 82 prohibits any abuse by one or more undertakings of a dominant position that distorts trade between member states. Such abuse could consist of setting unfair prices, limiting production or markets, applying dissimilar conditions, and making the conclusion of contracts subject to acceptance of supplementary obligations. Dominance is presumed to mean more than 50 percent of market share.

Clearly, EU antitrust law would have little effect without practical measures to implement it. Accordingly, in 1962 the Council adopted a regulation giving the Commission extensive powers of investigation, adjudication, and enforcement.[3] The Commission's ability to counter infringements depends to a great extent on the information at DG IV's disposal. Most companies under investigation cooperate with the Commission, however grudgingly. In the event that some would not, the 1962 regulation authorized Commission officials to arrive unannounced at businesses throughout the Community and conduct immediate on-site investigations. Apart from a flurry of activity in the late 1970s, the Commission shied away from doing anything of the sort. Only after the launch of the single market program did DG IV's "trustbusters" once again go on the offensive, under the energetic leadership of successive competition commissioners Peter Sutherland (1985–1989), Leon Brittan (1989–1993), and Karel van Miert (1993–2000).

Nevertheless, it would be misleading to imagine Commission officials conducting dramatic dawn raids. Unannounced on-site inspections take place during normal working hours and are the exception, not the rule. However, the unexpected arrival of Commission officials usually yields otherwise unobtainable evidence of wrongdoing. In 1980, the Court of Justice (ECJ) upheld the Commission's power to order and carry out investigations without warning companies in advance; since then it has upheld the Commission's right, once inside a company, to carry out an active examination of its files and records without hindrance or restriction.

New cases under Articles 81 and 82 average about 500 a year. Approximately 70 percent are notifications by undertakings seeking approval of a practice subject to Commission review, about 20 percent are complaints, and the remainder are cases where the Commission acts on its own initiative. The Commission resolves most of these cases informally, before ever carrying out exhaustive investigations. If the Commission decides to take formal action, it sends the firm in question a detailed statement of objections. Firms are entitled to respond in writing and to present their case (including witnesses) at a hearing. Not least because of the political sensitivity of some cases and the possibility that firms will appeal to the ECJ, the Commission deliberates carefully before reaching a decision.

If it concludes that there is an infringement, the Commission may impose a fine—not exceeding 10 percent of the firm's total turnover. Substantial though that amount seems—the Commission routinely imposes fines in the tens of millions of euros—it is often insufficient to deter large firms from conducting other abusive practices. As Leon Brittan once remarked, "Some firms seem to regard [Commission] fines as just another overhead."[4]

The Tetra Pak case is a good example of Commission action against abuse of a dominant position. Tetra Pak, a Swedish company based in Switzerland, is the largest supplier of packaging (cartons) for milk and fruit juices. In some cases the company enjoyed a virtual monopoly (95 percent of the market) for machinery and for packaging of "long-life" liquids. A lengthy Commission investigation, based on a competitor's complaint, revealed that Tetra Pak's marketing policy, customer contracts policy, and pricing policy had deliberately infringed Article 82. The Commission ordered Tetra Pak to end its anticompetitive behavior and imposed a fine of ECU 75 million on the firm.[5]

Mergers

The original TEC said nothing about mergers and acquisitions. However, an extensive body of EC case law built on the celebrated *Continental Can* (1972) case extended the scope of Article 82 to include structural changes brought about by mergers and acquisitions. Accordingly, a firm contravened Article 82 if it created or strengthened a dominant position by means of a takeover or merger. Yet the EC's limited merger control was reactive (it applied only to cases where a dominant market position had already been established). Although merger-control reform had been on the EC's agenda since 1973, little progress was made until a plethora of mergers and acquisitions took place in the mid-1980s at the outset of the single market program.

The number, size, and speed of 1992-induced mergers gave the Commission a legitimate pretext upon which to press national governments to cede more regulatory authority to Brussels. Member states appreciated the threat that uncontrolled EC-wide mergers posed to the emerging single market and the advantage for big businesses of dealing with one European competition authority rather than several national ones. Nevertheless, member states disagreed on the criteria for Commission vetting and approval, with Germany and Britain—the countries with the strongest national competition authorities—putting up the strongest resistance. As a result, it was not until December 1989 that the Council adopted a regulation providing for the prior authorization of mergers, thus enabling the Commission to control the buildup of dominant firms.[6] The 1989 merger regulation constitutes a cornerstone of the EU's competition policy and single market program.

Based on a number of key principles and provisos, the regulation makes a clear distinction between mergers with an EU dimension, where the Commission has the power to intervene, and those that have their main impact on a particular member state. An EU dimension exists when all of the following are true:

- The firms involved have an aggregate worldwide turnover of more than €5 billion (5 billion euros).
- Each of at least two of the firms involved has an aggregate EU-wide turnover of more than €250 million.
- At least one of the firms involved has less than two-thirds of its aggregate EU-wide turnover within one particular member state (i.e., requirement of transnationality).

For mergers coming under the Commission's scrutiny the crucial test is that of dominant position, taking into account such factors as the structure of the markets concerned, actual or potential competition, the market position of the firms involved, the opportunities open to third parties, barriers to entry, the interests of consumers, and technical and economic progress. The regulation also includes compulsory prior notification by the firms concerned and a strict timetable for Commission decisionmaking. The Commission established a merger task force to implement the new regulation, which came into force in September 1990.

The number of mergers above the threshold for notification to the Commission dropped in the early 1990s following the initial single market boom but picked up rapidly in the late 1990s as a result of an EMU-induced trend toward further integration of markets and companies. On a single day in 1997, plans were announced for six mergers or acquisitions among major European companies involving business worth more than ECU 110 billion.[7] Most of the mergers dealt with by the Commission are in particularly dynamic business sectors like telecommunications, financial services, pharmaceuticals, and the media.

Of the approximately 140 notifications that it receives annually, the Commission clears the vast majority within a month. Only a handful go to a full-scale, four-month, second-stage investigation. If the Commission considers that a proposed merger is incompatible with the single market, it may insist on the merging companies offering "remedies," such as the sale of some European production facilities or other assets. Otherwise, the Commission can block the merger. Companies that ignore the Commission's ruling can be fined up to 10 percent of their turnover (subject to appeal to the ECJ).

A proposed joint venture known as MSG Media Service, between Bertelsmann, the Kirch Group, and Deutsche Telekom, was one of the first deals blocked by the Commission (in November 1994) under the merger regulation. According to the Commission, the venture would have led to the creation or strengthening of a dominant position in three markets, including those for pay-TV and cable networks.[8] The Commission blocked another deal involving Bertelsmann and Kirch in 1998—a planned German digital pay-TV venture—when Bertelsmann rejected a last-minute compromise with DG IV.[9] Bertelsmann's refusal to make more concessions allowed the Commission to claim that its decision to block the deal was unanimous, whereas the Commission was divided on the issue, not least because of intensive lobbying from the media giants involved and from German politicians.

The Swiss food group Nestlé's takeover of Perrier, France's largest mineral water supplier, is an early example of Commission authorization of a major acquisition subject to remedies. The merger task force challenged the deal on the grounds that it would give two companies, Nestlé and BSN, a duopoly of the lucrative French mineral water market. After four months of hard bargaining the Commission approved the merger in July 1992, when Nestlé agreed to give up control of about 20 percent of the French market.[10] Although the deal left Nestlé and BSN with more than 65 percent of the mineral water market, it set a precedent by allowing the Commission to challenge duopolies as well as monopolies.

From the outset, the Commission worked with representatives of industry, the legal profession, and national competition authorities to ensure that the merger regulation worked well. Firms seemed pleased to have a single EU-level procedure with which to deal instead of having to deal with a number of procedures at the national level. Most companies complied fully with the notification requirement. Indeed, many firms complained about the high level of the thresholds triggering notification, as those whose mergers and acquisitions fell below those thresholds had to deal with a number of national authorities rather than benefit from the Commission's "one-stop-shop." In an effort to increase transparency and improve efficiency, in December 1994 the Commission introduced a revised implementing regulation and a number of other administrative modifications. But it was only in February 1996 that the Commission suggested, in the face of considerable member state opposition, that the thresholds be lowered.

In May 1997, thanks to the prompting of the Dutch presidency, member states agreed to a major change in the merger regulation, but not involving a general reduction of the notification thresholds, as requested by the Commission. Too many national competition authorities, especially those in Britain and Germany, were jealous of the Commission's control over big competition cases. Nevertheless, the Council agreed to increase the Commission's role by giving it jurisdiction over mergers falling short of the turnover thresholds that require multiple notifications to national competition authorities (subject to new thresholds for these cases). The Council's intent was to obviate the need for companies in certain merger cases to notify and await approval from national authorities in several member states.

Subsidies and State-Sponsored Bodies

State Aids

Control of state aids such as direct subsidies, tax breaks, and public investments on nonmarket conditions are an even more politically sensitive subject than merger policy. Although member states agreed in Article 87 (formerly Article 92) TEC that state aid should be prohibited in most circumstances, in practice they have allowed themselves broad latitude under the exceptions included in the treaty—notably for aid to poorer regions—especially during economic recession and when facing political and social fallout from the precipitous decline of industries. Nor have they always informed the Commission in advance of plans to grant or alter aid. The mixed character of the European economy, where government ownership of industry is considered an acceptable instrument of economic development, means that the precise level of state support is often difficult to determine.

Like the lack of an EC-level merger policy, state aid was a chronic problem that became a major issue in the mid-1980s with the launch of the 1992 program. Article 88 (formerly Article 93) TEC authorized the Commission, in cooperation with member states, to monitor state aid closely. Article 89 (formerly Article 94) allowed the Council, acting by a qualified majority on a proposal from the Commission, to adopt appropriate regulations to prohibit market-distorting public assistance. A weak Commission and a deep recession combined in the 1970s virtually to end EC-level efforts to control state aid. With EC solidarity almost nonexistent and governments vying with each other to prop up infirm industries, state aid was rampant. From 1981 to 1986 member states reported between 92 and 200 cases of state aid each year; the EC acted against fewer than 10 percent.[11]

A potentially ruinous increase in state aid in the early 1980s, along with national rivalry in the provision of public support, strengthened the Commission's hand. In 1983 the Commission sent a communication to member state governments announcing that it would require them to refund any aid granted without prior notification to the Commission or a prior ruling by the Commission on the aid's compatibility with Article 87. The onset of the single market program further boosted the Commission's position.

Strict control of state aid became as vital as the vigorous application of antitrust law for the success of the single market. By subsidizing companies in their own countries, national governments distorted competition throughout the whole EC and put nonsubsidized companies at an obvious disadvantage. Yet governments were loath to surrender such a powerful political, economic, and social instrument. Competition commissioner Peter Sutherland led the Commission's offensive to tackle the state aid scandal, pointing out to member states the "inherent contradiction in working for the creation of an internal market by 1992 and denying the independent role and obligation of Community institutions to enforce Community [competition] law fairly, even when this is contrary to the wishes of a national government."[12]

Soon after taking over from Sutherland, Leon Brittan began a comprehensive review of state-aid policy with a view to ascertaining the real level of aid being granted, taking strong measures against the most anti-competitive and wasteful subsidies, and rolling back the general level of aid. The Commission lacked an implementing regulation for state aid comparable to the 1962 antitrust regulation. Based on case law, a more favorable political climate, and a number of specific actions, the Commission began to make an impression.

Brittan also launched a procedure to tackle the problem of aid being granted without prior notification to the Commission. Under his plan, the Commission would require a member state to supply full details of the alleged aid within thirty days, sooner in urgent cases. If the member state failed to reply or gave an unsatisfactory response, the Commission would make a provisional decision requiring the state to suspend application of the aid within fifteen days and initiate proceedings under Article 88.2 (formerly Article 93.2) to make the member state provide the necessary data. If the member state still failed to comply, the Commission could adopt a final decision of incompatibility and require repayment of the amount of state aid allocated. Should the member state refuse to abide by the Commission's decision, the Commission would refer the matter to the ECJ.[13]

Despite the Commission's apparent feistiness, state aid remains ubiquitous in the EU, amounting to over €100 billion annually. The four biggest member states—Germany, France, Italy, and Britain—account for a growing share of state aid, most of which therefore goes to the EU's better-off regions. The Commission receives approximately 600 notifications annually of new aid schemes or amendments to existing aid schemes and registers approximately 100 cases annually of unnotified schemes. Yet the

Commission raises no objection to the vast majority of these, either because of prevailing economic circumstances (e.g., the acceptability of national assistance to firms in economic difficulties during a recession or in need of restructuring to cope with globalization) or because of their contribution to EU objectives in other areas such as social, regional, or environmental policy. Of the cases it pursues, the Commission rarely makes a negative decision, although it occasionally attaches conditions to approvals.

A well-publicized and widely criticized state-aid case that the Commission approved conditionally involved the French government's proposed injection of ECU 3.5 billion of new capital into the state-owned airline Air France. The government notified the Commission in March 1994 that it intended to make the investment as part of a restructuring plan to restore the ailing airline to economic health by the end of 1996. Two months later the Commission began an inquiry to assess the plan's feasibility and its compatibility with the single market. In September 1995, the Commission approved the plan but attached conditions to ensure that it did not distort competition while aiding the airline's recovery. The Commission also insisted that this was the last state aid payable to Air France. A number of other airlines understandably attacked the Commission's decision. Six of them, led by the privatized and highly successful British Airways, brought a successful case against the Commission in the ECJ (although it was then too late to make Air France give the money back).

The Commission's questionable record of curbing state aid masks the undoubted value of having a state-aid watchdog at the European level. Without the Commission's vigilance, however weak, the problem of national subsidies would be far worse than it is. Intellectually, governments accept that in many cases subsidies are expensive, wasteful, and generally unavailing, but politically they find it difficult to kick the habit. Paradoxically, it is precisely as a political tool that the Commission's state-aid authority can prove most useful to governments. Once again the case of Air France provides a good example. In June 1998 Air France pilots went on strike to protest government efforts to cut their salaries in order to maintain the airline's renewed profitability. Instead of giving in to the strikers' demands—as French governments usually do—the government held firm and conveniently cited the Commission's "one time/last time" approval of the 1994 aid package as evidence that it could not bail out the airline again. Realizing that they were running Air France into the ground and that the government would not pick up the pieces, the pilots abandoned their strike and meekly went back to work.

Regulated Industries

European governments have traditionally sheltered certain industries from competition because of those industries' fundamental economic importance.

In particular, telecommunications, energy (electricity and natural gas), banking, insurance, and transport have usually been highly regulated and in many cases were wholly or partly government-owned. In close association with the single market program, the Commission began in the early 1990s to apply competition law to liberalize those sectors, often in the teeth of fierce member state opposition.

Article 86 (formerly Article 90) TEC provides for the full application of treaty rules, including those on competition and free movement of goods and services, to companies owned by or in a special relationship with member states—except where the application of such rules would prevent the companies from carrying out their public service obligations. The Commission applies Article 86 by adopting appropriate directives or decisions without Council approval. The ECJ has upheld the Commission's right to do so, spelling out in a number of important cases the extent to which member states may grant statutory monopolies or special rights. As a result, there is much less uncertainty now than in the pre–single market period about the proper application of Article 86.

The Domestic and International Politics of Competition Policy

As is obvious from many of the cases already mentioned, competition policy is an extremely sensitive subject for the Commission, which must balance concern for preventing market distortion with the need to avoid overreaching its own political (as distinct from legal) authority with member states. Although striving for integrity, the Commission cannot divorce from politics the process of implementing antitrust law, merger policy, control of state aid, and liberalization of regulated industries. Decisions are taken by the full college of commissioners, which must consider such things as political timing and the need to maintain the appearance of national and regional impartiality. Member states are quick to accuse the Commission of favoritism. Inevitably, commissioners come under intense pressure from their governments and from firms in their countries during contentious competition policy cases.

Since the merger regulation entered into force in 1990 the Commission has blocked on average only one merger a year. Some critics contend that this low rejection rate is due to the Commission's susceptibility to political pressure. Whether or not the Commission is politically vulnerable, controversial mergers generate an intense amount of lobbying. The Commission's first-ever rejection of a merger under the new regime—the 1991 bid by France's Aerospatiale and Italy's Aliena to take over Canadian aircraft manufacturer De Havilland—split the Commission with one side (including the president, Jacques Delors) arguing that the merger would boost European competitiveness by giving manufacturers a bridgehead in the

North American marketplace and the other side, led by Leon Brittan, claiming that the merger would give Aerospatiale and Aliena a near monopoly in the EU marketplace for turboprop commuter aircraft. Arguments inside the Commission mirrored contending national positions with the French and Italian governments lobbying hard on behalf of their firms in favor of the merger and other more market-oriented member states, which did not have a stake in the case, urging a strict interpretation of the merger regulation.

Despite its decision in the De Havilland and a small number of other high-profile cases, Euroskeptics cite the Commission's approval of most big mergers as a reason to curb the Commission's power. Frank Vibert, a leading British Euroskeptic, argued in 1995 that the Commission should be "unbundled" into various authorities, including one for competition.[14] A number of governments—not only Euroskeptical ones—suggested before the 1996–1997 intergovernmental conference (IGC) that responsibility for competition policy should be taken from the Commission and given to an independent EU competition authority along the lines of Germany's *Bundeskartellamt*. Claus-Dieter Ehlermann, the formidable former head of DG IV, accepted the idea in principle but argued that it should not be implemented until the EU's political development made it more likely that such an office could be fully independent, or at least manifestly more independent that DG IV appeared to be.[15] In the event, the possibility of curbing the Commission's responsibility for competition policy was not pursued at the IGC.

The De Havilland decision is also an interesting case study because its politics transcended the EU with the Canadian government lobbying hard in favor of the proposed deal. A number of other high-profile cases involving U.S. companies demonstrate the extraterritorial nature of EU competition policy and the extent to which foreign governments often try to influence the outcome (EU competition rules apply to all companies operating in or having an impact on the EU marketplace regardless of whether they are based inside or outside the EU).

U.S.-EU friction over competition policy is a staple of the transatlantic relationship, with the U.S. government and U.S. companies highly critical of what they see as an EU competition policy that favors indigenous companies, often at the expense of their U.S. rivals. Although EU competition law is based on U.S practices and principles, Americans generally have a dim view of its partiality. As long ago as the mid-1980s, a protracted Commission investigation of IBM fueled "the prevalent American conception . . . that the EC's antitrust policy . . . invariably protects Community industries which are important for the achievement of social and economic goals and . . . promotes anti-competitive business agreements."[16]

U.S. antitrust authorities also vet mergers involving EU companies. Because of their mutual interest in megamergers, the Commission and its

U.S. counterpart concluded an agreement in 1991 to cooperate on competition cases (the ECJ threw out the agreement in 1994 because the Commission had exceeded its external relations competence; the agreement finally came into effect in 1995 when the Commission *and the Council* enacted the necessary legislation). In general, the U.S.-EU competition accord has operated well. For instance, the U.S. Justice Department authorized a merger between the U.S.-based paper industry giants Kimberly-Clark and Scott Paper, to which the Commission gave its approval in February 1996 subject to certain conditions. Similarly, after the U.S. authorities had imposed tough conditions the Commission approved with only one condition the merger between Swiss pharmaceutical and chemical giants Ciba-Geigy and Sandoz to create Novartis, the world's second-largest producer in the pharmaceuticals, animal health, and seed sector.

Cooperation between U.S. and EU competition authorities broke down spectacularly in mid-1997 when the Commission threatened to block a merger between Boeing and McDonnell Douglas despite the U.S. Federal Trade Commission's unconditional approval of it on July 1. The Commission objected to the deal on the grounds that the new firm would dominate the European market for large airliners, that Boeing's civil business might enjoy defense spillovers, and that Boeing had exclusive twenty-year contracts with a number of U.S. airlines. Boeing took steps to allay the Commission's first two concerns but argued that the third concern was beyond the scope of the merger and was not an issue with the U.S. airlines involved in the contracts. Instead, Boeing pointed out that a challenge to its exclusive contracts was in the interests only of its archival, Airbus.

Airbus is a dirty word in the United States, where it is synonymous with Europrotectionism and subsidization. The involvement of Airbus in the dispute, however indirectly, raised the political stakes. Despite intense pressure from Washington, including threats of a trade war, competition commissioner Karel van Miert obstinately refused to approve the deal unless Boeing made extra concessions. Boeing did so at the last moment, agreeing neither to sign any new exclusive contracts for ten years nor to enforce the deals it had signed. This paved the way for Commission approval of the merger, but at a cost of casting the Commission once again as an unswerving supporter of Airbus and of endangering cooperation between the United States and the EU in competition policy.

INDUSTRIAL POLICY

At one extreme, industrial policy means government intervention to underwrite specific enterprises or sectors whose survival the government deems essential for socioeconomic or strategic reasons. The instruments of such a policy include "soft" loans, grants, tax concessions, guaranteed procurement contracts, export assistance, and trade barriers. In the days before the homogenization of political ideology, left-wing governments were usually identified as zealous proponents of government intervention in industrial affairs. France in the 1960s was often taken as a classic example of economic interventionism, although at the time France had right-wing governments. Thus nationalism as much as ideology may underpin the pursuit of an interventionist industrial policy.[17]

A laissez-faire approach is the other extreme form of industrial policy and is often associated with right-wing governments. Even if they deliberately eschew direct intervention, however, governments have a major impact on industrial planning and production. Public contracts and defense-related procurement are obvious ways in which all governments, regardless of political persuasion, intentionally or unintentionally assist national manufacturers.

When it came into being in 1958, the EC inherited a strong interventionist ethos. Indeed, the CAP is a classic example of an intrusive industrial policy in the agricultural sector. But member states agreed to share responsibility for agriculture for peculiar political reasons and because the agricultural sector was in serious social and economic decline. By contrast, member states retained as much power as possible over other sectors, including the right to nurture "national champions"—national industries that could compete internationally. Although it dealt with certain aspects of regional policy and social policy, the Treaty of Rome therefore included few provisions for an interventionist, EU-level industrial policy.

Nevertheless, the treaty embodied an industrial policy in the broader sense of mapping out a strategy for industrial development. The projected internal market and related competition law were intended to create an economic framework conducive to industrial growth. In the prosperous 1960s, however, governments had little incentive to go beyond a rudimentary common market, and in the recessionary 1970s they resorted to restrictive practices to protect national champions. Following the agriculture precedent, national governments allowed the EC to intervene directly only in those industries in serious economic trouble: steel, shipbuilding, and textiles. Especially in the early 1980s, the EU provided various kinds of assistance to help such sunset industries restructure and survive.[18]

Steel, textiles, and shipbuilding were old, declining industries. The EC's high-technology sector (including computers, consumer electronics, and telecommunications) was new, yet it was also in trouble. *Le Défi Américain* (The American Challenge), the title of a popular book by Jean-Jacques Servan-Schreiber, seemed to sum up the problem. Throughout the 1960s, Europeans had fretted about a supposed "technology gap" between themselves and the United States. *The American Challenge* confirmed their fears by portraying the United States as a powerful predator encroaching on Europe's weak and fragmented market in the increasingly lucrative and strategically important high-technology sector.[19] Compared to American industry's enterprise, advantage of scale, and international ambition, European firms seemed severely handicapped.

For the next decade European governments responded to the U.S. challenge largely by supporting national champions—huge firms that enjoyed a virtual monopoly in their country's sizable public-sector markets. France, with a well-deserved reputation for intervention, was not the only culprit. Despite its supposed inclination toward market liberalism, Germany also promoted national champions, as did Britain under Labour leadership for much of the 1970s. Yet by the early 1980s the transatlantic technology gap had widened and a new chasm was opening between Western Europe and Japan. Poor economic performance during the previous decade exacerbated Europe's predicament. With little economic growth, industries had no incentive to invest heavily in research and development. Nor did the limited and relatively small size of their domestic markets encourage new initiatives.

At the same time European companies had undertaken a number of collaborative ventures, notably in aircraft manufacturing and marketing. Concorde, the joint Anglo-French effort to produce a supersonic passenger plane, is the most obvious and expensive example. In the early 1960s France and Britain also began to collaborate on Airbus, a project to produce short- to medium-range, wide-bodied passenger aircraft. Germany joined the consortium in 1966 and Britain departed in 1968. Despite its success in the 1980s and 1990s, Airbus began badly with numerous cost and time overruns. Whereas Concorde was already in service by the late 1960s, the first Airbus still remained on the drawing board. Only in the mid-1970s, when Airbus broadened its base to include Dutch and Spanish participation and received its first non-European orders, did the venture really take off.

The EC did not participate in those collaborative projects, although in 1967 the Commission established the Directorate-General for Industrial Affairs (DG III) to encourage cross-border cooperation. DG III's birth reflected a growing awareness of the need to concentrate resources and promote intra-EC industrial alliances. Early EC efforts to increase European competitiveness were not confined to the member states, however. In 1971 the Community joined with neighboring Western European countries to launch COST (European Cooperation in the Field of Scientific and Technical Research), an institutional framework and source of funds for joint research projects in such areas as informatics and telecommunications.

Despite such efforts, by the end of the 1970s Europe's high-technology sector seemed as badly off as before. Political and ideological problems beset both endeavors. National governments disputed the wisdom and practicability of cross-border industrial cooperation. Within the Commission, DG IV (competition) kept a close eye on DG III's interventionist proclivities.

Yet the EC's acute industrial difficulties, the soaring cost of research and development, the increasing importance of new technologies—especially in microelectronics and semiconductors—and the continuing U.S. and Japanese threat convinced many European manufacturers, politicians, and government officials that closer collaboration under the EC's auspices held the key to European industry's survival and success. By contrast, the notion of national champions became increasingly outmoded.

Etienne Davignon, Commission vice president with responsibility for industrial affairs between 1981 and 1985, took the lead in promoting EC-wide technological collaboration. By cultivating the CEOs of major European manufacturers in the high-technology sector, Davignon developed a powerful industrial support group for cross-border collaboration. European industrialists were especially receptive to Davignon's ideas because of renewed economic recession and the evident failure of the national champion approach. This was the background to the launch of the EC's first research and development (R&D) programs.

Despite their limited impact on European industrial competitiveness, these early R&D programs satisfied European industrialists that the Commission was a constructive and competent partner. Commission-industry collaboration, in turn, led to awareness on both sides of the EC's potential for economic revival in Europe. If the Commission could bring industrialists together to improve Europe's competitiveness, why could it not help end the fragmentation of Europe's own market by breaking down the plethora of nontariff barriers that impeded intra-EC business and trade? Why not use the Commission's authority to promote liberalization, harmonization, and standardization? Instead of interpreting industrial policy in an interventionist light, why not see it in broader terms as a way to help level the playing field for manufacturers across the EC? Thus Davignon's endeavors to promote industrial competitiveness contributed to a growing momentum in the early 1980s for completion of the single market.

Indeed, by giving European industry "a political program on which it could finally base concrete action plans for restructuring operations, for increasing economies of scale, and for improving the efficient use of vital resources,"[20] completion of the single market became an integral part of the EC's industrial strategy. Martin Bangemann, the commissioner with responsibility for industrial affairs, argued that the competitive discipline imposed by the single market would be the best medicine possible for European manufacturers.[21] In the sense that it opened up enormous opportunities for European industry, not least by forcing many national champions to restructure radically, the single market program became the most important instrument of EC industrial policy in the late 1980s.

The single market program also represented a triumph for economic liberalism and a setback for state interventionism. The aggressive application of competition policy reinforced that point. As the Commission observed after the De Havilland case, "a rigorous competition policy is an essential element in the Community's industrial policy. Maintaining effective competition is one of the key factors in ensuring that Community industry is successful."[22]

Yet the Commission's aggressive pursuit of competition policy as a means of opening up the marketplace—and therefore as an integral part of the EC's industrial strategy—appeared to thwart the emergence not only of national champions but also of Eurochampions (European firms that could compete and win globally). The problem seemed especially acute in the electronics sector, which encountered serious difficulties in the early 1990s despite market liberalization and the allocation of considerable amounts of R&D funding by the EC. Pressure from European electronics companies for the Commission to dispense old-fashioned industrial assistance became intense, not least because the French government owned two of them (Bull and Thomson).

In response to pressure from the French and other protectionists, and in an effort to lay the ground rules for a post–single market industrial strategy, the Commission produced a key discussion document in November 1990 on competitiveness. Following a contentious internal debate that split the college along national and ideological lines, the Commission declined to offer any industrial policy measures in the traditional (i.e., interventionist) sense of the term. Instead, in a decisive reiteration of prevailing economic orthodoxy, it issued guidelines rejecting sectoral policies as ineffective and stressing that the EC's role should be to maintain a competitive environment. In elaborating on this position, the guidelines accomplished two important Commission objectives: establishing a coherent philosophical framework to justify the policies the Commission was already pursuing in the realm of market integration and dashing expectations that the EC would act to support and protect a given sector, no matter how strategic.[23]

In the Commission's analysis, the role of government (hence that of the EC, with due regard for subsidiarity) should be limited to providing, first, a competitive business climate and, second, "catalysts to encourage firms to adjust rapidly to changing circumstances." The need for a competitive environment as an industrial policy objective implied vigorous competition policy—including strict control of state aid—in addition to macroeconomic stability. Moreover, it suggested a relatively open trade policy to allow European firms to become seasoned international competitors. Other prerequisites for competitive industry included a tough environmental policy, greater economic and social cohesion, and a higher educational level among workers.

The guidelines found a convenient niche in this framework for the single market as the EC's chief catalyst for structural adjustment. It noted the benefits, inter alia, of common standards, mutual recognition, open procurement, the abolition of quotas, and the development of Trans-European Networks to promote rapid structural adjustment and offer greater economies of scale. On the R&D side, the paper suggested that the EC should aim not only to develop but also to diffuse generic technologies—encouraging greater use of information technology, an area where Europeans lagged behind both as producers and as consumers.

Emphasizing the importance of a competitive business climate in which firms make key decisions, the paper stressed that EC assistance would be "horizontal" rather than industry-specific and would consist largely of policing the marketplace to guard against protectionism and private market power. The Commission also reiterated the current conception of industrial policy as a combination of environmental, social, regional, and competition policies contributing to a level playing field for European manufacturers as well as an aggressive trade policy to ensure that the international economic environment was as fair as possible.

The Commission proposed to follow up this broad conceptual framework with a series of papers applying its principles to various troubled sectors (notably electronics, autos, textiles, and aerospace), together with an analytical paper on industrial competitiveness and environmental regulation. The first testing ground for the Commission's noninterventionist stance was the European electronics industry, battered by foreign competition and holding on to less than half of its own domestic market. After a spirited tussle between the market-oriented DG IV (competition) and the largely French-influenced (and therefore protectionist) DG XIII (technology), the Commission produced a relatively noninterventionist paper that blamed the feeble state of Europe's electronics industry on market fragmentation and high capital costs.[24] It also advocated the development of TENs, better training, more market-oriented EC-level R&D, and completion of the Uruguay Round of trade negotiations as suitable approaches to resolving the industry's problems. Predictably, the Commission's paper infuriated the French and many in the private sector who wanted outright financial assistance and protection.

The Commission's position against demands for a more interventionist approach was strengthened by a coalition of member states with no national champions to protect. Transcending north-south differences, Britain, Ireland, Spain, and Portugal feared that protection of European industry would hamper foreign investment in their countries, harm consumers, and divert scarce EC resources to giant firms in France, Germany, and the Benelux (Belgium, the Netherlands, and Luxembourg). In the event, it was far from clear where new sectoral subsidies could come from, either in EC or member state budgets. France suggested redeploying existing EC funds, to which an unsympathetic commissioner cleverly countered that the EC should start with the CAP. In a clear victory for the free marketeers, in November 1991 the Council adopted a resolution along the lines of the Commission's paper.[25]

Subsequent Commission papers met a much less stormy reception. Perhaps all sides had learned the pitfalls of trying to push an overtly interventionist policy in the EU context. The debate over electronics clearly demonstrated that conflicting member state interests made it impossible to support sectoral initiatives at the EU level, to say nothing of the substantial new funding that such policies would require. Despite their panic at the thought of fully opening markets to the Japanese in 1999 (the long grace period was itself a concession to the need for structural adjustment among overprotected national champions), European auto producers were unable to wring much more from the Commission than some modest worker-training proposals for firms in poorer regions. The Commission applied the same principles to other sectors with increasing confidence and decreasing backlash from firms and member states.

Reflecting the ongoing debate on industrial policy, the TEU contained a new title (Title XIII, now Title XVI, TEC) on the subject. Like the language in the Commission's 1990 paper, the treaty's provisions on industrial policy are vague, calling on the EU and its member states "to ensure that the conditions needed to make Community industry competitive are met in a system of open and competitive markets." In order to achieve the objectives of structural change, a favorable business environment, and better exploitation of innovation and research, the treaty stipulates that the Council "may adopt specific measures in support of action taken by member states." However, the Council may act only unanimously, effectively denying the EU more authority in the area of industrial policy.

Later Commission initiatives, ranging from the white paper *Competitiveness, Growth, and Employment* (1993) to a communication entitled *Industrial Competitiveness Policy for the European Union* (1994) suggest that the debate about industrial policy in the EU has gone well beyond the old interventionist/laissez-faire arguments. Despite renewed recession in the mid-1990s, a widening trade deficit with Japan, and growing economic nationalism on both sides of the Atlantic, classical interventionists have mostly failed to make their voices heard. The difficulty of designing a sectoral policy that could give real benefits to the affected sector without distorting competition, retarding cohesion, and drawing fire from member states whose industries would be disadvantaged is the most compelling reason the horizontal approach is unlikely to be abandoned, especially in view of the TEU's highly restrictive language on industrial policy. Moreover, there is a general consensus in the Commission and among member states—including France, even under a Socialist government following the 1997 elections—that industrial policy should provide an umbrella for a range of measures aimed at boosting growth, prosperity, and jobs. Of these, R&D programs are almost the only holdover from the early days of industrial policy.

RESEARCH AND DEVELOPMENT

R&D is essential for industrial development and economic growth. Although most R&D spending should and does come from the private sector, even ardent free marketeers concede that R&D is one of the few areas (along with education and infrastructure) in which government intervention is necessary. Just as private R&D spending in most industrial sectors is essentially an indicator of corporate confidence, public spending on R&D is an indicator of the government's faith in a country's future economic performance.

EC involvement in R&D originated in a provision of the Atomic Energy Community treaty that led to the establishment of the Joint Research Center (JRC) in Ispra, Italy, in 1958. There are now seven institutes within the JRC system; they are located in five member states (Belgium, the Netherlands, Germany, and Spain, as well as Italy) conducting research on subjects such as the environment, nuclear measurement, advanced materials, informatics, and safety technology. Though funded by the EU and accountable to the Commission, the JRC is administered by an independent board.

Although the Commission established a directorate-general for science, research, and development (DG XII) in 1967 and issued a number of calls for EC-level R&D programs in various industrial sectors, it was only thanks to Davignon in the early 1980s that the Commission took a major step forward. In May 1982 the Commission unveiled a proposal for the European Strategic Program for Research and Development in Information Technology (ESPRIT), which the Council, already lobbied by Davignon's collaborators in European industry, approved the following June.[26] ESPRIT called for major European manufacturers, smaller firms, universities, and institutes throughout the EC to collaborate on "pre-competitive" (basic) research. That distinction helped to reduce friction between the industrial participants and satisfy the concerns of the Commission's competition watchdog. A pilot scheme of thirty-eight projects, funded jointly by the EC and the private sector, got under way in 1983 and constituted "the first step toward the development of a genuine, long-term European industrial policy."[27]

Within a short time the EC launched not only a full-fledged ESPRIT but also related research initiatives with catchy names such as RACE (advanced communications technologies), BRITE/EURAM (industrial technologies and advanced materials), and BAP (biotechnology). Later in the 1980s the Community launched BRIDGE (biotechnology), ECLAIR (linkage of agriculture and industry), FLAIR (agro-industry), and COMETT (education and training for technology). In 1985 the EC became a founding member of EUREKA, a French-led effort to develop European technology as a response to the U.S. Strategic Defense Initiative.[28]

These early R&D initiatives helped develop momentum for completion of the single market program, which the SEA made possible. The SEA also gave the EC a new and explicit basis for R&D policy (Articles 163–173, formerly Article 130f–q, TEC). With the aim of "strengthening the scientific and technological base of European industry and [encouraging] it to become more competitive at an international level," the SEA stipulated that the Council should unanimously adopt "multiannual framework programs" (MFPs) as the main instrument of R&D policy. MFPs would delineate the main scientific and technological objectives of R&D policy and define priorities. They would be implemented by a series of specific subprograms, most involving EC-industry cost sharing. The only important change to R&D policy in the TEU concerned decisionmaking: Henceforth MFPs would be adopted jointly by the Council and the EP using the codecision procedure. A further decisionmaking change in the Amsterdam Treaty dropped the unanimity requirement for the adoption of MFPs by the Council.

Activities under the MFP umbrella range from the work of the Joint Research Center to research undertaken by research centers and universities where the EU covers 50 percent of the costs (up to a certain ceiling). The essential perquisites for EU funding are that the research be of a precompetitive nature and involve at least two organizations in two different member states. In practice, most projects involve about eight partners with EU financing amounting to several million euros. In addition to the member states, four other countries—EEA members Iceland, Norway, and Liechtenstein, plus Israel—participate fully in the MFPs, to which they contribute financially. The candidate countries in Central and Eastern Europe have limited access to the MFPs, as have southern Mediterranean and some other developing countries.

The EU publishes requests for proposals for research projects four times a year in the *Official Journal*. Proposals are evaluated by independent scientific and technical experts who try to ensure unofficially that organizations in all member states are involved to some extent or other in the MFPs. The Commission runs a network of "innovative relay centers" (Eurospeak for information offices) throughout the EU to promote academic and business awareness of and involvement in the MFPs. The relay centers devote a lot of attention to small and medium-sized enterprises (SMEs), which might otherwise feel shut out of the process.

The fifth MFP, negotiated in 1998 to cover the period 1999–2002, sets out four thematic programs and key action areas that, given prevailing concerns about jobs and social exclusion, seek to address specific employment and social problems:

- quality of life (with a special emphasis on food safety and public health)
- information society (focusing, among other things, on systems and services such as health care, public administration, and transport)

- competitive and sustainable growth (including innovative products and processes)
- energy, environment, and sustainable development (climate change, biodiversity, urbanization, etc.)

Money—not objectives or priorities—has been the biggest obstacle confronting the framework programs. Member states support EU R&D policy but want to limit spending on it (as on other EU policy areas). The Commission and EP, the other key players in the MRP decisionmaking process, inevitably push for a higher budget than the Council is willing to countenance. The difference between both sides in the 1998 negotiations was a whopping ECU 2.3 billion (the Council agreed on a budget of 14 billion; the Commission and EP held out for 16.3 billion). The Commission argued that the Council's figure was ECU 0.5 billion less than the budget of the fourth MFP in real terms; the Council countered that at a time of fiscal retrenchment, ECU 14 billion was a generous amount of money. The Council also pointed out that the Commission could use its R&D budget more effectively by making procedural improvements and taking cost-cutting measures.

Even with the higher budget, R&D spending in the EU would still be less than in the United States. Moreover, EU spending is only a small part (about 4 percent) of total EU-wide spending on R&D; hence the need for greater coordination between national- and EU-sponsored R&D programs to ensure consistency and value for money. Despite a call in the TEU and frequent appeals by the Commission for more concerted national-EU action, there is still plenty of room for improvement.

Rapid globalization, the EU's increasing economic openness, and faster technological obsolescence are the greatest challenges facing EU R&D policy. Despite nearly twenty years of EU support for high-technology R&D and despite also having some global leaders in the high-technology sector, the EU continues to lag far behind the United States in biotechnology and information technology. Although R&D policy was never intended as a panacea for Europe's high-technology sector or as a substitute for industrywide restructuring, it seems reasonable to observe that EU-sponsored projects have so far produced little commercially useful technology (perhaps because of the emphasis on precompetitive research). In any event, R&D is only one element of an overall strategy to boost EU competitiveness, the most important being the single market program.

TRANS-EUROPEAN NETWORKS

The TEU contained a new title (Title XII, now Title XV, TEC) on the establishment of Trans-European Networks in the areas of transport, telecommunications, and energy infrastructures. The purpose of the TENs was to make the most of the single market and to further economic and social cohesion by "promoting the interconnection and the interoperability of national networks as well as access to such networks" (Article 154, formerly Article 129b). In other words, the TENs were intended to complete the EU's patchy infrastructural networks, thereby improving competitiveness, creating jobs, and reinforcing cohesion.

The TENs were a typical Delorian product: grandiose, ambitious, and expensive. For that reason they were completely out of keeping with the political and economic mood in Europe during and after the TEU ratification crisis. Politically, the putative EU was unpopular; economically, recession and financial retrenchment were not conducive to massive public spending. Undaunted, Delors submitted a paper to the European Council in Copenhagen in June 1993 in which he stressed the need to develop transport and telecommunications infrastructures, observing almost casually that "an overall total of ECU 30 billion a year [over a ten year period] seems to be a realistic minimum target for expenditure in this field."[29] A figure of that magnitude would surely have caught the European Council's attention, although few of the heads of state and government would have read the paper and Delors may not have mentioned it in his oral presentation.

What followed during the next three years was an interesting example of the difference between European Council rhetoric and political reality. The European Council invited Delors to prepare a white paper on a medium-term strategy for competitiveness, growth, and employment. In it, Delors emphasized the TENs as an important instrument to promote growth and combat unemployment in the EU.[30] Having discussed the white paper at their summit in Brussels in December 1993, the heads of state and government gave "strong political impetus" to completion of the TENs and set up two high-level groups of personal representatives—one under the chairmanship of Commissioner Christophersen to explore specific transport projects, the other under Commissioner Bangemann to examine information infrastructure and the information society.[31]

Meeting in Corfu six months later, the European Council endorsed the Christophersen group's interim report, including a list of eleven major priority projects that, despite their size, seemed economically viable and likely to be completed rapidly. Another six months later, at its meeting in Essen, the European Council approved the Christophersen group's addition of three more projects, making a total of fourteen transport networks and ten telecommunications networks.

Despite continued rhetorical support for the TENs, it was obvious that the European Council's enthusiasm was waning. Undoubtedly the heads of state and government wanted to accelerate big road, rail, and telecommunications projects for symbolic as well as substantive reasons, but funding—even on a far more manageable scale than Delors's original estimate—was an insurmountable problem. Contributions from the structural funds, Cohesion Fund, European Investment Bank, and the recently established

European Investment Fund could cover only a small part of the projected cost. National governments were strapped for cash and there was no question of going above the EU's budget ceiling. The Commission and member states were eager to secure private-sector support, but few investors were interested. Delors's suggestion of raising a huge commercial loan received short shrift from national governments in the grip of EMU-induced budget discipline and debt reduction.

Jacques Santer, Delors's successor, championed the TENs at subsequent European Councils, but to little avail. In September 1995 the Council adopted a regulation enabling the Commission to commit a relatively derisory ECU 274 million to the TENs (ECU 240 million for transport, ECU 22 million for telecommunications, and ECU 12 million for energy). A year later, Santer tried at the Florence summit in June 1996 to get the European Council to commit ECU 1 billion of surplus funds from the CAP budget, but the heads of state and government had other ideas for the money, some of which they used to compensate farmers for losses as a result of the bovine spongiform encephalopathy (mad cow) crisis. Nevertheless, the European Council reiterated its conviction that "the trans-European networks . . . can make a vital contribution to job creation and competitiveness."[32] Thereafter, TENs receded far into the background of European Council deliberations, although they reappeared at the special jobs summit in Luxembourg in November 1997 when the heads of state and government noted that the European Investment Bank was "prepared to grant a long grace period" for the TENs and to "provide further support for the creation of appropriate public-private partnerships."[33]

Although some TENs-related projects have begun, the scale of the operation is nowhere near what Delors envisioned. Whether this outcome represents a lost opportunity for European competitiveness is debatable. Undoubtedly the EU needs improved infrastructures, but the scale of Delors's scheme may have been excessive. Certainly its political cost was unacceptable to the European Council, notwithstanding a lot of rhetoric to the contrary. In the meantime, national investment on infrastructural development picked up as the EU emerged from recession, and the EU itself continued to spend money on transport through the structural funds and R&D framework program. These measures may not be adequate to boost growth and employment on the scale imagined by the Commission, but full-fledged TENs are a political impossibility.

EMPLOYMENT

Since the mid-1990s the EU has enjoyed respectable levels of economic growth; yet unemployment continues to hover around 11 percent of the workforce. Persistently high unemployment rose dramatically in the early

1990s with devastating effect for the EU. A former secretary-general of the Commission estimated that unemployment benefits cost EU member states almost ECU 200 billion a year, requiring high levels of taxation that drain the public purse.[34] Politically, double-digit unemployment undermines the EU's legitimacy—after all, the single market program and EMU promised to deliver economic growth *and* jobs. Far from delivering jobs, the post-Maastricht process of EMU was widely seen to have exacerbated unemployment.

The Commission has been sensitive to employment since the late 1980s, when it produced the first of its annual reports on the subject. European Councils started paying attention to unemployment in the early 1990s, issuing ritualistic denunciations of it in successive summit communiqués. Delors's 1993 white paper, *Employment, Growth, and Competitiveness,* dealt explicitly with the challenge of job creation, prompting an EU-wide debate on the issue in the mid-1990s. Santer took up the cause when he took over the Commission presidency, proposing in January 1996 a "confidence pact on employment" to boost jobs by improving the single market, curbing state aids, strengthening education and vocational training, and helping SMEs. This proposal was mostly a repackaging of existing ideas, including the proposal to fund the cherished TENs. Discussion of the TENs distracted attention from the pact's other proposals, which were in any case covered by existing policies.

Concern about unemployment reached the top of the EU's political agenda in 1997 and 1998, when unemployment in France and Germany peaked. French prime minister Lionel Jospin, a Socialist, won the May 1997 parliamentary elections on a pledge to cut unemployment; French president Jacques Chirac, a conservative, sought to outdo Jospin in proclaiming the importance of job creation. In Germany, Chancellor Helmut Kohl's attention grew more and more focused on unemployment in the run-up to the September 1998 federal elections.

The EU's high unemployment level disguises the fact that unemployment rates vary greatly from member state to member state, reflecting the diversity of economic policies among member states themselves. Most member states have economic policies that guarantee a high rate of structural unemployment (Britain, which undertook painful economic reforms in the 1980s and which now has low unemployment, is a striking exception). Labor market rigidities include high minimum wages, generous employment benefits that last for long periods, weak tests for claiming unemployment benefits, and strong trade union bargaining power. Industrial rigidities include an inability to grow small firms quickly into big ones and, at the other extreme, an inability to downsize quickly (by firing workers).

The cure for high EU unemployment should therefore be obvious: lower and shorter-lasting unemployment benefits, stricter tests for receipt of benefits, lower payroll taxes and other statutory charges, greater wage flexibility, less job protection, and the provision of earned-income tax credits. Taken together, these recommendations read like a recipe for what many Europeans decry as the callous Anglo-Saxon economic model, which, precisely because of its supposed social consequences—growing income inequalities, the emergence of a "working poor" underclass, and the lack of a social safety net—a majority of EU member states are loath to embrace. However, the United States does have an enviable record of sustained economic growth and low unemployment without inflationary pressure. Millions of working poor may be an indictment of the U.S. economic system, but the EU's millions of long-term, socially excluded unemployed also reflect poorly on the gentler European model.

Intellectually, most national governments, of whatever ideological stripe, are moving toward the U.S. model, hoping to find a middle way between it and the classical European model. The Netherlands may have found that middle way, but what works for a small country with a culture of consensus may not work for large countries like France and Germany. The French government appears to be going backward by mandating a thirty-five-hour work week and creating public-sector jobs. In fact, Jospin would like to move more in the opposite direction but faces considerable political constraints, not least his ambition for the presidency of France. The conservative German government failed to introduce potentially employment-enhancing tax reforms in 1997 and 1998 because of its weak hold on power and the new Social Democrative-Greens government was not inclined to revisit the issue.

Lack of EU competence for social security and related areas, as well as the diversity of economic systems and the vagaries of political circumstances among member states, precludes the adoption of EU measures to take the reforms necessary to translate economic growth into large-scale job creation. Yet Social Democratic governments (in the majority in the EU) pushed during the 1996–1997 IGC for an EU initiative on employment, not least to show their constituents that European integration means more than EMU and its attendant jobs squeeze. Precisely because such an initiative could not tackle the fundamental causes of high unemployment, however, it was bound to be more rhetorical than substantive.

In the event, the Amsterdam Treaty modified the EU's objectives to include "a high level of employment" (Article 2 TEC) and affirmed the necessity for "coordination between (member state) employment policies . . . with a view to enhancing their effectiveness by developing a coordinated strategy for employment" (Article 3.1 TEC). Competence for employment policy would remain at the national level, but the European Council would develop "common guidelines" based on input from various EU institutions and bodies. The Commission would monitor compliance with these guidelines, leaving it up to the European Council to slap noncompliant member states gently on the wrist. The Amsterdam Treaty also included provision for small "incentive measures" to encourage joint employment policy initiatives among member states.

At French insistence (largely as a reaction against the prevailing emphasis on the budget-cutting EMU stability pact), the European Council held a special jobs summit in Luxembourg in November 1997, soon after the Amsterdam Treaty was concluded. Although the European Council inevitably hailed the outcome as a success, there was little likelihood that it would make a serious dent on unemployment. The "new approach" agreed to at the summit involved member states submitting national employment action plans for annual peer review. These would follow common guidelines focusing on employability, entrepreneurship, adaptability of individuals and enterprises, and equal opportunity. The European Council also discussed job training for young or long-term unemployed and endorsed an initiative by the European Investment Bank making up to ECU 1 billion available to support high-technology and high-growth SMEs.[35]

Britain put employment at the top of its presidential agenda in early 1998, stressing a flexible rather than legislative approach. At the concluding summit of Britain's presidency, held in Cardiff in June 1998, the European Council discussed for the first time the member states' annual employment action plans. This was a painless process based on earlier assessments of the action plans by the Commission and the Council. Apart from some genial statements about the contents of the existing plans, the European Council adjured the Social Affairs and Economic and Finance Councils "to continue to work together to exchange best practice . . . [and] to develop peer group evaluation" of future plans.[36]

Clearly, measures at the EU level to combat unemployment are largely declamatory. They are intended more to appease a critical but uncomprehending public than to tackle the fundamental roots of Europe's high joblessness. Nevertheless, most national governments are beginning to introduce more wage and labor flexibility, however haltingly. The advent of monetary union increases the pressure on them to do so. Ironically EMU, which supposedly exacerbated unemployment in the mid- and late 1990s, may help to reduce it substantially in the early 2000s.

NOTES

1. Dean Acheson, *Present at the Creation: My Years in the State Department* (New York: Norton, 1969), p. 383.

2. Leon Brittan, "Competition Law: Its Importance to the European Community and to International Trade," speech at the University of Chicago Law School, April 24, 1992, p. 8.

3. Council Regulation 17/62, *Official Journal of the European Communities* [*OJ*] 62, no. 87, special edition (1959). 1959-62/87.

4. Leon Brittan, *European Competition Policy: Keeping the Playing Field Level* (Brussels: CEPS, 1992), p. 18.

5. *OJ* L 72, March 18, 1992, p. 1.

6. Council Regulation 4064/89, December 21, 1989, *OJ* L 395, December 30, 1989, p. 1.

7. Reported in the *Economist*, October 18, 1987, p. 61. The day in question was October 13.

8. Bull. EC 11-1994, point 1.2.34.

9. Bull. EC 5-1998, point 1.3.

10. Bull. EC 7-1992, point 1.3.47.

11. See European Parliament, *Fact Sheets on the European Parliament and the Activities of the European Community* (Luxembourg: Office for Official Publications of the European Communities [OOP], 1991), p. 1.

12. Peter Sutherland, "The European Community: Unity Without Tears," in *Times* (London), October 22, 1988, p. 10.

13. See Brittan, *Competition Policy,* pp. 48–50.

14. Frank Vibert, "The Case for 'Unbundling' the Commission," in Etienne Davignon et al., *What Future for the European Commission?* (Brussels: Philip Morris Institute for Public Policy Research, 1995).

15. Claus-Dieter Ehlermann, "Case for a Cartel Body," *Financial Times,* March 7, 1995, p. 10.

16. J. Patrick Raines, "Common Market Competition Policy: The EC-IBM Settlement," *Journal of Common Market Studies* 24, no. 2 (December 1985): 137.

17. See Sherill Brown Wells, *French Industrial Policy: A History, 1945–81* (Washington, DC: Office of the Historian, U.S. Department of State, 1991), pp. 61–80.

18. Commission, *The European Community's Industrial Strategy* (Luxembourg: OOP, 1983), p. 47.

19. Jean-Jacques Servan-Schreiber, *Le Défi Américain* (Paris: Denoel, 1967).

20. Walter Grunsteidl, "An Industrial Policy for Europe," *European Affairs* 3, no. 90 (fall 1990): 19.

21. See Martin Bangemann, *Meeting the Global Challenge: Establishing a Successful European Industrial Policy* (London: Kogan, Page, Pounds, 1992), p. 8.

22. Quoted in Commission, *21st Report on Competition Policy* (Luxembourg: OOP, 1992), p. 22.

23. Commission, *Industrial Policy in an Open and Competitive Environment: Guidelines for a Community Approach,* COM(90)556 final, November 16, 1990.

24. SEC(91)565, April 3, 1991.

25. EC Council Resolution, November 18, 1991.

26. See Bull. EC 5-1982, point 2.1.152; Bull. EC 6-1983, points 2.1.268 to 2.1.269.

27. Grunsteidl, "Industrial Policy," p. 17.

28. See Margaret Sharp, "The Single Market and European Policies for Advanced Technologies," in Colin Crouch and David Marquand, eds., *The Politics of 1992: Beyond the Single European Market* (Oxford: Basil Blackwell, 1990), pp. 100–120.

29. Copenhagen European Council, "Presidency Conclusions," Annex 1, "Orientations for Economic Renewal in Europe," Bull. EC 6-1993, point 1.4.

30. Commission, *Growth, Competitiveness, Employment: The Challenges and Ways Forward into the 21st Century,* COM(93)700.

31. Commission, *1994 General Report,* point 321, p. 110.

32. Florence European Council, "Presidency Conclusions," Bull. EC 6-1996, point 1.4.

33. Luxembourg European Council, "Presidency Conclusions," Bull. EC 11-1997, point 1.6.

34. David Williamson, "The European Union: New Money, New Treaty, New Members," *The European Union: Speeches,* www.eurunion.org/news/speeches/971211dw.htm.

35. Luxembourg European Council, "Presidency Conclusions," Bull. EC 11-1997, point 1.6.

36. Cardiff European Council, "Presidency Conclusions," Bull. EC 6-1998, points 1.2 to 1.4.

15

Beyond the Marketplace

Like the Single European Act (SEA), the Treaty on European Union (TEU) and the Amsterdam Treaty included articles on a wide range of policies and programs relating to market integration but warranting collective member state action in their own right. These include environmental policy, social policy, cohesion policy, and cooperation on Justice and Home Affairs (relating to the free movement of people). Although closely associated with the 1992 program, those policy areas promote important objectives that go well beyond the marketplace. Regardless of the single market, it is important for Europeans to breathe cleaner air, enjoy equality in the workplace, reduce regional disparities, and move freely from one member state to another. Apart from strengthening the EU socially and economically and enhancing the quality of life, the successful implementation of such policies supposedly imparts a sense of community and solidarity, thereby contributing to the construction of a "citizens' Europe."

ENVIRONMENTAL POLICY

Although not originally mentioned in the Treaty of Rome, environmental policy is now one of the most important and highly regulated areas of EU competence. Growing popular distress about environmental degradation, the impact of a number of heavily publicized environmental disasters, and the politicization of the environmental movement in the 1970s and 1980s account for the EU's increasing involvement in the area. At the same time, fearing that national environmental measures would distort the single market, governments strengthened the EC's environmental policymaking power as a corollary to the 1992 program. A number of global concerns—climate change, depletion of the ozone layer, dwindling natural resources, and excessive pollution—increased the EU's involvement in international environmental affairs. As a result, environmental policy has been at the top of the EU's political and economic agenda throughout the 1990s.

General Development

Early EC environmental legislation tended to be narrow and technical, justified either as an internal market measure or on the basis of a vague commitment in the preamble of the Treaty of Rome to improve "the living and working conditions" of people in the EC. Examples include a 1967 directive on the classification, packaging, and labeling of dangerous substances and 1970 directives on noise levels. As the environmental movement gathered momentum throughout Western Europe, however, national governments and the Commission developed a keen interest in environmental issues. Accordingly, at their summit in Paris in October 1972, the heads of state and government took the unprecedented step of calling for an EC environmental policy.

Within a year the Commission proposed and the Council adopted the first Environmental Action Program (EAP). This and the second EAP (1977) listed various measures that were essentially corrective in nature. Subsequent EAPs (1982, 1987, and 1993) emphasized preventive measures. Reflecting the economic malaise of the early 1980s, the third EAP specifically called for environmental action that would contribute to economic growth and job creation through the development of less-polluting industries. It also advocated a European-level environmental impact assessment procedure and, for the first time, offered some EC financing for environmental projects.

Reflecting the growing importance of environmental policy in the EC, in 1981 the Commission established a separate directorate-general—DG XI—to deal with environmental issues. Although smaller than other major DGs, DG XI quickly acquired a reputation for activism and as a main channel for environmental groups to pressure the Commission to pursue "greener" policies. This reputation often put DG XI at odds with its powerful counterparts engaged in economic and internal market activities. Among the member states, the so-called green troika of Denmark, Germany, and the Netherlands pushed hardest for environmental legislation at the European level, and the poorer southern countries put up most resistance at the legislative and implementation stages.[1]

The 1985 intergovernmental conference (IGC), held on the eve of the EC's Iberian enlargement, gave national governments an opportunity to incorporate environmental policy into the treaty. Accordingly, the SEA devoted an entire section (Article 130r–t, now Articles 174–176, TEC) to environmental policy and included in its single market provisions a new article on environmental protection (Article 100a.4, now Article 95.4, TEC). Whereas Article 130r.1 (now Article 174.1) gave the EC wide scope for environmental action, Article 130r.4 seemed to limit that scope by invoking, for the first time in the EC treaty, the principle of subsidiarity (member states deleted Article 130r.4 when they included a general subsidiarity clause in the TEU). Moreover, Articles 100a (now Article 95) and 130 (now Article 170) used different decisionmaking procedures to achieve essentially the same result.

Little wonder that the SEA's environmental provisions seemed "confusing, ambiguous, and contradictory."[2] Yet to a great extent they worked. Based on the SEA and on the designation of 1987 as the European Year of the Environment, the EC developed new environmental principles and measures in its fourth EAP (1987). References to environmental policy in successive European Council communiqués testified to growing public concern about the issue. At the macro level, the Commission pursued a new approach, making environmental policy an integral part of all other policies—notably economic, industrial, transport, energy, agricultural, and social—whether at the national or European level. At the micro level, the Commission worked on priority areas such as atmospheric and marine pollution, waste management, biotechnology, and enforcement of environmental legislation.

The TEU reiterated the importance of taking environmental policy into account when formulating and implementing other EU policies. In addition, the treaty assuaged the concerns of poorer member states by allowing temporary derogations and/or financial support from the Cohesion Fund to compensate them for environmental measures involving disproportionately high costs. However, the TEU's most important environmental provisions relate to the decisionmaking process. Article 130s (now Article 175 TEC) specified three legislative methods: the cooperation procedure (for most environmental measures); unanimity in the Council (for specified measures); and the codecision procedure (for general action programs).

Written with the TEU in mind, the EC's fifth EAP, covering the period 1993–2000, noted a "slow but relentless deterioration . . . of the environment" despite two decades of EC action. The report advocated "sustainable development," defined in general terms as that which "meets the needs of the present without compromising the ability of future generations to meet their own needs." More specifically, the report called for waste reduction through reuse and recycling, lower energy use, a change of general consumption patterns, integrated pollution-control measures, environmentally friendly transport, and industrial risk assessment. It identified five target sectors: industry, energy, transport, agriculture, and tourism. One of the report's most striking aspects was a shift in the EU's general approach from purely regulatory measures (e.g., emissions limits) to an emphasis on economic and fiscal measures (including taxes, incentives, and subsidies through the structural funds).

In 1992 the EU established the Financial Instrument for the Environment (LIFE) to contribute to the development and implementation of EU environmental policy. Under the terms of the program, the EU cofinances environmental activities in member states and in third countries bordering the Mediterranean and the Baltic Sea (except for countries with which the EU has Europe agreements). In its second phase, covering the years 1996–1999, LIFE made ECU 450 million available to a wide range of environmental projects.

Due mostly to pressure from the Netherlands and the two new Nordic member states, negotiations on environmental policy at the 1996–1997 IGC focused on three main issues: heightening environmental awareness by stressing the need for sustainable development; extending codecision; and introducing higher environmental standards than provided for in the EU's harmonization measures. Accordingly, the Amsterdam Treaty included a general stipulation (Article 6 TEC) that "environmental protection requirements must be integrated into the definition and implementation of . . . Community policies and activities . . . in particular with a view to promoting sustainable development"; it also extended the codecision procedure to environmental policymaking (Article 175 TEC) and altered Article 95 TEC to allow exceptions to EU rules because of environmental considerations as long as proposed national measures are based on new scientific evidence and the problem being addressed is specific to the member state proposing the exceptional measures. The treaty explicitly gives the Commission the right to reject such measures even if they are not found to be a means of arbitrary discrimination or a disguised restriction on trade. However, Commission review of these measures must be completed within a six-month time limit or they are approved by default. Whether the Commission will routinely be able to rule on complex scientific dossiers and make the related ethical or social judgments within this period remains to be seen; one commentator suggested that the time limit would at least force the Commission to develop procedures for a more systematic approach to these issues.[3]

Key Legislation

Environmental legislation enacted at the EU level now exceeds the quantity and generally exceeds the quality of environmental legislation enacted at the national level. EU environmental legislation has developed unevenly, varying from measures on specific problems to directives on catchall issues. In the mid-1990s EU environmental legislation developed along two main lines: (1) the proposal of framework directives such as those on air quality and the ecological quality of water and (2) the consolidation or revision of existing directives such as those on environmental impact assessments, the prevention of major accidents involving dangerous substances (the so-called Seveso directive), and the quality of bathing water.

General

• *Seveso directive:* After much debate following a major industrial disaster in Seveso, Italy, in 1977, the Council adopted a directive (82/501/EC) aiming to ensure that manufacturers using dangerous materials, as well as local authorities, have adequate contingency plans to limit the environmental impact of accidents. A revised and updated Seveso directive (96/82/EC), adopted in December 1996, retained the basic principles of the original directive but added new requirements and measures to achieve more consistent implementation.

• *Environmental impact assessments:* In 1985 the Council adopted a directive (85/337/EC) requiring member states to demand environmental impact assessments (EIAs) before approving projects that by virtue of size, nature, or location are likely to have a significant impact on the environment. Assessments are mandatory for certain types of industrial and infrastructural projects, and other types of activity may be subject to EIAs at the discretion of member states.

• *European Environment Agency (EEA):* A 1990 regulation (1210/90/EEC) created the European Environment Agency to collect and disseminate reliable data on the environment, thereby partially filling the information gap that had plagued EU efforts to formulate and enforce environmental policy. A dispute over the siting of European agencies, eventually resolved at the Brussels summit in October 1993, delayed formal establishment of the Environment Agency until October 1994, when it opened in Copenhagen.

• *Ecolabeling:* In 1992 the Council adopted a regulation laying out rules for a scheme to award "ecolabels" to environmentally friendly products, ranging from detergent to refrigerators.

• *Ecoauditing:* In March 1993 the Council adopted a regulation (1836/93) setting out the rules for the EU Eco-Management and Audit Scheme, which became fully operational in April 1995. Under the voluntary regulation, participating companies improve and periodically assess their environmental performance, provide adequate public information, and submit their systems and public statements to a review by a panel of independent experts. In return, companies are allowed to use a logo indicating their participation in the scheme.

• *Integrated pollution prevention and control (IPPC):* In December 1996 the Council adopted a directive (96/61/EC) obliging member states to install regulatory systems that would issue a single permit to enterprises covering all types of emissions (air, water, and soil). This directive obliges regulatory authorities to evaluate the overall effect of a given operation on the environment not only by using criteria based on environmental quality standards but also by comparing emissions levels to those possible with the "best available technology."

Habitats, Ecosystems, and Wildlife

• *Convention on Trade in Endangered Species (CITES):* A 1982 directive instituted a system of licensing to implement the 1973 international Convention on Trade in Endangered Species. In response to the impending elimination of border controls, in 1992 the Commission proposed further measures to improve internal implementation of CITES rules, resulting in a Council regulation (338/97) of December 1996.

• *Wild birds directive:* This directive (79/409/EC), updated six times between 1981 and 1994, is designed to protect more than 100 "particularly vulnerable" species of birds and their habitats. The directive also restricts hunting of additional species, but this provision is widely disregarded in certain member states (especially France) because of the strength of hunting lobbies.

• *Habitats directive:* In May 1992 the Council adopted a directive (92/43/EEC) establishing a general program for the protection of natural habitats. It was to be composed of a "coherent European ecological network," called "Natura 2000." The EU may designate sites as special conservation areas even if they have not been proposed by member states.

Air

• *Motor vehicle emissions:* Responding to steadily increasing volumes of motor vehicle traffic and to public concern, EU standards have become stricter over time; as a result, emissions have been reduced by an astounding 80–90 percent per car since 1980.

A 1970 directive (70/220/EC) began the process by setting technical standards for emissions of CO_2 and unburned hydrocarbons for most gasoline-powered vehicles. The 1970 directive was based on "optional harmonization": Member states were not obligated to implement the standards set forth in the directive but had to approve vehicles from other member states that met those standards. In a series of directives designed to ensure that lead-free gasoline was available throughout Europe at competitive prices, the EC also took action to lower emissions of lead by motor vehicles.

Although the Council amended its landmark 1970 motor vehicle emissions directive several times, the standards set by the amendments lagged behind those set in other large markets, notably the United States. The Commission and Council entered into an extended debate over updating EC emission standards in 1988 and 1989 with member states split over whether to introduce stricter standards for small cars (there was strong opposition from France and Italy, whose producers would be most affected). Eventually, bowing to pressure from the EP and the Dutch government, the Council adopted a directive (89/458/EC) requiring cars marketed in the

EU after January 1, 1993, to meet standards equivalent to those prevailing in the United States (in other words, all new cars must be equipped with catalytic converters).

A subsequent directive (91/441/EC) further tightened standards and called on the Commission to propose even stricter guidelines by mid-1996. The Commission did so, but the Council and the EP failed to reach agreement by the end of 1997, as stipulated in the 1991 directive. Apart from setting strict auto standards, the Commission has also concluded that further improvements in vehicle emissions will have to come from sources other than cars themselves (e.g., new fuel mixes, better mandatory maintenance and inspection, and reduction in the use of cars).

• *Other air-quality directives:* Other legislation covering air pollution can be divided roughly into two categories: air-quality standards and emissions limits. Following serious damage caused by acid rain to many European forests and the resulting public outcry, in the late 1970s the EC took action to limit emissions of sulfur dioxide (SO_2) and nitrous oxide (NO_2). Emissions of lead and other pollutants are also restricted, and plants are required to use the best available technology "not entailing excessive costs."

• *Protection of the ozone layer:* As concern grew over the effect of widely used chlorofluorocarbons (CFCs) on the earth's protective ozone layer, the EC took steps to limit use of CFCs in the early 1980s. The Commission and member states participated in the negotiation of the 1985 Vienna Convention for the Protection of the Ozone Layer, the 1987 Montreal Protocol (which created a mechanism for limiting use of CFCs and other ozone-damaging chemicals), and subsequent protocols tightening these restrictions and accelerating the phaseout of some substances. Regulations in 1991 (594/91) and 1994 (3093/94) on substances that deplete the ozone layer implemented the Montreal Protocol.

• *Climate change and CO_2 emissions:* Amid rising public concern about the prospect of global warming and scientific findings that it could cause rising sea levels and other disasters, the EC committed itself in 1990 to stabilizing emissions of carbon dioxide at a 1990 benchmark level by the year 2000.

As the key element in its strategy for achieving that goal, the Commission proposed a combined EU tax on energy and CO_2 emissions to be imposed by national governments. The proposed measure, which would have raised energy prices by the equivalent of $10 per barrel of oil over a ten-year period, inevitably engendered strong opposition in many quarters. Environment ministers cautiously endorsed it, but industry and finance ministers showed less enthusiasm. Aside from industry opposition, the main problems with the proposal were the technical difficulties of designing the tax itself and the political issue of exemptions for poorer member states. Although several member states have adopted CO_2 taxes, and despite a 1995 Commission amendment to its proposal making adoption of the tax voluntary, the EU CO_2 tax proposal itself appears to have become a dead letter. Perhaps as a result, or perhaps because of other factors such as economic growth, the EU stands little chance of achieving its goal of stabilization by the year 2000.

Water

The Commission divides legislation on water into three categories: quality objectives or other requirements; industry or sector regulations; and limits on the discharge of dangerous substances.

Building on a 1976 framework directive (76/464/EC), the EC enacted most of its legislation on water quality during the next decade and passed updated legislation in the 1990s. The framework directive identified substances deemed to pose a threat to the environment, dividing them into a "blacklist" (carcinogens and other dangerous substances, such as mercury or cadmium, for which discharges *are prohibited*) and a "graylist" (certain other metals and substances that affect the taste or smell of water, for which discharges *should be restricted*).

In addition, major horizontal directives (all of which were amended at least once in the 1990s) cover the quality of drinking water (80/778/EC), bathing water (71/160/EC), discharges to groundwater (80/68/EC), quality of water containing freshwater fish (78/659/EC) and shellfish (79/923/EC), surface water for drinking (75/440/EC), and treatment of urban wastewater (91/271/EC). In the Commission's view, the urban wastewater directive represents a departure from the traditional emphasis on quality standards and discharge limits and embodies a more general approach to confronting water pollution. It requires member states to provide for treatment of all urban wastewaters within a specific time frame (tailored to individual states and regions).

Eager to consolidate various water-quality initiatives, in February 1996 the Commission issued a communication on EU water policy, setting out objectives, principles, and proposed measures. Chief among these was a framework directive for water resources, proposed by the Commission in February 1997, laying down quality standards to be achieved by December 2007. Perhaps because of the far-off target date, the other EU institutions have been slow to act on it.

Waste

The EU began regulating waste disposal (hazardous and nonhazardous) in 1975 with adoption of a framework directive (75/442/EC, amended in 1991) that defined waste in general terms ("any substance disposed of by the holder") and required member states to designate competent authorities and set up permit systems for waste disposal. A series of directives dealing with specific areas of waste disposal, relating mainly to hazardous wastes, followed the original framework directive:

• *Toxic and dangerous waste (1978):* This directive required member states, producers, holders, and disposers of toxic wastes to keep close track of the movement and disposal of those wastes through the use of permits and extensive documentation. A subsequent Council directive (91/689/EC) defined hazardous waste, established general requirements for facilities that deal with it, tightened documentation requirements to include registration of all wastes discharged at waste sites, established a consignment note system for transfer of such wastes, and restricted mixing hazardous wastes with each other or with nonhazardous wastes.

• *Transfrontier shipment of hazardous waste (84/631/EC):* This directive created a system of compulsory prior notification and authorization for transport of hazardous wastes across national borders, including uniform documentation requirements.

• *Specific wastes:* A series of directives since the mid-1970s regulate treatment and disposal of specific types of waste, including polychlorinated biphenyls (PCBs) and polychlorinated terphenyls (PCTs), waste oils, asbestos, batteries and accumulators, and waste arising from the manufacture of titanium dioxide.

The Commission made its first foray into reduction of nonhazardous waste with a directive (85/339/EC) requiring member states to draw up a four-year program to reduce the contribution of beverage containers to the waste stream. In 1989, with the release of a communication on EC strategy for waste management, the Commission took a broader approach, promising to make a series of proposals covering multiple aspects of waste management, including

- stricter controls on the movement of all waste and ratification of the Basel Convention and OECD decision on transboundary movement of waste
- a directive on civil liability for damage caused by waste
- directives on uniform site design for landfills and standards for incineration of hazardous waste
- a proposal on recycling waste packaging

Among these, the directive on shipments of waste (93/259/EC) is probably the most important. Numerous disputes over EU competence and national sovereignty (including whether shipments within member states should be covered and whether a member state could ban imports of waste from another member state) delayed adoption for well over a year. In its final version, the regulation covers shipments between states only, although it obliges governments to establish "an appropriate system" for control of shipments within their own borders and to notify the Commission of that system. In keeping with the "proximity" principle (wastes should be disposed of as near as possible to where they were generated), the Commission conceded that member states should be allowed to ban waste imports systematically except in cases that involve specialized wastes coming from small member states.

Other elements of the Commission's strategy were even harder to enact. The draft directive on civil liability for damage caused by waste made little progress in the Council and was eventually subsumed into a green paper on remedying environmental damage, released by the Commission in March 1993. It reemerged in March 1997 in a Commission proposal for a new directive, which worked its way through the legislative process in 1998. The directive on incineration was enacted in December 1994 (94/67/EC); the directive on landfills was proposed in March 1998 and, like the proposed directive on civil liability, worked its way through the EU system in 1998 and 1999.

The Commission began to advocate common rules for packaging and packaging waste starting in 1992 after Germany adopted legislation threatening to disrupt the single market by requiring producers to take back, or guarantee recycling of, all packaging waste from consumer products sold in Germany. Initially, the Commission called for recycling 60 percent of each type of packaging waste and energy recovery (incineration) of a further 30 percent, in each member state, within ten years. The proposal also required extensive tracking of waste generation and disposal trends in the packaging area while leaving precise methods of implementing the targets to individual member states. Initially, the proposal provoked lively controversy with some member states complaining that the directive was too lax and industry objecting that the targets were technologically unreachable for certain types of materials. The debate grew more tense as it became clear that Germany was meeting its seemingly admirable recycling goals via massive exports of used packaging materials, threatening to destroy national recycling systems by driving prices below cost throughout Europe. After an arduous discussion with the EP and a host of interest groups, in December 1994 the Council finally adopted a much more modest directive requiring member states to reach targets of between 50 percent and 65 percent recovery (a figure covering both recycling and incineration) of packaging waste with a further minimum level of between 25 percent and 45 percent for recycling alone and a minimum of 15 percent recycling of each type of packaging material by mid-2001. These targets will be upgraded within ten years; meanwhile member states are free to exceed them as long as they do not produce "excessive" waste exports (i.e., disrupt the status quo elsewhere).

Problems of Enforcement

Enforcement is a critical problem in the search for an effective EU environmental policy. Differing legal regimes, economic concerns, degrees of public concern, and levels of political interest among member states have contributed to uneven implementation of environmental directives throughout the EU. Until the European Environment Agency became fully operational in 1995, the Commission was hampered by a dearth of reliable data on the state of the environment in Europe. Yet the Commission remains constrained by its reliance on national governments for the information needed to pursue some infringement proceedings.

The Commission generally paints a gloomy picture of enforcement of EU environmental rules by the member states; only Austria and the Nordic countries escape criticism. Problems range from egregiously late transposal of EU measures to failure to conform to standards established in EU legislation to nonsubmission of required reports.

The EIA directive is often disregarded. It has also been a fruitful source of conflict between the Commission and the member states, not least because it allows environmental organizations to appeal to another, highly visible authority the action (or inaction) of their own governments regarding local development issues. The Commission has brought infringement proceedings against a majority of member states for failure to implement EIAs in full and complained seven years after adoption of the EIA directive that "even where the procedure laid down by the directive is formally complied with, impact studies are often of a mediocre quality and almost always underestimate the harm to the environment."[4]

The politically contentious EIAs erupted into a public row in October 1991 when the British government reacted vehemently to a letter of infringement from the Commission concerning the siting of a new road. The incident elicited British foreign secretary Douglas Hurd's famous charge that the Commission was intruding into "every nook and cranny" of daily life.[5] The ensuing controversy added fuel to the debate on subsidiarity and on ratification of the TEU.

In areas covered by substantive legislation (air, water, waste, etc.), the Commission considers the situation to be least satisfactory where EU legislation lays down obligations to plan ahead. Water quality is a prime example: Many member states simply have not undertaken the massive public investment programs necessary to meet the standards to which they agreed in the Council. This failure is especially evident with respect to the drinking and bathing water directives, where concentrations of certain pollutants routinely exceed EU norms, sometimes with the explicit permission of national authorities. There are a number of flagrant abuses in the area of air quality (Athens comes immediately to mind), although the problem here is often lack of information on the real situation in member states.

In addition to the usual plethora of disputes over conformity of implementing legislation, a key problem in the area of waste is violation of control and documentation rules by waste shippers and an increase in uncontrolled or illegal tips or landfills. The Commission is far from certain that member states are disposing of waste in accordance with EC law. In the area of nature protection, the Commission cites continual problems with member states over their failure to designate adequate numbers of special preserves, as well as the persistence of hunting regulations that violate the directives on protection of wild birds and other wildlife.

The Environment and Enlargement

The Eftan enlargement of 1995 brought into the EU new member states with a bullish approach to environmental issues regionally and globally. Accession negotiations on the environment "chapter" were especially contentious because standards were generally higher in the applicant states: Negotiators strove to reconcile the applicant states' desire to maintain their higher standards until EU standards reached an equivalent level with the EU's desire to maintain the free movement of goods in the single market. The so-called third-option alternative provided an acceptable compromise. It promised a review of EU environmental directives within four years of enlargement, during which time the new member states could maintain their higher standards.[6] The issue of higher environmental standards in the new member states became bound up in negotiations at the 1996–1997 IGC resulting in a revised Article 95 (see above).

The problem with the environment dossier in the next round of enlargement negotiations, which began in March 1998, is the opposite of what it had been during the Eftan negotiations. After decades of Soviet-style economic planning and performance, the Central and Eastern European applicants have abysmally low environmental standards. Although air and water pollution levels in Central and Eastern Europe dropped significantly in the 1990s thanks to the collapse of the heavy-industry and mining sectors, the applicant states have a long way to go to meet EU requirements. Nuclear contamination and the risk of nuclear accidents are particularly worrisome and expensive to rectify.

The Europe agreements between the EU and the Central and Eastern European states stipulated in general terms that the associated countries' economic policies must be guided by the principle of sustainable development and take full account of environmental conditions. Beyond that, the Commission's 1995 white paper on integrating the applicant states into the internal market covered only a small fraction of the EU's environmental *acquis*. In its opinions on the Central and Eastern European states' membership applications, the Commission included an assessment—often bleak—of the environmental situation in each of the applicant countries. The applicant states' difficulties with conforming to the environmental *acquis* and their inevitable requests for derogations will likely complicate the enlargement negotiations.[7]

The EU's Role in International Environmental Affairs

Almost from the beginning, EU environmental policy acquired an international dimension. Realizing that pollution knew no bounds and that environmental degradation was a global problem, in 1973 member states undertook (as part of a "gentleman's agreement" on environmental issues) to coordinate their international positions. On that basis, the EU became increasingly involved in worldwide environmental affairs.

The SEA authorized the EC to enter into international agreements on environmental issues "with third countries and with . . . relevant international organizations," and the fourth EAP called on member states and the EC to participate actively on the international stage to protect the environment. As a result, the EU is now party to a number of international and regional conventions on the environment. The EU also participates in environmental activities with the OECD, the UN Environment Programme, and the Economic Commission for Europe. In addition, environmental criteria are integral to EU assistance to the countries of Central and Eastern Europe and the southern Mediterranean, and to EU development policy (for instance, the Lomé Convention provides for general environmental cooperation and includes a specific ban on exports of hazardous waste to African, Caribbean, and Pacific countries).

The EC and the member states participated in the Rio Conference in June 1992, which adopted three basic texts: the Rio Declaration on the Environment and Development (general principles relating to the environmental implications of economic development), Agenda 21 (a comprehensive work program covering virtually every aspect of environment and development), and a nonbinding statement on forest principles. The EC and the member states signed the UN Framework Convention on Climate Change and the Convention on Biodiversity, both of which emerged from negotiations begun well before the Rio Conference.

Of all the issues discussed at Rio, climate change is likely to remain the biggest bone of international contention in the years ahead. Beginning with its 1990 commitment to stabilizing carbon dioxide emissions (which required richer member states to reduce emissions), the Commission has attempted to stake out a position for the EU as a leader in reducing emissions of greenhouse gases and to exert moral pressure on others (mainly the United States) to follow the EU example. In practice, most member states found it impossible to meet their virtuous-sounding targets; the exception, Germany, was able to post impressive reductions after reunification led to the shutdown of most East German soft-coal electricity generating plants. The Commission's failure to persuade member states to adopt a Community-wide CO_2 tax in the early 1990s further widened the gap between rhetoric and results.

Nevertheless, the EU entered into negotiations leading up to the Kyoto Conference on Climate Change in December 1997 with the ambitious proposal that industrial countries reduce emissions by 2010 to 15 percent below 1990 levels of three greenhouse gases; the proposal imposed no targets on developing countries. The EU's biggest trading partners declined to follow this lead. The United States, which has some of the highest per capita emissions, proposed stabilization, and the Japanese offered a 2.5 percent cut. Everyone disagreed as to which gases should be included. The United States opposed the exclusion of developing countries; indeed, the U.S. Congress went so far as to threaten rejection of any deal not including developing-country commitments. Another contentious issue was the means by which countries could take credit for gains occurring elsewhere. The EU proposed a "bubble" allowing EU countries, including new entrants, to take collective credit for any reductions; the United States pushed for "joint implementation" that would allow it to take credit for reductions achieved through U.S. investment in Russia and other fuel-inefficient countries.

The debate over developing countries sets up a moral argument against an economic one: Should developed nations atone for their overconsumption through expensive emissions reduction measures, or should they be let off the hook by paying for cheaper measures that would achieve the same results in developing countries? EU officials, especially Commissioner Ritt Bjerregaard, argued for the former. Essentially, however, both the "bubble" and "joint implementation" achieve the latter by allowing the United States to take credit for improvements in Russia and the EU to pocket reductions occurring in Central and Eastern Europe as new EU entrants phase out inefficient coal-generating methods.

In the end, the EU reduced its target to 8 percent reductions below 1990 levels in six greenhouse gases between 2008 and 2012, accompanied by commitments of 7 percent for the United States and 6 percent for Japan and Canada with provisions allowing for both EU bubble and joint implementation as well as for emissions trading and a "clean-development mechanism" to attract private-sector investment to developing countries in return for tradable emissions credits. Whether any participants will achieve their targets remains to be seen: Accelerating economic growth in parts of Europe will also cause an increase in emissions that will be difficult to control without drastic fiscal measures or unforeseeable technological advances.

SOCIAL POLICY

The EU's social policy builds on a long history and a strong tradition of social legislation in the member states. Only Britain, during eighteen years of Conservative government (1979–1997), disputed the philosophical underpinnings of the EU's social policy agenda. Thus Brussels became the battleground for ideological, political, and economic disputes over such issues as women's rights, workers' rights, and, especially, "industrial democracy"—employee participation in company decisionmaking. More than simply trying to improve working and living conditions in the EU, the Commission has aggressively advocated social policy as a means of promoting a "people's Europe." Because legislation on social issues potentially affects the everyday lives of almost everybody in the EU, a progressive social policy is a useful means by which the Commission can stress the relevance of European integration.

From the Treaty of Rome to the Single European Act

The TEC contains a number of social policy provisions. Articles 39–43 relate to labor mobility, one of the prerequisites for a fully functioning internal market. Article 141 contains a binding obligation on member states to offer equal pay for equal work performed by men and women, and Articles 146–148 set up the European Social Fund to help achieve the EU's social policy objectives, most of which (apart from the treaty's specific provisions) are mentioned in the preamble, Article 2, Article 136 (improved living and working conditions), and Article 137 (close cooperation among member states on labor issues).

The EU built the first phase of its social policy in the 1960s almost entirely on Articles 39–43. However, movement of labor and the professions remained restricted for another twenty years, until the momentum of the single market program finally made it possible to resolve outstanding issues. In the meantime, broader aspects of social policy got off to a good start in the early 1970s thanks to the Europhoria generated by the 1969 Hague summit and thanks also to the leadership of Willy Brandt, Germany's Social Democratic chancellor. Accordingly, the heads of state and government reiterated their commitment to a comprehensive and effective social policy at the 1972 Paris summit.

Given the economic setbacks about to beset the EC, the Paris summit was a false dawn. Like other EC activities, social policy suffered from the political retrenchment that followed. Yet the initial impression was misleading. Buoyed by the Paris summit's endorsement of an active social policy, in 1974 the Commission proposed and the Council accepted the EC's first social action program. This program included wide-ranging measures to achieve full employment, better living and working conditions, worker participation in industrial decisionmaking, and equal treatment of men and women in the workplace.

A flurry of activity followed, but the legislative output was disappointing. Successful measures included directives on workers' information and consultation rights and on equal pay and equal treatment for women. The fifth company law directive and the European Company Statute—

company law measures that included provisions for worker participation—became bogged down in disputes among member states and trade unions over which model of industrial democracy to use. Apart from its legislative agenda, the EC established two institutions—the European Foundation for the Improvement of Living and Working Conditions and the European Center for the Development of Vocational Training—to conduct research on social issues. Nevertheless, the EC's performance paled in comparison with the promise of the Paris summit and the first social action program. It was a sad commentary on what followed that a leading scholar on the subject described the mid-1970s as "probably the high-tide of European social policy."[8]

The infamous Vredeling draft directive of 1980 showed how politically out of touch the Commission had become not only on the issue of worker participation but on social policy in general. Popularly known by the name of the commissioner for social affairs, the directive proposed to expand workers' information and consultation rights in multinational companies. Whereas previous proposals relating to information and consultation in the workplace had largely followed current member state practices, the Vredeling directive went well beyond existing provisions at the national level by requiring multinationals to give employees details of the company's entire operations, including those outside the EC.

Lingering Eurosclerosis fueled a powerful political backlash against the Vredeling directive. Fresh ideological winds also boded ill for social policy in the EC, with a right-wing reaction against excessive government intervention in economic and social affairs. In the prevailing political climate, few national governments supported as active a social agenda as the Commission proposed. Thus a combination of renewed economic recession and emerging market forces pushed social policy onto the back burner in the early 1980s and helps to explain why the single market program initially lacked a social dimension.

The 1985 White Paper touched on social policy only in relation to the free movement of people (workers and professions). The SEA went farther, affirming in its preamble the need to "improve the [EC's] economic and social situation by extending common policies and pursuing new objectives" and by including a new title on economic and social cohesion. Moreover, the SEA introduced qualified majority voting for legislation on "the health and safety of workers" (Article 118a, now Article 137, TEC). Not only did the health and safety area produce the largest and most important body of social policy legislation in the late 1980s and early 1990s but the majority voting provision for health and safety legislation opened a loophole through which the Commission tried to enact other social measures. This effort led to a number of legal challenges, most notably by the British government against the Council's adoption in December 1993 of the "working time" directive, which sets a maximum forty-eight-hour work week (with many exceptions), as a health and safety measure (needing only a qualified majority to pass) rather than as a social policy measure (needing unanimity). In its judgment, the European Court of Justice (ECJ) rejected Britain's challenge by ruling that the principal aim of the directive was, indeed, to promote the health and safety of workers (for that reason the Court struck down the directive's provision that the minimum weekly rest day should be a Sunday: Why, the Court asked, was Sunday more relevant to the health and safety of workers than any other day of the week?).[9]

The SEA also obliged the Commission to endeavor "to develop the dialogue between management and labor at Community level which could, if the two sides consider it desirable, lead to relations based on agreement" (Article 118b, now Article 139). This put an additional stamp of approval on the "Val Duchesse process," begun in 1985 when the Commission convened a meeting in Val Duchesse outside Brussels to encourage the "social partners" to develop a working relationship in order to provide an informal input into the EC's legislative process. Management is represented at the EU level by the Union of Industrial Employers' Confederations of Europe (UNICE); labor by the European Trade Union Confederation (ETUC). UNICE has always been more coherent, better organized, and far more affluent than ETUC. Indeed, the Commission has consistently bolstered ETUC in order to provide a counterweight on the labor side to UNICE on the management side. The European Center of Public Enterprises (CEEP), representing public servants, is the third of the EU-recognized social partners.

The SEA had an indirect impact on the European Social Fund (ESF): The member states' commitment in the SEA to economic and social cohesion led them in 1988 to overhaul and substantially increase the structural funds. By acquiring new missions and more money, the ESF was a beneficiary of that reform. Thus the ESF became an instrument used to fight long-term unemployment and facilitate the integration of young people into the workforce, largely through vocational training and subsidies for recruitment in newly created jobs and for the creation of self-employment opportunities. The ESF's role in promoting social and economic cohesion is discussed in this chapter in this section on cohesion.

The Social Charter

In an effort to ameliorate the possible adverse effects of economic liberalization and to counter criticism that completion of the single market by the end of 1992 would benefit only businesspeople, in 1988 Commission president Jacques Delors—a man of the left and a former trade union official—began what he called a "careful consideration of [the single market's] social consequences." Delors explored the social dimension of the 1992 goal, calling it one of the SEA's priorities and a "key to the success of the large market."[10] With the obvious exception of British prime minister Margaret Thatcher—a woman of the right and a union buster—most government leaders, whether Social Democrats or Christian Democrats, supported Delors. Some sympathized with the ideological underpinnings of a social dimension and saw an EC-level initiative as a way to improve social policy at home without losing competitiveness abroad. They also feared "social dumping," the possibility that member states with higher labor costs would lose market share to other member states with lower labor costs or, worse, that firms would relocate from the former to the latter.

With the single market well on track and the economy booming, political support for an active social policy began to gather speed. Meeting in Hanover in June 1988, the European Council stressed the social dimension's relevance for the 1992 program. The presidency conclusions noted that as the internal market had to be conceived "in such a manner as to benefit all our people," it was necessary to improve working conditions, living standards, protection of health and safety, access to vocational training, and dialogue between the two sides of industry.[11]

Buoyed by the European Council's support, the Commission attempted to give substance to the social dimension in a working paper released in September 1988.[12] Using a format similar to its famous White Paper on the single market, the Commission outlined the intellectual and economic rationale for a social dimension and listed eighty possible measures (but without a timetable for implementation). Proposals covered the familiar and the new with an emphasis on creating conditions necessary to bring about worker mobility, an essential attribute of an integrated market.

Inspired by similar declarations from the Council of Europe, the International Labor Organization, and the OECD and eager to dramatize the single market's social dimension, Delors proposed a charter of basic social rights, asking the Economic and Social Committee (ESC) for its opinion. Although less concerned about making a symbolic declaration than about taking concrete measures to protect social rights without lowering economic performance, the ESC's report contributed to the political momentum behind Delors's initiative; so, too, did the French government's determination to push social policy during its 1989 Council presidency. In October of that year the Commission produced the *Community Charter of the Fundamental Social Rights of Workers (Social Charter)*. Despite more pressing issues, such as discussions about economic and monetary union and reaction to events in Central and Eastern Europe, eleven of the twelve heads of state and government adopted the Social Charter at the Strasbourg summit in December 1989 (Thatcher was the lone dissenter).[13]

Following a preamble that outlined the development of social policy at the European level, the Social Charter listed twelve categories of workers' fundamental social rights:

- freedom of movement
- employment and remuneration

- improvement of living and working conditions
- social protection
- freedom of association and collective bargaining
- vocational training
- equal treatment for men and women
- information, consultation, and participation for workers
- health protection and safety at the workplace
- protection of children and adolescents
- protection of elderly persons
- protection of disabled persons

According to the social affairs commissioner, the Social Charter formed "a keystone of the social dimension in the construction of Europe, in the spirit of the Treaty of Rome supplemented by the Single European Act."[14] Being entirely hortatory, however, it lacked binding legal force. Nevertheless, the charter's importance should not be underestimated: In addition to identifying the EC's social agenda during and beyond the single market program, the Social Charter had political support at the highest possible level.

Yet the Social Charter never had much popular appeal. Despite its potential to improve the lives of millions of Europeans, from the outset it seemed too lofty and remote. Persistently high unemployment contrasted with the charter's rhetoric and threatened to erode popular support for the single market program itself. Potential popular disaffection offered a powerful impetus for member states to focus on the nuts and bolts of social policy in the late 1980s. Thus although it endorsed the Social Charter at the Strasbourg summit, the European Council stressed that "integration of unemployed young persons into working life and the fight against long-term unemployment . . . [partly through] vocational training . . . constitute decisive aspects of the Community social dimension."[15]

Hence there was a political imperative to put legislative flesh on the Social Charter as soon as possible. Indeed, the charter's brief concluding section called on the Commission to submit proposals to implement those rights for which the EC had competence to enact legislation. Sensitive to the subsidiarity principle, the Commission was careful not to encroach upon aspects of social policy that could best be dealt with at the national level. Nor did it want governments to use subsidiarity as a way to avoid legislation, either in national capitals or in Brussels. Accordingly, the Commission's "action program" sought to strike a balance between what was desirable, what was appropriate, and what was feasible at the European level.[16]

Of the action program's forty-seven measures, only seventeen were new. The predominance of preexisting measures testified to the EC's poor record of social policy legislation. Inevitably, familiar proposals dealing with industrial democracy, women's issues, and vocational training resurfaced in the action program; their proponents hoped that the momentum generated by the Social Charter would somehow carry them through. Aware of the huge stumbling block posed by the unanimity requirement for most social legislation, the Commission resorted in many cases to instruments other than legally binding directives or recommendations. The Social Charter also called on the Commission to prepare an annual report on its implementation. Those reports—the first of which appeared in December 1991—are an indispensable guide to the state of social policy in the EU.

The Commission soon prepared proposals on virtually all of the measures listed in the action program. In keeping with the principle of subsidiarity, only twenty-eight of the Commission's proposals required legislation at the EU level. The Council's treatment of those measures demonstrated the continuing controversy surrounding social policy, notwithstanding the rhetoric of successive summits. By the end of 1992 the Council had adopted only fifteen of the proposals, resulting in eight directives (including two based on unanimity) concerned primarily with the less contentious question of health and safety at work. As the Commission coyly put it in its second report on the Social Charter, "Discussions on most of the proposals for directives on important matters have not made sufficient progress to enable a final text to be adopted."[17] In other words, at least one member state—usually but not always Britain—had prevented the Council from reaching unanimity on key draft directives covering such issues as the length of the workweek, atypical work, European works councils, and transport for the disabled.

The Social Charter and ensuing action program represented the high point of EU activism in the realm of social policy. Far from being an impartial civil service, the Commission had consistently acted as a lobbyist and pushed a progressive agenda. The Commission in general, and the social affairs directorate-general (DG V) in particular, had cogent political and bureaucratic reasons to advance EC social policy. For its part, the EP traditionally took a strong stand in support of women's rights, industrial democracy, and other staples of EU social policy. The EP's Social Affairs Committee produced numerous reports on social issues focusing especially on improving the conditions of the most vulnerable groups in society: the disabled, migrant workers, and the poor. The Economic and Social Committee had been established in order to institutionalize discussions between workers' and employers' representatives on a range of social and economic issues. Apart from its involvement in early deliberations on the Social Charter, however, the ESC was conspicuous by its absence from the high-level social dialogue launched in 1985 and by its marginal impact on the EC's social legislation.

The Social Protocol

Given Britain's intense opposition to the Social Charter in particular and to social policy in general, it was not surprising that the 1991 IGC on political union almost foundered on the social chapter, a package of social policy provisions, based on the Social Charter, that other member states wanted to include in the TEU. Prime Minister John Major adamantly opposed the social chapter at the Maastricht summit in December 1991. Realizing the extent of Major's intransigence, Delors (using German chancellor Helmut Kohl as an intermediary) suggested removing the social chapter entirely from the treaty and replacing it with a protocol on social policy (the social protocol) attached to the treaty.

All twelve member states subsequently signed the social protocol, which authorized eleven of them (Britain being the exception) to proceed along the lines laid down in the Social Charter and to use the EU's institutions and decisionmaking procedures for that purpose. Britain would not take part in relevant Council deliberations or decisionmaking; in such cases the Council would decide by a qualified majority recalculated to take account of Britain's nonparticipation. Needless to say, any legislation adopted via the social protocol would not apply to Britain. However, Britain remained subject to the social policy provisions of the Treaty of Rome as revised by the SEA and by the TEU (apart from the social protocol). The three member states that joined the EU in 1995 happily subscribed to the social protocol; the threshold for a qualified majority in the Council with respect to social policy decisionmaking was recalculated accordingly.

The social protocol included

- revised policy objectives, such as the promotion of employment
- an extension of qualified majority voting procedures to cover proposals on working conditions, consultation of workers, and equality between men and women with regard to labor market opportunities and treatment at work
- unanimous decisionmaking in areas such as social security, termination of employment, and third-country worker protection
- a greater role in the formulation of social policy for the employers' and employees' representatives

The social protocol also reinforced the role of the social partners and provided for collective agreements at the European level. Specifically, if management and labor reached an agreement on certain social policy issues, the Commission could submit that agreement to the Council, which could enact it into Community law by qualified majority vote.

The social protocol's possible implications for European integration were a cause of great concern in the early 1990s. The protocol apparently set a precedent for a two-tier EU, a development inherent as well in the treaty's provisions for EMU. There were additional fears that Britain's exclusion from certain labor legislation would distort competition and have a negative impact on the single market. Fears of social dumping seemed justified even before ratification of the TEU when Hoover announced its decision to relocate a manufacturing plant from France to Scotland (in fact, the decision was based on a variety of considerations).[18]

Concern about the political and economic implications of Britain's exclusion from the social protocol dampened the Commission's ardor for using it to introduce new social policy legislation. Thus the Council enacted only two directives under the auspices of the social protocol. The first, on European works councils (mechanisms for worker information and consultation in large companies), followed the social partners' failure to negotiate a collective agreement on the subject. The Commission then submitted a new legislative proposal that sailed through the Social Affairs Council, in which Britain did not participate. The proposal was adopted in September 1994 (94/45/EC). The lesson of the works councils directive was not lost on the social partners. The next time they had an opportunity to reach a collective agreement under the social protocol—on establishing a worker's right, regardless of gender, to unpaid parental leave or time off for other important family reasons—they did so within the requisite nine-month period. Their agreement of December 1995 to a minimum three months unpaid leave in all member states (except Britain, of course) was quickly translated into law by a Council directive of March 1996 (96/34/EC).

Because these directives did not apply to Britain, their enactment emphasized both the peculiarity of EU social policy and Britain's increasing isolation in the EU. Other member states wanted to end the anomaly of the social protocol at the 1996–1997 IGC but knew that there was no hope of doing so as long as Britain's Conservative Party remained in power. Labour's victory in the May 1997 general election settled the issue. Within days, the new government announced its support for bringing the social protocol into the treaty proper, thereby ending both British exceptionalism and differentiated integration with respect to social policy. The Amsterdam Treaty's incorporation of the social protocol into the EC treaty restored the unity and coherence of EU social policy. The government also announced its willingness to abide by the two directives adopted under the social protocol, prompting the Commission to introduce proposals for legislation to extend the European works councils and parental leave directives to Britain.

The Changing Nature of EU Social Policy

The Labour government's embrace of the social protocol implied a sea change in Britain's approach. Yet the new government's position on the substance of social policy was not that different from that of the old government. Whereas the Conservatives opposed social policy on ideological grounds and had painted themselves into a corner politically, Labour took a pragmatic approach. Labour did not like every aspect of EU social policy but saw no reason for British exclusion from an important area of EU activity.

Other member states had also grown more pragmatic in their approach to social policy. By the mid-1990s, with unemployment at the top of the EU's agenda, there was little support any more for old-fashioned social policy. The Commission lost much of its zeal following Delors's departure, emphasizing instead the flexible and employment-enhancing nature of selective social policy measures. Significantly, the Amsterdam Treaty's revised title on employment (Title VII TEC) avoided "anything that might smack of a social approach to employment" and was "inserted next to [the title on] economic and monetary union, not social policy."[19] Under the circumstances, the Labour government's acceptance of the social protocol was an easy way to repudiate the previous government's EU policy without endorsing a radical social policy agenda.

A more restrained approach was clearly evident in the Commission's 1994 white paper on the development of social policy in the period 1995–1999.[20] In keeping with prevailing concerns over employment and competitiveness, the white paper argued rather defensively that social policy was not an obstacle to economic growth but was a key element of it. The white paper's main themes were job creation, labor mobility, equal opportunity, and the integration of social and economic policies. In its subsequent social action program, the Commission was careful not to propose a lengthy new legislative agenda.[21] By relying less on legal instruments to protect and strengthen workers' rights and more on discussion and conciliation, the program signaled not only a shift in the direction of EU social policy but also the Commission's increasing aversion to interventionism. Despite its incorporation of the social protocol and despite also including an explicit reference to fundamental social rights, the Amsterdam Treaty further reflects the toning down of EU social policy. Thus the social protocol was incorporated into the treaty largely unchanged, and unanimity was still required in certain policy areas.

EDUCATION

Despite its economic importance for the EU as a whole and its political potential for inculcating a sense of "Europeanness," education remains predominantly the preserve of national governments. Nevertheless, the TEU formally introduced education and youth programs as new areas of EU competence. According to Article 149 TEC, the EU is to support and supplement action taken by member states in areas such as cooperation between educational establishments, student and teacher mobility, youth exchanges, and language teaching. To that end, the Council adopts "incentive measures" using the codecision procedure and makes recommendations via qualified majority voting on proposals from the Commission.

Formal involvement in education policy came on the heels of highly successful educational and exchange programs organized by the EU since the late 1980s, including

- Erasmus (European Community Action Scheme for the Mobility of University Students: This program encourages student and faculty exchange. Since its inception in 1987, the Erasmus program has involved over 75,000 students and 1,500 higher-education institutions in all parts of the EU. The program offers grants to facilitate exchanges, curriculum development, and a badly needed course credit-transfer system.
- Lingua (Action Program to Promote Foreign Language Competence in the European Community): To a great extent an Erasmus companion program, Lingua provides financial support to encourage second- and third-language acquisition.
- Tempus (Trans-European Mobility Scheme for University Students: This program links universities in Eastern and Western Europe and the United States. Tempus funds joint research projects in a wide variety of disciplines.

Since 1995, these educational programs have been organized and funded under the umbrella of the so-called Socrates program.

COHESION POLICY

Cohesion—the reduction of economic and social disparities between richer and poorer regions—is a fundamental objective of the EU. Not only do such disparities threaten the integrity of the single market and EMU but their existence is incompatible with the sense of community and solidarity that supposedly infuses the movement for European integration. Indeed, an unusual blend of idealism and pragmatism has motivated the quest for cohesion, especially since the EC's Mediterranean enlargement in the 1980s. Yet concerns about the management and utility of structural and cohesion funds (the means by which cohesion is promoted) and the possible cost of cohesion in an EU encompassing the economically underdeveloped countries of Central and Eastern Europe have cast the future of cohesion policy in doubt.

Cohesion policy—encompassing regional policy (to reduce spatial disparities, regenerate old industrial areas, and assist rural development), aspects of social policy (to combat long-term unemployment and foster vocational education and training), and a small part of the Common Agricultural Policy (to assist rural development)—developed relatively late in the EU's history. The preamble of the Treaty of Rome mentioned the need to reduce regional disparities, but the treaty itself included few redistributive mechanisms. The European Social Fund (ESF) and the European Investment bank (EIB), both established by the treaty, were not intended primarily to promote cohesion but were nonetheless expected to help the EC's poorer regions. Similarly, Article 92.3 (now Article 87.3) TEC declared that national subsidies (state aids) were compatible with the common market if they promoted "the economic development of areas where the standard of living is abnormally low or where there is serious underemployment."

Apart from those concessions, the prevailing attitude in 1957—enunciated in Article 2 (unchanged) TEC—was that the common market would, of its own accord, "promote throughout the Community a harmonious development of economic activities" and thereby lessen disparities between regions. After all, the treaty was a package deal to distribute losses and gains among member states, not to redistribute resources between rich and poor regions. In any case, with the notable exception of the south of Italy, regional disparities in the EC of six member states were not as striking as in the enlarged EC of nine, ten, and twelve member states or in the EU of fifteen member states.

Successive enlargements therefore increased regional disparities with regard to income, employment, education and training, productivity, and infrastructure. The EC's growing regional differences manifested themselves in a north-south divide with Ireland included in the southern camp. The spatial characteristics of the EC's regional imbalance conformed to the core-periphery concept used by economists and social scientists to analyze inequalities between or among regions. As a result, the EC built its structural policy largely on the assumption of a poor periphery (Scotland, Ireland, Portugal, central and southern Spain, Corsica, southern Italy, Greece, and—after 1990—eastern Germany) and a rich core (southern England, northeastern France, the low countries, northwestern Germany, and northern Italy).

Protocol 30 of Ireland's accession treaty (1972) emphasized the need to end regional disparities in the EC, but the European Regional Development Fund (ERDF) was established only in 1975, largely to compensate Britain for its poor return from the CAP. The EC began coordinating member states' regional aid schemes in the late 1970s, although its own regional aid policy remained rudimentary. The extent of the EC's failure to redress regional imbalances became more apparent after Greek accession in 1981 and in the run-up to Spanish and Portuguese accession in 1986. Concern that the EC's existing disadvantaged regions in southern Italy and

Greece would suffer as a result of Iberian enlargement sparked a row in early 1985 over Integrated Mediterranean Programs (IMPs). By taking personal responsibility for resolving the IMP issue, newly installed Commission president Delors signaled the enhanced importance of structural policy during his administration.

Economic, political, and moral arguments underpinned the Commission's efforts to promote cohesion in the aftermath of the EC's second and third enlargements. Delors had long been aware of a growing rich-poor divide in the EC, which the accession of Spain and Portugal would greatly exacerbate. The Commission's program for 1985 cautioned that regional disparities "could become a permanent source of political confrontation" and urged that the south be given "a fairer share of the benefits of economic development."[22] Delors warned the EP in March 1985 that enlargement negotiations with Greece, Spain, and Portugal had "revealed a tension in Europe which is, let's face it, a tension between north and south. It stems not only from financial problems but from a lack of understanding, from a clash of culture, which seems to be promoting certain countries to turn their backs on the solidarity pact that should be one of the cornerstones of the Community, solidarity being conceived not in terms of assistance, but rather as an expression of the common-weal, contributing to the vigor of the European entity."[23]

The single market program greatly boosted the Commission's and the poorer countries' arguments in favor of a vigorous cohesion policy. The gradual worsening of regional disparities since the 1960s suggested that market liberalization would broaden rather than narrow the EC's rich-poor divide. Advocates of a stronger structural policy exploited uncertainty about the distributional consequences of the single market program to press their claims for cohesion. Fear that the single market would make rich regions richer and poor regions poorer and that the dynamic of market liberalization would intensify existing disparities led to an explicit link between cohesion policy and the 1992 program. In the Commission's words, "The reduction of disparities and the strengthening of economic and social cohesion should go hand in hand with the implementation of the large internal market."[24]

Apart from the "solidarity principle," the likely economic and political impact of greater regional disequilibrium strengthened the case for cohesion. The EC would not prosper, let alone survive, if excessive disparities caused poorer member states to block legislation and impede completion of the single market. Accordingly, during the 1985 IGC the Commission advocated a substantial redistribution of resources to the EC's less prosperous regions. Although one of the attractions of the single market program for a financially strapped EC was its relative lack of cost, the Commission's emphasis on cohesion raised the prospect of a sizable budgetary hike. The IGC deferred until later a decision about increasing the amount of structural funds, EIB loans, and other forms of assistance for poorer regions but committed member states to promoting economic cohesion and reducing regional diversity.

As a result, the SEA added a title on economic and social cohesion to the TEC (now Title XVII). This title committed the EC to "reducing disparities between the various regions and the backwardness of the least favored nations," called for coordination between other EC policies and cohesion, and obliged the Council to reform the structural funds within a year of the SEA's implementation on the basis of a Commission proposal. Delors subsequently described the revised treaty's provisions on structural policy as one of the SEA's "fundamental objectives."[25]

Delors I and Reform of the Structural Funds

In February 1987 the Commission introduced a five-year budgetary package to control agricultural spending, increase the EC's own resources, and impose budgetary discipline. The so-called Delors I package also proposed reform of the structural funds (the financial instruments of cohesion policy), a doubling in real terms of the resources available through them (making a total of ECU 60 billion from 1989 to 1993), and a particular focus on regions with a per capita income below 75 percent of the EC average. Just as Delors had used the voluminous Cecchini Report to bolster his arguments in support of the single market, he now cited the Padoa-Schioppa Report to make a compelling case for reform of the structural funds. Published in April 1987, the report assessed the "implications for the economic system of the Community of . . . [the] adoption of the internal market program and the latest enlargement." One of its major conclusions pointed out "the serious risks of aggravated regional imbalances in the course of market liberalization" and, in a memorable phrase, warned that "any easy extrapolation of 'invisible hand' ideas into the real world of regional economics in the process of market opening would be unwarranted in the light of economic history and theory."[26]

This was grist to Delors's mill and strengthened the southern countries' determination to win a sizable redistribution of resources. As a staunch Conservative, however, Thatcher instinctively rejected Padoa-Schioppa's advocacy of guiding the "invisible hand." In her view, market liberalization throughout the EC would foster rather than hinder economic development in the southern member states. Kohl sympathized with the southern states but knew that Germany would have to contribute most of the proposed budgetary increase. Thus the battle lines were drawn for a protracted dispute that, thanks to Kohl's largesse, the European Council eventually resolved at the special Brussels summit in February 1988. A delighted Delors called the European Council's decision to double the structural funds by 1993 "a second Marshall Plan."[27] Despite Thatcher's misgivings, the northern countries' endorsement of the Delors I package demonstrated their acceptance of redistributional solidarity as part of market integration.

Having agreed to double the combined size of the three structural funds—the ERDF, the ESF, and the Guidance Section of the CAP's European Agricultural Guarantee and Guidance Fund (EAGGF)—the Council adopted regulations in June and December 1988 reforming the EC's cohesion policy. Substantially increasing the structural funds was not enough to redress regional imbalances. As Delors told the EP in January 1988, "Cohesion is not simply a matter of throwing money at problems. . . . It implies rather a willingness to act at Community level to redress the disparities between regions and between different social groups."[28] Accordingly, the 1988 reform sought to turn the structural funds into effective instruments of economic development. That transformation involved welding the EC's regional policy and aspects of EC social and agricultural policies into a powerful mechanism to narrow the north-south divide.

The 1988 reform radically revised structural policy by introducing a number of new principles and procedures and strengthening existing ones.

- *Additionality:* Structural funds must add to, not substitute for, member state public expenditure.
- *Partnership:* The partnership principle is the key to involving regions, not just national governments, in formulating and implementing structural policy. Because EC operations complement corresponding national measures, there must be close consultation and cooperation among the Commission, member states, and regional or local bodies at all stages of a structural program. Eligible member state plans for regional assistance are incorporated into Community Support Frameworks (CSFs): contractual agreements between the Commission and national and regional authorities. CSFs set out the program's priorities, type of aid, methods of financing, and so on. Moreover, the Commission can take the initiative and propose that member states and regions participate in operations of particular interest to it. Operational programs usually last five years.
- *Programing:* The structural funds reform involved a major switch from project-related assistance to program assistance and decentralized management. This change put the emphasis on planning and continuity rather than on ad hoc activities. Under the old system the Commission dealt with thousands of separate projects; under the new system the Commission oversees a much smaller number of CSFs.
- *Concentration:* Instead of spreading the EU's financial resources widely and ineffectively, structural funds were refocused on a few major objectives. Functional and geographic concentration restricts assistance to five priorities:

  Objective 1. Assist "regions whose development is lagging behind." These are regions with a per capita GDP of less than 75 percent of the EU average and include all of Greece and Portugal, large parts of Spain, and southern Italy, Corsica, and the French overseas departments. Technically the island of Ireland is still an Objective 1 region, although by the late 1990s the Irish Republic's GDP approached 90 percent of the EU average. Objective 1 regions account for about 20 percent of the EU's population. Funding source: ERDF, ESF, EAGGF Guidance Section, EIB, and the European Coal and Steel Community (ECSC). The EU spends almost 80 percent of the ERDF (by far the largest structural fund) on Objective 1 projects.

Objective 2. Promote economic conversion and modernization in declining industrial areas, including about sixty sites in nine member states, notably Britain, Spain, France, and Germany. The EU mostly helps small and medium-sized enterprises in new economic sectors. Funding source: ERDF, ESF, EIB, and ECSC.

Objective 3. Combat long-term unemployment by assisting workers over twenty-five, anywhere in the EU, who have been unemployed for more than one year. Funding source: ESF, EIB, and ECSC.

Objective 4. Integrate young people, anywhere in the EU, into the workforce. Funding source: ESF, EIB, and ECSC.

Objective 5. Adjust agricultural structures (with a view to CAP reform, aims to adjust production, processing, and marketing structures in agriculture and forestry). Funding source: EAGGF Guidance Fund.

The 1988 structural funds reforms had political as well as economic implications, as the principles of concentration and partnership allowed the Commission to work closely with regional authorities, often bypassing national governments. The Commission used these contacts "to act as a lever for regions that are not yet traditionally recognized"[29] and to promote the emergence of new "Euroregions" that straddle national frontiers. Most regions opened offices in Brussels and became active in the Assembly of European Regions, a Brussels-based interest group. Increasingly, therefore, the formulation and implementation of cohesion policy strengthened regionalism in Europe and contributed to the emergence of multilevel governance in the EU.[30]

The Treaty on European Union

Moves toward EMU in the late 1980s raised concerns among the poorer countries similar to those prevalent at the outset of the single market program. For Delors, the architect of structural policy reform, EMU was inconceivable without a sizable increase in assistance for disadvantaged regions. The 1989 Delors Report pointed out that because EMU would deprive member states of their ability to devalue, it could worsen the balance-of-payments difficulties of poorer countries. Indeed, the need for member states to harmonize their budgetary policies, coupled with a loss of exchange rate flexibility, portended serious problems for less-developed regions.[31]

During the IGC on political union, Ireland, Spain, and Portugal attached the highest priority to strengthening structural policy and called for a new framework to enable the putative EU to promote cohesion in the context of closer political and economic integration. Predictably, the three countries asserted that in the absence of mechanisms to redistribute the benefits of EMU, the more central and prosperous regions would gain disproportionately. Using moral, political, and economic arguments honed during the Delors I debate, the poorer countries claimed that failure to meet their demands could undermine the EU's foundations. Felipe González, the Spanish prime minister and the poor countries' standard-bearer, fought tenaciously in the run-up to the Maastricht summit to win a greater commitment to cohesion in the TEU.

From the poorer countries' point of view, the redistributive provisions of the TEU were highly satisfactory. Articles 2 and 3 (unchanged) TEC, which enumerated the EU's tasks and activities, specifically mentioned cohesion. Amendments to Article 130a–e (now Articles 158–162) TEC listed rural development as an objective of structural policy; stipulated that the Commission must report every three years on progress made toward achieving cohesion; and provided a framework for extending and deepening EU policies and actions to promote cohesion in parallel with the degree of political, economic, and monetary integration in the EU.

Article 130d (now Article 161) TEC stipulated that the Council, acting unanimously on a proposal from the Commission and after obtaining the EP's assent, would set up the Cohesion Fund by the end of December 1993 to contribute to projects on the environment and on transport infrastructure. The purpose of the Cohesion Fund was to reconcile the apparent contradiction in the treaty between the budgetary rigor necessary for convergence and the budgetary lenience inherent in cohesion.

At Spain's insistence, a special protocol supplemented the treaty's cohesion provisions. Apart from agreeing to review the size of the structural funds and to permit greater flexibility to meet new needs, the protocol specified that the Cohesion Fund would be for the benefit of member states with a per capita GDP of less than 90 percent of the EU average and a program designed to achieve convergence. In effect, that meant Spain, Portugal, Ireland, and Greece. Without mentioning a figure, the protocol earmarked 85–90 percent of the fund to support environmental and transport projects.

The TEU also reinforced the trend toward regionalism in the EU by establishing a new consultative body, the Committee of the Regions (COR).

Delors II

In a repeat of its 1987 performance, in February 1992 the Commission sent the Council a budget package for the years 1993–1999.[32] In order to meet the additional cost of implementing the TEU, the Commission proposed increasing the EC's budgetary ceiling from 1.2 to 1.37 percent of GDP by 1997 (an annual budgetary growth rate of 5 percent), including an allocation of ECU 11 billion for cohesion. The Commission also proposed improving structural fund operations. Together with the Cohesion Fund, a projected 66 percent increase in Objective 1 funding would boost EU financial support for Spain, Portugal, Ireland, and Greece by 100 percent. Some of the new spending on Objective 1 would go to the five new German states (the former East Germany), which had received a special structural funds appropriation for 1991–1993. Other objectives would receive a 50 percent increase in funding. Assistance for "regions dependent on fishing" would become Objective 5(a) (fisheries), and Objective 5(b) would be established to support certain "rural areas" in the EU.

Circumstances in 1992 were hardly propitious for such an ambitious proposal. In its first-ever Council presidency, Portugal made little headway on Delors II. Meeting in Lisbon in June, the European Council agreed only to postpone a decision on it until the Edinburgh summit six months later. Britain, in the Council presidency for the second half of 1992, had little sympathy with Delors II and fretted about the future of its budget rebate. A deepening economic recession, and Germany's effort to meet the costs of unification, put the future of Delors II further in doubt.

Ironically, the TEU ratification crisis—another gloomy development—may have saved Delors II. Battered by a year of economic and political setbacks, government leaders wanted to establish at Edinburgh their ability to act decisively in the EU's interest. As one observer noted, it was imperative for the EU "to avoid the high costs of a failure whose repercussions would have extended well beyond the budgetary arena."[33] The Delors II package was also an ideal opportunity to demonstrate that redistributional solidarity had survived the year's setbacks. Once again, González represented the southern countries' interests, and after intense bargaining at the Edinburgh summit, Kohl conceded on most issues. The new financial perspective more than doubled EU assistance for the least-prosperous countries (to €30 billion [30 billion euros] in 1999). As the southern member states must have known, with the Central and Eastern European states knocking on the EU's door, Delors II was probably their last chance to get a big share of the EU budget. Paradoxically, in view of imminent cutbacks in cohesion spending, as a result of the accession of Finland and Sweden the EU created another new priority—Objective 6—applicable from January 1, 1995, for the development of regions in those countries with very low population densities.

Beyond Delors II

Structural and cohesion funds account for more than one-third of the EU's annual budget of nearly €100 billion. Structural funds have risen from

ECU 18 billion in 1992 to €31 billion in 1999 (at 1992 prices). The Cohesion Fund cost €14.5 billion between 1994 and 1999.

Is the money well spent? Apart from problems with the management of structural and cohesion funds, economists disagree on the usefulness of cohesion policy. Empirical evidence is difficult to distill because of the multifaceted nature of economic growth and decline. Thus a comprehensive Commission report on cohesion policy, covering the period 1983–1993, concluded that the north-south economic divide in Europe is closing, but the gap between rich and poor regions is growing, notably in Britain.[34] But the poorer member states' economic improvement is due to a number of factors, not least EU-wide growth in the late 1980s and macroeconomic policy reforms in the mid-1990s. Thanks to annual growth well in excess of 5 percent and to sound economic management, Ireland's per capita GDP rose from 63.6 percent of the EU average in 1983 to 89.9 percent in 1995. Spain moved up from 70.5 percent in 1983 to 76.2 percent in 1995, a slight drop from 1993. Portugal climbed from 55.1 to 68.4 percent, but Greece raised its per capita income only from 61.9 to 64.3 percent despite receiving hundreds of millions of ECUs in aid. The key to economic development in the poorer member states would appear to be a combination of sensible macroeconomic policies, a favorable international economic climate, large allocations of well-managed transfers from Brussels, and closer coordination in the formulation and implementation of regional policy at the European and national levels.

Yet the future of cohesion policy is in doubt. Rich member states resent generous financial transfers to countries that either are doing well economically (Ireland has the highest growth rate in the EU) or seemingly abuse regional aid (Greece has a reputation for fraud and mismanagement). The Commission's arguments that cohesion is working and that net contributors to the budget such as Germany and the Netherlands benefit from extra public works contracts and other business in the recipient countries are unlikely to assuage cash-strapped "donor" governments.

The cost of cohesion in an enlarged EU with numerous poor Central and Eastern European member states is potentially prohibitive. Nevertheless, in *Agenda 2000,* its strategy for enlargement and internal policy reform, the Commission proposed keeping EU funding for economic and social cohesion at 0.46 percent of the EU's GDP, amounting to €275 billion over the period 2000–2006; €45 billion would be earmarked for the new member states—which are likely to join only toward the end of the financial perspective—including €7 billion in preaccession aid. The Commission also proposed reducing the structural fund objectives to three: a strengthened Objective 1, a redefined Objective 2, and a new Objective 3 (developing a strategy for human resources). In addition to some badly needed administrative and managerial reforms, the Commission further recommended reducing the proportion of the EU population covered by the structural funds from 51 percent to between 35 and 40 percent.

Although the Commission's scenario was modest by the standards of many other estimates of the financial impact of enlargement, *Agenda 2000* generated controversy in existing and prospective member states. Net contributors to the EU budget want to pay less; recipients of large-scale donations from the structural and cohesion funds want to maintain or increase their share; and prospective member states want more than the EU is likely to offer. The inevitable row over future cohesion funding began in earnest in March 1998 when the Commission followed up on *Agenda 2000* with precise legislative proposals. Almost every member state—not only the poorer ones—pleaded for special treatment. With federal elections looming and popular dislike of the EU running high, Kohl denounced any reform of cohesion policy that could reduce financial transfers to eastern Germany.

Gerhard Schröder, Kohl's successor, kept up the pressure for reform and also to protect Germany's interests. Schröder's effectiveness was impaired, however, by his relative inexperience and by Germany's presidency of the Council during the last stages of the *Agenda 2000* negotiations (as Council president, Germany had to moderate its own position while striving to end the negotiations by the agreed-upon deadline of March 1999). As a result, Schröder made generous concessions to Spain and Britain during the final negotiating session at the Berlin summit of March 24–25. Despite expectations to the contrary, the *Agenda 2000* agreement therefore failed to bring about major reform of cohesion policy. With enlargement still several years away, member states were not sufficient pressure to bit the political bullet and radically overhaul one of the EU's most costly and controversial policies.

JUSTICE AND HOME AFFAIRS

Cooperation among member states on Justice and Home Affairs (JHA)—a range of activities pertaining to internal security—began in the mid-1970s in response to a wave of terrorism in Western Europe. Based on their experience of foreign policy cooperation, member states decided to set up a committee of senior officials from national ministries to share information on terrorist organizations and activities. By virtue of its mission and the secrecy inherent in security cooperation, the so-called Trevi group worked unobtrusively on the margins of the EC.

It is impossible to assess the contribution of the Trevi group to antiterrorism. But procedurally at least it brought justice and interior ministries into the fold of European integration, albeit on an informal and intergovernmental basis. There was something of a spillover effect as the Trevi group extended its scope from terrorism to other transnational security threats, including organized crime and soccer hooliganism. Nevertheless, the group remained peripheral to the EC's main activities and methods of operation.

That began to change in the mid-1980s with the launch of the single market program. The Single European Act of 1986 called for completion of the single market—"an area without internal frontiers, in which the free movement of goods, persons, services and capital is ensured"—by the end of 1992. Of these "four freedoms," free movement of people was particularly problematic because it implied the introduction of a host of difficult accompanying measures dealing with political asylum, immigration, and visas for third-country nationals as well as better police networks and external border measures directed against terrorism, drug smuggling, and other criminal activity. Such measures—unlike those necessary to implement the free movement of goods, services, and capital—were mostly unknown territory for the EC. Having laid some of the groundwork for police cooperation, government ministers asked the Trevi group to consider the broader security implications of a frontier-free EC. However, the large and equally contentious area of immigration and asylum had yet to be addressed comprehensively.

Schengen

Buoyed by general enthusiasm in the mid-1980s for deeper integration, the EC's geographically core countries (France, Germany, Belgium, the Netherlands, and Luxembourg) took the first steps toward abolishing all frontier formalities between them. First France and Germany signed an agreement in July 1984 to reduce border checks; then the five countries signed a more far-reaching agreement in June 1985, in the town of Schengen in Luxembourg. The so-called Schengen agreement launched a lengthy series of meetings and negotiations to identify and implement the numerous measures to abolish internal frontiers and establish a common external border around the signatory states. Major challenges included setting visa requirements, dealing with asylum applications, combating illegal immigration, improving police cooperation in order to counter terrorism and other crime, and physically reconfiguring airports in order to segregate passengers traveling within Schengenland from those on other flights.

The subsequent SEA with its call for free movement should have made Schengen redundant. Indeed, the EC established an Ad Hoc Group on Immigration (under Trevi) at the end of 1986 to plan the abolition of internal border controls. But three member states—Britain (for reasons of history and national sovereignty), Ireland (because it wanted to keep a common travel area with Britain), and Denmark (because of the possible impact of free movement in the EC on free movement among Nordic countries)—did not subscribe fully to the SEA's call for unrestricted travel.

To be precise, they subscribed to the free movement of member state nationals, but not nationals of third countries. As it would have been impossible to distinguish between member state and non–member state nationals without checks at intra-EC borders, Britain, Ireland, and Denmark insisted on keeping some frontier controls even after completion of the single market. As a result the Schengen states continued their preparations to establish an area inside the EC in which people could move freely. Here was a striking example of differentiated integration.

The other member states—those neither in the Schengen group nor opposed to free movement—wanted to join Schengen and resented their exclusion from it. Italy, the only original EC member state not in the group, was especially miffed. The Schengen countries held out the prospect of expanded membership, hoping that Schengen would eventually be incorporated into the EC itself. Yet they were reluctant to allow Italy, Greece, Portugal, and Spain into the fold until confident of those countries' willingness and ability to impose rigorous border checks.

It took nearly five years for the Schengen five to conclude a convention (also called Schengen II) to implement the measures necessary to ensure that "internal borders may be crossed at any point without any checks on persons being carried out" (Article 2). Key issues and features included the following:

- *Visas:* The convention aimed at harmonizing immigration law in order to devise a common list of third countries whose nationals needed a visa to enter Schengenland and common rules for granting or denying visas, as well as agreement on a common visa stamp or sticker.
- *Illegal immigration:* Given the size and nature of Schengen's external borders, combating illegal entry posed a large and potentially expensive challenge. Moreover, the expense of securing external borders would have to be shared by those countries (like Belgium and the Netherlands) whose borders diminished or disappeared because they were subsumed into a large free-travel area. The issue of illegal immigration grew increasingly sensitive in the late 1980s after the collapse of communism in Central and Eastern Europe, when a tide of illegal immigrants was expected to inundate the West.
- *Asylum:* For historical reasons (memories of Jews fleeing Germany and being denied refuge in other European countries were still vivid), asylum was a particularly sensitive issue on the Schengen agenda. There was little controversy about the definition of asylum or about how asylum seekers should be treated (EC member states had signed the relevant international agreements on the subject: the Geneva Convention and the New York Protocol). The main challenge was to prevent an individual from submitting more than one asylum request in more than one country, either serially or simultaneously. Accordingly, the Schengen Convention

included criteria to determine which state should deal with which asylum application. It also outlined a system for tracking asylum seekers within the Schengen area.

• *Police cooperation:* There was already a high degree of cooperation among Schengen police forces, although mostly on a bilateral and informal basis. Media coverage of the Schengen negotiations occasionally raised the specter of a common European police force snuffing out national sovereignty and disregarding individuals' rights. No national government contemplated a supranational police authority, although cooperation would have to include an EC-wide system for exchanging information and intelligence (this was the genesis of EUROPOL, the European police agency). Given the sensitivity surrounding police cooperation, especially at the operational level, provisions dealing with issues such as cross-border surveillance and "hot pursuit" were hedged with limitations and qualifications.

• *Judicial Cooperation:* Negotiations about judicial cooperation contained the same pitfalls as those about police cooperation, although the convention contained a number of provisions to increase contacts and strengthen cooperation among judicial authorities, especially on the sensitive issue of extradition.

• *Schengen Information System (SIS):* The Schengen Convention included provision for the Schengen Information System, headquartered in Strasbourg and linking relevant databases in participating states. Access to the SIS at border posts and other locations would allow officials to retrieve information quickly on missing persons, arrest warrants, false passports, stolen vehicles, and so on. Without the SIS, Schengen simply could not function. Yet the development of the SIS further alarmed the sovereignty-conscious as well as civil libertarians. Inevitably, strict privacy and confidentiality laws were put in place to govern the system's content and use. Apart from political and legal problems, the technical difficulty of linking so many different national systems delayed completion of the SIS and contributed to the delay in implementing the Schengen Convention.

• *Institutional Structure:* The Convention established an institutional structure (outside the EC framework) to manage its operation and future development, including an executive committee at the ministerial level, a central negotiating group of senior officials, and numerous working groups.

The Schengen Convention was to have come into effect in January 1990, three years before completion of the single market program. However, growing fears of mass immigration from Central and Eastern Europe prompted second thoughts about the abolition of member state controls. France announced that it would continue border checks on non-EC nationals (which, by implication, meant some border control of all individuals entering the country). Much to the relief of its Schengen partners, in December 1989 Germany postponed signing the convention because of uncertainty about the rights of East Germans to travel in the Schengen zone. After renewed negotiations the convention was eventually signed in June 1990, although its implementation was delayed for several years, partly for political reasons and partly because of the difficulty of organizing the SIS.

Thus by the time the single market was to have been fully implemented, in December 1992, free movement of people was still a chimera even among the Schengen states. Despite successive European Council statements about the need for free movement of people, the Commission's efforts to achieve that goal within the EC itself merely elicited a suggestion that member states allow EC nationals to show, but not hand over, their passports at intra-EC borders—a maneuver derisively known as the "Bangemann wave" (named after the internal market commissioner Martin Bangemann). Seeing no point in hauling disobedient member states before the ECJ, the Commission shifted to a lame emphasis on the need for "confidence building" to occur before passport checks could be eliminated throughout the EC and once again urged the European Council "to ensure that the goals of [the EC treaty] in the area of the free movement of persons are realized."[35]

Using the Schengen process as a precursor to EC-wide action on the free movement of people, the Ad Hoc Group on Immigration drafted provisions of the Schengen Convention into two separate international conventions that all member states signed in 1990: the Dublin Convention on Asylum and the External Borders Convention. The fact that these conventions were drafted intergovernmentally without reference to the EC's supranational institutions demonstrated the continuing sensitivity for member states of JHA issues. In the event, problems of sovereignty and a territorial dispute between Britain and Spain over Gibraltar indefinitely delayed ratification of the Dublin Convention and the External Borders Convention.

Continuing concern about uncontrolled immigration and a variety of country-specific concerns—ranging from widespread criticism of Luxembourg's bank secrecy laws to French criticism of the Netherlands' policy on soft drugs—demonstrated the degree of disarray on JHA issues even among Schengen states. Nevertheless, work continued on implementing the Schengen Convention, to which Italy acceded in November 1990, Portugal and Spain in June 1991, and Greece in November 1992. By that time the process of European integration had accelerated due to the success of the single market program and the unification of Germany. Indeed, many of Schengen's objectives were incorporated into the TEU, although Schengen continued to exist independently of the EU.

The TEU

Given the topicality of JHA in the late 1980s and the desire of some member states, notably Germany, to strengthen the EC's competence in that regard (ultimately by bringing Schengen into the treaty), JHA was a major item on the agenda of the 1991 IGC that resulted in the TEU. Yet doubts about free movement of people and difficulties surrounding the Schengen Convention augured ill for the JHA negotiations. In the event, proponents of supranationalism, including the Commission, spent most of their political capital on issues such as EMU and institutional reform rather than on the relatively unpromising JHA, which was included in the treaty as a separate intergovernmental pillar (i.e., the Third Pillar, next to the supranational EC and intergovernmental foreign and security policy pillars).

Nevertheless, JHA issues were not rigidly segregated from the EC proper. Indeed, the establishment of Union citizenship reinforced the salience of JHA for the development of the EU as a whole (a new Article 8a, now Article 18, TEC asserted that "every citizen of the Union shall have the right to move and reside freely within the territory of the member states"). Accordingly, a new Article 100c (later incorporated by the Amsterdam Treaty into Title IV TEC) gave the Council, acting unanimously on a proposal from the Commission, power to determine those countries whose nationals needed a visa in order to enter the territory of the EU, and to adopt measures for a uniform visa format. A new provision for action to prevent drug dependence, in Article 129 (now Article 152) TEC (on public health), brought another JHA matter into the EC pillar. And in the Third Pillar itself, member states agreed to act "without prejudice to the powers of the European Community" (Article K.1, now Article 29, TEU).

The Third Pillar

However, the bulk of the TEU's JHA provisions were located in a new title at the end of the treaty, the first article of which (now Article 29) listed nine areas of "common interest" subject to intergovernmental cooperation:

- asylum
- the crossing of external borders
- immigration
- combating drug addiction
- combating fraud on an international scale
- judicial cooperation in civil matters
- judicial cooperation in criminal matters
- customs cooperation
- police cooperation

Being closer to the core of national sovereignty, the last three areas are qualitatively different from the rest. Accordingly, they were not included in the so-called *passerelle* (gateway) provision that allowed for the transfer of Third Pillar issues to the First Pillar (a provision included in the treaty as a sop to supranationalists). Although the *passerelle* provision was not used during the brief lifetime of the unreformed TEU, the exclusion of police, customs, and most judicial cooperation from it meant that whatever the outcome of the 1996–1997 IGC, these areas would definitely remain in the intergovernmental Third Pillar.

The TEU established three instruments for the implementation of JHA policy: joint positions, joint actions, and conventions. Joint positions and joint actions resembled similar instruments established in the TEU's pillar for foreign and security policy but were even less precisely defined. As the Dublin Asylum Convention and the External Borders Convention illustrated, conventions were already a familiar though unproductive feature of JHA cooperation among member states. Not surprisingly in an intergovernmental pillar, the JHA Council (of JHA ministers) would have to act unanimously except on procedural matters and when deciding on measures to implement joint actions.

Article K.4.1 established a coordinating committee (still popularly known as the K.4 Committee although Article K.4 became Article 36 as a result of the Amsterdam Treaty) of senior member state officials to work on JHA issues and prepare JHA Council meetings (in collaboration with the Committee of Permanent Representatives). The TEU stipulated that the Commission would be "fully associated" with the work of the Third Pillar. However, the Commission was given a nonexclusive right of initiative in the first six policies of common interest to member states and denied any right of initiative in the remaining three areas. As for the EP, the TEU used weak verbs like "inform" and "consult" to describe its limited involvement in the Third Pillar. Paradoxically, the EP's almost nonexistent role opened a democratic deficit in an important policy sphere at precisely the time when member states were moving toward greater parliamentary accountability of EU affairs. The ECJ's absence from the Third Pillar caused a similar "judicial deficit," although the TEU gave the Court authority to interpret the provisions of JHA conventions subject to member state approval on a case-by-case basis.

A final article in the original Third Pillar stipulated that "the provisions of this Title shall not prevent the establishment or development of closer cooperation between two or more Member States in so far as such cooperation does not conflict with, or impede, that provided for in this Title." In other words, national governments acknowledged that differentiated integration would continue to be a feature of cooperation on JHA among member states.

From Maastricht to Amsterdam

Accordingly to a senior Commission official, the Third Pillar got off to "a misleadingly good start."[36] Officials and ministers busied themselves preparing a work program and an action plan, which the European Council endorsed at the Brussels summit in December 1993.[37] But the sudden flurry of activity could not disguise the fact that the work program consisted mostly of old, repackaged items and that the action plan was condemned to inactivity as long as unanimity remained the norm. The EP immediately denounced the Third Pillar as an insult to the Community method and pressured the Commission to involve itself as aggressively as possible in JHA affairs. Already reeling from the TEU ratification crisis, initially the Commission preferred a less confrontational approach. In an effort to move things along and establish its own credibility in a hostile intergovernmental environment, the Commission sent the Council general communications rather than proposals for legislation on Third Pillar issues. Nevertheless, the Commission did not hesitate to take the initiative under the then-extant Article 100c TEC, resulting in a regulation in May 1995 on a uniform format for visas and another in September 1995 establishing a legally binding list of countries whose nationals needed a visa to enter the EU.

Given the history of cooperation on JHA, the cloak of confidentiality that shrouded the new JHA Council and K.4 Committee, the imprecision of JHA instruments, and the ability of member states to veto decisions, inevitably there was little or no headway on issues covered by the Third Pillar. Yet public support for EU-wide measures to combat illegal immigration and organized crime was remarkably high despite widespread hostility during and after the TEU ratification crisis toward the EU and its institutions. Within the Schengen framework at least, despite differences of opinion and occasional political grandstanding, JHA ministers and officials made some progress. In March 1995 the Schengen Convention finally became operational for seven of its signatory states (Italy and Greece needed to make additional adjustments; new member state Austria, which signed up in April 1995, also needed a lengthy transition period).

The fate of EUROPOL, which occupied more time and got more attention than any other Third Pillar issue in the mid-1990s, demonstrated the continuing difficulty of making progress within the EU in the field of JHA. Although ministers reached political agreement in June 1993 to establish EUROPOL, the necessary implementing convention became a major battleground in the war between intergovernmentalists and supranationalists. Germany and the Benelux countries insisted on a role for the ECJ; Britain, supported to some extent by Denmark and (after January 1995) by Sweden, fiercely resisted. In the meantime, in deference to public anxiety about transnational drug dealing, EU member states launched the EUROPOL Drugs Unit (EDU) in January 1994 in a renovated police barracks in The Hague. The EDU did not undertake any operations itself but supported operations involving two or more member states by facilitating access to information, intelligence, and analysis. The EDU's strengths were its highly sophisticated computer links and the discretion and personal contacts of its national liaison officers.

As the dispute over the EUROPOL Convention dragged on, member states progressively broadened the EDU's scope to cover also trafficking in stolen vehicles, illegal immigration, trafficking in human beings, and money laundering. In effect, the EDU was EUROPOL under a modified name (it lacked competence only for terrorism and other serious crimes such as kidnapping and arms trafficking). France wanted to resolve the EUROPOL row during its Council presidency in early 1995 but failed at the June 1995 Cannes summit to overcome British opposition to ECJ involvement in EUROPOL's affairs. The dispute then became bound up politically in an equally embittered row over bovine spongiform encephalopathy (BSE), before being resolved at the Florence summit in June 1996 by an agreement enabling the ECJ to give preliminary rulings on the interpretation of the EUROPOL Convention.[38]

Public support for EU efforts to enhance internal security, together with disappointing progress to date on the Third Pillar, emboldened the Commission and like-minded member states in the run-up to the 1996–1997 IGC. Nevertheless, the pre-IGC Reflection Group was divided on how to strengthen and reorganize the EU's involvement in JHA. Not all member states favored extending Community competence over part of the Third Pillar or incorporating Schengen into the EU, albeit "by means of flexible arrangements."[39]

Given its political and procedural complexity, JHA was one of the most thoroughly discussed issues at the IGC itself. Germany and the Benelux countries (supported by the Commission and the EP) advocated moving the first six areas of common interest listed in the Third Pillar of the TEU into the First Pillar (i.e., the TEC) and bringing the Schengen *acquis* (more than 3,000 pages of rules and regulations that had accrued since the launch of the Schengen process in 1985) into the *acquis communautaire*. Having joined Schengen in 1996, the Scandinavian member states did not demur (non–EU member states Iceland and Norway became associate members of Schengen), although Denmark insisted on an opt-out from JHA provisions that were moved to the First Pillar. Only Britain continued to object to a radical restructuring of JHA in the Amsterdam Treaty, an objection that ended when the more pro-EU Labour Party formed a new government in May 1997. Nevertheless, like the Danish government, even the new British government insisted on an opt-out from JHA provisions moved to the First Pillar.

The Amsterdam Treaty

Thanks in large part to the change of government in Britain and to aggressive Dutch chairmanship of the concluding stages of the IGC, the Treaty of

Amsterdam included radical changes in the realm of JHA. The most striking innovation was the wholesale transfer into the First Pillar (new Title IV TEC) of responsibility for visas, asylum, immigration, and other policies related to the free movement of people. Provisions for police cooperation and judicial cooperation on criminal matters remained within a truncated Third Pillar. Whether taken under the auspices of the First or Third Pillar, JHA measures would help realize a new objective of the EU: "to maintain and develop . . . an area of freedom, security, and justice" (new Article 2 TEU). Moreover, member states agreed to take such measures during a specific time frame: "within a period of five years after the entry into force of the Treaty of Amsterdam" (Article 61 TEC).

New First Pillar Provisions

Scope. Articles 62–65 TEC deal with border controls and visas; asylum, refugees, and immigration, and judicial cooperation in civil matters.

Institutional involvement. The decisionmaking procedures outlined in Article 67 TEC severely mitigate the impact of moving these areas into the First Pillar: During the five years leading up to the establishment of an area of freedom, security, and justice, the Council acts by unanimity; the Commission has only a shared right of initiative; and the EP is consulted only on proposed legislation. In other words, decisionmaking on the free movement of people remains intergovernmental rather than supranational. After the transitional period, the Commission will acquire an exclusive right of initiative and the Council will decide whether to use the codecision procedure to enact legislation on the free movement of people—but the Council must make that decision unanimously. Finally, the role of the ECJ is restricted in relation to JHA areas now included in the First Pillar.

Instruments. The use of First Pillar instruments such as directives and regulations should improve the implementation of EU policy in those JHA areas transferred from the Third Pillar. However, the perpetuation of intergovernmental decisionmaking means that directives and regulations will not be easy to enact.

Opt-Outs. Determined to maintain control over its own borders, Britain won an opt-out from the EC's new provisions on the free movement of people. Willing in principle to accept those provisions but constrained in practice by a desire to maintain a Common Travel Area with Britain, Ireland also opted out. Although both countries may decide on a case-by-case basis to adopt legislation on First Pillar JHA issues (i.e., they may selectively opt back in), they cannot prevent other member states from adopting such legislation. Because its hands were tied politically by earlier TEU opt-outs, the Danish government reluctantly opted out also from Title IV. Unlike Britain and Ireland, Denmark can opt back in on a case-by-case basis, but only by accepting Title IV legislation in its entirety.

The Truncated Third Pillar

Scope. A revised Article 29 TEU relates the activities of the Third Pillar—now confined to police cooperation and judicial cooperation on criminal matters—to the goal of giving EU citizens "a high level of safety" within the putative area of freedom, security, and justice. It also mentions the prevention of "racism and xenophobia," although this subject is not developed elsewhere in the treaty. Article 30 TEU outlines the extent of common action in the field of police cooperation; Article 31 TEU does so for judicial cooperation on criminal matters.

Institutional involvement. As the Third Pillar is an intergovernmental one, the roles of the Commission, EP, and ECJ remain limited. Nevertheless, the Commission gained the right of initiative (shared with member states) in all areas, and the EP gained the right to be consulted on most issues.

Instruments. Article 34 TEU outlines a range of new and revised Third Pillar instruments:

- *Common positions* define the approach of the EU to a particular matter.
- *Framework decisions* are binding on member states as to the results to be achieved, but member states themselves decide how to implement them. They are to be used to approximate laws and regulations among member states. The more "progressive" member states hope that framework decisions will replace conventions—often negotiated but rarely implemented—as the main Third Pillar instrument.
- *Decisions* are similar to framework decisions but are to be used to achieve JHA objectives other than by harmonizing member state laws and regulations.
- *Conventions* are still available in the Third Pillar but, once adopted by at least half of the member states, may enter into force for those member states. The Council may adopt measures to implement conventions by a two-thirds majority.

Flexibility. Differentiated integration has always been a feature of cooperation on JHA among EU member states (even including some non–member states). Article 30 TEU includes a flexibility clause that allows member states wanting to cooperate more closely to do so using EU institutions, procedures, and mechanisms. The Council may authorize closer cooperation, acting by a qualified majority at the request of the member states concerned. As in similar flexibility provisions in the Second Pillar (cooperation on foreign and security policy), Article 30 has an "emergency brake": By invoking "important and stated reasons of national policy," a member state may prevent the Council from voting to authorize closer cooperation. Although the Council may then vote to refer the matter to the European Council for a decision by unanimity, it seems unlikely that a member state that pulled the emergency break in the first place would release it because the issue had been pushed up to the level of the heads of state and government.

Schengen

In view of the Amsterdam Treaty's provisions for an area of freedom, security, and justice, including a flexibility clause for closer collaboration on JHA issues, there was no need to continue Schengen's separate existence. Accordingly, a protocol attached to the treaty provided for Schengen's incorporation into the EU framework with special provision (in a separate protocol) for non–Schengen members Britain and Ireland to accept some or all of the Schengen *acquis*. Having recently joined Schengen, Denmark was in the peculiar position of opting out of the JHA provisions into which Schengen was about to be folded. Denmark's situation was further complicated by the fact that non–EU members but fellow Nordic Union members Iceland and Norway remained fully associated with the Schengen *acquis* following its incorporation into the EU. The inelegant solution to Denmark's dilemma was a clause in the "Danish protocol" stipulating that within six months of the Council taking a decision that built on the Schengen *acquis,* Denmark would decide whether to incorporate that decision into national law.

CONCLUSION

The establishment of an area of freedom, security, and justice within five years of the Treaty of Amsterdam coming into effect, and nearly twenty years after a handful of member states signed the Schengen agreement, would be a major achievement for the EU and a major benefit for its citizens. Will it happen? The record of cooperation on JHA is not encouraging. Although the extension of Community competence to the free movement of people is a far-reaching step, the perpetuation of intergovernmental decisionmaking procedures suggests that progress will be patchy in the First Pillar. And if member states agree to act in what remains of the intergovernmental Third Pillar, they may not be willing to do so by adopting framework decisions, the most powerful instrument in the Third Pillar's arsenal.

The projected date for the establishment of an area of freedom, security, and justice (2004) coincides with the likely date of the next enlargement. The applicant countries are attempting to incorporate the Schengen *acquis* as part of their preaccession strategies. Most lack the administrative capacities and financial resources to do so. As a result, enlargement could delay the establishment of an area of freedom, security, and justice; or the establishment of an area of freedom, security, and justice could delay enlargement. More than likely enlargement will go ahead, but the putative area of freedom, security, and justice will not immediately encompass the new member states. With Britain and Ireland opting out in the West and some new member states unable to meet JHA requirements in the East, differentiation will continue to characterize the EU's efforts to bring about the free movement of people.

NOTES

1. See Alberta Sbragia, "The Push-Pull of Environmental Policy-Making," in Helen Wallace and William Wallace, *Policy-Making in the European Union,* 3d ed. (Oxford: Oxford University Press, 1996), pp. 235–256.
2. Ida Johanne Koppen, *The European Community's Environment Policy: From the Summit in Paris, 1972, to the Single European Act, 1986,* EUI working paper no. 88/328 (Florence: EUI, 1988), p. 62.
3. Michael Petit, *The Amsterdam Treaty*, Harvard Law School working paper (Cambridge: Harvard Law School, 1997), p. 14.
4. EP written question 1337/92, *Official Journal of the European Communitites* [*OJ*] C 40/26, February 15, 1992.
5. Quoted in *Financial Times,* January 10, 1992, p. 2.
6. Francisco Granell, "The European Union's Enlargement Negotiations with Austria, Finland, Norway, and Sweden," *Journal of Common Market Studies* 33, no. 1 (March 1995): 129.
7. Commission, *Agenda 2000: For a Stronger and Wider Europe,* Brussels, July 16, 1997, COM(97)2000 final.
8. Beverly Springer, *The Social Dimension of 1992* (New York: Praeger, 1992), p. 39.
9. Council Directive (EC) 93/104, November 13, 1993, concerning certain aspects of the organization of working time.
10. Jacques Delors, speech to the European Parliament outlining the Commission's program for 1988, January 20, 1988. Bull. EC S/1-1988, p. 12.
11. Bull. EC 6-1988, "Presidency Conclusions," point 1.1.1.
12. Bull. EC 9-1988, points 1.1.1 to 1.1.6.
13. Bull. EC 12-1989, "Presidency Conclusions," point 1.1.10.
14. Commission, *Social Europe: First Report on Application of the Social Charter of Fundamental Social Rights for Workers* (Luxembourg: Office for Official Publications of the European Communities [OOP], 1992), p. 5.
15. Bull. EC12-1989, "Presidency Conclusions," point 1.1.10.
16. COM(89)568 final, November 29, 1989.

17. COM(92)562 final, December 23, 1992.
18. See *Financial Times,* February 5, 1993, p. 1.
19. Petit, *The Amsterdam Treaty,* p. 18.
20. COM(94)333.
21. COM(95)134.
22. "Commission's Program" for 1985, Bull. EC S/1-1985, p. 15.
23. Bull. EC S/4-1985, p. 5.
24. Commission, *From the Single Act to Maastricht and Beyond: The Means to Match Our Ambitions,* Bull. EC S/1-1992, p. 9.
25. Jacques Delors, speech to the European Parliament, January 20, 1988, in Bull. EC S/1-1988, p. 11.
26. Tommaso Padoa-Schioppa et al., *Efficiency, Stability and Equity: A Strategy for the Evolution of the Economic System of the European Community* (Oxford: Oxford University Press, 1987), pp. 3, 4, 10.
27. Quoted in the *Economist,* February 27, 1988, p. 41
28. Jacques Delors, address to the European Parliament, January 20, 1988, Bull. EC S/1-1988, p. 11.
29. Commission, *Reform of the Structural Funds: A Tool to Promote Economic and Social Cohesion* (Luxembourg: OOP, 1992), p. 18.
30. See Liesbet Hooghe, ed., *Cohesion Policy and European Integration: Building Multi-Level Governance* (Oxford: Oxford University Press, 1996).
31. Jacques Delors, *Report of the Committee for the Study of Economic and Monetary Union* (Luxembourg: OOP, 1989).
32. Commission, *Maastricht and Beyond.*
33. Michael Shackleton, "The Community Budget After Maastricht," in Alan Cafruny and Glenda G. Rosenthal, eds., *The State of the European Community*, vol. 2, *The Maastricht Debates and Beyond* (Boulder: Lynne Rienner, 1993), p. 387.
34. Commission, *Cohesion Report*, COM(96)542 (Luxembourg: OOP, 1996).
35. Copenhagen European Council, "Presidency Conclusions," Bull. EC 6-1993, point 1.4.
36. John Adrian Fortescue, "First Experiences with the Implementation of the Third Pillar," in R. Bieber and J. Monar, eds., *Justice and Home Affairs in the European Union* (Brussels: European Interuniversity Press, 1995), p. 23.
37. Bull. EC 13-1993, "Presidency Conclusions," points 1.1 to 1.6
38. Florence European Council, "Presidency Conclusions," Bull. EC 6-1996, point 1.6.
39. The Reflection Group Report is published in European Parliament, *White Paper on the 1996 IGC,* vol. 1, *Official Texts of the EU Institutions* (Luxembourg: European Parliament, 1996), pp. 149–212.

16

Economic and Monetary Union

There have been three major monetary policy initiatives in the history of European integration: the Werner Plan to achieve Economic and Monetary Union (EMU) by 1980; the European Monetary System (EMS), launched in 1979; and the Delors Report of 1989 and ensuing intergovernmental conference (IGC) on EMU. All were due, in part, to deliberate decisions to "relaunch" European integration. Unlike the third initiative, the two earlier ones were also a response to international currency crises or challenges. In the case of the Werner Plan, international exchange rate fluctuations, culminating in the collapse of the Bretton Woods system, impelled the EC to act; in the case of the EMS, the destabilizing impact of foreign currency movements, notably the dollar, had the same effect.

By comparison, the 1991 IGC took place at a time of stable exchange rates between member state currencies, thanks in part to the relative success of the EMS. Moreover, in marked contrast to the 1970s, the late 1980s was a period of economic buoyancy in the EC as the single market program boosted business confidence and set the stage for deeper integration. The circumstances seemed particularly propitious not only for a new monetary initiative but also for the achievement of economic union, which in the EU means not a common economic policy for all member states but the existence of a single market plus close coordination of member states' economic policies. A three-stage plan for EMU was the centerpiece of the Treaty on European Union (TEU), concluded at the Maastricht summit in December 1991.

The politics of EMU dominated the 1990s. Would a majority of member states meet the convergence criteria on time to launch Stage III of EMU (the single currency) in 1997? Would France and Germany, the key EMU participants, be among the member states to meet the criteria by 1999? Would skeptical European publics accept the kinds of austerity measures necessary in order to qualify for Stage III? Would they endure the high unemployment that seemed an inevitable accompaniment of EMU?

Would EMU continue to divide Britain's (then) ruling Conservative Party? Would Britain's (then) opposition Labour Party overcome its differences on EMU and be able to present itself as a credible alternative government? Would mainstream political parties on the Continent exploit popular concern about the loss of national currencies and play the anti-EMU card?

Despite a poor economic climate in the mid-1990s and despite having missed the 1997 target date, a majority of member states indeed qualified for the 1999 deadline for the launch of Stage III. By that time Helmut Kohl, the architect of EMU, was out of office in Germany, although only indirectly because of EMU. By that time also the Conservatives were out of office in Britain, having been replaced by an EU-friendly Labour government. However, the new government decided to exercise Britain's opt-out from Stage III despite having met the criteria for participation in it. If Labour wins the next election (due by early 2002 at the latest), it will call a referendum on whether belatedly to join "euroland" (providing that the single currency is a success). Divisions within the Labour Party on EMU, conveniently covered up during the 1997 election, will most likely have reemerged with a vengeance by then.

THE NEW IMPETUS FOR EMU

In October 1990 an exuberant Jacques Delors, president of the Commission, declared emphatically that "we need a single currency before the year 2000."[1] The necessity of EMU was debatable on economic grounds, but Delors's remark demonstrated his personal drive and political ambition. As finance minister in 1983, Delors had convinced French president François Mitterrand to reverse his socialist economic policy and commit France uncompromisingly to the exchange rate mechanism (ERM) of the EMS, arguably saving both the French government and the EMS in the process. The Single European Act (SEA) and the successful launch of the single market program in the late 1980s greatly enhanced Delors's standing and provided a powerful new impetus for EMU. It was no coincidence that Delors chaired the committee charged by the European Council with plotting a path to EMU or that the committee's influential report unofficially bore his name.

Market Integration and Monetary Union

By advocating EMU, Delors championed a long-standing objective of European integration. The Treaty of Rome's goal of market integration and espousal of "ever closer union" implicitly endorsed EMU. Yet the treaty contained few provisions for economic and monetary coordination, partly because of the political constraints on European integration in the late

1950s in the aftermath of the failed European Defense Community initiative. In addition, the fully functioning fixed exchange rates of the Bretton Woods system, to which the member states belonged, made monetary union unnecessary.

Predictably, the EC's first overt espousal of EMU came at a time of international financial upheaval in the late 1960s, culminating in the breakdown of the Bretton Woods system. A call by EC leaders in 1972 for EMU by 1980 nevertheless proved unrealistic. More than a decade later, in the preamble of the SEA, member states reaffirmed their commitment to "the progressive realization of economic and monetary union." The SEA's modest provisions for an EC monetary capacity and pointed reference to "the experience acquired in cooperation within the framework of the European Monetary System" provided a modest political push toward EMU.

The single market program, which took off with the SEA, greatly advanced the goal of EMU. Exchange rate fluctuations seemed inconsistent with and contradictory to the objectives of the single market. In the early 1980s, before the launch of the single market program, a group of influential academics had argued that "a common market with common policies can be viable in the long run only within a coherent framework of macroeconomic and monetary policies."[2] With the 1992 program off to a strong start, the symbiotic relationship between it and EMU became a new orthodoxy. In his influential report on the single market program's implications for the European economy, Tomaso Padoa-Schioppa strongly endorsed the link between completing the single market and embarking on EMU.[3]

By the end of the 1980s, market integration as a rationale for EMU was almost unquestioned. A communication by the Commission in August 1990 developed the link: "A single currency is the natural complement of a single market. The full potential of the latter will not be achieved without the former. Going further, there is a need for economic and monetary union in part to consolidate the potential gains from completing the internal market, without which there would be risks of weakening the present momentum of the 1992 process."[4] The Commission's much-quoted cost-benefit analysis of EMU appeared two months later. Its title, *One Market, One Money*, reinforced the 1992-EMU connection and became a mantra for advocates of a single currency.[5] A Commission publication, prepared by the information directorate-general, maintained that "the creation of a single currency is a natural and necessary attribute of a smoothly functioning single market."[6]

The EMS, which had helped to make the single market possible, provided another impetus toward EMU in the late 1980s. Padoa-Schioppa pointed out that with complete capital mobility (a feature of the single market), the ERM and the existing degree of monetary policy coordination would be insufficient to promote price stability and ensure orderly trade relations among member states. "In a quite fundamental way," Padoa-Schioppa concluded, "capital mobility [1992] and exchange rate fixity [the EMS] together leave no room for independent monetary policies."[7] Put another way, a unified market with a free flow of capital could put the EMS under unbearable pressure.

Member states would discover the extent of that pressure during the currency crisis of 1992. In the meantime, the perceived success of the EMS in the late 1980s increased the momentum for EMU. Given the stability of the ERM since early 1987, when the last general alignment had occurred, the EMS tended to be seen as a forerunner of EMU. Further economic convergence, it seemed, would reinforce exchange rate stability and turn the EMS into a quasi–monetary union. Therefore, moving from the EMS to EMU seemed logical and relatively effortless. As commissioner Leon Brittan remarked in October 1990, "The ERM is the kernel of the future single European currency."[8]

Brittan's audience of businesspeople was predisposed to the idea of monetary union thanks to the success of both the EMS and the single market program. In 1990, management consultants Ernst and Young conducted a survey for the Commission that showed widespread optimism in business circles about the economic impact of monetary union combined with completion of the single market.[9] The experience of working together in the ERM also reconciled many government officials and politicians to the prospect of EMU. Twenty years earlier Leo Tindemans had reported regretfully that there was not enough trust between member states to transfer responsibility for EMU to a central authority.[10] Without doubt, participation in the EMS had helped member states to overcome such distrust.

The Delors Report

The decisive Delors Report did not take an explicit stand on whether monetary union was necessary to ensure the success of the single market. Nor did it develop a cost-benefit analysis of EMU. Instead, the committee of central bank governors of the (then twelve) member states, two commissioners, and three independent experts outlined what EMU would look like and devised specific steps that could result in its achievement. Taking a lead from the Werner Report, the Delors Report defined monetary union as "the assurance of total and irreversible convertibility of currencies; the complete liberalization of capital transactions and full integration of banking and other financial markets; and the elimination of margins of fluctuation and the irrevocable locking of exchange rate parities."[11] Although the committee did not explicitly endorse a single currency, its definition of monetary union necessarily involved a centralized monetary policy for the Community.

The report identified four basic elements of economic union:

1. a single market, within which persons, goods, services, and capital can move freely
2. competition policy and other measures aimed at strengthening market mechanisms
3. common policies aimed at structural change and regional development
4. macroeconomic policy coordination, including binding rules for budgetary policies

Three of these were already being put in place:

1. The single market program was in full swing.
2. The importance of an effective competition policy to create a "level playing field" in the single market was uncontested.
3. Member states had agreed in February 1988 that a huge increase in regional development assistance was necessary to make a success of the single market. A decade earlier, the EC had offered financial assistance to poorer countries participating in the ERM and, for the same reason, would establish a sizable Cohesion Fund in 1992 for disadvantaged member states hoping to embark on EMU.

Only macroeconomic coordination would represent a noticeable new departure. Although economic union would not necessitate a common economic policy, the Delors Report stressed the need for centralized control over national fiscal policies in order to operate EMU successfully. Specifically, the report advocated effective upper limits on the budget deficits of individual member states, no recourse to direct central bank credit and other forms of monetary financing, and limited recourse to borrowing in non-EC currencies.[12]

The Delors Report proposed a federal European System of Central Banks (ESCB) made up of a central institution (a "Eurofed") and constituent national central banks to formulate and implement a common monetary policy. Reflecting both the influence of Karl-Otto Pöhl, president of the Bundesbank (German central bank) and a member of the committee, and a high degree of satisfaction with the existing EMS, the report emphatically identified price stability as the ESCB's primary objective. Like the Bundesbank's directorate, the ESCB's council would be rigidly independent of government influence or control.

The Delors Report is best known for proposing a three-stage approach to EMU:

- Stage I: free capital movement in the EC and closer monetary and macroeconomic cooperation between member states and their central banks

- Stage II: launch of the ESCB to monitor and coordinate national monetary policies; stronger supervisory powers for EC institutions, notably the European Parliament (EP) and the Council; and a progressive narrowing of margins of fluctuation within the exchange rate mechanism
- Stage III: establishment of "irrevocably fixed" exchange rate parities; granting of full authority monetary policy to EC institutions

A phased approach was inevitable. Nor were the contents of each stage surprising. Mindful of the embarrassment caused by the EC's commitment in 1972 to achieve EMU by the end of the decade, the Delors Report did not adopt a timetable for a renewed effort to achieve EMU. Instead, the report merely recommended that Stage I start no later than July 1, 1990, when capital movements were due to be liberalized anyway as part of the single market program.

Toward the Treaty on European Union

The Delors Report sparked a lively debate. The most explosive political point, inherent in any discussion of EMU, centered on the question of national sovereignty. Most ERM participants had already lost control over national monetary policy. By the late 1980s their currencies were pegged to the mark, the system's unofficial anchor. The Bundesbank formulated monetary policy in the EMS, and member states reaped the political and economic rewards of low inflation and stable exchange rates. In effect, Germany's partners in the EMS gave up using interest rates and nominal exchange rates as instruments of national policy. In any case, prevailing opinion in the 1980s held that using devaluations to tackle such problems as declining demand for a country's products was both ineffective and likely to fuel inflation.

As far as monetary union was concerned, most ERM participants stood to regain sovereignty rather than lose it. By joining a federal monetary system, they would wrest some power back from the Bundesbank. This was the reasoning behind French finance minister Edouard Balladur's influential advocacy of EMU in early 1988. By the same token, Germany should have been the least happy about monetary union. Indeed, the Bundesbank had serious concerns about surrendering its virtual monopoly of decisionmaking, at least until it could be sure that an alternative arrangement offered as good a prospect of price stability as did the existing mechanism. But the German government, which in any event supported monetary union for political reasons, could hardly argue in favor of maintaining a monopoly over monetary policy in the EC.

Economic union would involve less centralization of power than would monetary union because a single economic policy did not seem essential. Sensitive to the political climate of the late 1980s, the Commission claimed that "the Community's involvement in economic decision-making should be based on a balance between subsidiarity and parallelism [between the economic and monetary parts of EMU]."[13] Whereas economic policy could be formulated at different levels of government, responsibility for monetary policy would rest squarely with a new EC institution, the European Central Bank (ECB).

The debate over national sovereignty was loudest in Britain, where the economic benefits of EMU were also least apparent. In a speech to the House of Commons in January 1991, the chancellor of the exchequer (finance minister) explained that safeguarding the "sovereign right of Parliament" would be one of his priorities in the forthcoming IGC on EMU.[14] Even before the IGC began, Prime Minister Margaret Thatcher complained in July 1991 that the ERM, into which she had reluctantly brought Britain the previous October, was "tearing the heart out of parliamentary sovereignty." As for EMU, handing over responsibility for monetary policy to the putative ECB would reduce "national finance ministers to the status of innocent bystanders at the scene of an accident."[15]

The question of sovereignty also hinged on powerful political symbols. Money was both a means of transacting business and a badge of national identity or, in the event of a single currency, a symbol of European unity. As a compromise, Leon Brittan suggested keeping existing coins and bank notes and simply denominating their ECU value on one side.[16] A number of countries designed new currency along those lines. As the TEU ratification crisis would show, attachment to the national symbolism of money ran deep throughout the EC, especially in Germany, where the mark epitomized postwar prosperity and stability.

The Commission did not try to calculate the political costs or benefits of EMU apart from an oblique reference to possible "psychological" problems.[17] Member states would have to reach their own conclusions, but for most it was clear that the anticipated benefits of EMU outweighed the intangible political costs. Not only had most countries already sacrificed national sovereignty by participating in the ERM but some—notably Italy—saw future EC curbs on national fiscal policy as the only way to cut their exorbitant budget deficits.

Instead, the Commission focused on economic losses and gains, identifying the elimination of transaction costs and exchange rate vulnerability, resulting in greater trade and investment, as a major advantage. The Commission estimated that EC-wide savings on transaction costs could amount to as much as 0.3 to 0.4 percent of GDP.[18] Yet the Commission conceded that the EC was not an "optimum currency area" in which labor would move freely in order to offset country-specific shocks; nor would Brussels have a fiscal system capable of making income-stabilizing transfers. Given that economic shocks would continue to affect each member state differently, that labor would remain relatively immobile because of cultural and linguistic barriers, and that the EC would not acquire a sizable fiscal system, the advantages of EMU seemed far from obvious. Based on additional analysis applied to the EC's actual structure and situation, however, the Commission not surprisingly concluded that "the case [for EMU] can stand powerfully on economic criteria alone."[19]

The Commission's arguments failed to impress some influential economists on both sides of the EMU debate. Peter Kenen, professor of economics and international finance at Princeton University and a supporter of monetary integration, regretted that *One Market, One Money* did not prove conclusively "that the benefits would exceed the costs," its title being "as close as the study came to making a case for EMU."[20] Martin Feldstein, professor of economics at Harvard University and an opponent of EMU, refuted the assertion that a single market needs a single currency, let alone monetary union. Feldstein argued that monetary union would not necessarily increase trade and that the success of the EMS weakened the anti-inflationary argument for EMU.[21] Perhaps the Commission should have produced an aggregate estimate of the impact of EMU, along the lines of the Cecchini Report on the single market. The Commission explained in August 1990, however, that the nature of EMU, conditional as it was on "the responses of governments as well as private economic agents," made such an approach unfeasible.[22]

In the event, as Feldstein noted disapprovingly, the main push for EMU was political, not economic. It emanated mainly from Paris, Brussels, and Bonn. Indeed, the conclusions of successive European summits in the late 1980s chronicled the seemingly unstoppable political pressure that had developed for EMU:

- It was striking that in June 1988 the European Council charged the Delors Committee not with exploring the rationale for EMU but with suggesting concrete steps for achieving it.[23]
- Twelve months later, in Madrid in June 1989, the European Council reiterated its "determination progressively to achieve economic and monetary union," endorsed the Delors Report as a basic blueprint for EMU, and decided to launch Stage I of EMU on July 1, 1990.[24]
- At the Strasbourg summit in December 1989, Mitterrand noted that the necessary majority existed to convene an IGC on EMU.[25]
- The European Council decided in June 1990 to begin the IGC six months later in Rome, with a view to concluding and ratifying a treaty before the end of 1992.[26]
- Finally, at an extraordinary summit in Rome in October 1990, two months before the launch of the IGC, eleven of the twelve heads of state and government—Thatcher was the odd one out—agreed to begin Stage II of EMU on January 1, 1994.[27]

The Treaty on European Union

The ensuing TEU duly adopted a three-stage process for the completion of EMU but differed from the Delors Report in a number of important respects, not least by affirming a single currency (and not simply fixed exchange rates) as EMU's ultimate goal. The single currency would be launched at the beginning of Stage III, for which the TEU set a deadline of January 1, 1999. A European Monetary Institute (EMI) would be established at the beginning of Stage II to make technical preparations for Stage III and monitor member state compliance with the requirements for participation in it. The EMI council would consist of national central bank governors, although the council president would be "selected from among persons of recognized standing and professional experience in monetary or banking matters" from outside the governors' circle.

According to the treaty, member states wishing to participate in Stage III would have to meet a number of criteria intended to ensure "a high degree of sustainable [economic] convergence" (Article 121, formerly Article 109j, TEC). There were four so-called convergence criteria:

- *Price stability:* an average inflation rate not exceeding by more than 1.5 percent that of the three best-performing member states
- *Budgetary discipline:* a government financial position that does not include an excessive deficit (a protocol attached to the treaty provided two reference values: a budget deficit of less than 3 percent of GDP and a public debt ratio not exceeding 60 percent of GDP)
- *Currency stability:* observance of normal fluctuation margins of the ERM for at least two years with no devaluations
- *Interest rate convergence:* an average nominal long-term interest rate not exceeding by more than 2 percent that of the three best-performing member states

Before the end of 1996 the Council—meeting at the level of heads of state and government—would assess the degree of economic convergence among member states. If they decided that a majority of member states met the convergence criteria, the heads of state and government could set a date in 1997 or 1998 for the launch of Stage III. If they decided by the end of 1996 that a majority of member states failed to meet the criteria, the heads of state and government would make another assessment before July 1, 1998. Member states meeting the criteria at that time, regardless of whether they constituted a majority, would go ahead and launch Stage III on January 1, 1999.

From the beginning of Stage III (whether in 1997, 1998, or 1999), exchange rates between participating countries would be irrevocably fixed and a single currency (later named the euro) introduced. The ESCB, consisting of the ECB and national central banks, would replace the EMI on the eve of Stage III and formulate the participating states' single monetary policy. National central banks would thus become branches of the ECB and carry out operations necessary to implement a single monetary policy.

According to the treaty, the primary objective of the ESCB is to maintain price stability (i.e., to fight inflation). In the tradition of the Bundesbank, it is independent of member state governments and other EU institutions (Articles 107 and 108, formerly Articles 106 and 107, TEC). The ESCB's governing council, consisting of the ECB's executive board (selected by the European Council) and governors of the national central banks, is the ESCB's highest decisionmaking body, responsible for monetary policy, foreign exchange operations, management of the official foreign reserves of member states, and smooth operation of a payments system. The executive board manages monetary policy on a day-to-day basis in accordance with decisions and guidelines laid down by the governing council.

Clearly, the treaty's provisions for EMU were comprehensive and complicated. But would they work? In a reply to Feldstein's criticism of EMU, a number of eminent European economists described the endeavor as "full of calculated risk [but] a risk worth taking."[28] The authors of the treaty had tried to minimize the risk by elaborating what they considered to be sound institutional and procedural prerequisites, although the convergence criteria seemed arbitrary and not necessarily related to the conduct of sound monetary policy. Given the politics of European integration and the unpredictability of global economics, the treaty's provisions for EMU could hardly have been flawless. Inevitably, the following few years put the treaty and its framers to the test.

TOWARD THE SINGLE CURRENCY

The TEU and ERM Crises

Although Stage I had begun without fanfare in July 1990, the post-Maastricht path to EMU got off to the worst possible start. Not only was the TEU's future cast in doubt by the June 1992 Danish referendum result and the ensuing ratification crisis but a related ERM crisis that erupted in September 1992 and crested in July 1993 shattered public confidence in the possibility that EMU could ever be achieved. Throughout 1992 the mark rose steadily as high German interest rates attracted funds from the United States, where interest rates were low and the dollar continued to depreciate. As the mark climbed in value, weaker EC currencies fell to the floor of their ERM bands. Certain currencies—notably the Italian lira and the British pound—were inherently weak and ripe for devaluation. Dealers sensed that a realignment of the ERM was imminent. The TEU had itself encouraged speculation about an inevitable realignment or series of realignments before the advent of fixed exchange rates. Such speculation, in turn, tended further to strengthen strong currencies and weaken weak ones.

Of more immediate concern, the Bundesbank was less and less inclined to prop up weak currencies. In July and August, the Bundesbank spent a small fortune trying to keep the lira above its ERM floor. Convinced of the Bundesbank's unwillingness or inability to support the lira indefinitely, dealers moved large amounts of money out of the Italian currency and into the mark. Similar concerns about sterling led to massive sales of the pound and purchases of the mark. Ironically, the removal of exchange controls as part of the single market program contributed to the imminent crisis by making it possible to move money freely around the EC.

The evolution of the EMS into what looked like a fixed-rate regime exacerbated tension. The frequency of realignments before 1987 (thirteen altogether) and absence of them afterward gave the impression that the EMS had turned into a quasi–currency union. Except in Germany and some other "core" currency countries, realignment became a dirty word, synonymous with political indecision and economic frailty. The pound had joined the ERM in October 1990 at a high benchmark central rate (2.95) against the mark; but it was politically impossible for the British government to contemplate realignment, especially with a general election in the offing.

Although the TEU prompted speculation about the inevitability of realignments before EMU, most governments feared that a parity change would affect their credibility, undermine confidence in the convergence criteria, fuel inflation, and thereby make EMU harder to achieve. Realignments appeared to be incompatible with the treaty's convergence strategy and with the goal of EMU; as a tool of macroeconomic management, they seemed anachronistic at a time when the EC was moving toward a single monetary policy. For all of those reasons, governments unwisely but understandably endured mounting pressure in the ERM, often at a cost of high interest rates and declining competitiveness.

Matters came to a head in mid-September 1992, partly because of the negative result of the Danish referendum and the unpredictability of the upcoming French referendum. First the Finnish markka, unofficially linked to the ERM, collapsed under the strain of huge speculative attacks. The Swedish krone, also unofficially linked to the ERM, was next. In the EMS, the Italian and British governments desperately shored up their ailing currencies with noticeably unenthusiastic German support.

An informal meeting of finance ministers in early September 1992 presented an opportunity to defuse the looming crisis and avert imminent disaster. Instead, the meeting ended in acrimony as Britain blamed the Bundesbank for the EC's high interest rates, economic ills, and currency turbulence. Helmut Schlesinger, the Bundesbank president, promised only that Germany would not raise interest rates further. As for a possible realignment, Schlesinger neither proposed a devaluation of sterling nor suggested a new parity for the pound. Had he done so, it is doubtful in any case that Britain would have gone along with it.

The surprise realignment of September 13, involving a 7 percent devaluation of the lira, did not affect the pound's parity in the ERM. More money flowed out of sterling as dealers sought a safer haven and speculators renewed their attacks. Two days later the pound closed just above its ERM floor. Reports of Schlesinger's support for a broader realignment made the pound's position untenable. Having spent billions trying to prop up the pound, the British government pulled sterling out of the ERM on "Black Wednesday," September 16. Unable to stanch further speculative flows despite the Bundesbank's decision to cut interest rates, Italy followed suit.[29] In a preemptive move, Spain devalued the peseta by 5 percent against the remaining ERM currencies.

Opinion polls showing a possible French rejection of the TEU increased attacks against the franc, which were already acute. The French "yes," regardless of the margin, failed to stem the flow of funds out of the franc. Only concerted efforts by the French and German governments and central banks averted a disaster in late September and prevented a French devaluation. Currency turbulence continued in late 1992 and early 1993 with the franc again under pressure, Spain and Portugal devaluing by 6 percent on November 23, and Ireland devaluing by 10 percent on January 30.

The currency crisis contributed to the contemporaneous TEU ratification debacle by undermining public confidence in the EMS and, by extension, in deeper European integration. With the pound outside the ERM and the Danish krone still inside but under growing pressure, public opinion in Britain and Denmark—already bitterly divided over Maastricht—hardened against ratification. Although the treaty survived, the EMS crisis had other consequences for EMU. Britain's and Italy's abrupt departure from the ERM made it seem highly unlikely that either country would rejoin in time to participate in Stage III of EMU. Of course, Britain's participation was already doubtful for political reasons, Italy's for economic reasons. Yet the embarrassing events of September 1992 had diametrically opposite consequences for both countries. Whereas the ERM crisis indeed strengthened British antipathy to EMU, it convinced many Italians that the solution ultimately lay in EMU itself. As a result, Italy's humiliating exit from the ERM in 1992 strengthened the country's resolve to meet the convergence criteria and join the single currency in 1999.

Elsewhere in the EC, the crisis shook confidence in the EMS but did not undermine the foundations of the system or seriously weaken intellectual and political support for EMU. Government officials pointed out that the crisis merely restored the EMS to its original state: a system of fixed but adjustable exchange rates. Wim Duisenberg, president of the Dutch central bank and later president of the ECB, put the situation in perspective: "What crisis?" he asked in January 1993. "The problem was that we had forgotten how to realign."[30]

Duisenberg spoke too soon. Currency turmoil peaked in July, not January, 1993. On July 29, when the Bundesbank decided not to make an eagerly awaited cut in interest rates, other EMS currencies—notably the franc—came under huge pressure. Angered by French criticism of German monetary policy, the Bundesbank conspicuously failed to provide the massive assistance necessary to prop up the franc. After an emergency meeting on August 1, 1993, EC finance ministers announced that apart from the Dutch guilder, which would stick to its original 2.5 percent band, EMS currencies would float within a 15 percent band around their parity with the mark.

Staying the Course

Most government officials and politicians defended the EMS tenaciously during the protracted crisis. After a meeting on September 28, 1992, finance ministers issued a joint communiqué describing the EMS as a "key factor of economic stability and prosperity in Europe."[31] Not surprisingly, the Commission claimed at the height of the crisis that "only a single currency will put an end to [the] waves of speculation which we have witnessed over the last weeks."[32] The OECD concurred, suggesting that "rather than casting doubt on the prospect for monetary unification, recent events should strengthen the EC members' resolve to conclude EMU as quickly as possible."[33]

Currency turmoil may have strengthened the rationale for EMU, but it widened the already growing gap between political and public opinion in most member states. Ordinary mortals could comprehend neither the complexities of the ERM nor the reasons for its existence. To most of them, the currency crisis had shown the impracticability, if not the impossibility, of currency union. Not only had the TEU ratification and ERM currency crises damaged public confidence in EMU but deep recession and growing economic divergence made it unlikely that member states would satisfy the prerequisites for EMU within the stipulated period.

Most striking, Germany's high interest rates forced other ERM participants to pursue equally tight monetary policies, which exacerbated the EU's economic downturn and made the convergence criteria harder to meet. The Bundesbank's decision less than a week after the Maastricht summit to raise interest rates by 0.5 percent was widely denounced as an affront to the spirit of EMU and an egregious example of its blatant "Germany first" approach. Of course, the Bundesbank's duty was solely to Germany and not at all to the wider Community. Nevertheless, the persistence of high German interest rates in the mid-1990s suggested that the Bundesbank would continue to subordinate wider European interests to German policy interests, possibly to the detriment of convergence among member states. Inasmuch as the Bundesbank wanted to warn the EU, the message was that high inflation could not be tolerated and that a form of monetary Darwinism would weed out the noncharter members of EMU.

Germans like to point out that their experience of hyperinflation in the early 1920s forged an anti-inflationary consensus that accounted for the Bundesbank's preoccupation with price stability and determination to make it the primary objective of the ECB. The Bundesbank always argued that there was no trade-off between inflation and employment. As Pöhl insisted in 1977, well before becoming Bundesbank president, "Inflation does not reduce unemployment. On the contrary, it is one of its major causes."[34] Economic theory and empirical evidence bear out the Bundesbank's point, except in the short term. And in the short term of the mid-1990s, as the Bundesbank pursued a tight monetary policy at a time of deep economic recession, unemployment rose alarmingly in most member states. This outcome further eroded support for EMU by creating the impression that a future ECB, like the present Bundesbank, would pursue price stability regardless of the EU's unemployment level.

High interest rates exacerbated the economic situation by increasing the cost of borrowing money, thereby reducing investment. With unemployment rising and consumer spending declining, governments took in less revenue through direct and indirect taxation and paid out more money in unemployment and other benefits. This situation made it impossible for governments to bring down deficits and debts toward the TEU-stipulated reference points. In many cases, not least in postunification Germany, public-sector borrowing rose at a time when, according to the EMU timetable, governments should have been exercising strict budget discipline.

Thus in the mid-1990s, EMU seemed an unlikely prospect. Few member states could satisfy the government finance criterion; most member states' inflation rates ranged outside the targeted band of not more than 1.5 percent of the EU's three best performers; and although interest rates had converged, they had done so at an unacceptably high level. Ironically, only the currency stability criterion was unproblematic, but not uncontroversial. The TEU stipulated that ERM participants should stay within "normal" fluctuation margins. In 1991, when the treaty was drafted, the prevailing 2.5 percent margin was presumed to be normal. But in August 1993, in the aftermath of the currency crisis, finance ministers widened the band to 15 percent. By claiming that "normal" now meant 15 rather than 2.5 percent, finance ministers fudged one of the conversion criteria and in effect removed exchange rates as a factor in the EMU equation.

It was little wonder, under the circumstances, that a single currency seemed unlikely to be introduced before the end of the century. The first edition of this book, written in 1994, concluded that "with Europe in the grip of recession and the ERM in disarray, it is difficult to see EMU coming into being within the Maastricht Treaty time frame.[35] Meeting in Madrid in December 1995, the European Council abandoned the goal of launching Stage III in 1997. Despite the European Council's earlier-than-expected decision, both the EMI and the Commission had statuary obligations to produce reports in 1996 on progress toward convergence. Whereas the Commission in its report stressed the positive progress that had already been made toward meeting the criteria, the EMI in its report emphasized the distance that member states still had to travel.[36] Together with the subsequent formal decision that Stage III could not be launched in 1997, the reports fed prevailing skepticism about the feasibility of EMU at any time in the foreseeable future.

Technical Preparations

Although the European Council abandoned 1997 as a starting date for Stage III of EMU, it nevertheless affirmed its commitment to starting Stage III in January 1999. At the time, the European Council's optimism about 1999 seemed far-fetched. Yet in retrospect, the Madrid summit of December 1995 was a turning point in the EMU's fortunes. The summit's significance lies not only in the affirmation of the 1999 deadline—after all, European Councils are notorious for their optimistic announcements—or in the decision to name the new currency the euro but in the adoption of a technically detailed post-1999 scenario for switching to the single currency. EMU could come about only by political will and administrative fiat. The Madrid summit showed that despite popular indifference or even opposition to EMU, political will existed in abundance. Moreover, deep administrative foundations were being laid regardless of prevailing Europessimism.

The abundance of political will was all the more surprising in view of otherwise weak leadership in the aftermath of the TEU ratification debacle. Apart from prevailing public skepticism about further integration, few governments enjoyed large parliamentary majorities. This was especially true of Germany, where Kohl had narrowly won the October 1994 election and was hampered not only by a small majority in the Bundestag but also by a Social Democratic majority in the Bundesrat (upper house). Yet Kohl pursued EMU with a passion, staking his political future and his place in history on its achievement. Kohl's obsession with EMU was partly emotional and partly rational—emotional in that despite his equivocation in the late 1980s, he had advocated EMU unhesitatingly during and after the IGC and rational in that he strongly believed that EMU was essential for Germany's and Europe's political and economic welfare.

Mitterrand shared Kohl's conviction, but Mitterrand's presidency ended in May 1995. Jacques Chirac, Mitterrand's successor, had been ambivalent about EMU during the presidential election campaign, having earlier called for a referendum in France to endorse the single currency. As a neo-Gaullist, Chirac was not well disposed toward deeper European integration. Once in office, however, Chirac realized that France had no choice but to press ahead with EMU. Chirac's relationship with Kohl would never be close, and Chirac's stubbornness over the selection of the ECB president would later cast a shadow over the launch of Stage III. But on EMU itself Chirac proved resolute. Although Franco-German relations lost their coziness after Mitterrand's departure from the Elysée Palace in 1995, the Franco-German tandem continued to advocate EMU and take the unpopular steps necessary to achieve it.

While Kohl, Chirac, and other EU leaders used European Councils as media-saturated opportunities to press ahead with EMU, administrative work proceeded apace in national central banks, the Commission, and the new EMI. Although EMU threatened to turn them into branch offices of the ESCB, national central banks—including the Bundesbank—relished the intellectual and analytical challenges of preparing for Stage III. The Commission had a more obvious bureaucratic incentive to lay the groundwork for EMU. Indeed, at the height of EMU skepticism in early 1995, the Commission issued a detailed green paper on technical aspects of launching the single currency.[37]

As stipulated in the treaty, the EMI bore the brunt of the administrative work necessary to ensure EMU's success. The EMI had been set up at the beginning of Stage II, in July 1994. The institute's location, a highly political decision, provoked a row between France and Germany. At Kohl's insistence, the European Council decided at a special summit in October 1993 to locate the EMI in Frankfurt, seat of the Bundesbank and a symbol for Germans of sound monetary policy. Alexandre Lamfalussy, former president of the Bank of International Settlements in Basel, was appointed the EMI's first president.

The EMI was neither an extension of the Committee of Central Bank Governors, which it replaced, nor a synonym for the ECB, which it preceded. Instead, the EMI had two main tasks: make technical preparations for Stage III of EMU and help coordinate member states' monetary policies. The foremost technical preparation was to specify, by the end of 1996, the regulatory, organizational, and logistical framework for the ESCB (including the ECB), which would come into existence on the eve of Stage III. Thus the EMI drafted the "changeover scenario" that the European Council adopted in December 1995, developed monetary policy instruments and procedures, prepared the TARGET cross-border payment system, and compiled EU-wide statistics. In addition, the EMI had to strengthen cooperation among national central banks in an effort to coordinate national monetary policies. Here the EMI was powerless to make decisions, as member states remained responsible for their monetary policies

Table 16.1 Key EMU Decisions and the Changeover to the Euro, 1995–2002

Event	Actions
Madrid European Council, December 1995	Decision on the changeover timetable and the name "euro."
Amsterdam European Council, June 1997	Agreement on Stability and Growth Pact, ERM II.
Brussels Council, May 1998	Decision on participating member states in Stage III of EMU. Fixing of bilateral conversion rates. Decision on president and executive board of the European Central Bank.
June 1, 1998	European Central Bank set up in Frankfurt, replacing the European Monetary Institute, under presidency of Wim Duisenberg. European System of Central Banks also set up.
January 1, 1999	Start of Stage III—irrevocable fixing of exchange rates and entry into force of relevant legislation.
From January 1, 1999	Execution of single monetary policy, foreign exchange operations in euros, operation of TARGET payment system, new public debt to be issued in euros.
January 1, 1999, to January 1, 2002	Exchange at par value of currencies with irrevocably fixed exchange rates. Assistance with an "orderly changeover."
By January 1, 2002, at latest	Start circulation of euro banknotes and coins.
By July 1, 2002, at latest	Cancel legal tender status of national banknotes and coins.

until the beginning of Stage III. Nevertheless, the EMI board's monthly debates and regular reports on monetary policy and economic performance in the EU helped nudge member states toward compliance with the convergence criteria.

Between the technical level of the national central banks, the Commission's services, and the EMI on the one hand and the highest political level of the European Council on the other, the Council of Economic and Finance Ministers (ECOFIN) and its preparatory monetary committee played a key role in bringing about Stage III. ECOFIN had an obvious vested interest in ensuring the venture's success. In a post-EMU world, the coordination of national economic policies would assume greater political importance. As a result, ECOFIN's stature would rise, especially vis-à-vis that of its main rival in the EU pecking order, the General Affairs Council (foreign ministers).

The European Council asked ECOFIN in December 1995 to study two issues central to EMU's success. One was the problem posed by the fact that some member states would not participate initially (if ever) in Stage III. The other, at Germany's insistence, was to ensure the sustainability of

EMU through the continuation of budgetary discipline *after* the launch of Stage III. Based on contributions from the Commission and the EMI, ECOFIN proposed a revised exchange rate mechanism (dubbed ERM II) to regulate relations between the euro and nonparticipating member state currencies and a stability pact to ensure budgetary discipline after the launch of the euro.

The ERM II proposal was relatively straightforward and uncontroversial. The European Council adopted an ERM II framework in December 1996 and a resolution setting out the mechanism's principles and fundamentals in June 1997. Modeled on the existing ERM, ERM II would allow relatively large fluctuation margins (15 percent) for noneuro currencies in relation to the euro. The ESCB and the central banks of noneuro member states would intervene if necessary to maintain currency parities within the fluctuation limits.

Sustainability, Employment, and Oversight

By contrast with ERM II, the proposed stability pact caused a political storm. Bearing an obvious German imprint, the draft agreement threatened automatic penalties for euro-zone countries running excessive budget deficits. Like the TEU's budget deficit criterion for participation in Stage III, the proposed stability pact defined "excessive" as above 3 percent of GDP. By 1996, when the proposal was being drafted and debated, member states were cutting budgets in order to bring deficits below the 3 percent ceiling. As budget cuts resulted in less government hiring, fewer and smaller business subsidies, and lower expenditure on public works, unemployment inevitably increased. As budget cuts also resulted in less generous social welfare programs, unemployment became less congenial for many Europeans. These developments reinforced a popular perception that EMU itself caused unemployment and worsened the plight of the unemployed.

Nowhere was this perception stronger, and nowhere was a government more sensitive to its political repercussions, than in France. Chirac's pre-presidential ambiguity about EMU was due largely to the domestic political risk of embracing EMU enthusiastically. Once elected, Chirac would take the credit for EMU if and when it succeeded. In the meantime, Alain Juppé, his prime minister, took the blame for unpopular austerity measures. Already French workers had rioted in Paris in December 1995, protesting proposed changes in the social security system. In deference to French sensitivity, Germany watered down the terms of the proposed stability pact, making fines not automatic but subject to approval by governments. Also in deference to the perception that EMU was imposing a fiscal straitjacket that destroyed jobs, ECOFIN renamed the proposed agreement, which the European Council adopted in Dublin in December 1996, the *stability and growth pact.*

Eager to have a government whose term would coincide with the remainder of his seven-year presidency, the latter part of which would include the launch of Stage III and the changeover to the euro, Chirac brought forward the date of parliamentary elections from March 1998 to March 1997. Chirac miscalculated badly: Juppé paid for his unpopularity in the polls, and Lionel Jospin, Chirac's Socialist opponent in the earlier presidential election, formed a new government. Not only did France now enter a new period of *cohabitation* (whereby the presidency and government were held by opposing political parties) but Jospin was outspoken in his criticism of EMU.

One of Jospin's first steps as prime minister, at the Amsterdam summit in June 1997, was to demand a renegotiation of the stability and growth pact. This irked the Germans and delayed discussion of the summit's most pressing business: the Amsterdam Treaty. Jospin succeeded only in having the European Council adopt a separate resolution on growth and employment that stressed member states' determination to keep employment firmly at the top of the political agenda. The European Council also decided to hold an extraordinary summit in Luxembourg in November 1997 to discuss job creation.[38]

A call by Jospin for an "economic government" to watch over the supposedly independent ECB caused even greater alarm in Frankfurt and Bonn. Germany and like-minded member states had no intention of undermining the ECB's independence or commitment to price stability, although they saw in Jospin's proposal an opportunity to establish a forum for discussions among euro-zone countries about such key issues as maintaining fiscal discipline, coordinating taxation policy, and setting the euro's exchange rate. Accordingly, the European Council agreed in December 1997 to form a "Euro-X" council of finance ministers (Euro referring to the single currency, X to the variable number of participating member states).

The EMU Juggernaut

The controversy surrounding the stability and growth pact and the Euro-X council demonstrated both the increasing politicization of EMU and the increasing likelihood that it would be launched on time. As late as 1996 most political pundits argued that Stage III would have to be deferred beyond 1999; by mid-1997 prevailing opinion was that Stage III would begin on time but with a minority or at most a small majority of member states. By late 1997 this view had given way to the conviction that Stage III would begin on time with eleven member states, that is, with all the member states that wished to participate, minus Greece (Britain, Denmark, and Sweden opted out for political reasons).

The growing conviction that EMU would be launched on time was due to a number of factors:

- the manifest determination of France and Germany to meet the convergence criteria by hook or by crook
- the impact of economic recovery
- the acquiescence of public opinion
- detailed and credible technical preparations by the EMI and other bodies
- the seriousness with which large banks and businesses took the EMU venture

French and German efforts to meet the convergence criteria by engaging in what some critics derided as "creative accounting" reinforced the impression that Stage III would be launched in 1999 at all costs. France's creative accounting was successful; Germany's was a failure. The Commission allowed France to apply a huge one-off payment from France Telecom in 1997 against the country's deficit; the Bundesbank rejected the finance minister's effort to revalue Germany's gold reserves in May 1997 and apply the proceeds against the country's deficit. These stratagems demonstrated both countries' determination to meet the most difficult convergence criterion, if necessary by subterfuge. Given that the decision as to which countries met the criteria would be a political one and that the political establishments of most member states had set their sights on the starting date of January 1, 1999, it became increasingly obvious that Stage III would be launched on time. Unless certain of EMU's punctual launch, France and Germany would not have argued so hard over the terms of the stability and growth pact or of the Euro-X council.

The TEU's criteria for the measurement of "excessive deficit" gave member states ample wriggle room. The 60 percent reference point for national debt could be exceeded if "the ratio [of debt to GDP] is sufficiently diminishing and approaching [60 percent] at a satisfactory pace." Similarly, the 3 percent reference point for budget deficit could be relaxed if the ratio (of deficit to GDP) declined "substantially and continuously and reached a level that comes close to [3 percent]," or if the excess "is only exceptional and temporary and the ratio remains close [to 3 percent]" (Article 104, formerly Article 104c, and the excessive deficit procedure protocol, TEC).

Yet the budget deficit criterion of 3 percent became a rigid yardstick for measuring member states' eligibility for EMU. That was not only because the 3 percent figure had been bandied about more than any other in the EMU debate but also because opponents of EMU, especially in Germany, had seized on it as the absolute limit for the budget deficit of an aspiring Stage III participant—hence the French and German governments' extraordinary measures to get their deficits below the 3 percent ceiling.

Even with recourse to such measures as privatization and gold-reserves revaluation, neither France nor Germany looked likely in early

1997 to come under the 3 percent ceiling. If one or both of them proved unable to participate in EMU, the entire project would collapse. By mid-1997, however, Europe's economic recovery began to have an impact on the member states' budget deficits. It seemed that France, Germany, and most other member states would confound the skeptics and meet the 3 percent standard. The Commission's fall 1997 economic forecast bore out this rosy scenario and strengthened the growing conviction that EMU would start with a large majority of member states.[39]

Most surprising of all was the likelihood that Portugal, Spain, and Italy, countries with a tradition of lax monetary policy and financial profligacy, would make the first cut. Even strong supporters of EMU derided the Mediterranean countries' possible participation in it. Snide comments by German officials about Italy's ineligibility for EMU strained relations between both countries. Yet whereas the German government had sneakily tried to revalue the Bundesbank's gold reserves in order to meet the convergence criteria, Italy's center-left Olive Tree coalition government had taken such politically courageous steps as introducing tough austerity measures and levying a special tax to help cut the budget deficit. For Italy, then in the throes of post–Cold War political upheaval, failure to make the EMU grade came to be seen as a potential national disaster.

Germany's concerns about Italy, shared by most northern countries, pertained especially to sustainability. Even if Italy met the convergence criteria, would it sustain the 3 percent budget deficit ceiling after 1999? Opponents of Italy's participation may have had legitimate concerns, but attempting to keep Italy out of Stage III on grounds of nonsustainability would have implicitly acknowledged the worthlessness of the stability and growth pact, which the European Council had already adopted to deal with this issue.

A technical announcement by ECOFIN in September 1997 that finance ministers would fix conversion rates between single currency countries several months earlier than stipulated in the treaty strengthened political opinion that EMU was firmly on track. Instead of waiting until the end of 1998, ECOFIN would agree on the conversion rates in early May 1998, when the heads of state and government were due to select countries for participation in Stage III. Although intended to deter speculative attacks on prospective participants' currencies in the run-up to January 1, 1999, inevitably the announcement boosted political confidence in EMU's prospects.

One of the most surprising aspects of the developing EMU juggernaut was the degree of public acquiescence in it. The TEU ratification crisis had exposed a high degree of public opposition to deeper integration, which many observers expected to crystallize around EMU. Moreover, the popular equation of EMU with austerity and unemployment seemed destined to spark anti-EMU protests at the polling booth and in the streets. Yet apart from demonstrations in France in December 1995 and the Juppé government's defeat in

May 1997, public concern about EMU failed to manifest itself. Clearly, the degree of public opposition to EMU, and the extent to which ordinary Europeans would demonstrate such opposition, had been exaggerated.

In reality, the pain of EMU was unevenly spread and reaction to it differed widely among aspiring participants. Luxembourg was already a model of fiscal rectitude. Belgium considered that EMU membership was its birthright and so did not bother to tackle seriously its bloated public debt. Alone of the Nordic member states, Finland was highly motivated to participate in EMU. The criteria caused little pain in Ireland and the Netherlands, which had already embarked on economic restructuring and were enjoying strong economic growth. The convergence criteria caused a lot of pain in Italy, Portugal, Spain, and Greece, but these countries badly needed a pretext to put their public finances in order and at the same time feared the humiliation of not coming up to EMU standards.

Only in France and Germany, the EU's core countries, might hostile public opinion have jeopardized EMU. France seemed especially vulnerable because of its tradition of government surrender in the face of violent political protest. Nor did the election of Jospin, who had made lavish campaign promises, seem auspicious. In the event, economic recovery made it possible for Jospin to square the circle of EMU-inspired austerity and Socialist extravagance. Anti-EMU protests never materialized, and the government did not have to put its EMU commitment to the ultimate political test of facing down demonstrators.

In contrast to France, Germany's political tradition is one of obedience. That helps to explain why, despite numerous polls showing how unhappy the majority of Germans were to give up the mark, a powerful anti-EMU movement failed to materialize during the 1998 federal election campaign. Germans confined their protests to writing letters to the editor and bringing a case before the Constitutional Court. Most Germans reckoned that the political consequences of abandoning EMU were potentially more destabilizing than the economic consequences of staying the course. The opposition Social Democratic Party (SPD) learned that lesson in local elections in 1997, when anti-EMU SPD candidates lost decisively. Gerhard Schröder, who emerged in early 1998 as the SPD contender for the chancellorship (and who beat Kohl in the September 1998 election), took the lesson to heart by abandoning his earlier equivocation about EMU.

With the realization by late 1997 that opposition to EMU was muted and that most member states would meet the convergence criteria, the procedure for selecting Stage III participants in 1998 lost its political edge. On February 28, 1998, member states released data showing a high degree of nominal convergence.

Based on these figures, of the twelve countries hoping to participate in Stage III only Greece would fail to qualify because its budget deficit was a full percentage point above the reference point. (By devaluing its currency

Table 16.2 Member State Finances in February 1998

Member State	Public Deficit[a] (as % of GDP)	Public Debt (as % of GDP)	Participation in EMU Stage 3?
Belgium	2.1	122.2	y
Denmark	–0.7	64.1	n[b]
Germany	2.7	61.3	y
Greece	4.0	108.7	n[c]
Spain	2.6	68.3	y
France	3.0	58.0	y
Ireland	–0.9	67.0	y
Italy	2.7	121.6	y
Luxembourg	–1.7	6.7	y
Netherlands	1.4	72.1	y
Austria	2.5	66.1	y
Portugal	2.5	62.0	y
Finland	0.9	55.8	y
Sweden	0.4	76.6	n[b]
Britain	1.9	53.4	n[b]
TEU limits	3.0	60.0	

Source: Agence Europe, February 28, 1998.
Notes: a. Negative donates a budget surplus.
b. Country has chosen not to participate for domestic political reasons.
c. Country failed to meet convergence criteria.

and joining the ERM on March 14, 1998, Greece signaled its determination to join Stage III perhaps as early as January 2001, subject to continued deficit and inflation reduction.) Britain, Denmark, and Sweden, which had decided not to adopt the single currency, came in well under the 3 percent ceiling. By contrast, France reported a deficit of 3.02 percent, sufficiently close to the reference point to assuage critics and opponents of EMU. The member states' figures on national debt were less impressive with Belgium, Italy, and Greece coming in well above 100 percent (the reference point being 60 percent).

In their respective convergence reports, published on March 25 (the anniversary of the signing of the Treaty of Rome), the EMI and the Commission drew attention to these large debts and adjured member states to accelerate economic reform and restructuring. In particular, the EMI warned that "decisive and sustained corrective policies of a structural nature" were necessary in most countries. Nevertheless, both reports recommended that eleven member states begin Stage III in January 1999.[40] At the same time, the Commission's spring economic forecast predicted strong economic growth throughout the EU despite the possible impact of the Asian economic crisis.[41]

The Commission and EMI recommendations, obligatory under the terms of the TEU, made it inevitable that the heads of state and government, meeting in Brussels on May 2, 1998, would formally select the same eleven member states for participation in Stage III. Only twelve months earlier, the Brussels summit was expected to be contentious because of the possibility that the heads of state and government would have to decide on the composition of euroland by qualified majority vote. By early 1998, however, consensus on the composition of euroland threatened to rob the summit of all drama. In the event, the Brussels summit was highly memorable because of a drama of a different kind: a bitter row between Chirac and Kohl over the presidency of the ECB that overshadowed the formal selection of the single currency countries.

The Duisenberg Row

The row originated in a decision by central bank governors in May 1996 to appoint Wim Duisenberg to succeed Lamfalussy as head of the EMI on the understanding that Duisenberg would then become president of the ECB. Although the ECB was to be independent of national influence, the choice of ECB president was nonetheless a political decision. The TEU acknowledged that fact by giving the European Council responsibility for selecting the ECB president. Realizing that the European Council would formally appoint the ECB president several months before the launch of Stage III, in May 1996 the central bank governors got their national leaders' approval of Duisenberg's eventual succession to the ECB presidency.

Chirac was unhappy about Duisenberg's selection both because Duisenberg was clearly the German government's candidate (having won the battle to locate the ECB in Frankfurt, Germany could not also have pushed one of its own nationals to head the new bank; Duisenberg was the next best thing) and because the selection procedure smacked of unelected central bankers usurping the prerogative of elected government leaders. Chirac grumbled at the time but objected publicly to Duisenberg's otherwise uncontested nomination only in November 1997, when he nominated Jean-Claude Trichet, governor of the Bank of France, for the job.

Thereafter the issue was Chirac's insistence on a Franco-German trade-off: a German location for the ECB (already decided) and a French president for the ECB (not yet decided). Ironically, Chirac did not much like Trichet, who as head of the Bank of France had pursued an independent monetary policy. As far as Chirac was concerned, Trichet's strengths were that he was a member of the central bankers club and, more important, that he was French.

To everyone's surprise, Chirac pursued this nakedly nationalistic position to the end, compromising only to the extent that Duisenberg could begin the ECB presidency's first eight-year term but would have to step down for Trichet halfway through. Chirac held out for a written commitment by Duisenberg to resign on January 1, 2002. After ten hours of bitter negotiation, which Kohl described as among the most difficult in his lengthy EU experience, Chirac accepted a decision by Duisenberg, supposedly reached "of my own free will . . . and not under pressure from anyone," to step down sometime after mid-2002.[42] As part of the compromise, the European Council agreed that another Frenchman would become Duisenberg's vice president and that Trichet would succeed Duisenberg for a full eight-year term.[43]

The outcome of the Brussels summit suggested that the ECB's independence was compromised even before the bank came into being and that the French government would attempt to interfere in European monetary policymaking. Such concerns were largely assuaged by Duisenberg's robust performance at a hearing in the EP the following week and by the composition of the ECB's governing board; all are experienced, independent-minded central bankers. The significance of Chirac's behavior was what it portended not for EMU but for Chirac's relations with his EU partners. Apart from insulting his fellow heads of state and government, Chirac further undermined Kohl's chances of reelection in September 1998. Nor should Chirac's conduct be dismissed as "typically French." Although the French are generally not self-conscious about advocating national interests, Chirac's definition of the national interest is unusually narrow and his behavior is generally impulsive and idiosyncratic.

WILL EMU WORK?

The short answer to the question "Will EMU work?" is yes, it *will* work because a majority of Europeans have decided that it *must* work. During the transition stages, member states displayed a determination to make it happen; new and existing administrative bodies demonstrated the necessary expertise to bring it about; and public opinion showed surprising compliance with it. Having concluded during the transition stages not only that EMU was feasible but also that the political and economic costs of failure were greater than the costs of success, politicians, technocrats, and ordinary Europeans alike were bound to conclude after the launch of Stage III that the costs of maintaining the single currency are considerably less than the costs of its collapse.

Nevertheless, the challenges of managing the single currency and generating public support for it are considerable. At one level, acceptance of the single currency will most likely prove surprisingly easy. Few people will mourn their national currencies. As long as the new currency is a strong one that is not eroded by inflation, the public will quickly come to terms with it.

The strength of the currency, in turn, will depend on prevailing international circumstances and on the judgment and credibility of the ECB, whose board consists of highly reputable and experienced former national bankers. Governments may try to pressure individual members, but the likely loss of credibility resulting from public knowledge of a board member's surrender to such pressure serves as a strong deterrent. There is no guarantee that board members will not succumb privately to national pressure, although obvious nationalistic behavior is unlikely to escape their colleagues' notice and opprobrium.

The fate of the ECB depends not only on its integrity and independence but also on its effectiveness and legitimacy. The euro's value is a prime determinant of the ECB's credibility. But managing the single currency, like preparing for it, imposes costs that are unevenly spread among member states and that vary over time. Given the diversity of national economic and financial systems, a euro-zone-wide monetary policy cannot fit each member state equally well. Monetary tightening affects member states in different ways and at different times.[44] An economic shock in one member state may prompt a monetary response that disadvantages another member state; alternatively, the ECB's refusal to respond to a regional economic shock could undermine support for the ECB in that part of euroland. Without financial transfers to compensate those parts of euroland in recession and with little cross-border labor mobility and strong constraints on the use of national fiscal instruments, the ECB's response to asymmetrical shocks assumes even greater importance.

Those who are disadvantaged by prevailing monetary policy will direct their anger at "Brussels" and "Frankfurt." Inevitably, the ECB's legitimacy will be called into question. This problem relates to a wider, longstanding one of democratic accountability and representation in the EU. Nevertheless, the legitimacy of the ECB is especially troublesome because of the necessity to maintain its political independence and also because its decisions will have a profound impact on economic activity throughout euroland.

Public doubts about the bank's legitimacy make it imperative for ECB board members to give frequent speeches, interviews, and press conferences about the bank's policy goals and instruments, within the bounds of confidentiality. The EP is the ECB's obvious official interlocutor at the European level. Regular meetings with the EP's Committee on Economic and Monetary Affairs may help to personalize the ECB and build public support for its actions. Yet it will be difficult to build the legitimacy of the ECB on that of the EP, which, despite being directly elected, is neither well liked nor well understood in the EU.

EMU will most likely work at least in the narrow sense of the euro's survival. Beyond that, EMU has the potential to succeed by prompting economic restructuring, boosting employment, and propelling growth. As Commission president Jacques Santer commented during the selection of the eleven euro countries in early 1998, the euro is "not an end in itself but an instrument to spur and sustain economic growth into the next century."[45] A small degree of economic growth is likely to follow in the wake of EMU because of the abolition of currency conversions between participating countries and because of greater price transparency, although proponents of EMU have exaggerated the cost of currency conversions and the prospect that their abolition will spur cross-border trade. Nevertheless, the eradication of bank charges and commissions, as well as of personnel and other costs relating to currency management and hedging, will save exporters money. Similarly, the removal of currency barriers will stimulate some additional cross-border trade. A rise in business and consumer spending may also follow a fall in prices in some member states due to price transparency across borders. Yet prices are unlikely to converge in the euro zone because of vastly different tax rates among member states.

Whether EMU spurs greater economic growth and makes a serious dent in unemployment depends not only on the global economic situation but also on whether EMU results in major economic and financial restructuring. EMU will generate momentum for such restructuring, but individual national responses will depend on political and cultural considerations. The follow-on debate about a possible overhaul of taxation, subsidies, and labor market policies touches a raw nerve in France, especially because of the implication that EMU is incompatible with the much-vaunted European model of society and is a stalking horse for the despised Anglo-Saxon model. Stereotypically, the European model, based on a fusion of capitalism and socialism, values solidarity and cohesion; the Anglo-Saxon model, based on naked capitalism, thrives on individualism and greed.

Even without EMU, the European model as idealized in France and elsewhere is unsustainable. Domestically, welfare costs impose a huge economic burden; internationally, liberalized trade and free capital movements are irreconcilable with overregulation of the workforce and marketplace. The high cost of hiring and firing workers accounts in large part for double-digit unemployment in parts of Europe, yet calls for welfare and labor market reform evoke a defensive, ideological response not only in France but also in Germany following the Social Democrats' September 1998 election victory.

A more realistic version of the European model exists in the Netherlands, which has enjoyed high employment and low inflation since the mid-1990s. The ingredients of the Dutch model are social partnership, wage moderation, budget discipline, and gradual welfare reform. The German model is traditionally closer to the Dutch than to the French model, but the high costs of unification and weak domestic leadership made it impossible in the late 1990s for the Christian Democratic government to emulate the Dutch entirely. By contrast, Germany's Social Democratic government may be unable to resist the temptation to try to cut unemployment through government spending rather than through taxation, labor market, and other reforms, despite the constraints of the stability pact. If so, EMU may succeed in a narrow sense, but will not achieve its full potential.

NOTES

1. Interview in *Wall Street Journal,* October 29, 1990, p. 1.

2. Karl Kaiser et al., *The European Community: Progress or Decline?* (London: RIIA, 1983), p. 13.

3. Tomaso Padoa-Schioppa, ed., *Efficiency, Stability and Equity: A Strategy for the Evolution of the Economic System of the EC* (Luxembourg: Office for Official Publications of the European Communities [OOP], 1987), p. 8.

4. Commission, *Economic and Monetary Union* (Luxembourg: OOP, 1990), p. 11.

5. Commission, *One Market, One Money: An Evaluation of the Potential Benefits and Costs of Forming an Economic and Monetary Union* (Luxembourg: OOP, 1990), p. 9.

6. Commission, *From Single Market to European Union* (Luxembourg: OOP, 1992).

7. Padoa-Schioppa, *Efficiency,* pp. 3, 13.

8. Leon Brittan, speech to the British Chamber of Commerce in Germany, October 31, 1990.

9. See Commission, *One Market,* p. 10.

10. Bull. EC S/1-1976, p. 20.

11. Committee for the Study of Economic and Monetary Union, *Report on Economic and Monetary Union in the European Community (Delors Report)* (Luxembourg: OOP, 1989), pp. 18–19.

12. *Delors Report,* p. 24.

13. Commission, *Economic and Monetary Union,* p. 21.

14. *Hansard,* 184/41, Cols. 470–479, January 24, 1991.

15. Quoted in *Manchester Guardian Weekly,* July 7, 1991, p. 6.

16. Leon Brittan, speech to the British Chamber of Commerce in Germany, October 31, 1990.

17. Commission, *Economic and Monetary Union,* p. 17.

18. Commission, *One Market,* p. 251.

19. Ibid., pp. 28–29.

20. Peter Kenen, "Speaking Up for EMU," *Financial Times,* July 28, 1992, p. 15.

21. Martin Feldstein, "Europe's Monetary Union: The Case Against EMU," *Economist,* June 13, 1992, pp. 19–22.

22. Commission, *Economic and Monetary Union,* p. 11.

23. Bull. EC 6-1988, "Presidency Conclusions," points 1.1.1 to 1.1.4, and 3.4.1.

24. Bull. EC 6-1989, "Presidency Conclusions," point 1.1.11.

25. Bull. EC 12-1989, "Presidency Conclusions," point 1.1.11.

26. Bull. EC 6-1990, "Presidency Conclusions," point 1.10.

27. Bull. EC 10-1990, "Presidency Conclusions," points 1.2 to 1.6.

28. Paule de Grauwe, Daniel Gros, Alfred Steinherr, and Niels Thygesen, "Reply to Feldstein," *Economist,* July 4, 1992, p. 67.

29. See "The ERM Crisis," *Financial Times,* December 12–13, 1992, p. 2.

30. Quoted in *Financial Times,* January 15, 1993, p. 2.

31. Council press release 8854/92, September 28, 1992, 1604th Council Meeting.

32. Henning Christopherson, speech to the European Institute, Washington, D.C., September 21, 1992.

33. OECD, *Financial Market Trends,* October 1992, p. 16.

34. Quoted in *Financial Times,* May 17, 1991, p. 18; Pöhl inserted this phrase into the final communiqué of the 1977 G7 summit.

35. Desmond Dinan, *Ever Closer Union? An Introduction to the European Community* (Boulder: Lynne Rienner, 1994), p. 435.
36. Commission, *Report on Convergence in the European Union in 1996,* COM(96)560, November 6, 1996; European Monetary Institute, *Progress Towards Convergence* (Frankfurt: EMI, November 1996).
37. Commission, "Green Paper on Technical Preparations for the Single European Currency," COM(95)333.
38. Amsterdam European Council, "Presidency Conclusions," Bull. EC 6-1997, point 1.1.10.
39. Commission, *European Economy*, Supplement A, No. 10 (October 1997).
40. Commission, *Euro 1999: Progress Towards Convergence* (Luxembourg: OOP, 1999); and European Monetary Institute, *Convergence Report* (Frankfurt: EMI, 1998).
41. Commission, *European Economy*, Supplement A, no. 3/4 (March-April 1998).
42. Associated Press, May 4, 1998.
43. See Lionel Barber, "The Euro: Single Currency, Multiple Injuries," in *Financial Times,* June 10, 1999, p. 10.
44. See R. Ramaswamy, and T. Sloek, "The Real Effects of Monetary Policy in the European Union: What Are the Differences?" IMF working paper 97/160, December 1997.
45. Quoted in the *International Herald Tribune*, March 26, 1998, p. 4.

17

External Relations

With a population of 375 million and a GDP of $8,600 billion, the EU is a leading global economic actor. Most "third countries" (nonmember states) have diplomatic missions in Brussels accredited to the EU. The Commission negotiates on member states' behalf in the World Trade Organization (WTO), participates in the work of the Organization for Economic Cooperation and Development (OECD), coordinates assistance to the countries of Central and Eastern Europe and the former Soviet Union, and has over 100 diplomatic missions and offices around the world. The Commission president meets regularly with the president of the United States and other world leaders and attends the annual summits of the seven most industrialized countries (G7); commissioners frequently visit and receive government ministers from nonmember states to discuss trade, environmental, labor, and other economic issues.

Despite its high international profile and considerable economic weight, the EU lacks commensurate political power. The EU's Common Foreign and Security Policy (CFSP) is far weaker than its Common Commercial Policy (CCP). Despite this glaring imbalance, efforts to strengthen the CFSP, let alone develop a common defense policy, have proved unavailing. At a time when most member states are adopting a common monetary policy and a common currency, and at a time also of instability on Europe's periphery, the EU's inability to share sovereignty in the realm of security and defense is especially glaring.

COMMON COMMERCIAL POLICY

The Common Commercial Policy (CCP) gives the EU exclusive competence for external trade relations. The CCP is the external manifestation of the customs union, itself the foundation upon which the single market and EMU were built. The common external tariff (CET), established in

July 1968 upon completion of the customs union, is a key regulatory instrument of the CCP. Technically the CCP was not complete until the single market became (almost) fully operational in 1992, putting an end to long-standing quota restrictions and other controls that individual member states had imposed against certain imports (mostly textiles, cars, and consumer electronics) from third countries. According to the Commission, the single market program meant, among other things, "putting in place the final elements of the CCP."[1]

The original Articles 110–116 of the Treaty of Rome (now Articles 131–135 TEC) outlined the CCP. Article 110 declares the CCP's guiding principle: "to contribute, in the common interest, to the harmonious development of world trade, the progressive abolition of restrictions on international trade, and the lowering of customs barriers." To that end the EU has developed a network of highly institutionalized multilateral, interregional, and bilateral trading relationships involving almost every country in the world.

The Institutional Context

Article 133 (formerly Article 113) authorizes the Commission to conduct the EC's external trade relations subject to direction from the Council (using qualified majority voting). It remained essentially unchanged through successive treaty reforms. Article 300 (formerly Article 228) gives the EC the authority to conclude international agreements (with the Council acting, as in Article 133, by qualified majority vote). Although the TEU amended Article 300 in order to give the European Parliament (EP) a greater role in concluding international agreements (by way of the assent procedure), the EP continues to be excluded from commercial agreements.

Two key controversies have dominated the implementation of Articles 133 and 300. The first is the nature and conduct of the Commission-Council relationship; the second is the extent of EC competence given the emergence of new trade issues and the rapidly changing international trade agenda. Both are classic examples of the struggle between supranationalism and intergovernmentalism in the EU system.

Article 133 describes the Commission-Council relationship by stipulating that the Council must approve Commission proposals to implement the CCP and must also approve Commission recommendations to open negotiations for agreements with third countries (in both cases acting by a qualified majority). In addition, Article 133 provides for "a special committee appointed by the Council to assist the Commission" with its negotiations "within the framework of such directives as the Council may issue to it." This is the famous 113 Committee (it is still known by the original treaty article number) of member state civil servants that meets regularly with Commission officials to approve the Commission's negotiating strategy and proposals. Similarly, Article 300 authorizes the Commission to negotiate international agreements subject to the Council's oversight.

The Commission has a love-hate relationship with the 113 Committee, whose presence behind the scenes ensures that Commission negotiators stick to the agreed-upon Council position. The committee's existence inherently strengthens the Commission's negotiating position because third countries know that the Commission has the committee's—and therefore the Council's—support. On the other hand, the committee's existence reduces the Commission's room for maneuver. Either way, the Article 133 regime means that the Commission is always involved in parallel sets of negotiations: with member states (through the 113 Committee) to agree upon and (when necessary) adjust a negotiation position and with third countries to conclude a trade accord.

Inevitably the Commission tries to maximize its influence and input and frequently exceeds its negotiating brief. Sometimes the 113 Committee is too intrusive; at other times it is surprisingly lax and can be "captured" by the Commission. How much the Commission gets away with usually depends first and foremost on the political and economic importance of the negotiations. Other factors that determine the Commission's degree of flexibility in the conduct of external trade negotiations include the complexity of the issues under discussion (the Commission has a long institutional memory and a high level of expertise); the stature of the trade policy commissioner and of the country in the council presidency; the Commission's willingness and ability to take initiatives, build coalitions of member states, and mobilize interest groups; the timing of the negotiations and the pressure (or nonpressure) for agreement; the involvement of various sectoral councils as well as the General Affairs Council (which has overall authority for trade policy); and the busyness of the Commission's own political agenda.

Member states started to dispute the extent of Community competence for trade relations as trade began to account for a growing share of GDP and as the international economic system grew more complex. When the original version of Article 133 was drafted, trade barriers consisted mostly of tariffs and quotas. Subsequently, regulatory barriers such as standards, conformity testing, certification, and product approval assumed paramount importance. At the same time, trade in goods lost its primacy to trade in services, and issues such as investment and the environment impinged more and more on the international trade agenda. The acceleration of technological change introduced new products (such as genetically modified organisms) and new processes (such as electronic commerce). Sometimes new products necessitated a reconfiguration of existing services (such as the impact of cell phones on the provision of telephone service).

The Commission consistently interpreted Articles 133 and 300 flexibly, arguing that the Community retained exclusive competence for trade relations regardless of these developments. Partly because of institutional rivalry, but mostly because the economic stakes were so much higher, member states (through the Council) took a more rigid view of Article 133. There were frequent spats between the Council and the Commission in the 1980s, but matters came to a head during the final stages of the Uruguay Round of the GATT in the early 1990s. When member states questioned the Commission's competence to conclude agreements on trade in services and trade-related aspects of intellectual property rights, the Commission responded by requesting a ruling from the European Court of Justice (ECJ). Much to the Commission's surprise, the ECJ interpreted Article 133 conservatively and ruled against the Commission.[2]

The Commission unsuccessfully attempted at the 1996–1997 IGC to extend the scope of Article 133 to cover trade in services and intellectual property rights. By stipulating in the revised article that the Council could decide in future *by means of unanimity* to extend Article 133, national governments effectively maintained the status quo. Nor did they accede to a request from the EP to change Article 133 in order to give the EP a formal role in CCP decisionmaking. Although the EP has an influential external trade relations committee and frequently passes resolutions and sends delegations to major trade negotiations, Articles 133 and 300 limit the conduct of the CCP to the Commission and the Council.

The Commission had long complained to the Council that the 133 regime made the EU a difficult and complicated trade partner for third countries to negotiate with. In the Commission's view, mixed (i.e., joint EU and member state) competence for new trade issues compounded the problem. The Commission is not usually solicitous of third countries, but it has a point about the complexity of their dealings with the EU. For instance, in the WTO committee on trade in goods, the Commission alone represents the EU. In the services and intellectual property committees, by contrast, the Commission and member states negotiate jointly on behalf of the EU. Third countries may find this strange, but they come to terms easily with it. Similarly, third countries have reconciled themselves for a long time to the 133 regime and have learned to exploit it on occasion by lobbying the 113 Committee before key negotiating sessions.

Perhaps a more serious problem for third countries, but one to which the Commission does not draw attention, is the proliferation of trade-related directorates-general and portfolios within the Commission itself. This is due not to a rational division of labor but to the oversupply of commissioners in a system in which big countries send two commissioners each to Brussels and small countries send one commissioner each. Even when the number of commissioners is limited to one per member state, impending enlargement ensures that the Commission will always be bigger than the optimum number of portfolios (the Amsterdam Treaty limits the number of commissioners to twenty, the Commission's current size).

Hence there is the prospect of a continuing division of responsibility within the Commission for external economic relations.

The Development of EU Trade Policy

The single market program of the late 1980s was a crucial event in the development of EU trade policy. To the Commission's dismay, external reaction to the 1992 agenda was far from favorable. "Fortress Europe" became a catchphrase in the United States and elsewhere to signal concern about the implications for nonmember states of greater market integration. The EU had given little thought to the external perception of the internal market and responded to international criticism by emphasizing its commitment to free trade and open markets. In an effort to allay growing concern beyond the EC's borders, the European Council proclaimed in December 1988 that "the single market will be of benefit to Community and non-Community countries alike, by ensuring continuing economic growth. The internal market will not close in on itself. 1992 Europe will be a partner and not a fortress Europe."[3]

The phrase "partner Europe" lacked the resonance and appeal of "fortress Europe"; nor were the EC's trading partners convinced that the post-1992 European market would be as accessible as the European Council promised. The contemporaneous Uruguay Round seemed a fortuitous chance to test the EC's resolve to maintain a liberal international trading system and for the EC to leverage concessions from its trading partners based on the single market's purported benefits. The tortuous course of the Uruguay Round, however, sent mixed signals about the EU's commitment to global trade liberalization (negotiations almost collapsed because of EU agricultural protectionism). In the event, market integration and external trade liberalization have been mutually reinforcing for the EU, resulting in improved market access for external suppliers and increased exposure of the EU economy to global competition.

The EU's trade policy is reasonably open, with the exception of the agricultural and (for cultural reasons) audiovisual sectors. Apart from films and farm products, third countries complain most about limited market access for items such as textiles, clothing, and cars. The EU's average industrial tariff is about 10 percent (the EU's main trading partners generally have a lower rate) but is declining to about 3 percent as a result of Uruguay Round commitments. Other trade-related concerns of third countries include the impact of EU enlargement into Central and Eastern Europe (concerns about trade diversion have been a feature of every EU enlargement); the impact of the EU's growing network of preferential and regional agreements on the multilateral system; the frequency and severity of EU antidumping actions in sensitive sectors such as electronics, steel, and textiles; and the trade-restricting impact of EU health, safety, and environmental directives. For its part, the EU has always been willing to negotiate compensation for countries that encounter new or higher trade barriers in their dealings with new EU member states (although the EU has not always conducted such negotiations with alacrity); argues that there is no inconsistency between progressive multilateral liberalization and the conclusion of preferential trade agreements; doggedly defends its recourse to antidumping measures under agreed WTO rules; and claims that its health and safety legislation is not politically inspired but is based on sound scientific advice or, more weakly, "consumer preference."

In December 1996 the EU signaled a tough approach to third-country trade barriers by launching a "Market Access Strategy."[4] This approach involves identifying persistent barriers to European exports and deciding how best to combat them using existing instruments. The initiative included establishing a new database with information on all trade barriers faced by EU firms in foreign markets, broken down by sector and country. Although largely a domestic public relations exercise, the strategy provides a useful overview of the conduct of EU trade policy.

The WTO

The WTO came into being on January 1, 1995, nearly fifty years late. In the immediate post–World War II period, the United States had proposed setting up the International Trade Organization (ITO) as the third pillar of a new liberal international economic system—the other two were the World Bank and the International Monetary Fund. The proposed ITO was stillborn because the U.S. Senate failed to ratify its founding treaty (the Havana Charter of 1950). Thus the GATT, which had been launched in January 1948 as an interim measure until negotiation and ratification of the ITO, became by default the key forum for international trade liberalization. Only at the end of the Uruguay Round—the longest, most complicated, and most contentious "round" of multilateral trade liberalization negotiations held under the auspices of the GATT—did the GATT's "contracting parties" (i.e., members) establish a successor organization. In deference to the United States, the new organization was called the WTO instead of the ITO.

The WTO is much weightier than the interim (although long-lived) GATT ever was. Regular ministerial meetings give the WTO a political prominence that the GATT conspicuously lacked. Substantively, the WTO encompasses not only the old GATT, but also the General Agreement on Trade in Services (GATS) and the Trade-Related Aspects of Intellectual Property Rights (TRIPs) agreement, both of which were negotiated as part of the Uruguay Round and came into effect when the WTO became operational. One of the WTO's most important innovations is the Dispute Settlement Body (DSB) and Appellate Body to resolve disputes between contracting parties. This is a major improvement on the GATT system of dispute resolution, which, because it operated on the basis of unanimity, was weak and generally ineffective. The EU strongly supported establishing a DSB and an Appellate Body not only because their rulings would be binding, but also because they could be used to check unilateral action by the United States.

The EU is one of the WTO's two heavyweight boxers; the other is the United States. Japan is less weighty but nonetheless influential. The EU, United States, Japan, and Canada form the Quad, an informal group of the WTO's most powerful players. Paradoxically, the EU is not a WTO contracting party (nor was it ever a contracting party to the GATT). Only by virtue of its member states' treaty obligations to act as one in the international trade arena (an obligation that yields solid political and economic advantages) is the EU a de facto WTO member.

The EU sought to put its stamp on the new WTO by taking an aggressive approach to procedural and institutional issues. For instance, the EU successfully insisted that "its candidate" (Renato Ruggiero, the former Italian trade minister) become the WTO's first secretary-general and unsuccessfully insisted on two "EU seats" on the supposedly nonpartisan Appellate Body (the EU agreed to only one seat when the United States did likewise). In both cases, the EU thought of itself as acting not only in the EU's interests but also against U.S. interests.

The EU adopted a three-pronged approach to the WTO in the late 1990s. One was simply to carry out its commitments under the Uruguay Round and related agreements. These included implementing the Agreement on Textiles and Clothing (ATC), which entered into force with the WTO agreement and applies GATT rules to a sector undergoing considerable restructuring in the EU (notably Portugal); reducing tariffs on industrial goods on a year-by-year basis; phasing out remaining quantitative restrictions on imports; and cutting levies and price supports for agricultural products.

Another part of the EU's approach to the WTO has been to use the dispute-resolution mechanism as a major trade policy instrument (the EU is the complainant far more often than it is the defendant). The EU has won some high-profile cases and lost a few as well. For instance, the EU lost a big case against its banana-import regime, which discriminates against larger, cheaper Latin American bananas in favor of more expensive, poorer-quality bananas from countries that are party to the EU's Lomé Convention (an aid and preferential trade program for former European colonies in Africa, the Caribbean, and the Pacific). The EU also lost a case brought by the United States against its ban on hormone-treated beef because the ban was not based on scientific evidence (and therefore contravened international trade rules). Both cases caused considerable political upset in the EU. Nevertheless, as trade commissioner Leon Brittan observed of the new dispute-resolution mechanism, "it is vital for Europe to be able to take the rough with the smooth."[5]

Involvement in the WTO's work program for further multilateral liberalization, which includes unfinished GATT business as well as new initiatives, is the third, most far-reaching aspect of the EU's WTO policy. Highlights include:

• *Telecommunications:* The EU was in the forefront of efforts to reach a WTO agreement on the liberalization of global telecommunications markets. When the United States pulled out of the talks—largely for domestic political reasons—shortly before the initial deadline of April 30, 1996, it and the EU agreed to prolong negotiations until February 15, 1997. Prospects for a successful conclusion of the talks received a political boost at the inaugural WTO ministerial meeting in Singapore in December 1996. Although discussion went down to the wire, sixty-nine countries (including the EU Fifteen) signed the agreement at WTO headquarters in Geneva before the deadline expired. The agreement opens voice telephony, electronic data transmissions, telex, and fax services to global competition and covers all means of service (cable, fiber optics, radio, and satellite). For the first time in a global accord, the agreement also included a commitment to basic competition policy principles. Implementation of the agreement on January 1, 1998, and the granting of temporary derogations for some countries mirrored the calendar for the EU's own liberalization of telecommunications.

• *Information technology:* The EU and the United States sought the Information Technology Agreement (ITA) in order to eliminate tariffs on a host of nonconsumer electronic products including telecommunications equipment, computers, computer chips, and software. The EU pushed for the ITA partly to counter what it perceived as the discriminatory aspects of the U.S.-Japan semiconductor accord. In late 1996 the U.S. trade representative accepted a Commission proposal to postpone a meeting of the U.S.-Japan semiconductor industry council until March 1997, by which time the EU hoped to conclude the ITA. After hectic negotiations, an ITA was reached at the Singapore ministerial meeting by the EU Fifteen plus twelve other countries (including the United States), which together accounted for over 80 percent of global information technology trade.

• *Financial services:* The EU was instrumental in achieving an interim multilateral agreement on financial services in July 1995, covering the period until December 1997, despite U.S. withdrawal from the talks because of dissatisfaction with the market-opening offers on the table, especially from emerging economies. The agreement promised foreign access (in varying degrees) to the banking, insurance, and securities sectors in more than ninety countries (covering 90 percent of all international financial business). The EU trumpeted its ability to lead the talks to a successful conclusion, regardless of the U.S. walkout, as a major international achievement. The EU's triumphalism in 1995 put it under considerable pressure to help translate the interim agreement into a permanent arrangement before the end of 1997 that included the United States. Although prospects for doing so seemed to fade in the closing stages of the talks as the Asian economic crisis distracted some of the Asian countries' attention and dimmed their enthusiasm for market liberalization, a permanent agreement was secured at the last moment (in December 1997) with the full participation of the United States.

• *Foreign direct investment (FDI):* The EU has long taken the lead in calling for binding multilateral rules to cover FDI, the means by which entrepreneurs establish new firms or buy existing ones in other countries. The Commission sees FDI as "the second pillar of the international economy" (trade being the first).[6] Although the General Agreement on Trade in Services and the Agreement on Trade-Related Investment Measures (TRIMs) have a bearing on FDI and are under the WTO umbrella, the EU has been keen to negotiate a comprehensive multilateral agreement that would range from investment rules to environmental protection and sustainable development. However, the complexity and political sensitivity of many FDI-related issues have thwarted the Commission's initiatives to promote a global regime. The most ambitious effort to date has taken place not in the WTO but in the OECD, where negotiation of the proposed Multilateral Agreement on Investment (MAI) has been deadlocked for some time. Growing controversy over the provisions of the MAI, which many private pressure groups and some government officials perceived as a threat to national sovereignty, the environment, and sundry other entities forced OECD members to shelve negotiations in May 1998.

Conditional support for China's and Russia's WTO membership is a separate issue on which the EU has taken a lead. By contrast with the United States, which rejects China's candidacy outright until well-documented trade barriers have been lifted, the EU supports China's accession to the WTO, ostensibly as a means of encouraging economic reform by locking China into a rule-based organization. Critics contend that the EU also has selfish motives, perhaps hoping that China will look more favorably on European exporters and investors. The question of Russia's WTO membership also divides the United States and the EU, although not as sharply and not with ideological overtones. Whereas the EU is sympathetic to Russia's application, the United States holds that Russia has a long way to go before it develops a market economy with a trade regime that complies with rigorous WTO rules. Without agreement between the United States and EU, neither China nor Russia will be admitted to the WTO.

The WTO is committed under the terms of the Uruguay Round and the GATS to opening two new sets of negotiations, on agriculture and on services, no later than the year 2000. The EU—more specifically Leon Brittan—would like instead to have a single, broader, more inclusive Millennium Round, similar to the Uruguay Round but shorter and less acrimonious. Knowing that it will be pressed to make concessions on agriculture, the EU wants in turn to be able to leverage concessions in other areas by conducting the agricultural negotiations in the context of a multifaceted trade round. As Brittan sees it, "the more horses there are to trade, the more logical it becomes to trade them within the same market."[7]

Few other WTO players, including some EU member states, share the Commission's enthusiasm for a grand Millennium Round of trade liberalization talks. Post–Uruguay Round fatigue is still prevalent, and the WTO has plenty on its plate already. Denied congressional authorization for "fast track" trade talks, the U.S. administration has little appetite for a Millennium Round. Nor would a commitment to begin such a round be a likely vote winner in the 2000 presidential election. Under the circumstances, the EU may have to limit its ambitious WTO agenda to the organization's existing obligations and work program.

Interregional and Bilateral Relations

The EU has developed an intricate web of interregional and bilateral contacts covering commercial and political relations with almost every country in the world. Most of these are highly institutionalized, often involving annual summit meetings, ministerial meetings, meetings of high-level officials, and interparliamentary relations. Given the size of the U.S. economy and its importance for the EU, U.S.-EU relations are examined in Chapter 18. The following sections outline the EU's other major interregional and bilateral external economic relationships.

Non-EU Europe

The European Economic Area. The European Economic Area (EEA) extends the EU's single market to three of the European Free Trade Association's members: Iceland, Liechtenstein, and Norway. EFTA's other member, Switzerland, chose not to join the EEA after a referendum on the issue in December 1992. When the EEA came into being in January 1994, Austria, Finland, and Sweden were also EFTA members; their accession to the EU in January 1995 therefore robbed the EEA of much of its significance. Despite the huge imbalance between its EU and EFTA members, the EEA is nevertheless the most highly institutionalized and integrated external economic arrangement involving the EU. Substantively, the EEA covers the single market *acquis* plus competition policy. Institutionally, the EEA includes a council composed of government ministers and commissioners (meets twice a year), a joint committee composed of high-level representatives of the

Commission and the EEA member states (meets at least monthly), a joint parliamentary committee composed of members of the EP and the national parliaments of the EFTA states (meets twice a year), and a consultative committee composed of representatives of employers' and workers' groups (meets twice a year). The EEA was to have included a supranational court, but the ECJ ruled in December 1991 that the establishment of such an institution would have contravened EC law because of its supremacy over the ECJ. As a result, disputes between the EU and EFTA parties to the EEA must be settled politically in the EEA council. Regardless of the defection of three countries from EFTA to the EU, and Switzerland's decision not to join either the EEA or the EU, with 380 million people and 40 percent of global trade the EEA is the world's largest commercial bloc. (The history and development of the EEA are examined in Chapter 7.)

Europe agreements. Europe Agreements are individual association agreements between the EU and the countries of Central and Eastern Europe that are candidates for EU membership. The nomenclature emphasizes the closeness of the EU's relations with the recently independent Central and Eastern European states. Substantively, Europe agreements go beyond most association agreements by embracing a considerable amount of the *acquis communautaire* and a high degree of political cooperation. Institutionally they resemble association agreements more closely, having association councils at the ministerial/Commission level, association committees at the high-official level, and EP–associated country parliamentary committees. (Europe agreements are examined in the context of EU enlargement in Chapter 7.)

Russia. Political and economic relations are especially hard to disentangle in the case of the EU's dealings with Russia. Politically, a stable Russia is essential for European security and for the success of EU enlargement; economically, the EU is Russia's main Western partner. Without more trade and investment Russia could collapse politically; without more political stability and structural reform EU trade and investment in Russia cannot reach its full potential.

The disintegration of the Soviet Union in December 1991—coincidentally, during the second day of the Maastricht summit—presented the EC with a major political and economic challenge. Two years earlier, the EC had concluded a trade and cooperation agreement with the Soviet Union, a "modest and prudent first step" in developing an economic and political relationship.[8] In the following year, with German unification a reality and the Soviet Union on the verge of collapse, it was more important than ever for the EC to involve Russia in the emerging post–Cold War European system. As a grudging host to several hundred thousand Soviet troops, Germany especially wanted the EU to pursue a positive, constructive policy in the East. Accordingly, in December 1990 the European Council approved emergency food aid and an ambitious technical assistance program for the Soviet Union.[9]

Events in the early 1990s severely strained the EU's relations with Russia. Brussels protested against Russian repression in the Baltic states in January 1991 and fretted about the apparent ascendancy of conservative Communists in the Kremlin. Yet the Commission opened an office in Moscow later in 1991, just in time to observe at close quarters the failed military coup in August, Boris Yeltsin's triumph over Mikhail Gorbachev, and the rapid dissolution of the Soviet Union. In 1992 the EU reorganized its aid to Russia and other former Soviet republics in a program called Technical Assistance for the Commonwealth of Independent States (TACIS) and laid the foundations for a longer-term, more substantive relationship. This approach bore fruit in a political declaration issued in Brussels in December 1993 and a partnership and cooperation agreement signed by Russia and the EU during the European Council in Corfu in June 1994. The EU's overall objectives were to bolster political and economic reform in Russia and win Russian support for—or at least acquiescence in—EU enlargement in Central and Eastern Europe. However, a succession of trade disputes, coupled with Russia's brutality during Chechnya's secessionist war in 1995, held up ratification of the partnership and cooperation agreement, delayed conclusion of an interim agreement, and caused considerable tension in EU-Russia relations.

Although Russia's prime minister once remarked that Russia would apply for EU membership, neither Russia nor the EU seriously considered that Russia would ever become an EU member state. Were the EU to enlarge eastward beyond Poland, French prime minister Balladur remarked in November 1994, "it would become unbalanced, doomed to paralysis and ineffectiveness."[10] A key Commission report on relations with Russia, published in 1995, envisioned an emerging Europe based on the EU in the West and Russia in the East, with most of the former Soviet republics gravitating toward "Russian" Europe.[11]

Nevertheless, for Russia, struggling to come to terms with the Soviet Union's demise, resentful of the United States as the world's sole superpower, and on the verge of economic collapse in 1998, relations with the EU assumed special importance. Only the EU could give Russia the political respect and, more important, the economic assistance and market access that were indispensable for putting the country back on its feet. EU-Russia relations steadily improved in the late 1990s, especially in terms of trade and aid. In return, Russia did not attempt to block EU enlargement. Moreover, without the EU's considerable economic assistance and political support, it is doubtful that Russia would have dropped its resistance to NATO enlargement.

Ukraine. Strategic considerations also account for the high degree of EU interest in Ukraine. A country larger and more populous than France, Ukraine's continuing independence helps prevent the reemergence of a Russian empire in Eastern Europe, as distinct from a Russian zone of influence. The EU has provided considerable economic assistance to Ukraine, largely through the TACIS program. The EU has a particular interest in closing down the Chernobyl nuclear power station (if possible by 2000), site of a major disaster in 1986 and still considered unsafe. The EU signed a partnership and cooperation agreement (PCA) with Ukraine on June 14, 1994, only days before signing a similar agreement with Russia. The EU-Ukraine PCA became operational only in March 1998, after extensive ratification delays on both sides. Despite good EU-Ukraine political relations, Ukraine's failure to restructure its economy stymies Western investment in the country and threatens the political independence that Ukraine and the EU want, above all, to maintain.

Turkey. Turkey is an applicant (but not an active candidate) for EU membership and has a customs union with the EU (covering industrial products only) that came into effect in January 1996. Negotiations to establish the customs union were dogged by disputes over copyright, dumping, textile quotas, and tariff and nontariff barriers. The final agreement did not include a concession that Turkey most wanted: free movement of Turkish labor inside the EU. Nor did it extend to Turkey many of the single market's other benefits. For Turkey, therefore, the customs union is an unacceptable substitute for full membership. As a consolation, the EU promised financial assistance, ostensibly to restructure Turkish industry, but Greece has consistently blocked delivery of the aid package. (The politics of EU-Turkey relations are examined in Chapter 7.)

The Mediterranean Region

For historical, strategic, and economic reasons, the EU has always had a unique relationship with neighboring Mediterranean countries. To emphasize the importance of that relationship, the heads of state and government adopted the Global Mediterranean Policy (GMP) at their 1972 Paris summit. Although the EC had already concluded a variety of trade agreements with a number of Mediterranean countries, the GMP promised to deepen and broaden the EC's involvement in the region. Yet the grandiloquent GMP sounded more impressive than it really was. Economic recession later in the 1970s diminished the EC's ambitious plans for the Mediterranean basin. The accession of Greece, Spain, and Portugal in the 1980s both strengthened the EC's Mediterranean orientation and strained its economic relations with nonmember Mediterranean countries by further restricting access to the EC marketplace for Mediterranean products.

In the late 1980s, southern Mediterranean countries fretted about the economic consequences of the single market program and feared that massive financial transfers to Greece, Spain, and Portugal as part of the single market initiative (and later as part of the EMU initiative) would further widen the economic divide between member and nonmember Mediterranean states. The EU's growing preoccupation with developments in Central and Eastern Europe in the early 1990s almost blinded Brussels to developments in the Mediterranean region, where economic and political instability also threatened the EU's security. Anxiety about a possible influx of immigrants from the East finally drew the EU's attention to the reality of mass migration from the south.

Despite the launch more than two decades earlier of the GMP, the EU's relations with most Mediterranean countries remained precarious. The situation in the western Mediterranean was especially sensitive. In October 1987 the Council rejected Morocco's application for EC membership on the self-evident grounds that Morocco was not a European country. Relations with Morocco deteriorated further in the early 1990s after the EP voted down ECU 463 million in credit and aid under a cooperation agreement because of Morocco's poor human rights record. Morocco responded by freezing its agreement with the EC and jeopardizing a four-year fishing accord vital to Spain's large fleet. The crisis was resolved only after the Council agreed to explore a wide-ranging free trade agreement with Morocco, possibly including also Algeria and Tunisia.

At the other end of the Mediterranean, political problems also overshadowed the EC's economic relations with Israel, which are based on a 1975 free trade agreement that finally became fully operational in 1989. Israel desperately wanted to upgrade its economic relations with the EU, its main trading partner, but until the September 1993 Israel–Palestine Liberation Organization (PLO) Accords, political obstacles proved insurmountable. The EU was extremely critical of Israel's hard line in the Occupied Territories, and Israel objected to full EU participation in the Middle East peace process. Neighboring countries with which the EU has trade agreements dating from the 1970s—Syria, Egypt, Jordan, and Lebanon—also sought closer economic relations with Brussels but objected to further EU trade concessions to Israel.

These and other worrisome regional developments were the backdrop against which the Commission worked in the mid-1990s to devise a new Mediterranean strategy. The Commission eventually came up with a typically ambitious proposal to establish a huge free trade area stretching from Morocco in the west to Turkey in the east; altogether it would embrace twelve Mediterranean countries. Negotiations between the EU and the so-called MED (Mediterranean) 12 (Algeria, Cyprus, Egypt, Israel, Jordan, Lebanon, Malta, Morocco, Syria, Tunisia, Turkey, and the autonomous Palestinian territories) culminated in a declaration issued at an EU–MED

12 summit in Barcelona in November 1995. The Barcelona Declaration—the cornerstone of the EU's new Mediterranean policy—covers a wide range of issues beyond commercial relations. Chief among these are steps to enhance regional security and to strengthen EU–MED 12 cultural and educational ties.[12]

Nevertheless, economic and financial affairs are at the heart of the new Euro-Mediterranean partnership, and the success of the Barcelona Declaration depends on the EU's ability to promote regional development. The main vehicle for this is the proposed free trade area, due to be completed by 2010. Although the target date remains a long way off, establishing a free trade area involves negotiating separate association agreements between the EU and the MED 12 countries and negotiating similar agreements among the MED 12 countries themselves. Given the political volatility of the region and the degree of animosity between some of the MED 12 countries (Israel and Syria are barely at peace with each other), it is hard to see how the free trade area will come into being. Nor are relations between each of the MED 12 countries and the EU on an equal footing. For instance, Cyprus is negotiating EU membership, Turkey has a customs union with the EU but is sulking because the EU shelved its membership application in 1998, and Syria is a difficult and elusive partner. Thus the apparent symmetry of EU–MED 12 relations disguises a series of bilateral relations that range in their conduct from friendly to frigid.

The Barcelona Declaration's ultimate goal therefore seems unattainable, although the Barcelona process serves a useful purpose by keeping the EU focused on the Mediterranean region. Frequent follow-up meetings, including biennial summits, monitor the state of EU-Mediterranean relations and sustain the momentum for closer political and economic cooperation. Nevertheless, as far as the EU is concerned, commercial considerations are secondary to political and security ones. EU trade concessions to neighboring Mediterranean countries are worth the potential benefit of enhanced regional stability, although the EU's own Mediterranean member states may balk at paying the price.

South Africa

South Africa is a special case for the EU in a number of respects. Member states were embarrassingly divided on the question of sanctions against South Africa during the apartheid years, especially after the escalation of violence there in the mid-1980s. After the collapse of apartheid, South Africa became one of the few positive CFSP case studies as member states rallied in support of the new regime. Economically, relations with the new South Africa were problematical because of the country's size and its peculiar status as both a developed and developing country (depending on the sector). South Africa wanted to join the Lomé Convention, but the existing Lomé countries feared being crushed by South African competition, and the EU feared a WTO challenge from non-Lomé trading partners. Accordingly, in 1997 South Africa became a "qualified member" of Lomé under a special protocol attached to the convention. Whereas South Africa enjoys some benefits of Lomé membership, it is excluded from the convention's special trade regime. EU–South African trade is governed instead by a bilateral agreement that provides for the eventual establishment of a free trade area.

Asia

In July 1994, largely at the behest of Leon Brittan, the Commission issued a position paper advocating a new EU strategy toward Asia.[13] Based on political and economic arguments, the communication urged greater EU involvement in Asia through closer bilateral and multilateral relations. The European Council endorsed the Commission's communication and called for closer EU cooperation with Asian countries and regional organizations, notably the Association of Southeast Asian Nations (ASEAN), with which the EU has had relations since 1972.[14] ASEAN consists of Brunei, Burma, Indonesia, Malaysia, the Philippines, Singapore, Thailand, and Vietnam.

The European Council's endorsement of greater EU involvement in Asia might have gone the way of many other European Council statements but for the Commission's activism, again based largely on Brittan's determination to promote the EU's external relations and his interest in the region. The Commission's seeming proactivism was nonetheless partly a reaction against renewed U.S. economic interest in Asia, notably through Washington's rejuvenation of the Asia Pacific Economic Cooperation group (APEC), a loose association that spans the Pacific from Canada to Korea and includes the ASEAN countries.

The EU's new approach toward Asia manifested itself most obviously in an intensification of contacts with China and in the launch of a new, biennial summit attended by EU, ASEAN, Chinese, Japanese, and South Korean government leaders. The first such Asia-Europe Meeting (ASEM) took place in Bangkok in March 1996, the second in London in March 1998 (the third is scheduled for Seoul in 2000). One of the goals of holding ASEMs is to have a freer and less formal exchange than happens at most summit meetings, although the large number of participants and the attendant linguistic muddle inevitably inhibit conversation.

The EU's new Asia strategy has been overshadowed by disagreements with the Asian countries over social policy, environmental issues, and human rights abuses in East Timor and Burma. The onset of the Asian financial crisis in 1997 and 1998 also dampened the EU's new approach and prompted complaints from Asian countries that the EU was more concerned about safeguarding EMU than with helping Asia to recover. Although overshadowed by many such recriminations, ASEM 2 (the 1998 meeting) at least provided an opportunity to involve the EU in the Asian crisis and exchange ideas on how best to restore financial health to the region.

Japan

Despite having slipped into recession in 1998, Japan remains an economic giant. The United States, the EU, and Japan together dominate the global economy. Yet the EU-Japan relationship is the weakest side of the trilateral U.S.-EU-Japan relationship. Until recently, relations between the EU and Japan were almost exclusively economic, whereas both have had robust political and economic relations with the United States. Japan's weak political relationship with the EU is due not simply to its geographical distance from Europe but primarily to disputes over Japan's protected domestic market and huge trade surplus with the EU.

In 1990 the Japanese ambassador to the EC complained pointedly that during the previous year the Commission president had met the U.S. president five times but had met the Japanese prime minister only once.[15] After the United States and the EC concluded the Transatlantic Declaration in November 1990, Japan pressed the EC for a similar accord. The epilogue and prologue to the EC-Japan Declaration, eventually concluded by the Commission president, Council president, and Japanese prime minister in July 1991, illustrate the extent of the EU's concern about Japanese trade practices. French insistence on references to reciprocity and "balance" at a time when Japan's trade surplus with the EC had grown sharply delayed the declaration. Eventually, France accepted a Commission compromise calling for the EC and Japan to have "equitable access to their respective markets and to remove obstacles, whether structural or other, impeding the expansion of trade, on the basis of comparable opportunities."[16]

The declaration established an institutional framework for annual meetings between the Japanese prime minister, the Commission president, and the Council president, as well as regular meetings between Japanese ministers and EC commissioners. But those provisions, and the declaration's lofty rhetoric about "a deeper partnership based on the common ideals of freedom, democracy, and the rule of law," could not alter the reality of an unhealthy trade imbalance. Japan's expanding trade surplus, especially in electronics and cars, continued to alarm the EU. Shortly after publicly issuing the joint declaration, the Commission and the Japanese government announced that they had concluded an export-restraint agreement—euphemistically called "Elements of Consensus"—to limit the number of Japanese cars entering the European market until the year 2000.

The auto agreement culminated two years of arduous negotiations within the Commission, among member states, and between the Community and Japan. Five member states—Britain, France, Italy, Portugal, and

Spain—had long-standing quotas on Japanese car imports, which the single market program was about to bring to an end. To compensate the countries concerned, the Commission, under intense pressure from most European car manufacturers, proposed a post-1992 transitional period of voluntary restraints on Japanese car sales in the EU. By allowing direct imports from Japan of 1.23 million vehicles in 1999, compared with 1.24 million in 1989, the deal effectively froze until the end of the decade the annual level of direct exports of cars and light trucks from Japan to the EU.[17] After 1999, the EU car market will supposedly be fully liberalized. As a classic example of a voluntary export restraint in a sector where Japan has a strong competitive advantage, the EU-Japan auto agreement is a key element in the EU's strategy toward Japan.[18]

The auto agreement was controversial not only because of its protectionism but also because of uncertainty about its impact on cars produced by Japanese "transplants" in the EU. Located chiefly in Britain, these Japanese-owned factories have revolutionized car manufacturing in Europe and captured a substantial share of the market. The British government claimed that the car agreement did not impose a ceiling on transplant production in the EU, strongly protectionist French and Italian car manufacturers reached the opposite conclusion, and the Commission sat on the fence by citing vague "working assumptions" for transplant output. Once the agreement became operational in 1993 and the protectionist demands of Continental carmakers increased, the market share of Japanese transplants became an even more sensitive issue. Largely because of the growth of transplant production, the Japanese quotas were rarely filled. Free-traders in the EU interpreted this to mean that the agreement was redundant and should not be renewed in 1999; protectionists argued instead that the agreement should be renewed because it provides a useful framework for dealing with possible future problems.

Although the auto agreement was implemented in the early 1990s, the fledgling political relationship between Japan and the EU continued to suffer from mutual misunderstanding and mistrust. Japanese investment in the EU remained far in excess of EU investment in Japan, and the trade surplus widened further in Japan's favor. This led to calls from European industry for retaliatory measures against alleged dumping of Japanese products and for EU efforts to break down supposed structural impediments to entry into the Japanese market. As a result, the EU intensified its market-opening efforts, for instance by launching a "deregulation dialogue" with Japan in 1994.

Under the circumstances, a Commission communication of March 1995 on relations with Japan was surprisingly optimistic. The Commission claimed to have found a "new and more focused approach" to the problem of market access that was "now producing results." The Commission could not resist comparing its approach favorably to that of the United States, commenting that "unilateral trade sanctions are a destabilizing factor in world trade."[19]

Bilateral economic relations indeed warmed up as Japan's trade surplus with the EU fell sharply and as the EU made inroads into the Japanese marketplace. The resolution of two long-standing trade disputes between the EU and Japan in late 1996 and early 1997—one on Japan's insufficient music copyright protection, the other on Japan's discriminatory liquor taxes—improved relations further. In both cases the WTO had ruled in the EU's favor, but Japan had not implemented the required changes fully. But tension rose again during the Asian economic crisis when Japan resumed its export-led growth strategy with the assistance of a greatly depreciated yen. There was still hope, however, that the Asian crisis and the continuing deterioration of the Japanese economy would provide the shock necessary to convince Japan to undertake the kinds of structural reforms upon which a sound economy and a satisfactory relationship with the EU and its other trading partners can be built.

China

Historically, Communist China never shared the Soviet Union's squeamishness about dealing with the capitalist EC. China and the EC agreed to establish diplomatic relations in 1975 and signed a trade and economic cooperation agreement in 1978. So vigorous was their economic relationship that in 1985 China and the EC signed a new agreement to provide for more comprehensive cooperation. Three years later the Commission opened a delegation (embassy) in Beijing.

The EC's cozy relationship with China came to an abrupt end in June 1989, when the Chinese government ruthlessly suppressed the pro-democracy student demonstrations in Tiananmen Square. The European Council condemned China's repression, suspended high-level bilateral meetings, postponed new cooperation projects, and cut existing programs.[20] Over a year later, the EC decided gradually to normalize relations with China, although the dilemma between upholding human rights and enhancing bilateral trade continued to confound member states.

As a key component of its new strategy toward Asia, in 1995 the EU developed a "comprehensive, independent, and consistent long-term strategy" for relations with China, an emerging economic and political powerhouse.[21] By that time China had become the EU's fourth largest export market and fourth largest supplier. Eager to maximize trade and investment opportunities for Europeans in China, and eager also to raise the EU's international profile, Brussels intensified its "constructive engagement" with Beijing. The ASEM process further demonstrates the EU's and

China's interest in each other and in broader Asian affairs. In 1998 the Commission launched yet another initiative, covering a range of political and economic issues, to strengthen and deepen relations with China.[22]

Despite the progressive strengthening and deepening of contacts during the past two decades, EU-China relations have always been touchy. Negotiations to reduce quotas and other barriers to trade have been difficult and prolonged. Although the EC was one of the earliest major trading partners to grant China fully unconditional most-favored-nation (MFN) status (nondiscriminatory tariff access for China's goods and services), the EU resents what it sees as continuing barriers to European exports. Disputes abound, involving frequent use by the EU of antidumping measures. China's disregard for intellectual property rights was a major irritant in EU-China relations. Although China now has intellectual property laws in place (thanks largely to U.S. pressure), problems of enforcement remain. A long-standing dispute over maritime transport was finally resolved to the EU's satisfaction and, as the EU likes to point out, to the benefit of China's other trading partners as well.

The EU's interest in China also encompasses humanitarian and environmental concerns. Thus the EU wants to help China feed its burgeoning population, make better use of its natural resources, reduce environmental damage (due especially to China's huge coal consumption), and alleviate rural poverty. The EU promotes these objectives through direct financial and technical assistance, support for nongovernmental organizations (NGOs) working in China, and humanitarian aid through the European Community Humanitarian Office (ECHO).

Overall, the EU's policy toward China is quite ambitious. Apart from commercial, environmental, and humanitarian concerns, the EU seeks to promote regional stability and global prosperity by achieving "smooth and gradual integration of China into the world economy." The Commission and member states are trying to achieve greater coordination of EU activities and national policies relating to China, and a higher EU profile in China and throughout Asia. However, China's unpredictability, prickliness, and opacity may make these objectives difficult to attain.

Latin America

The EU has extensive relations with individual Latin American countries and regional groupings, notably with the Rio Group and with Mercado Común del Cono Sur (or the Common Market of the Southern Cone—Mercosur), a customs union including Argentina, Brazil, Paraguay, and Uruguay. Indeed, a December 1995 agreement between the EU and Mercosur was the first ever between two customs unions.[23] The EU's rapidly developing relations with Mexico—on the basis of an agreement signed in December 1997, the EU and Mexico began negotiations to establish a free trade area—could provide an entrée for the EU to the North American Free Trade Agreement (NAFTA).

The EU's relations with Latin America date from the early 1960s, and were based in part on close cultural, historical, and social ties between the two regions. For that reason, Euro–Latin American relations should have received a huge boost when Spain and Portugal joined the EC in 1986. Instead, the EC's dealings with Latin America continued to languish because of the region's economic stagnation, high indebtedness, and political instability. Nevertheless, Spain's bridge building across the Atlantic helped restore diplomatic relations between Argentina and the EC, broken off in 1982 during the Falklands/Malvinas War. A gradual rapprochement in EC-Argentina relations led to a cooperation agreement in April 1990; three months later Argentina further improved its standing with the EC by restoring diplomatic relations with Britain.

Yet it was only later in the 1990s, when democracy took hold throughout most of Latin America, that prospects for close EU–Latin American relations improved. Latin America began to attract European investment and trade missions. Once again Spain took the lead within the EU, especially during its Council presidency in late 1995. As a result, in December 1995 the Council approved a Commission communication on ways to strengthen EU–Latin American relations during the period 1996–2000.[24] Meeting in Madrid later that month, the European Council endorsed the Council's decision and called for deeper EU ties with Latin American countries and regional organizations.[25]

The EU's new approach toward Latin America was similar to, but less prominent than, its new approach toward Asia. Although reflecting different regional concerns and internal EU dynamics, both initiatives were nonetheless part of a broader strategy to raise the EU's profile as a global political and economic actor. The stakes in Latin America are smaller than in Asia because of Latin America's lesser economic importance and its traditionally close (although rocky) relationship with the United States. Ironically, although EU trade with Latin America has risen since the mid-1990s, its proportion of total EU trade has continued to decline.

DEVELOPMENT POLICY

The Lomé Convention, a trade-and-aid agreement between the EU and seventy-one African, Caribbean, and Pacific (ACP) countries, is the EU's flagship development program. The convention was negotiated in accordance with Articles 182–188 (formerly Articles 131–136) TEC, dealing with overseas countries and territories. Apart from Lomé, the EU has always been a major provider of international development assistance, ranging from food aid to technical support to financial donations. Yet "development cooperation" was given a treaty base only in the TEU. According to Articles 177–181 (formerly Articles 130u–y) TEC, the EU's objectives in this area are to foster sustainable economic and social development in the world's poorer countries; to promote their smooth and gradual integration into the global economy; to campaign against global poverty; and to develop and consolidate democracy, the rule of law, and respect for human rights.

Among other things, the relevant treaty articles adjure member states to coordinate their own development policies with that of the EU. Indeed, the persistence of separate member state development policies (some member states contribute more development assistance than does the EU itself, and EU development assistance amounts to less than 20 percent of what the member states contribute altogether) is a reminder of member states' unwillingness to surrender policy instruments in the international sphere. Most member states want to maximize their own international influence while benefiting also from a collective effort. In the case of development assistance in particular, most member states have specific preferences and agendas that are best pursued individually rather than collectively.

The fact that the European Development Fund (EDF), used to finance the Lomé Convention, is not part of the EU budget is another peculiarity of EU development policy. Because the member states are also signatories of the convention in their own right (Lomé is a "mixed" agreement) and want to control spending as much as possible, the EDF is not included in the development-cooperation section of the EU's general budget, much to the chagrin of the EP. Yet this does not result in greater efficiency: Intergovernmental negotiations to renew the EDF can be contentious and extend beyond the stipulated deadline, and lengthy national ratification procedures often delay implementation of the new agreements. Apart from the EDF, European Investment Bank loans to countries in the Mediterranean region, Asia, and Latin America that have concluded cooperation agreements with the EU are an integral part of the EU's development policy.

Institutionally, the Commission's role in development policy is complicated by the fact that its staff is too small to manage such a large policy area, responsibility for which, paradoxically, is spread among three commissioners in charge of two directorates-general and one special service: DG IB (southern Mediterranean, Middle East, Latin America, and South and Southeast Asia); DG VIII (development); and ECHO. The EP's influence over development cooperation has increased over time, partly because of many parliamentarians' personal interest and expertise in the area and partly for institutional reasons: Although the EDF is not part of the EU budget, the EP has a degree of control over parts of the development budget; the assent procedure covers development-related international agreements (such as Lomé); and under the Amsterdam Treaty development policy decisionmaking is subject to the codecision procedure.

Lomé

The Lomé Convention originated in a provision of the Treaty of Rome allowing non-European countries and territories that had a "special relationship" with member states to become associated with the EC. "Special relationship" was a euphemism for being a current or former colony. Initially most such countries or territories were French-African; the EC concluded the first and second Yaoundé Conventions with them in 1963 and 1969, covering mostly development assistance. Britain's impending accession to the EC in the early 1970s, together with Dutch and German pressure for a new Community approach to the Third World, led to a revision of the French-inspired principles underlying the Yaoundé Conventions. Instead of a traditional donor-recipient relationship, the EC strove for a novel partnership with forty-six developing countries—including numerous British former colonies—in Africa, the Caribbean, and the Pacific. EC-ACP negotiations began in July 1973 and ended in February 1975 when both sides signed a new convention in Lomé, the capital of Togo.

The Lomé Convention was inspired as much by the prevailing vogue for a New International Economic Order as by the member states' desire to favor former colonies. The convention included a development assistance package; a system of generalized preferences in trade (practically all products originating in the ACP countries were given free access to the EC, in return for which the ACP states had to give the EC only most-favored-nation status); the System for the Stabilization of Export Earnings from Products (STABEX) to guarantee ACP export prices regardless of fluctuations in world commodity prices; and a host of innovative aid and technical assistance programs. The convention also established an elaborate institutional framework, which now includes an ACP-EC council (composed of members of the Council, the Commission, and a government minister from each of the ACP countries), and an ACP-EP joint assembly. The number of countries in the ACP grouping increased over the years to seventy-one by 1999 (including South Africa as a qualified member and including some of the world's poorest countries). The Lomé Convention was renegotiated every five years and redesignated accordingly (i.e., Lomé II covered the period 1980–1985 and Lomé III, 1985–1990). Lomé IV, negotiated in December 1989, covers a ten-year period, although its midterm review in 1995 was tantamount to an extensive renegotiation (hence after 1995 Lomé IV became known as Lomé IV B).

The EU's dealings with the heterogeneous and economically diverse ACP states have never been easy. Despite the much larger number of countries on the ACP side, the EU's immensely greater wealth and international influence, together with the inherent tension between former colonial powers and their former colonies, made for a difficult EC-ACP relationship. The EU complains that the ACP countries demand too much, and the ACP countries complain that the EU offers too little. Negotiations for successive Lomé Conventions in the recessionary 1970s and economically uncertain 1980s grew more and more edgy. In the late 1980s, the ACP states feared that the EU's preoccupation with the single market program, obduracy in the Uruguay Round, and increasing involvement in Central and Eastern Europe meant that Brussels had lost interest in Third World issues.

Following arduous negotiations in 1989, Lomé IV included a number of important innovations apart from its ten-year time frame. While retaining its predecessors' relatively complex structure and comprehensive provisions, Lomé IV included greater emphasis on human rights (and especially on women's rights); environmental protection; regional economic integration; and the need for overall, self-reliant, and self-sustained development. Provisions to help ACP countries manage their existing debt and avoid additional debt were another novelty in Lomé IV (ACP debt had more than doubled in the 1980s).

Changes in the international political and economic system in the early 1990s, together with awareness on the EU's part that Lomé had not succeeded in restructuring the economies of the ACP states, led to a difficult midterm review of the fourth convention. With the Cold War well and truly over, member states began to take seriously their demands for democratization and good governance in Third World countries instead of merely using such rhetoric to disguise support for authoritarian, anti-Communist regimes. Economically, the process of liberalization and globalization rendered traditional trade-and-aid assistance even less effective than in the past, and in some cases incompatible with the Uruguay Round agreement and WTO rules (the banana regime is an obvious example). The 1995 review reflected some of these changes. For instance, a new article inserted in the convention declared that "respect for human rights and democratic principles and the rule of law, which underpins relations between the ACP states and the Community and all the provisions of the Convention, and governs the domestic and international policies of the Contracting Parties, shall constitute an essential element [of Lomé IV B]." At the same time, a general EMU-induced climate of fiscal restraint made it more difficult for member states to renegotiate the terms of the EDF to pay for the revised convention. A last-minute French concession—made primarily to save the Cannes summit of June 1995—resulted in a new EDF, thereby bringing the Lomé review to an end.

Continuing concern about Lomé's suitability and effectiveness overshadowed the run-up to the convention's renegotiation in 1999. Following an intensive internal debate in 1996 and 1997, the Commission suggested moving away from an all-embracing Lomé agreement toward separate economic cooperation and partnership agreements with groups of African, Caribbean, and Pacific countries. As it is, most Lomé recipients have little in common with each other. The Commission argues that geographical differentiation would improve the effectiveness of EU assistance and accelerate the integration of recipient countries into the global economy. Whether genuinely unconvinced by the Commission's arguments or simply afraid of the future, many ACP countries cling to the Lomé framework and oppose what they see as EU efforts to break up supposed ACP solidarity.

More controversial than the possible regionalization of Lomé is the Commission's increasing emphasis on political conditionality for future EU assistance. In the Commission's view, the EU should support only countries that—apart from being economically needy—respect democracy, govern themselves well, and fight corruption. In effect, the Commission wants to establish a political climate conducive to a successful development policy. Just as they oppose the regionalization of Lomé assistance, many ACP countries resent Commission efforts to impose political preconditions, pointing out that Lomé IV B already contains commitments to democracy and good governance.

In the meantime, the deteriorating economic situation in most Third World countries has put Lomé under further pressure. Looking beyond Commission statements about sound management and good governance, many ACP countries see an EU that is preoccupied with monetary union and enlargement and whose international interests are limited to maximizing trade with developed countries. On the EU side, there is a reluctant acknowledgment that Lomé was a worthy but failed experiment in development assistance and that the time has come to construct new models and new relationships. As a result, Lomé is unlikely to survive in its present form.

Generalized System of Preferences

The EU grants duty-free access for industrial goods and some agricultural produce from a number of developing countries. The EU introduced a new dimension to its Generalized System of Preferences (GSP) regime in the late 1990s by providing additional trade benefits to countries that meet core labor and environmental standards (such as International Labor Organization standards for the protection of workers' rights and International Tropical Timber Organization standards for tropical wood products). Some GSP beneficiaries, such as Brazil, Pakistan, and Indonesia, have expressed concern about EU intrusion into their internal affairs and about EU conditionality regarding their continued eligibility for preferences. The EU points out that it is not limiting the GSP regime but is instead offering special incentives for developing countries to comply with internationally set social and environmental standards.

Humanitarian Assistance

Apart from contractual development assistance agreements such as Lomé, the EU dispenses large amounts of aid unilaterally. In 1992 the EU established the European Community Humanitarian Office to provide emergency humanitarian and food aid wherever needed around the world. By the end of the 1990s ECHO had funded nearly 2,000 projects in over eighty countries on four continents. ECHO operates through a wide range of partners, including nongovernmental organizations, which administer nearly 60 percent of ECHO funding, and UN agencies, which administer over 25 percent. ECHO's high dependence on NGOs reflects both a dearth of Commission officials on the ground in recipient countries and the Commission's frequent need to try to circumvent corrupt recipient governments. Ironically, the EU itself stands accused of major fraud and mismanagement in the conduct of ECHO affairs.

THE COMMON FOREIGN AND SECURITY POLICY

The CFSP is not a common policy like the Common Commercial Policy. In other words, the member states have not pooled responsibility for foreign and security policy, let alone defense policy, in the EU. Foreign and security policy is neither an exclusive EU competence nor an area of mixed EU–member state competence. Instead, foreign and security policy remains the responsibility of the member states, which have set up an elaborate system at the EU level in an intergovernmental pillar of the TEU to coordinate their policies more closely and to attempt to devise common strategies, reach common positions, and take joint actions on a wide range of issues.

The CFSP evolved out of European Political Cooperation (EPC), a mechanism for foreign policy coordination among member states that dates from the early 1970s. EPC transmogrified into the CFSP, like a caterpillar into a butterfly, during the 1991 IGC that resulted in the TEU. Unlike a beautiful butterfly, however, the CFSP is cumbersome and colorless and has had great difficulty getting off the ground. Under the circumstances, it is surprising that member states use the resonant and value-laden word "common" to describe foreign and security policy cooperation in the EU. Perhaps the word was chosen carelessly, or perhaps it was chosen deliberately in the hope of spurring member states to match deeds and words by eventually formulating and implementing a truly joint foreign and security policy. In any case, the nomenclature is misleading and generates unrealistic expectations inside and outside the EU about the CFSP's capabilities. Given the divergence of member states' foreign and security policy interests and orientations and the weakness of CFSP instruments and mechanisms, the CFSP cannot be as formidable as its name implies.

Does the EU need a CFSP? There are compelling reasons (although their validity may be disputed) for the existence of EU policies in almost every other sphere. Even in the contentious area of monetary policy (an area, like foreign and security policy, at the core of national sovereignty and identity), there are cogent arguments in favor of establishing a European central bank and launching a single currency. Powerful national political interests and trans-European business interests are firmly behind the venture (this does not mean that EMU is a good thing, only that it has considerable political momentum). CFSP and a common defense policy, its logical corollary, lack comparable political and economic support. Intellectually, most member states see the advantage of coordinating their foreign and security policies, but politically the costs—in terms of the presumed loss of national influence and prestige (notably for big member states) and the possible impact on transatlantic diplomatic and military relations—are too high for member states to risk taking the plunge by attempting to give the EU political and military weight commensurate with its economic clout.

The need to counterbalance the EU's economic weight with proportionate political power is one of the main arguments used by proponents of a truly common foreign, security, and eventually defense policy. With the EU throwing its weight around in the WTO, for instance, it seems anomalous that the EU hardly has a presence in the UN. As Hans van den Broek, the commissioner for external political relations, put it, "The voice of Europe will only be heard in world affairs if there is a single voice" (the metaphor most frequently used by academics and officials to describe the rationale for foreign and security policy cooperation is the need for the EU "to speak with one voice").[26] A logical implication of van den Broek's remark is that there should be a single EU seat in the Security Council, a development that Britain and France, permanent Security Council members, are unlikely to support. As it is, Article 19.2 TEU declares that member states that are permanent members of the Security Council (i.e., Britain and France) "will . . . ensure the defense of the positions and the interests of the Union." Yet Britain and France often disagree on issues before the Security Council. In December 1998, for instance, they took diametrically opposite positions on whether to use force against Iraq during the UN inspection crisis.

It is difficult enough to compose a single EU voice, but a single EU voice *to which others will listen* must come from a militarily muscular body. Individual member states have some military muscle, and collectively the EU has the potential to become a formidable military power. Yet political and historical realities militate against the prospect of the EU ever acquiring the kind of diplomatic and military might to match its undoubted economic influence. Although willing to collaborate closely on a range of foreign policy issues, member states jealously preserve certain foreign policy–related prerogatives, notably in the domain of "hard" security and defense.

This is not to argue that the EU should never attempt to exert diplomatic pressure. Indeed, economic power alone gives the EU considerable political leverage, as the conditionality clauses of EU agreements with third countries (individually or interregionally) clearly show and for which Article 301 TEC (sanctions against third countries) provides. Closer to home, instability in the southern Mediterranean, Middle East, and the Balkans make it incumbent upon the EU to use every means possible to promote security and stability there. In this case van den Broek is right to argue that post–Cold War changes in the EU's strategic situation necessitate close foreign, security, and defense policy cooperation among member states.

Yet complaints from the Commission about the limits of EU influence in two regional conflicts—the Middle East and the Balkans—demonstrate the Commission's inability to understand or accept the realities of the international political system and of the EU's role in it. In both cases, the Commission and others complain that despite contributing more money than any other organization or country (notably the United States) for reconstruction and development in Palestine and Bosnia, the EU is less influential politically in those regions than is one other international actor (pointedly, the United States). As successive Middle East wars and as the war in the former Yugoslavia proved, however, political influence in such volatile regions and situations derives not from economic weight but from a potent combination of economic weight and military might.

A final reason given by van den Broek for a CFSP is peculiarly formalistic: "The [TEU] contains a binding commitment . . . to develop a CFSP. . . . This is a legal commitment which all member states have accepted and are bound to respect."[27] Van den Broek's argument raises a question similar to the earlier one about nomenclature. Why did member states undertake obligations that they are obviously unwilling to carry out? The answer would seem to be that the ideal of a CFSP is more appealing than the reality of sharing sovereignty in such a sensitive political area, especially in the absence of powerful political or economic pressure to do so.

From EPC to CFSP

Member states launched EPC in response to a call by the heads of state and government, meeting in The Hague in 1969, to deepen European integration at a time of impending enlargement lest a "wider" EC become politically "weaker." The launch of *Ostpolitik* (Germany's policy of reconciliation with the countries of the Sovier bloc) at about the same time provided a strong impetus for member states to exchange more information and to attempt to coordinate their policies toward Central and Eastern Europe and the Soviet Union. The 1973 Middle East war and subsequent Euro-Arab dialogue had a similar impact on the development of EPC. Indeed, the so-called Venice Declaration of June 1980, in which member states publicly recognized the special position of Palestine in the Arab-Israeli conflict, showed how closely member states coordinated their Middle East policies and how radical their joint position could be.[28]

The Conference on Security and Cooperation in Europe (CSCE), which began in the early 1970s and culminated in the August 1975 Helsinki Final Act, helped greatly to forge an international identity for the EC and to promote EPC. Member states indicated at an early stage of the CSCE process that they would act as a group and be bound collectively by CSCE commitments. Member states fared best in negotiations on "Basket Two" (economic cooperation) and "Basket Three" (human rights) of the CSCE's agenda. There was never an EC delegation in the CSCE, and the Community itself could not make proposals, but Commission officials, attached to the national delegation of the Council presidency, participated fully in the negotiations.

EPC procedures were based on the Luxembourg Report of 1970 and the Copenhagen Report of 1973, which identified four levels for conducting political cooperation:

- meetings of the heads of state and government (later institutionalized as the European Council) to provide overall direction
- meetings of foreign ministers "in EPC" as opposed to the General Affairs Council (an artificial distinction that was later dropped) to prepare and follow up on summit meetings and to deal with foreign policy issues on a regular (monthly) basis
- meetings of the Political Committee (foreign ministries' political directors) to prepare and follow up on foreign ministers' meetings
- meetings of working groups (midlevel foreign ministry officials) to exchange views and prepare reports on a variety of geographical and functional issues, and of the group of European correspondents (junior foreign ministry officials) to liaise between foreign ministries and prepare meetings of the Political Committee

National foreign ministries set up Coreu, a secure communications system, exclusively for the conduct of EPC business.

The Council presidency chaired EPC meetings at all levels. There was no voting; instead, lengthy negotiations in a search for consensus created informal pressures to agree. Consensus became one of EPC's fundamental rules. As in other policy areas, although no one wanted to be outvoted, no one wanted to be isolated either. A strong tendency therefore developed to follow the opinion of the majority. Unofficial and subtle linkages between EPC and other policy areas reinforced this tendency despite obvious exceptions (for most of the 1980s, for instance, the Greek government had scant regard for EPC consensus building).

In the early 1980s, when the EC's external relations were every bit as problematical as its internal development, EPC's procedural limits became obvious. The onset of the "second Cold War"—the sudden heightening of East-West tension in the late 1970s after a decade of relatively benign relations—tested the EC's ability to act internationally. EPC proved an inadequate mechanism, especially in response to sudden crises such as the Soviet invasion of Afghanistan in December 1979. Two years later, following the imposition of martial law in Poland, the member states met more promptly in EPC to try to coordinate their response, but it was not until March 1982 that the EC imposed limited sanctions against the Soviet Union.

A worsening East-West climate and member states' slow response to international crises led to a number of initiatives in the early 1980s to improve EPC and broaden its agenda to encompass security and even defense issues. The 1981 London Report introduced minor procedural reforms but limited EPC discussions to "the political aspects of security." Hans-Dietrich Genscher, Germany's foreign minister, and Emilio Colombo, Italy's foreign minister, launched a joint initiative in November 1981 to strengthen the EC's institutional structure and to extend EC competence in external relations. Officially called the "Draft European Act," the Genscher-Colombo proposals sought to end the distinction between EPC and EC external economic policy and to make it possible for member states "to act in concert in world affairs so that Europe will increasingly be able to assume the international role incumbent upon it."[29]

Foreign ministers acting at the behest of the European Council failed to find a way forward and could not concur on the relatively mild foreign and security policy proposals contained in the Genscher-Colombo proposals. Some member states (such as Britain and the Netherlands) were wary of developing an EC-based security structure that might have upset Washington; others (such as Ireland, Denmark, and Greece) faced domestic political constraints. Consequently, the foreign ministers' report, presented at the Stuttgart summit in June 1983, was a classic compromise. It resulted only in the "Solemn Declaration on European Union," a vague proclamation of the EC's international identity.[30]

Member states soon had a better opportunity, during the 1985 IGC, to revamp EPC. Once again emphasizing the distinctiveness of EPC from other EC activities, the Political Committee considered foreign and security policy in a separate IGC working party. EPC's evolution since the early 1970s, together with a number of member state proposals, formed the basis of its discussions. All member states agreed on the need to make the EC's external economic policy and the member states' foreign policies more consistent with each other. Other ideas included formalizing EPC in the Treaty of Rome, strengthening cooperation procedures, providing an EPC secretariat, and incorporating military and defense issues. Neutral Ireland shied away from going too far down the defense road, as did pacifist (though NATO member) Denmark and idiosyncratic (though also NATO member) Greece.

Title III of the ensuing SEA dealt exclusively with EPC. Procedural improvements included associating the Commission fully with EPC, ensuring that the EP was "closely associated" with it, creating a mechanism for convening the Political Committee or the General Affairs Council within forty-eight hours at the request of at least three member states, and establishing an EPC secretariat in Brussels. The SEA also stipulated that "the external policies of the EC and the policies agreed in Political Cooperation must be consistent" and charged the presidency and the Commission with ensuring such consistency. However, EPC remained largely intergovernmental and was not subject to judicial review by the ECJ.

Revolution in Central and Eastern Europe and the abrupt end of the Cold War brought security concerns to the top of the EC's agenda. Simultaneously, the Commission's leadership of the G24 aid effort in Central and Eastern Europe helped to narrow the conspicuous gap between EPC and the EC's external economic relations. A paper on Central and Eastern Europe prepared collectively by the Council presidency, the Commission, and the EPC secretariat for the June 1989 Madrid summit set an important precedent in joint EC-EPC policymaking. Thereafter, "the Community and its member states" became standard usage in EPC documentation.

With the imminence of German unification in 1990, there was near unanimity among member states on the need to reform EPC. Indeed, member states decided to convene an IGC on political union largely for that reason. By developing a CFSP, member states and the Commission hoped to enhance European security at a potentially destabilizing time, boost the new EU's international standing, and bind external economic and political policymaking more closely together.

Article C (now Article 3) TEU optimistically called for consistency between the EC and the CFSP pillars of the EU and charged the Commission and the Council with achieving that goal. The treaty's CFSP provisions were contained in a new series of articles (J.1 to J.11, now 11–28). The first of these set out the CFSP's objectives in typical hortatory style: to safeguard the common values, fundamental interests, and independence of the EU; to strengthen the security of the EU and its member states in all ways; to preserve peace and strengthen international security in accordance with the principles of the UN charter and the CSCE; to promote international cooperation; and to develop and consolidate democracy and the rule of law and respect human rights and fundamental freedoms.

The TEU introduced two novel instruments to implement the CFSP:

- *common positions* to establish systematic cooperation on a day-to-day basis
- *joint actions* to allow member states to act together in concrete ways based on a Council decision as to the specific scope of such actions, the EU's objectives in carrying them out, and (if necessary) the duration, means, and procedures for their implementation

The success of the CFSP would depend in part on how these instruments were adopted. Some member states advocated the use of qualified majority voting (QMV); others were adamant that unanimity should remain the norm. The TEU struck a clumsy compromise by providing for QMV for the implementation of joint actions, which the Council first had to adopt on the basis of unanimity.

Article J.9 (now Article 18) stipulated that the Commission would be fully associated with the work of the CFSP, although it would not have an exclusive right to submit proposals. Article J.7 (now Article 21) contained a weaker commitment to involve the EP with the CFSP. Given that the CFSP occupied an intergovernmental pillar, from which the ECJ was excluded, there was no way of enforcing member state compliance with these or any other CFSP provisions.

Defense

The outbreak of the Gulf crisis—caused by Iraq's invasion of Kuwait—in August 1990, in the run-up to the IGC on political union, focused additional attention on the importance of transforming EPC into CFSP and drew attention specifically to a possible defense dimension. Despite having reacted promptly and forcefully within the limits of its ability to news of the Iraqi invasion, the EC soon came in for criticism, especially in the United States, for its inability to do more. To some extent the EC was a victim of its own success. Prevailing Europhoria and pervasive discussion of a putative CFSP had raised unrealizable expectations about the EC's capacity to take concerted international action, especially involving the use of force. Accordingly, the inadequacy of the EC's overall performance in the crisis revealed more than merely the limits of EPC. A marked divergence of opinion among member states on the advisability of using force against Iraq demonstrated the difficulty of their ever developing a common security policy with a defense component. Reactions varied from Britain's instinctive acquiescence in the U.S. line to Spain's strong support for military action to France's unilateral diplomatic démarche to Germany's hiding behind a supposed constitutional ban on sending troops outside the NATO area to Ireland's whining about the limits of "neutrality."[31]

To the extent that they wanted to cooperate militarily during the Gulf crisis, the Western European Union (WEU) provided a ready-made mechanism for member states to do so. The WEU also had great potential for long-term EC defense cooperation, not least because the United States was not a member. In 1984, during the height of renewed U.S.-Soviet tension, the then seven members of the WEU—Britain, France, Germany, Italy, Belgium, the Netherlands, and Luxembourg—had revived the moribund organization in order to assert their security and defense identity. Three years later the WEU's platform on European security emphasized the organization's commitment to European integration, especially in the context of the SEA. With member states striving for a CFSP as an element of political union and some of them eager to cooperate militarily in the Gulf, the WEU (which Portugal and Spain had subsequently joined) inevitably returned to the forefront of the debate on European security during the early 1990s.

France, then in the WEU presidency, invited all EC member states to attend a WEU meeting in August 1990 to discuss possible military action in the Gulf. Not by chance, the meeting was held on the same day and in the same place as a meeting of the General Affairs Council to discuss political aspects of the crisis. Italy, then in the Council presidency, took the far-reaching step of suggesting a merger between the EC and the WEU. Then, as later, Italy's proposal proved too radical for most member states. Meeting in Rome in October 1990, the European Council merely "noted a consensus to go beyond the present limits in regard to security" but could not agree on the putative CFSP's scope, content, and procedure or the WEU's role in it. The European Council was careful to state, however, that the CFSP would "be defined . . . without prejudice to the obligations arising out of the security arrangements to which Member States are party"—that is, without undermining NATO.[32]

As expected, negotiations about security and defense proved especially arduous during the 1991 IGC. The outbreak of war in Yugoslavia in June 1991 highlighted the difficulty of reconciling member states' notoriously discordant positions. Few member states supported establishing a full-fledged EU defense policy (neutral Ireland and pacifist Denmark especially bristled at the "D-word"). Nevertheless there was near unanimity about at least establishing an EU defense identity and about using the WEU to do so. This led to difficult negotiations about the precise relationship between the EU, the WEU, and NATO. "Atlanticist" countries such as Britain, the Netherlands, and Portugal—staunch NATO supporters—traditionally shied away from initiatives that might weaken, or appear to weaken, the Atlantic Alliance. The end of the Cold War, doubts about NATO's future, and uncertainty about the United States' role in Europe complicated the issue and increased the Atlanticists' reluctance to forge too close a link between the EU and WEU. "Europeanist" countries—notably France—argued the contrary case, making the old point that a stronger European pillar would bolster the alliance and the new point that with the end of the Cold War, Europe needed to develop its own defense organization because the United States would quickly reduce its military involvement on the Continent. Germany sided instinctively with the Europeanists but, at least as long as Soviet troops remained in the eastern part of the country, opted pragmatically for the Atlanticists.

Inevitably, the TEU struck a compromise between the Europeanists and the Atlanticists. Article J.4 (now Article 17) allowed for "the eventual framing of a common defense policy, which might in time lead to a common defense." Although hedged with qualifications about a future defense policy, the unequivocal use of the D-word represented a new departure by the member states. Article J.4 also recognized the WEU as "an integral part of the development of the European union" and authorized the Council, acting on the basis of unanimity, to ask the WEU "to elaborate and implement [the EU's] decisions and actions . . . which have defense implications."

A declaration attached to the treaty explained the member states' intention to "build up WEU in stages as the defense component of the Union." However, the declaration also spelled out the WEU's relationship to NATO, citing the WEU's future development "as a means to strengthen the European pillar of the Atlantic Alliance." The treaty's language allowed both sides in the defense debate to claim victory. Yet a TEU commitment to review defense arrangements at the 1996 IGC hinted that the EU's defense identity would increasingly assume a Europeanist rather than an Atlanticist appearance.

From Maastricht to Amsterdam: The Disappointing Development of CFSP

The CFSP got off to a bad start. Even before the heads of state and government put the finishing touches on the TEU at the Maastricht summit, there was a feeling among negotiators and observers that the treaty's CFSP provisions were flawed. For that reason, the TEU included specific provisions for a review of the CFSP at the IGC due to take place in 1996. Some optimistic officials may have hoped that such a review would give the CFSP a supranational character; most simply wanted to be able to iron out the CFSP's institutional and procedural wrinkles within a few years of the treaty becoming operational.

Even though implementation of the CFSP was delayed by the TEU ratification crisis, member states and EU institutions lost little time preparing to put the TEU into effect. At its meeting in Lisbon in June 1992, the European Council endorsed a foreign ministers' report outlining EU policy toward certain countries or groups of countries and "domains within the security dimension" that could be subject to joint action. These included the Organization for Security and Cooperation in Europe (formerly the Conference on Security and Cooperation in Europe) process; disarmament and arms control, including confidence-building measures; nuclear nonproliferation issues; and economic aspects of security, in particular control of the transfer of military technology to third countries and control of arms exports.[33] Once the time came to adopt common positions and joint actions, however, there was considerable confusion among member states, the Council secretariat, and the Commission about the difference between the two instruments and the advisability of choosing one rather than the other in any given situation. In the meantime member states seemed wedded to high-sounding but harmless declarations, which had been a feature of EPC but were not provided for in the CFSP.

Eventually the Council settled on a formula whereby common positions would be used to set out an agreed-upon approach to an issue and joint actions to make concrete commitments or undertake specific initiatives. The European Stability Pact, proposed by French prime minister Edouard Balladur as a means of promoting harmonious relations between the countries of Central and Eastern Europe, became one of the EU's first joint actions in 1994. The so-called Balladur Plan is a good example of a joint action not only because it was a discreet, focused, and manageable initiative but also because it worked (the OSCE subsequently took over responsibility for its implementation). Another joint action (in 1995) involved an EU reconstruction and reconciliation effort in Mostar, a city in Bosnia bitterly divided between Croats and Muslims. This was the only time that the EU called upon the WEU to help implement a CFSP decision, although the Council made its request of the WEU in October 1993, a month before the TEU came into effect, and the operation was a civilian rather than a military one (the WEU provided a small police force).

Despite these successful joint actions (Mostar was successful only in the procedural sense; the EU's involvement was a dismal failure), most other joint actions and common positions are less clear cut and less impressive. Even more striking are the joint actions and common positions that the EU should have taken but never did. In its submission to the pre-IGC Reflection Group in 1995, the Commission complained about the variety of joint actions—ranging from ad hoc operations such as election monitoring in South Africa to regulatory matters such as control of dual-use (civil/military) goods to diplomacy (the Balladur Plan) to the deployment of substantial resources such as convoying humanitarian aid in Bosnia—and their reduced scope when compared to what the European Council had requested the Council to do.[34]

The problem was both procedural and political. Despite possible recourse to QMV to implement joint actions, member states stuck doggedly to unanimity. Thus the consensus principle of EPC permeated the CFSP, thwarting effective decisionmaking and in some cases keeping worthy foreign and security policy issues off the EU's agenda. Within a year of the TEU becoming operational, Commission president Jacques Delors declared that the CFSP "is not working. . . . This is not simply a question of political will. Objectives must be realistic and decisionmaking powers and actions effective, which is not the case."[35]

Other challenges confronting the new CFSP ranged from the difficulty of setting up the CFSP unit in the Council secretariat to the nature of the Council presidency, to the tendency of member states to go it alone on issues of particular national interest. The problem with the CFSP unit was not administrative but cultural: Officials seconded to the unit from member state foreign ministries had a completely different outlook than their colleagues drawn from the Council secretariat itself. Whereas the former had a national perspective, the latter had a European (although not necessarily a supranational) one. It took at least two years for the new unit to establish itself bureaucratically in the Council secretariat and for its mixed group of officials to begin to work harmoniously together.

The problem with the presidency was multifaceted: Some presidencies threw themselves wholeheartedly behind the CFSP; others had different priorities. The Greek presidency in early 1994 distinguished itself by pursuing foreign policy interests that ran counter to the EU's own interests (notably by refusing to recognize the former Yugoslav republic of Macedonia and imposing sanctions against it, in response to which the Commission took Greece—the Council presidency—before the ECJ). Lack of continuity due to the biannual presidential rotation inevitably affected the implementation of CFSP and weakened the EU's external representation.

The Yugoslav Debacle

Unprecedented challenges confronting the EU in the early 1990s exacerbated the CFSP's procedural problems. The greatest challenge came from Yugoslavia, where Europe's first post–Cold War conflict erupted in June 1991. Initially the Yugoslav army fought a short, unsuccessful war against secessionist Slovenia. Later that summer, Serbia (Yugoslavia's dominant republic) launched a war of territorial expansion in neighboring Croatia, which had also seceded from the Yugoslav federation. The new round of fighting unleashed a ferocity last seen in Europe during World War II. In April 1992 fighting spread to Bosnia, where both Serbia and Croatia wanted to expand but where mutual hatred of Serbia turned Bosnian Muslims and Croatian nationalists into temporary allies. Although all sides committed atrocities, Serbia's ruthless siege of Sarajevo, Bosnia's capital, seemed especially callous. Nightly news film of maimed and murdered Bosnians, victims of Serb sniper and artillery attacks, sickened the outside world. Evidence of Serb "ethnic cleansing" in Bosnia recalled Europe's nightmare of World War II and made an even more compelling humanitarian case for EC intercession in the conflict.

Coincidentally, a European Council had opened in Luxembourg on the same day that fighting first broke out in Yugoslavia. The troika of foreign ministers (from the current, immediately preceding, and immediately succeeding presidencies) left Luxembourg on a dramatic overnight peace mission to Belgrade, returning to report to the heads of state and government before the summit's end. A remark by van den Broek, then foreign minister of the Netherlands and a member of the troika, revealed the confidence and conviction that pervaded the EC's early peacekeeping efforts: "When we went on this mission to Yugoslavia, I really had the feeling that the Yugoslav authorities thought that they were talking to Europe, not just to a country incidentally coming by but to an entity whose voice counts."[36]

The instruments available to the embryonic EU included arbitration, inspection, diplomatic recognition or nonrecognition of the warring parties, and economic sanctions and inducements. The EU could neither take nor threaten to take military action, although individual member states and the WEU could. In practice, the EU was hampered by deep divisions among its member states. Although most member states instinctively sympathized with Croatia and especially with Bosnia, both victims of Serb aggression, Greece sympathized with Serbia, with which it had close cultural and religious ties. Greece also blocked EU recognition of neighboring Macedonia unless the former Yugoslav republic, having stolen "a historically Greek name and feeding long-nourished appetites for Greek territory" changed its name.[37] The most divisive row over recognition or nonrecognition of a breakaway Yugoslav republic, however, centered on Croatia.

Due to mounting domestic pressure, Germany began to press for EU recognition of Croatia and Slovenia in the fall of 1991. Few member states disputed Slovenia's right to self-determination, but the fate of a large Serbian minority in Croatia raised concerns about Croatia's claim. Moreover, a majority of member states doubted that fragmentation of the Yugoslav federation would ultimately resolve the conflict and feared that diplomatic recognition would encourage, not discourage, Croatian and Serbian irredentism. Matters came to a head at a General Affairs Council on December 16. After ten hours of fierce debate, the foreign ministers drew up criteria for the recognition of new states in Yugoslavia and the former Soviet Union.[38] Germany wanted to recognize Slovenia and Croatia immediately but agreed not to act until January 15, 1992.

Germany's unilateralism made nonsense of the newly established procedures for recognizing breakaway republics and set a bad precedent for closer cooperation on foreign and security policy. Unable to change Germany's mind and fearing a damaging split on a major international issue immediately after the Maastricht summit, the other member states agreed also to recognize Slovenia and Croatia, arguably at the cost of provoking Serb aggression in neighboring Bosnia.[39]

The EU's high hopes of mediation in the former Yugoslavia were an early victim of these and other disputes among member states over how best to respond to the conflict. Initial EU intervention during fighting in Slovenia had resulted in the Brioni Accords of July 1991, which committed all sides to a "peaceful and negotiated solution." The escalation of hostilities in Croatia prompted the EU to convene a peace conference in September 1991 in The Hague and apply intense pressure on Serbia to attend. Serbia duly showed up, but its intransigence at the conference table and belligerence on the battlefield undermined the EU's arbitration efforts.

EU mediation fared little better following the spread of hostilities to Bosnia. Persistent Serbian deception discouraged Lord Carrington, the EC mediator, to the point of resignation. A strong public reaction against Serbian atrocities redoubled the EU's diplomatic offensive, culminating in the joint UN-EU–sponsored London Conference of August 26, 1992. Leaders of all six Yugoslav republics and a host of foreign ministers (including those of the UN Security Council countries) attended. The London Conference developed "peace principles," an "action program," and a negotiating framework for six working groups, which deliberated for the rest of the year in Geneva. The Geneva talks, in turn, ended at a conference in January 1993, at which Lord Owen (Carrington's successor) and Cyrus Vance (his UN counterpart) produced a comprehensive EU-UN peace plan for Bosnia.

This was the high point (or possibly the low point) of EU mediation in the conflict. Bosnian Muslims' unwillingness to accept a proposal that seemed to reward Serbian aggression, Bosnian Serbs' reluctance to cede control over any part of their recently acquired enclaves, and Croatia's determination to grab more territory in Bosnia doomed the painstakingly prepared Owen-Vance Plan, as did the pointed lack of U.S. support for it. With its mediation effort in tatters, EU involvement in the Bosnian conflict was reduced to providing humanitarian assistance, although individual member states also sent troops under UN auspices to protect so-called safe areas.

The failure of CFSP with regard to the Yugoslav war became even more evident in April 1994 with the establishment of the Contact Group, consisting of Britain, France, Germany, Russia, and the United States, to "manage" the Yugoslav situation. Although the three EU member states in the group (later joined by Italy) supposedly represented the EU, in fact they were included because of their size and influence and represented only themselves. The establishment of the Contact Group and the lack of formal EU membership in it harked back to the old days of great-power politics and caused considerable resentment among other member states, especially those (like the Dutch) with a sizable contingent of troops in Bosnia.

The Bosnian war reached its denouement in the summer and fall of 1995 when Serbian atrocities in Sarajevo and Srebrenica finally compelled the United States to act militarily. Heavy NATO bombardment of Serbian positions in August 1995 finally brought the Serbs to their senses. The United States followed up diplomatically by convening a peace conference in Dayton, Ohio, at which a settlement was hammered out. In order to emphasize the transatlantic nature of the peace initiative, the so-called Dayton Accords were formally signed in Paris in November 1995. Yet this move could not disguise the predominantly U.S. stamp on the peace process and the failure of EU efforts to end the fighting in the former Yugoslavia during the preceding four years.

Although unique in many respects, the Yugoslav war provided a lesson in the limits of EU involvement in post–Cold War conflict resolution. The Balkans' history of instability, which had dragged the great powers into World War I and which, as German unification reminded everyone, cast a long shadow over twentieth-century Europe, complicated the EU's response to the fragmentation of Yugoslavia. Yet it is an exaggeration to claim that "unlike the situations in 1914 and 1939 . . . Europe [has been spared] a wider conflagration as a result of the policies of the EU and other key principal actors."[40] Undoubtedly, Germany's support for Croatian independence in 1991 jogged memories of Nazi support for Fascist Croatia fifty years previously and sparked an ugly media reaction in France.[41] Similarly, France's instinctive sympathy for Serbia in 1991 echoed its support for Serbia during World War I. But the democratization of Germany (and Italy) since 1945, the demise of aggressive nationalism in Western Europe, and Western European solidarity during the Cold War—to which the EC certainly contributed—ensured that the Yugoslav war did not risk pitting EU member states against each other (although, as a Balkan country, Greece almost became embroiled in the conflict).

The impossibility of sending large numbers of German troops to Yugoslavia was a more pertinent legacy for the EU of recent Balkan and European history. Britain's "Northern Ireland syndrome" made the government in London extremely cautious about intervening militarily in Yugoslavia apart from providing limited humanitarian assistance under UN auspices. Of the EU's three "great powers," only France appeared willing to take some form of military action, but not alone. The member states' reluctance to use force not only limited their policy options during the crisis but also hindered the development of an EU "defense identity" during the early years of the CFSP's existence.

Far from reflecting well on the EU, the Yugoslav war emphasized deep foreign policy differences among member states and showed the limits of EU international action.[42] More than any other event or development since the end of the Cold War, Yugoslavia demonstrated the extent to which "the dominant foreign policy reflex in Western Europe [continued to be] national, not communitarian."[43] The EU's ineffectual involvement also sapped popular support for European integration and for the fledgling CFSP. The EU's performance had a similarly debilitating effect on opinion in the United States. A rash boast in early July 1991 by Jacques Poos, Luxembourg's foreign minister and Council president-in-office, that "this is the hour of Europe, not the hour of the Americans," gave explosive ammunition to critics of the EU, especially those in Congress.[44]

Initial intervention in Yugoslavia may have given the embryonic EU a sense of identity and self-importance, but the EU's subsequent arbitration efforts seriously undermined its international standing and foreign policy effectiveness. Nor would the EU have performed better had the

CFSP been in place earlier. The problem lay not simply in a lack of mechanism or structure but rather in profound historical differences compounded by a radical contextual change caused by the end of the Cold War. The Yugoslav crisis was a salutary lesson in the limits of European integration, specifically in the difficulty of sharing sovereignty in the sensitive areas of security and defense.

CFSP Reform

Planning for the 1996–1997 IGC took place in the shadow of the Yugoslav debacle. Painfully aware of the weakness of the CFSP, member states now had an opportunity to make procedural and institutional reforms. As the work of the pre-IGC Reflection Group showed, however, the precise nature of those reforms was highly contested. The lessons of Yugoslavia were not sufficient to weaken the remaining ramparts of national sovereignty in the foreign policy field; nor did member states interpret them uniformly. Accordingly, at the outset of the IGC there was consensus among national governments only on what the CFSP-related negotiations should cover: instruments; decisionmaking, representation, planning and analysis, the budget, and the ever-present issue of EU-WEU relations.

Instruments

In an effort to clarify and enhance the means available to make a success of the CFSP, the Treaty of Amsterdam (Article 12 TEU) identifies four policy instruments:

- *Principles and guidelines* (adopted by the European Council) provide general political direction.
- *Common strategies* (adopted by the European Council) establish an umbrella under which the Council may adopt joint actions and common positions by QMV (except those with military and defense implications). Common strategies set out "the objectives, duration, and the means to be made available by the Union and the Member States" in areas of mutual interest.
- *Joint actions* (adopted by the Council) are further refined to address specific situations requiring "operational action," including a revised list of their possible contents. The Council may request the Commission to submit proposals to ensure the proper implementation of joint actions.
- *Common positions* (adopted by the Council) have also been further refined to "define the approach of the Union to a particular matter of a geographical or thematic nature."

In effect, joint actions and common positions became tools to implement common strategies, the key CFSP device.

Decisionmaking

As in the past, the clarity and effectiveness of these instruments depends on the quality and capacity of the decisionmaking process. Also as in the past, few member states were willing to give up unanimity in all areas of CFSP. Nevertheless there was a widespread acknowledgment during the IGC of the need to provide greater scope for QMV and to allow a majority of member states to act on sensitive international issues even if a minority did not want to participate in such action. As a result, the treaty incorporated two new decisionmaking formulas:

- *Constructive abstention:* As long as they do not constitute more than one-third of weighted votes in the Council, member states may abstain from a decision taken unanimously by the other member states. The abstaining member states accept that the decision is binding on the EU but need not apply the decision themselves.
- *Emergency brake:* Where decisions may be taken by QMV (e.g., the adoption of joint actions), a member state may declare "for important and stated reasons of national policy" its opposition to a vote being taken on such a decision. In that case, the Council may decide, by QMV, to refer the matter to the European Council, which can then decide the matter unanimously. The presumption seems to be that a recalcitrant member state would succumb to peer pressure in the European Council and go along with the otherwise contested decision. In reality, if a member state feels strongly enough about an issue to pull the emergency brake in the first place, other member states are unlikely to vote the matter up to the European Council. Even if they did, the European Council would hardly be able to reach a unanimous decision.

These reformed decisionmaking procedures are more complicated than the original ones without necessarily being an improvement on them. Not only is the emergency brake a throwback to the Luxembourg Compromise but the codification of abstentionism and the introduction of various restrictions and qualifications seems likely to reduce rather than enhance the CFSP's effectiveness. How could a conference convened in large part to improve CFSP decisionmaking have produced such a monster? A leading scholar has speculated that "some of the 'Community-minded' member states are by now so desperately attached to majority voting as an ideology that they are prepared to pay any price for any sort of progress, even if this means sacrificing long-defended principles."[45]

Representation

As a solution to the problem of external representation, member states agreed to the establishment of the position of High Representative for the CFSP to "contribute" to the formulation and implementation of policy and to "assist" the work of the Council, all the while acting at the "request" of the Council presidency. These weak verbs suggest that the High Representative will be no more and no less than a particular presidency wants him or her to be. The High Representative's day job is secretary-general of the Council secretariat. The High Representative forms part of a new troika, along with the Council presidency and the Commission, to represent the EU in international organizations and conferences.

Clearly, the presidency remains central to CFSP representation and to other aspects of the CFSP's operation. There could be a tendency on the part of large member states with greater resources at their disposal to make less use than smaller states of the High Representative. This is ironic in the case of France, which pressed hard during the IGC for the establishment of a more politically prominent High Representative. Had France succeeded, doubtless it would have fought as hard for the appointment of a French person to the job as it did for the appointment of a Frenchman to head the European Central Bank.

Planning and Analysis

Lack of planning and analysis was generally seen as one of the main weaknesses of the original CFSP. Accordingly, a declaration attached to the Amsterdam Treaty establishes the Policy Planning and Early Warning Unit in the Council secretariat, under the authority of the secretary-general (the High Representative). Although in principle a good idea, it is difficult to see how this innovation will greatly benefit the functioning of the CFSP. Much depends on the seniority and ability of the officials appointed to the new unit from the Commission, WEU, member states, and from the Council secretariat itself. Much depends also on the flow of information into the unit from member states. Despite being obliged to provide the unit with all relevant information, even of a confidential nature, member states are likely to keep certain things to themselves. The presidency may authorize the unit to present policy papers for the Council's deliberation. As in the case of CFSP representation, therefore, the effectiveness of the unit depends in part on the presidency's interests and orientations.

Budget

Under the original TEU, member states could charge CFSP operations either to their own budgets or to the EU's budget. Not surprisingly, member states invariably chose the latter but were unwilling to pay the political price of EP scrutiny of CFSP operational expenses. For the EP, effectively shut out of the TEU's intergovernmental pillars, such scrutiny provided a way to exert some influence over CFSP activities. Member states resolved the issue in the Treaty of Amsterdam by agreeing (Article 28 TEU) that most CFSP operational expenditures are to be charged to the EU budget (the major exceptions are those with military implications), thereby acknowledging an EP role. This treaty reform complemented an interinstitutional agreement on CFSP funding negotiated among the Council, Commission, and EP while the IGC was still in progress.

The WEU

Collaboration between the EU and WEU, as envisioned in the TEU, proceeded slowly and unspectacularly in the mid-1990s. In 1993 the WEU moved its headquarters from London to Brussels in order to be close to NATO and EU headquarters. The WEU established a closer working relationship with NATO than with the EU, where it was rarely represented at relevant meetings of the General Affairs Council. Nor, with the exception of the Mostar operation, did the EU call upon the WEU for assistance. Instead the WEU occasionally assisted NATO, for instance in Operation Sharp Guard (to enforce sanctions against Serbia in the Adriatic).

Reflecting the nature of post–Cold War security challenges, in 1992 the WEU adopted the so-called Petersberg Declaration, which, among other things, included peacekeeping, humanitarian, and rescue missions in the organization's mandate. The WEU also established a planning cell to prepare troop deployments for Petersberg and other tasks and to act as an operation headquarters in the event of a crisis.

The asymmetry between EU and WEU membership became more marked in 1995 when three neutral states—Austria, Finland, and Sweden—joined the EU. The WEU responded to this and another asymmetry of the European security architecture whereby not all European NATO members were members also of the WEU by bringing everybody under the same roof through different kinds of affiliations:

- *Full members (EU and NATO members):* Belgium, Britain, France, Germany, Greece, Italy, Luxembourg, the Netherlands, Portugal, Spain
- *Associate members (non-EU NATO members):* Iceland, Norway, Turkey
- *Observers (EU neutrals, plus neutralist but NATO-member Denmark):* Austria, Denmark, Finland, Ireland, Sweden

An additional category, associate partners, brought in the Central and Eastern European States (CEES).

NATO's close collaboration with the WEU, together with the Europeanists' support for NATO's continued primacy in European security affairs (after Bosnia, not even diehard Gaullists wanted a NATO-free Europe) took the edge off the formerly divisive Atlanticist/Europeanist cleavage among EU member states. Just as ardent Europeanists came to terms with NATO's post–Cold War role, the United States swung in the early 1990s from concern about the emergence of a CFSP to genuine support for the European Security and Defense Identity (ESDI). Indeed, in January 1994 NATO (and therefore the United States) endorsed the establishment of Combined Joint Task Forces (CJTF) to make available to NATO's European members "separable but not separate" NATO capabilities. In other words, the WEU could have NATO assets at its disposal for operations outside the NATO area in which the United States chose not to participate.

Defense-related negotiations at the 1996–1997 IGC centered once again on whether to merge the EU and the WEU. This time the implications of the outcome for transatlantic relations were not as serious as during the 1991 IGC, when the United States had launched a diplomatic offensive to prevent an EU-WEU merger from taking place. By 1996 there was still a discernible difference between Atlanticists and Europeanists (the former wanted to keep the EU and WEU apart; the latter wanted to bring them together), but the political ramifications of their positions were less profound for NATO's future.

The presence of four neutrals in the 1996–1997 IGC, instead of a single, apologetic neutral (Ireland) in the 1991 IGC, added a new factor to the equation. In the event, the neutrals and the Atlanticists (notably Britain and Denmark) prevailed, and the Amsterdam Treaty did not bring about an EU-WEU merger. Nevertheless, the Amsterdam Treaty incorporated the WEU's Petersberg tasks into the TEU (with the full support of the neutral member states), therefore raising the possibility of future EU-WEU peacekeeping operations. The NATO summit in Madrid in July 1997, held only a month after the EU summit in Amsterdam where the IGC came to an end, not only took a key decision about NATO enlargement but also stressed in its final communiqué NATO's primacy over the EU's efforts to develop a security and defense identity. Accordingly, Britain's acceptance in 1998 of a possible EU defense role was far less significant that it would have been in the run-up to the 1991 IGC, let alone earlier in the history of EPC.

CONCLUSION

Taken separately or together, the Amsterdam Treaty's reforms of EU trade policy and foreign and security policy are unimpressive. The EU after Amsterdam continues to be economically powerful but politically weak on the international scene. The treaty reworded Article C (now Article 3) TEU in order to emphasize the responsibility of the Council and the Commission for ensuring the coherence of EU external action, but without specifying how this could be done effectively. More significant, the extensive rewriting and restructuring of the TEU's CFSP provisions amount to no more than "piecemeal engineering."[46] The CFSP is still primarily intergovernmental and remains relatively isolated in the EU's Second Pillar. Despite being integral to the CFSP, the WEU is still an autonomous and insubstantial organization, and the prospect of a common EU defense policy is as remote as ever.

The effective maintenance of the pre-Amsterdam status quo in the post-Amsterdam EU is disappointing in view of the EU's impending enlargement and of continuing instability in the Balkans. Accession of a number of Central and Eastern European states and (possibly) Cyprus will further complicate the formulation and implementation of the CFSP. In the meantime, uncertainty about CFSP procedures makes it difficult for the applicant states to come to terms with the EU's *acquis politique*.

As for the Balkans, the collapse of law and order in Albania in 1997 and Serbian assaults in Kosovo in 1998 and 1999 further demonstrated the EU's inability to act swiftly and successfully to restore stability and stop aggression. Although the logic of integration indicates the indispensability of an EU role in the realm of foreign and security policy, the reality of events in the Balkans suggests that member states could be more effective if they acted singly or jointly outside the CFSP framework. Indeed, CFSP seems to provide political cover by allowing member states to be seen to be doing something about difficult problems on Europe's periphery, whereas in fact they are often content to stay on the sidelines or are willing to act militarily only in concert with the United States.

NOTES

1. Commission, *Europe: World Partner* (Luxembourg: Office for Official Publications of the European Communities [OOP], 1991), p. 11.
2. Commission, *1994 General Report* (Luxembourg: OOP, 1995), point 989.
3. Bull. EC 12-1988, "Presidency Conclusions," point 1.1.10.
4. Commission, *1996 General Report* (Luxembourg: OOP, 1995), point 768.
5. Leon Brittan, "Everybody Free Up, Please," in *The World in 1998* (London: The Economist, 1998), p. 55.
6. See Commission, "Investment as an Engine of Growth: A Need for Better Rules of the Game," in *European Union: World Trade (*Brussels: Commission, 1998).
7. Brittan, ""Everybody Free Up," p. 55.
8. John Pinder, *The European Community and Eastern Europe* (London: RIIA, 1991), p. 75.
9. Rome European Council, "Presidency Conclusions," Bull. EC 12-1990, point 1.31.

10. Quoted in *Le Monde,* November 30, 1994.
11. Commission, *The European Union and Russia: The Future Relationship,* COM(95)223.
12. Bull. EC 11-1998, point 2.2.12.
13. Commission, *Toward a New Strategy for Asia*, COM(94)314.
14. Essen European Council, "Presidency Conclusions," Bull. EC 12-1994, point 1.3.1.
15. Quoted in *Financial Times,* March 24, 1990, p. 3.
16. Bull. EC 7/8-1991, point 1.3.33.
17. The agreement is secret, but the *Financial Times* published details of it on September 23, 1991, p. 4, and September 26, 1991, p. 7.
18. See Dick K. Nanto, "The U.S.-EC-Japan Trade Triangle," in U.S. Congress, House Committee on Foreign Affairs, *Europe and the United States* (Washington, DC: Government Printing Office), p. 361.
19. Commission, *Europe and Japan: The Next Steps,* COM(95)73 final.
20. Madrid European Council, "Presidency Conclusions," Bull. EC 6-1989, point 1.2.24.
21. COM(95)279.
22. Commission, *Building a Comprehensive Partnership with China,* COM(98)181 final.
23. Commission, *1995 General Report,* point 926.
24. COM(95)495.
25. Madrid European Council, "Presidency Conclusions," Bull. EC 6-1989, point 1.2.25.
26. Hans van den Broek, "CFSP: The View of the Commission," in Spyros A. Pappas and Sophie Vanhoonacker, eds., *The European Union's Common Foreign and Security Policy: The Challenge of the Future* (Maastricht: European Institute of Public Administration, 1996), p. 23.
27. Ibid., p. 5.
28. See David Allen and Alfred Pijpers, *European Foreign Policy-Making and the Arab-Israeli Conflict* (The Hague: Martinus Nijhoff, 1984).
29. "Draft European Act," Bull. EC 11-1981, point 3.4.1. For an academic appraisal of Genscher-Colombo, see Joseph Weiler, "The Genscher-Colombo Draft European Act: The Politics of Indecision," *Journal of European Integration* 4, nos. 2 and 3 (1983): 129–153.
30. Bull. EC 6-1983, point 1.6.1.
31. See Pia Christina Wood, "EPC: Lessons from the Gulf War and Yugoslavia," in Alan Cafruny and Glenda Rosenthal, *The State of the European Community, Volume 2: The Maastricht Debates and Beyond* (Boulder: Lynne Rienner, 1993), pp. 227–244.
32. Rome European Council, "Presidency Conclusions," Bull. EC 10-1990, point 1.4.
33. Lisbon European Council, "Presidency Conclusions," Bull. EC 6-1992, point 1.2.4.
34. European Parliament, *White Paper on the 1996 IGC*, vol. 1, *Official Texts of the EU Institutions* (Luxembourg: European Parliament, 1996), p. 246.
35. Quoted in *Agence Europe,* October 15, 1994, p. 1.
36. Interview in *International Herald Tribune,* July 1, 1992, p. 2.
37. Embassy of Greece, *News from Greece*, 16/92, November 10, 1992, p. 1.
38. EPC press release P129/91, December 16, 1991.
39. EPC press release P9/92, January 15, 1992.
40. Roy Ginsberg, "The EU's Common Foreign and Security Policy: An Outsider's Retrospective on the First Year," *ECSA Review* (fall 1994): 14.

41. See, for instance, coverage of the Yugoslav war in *Le Monde* in August and September 1991.

42. For an insider's account of the EC's failure in Yugoslavia, see Henry Wynaents, *L'Engrenage* (Paris: Denoel, 1993). Wynaents was a senior Dutch diplomat involved in the EC's peace efforts.

43. Reinhardt Rummel, ed., *Toward Political Union: Planning a Common Foreign and Security Policy in the European Community* (Boulder: Westview Press, 1992), p. 298.

44. Quoted in *Financial Times*, July 1, 1991, p. 1.

45. Jörg Monar, "The European Union's Foreign Affairs System After the Treaty of Amsterdam: A 'Strengthened Capacity for External Action?'" *European Foreign Affairs Review* 2, no. 4 (winter 1997): 421.

46. The term "piecemeal engineering" is used by both Monar, "The European Union's Foreign Affairs System," p. 435, and Wolfgang Wessels, "The EU as an Actor in the International System: The CFSP After Amsterdam," paper presented at the Netherlands Institute of International Affairs, Clingendael, December 1997, p. 6.

18

U.S.-EU Relations

The United States has consistently (and genuinely) espoused European integration for strategic reasons. It saw the EC as an essential element of the post–World War II peace settlement and as an important contributor to the security of Western Europe during the Cold War. It now sees the EU as indispensable for the security and stability of post–Cold War Europe. Moreover, the United States and the EU enjoy the world's largest and deepest economic relationship; together they account for the majority of world GDP.

By and large, this relationship is healthy and stable. By contrast with the structural problems inherent in EU (and U.S.) relations with Asia, the U.S.-EU trade balance reliably reflects growth rates and macroeconomic developments on both sides of the Atlantic. Yet the underlying soundness of transatlantic economic relations is often obscured by friction between the world's two largest trading blocs. Indeed, economic dialogue between the United States and the EU has been dogged by persistent trade disputes, spillover from domestic controversies, and rivalry on the world economic stage.

Nor have U.S.-EU political relations been trouble-free. Despite U.S. support, inevitably the process of European integration contained the seeds of transatlantic political discord. Not surprisingly, the more recent emergence of a political dialogue between the United States and the EU, although an encouraging sign of a broader and more balanced transatlantic relationship, has been marked by mutual frustration and occasional unproductive rivalry.

UNDERLYING DIFFICULTIES

It has been popular in Europe to ascribe sour notes in the transatlantic relationship to American resentment of the emergence of a strong and united Europe and to the resulting decline in U.S. influence. The truth is more complicated. The uneasy relationship between the United States and the EU is a result of a number of inherent asymmetries in their structure and outlook. Whereas the United States and Europe undoubtedly have far more in common with each other than with any other world region, the devil, as always, is in the details.

From the U.S. perspective, the initial difficulties lay in the incremental, often untidy nature of European integration, which caused constant changes in the scope of the EC's agenda and in the character of its policy-formulating process. By contrast, bilateral, country-to-country relations were easily comprehensible: Both sides had a well-understood governmental structure and an easily identifiable set of issues. But in the case of the EC, who exactly had decisionmaking power, and where precisely was the boundary between Community and member state competence?

Understandably, the tenuous connection between the trade and commercial policies conducted by the EC and the geopolitical concerns of its member states made it impossible for the United States, a traditional nation-state, to achieve the normal trade-offs between political and economic goals. Despite early U.S. support for European integration, the frustrations of dealing with this unnatural compartmentalization of political and economic policy soured many U.S. policymakers on the EC and its institutional machinery. Increasing pressure on world agricultural markets imposed by CAP-generated surpluses and the steady erosion of U.S. agricultural exports to EC member states exacerbated the problems. Typically, disputes over European restrictions on agricultural imports—long the most visible element of the EC's international mandate—have been the biggest source of bilateral friction.

Other asymmetries have added to the difficulties of both sides in multilateral negotiations. The Commission's need to develop trade policy by negotiating with member states, a feature of the Common Commercial Policy (CCP), often results in lowest-common-denominator mandates that leave the Commission little room for maneuver in the multilateral sphere. By the same token, the U.S. administration's need to persuade Congress to accept the final package can leave an entire multilateral agreement in agonizing suspense for months or can lead to peculiar negotiating positions designed to placate a handful of powerful senators. Shifting boundaries between EU and member state competencies can lead to conflicting signals in areas such as aviation policy. Finally, although the United States and the EU dominate the world trading system, their international and regional priorities are different. The United States has enormous trading interests to protect around the Pacific Rim, and its troubled relationship with Japan has long been at the center of its trade policy. The EU, by contrast, is primarily a regional power: The bulk of its trade is with its neighbors, and its links with Asia, especially Japan, are substantially weaker than those of the United States. Furthermore, successive enlargements have steadily brought the EU's most important regional trading partners into the fold, and the hope of future enlargement causes others to refrain from challenging EU trade policies.

The growing role of the EU as a political actor has undoubtedly added needed depth to the relationship at a time when the simple verities of the Cold War have been replaced by messy and nearly unmanageable regional breakdowns. However, it has brought with it new difficulties generated by incompatible expectations and capabilities on each side. For U.S. policymakers, it was always easier to work with those European countries whose outlook and approach were similar to theirs and to rely on firm alliances with Britain, Germany, and others such as the Netherlands, ignoring opposition elsewhere in Europe. Although great-power groupings such as the G7 and the Contact Group continue to play a role in international management, the Common Foreign and Security Policy (CFSP) has made this traditional U.S. strategy harder to pursue.

Inevitably, in moments of crisis, the United States tends to go back to its old friends and bypass the EU decisionmaking structures so painstakingly developed. This tendency is exacerbated by the fact that EU political clout does not extend much beyond the power of the purse; although EU aid disbursements to Central and Eastern Europe, for example, dwarf those of the United States, the big decisions, such as on military intervention in Bosnia, remain the province of the nation-states. Although U.S. aid disbursements have steadily declined in real terms during the postwar era, the United States remains the military power of last resort.

Although a gross generalization, it also seems reasonable to observe that many Europeans are resentful of the United States because of its economic and military power and its cultural influence. EU officials are not entirely free of such prejudice, operating as they do on a vision of Europe that is always slightly ahead of reality. Moreover, many of them complain that Americans are only dimly aware of the EU. Certainly the great American public knows little about the EU, just as the great European public knows little about how the U.S. government works. However, academic study of the EU is as advanced in the United States as it is in Europe. As for U.S. officials and businesspeople, those who deal with the EU regularly know well how it works and what it does; the U.S. Mission to the EU and the EU Committee of the American Chamber of Commerce are among the most effective lobbyists in Brussels.

EU officials are especially irritated by what they see as the refusal of Americans who deal regularly with the EU to acknowledge the EU as a serious political actor, perceiving U.S. officials as either unwilling to see the EU as a political equal or as unable to comprehend the complexities of the CFSP. Indeed many U.S. officials are frustrated with the EU politically not because of the CFSP's opacity but because more often than not EU action fails to match EU rhetoric—hence, for instance, occasional intemperate remarks by U.S. officials about EU policy toward Bosnia and Kosovo, and vice versa. Although Europeans may retort that Americans do not appreciate the difficulty of reaching a common EU position, Americans believe with some justification that the EU cannot expect to be taken seriously as a political entity as long as the results of its foreign policy coordination efforts are so meager. The problem is not that U.S. officials are unfamiliar with the intricacies of the CFSP but that they are only too well aware of CFSP's procedural and political weaknesses.

To some extent, these problems and resentments have been tempered (or at any rate muffled) by the growing mutual engagement that has resulted from the EU's increasing powers and mandate. Since the beginning of the 1990s, leaders on both sides have tried to speed this process by a series of ever-more-ambitious initiatives intended to increase U.S.-EU cooperation and engagement across the board and to raise the profile of the relationship. These have been only partly successful. Through innumerable high-level meetings and rising piles of communiqués, they have created an aura of dynamism and progress and have provided political cover for some quiet compromises on especially touchy issues. They have been less successful, however, in resolving either the persistent irritants in the trade field or the fundamental differences in political priorities and social outlook that will continue to produce trade frictions, especially as trade is increasingly affected more by regulatory policy than by "traditional" protectionism.

THE DEVELOPMENT OF U.S.-EU RELATIONS

Despite early U.S. support for European unity, the development of European integration was bound to bring with it a degree of transatlantic discord. Economically, a strong EC caused a decline in U.S. market share within the EC itself and in some third countries. Since the early 1960s, the United States and the EU have been embroiled in disputes over alleged Europrotectionism and unfair EU practices in the international marketplace. Beginning with the so-called chicken and pasta wars, continuing with tit-for-tat restrictions on steel trade generated by domestic pressure to protect tottering industries and culminating in a decade-long dispute over hormones in beef, the history of U.S.-EU relations is replete with issue-specific disputes even as transatlantic trade and investment flourished.

Politically, an assertive EC might have challenged the United States' hegemony in Europe and global preeminence. Certainly French president Charles de Gaulle saw such a challenge as its main raison d'être. But the EC's member states never displayed a willingness, let alone ability, to form a political and military bloc that could rival the United States. During the Cold War, when Western Europe depended on U.S. military protection, it would have been foolhardy for Western European countries to risk antagonizing the United States by challenging its ascendancy in NATO (de Gaulle could afford to do so precisely because no other country would follow his lead). In the early 1970s EC member states launched European Political Cooperation (EPC); a decade later, during a resurgence of Cold War tension, some sought to extend EPC into the security domain. But Washington's frosty response, or some member states' anticipation of Washington's frosty response, helped restrict EPC deliberations to the "political and economic aspects" of security.

Ultimately, the change that swept across Europe in the wake of the Single European Act (SEA) offered the chance to breathe new life into transatlantic relations. Initially, however, American reactions baffled and annoyed EC policymakers caught up in a vision of a Europe without barriers. Businesspeople and some policymakers in the United States, their opinions of the EC shaped by the CAP as well as by limitless European subsidies for "national champion" and "Eurochampion" industries such as Airbus, were unimpressed by the stated aims of the single market. They charged that the single market would bring about a "fortress Europe" in which the fruits of economic integration would somehow be reserved for Europeans. Commission officials, perceiving themselves as the vanguard of a liberalizing force, were hurt and angry at this charge, although they unwittingly abetted it at the outset through a crude effort to use market integration as a bargaining chip in the banking sector. This move raised such an outcry among U.S. banks long established in Europe, supported by U.S. policymakers, that the Commission was forced to rewrite much of its initial draft directive.

Despite Commission resentment of it, ultimately U.S. pressure forced Commission officials to address the international consequences of their internal decisions. As a practical matter, the structure of the single market program would have made it difficult to deny its benefits to foreign players; foreign pressure made it necessary for the Commission to resist the temptation to try. Although rightly rejecting U.S. demands for "a seat at the table," the Commission agreed to beef up consultations with and develop greater institutional ties between U.S. and European standards-setting bodies as well as develop mutual recognition agreements that would allow manufacturers to sell in both EC and foreign markets without the need for additional certifications. Simultaneously, a second look at the internal market program itself persuaded many U.S. firms, especially those already established in Europe, that the single market presented more opportunity than threat. Ever eager to jump on a bandwagon, U.S. business became a cheerleader for European deregulation and elimination of internal barriers, and seminars on "1992" became a cottage industry among U.S. consulting firms.

At the same time, post-SEA changes in the EC's agenda and institutional structure complicated U.S.-EU relations procedurally. In terms of the EC's agenda, the most important changes were greater Community involvement in environmental policy, industrial policy, research, and science and technology. Institutional change was most marked in the increasing assertiveness and growing authority of the Commission. This was a perturbing development for the United States, where the name of the Commission itself evoked an unfavorable (and wholly unfair) image of all that was iniquitous about the EC: a bloated bureaucracy, an opaque administration, and an unaccountable authority. Who drafted proposals in the Commission? When were they circulated outside Commission headquarters? How could third countries express their points of view? The answers to those questions seemed to differ from one directorate-general to another.

Post–Cold War Transitions

The context of U.S.-EU relations changed dramatically with the end of the Cold War.[1] The United States responded to the revolution in Central and Eastern Europe with a fundamental review of policy toward the Continent. President George Bush articulated the result in two speeches in May 1989, and Secretary of State James Baker elaborated further in a famous speech in December of that year—one month after the fall of the Berlin Wall. The essence of the United States' "New Atlanticism" was a determination to preserve NATO regardless of the changes ahead, an appreciation of the potential of the Conference on Security and Cooperation in Europe (CSCE)—the CSCE later became the Organization for Security and Cooperation in Europe (OSCE)—and a recognition of the EC's importance as a political and economic anchor in post–Cold War Europe. At the G7 summit in July 1989, Bush manifested Washington's confidence in the EC by asking the Commission to coordinate Western aid to Hungary and Poland.[2] The acceleration of reform in Central and Eastern Europe—and the EU's ability to mobilize massive amounts of aid to help the process—further convinced the United States of the EC's political significance, especially as an essential underpinning for a united Germany, which Washington strongly supported.

Changing U.S. policy toward the EC and a continuing surge in the EC's political importance in the late 1980s provided the background to the Transatlantic Declaration. The United States accepted with alacrity a proposal by the Council presidency in early 1990 to formalize U.S.-EC relations. The appeal for the United States of such an arrangement grew throughout the year, as the EC responded to the complete collapse of communism in Central and Eastern Europe and the sudden inevitability of German reunification by calling for an intergovernmental conference (IGC) on political union in addition to the previously scheduled IGC on EMU.

The "Declaration on US-EC Relations," signed in Washington, D.C., in November 1990 by Bush and the presidents of the Council and Commission, seemed long on rhetoric and short on substance. Among the reasons for a solid U.S.-EC relationship, the declaration included a new factor: "the accelerating process by which the European Community is acquiring its own identity in economic and monetary matters, in foreign policy and in the domain of security." Yet apart from its general significance, the declaration's only tangible contribution to U.S.-EC relations was a strengthened framework for regular consultations to enable both sides to "inform and consult each other on important matters of common interest, both political and economic, with a view to bringing their positions as close as possible, without prejudice to their respective independence."[3]

Changes in the political atmosphere, however, had little effect on the long-standing problems and tensions in the economic relationship. No sooner had the EC signed the Transatlantic Declaration and launched the IGCs than the Uruguay Round negotiations of the GATT collapsed in Brussels in December 1990 over U.S.-EC differences.[4] The talks broke down in a swirl of mutual recriminations with the United States and the EC accusing each other of never having been serious about a successful conclusion. The EC especially objected to what seemed like excessive and high-handed U.S. demands for CAP reform at a time when the Commission had not completed its own internal negotiations on this supremely touchy issue. Some in Europe interpreted the EC's stance as evidence of a newfound willingness to "stand up" to the United States. In fact, there was more of the old Europe than the new in the EC's position, which resulted from a French veto of a last-minute compromise. For its part, the United States saw the failure of the Brussels talks as evidence of the EC's continuing intransigence and introversion. The EC seemed neither able nor willing to face up to its international responsibilities. Indeed, some member states appeared to exploit a domestic reaction against Washington's conduct at the Brussels talks to entrench their uncompromising positions.

What was less evident in the strife surrounding the final stages of the Uruguay Round negotiations was the extent to which it illustrated the duality of the economic relationship between the United States and the EU: a continuing pattern of intractable disputes obscuring a far larger set of common interests vis-à-vis the rest of the world. Well-publicized spats between the U.S. and European negotiators over the nuances of issues such as trade in services, intellectual property protection, and antidumping and subsidy rules suggested that the Uruguay Round was a struggle between titans with the rest of the world looking on. In fact, much of the force driving the talks came from the joint determination of the United States and the EU to restore the credibility of the GATT and drag the rest of the world into a liberalized trading system (developing countries, including several of the Asian "tigers," were by no means eager to open their domestic markets). A more muscular world trading regime would not only secure better market access for U.S. and European exporters; it could also contain transatlantic trade disputes that threatened to poison the broader economic and political relationship.

The emergence in May 1992 of a CAP reform package made possible the so-called Blair House agreement between the United States and the EU, which provided for gradual reduction and limitation of agricultural subsidies. This in turn paved the way for the belated conclusion of the Uruguay Round and the birth of the WTO in 1995. The conclusion of the round led to a respite in many long-running U.S.-EU skirmishes. Some issues, such as U.S. complaints about EU oilseed subsidies, were subsumed into WTO commitments under the Blair House agreement; others, such as disputes over beef hormones and bananas, went temporarily on hold until they could be revived as WTO cases under more stringent dispute-settlement rules.

Toward the New Transatlantic Agenda

The Transatlantic Declaration appeared little more than a transitional measure pending the results of the IGCs in December 1991 and the development of U.S.-EU relations in the post-Maastricht period. The already well-known Delors Plan had set the agenda for the IGC on EMU, the outcome of which was unlikely to cause much surprise in Washington. But the negotiations on the European Political Union (EPU) held out an entirely different prospect, including a possibility that the EC might finally extend its agenda to include "hard" security and defense.

As it was, the transition to a new political relationship with the EC proved difficult for the United States, which sometimes seemed alarmed, or at least discomfited, by the EC's rising political profile. On top of this, security and defense issues initially brought a new edge to transatlantic relations. Efforts by some member states during the IGC to give the EU a security dimension and, ultimately, a military capability provoked an intemperate U.S. response with warnings from Washington about the dangers of undermining NATO. Rather than being representative of U.S. policy toward European security in the post–Cold War period, however, this infamous U.S. outburst was a throwback to earlier, Cold War ways. Six years later, during the IGC that resulted in the Amsterdam Treaty, the United States fully supported the development of an EU security and defense identity.

Member states' apparent responsiveness to U.S. demands in 1991 not to risk undermining NATO by developing an EU defense identity suggested that the United States continued to wield considerable diplomatic clout and that member states took seriously the implied threat of a U.S. military withdrawal from Europe. Indeed, member states drew back from acquiring for themselves or the EU an independent defense capability and opted instead to use the WEU as a bridge between NATO and the EU. But their reasons for doing so were more diverse than simply succumbing to a

U.S. démarche. Regardless of Washington's position, member states could not agree among themselves so soon after the end of the Cold War about the form or content of an EU defense identity. Moreover, few were willing to surrender sovereignty in this area.[5]

From the U.S. perspective, the outcome of the 1991 IGCs was satisfactory. As expected, the EMU negotiations led to a general endorsement of the Delors Plan and a decision to establish a common monetary policy and single currency by 1999 at the latest. To the annoyance of EU politicians and officials, in the mid- and late 1990s their U.S. counterparts seemed indifferent or even hostile to EMU. In fact, the United States was reasonably sanguine about EMU; far from trying to thwart EMU and abort the euro, most Americans who thought about the issue seemed more enthusiastic about monetary union than the fabled European man in the street. At the same time, U.S. officials appreciated that the launch of the euro would have important repercussions for transatlantic relations (these are examined below).

As for political union, the TEU formally altered the EU's competence and institutional framework in ways that were not disadvantageous to the United States. The extension of Community competence in areas such as environmental and industrial policy for the most part formalized the status quo (the treaty's industrial policy provisions were not as damaging to the United States as they might have been had certain member states, notably France, had their way). Institutional changes introduced in the treaty, together with a vogue for transparency, promised to make the decision-making process more open and amenable to outside influence, a prospect welcomed by the United States. At the very least, the institutional provisions of the treaty did not require a radical reappraisal of the U.S. foreign policy apparatus for dealing with EC affairs.

Member states' differing and at times contradictory responses to the two major international crises during the course of the 1991 IGCs—the Gulf War and the outbreak of hostilities in Yugoslavia—made it even more difficult for them to agree on an EU-based security structure independent of the United States. By the same token, the EU's performance in both crises fueled doubts in Washington about the EU's ability ever to fashion a coherent foreign and security policy. As for Washington's own reaction to the Gulf War, the speed and success with which it dispatched a massive expeditionary force briefly overcame the self-doubt and insecurity that had characterized the United States since the declinism debate of the mid-1980s.[6]

Yet the United States' post–Gulf War triumphalism was succeeded by a growing preoccupation with domestic affairs at the expense of international interests. A faltering election campaign obliged Bush in late 1992 to devote more time and attention to domestic economic problems. The arrival of the Clinton administration, headed by the first U.S. president from the postwar generation, appeared only to increase European ambivalence over relations with the United States. In fact, there was little in the first months of the Clinton administration to suggest a turn away from Europe. Clinton's trade representative steered the United States through the final months of the Uruguay Round, and Clinton himself spearheaded a vigorous push to get congressional ratification of the results. Clinton's political-military advisers also promptly abandoned much of Bush's prickly resistance to the emergence of closer European cooperation within NATO. They obligingly stepped back to allow the nascent CFSP structure to deal with the civil war in the former Yugoslavia, an issue from which senior U.S. diplomats instinctively recoiled.

However, the administration's abrupt shift of attention to another Bush legacy, the North American Free Trade Agreement, and to the Pacific, with growing emphasis on the fledgling Asia Pacific Economic Cooperation (APEC) dialogue, rattled European leaders. The curious result of their anxiety was the sudden emergence in 1994 and 1995 of European calls for negotiation of the Transatlantic Free Trade Agreement (TAFTA). Its earliest advocates were not trade negotiators, exhausted after the Uruguay Round, but senior politicians such as German foreign minister Klaus Kinkel and British defense minister Malcolm Rifkind.[7]

The TAFTA idea never really amounted to more than a straw man. Under GATT rules, any free trade agreement must cover "substantially all trade." Thus negotiation of a TAFTA would require reopening of all the agricultural and other disputes that had plagued the Uruguay Round talks. This was hardly a recipe for greater transatlantic unity. The idea also raised worries among other WTO members that the United States and the EU would retreat to their own cozy condominium, creating the world's largest trading bloc and relegating the WTO to irrelevancy. However, the notion of a TAFTA served its purpose by putting the ball in the U.S. court; its failure to respond would be interpreted as a signal that the transatlantic relationship was deteriorating. U.S. officials therefore made encouraging, if vague, statements about the need for closer economic and political cooperation

In the event, when trade commissioner Leon Brittan took up the issue, he proposed something at once less and more than a TAFTA. The "transatlantic economic zone" was a highly flexible concept that would liberalize trade in certain areas while skipping over others. Its relation to existing WTO rules was ambiguous. U.S. policymakers, more legalistic in their outlook, were uneasy about the haziness of the concept and reluctant to be dragged into TAFTA negotiations through the backdoor. Nevertheless, Secretary of State Warren Christopher signaled U.S. willingness to go along with negotiation of a "transatlantic economic area" (described by one wag as "TEA for two") in the context of a broader bilateral effort to expand the Transatlantic Declaration (TAD) to include substantive cooperation to the existing consultation mechanisms. Thus the second grand bilateral initiative, the New Transatlantic Agenda (NTA), was born. Following short but intensive negotiations, it was signed by Clinton and the presidents of the Council and the Commission in Madrid in December 1995.[8]

The NTA was much more concrete than the 1990 TAD. To the usual rhetoric about common values, it added broad areas in which the United States and the EU were to make joint efforts in order to

- promote peace, stability, democracy, and development
- respond to global challenges relating to issues such as the environment, terrorism, and international crime
- expand world trade and promote closer economic relations
- build "bridges" across the Atlantic in the cultural and educational domain

The NTA further beefed up the schedule of mandatory meetings established under the TAD to include those of a "Senior-Level Group" charged with the task of adding substance to the twice-yearly, and increasingly perfunctory, U.S.-EU summits instituted under the 1990 declaration.

An accompanying action plan listed a number of short- and medium-term goals to achieve the NTA's objectives, ranging from the conclusion of issue-specific trade negotiations to closer educational cooperation. For the most part, the political game plan was heavily weighted with words like "cooperate," "reinforce," "pursue," and so forth reflecting the intractable nature, and resistance to schematization, of problems such as Bosnia, Cyprus, the Middle East, and the recurring crises in Africa. The few specifics involved referred mostly to participation in negotiations or conferences and implementation of various agreements already negotiated. Economic commitments were slightly more specific, covering both the multilateral issues of the day and continuing bilateral efforts.

Neither the NTA nor the action plan contained any reference to a free trade area. Instead, in addition to a host of promises to fulfill Uruguay Round commitments and strengthen the international system, the NTA and action plan called for a "new transatlantic marketplace" to be achieved by progressive reduction or elimination of bilateral trade barriers, stronger regulatory cooperation, and commitments to complete various negotiations then in progress. In short, the new transatlantic marketplace was less a radical departure from the past than an effort to breathe new life into a continuing process.

Nevertheless, the NTA included one real innovation on the economic front: the Transatlantic Business Dialogue (TABD), which brought together senior corporate officials to set an agenda for government negotiators. The TABD—the first truly transatlantic lobby—quickly showed its value in focusing the attention of trade negotiators on the bread-and-butter issues most important to those actually doing the trading; it placed a heavy emphasis on unglamorous but important tariff problems and standards, testing, and certification issues. Efforts to set up a transatlantic labor dialogue have been less successful; successive U.S.-EU summits have also called for transatlantic environmental and consumer dialogues.

Beyond formalizing and making obligatory meetings among senior officials that had already been taking place on an ad hoc basis, the NTA cannot be said to have substantially improved transatlantic cooperation. Although upcoming U.S.-EU summits have helped create pressure for progress on issues such as U.S. sanctions that affect European firms, the increasingly frantic meeting schedule has not necessarily facilitated lasting progress on otherwise intractable issues. Even the combined pressure of regular U.S.-EU summits and the persistent nagging of the TABD could not spur negotiators to complete the initial round of talks on mutual recognition agreements in less than six years, let alone come to a real meeting of the minds on the correct approach to Iran. More broadly, the TABD praised government officials in 1998 for achieving roughly a third of the concrete goals they had set themselves in the action plan, but it is debatable whether the outcome would have been much different without the trappings of the NTA.[9]

Reconciling the Security Dilemma

In the early 1990s, the United States and its main European allies (i.e., the EU's largest member states) resolved only temporarily the post–Cold War security dilemma of trying to maximize Europe's collective security identity and capability (the "Europeanist" position) and trying to maintain the status quo of U.S. preeminence in NATO (the "Atlanticist" position). The TEU provided an interim solution: The WEU would become both the prototypical defense arm of the EU and a vehicle through which the European pillar of NATO could be strengthened. This arrangement was up for grabs at the 1996–1997 IGC, where rivalry between Europeanist and Atlanticist member states was expected to resurface. In the event, by 1996 the EU was almost uniformly Atlanticist, whereas the United States had become somewhat Europeanist. In other words, based especially on the lessons of Bosnia and the Dayton peace settlement, erstwhile Europeanists saw the necessity for a strong U.S. military presence in Europe, whereas the United States pressed its European allies to strengthen their own capability to confront security threats in Europe's "backyard."

Agreement within NATO in January 1994 on the concept of Combined Joint Task Forces (CJTF)—an arrangement that would make NATO assets available to NATO's European members for operations outside the NATO area in which the United States did not want to participate—demonstrated a new transatlantic consensus on European security and the U.S. role in it.

Of greater political importance in the aftermath of the Bosnian debacle was the outcome of the NATO summit in Madrid in July 1997, which endorsed the EU's development of a security and defense identity but asserted NATO's primacy. Only a month before, when they concluded the IGC at the Amsterdam summit, member states agreed to incorporate WEU peacekeeping tasks into the CFSP, therefore raising the possibility of future EU-WEU peacekeeping operations. Unlike in 1991 (during the previous IGC), there was no U.S. diplomatic intervention during the 1996–1997 IGC to try to prevent a WEU-EU merger. In the event, member states themselves agreed, without much rancor, to keep the two organizations separate.

The Madrid NATO summit also endorsed the NATO membership applications of the Czech Republic, Poland, and Hungary. Yet the debate about NATO enlargement had angered many Europeans because of the U.S. administration's apparently high-handed approach to one of the most important security issues in post–Cold War Europe. Essentially, the United States alone decided which Central and Eastern European countries would joint NATO first, and when they would do so. Related suggestions in the U.S. Congress that EU membership was either a substitute for NATO membership or a consolation for those Central and Eastern European countries not initially admitted to NATO, together with criticism of the EU's slow enlargement process, demonstrated a profound misunderstanding in American political circles of the EU's nature and procedures. Although intensely irritating for Europeans, U.S. conduct of NATO enlargement and critical or erroneous comments about EU enlargement did not unravel the solid transatlantic consensus on the post–Cold War European security structure.

Old Wine in New Bottles?

The temptation to put old wine in new bottles—that is, to repackage the relationship—returns periodically to U.S. and EU officials, especially when the relationship appears to be in the doldrums. In the late 1990s, tensions over U.S. sanctions and new agricultural trade irritants were again on the rise. Growing congressional skepticism of multilateral trade initiatives and corresponding U.S. ambivalence about European proposals for a broad new Millennium Round increased European misgivings. In early 1998, therefore, Leon Brittan proposed to cap a long and brilliant career in the Commission with yet another bilateral initiative. This one, initially known as the New Transatlantic Marketplace (which had figured as one of the elements of the NTA of 1995) was carefully composed of elements, such as free trade in services, that both sides (and particularly the EU) could presumably accept. It conspicuously did not include any proposals in the traditionally touchy areas of agriculture and culture.

The U.S. response to Brittan's swan song was cautiously receptive; it met a much frostier reception in Europe. The French openly rejected the initiative on the grounds that it had not been vetted first by the member states. Others expressed concern about the advisability of some of the elements, especially efforts to achieve bilateral free trade in services at the expense of the multilateral process. As the Commission worked to finesse all these objections, the proposed New Transatlantic Marketplace was transmogrified and watered down into the Transatlantic Economic Partnership (TEP). Publicly unveiled at the May 1998 U.S.-EU summit, the TEP was worthy but anodyne. Its stated objective was the "intensification and extension of multilateral and bilateral cooperation." On the multilateral side, it affirmed that the two sides would cooperate to pursue a list of initiatives that for the most part were already under way in the WTO. On the bilateral side, the highlight was a promise to concentrate on "those barriers that really matter," especially regulatory barriers, with a nod to the efforts of the TABD. Following the NTA model, this rather general declaration was to be followed as soon as possible by a common action plan.

EMU: A New Dimension in U.S.-EU Relations

Coming to terms with the launch of the euro entails a major shift in the substance of the U.S.-EU dialogue. A relationship forged in the slow-moving and compartmentalized world of trade disputes will have to evolve substantially to cope with fast-breaking exchange rate and international capital movements. The traditionally close relationship among G7 finance ministers and central bankers, particularly between the United States and Britain, will have to give way to a more complex and probably less collegial interplay among EU finance ministers, the European Central Bank (ECB), and their U.S. counterparts. EU efforts to solve the conundrum of euroland representation in G7 summits suggest that for the short term, decisionmaking on the EU side will be cumbersome and plagued by disputes over who is to speak for whom; the risk is that European internal problems will irritate U.S. policymakers and confirm them in their tendency to act alone rather than coordinate with the EU in finding solutions to future financial crises. The continuing role of member state finance ministries in providing IMF resources and emergency financial assistance during crises will make the relationship even more complicated. Experience with CFSP so far suggests that in moments of stress, the United States will go back to its old friends for help rather than wait for the EU process to produce a response and that this tendency will irritate euroland's smaller members and the Commission.

In the long term, however, the two sides must and will engage as equal partners. The euro has more weight on the world scene than any of its European predecessors, even the mighty mark. Already, the advent of EMU has had a calming effect on EU investor expectations in the wake of the

Asian crisis. Over time, it will inevitably grow into a primary reserve currency, and the makers of EU currency policy will be key to addressing any global financial problem. The obvious solution would be to realign international institutions, especially the G7, to correspond with this new reality. However, European G7 powers have shown little inclination to do so. The G7 is an awkward and illogical grouping, a postwar historical artifact made even more ungainly by the partial grafting onto it of Russia in the 1990s. Membership in the G7 carries a certain glamour that members are reluctant to relinquish; proposals to make it more representative, or more compact, have fallen on deaf ears. Perhaps it will gradually become marginalized, replaced by informal contacts between the U.S. Federal Reserve and the ECB, on the one hand, and the Federal Reserve and a shifting group of EU finance ministries, on the other. New ad hoc groups may spring up; for example, the recently arrived G22 was set up in response to the Asian crisis and offers more scope for input from Asian and non-G7 European powers. In the meantime, the United States and the EU will have to draw upon forty years of experience and adjust again to the shifting nature of the relationship.

ENDURING DIFFERENCES

Despite relative harmony in transatlantic security relations and a new framework for political-economic relations (the NTA and its action plan), U.S.-EU trade disputes persist. Concrete progress in some areas—such as the conclusion of multilateral trade agreements on telecommunications and financial services; bilateral mutual recognition agreements in the area of standards, testing, and certification; agreement to work toward a global set of auto standards; and agreement in principle that electronic commerce should remain tariff-free—has been overshadowed by new and daunting problems such as regulation of genetically modified organisms and privacy-related restrictions on electronic data transmission. At one extreme, political-economic issues such as trade sanctions have generated serious tensions. At the other extreme, disputes related to product regulation for both safety and environmental reasons are proliferating. Far from being primarily technical in nature, many of these issues evoke emotional public responses that make them difficult for the EU to manage.[10] At the same time, traditional trade barriers such as quotas, tariffs and other forms of trade protection remain a periodic irritant in the relationship.

Traditional Issues: Tariffs and Quotas

The most prominent "traditional" dispute is the continuing row over EU banana quotas.[11] These quotas, long imposed by certain member states in order to favor former colonial banana growers, were extended in 1993 to the entire EU as part of the single market program, thus denying access by so-called dollar banana growers in Central America. Although the United States grows few bananas itself, U.S. corporations are among the major banana brokers; thus U.S. trade officials vigorously opposed the EU measures. A WTO case led to a judgment in May 1997, later confirmed by an appellate body, that the EU quotas were indeed illegal under WTO rules. The Commission, however, mindful of the vehement opposition from the old colonial powers to eliminating the preferential quotas, chose a legalistic response that adjusted the regime to meet some of the technical objections raised by the WTO panel over administration of the quotas while skirting the larger issue of the legality of the quotas themselves. To no one's surprise, the United States and Central America promptly objected again. Weary of the ensuing debate over whether a new panel was required to decide whether the new plan was also WTO-illegal (as seemed likely), the United States announced in October 1998 their intention to take retaliatory measures by January 1999 if the EU did not comply to their satisfaction with the initial judgment.

Based on past experience, other traditional trade issues are likely to continue to crop up as the EU enlarges. For instance, in the mid-1980s, U.S. objections to the loss of agricultural export markets in Spain and Portugal as a result of their accession to the EC were eventually satisfied by the establishment of special quotas for U.S. exports to Spain and Portugal outside of CAP limits. The application of EU tariffs to U.S. electronic components that had hitherto entered Austria, Finland, and Sweden duty-free became a source of transatlantic friction at the time of the 1995 enlargement before being resolved under the WTO Information Technology Agreement of 1997. The next rounds of EU enlargement may generate similar problems, although the United States refrained on political grounds from challenging the more dubious trade provisions of the EU's Europe agreements with the countries of Central and Eastern Europe. On another front, U.S. and EU antidumping actions, which impose tariffs on foreign producers supposedly selling below cost, continue to generate predictable complaints from the targets of those actions on both sides of the Atlantic. Antidumping actions and ensuing complaints are likely to increase in intensity in times of economic downturn.

Trade, Morality, and Extraterritoriality

Economic sanctions became an increasingly popular foreign policy tool in the United States during the 1990s. Despite their evident ineffectiveness, unilateral sanctions against such popular targets as Iran, Libya, and Cuba offered a seemingly low-cost way to express moral disapproval and, for the Congress, to assert control over foreign policy. This approach met with little support in Europe, where policymakers were reluctant to mix business with morality. Even in cases where there was broad agreement on sanctions, such as those imposed against the former republic of Yugoslavia, sanctions proved only moderately effective and depressingly easy to evade.

As U.S. sanctions measures proliferated, U.S. and EU policymakers increasingly clashed over their legality and efficacy. Faced with European refusal to go along with their efforts to punish rogue regimes, U.S. legislators became increasingly adept at devising measures that would punish foreign firms who rushed into markets in which U.S. firms were forbidden to trade or invest. In the case of the Iran-Libya Sanctions Act (sometimes known as the D'Amato Act), foreign firms investing in the petroleum sectors of the two target countries were threatened with action against their U.S. activities as well as smaller inconveniences such as visa denials for their executives. Likewise, the Helms-Burton (or "Libertad") Act proposed sanctions against firms of any nationality investing in Cuban property expropriated from U.S. citizens (a potentially vast category given U.S. dominance of the Cuban economy before the revolution and the large numbers of wealthy Cubans who fled to the United States).

In both cases, Europeans objected vehemently to what they termed extraterritorial measures that sought to impose not only U.S. moral standards but explicit U.S. policy decisions on others. (The issue of extraterritoriality had already plagued U.S.-European relations since the Reagan administration had attempted to impose sanctions on European firms participating in construction of a Soviet gas pipeline to Europe.) The EU went so far as to adopt "blocking legislation" that prohibited EU firms from complying with the requirements of U.S. sanctions law, leaving EU firms with operations in both countries in a legally uncomfortable situation. EU officials also repeatedly threatened to bring the Helms-Burton legislation before a WTO panel, which would almost certainly have rejected it.

Instead, officials on both sides seemed to recognize the potentially disastrous effects on transatlantic economic relations of a full-scale cycle of dispute and retaliation over this issue. In an initial effort to manage the dispute, Leon Brittan and Stuart Eizenstat, undersecretary for economic affairs at the State Department, hammered out an "understanding" in April 1997 to address issues of expropriated property in the framework of the OECD negotiations on the Multilateral Agreement on Investment (MAI). The hope that this would lead to a durable solution proved unfounded; rather than the MAI helping to solve the expropriated property issue, the expropriated property issue probably helped to sink the MAI, which ultimately foundered when attacks by Greens and consumer groups led to French withdrawal from the talks in the fall of 1998. At the May 1998 summit, however, the United States and the EU announced another carefully hedged "understanding" under which EU member state authorities would scrutinize new investments in Cuba and deny financial and other support, such as insurance cover, to investments involving certain kinds of illegally expropriated property. In return, the U.S. side would seek congressional authorization to waive Helms-Burton sanctions against EU firms. Given strong opposition in Congress to such a request, this was a tenuous prospect at best.

The dispute over sanctions came to a head in the spring of 1998, when the French oil firm Total announced its intention to develop Iran's South Pars oil field in cooperation with the French government. Total, one of the few major oil companies with negligible investment in the United States, had little to lose by defying U.S. legislation. This placed U.S. policymakers in a dilemma, as sanctions against Total would have no effect on Iran's access to foreign investment but would incur huge costs for U.S.-EU relations. The beginning of a tentative and oblique dialogue between the United States and Iran complicated the picture further. In the end, both sides agreed to back off. At the May 1998 U.S.-EU summit, Secretary of State Madeleine Albright announced that the United States would waive sanctions against Total and would work with Congress to modify the legislation in return for EU cooperation on issues such as thwarting Iranian efforts to acquire weapons of mass destruction.

Although there have been signs that U.S. legislators are beginning to question their promiscuous use of unilateral sanctions, the issue is unlikely to go away quickly, especially if EU leaders revert to the doctrinaire (if defensible) view that the United States must be forced to eliminate these measures forthwith or face a WTO challenge. Sanctions issues are important to EU business, but they have little resonance among the European public. Indeed, the Commission, which had long harped on a Massachusetts measure that sanctions firms doing business in Burma, was unexpectedly ambushed in the fall of 1998 by an EP resolution supporting Massachusetts and calling for EU sanctions against Burma.

Regulatory Issues: Standards, Science, and Consumer Anxiety

As arduous as sanctions-related questions have become, they pose less of a threat to transatlantic trade than do complex issues emerging from the regulatory arena. During implementation of the single market program, the United States and the EU haggled over procedures for the development of product standards, as well as procedures for testing and certifying those products, in various industrial sectors. The difficulty surrounding standards, testing, and certification was evident from the protracted negotiations of bilateral mutual recognition agreements in a limited number of sectors; the negotiations finally concluded in 1997, years after their scheduled dates of completion.

Difficult though they are, disputes over product standards are far less intractable than issues in which scientific results and popular attitudes have proved almost impossible to reconcile. Nowhere do U.S. and EU policymakers face greater challenges than in the area of food regulation, where issues of science, popular emotion, social judgments about acceptable level of risk, and regulatory responsibility have become hopelessly entangled. Regulatory issues ranging from the use of hormones in meat production to control of bovine spongiform encephalopathy (BSE) to the role of genetic engineering in grains have seemingly transcended their technical origins to become symbolic of larger anxieties over the pace of change and the role of science in modern life. In the process these issues have generated increasingly intractable trade disputes.

Some observers have seen in the rising tensions over food regulation a reflection of deep differences between the U.S. and European publics, for instance, in their conception of nature. A more modest explanation is that they reflect differences in public confidence in the efficacy of government regulation. Here, as in other areas, the structural asymmetry between the United States and the EU is an underlying cause of the tension. For example, despite complaints from business about its slowness and inefficiency, the U.S. Food and Drug Administration, in existence for the better part of the century, enjoys a broad degree of confidence among the American public. By contrast, the EU lacks a single politically independent and effective regulatory body that can play the role of public guardian. Commission officials have long argued that the system of mutual recognition and member state consultation (via various scientific advisory committees) is effective, but in practice Commission officials have limited control over the behavior of member-state regulatory agencies. The BSE scandal of the mid-1990s—which erupted when British scientists found a link between beef consumption and Creutzfeld-Jacob disease (CJD), a degenerative brain disease in humans—exposed the weakness of EU institutions and of EU-level regulatory oversight in the face of political pressure, seriously eroding public confidence in the process. Lacking credibility as impartial authorities in this area, EU and member state officials instinctively bow before every expression of public alarm over new processes or substances. As U.S. agriculture transforms itself with the aid of genetic-engineering techniques, the EU's reflexive response is bound to lead to serious disruptions in trade flows.

In retrospect, the U.S.-EC dispute in the 1980s over the use of hormones in beef was an indicator of problems to come. The dispute arose out of a public scandal in Italy, where farmers were found to have been dosing cattle with large amounts of certain hormones known to be dangerous and banned in both the EC and the United States. In an effort to respond to public indignation over a case involving egregious failure to enforce existing laws, EU policymakers decided to ban all use of any hormones in the production of beef (with an exception for "therapeutic" use), including a number of hormones that scientific studies had shown to be benign. Arguments based on scientific evidence were brushed aside with responses about "consumer preference" and the impossibility of proving that the use of any hormone was completely safe. After the GATT's weak dispute-settlement mechanism proved unable to resolve the quarrel, the United States retaliated against the EC for lost beef exports. When more stringent WTO rules took effect after 1995, the United States promptly hauled the EU back into dispute settlement. A WTO panel predictably concluded that the hormone ban was scientifically unfounded and thus inconsistent with WTO obligations. In response, the EU announced that it would gather scientific evidence to justify the ban, which had already been in effect for ten years. The paucity of such evidence so far suggests that this strategy will not succeed. Unfortunately, the EU has little political room for maneuver: After years of official denunciation of "hormone beef," public attitudes are firmly set and efforts to relax the ban would be politically suicidal in many member states.

When the next dispute arose, over use of BST, a hormone used to improve milk yields in cows, the Commission proposed to add a political escape clause to all scientific reviews of new substances. The so-called fourth criterion or fourth hurdle required that after passing the tests of safety, quality, and efficacy, new substances would be judged on socioeconomic grounds. (In the case of BST, the socioeconomic argument advanced was that its use would unfairly benefit large farmers and would add to already rampant overproduction in the dairy sector.) Policymakers and businesspeople in the United States, including the developer of BST, denounced this idea as a perversion of the role of regulators and a form of hidden protectionism.

Although the agricultural and veterinary provisions of the Uruguay Round agreement ruled out the use of the fourth hurdle and raised the burden of proof required for banning products on health grounds, regulatory issues in the agriculture area continue to play a growing role in U.S.-EU tensions. In particular, under intense pressure to respond forcefully to the BSE crisis, the EU hastily passed a broad-based ban in July 1997 on all products containing beef derivatives from any source. Only later did it emerge that the ban encompassed approximately $20 billion in transatlantic trade, much of it in the pharmaceuticals sector. A brief delay in implementation of the ban averted major disruptions in trading patterns and enabled the United States and the EU to settle down to an extended argument over who could qualify as "BSE-free" and which standards were to be used in making that decision.

Finally, the rapid entry of genetically modified crop varieties into U.S. agriculture has set the scene for long-running disputes over the pace of approval of genetically modified organisms (GMOs) in Europe and given rise to a contentious dispute over the appropriateness of requiring labels for all foods containing any trace of a genetically modified ingredient. The fundamental problem is a significant difference in public attitude. Americans for the most part seem reconciled to genetic engineering as a more modern form of plant breeding and accept scientific judgments on the safety of these products. Europeans for the most part are deeply suspicious of such "unnatural" products and either disbelieve the scientists or argue that it cannot be known for sure that GMOs are absolutely safe in every respect (this is a reflection of the well-known difficulty of proving a negative).

Much to the irritation of the United States, the EU has responded to these pressures by periodically adding extra steps to the already arduous approval process for GMOs laid out under its 1990 directive on the subject (Directive 90/220). Thus in addition to approval by all member states, GMOs must undergo additional scrutiny by the Commission's consumer affairs officials. In the meantime, new genetically modified crop varieties are approved and planted in the United States, which does not require genetically modified soybeans, for instance, to be separated from other varieties. The risk continues to grow, therefore, that dilatory EU approvals—or successful political and legal challenges from environmental groups—will cause a crisis in trade relations.

The Information Revolution: A New World of Disputes?

The rapid evolution of the Internet in the mid- and late 1990s, both as a business tool and as a commercial environment, presented new dilemmas and new potential sources of friction to U.S. and EU regulators. Perhaps the most serious was the problem posed for transatlantic data flows by the EU data privacy directive. This directive set up a regulatory structure to ensure that personal data were properly protected both by government authorities and by the private sector. As a corollary, it also prohibited transmission of personal data on EU citizens to countries in which adequate protection of data (by EU standards) did not prevail. The United States has no centralized regulatory structure protecting data privacy comparable to that set forth in the directive; it has traditionally relied on self-regulation by companies in this area. Thus the directive caused consternation among major firms both in the United States and in the EU, which feared that the law would prevent routine intracorporate transfer of data such as personnel and payroll records and could well hamper transactions such as airline reservations or electronic commerce. Efforts to come to a resolution whereby the EU would accept voluntary commitments by U.S. firms as adequate for the purposes of the directive had not made much progress by the time the directive entered into force in October 1998. Fortunately, however, the low level of implementation among member states and member state reluctance to cut off data flows without a greater effort to find a solution resulted in a decision to avoid action for an additional ninety days.

In other Internet-related areas, such as electronic commerce (i.e., the sale of products and services entirely via the Internet), prospects for true regulatory cooperation appear better. Relatively speaking, regulation of the Internet is a blank page, making it easier to avoid conflicts emerging from the clash of established regulatory structures and to come to a meeting of minds before positions are set. In December 1997, for example, the United States and the EU issued a joint declaration on electronic commerce, which helped set the agenda for OECD and WTO examination of the issues (with the United States and the EU starting out on the same side for a change). This fairly general document stated certain common principles, among them the need to keep regulation to a minimum and to avoid new taxes on Internet transactions.

However, electronic commerce entails difficult and potentially divisive legal issues such as the validity and authentication of electronic signatures. As another example of possible points of conflict, the "no new taxes" pledge does not solve the problem of collecting existing taxes such as VAT on electronic commerce. Governments are worried not only about loss of revenue but also about the inequities between electronic and nonelectronic traders of the same products that would result from an entirely tax-free Internet. Regimes set up to address this issue could well cause trade problems if not carefully coordinated, although such coordination is not always a given.

The inherent bias toward or against government involvement in new economic areas differs across the Atlantic, as it does among member states; for example, a number of U.S. firms reacted with alarm to a proposal by Commissioner Martin Bangemann to develop a "charter" for electronic commerce. Another tricky issue has been data encryption. Technology that allows private users to encrypt data transmissions over the Internet offers greater privacy and security to businesses and citizens but also presents serious problems for law-enforcement agencies. U.S. efforts to control export of encryption technology and ensure that "keys" that allow law officers to break codes would remain accessible to U.S. authorities caused friction with EU member states that resented the implication that ultimate control of all these technologies would remain in U.S. hands. A decision by the United States in late 1998 to ease these rules appeared to address most of these concerns.

CONCLUSION

In looking at the long, complicated, and fractious relationship between the world's two greatest powers, it is clear that permanent harmony is neither achievable nor, perhaps, desirable. In most important respects, the relationship is fundamentally sound. The overwhelming importance of the economic relationship and the slow but definite growth of a permanent institutional framework make it difficult to conceive of a major breakdown in U.S.-EU relations. However, many of the most visible disputes between the two arise from real differences in social and political outlook, ranging from the role of foreign policy in economics to the role of governments in ensuring public safety and managing scientific risk. These are unlikely to yield to any grand initiatives; convergence, if it occurs, will happen incrementally and over time.

A recurring theme in U.S.-EU economic dialogue has been the importance of regulatory cooperation, whereby the two sides try to find a common approach to regulatory issues, thus eliminating disputes in advance. This is clearly a rational approach that has particular promise in areas where both sides are not already burdened with long-standing institutional differences. It would be a mistake to imagine, however, that true convergence is possible in regulating the economies of two societies with vastly different histories, geographies, demographics, and social philosophies.[12]

One can argue that such an outcome is not even necessarily ideal. A single market is one of the guiding tenets of the EU, faced as it is with the challenge of fostering integration in the face of intractable linguistic and historical barriers. The United States, with a single language, a single currency, and a singularly mobile population, has been much more willing to tolerate certain residual regulatory barriers. And, in areas where it chooses to regulate, as a nation-state the U.S. has a federal regulatory apparatus far more powerful than anything sovereign European nation-states would be prepared to accept. Under the circumstances, it is hard to argue that the benefits of eliminating remaining trade barriers from a relationship in which the overwhelming majority of trade already flows unhindered would be greater than the costs of trying to impose a one-size-fits-all economic regime, even if such a regime could be devised.

Thus persistent effort to make incremental progress on hard issues (such as agricultural trade), coupled with a will to live through occasional acrimonious rows in the WTO without paralyzing other important areas of cooperation, is likely to remain the preferred formula for managing the U.S.-EU relationship. Periodic announcements of grand new initiatives are part of the picture and occasionally aid in achieving breakthroughs on particular issues. The risk, of course, is that an unending line of such initiatives will lead to meeting fatigue among policymakers and perhaps strain institutional resources with increasingly trivial processes such as "dialogues" among various social groups or redundant efforts to increase social and cultural exchanges. On balance, however, such initiatives appear to serve the important purpose of reaffirming that both sides still care about each other and that what they have in common far outweighs the remaining differences, irritating though they may be. As seen in the Uruguay Round, despite their differences the United States and EU are doomed to remain close collaborators, not only because of the importance of their bilateral relationship but also because of the need to defend their common interests and approaches in a world where democratic values and functioning market economies remain largely ideals rather than realities.

NOTES

1. For an overview of U.S.-EU relations in the post–single market and post–Cold War period, see Michael Calingaert, *European Integration Revisited: Progress, Prospects, and U.S. Interests* (Boulder: Westview Press, 1996), pp. 151–206; Kevin Featherstone and Roy H. Ginsberg, *The United States and the European Union in the 1990s: Partners in Transition* (New York: St. Martin's Press, 1996); and John Peterson, *Europe and America in the 1990s: The Prospects for Partnership,* 2d ed. (London: Edward Elgar, 1993).

2. Bull. EC 7/8-1989, points 1.1.1 to 1.1.5.

3. "Declaration on US-EC Relations," U.S. Department of State, November 11, 1990.

4. Bull. EC 12-1990, point 1.4.94.

5. On the U.S. démarche, see John Newhouse, "The Diplomatic Round: A Collective Nervous Breakdown," *New Yorker,* September 7, 1991, p. 92.

6. See Paul Kennedy, *The Rise and Fall of the Great Powers: Economic Change and Military Conflict from 1500 to 2000* (New York: Random House, 1987).

7. On the TAFTA and related proposals, see Ernest H. Preeg et al., "Policy Forum: Transatlantic Free Trade," *Washington Quarterly* 19, no. 2 (spring 1996): 105–133.

8. Bureau of Public Affairs, "The New Transatlantic Agenda and Joint EU-U.S. Action Plan," Department of State Dispatch 6, 49 (December 3, 1995).

9. *TABD News,* no. 2 (June 1998): 1.

10. For the background to these new disputes, see Miles Kahler, *Regional Futures and Transatlantic Economic Relations* (New York: Council on Foreign Relations, 1995); for a discussion of them in the WTO context, see Mary E. Footer, "The EU and the WTO Global Trading System," in Pierre-Henri Laurent and Marc Maresceau, eds., *The State of the European Union,* vol. 4, *Deepening and Widening* (Boulder: Lynne Rienner, 1998), pp. 317–336.

11. For the background to the dispute, see Christopher Stevens, "EU Policy for the Banana Market," in Helen Wallace and William Wallace, eds., *Policy-Making in the European Union,* 3d ed. (Oxford: Oxford University Press, 1996), pp. 325–352.

12. See David Vogel, *Barriers or Benefits: Regulation in Transatlantic Trade* (Washington, D.C.: Brookings Institution, 1997).

Appendix 1

Abbreviations and Acronyms

ACP	African, Caribbean, and Pacific
ACUSE	Action Committee for the United States of Europe
AER	Assembly of European Regions
APEC	Asia Pacific Economic Cooperation
ASEAN	Association of Southeast Asian Nations
ASEM	Asia-Europe Meeting
ATC	Agreement on Textiles and Clothing
Benelux	Belgium, the Netherlands, and Luxembourg
BSE	bovine spongiform encephalopathy
BST	bovine somatotropin
CAP	Common Agricultural Policy
CCP	Common Commercial Policy
CE	European conformity
CEAC	Conference of European Affairs Committees
CEDEFOP	European Center for the Development of Vocational Training
CEEP	European Center of Public Enterprises
CEES	Central and Eastern European States
CEN	European Standardization Committee
CENELEC	European Electrotechnical Standardization Committee
CET	common external tariff
CFCs	chlorofluorocarbons
CFI	Court of First Instance
CFSP	Common Foreign and Security Policy
CITES	Convention on Trade in Endangered Species
CJD	Creutzfeld-Jacob disease
CJTF	Combined Joint Task Forces
COPA	Committee of Professional Agricultural Organizations of the European Community
COR	Committee of the Regions

COREPER	Committee of Permanent Representatives
COST	European Cooperation in the Field of Scientific and Technological Research
CSCE	Conference on Security and Cooperation in Europe
CSFs	Community Support Frameworks
CTMO	Community Trademark Office
DG	Directorate-General
EAGGF	European Agricultural Guidance and Guarantee Fund
EAP	Environmental Action Program
EBRD	European Bank for Reconstruction and Development
EC	European Community
ECB	European Central Bank
ECHO	European Community Humanitarian Office
ECHR	European Convention for the Protection of Human Rights and Fundamental Freedoms
ECJ	European Court of Justice
ECOFIN	Council of Economic and Finance Ministers
ECSC	European Coal and Steel Community
ECU	European currency unit
EDA	European Democratic Alliance
EDC	European Defense Community
EDF	European Development Fund
EDU	European Democratic Union
EEA	European Economic Area
EEA	European Environment Agency
EEC	European Economic Community
EEIG	European Economic Interest Grouping
EFTA	European Free Trade Area/Association
EIA	environmental impact assessment
EIB	European Investment Bank
EIF	European Investment Fund
ELDR	European Liberal, Democratic, and Reformist Party
EMCDDA	European Montioring Center for Drugs and Drug Addiction
EMEA	European Agency for the Evaluation of Medicinal Products
EMI	European Monetary Institute
EMS	European Monetary System
EMU	Economic and Monetary Union
ENs	European Norms
EP	European Parliament
EPC	European Political Cooperation
EPP	European People's Party
EPU	European Payments Union

EPU	European Political Union
Erasmus	European Community Action Scheme for the Mobility of University Students
ERDF	European Regional Development Fund
ERM	exchange rate mechanism
ERT	European Round Table of Industrialists
ESC	Economic and Social Committee
ESCB	European System of Central Banks
ESDI	European Security and Defense Identity
ESF	European Social Fund
ESPRIT	European Strategic Program for Research and Development in Information Technology
ETSI	European Telecommunications Standards Institute
ETUC	European Trade Union Confederation
EU	European Union
Euratom	European Atomic Energy Community
EUROPOL	European police agency
FDI	foreign direct investment
FTAA	Free Trade Area of the Americas
G7	Group of Seven Most Industrialized Countries
G8	Group of Seven Most Industrialized Countries plus Russia
G24	Group of Twenty-Four Most Industrialized Countries
GAC	General Affairs Council
GATS	General Agreement on Trade in Services
GATT	General Agreement on Tariffs and Trade
GDP	gross domestic product
GDR	German Democratic Republic
GMO	genetically modified organism
GMP	Global Mediterranean Policy
GNP	gross national product
GSP	Generalized System of Preferences
IGC	intergovernmental conference
IMF	International Monetary Fund
IMPs	Integrated Mediterranean Programs
IPPC	integrated pollution prevention and control
ITA	Information Technology Agreement
ITO	International Trade Organization
JHA	Justice and Home Affairs
JRC	Joint Research Center
LIFE	Financial Instrument for the Environment
Lingua	Action Program to Promote Foreign Language Competence in the European Community
MAI	Multilateral Agreement on Investment

MCAs	monetary compensatory amounts
MED	Mediterranean
MEP	member of the European Parliament
Mercosur	Mercado Común del Cono Sur (Southern Cone Common Market)
MFA	Multifiber Arrangement
MFN	most-favored nation
MFPs	multiannual framework programs
MP	member of Parliament
MRAs	mutual recognition agreements
NAFTA	North American Free Trade Agreement
NATO	North Atlantic Treaty Organization
NGO	nongovernmental organization
NIEO	New International Economic Order
NTA	New Transatlantic Agenda
NTB	nontariff barrier
OECD	Organization for Economic Cooperation and Development
OEEC	Organization for European Economic Cooperation
ONP	Open Network Provisions
OSCE	Organization for Security and Cooperation in Europe
PCA	partnership and cooperation agreement
PCBs	polychlorinated biphenyls
PCTs	polychlorinated terphenyls
PES	Party of the European Socialists
PHARE	Poland-Hungary: Actions for Economic Reconstruction
PLO	Palestine Liberation Organization
QMV	qualified majority voting
R&D	research and development
SEA	Single European Act
SIS	Schengen Information System
SMEs	small and medium-sized enterprises
SPD	Social Democratic Party
STABEX	System for the Stabilization of Export Earnings from Products
TABD	Transatlantic Business Dialogue
TACIS	Technical Assistance for the Commonwealth of Independent States
TAD	Transatlantic Declaration
TAFTA	Transatlantic Free Trade Agreement
TEC	Treaty Establishing the European Community
Tempus	Trans-European Mobility Scheme for University Students
TENs	Trans-European Networks

TEP	Transatlantic Economic Partnership
TEU	Treaty on European Union
TRIMs	trade-related investment measures
TRIPs	Trade-Related Aspects of Intellectual Property Rights
TRNC	Turkish Republic of Northern Cyprus
UFE	Union for Europe
UNICE	Union of Industrial and Employers' Confederations of Europe
USSR	Union of Soviet Socialist Republics
VAT	value-added tax
WEU	Western European Union
WTO	World Trade Organization

Appendix 2

Renumbered Articles, Titles, and Sections of the Treaty on European Union

Previous Numbering	New Numbering	Previous Numbering	New Numbering
Title I	Title I	Article J.16	Article 26
Article A	Article 1	Article J.17	Article 27
Article B	Article 2	Article J.18	Article 28
Article C	Article 3		
Article D	Article 4	Title VI†	Title VI
Article E	Article 5	Article K.1	Article 29
Article F	Article 6	Article K.2	Article 30
Article F.1*	Article 7	Article K.3	Article 31
		Article K.4	Article 32
Title II	Title II	Article K.5	Article 33
Article G	Article 8	Article K.6	Article 34
		Article K.7	Article 35
Title III	Title III	Article K.8	Article 36
Article H	Article 9	Article K.9	Article 37
		Article K.10	Article 38
Title IV	Title IV	Article K.11	Article 39
Article I	Article 10	Article K.12	Article 40
		Article K.13	Article 41
Title V†	Title V	Article K.14	Article 42
Article J.1	Article 11		
Article J.2	Article 12	Title VIa‡	Title VII
Article J.3	Article 13	Article K.15*	Article 43
Article J.4	Article 14	Article K.16*	Article 44
Article J.5	Article 15	Article K.17*	Article 45
Article J.6	Article 16		
Article J.7	Article 17		
Article J.8	Article 18		
Article J.9	Article 19		
Article J.10	Article 20		
Article J.11	Article 21		
Article J.12	Article 22		
Article J.13	Article 23		
Article J.14	Article 24		
Article J.15	Article 25		

(continued)

Appendix 2 continued

	Previous Numbering	New Numbering
	Title VII	Title VIII
	Article L	Article 46
	Article M	Article 47
	Article N	Article 48
	Article O	Article 49
	Article P	Article 50
	Article Q	Article 51
	Article R	Article 52
	Article S	Article 53

Source: Conference of the Representatives of the Governments of the Member States, Treaty of Amsterdam.

Notes: *New Treaty of Amsterdam article.

†Title amended by the Treaty of Amsterdam.

‡New Treaty of Amsterdam title.

Appendix 3

Renumbered Articles, Titles, and Sections of the Treaty Establishing the European Community

Previous Numbering	New Numbering	Previous Numbering	New Numbering
Part One	*Part One*	*Chapter 1*	*Chapter 1*
Article 1	Article 1	*Section 1 (deleted)*	—
Article 2	Article 2	Article 12	Article 25
Article 3	Article 3	Article 13 (repealed)	—
Article 3a	Article 4	Article 14 (repealed)	—
Article 3b	Article 5	Article 15 (repealed)	—
Article 3c*	Article 6	Article 16 (repealed)	—
Article 4	Article 7	Article 17 (repealed)	—
Article 4a	Article 8		—
Article 4b	Article 9	*Section 2 (deleted)*	
Article 5	Article 10	Article 18 (repealed)	—
Article 5a*	Article 11	Article 19 (repealed)	—
Article 6	Article 12	Article 20 (repealed)	—
Article 6a*	Article 13	Article 21 (repealed)	—
Article 7 (repealed)	—	Article 22 (repealed)	—
Article 7a	Article 14	Article 24 (repealed)	—
Article 7b (repealed)	—	Article 25 (repealed)	—
Article 7c	Article 15	Article 26 (repealed)	—
Article 7d*	Article 16	Article 27 (repealed)	—
		Article 28	Article 26
Part Two	*Part Two*	Article 29	Article 27
Article 8	Article 17		
Article 8a	Article 18	*Chapter 2*	*Chapter 2*
Article 8b	Article 19	Article 30	Article 28
Article 8c	Article 20	Article 31–33 (repealed)	—
Article 8d	Article 21	Article 34	Article 29
Article 8e	Article 22	Article 35 (repealed)	—
		Article 36	Article 30
		Article 37	Article 31
Part Three	*Part Three*		
Title I	*Title I*	*Title II*	*Title II*
Article 9	Article 23	Article 38	Article 32
Article 10	Article 24	Article 39	Article 33
Article 11 (repealed)	—	Article 40	Article 34

(continued)

Appendix 3 continued

Previous Numbering	New Numbering	Previous Numbering	New Numbering
Article 41	Article 35	*Title IIIa‡*	*Title IV*
Article 42	Article 36	Article 73i*	Article 61
Article 43	Article 37	Article 73j*	Article 62
Article 44 (repealed)	—	Article 73k*	Article 63
Article 45 (repealed)	—	Article 73l*	Article 64
Article 46	Article 38	Article 73m*	Article 65
Article 47 (repealed)	—	Article 73n*	Article 66
		Article 73o*	Article 67
		Article 73p*	Article 68
		Article 73q*	Article 69
Title III	*Title III*	*Title IV*	*Title V*
Chapter 1	*Chapter 1*	Article 74	Article 70
Article 48	Article 39	Article 75	Article 71
Article 49	Article 40	Article 76	Article 72
Article 50	Article 41	Article 77	Article 73
Article 51	Article 42	Article 78	Article 74
		Article 79	Article 75
Chapter 2	*Chapter 2*	Article 80	Article 76
Article 52	Article 43	Article 81	Article 77
Article 53 (repealed)	—	Article 82	Article 78
Article 54	Article 44	Article 83	Article 79
Article 55	Article 45	Article 84	Article 80
Article 56	Article 46		
Article 57	Article 47	*Title V*	*Title VI*
Article 58	Article 48	*Chapter 1*	*Chapter 1*
		Section 1	*Section 1*
Chapter 3	*Chapter 3*	Article 85	Article 81
Article 59	Article 49	Article 86	Article 82
Article 60	Article 50	Article 87	Article 83
Article 61	Article 51	Article 88	Article 84
Article 62 (repealed)	—	Article 89	Article 85
Article 63	Article 52	Article 90	Article 86
Article 64	Article 53		—
Article 65	Article 54	*Section 2 (deleted)*	—
Article 66	Article 55	Article 91 (repealed)	
Chapter 4	*Chapter 4*	*Section 3*	*Section 2*
Article 67 (repealed)	—	Article 92	Article 87
Article 68 (repealed)	—	Article 93	Article 88
Article 69 (repealed)	—	Article 94	Article 89
Article 70 (repealed)	—		
Article 71 (repealed)	—	*Chapter 2*	*Chapter 2*
Article 72 (repealed)	—	Article 95	Article 90
Article 73 (repealed)	—	Article 96	Article 91
Article 73a (repealed)	—	Article 97 (repealed)	—
Article 73b	Article 56	Article 98	Article 92
Article 73c	Article 57	Article 99	Article 93
Article 73d	Article 58		
Article 73e (repealed)	—	*Chapter 3*	*Chapter 3*
Article 73f	Article 59	Article 100	Article 94
Article 73g	Article 60	Article 100a	Article 95
Article 73h (repealed)	—	Article 100b (repealed)	—

(continued)

Appendix 3 continued

Previous Numbering	New Numbering	Previous Numbering	New Numbering
Article 100c (repealed)	—	Article 113	Article 133
Article 100d (repealed)	—	Article 114 (repealed)	—
Article 101	Article 96	Article 115	Article 134
Article 102	Article 97	Article 116 (repealed)	—
Title VI	*Title VII*	*Title VIIa‡*	*Title X*
Chapter 1	*Chapter 1*	Article 116*	Article 135
Article 102a	Article 98		
Article 103	Article 99	*Title VIII*	*Title XI*
Article 103a	Article 100	*Chapter 1§*	*Chapter 1*
Article 104	Article 101	Article 117	Article 136
Article 104a	Article 102	Article 118	Article 137
Article 104b	Article 103	Article 118a	Article 138
Article 104c	Article 104	Article 118b	Article 139
		Article 118c	Article 140
Chapter 2	*Chapter 2*	Article 119	Article 141
Article 105	Article 105	Article 119a	Article 142
Article 105a	Article 106	Article 120	Article 143
Article 106	Article 107	Article 121	Article 144
Article 107	Article 108	Article 122	Article 145
Article 108	Article 109		
Article 108a	Article 110	*Chapter 2*	*Chapter 2*
Article 109	Article 111	Article 123	Article 146
		Article 124	Article 147
Chapter 3	*Chapter 3*	Article 125	Article 148
Article 109a	Article 112		
Article 109b	Article 113	*Chapter 3*	*Chapter 3*
Article 109c	Article 114	Article 126	Article 149
Article 109d	Article 115	Article 127	Article 150
Chapter 4	*Chapter 4*	*Title IX*	*Title XII*
Article 109e	Article 116	Article 128	Article 151
Article 109f	Article 117		
Article 109g	Article 118	*Title X*	*Title XIII*
Article 109h	Article 119	Article 129	Article 152
Article 109i	Article 120		
Article 109j	Article 121	*Title XI*	*Title XIV*
Article 109k	Article 122	Article 129a	Article 153
Article 109l	Article 123		
Article 109m	Article 124		
Title VIa‡	*Title VIII*	*Title XII*	*Title XV*
Article 109n*	Article 125	Article 129b	Article 154
Article 109o*	Article 126	Article 129b	Article 155
Article 109p*	Article 127	Article 129c	Article 156
Article 109q*	Article 128		
Article 109r*	Article 129	*Title XIII*	*Title XVI*
Article 109s*	Article 130	Article 130	Article 157
Title VII	*Title IX*	*Title XIV*	*Title XVII*
Article 110	Article 131	Article 130a	Article 158
Article 111 (repealed)	—	Article 130b	Article 159
Article 112	Article 132	Article 130c	Article 160

(continued)

Appendix 3 continued

Previous Numbering	New Numbering	Previous Numbering	New Numbering
Article 130d	Article 161	Article 143	Article 200
Article 130e	Article 162	Article 144	Article 201
Title XV	*Title XVIII*	*Section 2*	*Section 2*
Article 130f	Article 163	Article 145	Article 202
Article 130g	Article 164	Article 146	Article 203
Article 130h	Article 165	Article 147	Article 204
Article 130i	Article 166	Article 148	Article 205
Article 130j	Article 167	Article 149 (repealed)	—
Article 130k	Article 168	Article 150	Article 206
Article 130l	Article 169	Article 151	Article 207
Article 130m	Article 170	Article 152	Article 208
Article 130n	Article 171	Article 153	Article 209
Article 130o	Article 172	Article 154	Article 210
Article 130p	Article 173		
Article 130q (repealed)	—	*Section 3*	*Section 3*
		Article 155	Article 211
Title XVI	*Title XIX*	Article 156	Article 212
Article 130r	Article 174	Article 157	Article 213
Article 130s	Article 175	Article 158	Article 214
Article 130t	Article 176	Article 159	Article 215
		Article 160	Article 216
Title XVII	*Title XX*	Article 161	Article 217
Article 130u	Article 177	Article 162	Article 218
Article 130v	Article 178	Article 163	Article 219
Article 130w	Article 179		
Article 130x	Article 180	*Section 4*	*Section 4*
Article 130y	Article 181	Article 164	Article 220
		Article 165	Article 221
Part Four	*Part Four*	Article 166	Article 222
Article 131	Article 182	Article 167	Article 223
Article 132	Article 183	Article 168	Article 224
Article 133	Article 184	Article 168a	Article 225
Article 134	Article 185	Article 169	Article 226
Article 135	Article 186	Article 170	Article 227
Article 136	Article 187	Article 171	Article 228
Article 136a	Article 188	Article 172	Article 229
		Article 173	Article 230
Part Five	*Part Five*	Article 174	Article 231
Title I	*Title I*	Article 175	Article 232
Chapter 1	*Chapter 1*	Article 176	Article 233
Section I	*Section I*	Article 177	Article 234
Article 137	Article 189	Article 178	Article 235
Article 138	Article 190	Article 179	Article 236
Article 138a	Article 191	Article 180	Article 237
Article 138b	Article 192	Article 181	Article 238
Article 138c	Article 193	Article 182	Article 239
Article 138d	Article 194	Article 183	Article 240
Article 138e	Article 195	Article 184	Article 241
Article 139	Article 196	Article 185	Article 242
Article 140	Article 197	Article 186	Article 243
Article 141	Article 198	Article 187	Article 244
Article 142	Article 199	Article 188	Article 245

(continued)

Appendix 3 continued

Previous Numbering	New Numbering	Previous Numbering	New Numbering
Section 5	*Section 5*	Article 209a	Article 280
Article 188a	Article 246		
Article 188b	Article 247	*Part Six*	*Part Six*
Article 188c	Article 248	Article 210	Article 281
		Article 211	Article 282
Chapter 2	*Chapter 2*	Article 212	Article 283
Article 189	Article 249	Article 213	Article 284
Article 189a	Article 250	Article 213a*	Article 285
Article 189b	Article 251	Article 213b*	Article 286
Article 189c	Article 252	Article 214	Article 287
Article 190	Article 253	Article 215	Article 288
Article 191	Article 254	Article 216	Article 289
Article 191a*	Article 255	Article 217	Article 290
Article 192	Article 256	Article 218	Article 291
		Article 219	Article 292
Chapter 3	*Chapter 3*	Article 220	Article 293
Article 193	Article 257	Article 221	Article 294
Article 194	Article 258	Article 222	Article 295
Article 195	Article 259	Article 223	Article 296
Article 196	Article 260	Article 224	Article 297
Article 197	Article 261	Article 225	Article 298
Article 198	Article 262	Article 226 (repealed)	—
		Article 227	Article 299
Chapter 4	*Chapter 4*	Article 228	Article 300
Article 198a	Article 263	Article 228a	Article 301
Article 198b	Article 264	Article 229	Article 302
Article 198c	Article 265	Article 230	Article 303
		Article 231	Article 303
Chapter 5	*Chapter 5*	Article 232	Article 304
Article 198d	Article 266	Article 233	Article 305
Article 198e	Article 267	Article 234	Article 306
		Article 235	Article 307
Title II	*Title II*	Article 236	Article 308
Article 199	Article 268	Article 237 (repealed)	Article 309
Article 200 (repealed)	—	Article 238	Article 310
Article 201	Article 269	Article 239	Article 311
Article 201a	Article 270	Article 240	Article 312
Article 202	Article 271	Article 241 (repealed)	—
Article 203	Article 272	Article 242 (repealed)	—
Article 204	Article 273	Article 243 (repealed)	—
Article 205	Article 274	Article 244 (repealed)	—
Article 205a	Article 275	Article 245 (repealed)	—
Article 206	Article 276	Article 246 (repealed)	—
Article 206a (repealed)	—		
Article 207	Article 277	*Final Provisions*	*Final Provisions*
Article 208	Article 278	Article 247	Article 313
Article 209	Article 279	Article 248	Article 314

Source: Conference of the Representatives of the Governments of the Member States, Treaty of Amsterdam.

Notes: *New Treaty of Amsterdam article.

†Title amended by the Treaty of Amsterdam.

‡New Treaty of Amsterdam title.

§Chapter amended by the Treaty of Amsterdam.

BIBLIOGRAPHY

Acheson, Dean. *Present at the Creation: My Years in the State Department*. New York: Norton, 1969.
Adenauer, Konrad. *Memoirs, 1945–1966*. Chicago: Henry Regnery, 1966.
Anderson, Jeffrey J. *German Unification and European Union*. Cambridge: Cambridge University Press, 1999.
Archer, Clive, and Fiona Butler. *The European Union: Structure and Process*. 2d ed. New York: St. Martin's Press, 1996.
Armstrong, Kenneth, and Simon Bulmer. *The Governance of the Single European Market*. New York: St. Martin's Press, 1998.
Artis, Michael, and Norman Lee. *The Economics of European Union: Policy and Analysis*. Oxford: Oxford University Press, 1997.
Avery, Graham, and Fraser Cameron. *The Enlargement of the European Union*. Sheffield: Sheffield Academic Press, 1998.
Bache, Ian. *The Regional and Structural Policies of the European Union*. Sheffield: Sheffield Academic Press, 1998.
Baldwin, Richard E. *Towards an Integrated Europe*. London: Center for European Policy Research (CEPR), 1994.
Bangemann, Martin. *Meeting the Global Challenge: Establishing a Successful European Industrial Policy*. London: Kogan Page, 1992.
Barnes, Ian, and Pamela Barnes. *The Enlarged European Union*. London: Longman, 1995.
Baun, Michael. *An Imperfect Union: The Maastricht Treaty and the New Politics of European Integration*. Boulder: Westview Press, 1996.
———. *A Wider Europe: The Politics of European Union Enlargement*. Boston: Rowman & Littlefield, 1999.
Begg, Iain, and Nigel Grimwade. *European Union Own Resources*. Sheffield: Sheffield Academic Press, 1998.
Bianchi, Patrizio. *Industrial Policies and Economic Integration: Learning from European Experiences*. London: Routledge, 1998.
Bieber, Roland, and Jörg Monar, eds. *Justice and Home Affairs in the European Union*. Brussels: EIP, 1995.
Bieber, Roland, Jean-Paul Jacqué, and Joseph Wieler, eds. *An Ever Closer Union: A Critical Analysis of the Draft Treaty on European Union*. Luxembourg: Office for Official Publications of the European Communities, 1985.
Blondel, J., Richard Sinnott, and P. Svensson. *People and Parliament in the European Union*. Oxford: Clarendon Press, 1998.

Bomberg, Elizabeth. *Green Parties and Politics in the European Union.* London: Routledge, 1999.

Brinkley, Douglas, and Clifford Hackett, eds. *Jean Monnet: The Path to European Unity.* New York: St. Martin's Press, 1991.

Bulmer, Simon, and Andrew Scott, eds. *Economic and Political Integration in Europe: Internal Dynamics and Global Context.* Oxford: Blackwell, 1995.

Bulmer, Simon, and Wolfgang Wessels. *The European Council: Decision-Making in European Politics.* London: Macmillan, 1987.

Burgess, Michael. *Federalism and European Union: Political Ideas, Influences, and Strategies in the European Community, 1972–1987.* London: Routledge, 1987.

Button, Kenneth, Kingsley Haynes, and Roger Stough. *Flying into the Future: Air Transport Policy in the European Union.* London: Edward Elgar, 1998.

Button, Kenneth, Peter Nijkamp, and Hugo Priemus, eds. *Transport Networks in Europe: Concepts, Analysis and Policies.* London: Edward Elgar, 1998.

Cafruny, Alan, and Carl Lankowski, eds. *Europe's Ambiguous Unity: Conflict and Consensus in the Post-Maastricht Era.* Boulder: Lynne Rienner, 1997.

Cafruny, Alan, and Patrick Peters, eds. *The Union and the World: The Political Economy of a Common European Foreign Policy.* The Hague: Kluwer, 1998.

Cafruny, Alan, and Glenda Rosenthal, eds. *The State of the European Community, Volume 2: The Maastricht Debates and Beyond.* Boulder: Lynne Rienner, 1993.

Calingaert, Michael. *European Integration Revisited: Progress, Prospects, and U.S. Interests.* Boulder: Westview Press, 1996.

Calleo, David, and Eric Staal, eds. *Europe's Franco-German Engine.* Washington, DC: Brookings Institution, 1998.

Cecchini, Paolo. *The European Challenge 1992: The Benefits of a Single Market.* Aldershot: Wildwood House, 1988.

Chryssochoou, Dimitris. *Democracy in the European Union.* New York: St. Martin's Press, 1998.

Cini, Michelle. *The European Commission: Leadership, Organization, and Culture in the EU Administration.* Manchester: Manchester University Press, 1996.

Cockfield, Arthur. *The European Union: Creating the Single Market.* Chichester: John Wiley and Sons, 1994.

Coffey, Peter. *The Future of Europe.* Aldershot: Edward Elgar, 1995.

Connolly, Bernard. *The Rotten Heart of Europe: The Dirty War for Europe's Money.* London: Faber and Faber, 1995.

Coombes, David. *Politics and Bureaucracy in the European Communities.* London: Allen & Unwin, 1977.

Corbett, Richard. *The European Parliament's Role in Closer European Integration.* Basingstoke: Macmillan, 1998.

Corbett, Richard, Francis Jacobs, and Michael Shackleton. *The European Parliament.* 3d ed. London: Catermill, 1995.

Corcelle, Guy, and Stanley Johnson. *The Environmental Policy of the European Communities.* London: Kluwer, 1995.

Cram, Laura. *Policy-Making in the European Union: Conceptual Lenses and the Integration Process.* London: Routledge, 1997.

De Bassompierre, Guy. *Changing the Guard in Brussels: An Insider's View of the EC Presidency.* New York: Praeger, 1988.

De Gaulle, Charles. *Memoirs of Hope: Renewal and Endeavor.* New York: Simon & Schuster, 1971.

De Grauwe, Paul. *The Economics of Monetary Integration.* 3d ed. Oxford: Oxford University Press, 1997.

Dehousse, Renaud. *The European Court of Justice: The Politics of Judicial Integration.* New York: St. Martin's Press, 1998.

———, ed. *Europe After Maastricht: An Ever Closer Union?* Munich: LBE, 1994.

Deissenberg, Christophe, et al., eds. *European Economic Integration.* Oxford: Blackwell, 1998.

Den Boer, Monica, ed. *Schengen: Judicial Cooperation and Policy Coordination.* Maastricht: EIPA, 1997.

Delors, Jacques. *Le Nouveau Concert Européen.* Paris: Editions Odile Jacob, 1992.

———. *Our Europe: The Community and National Development.* London: Verso, 1992.

De Porte, Anton. *Europe Between the Superpowers: The Enduring Balance.* New Haven: Yale University Press, 1979.

De Ruyt, Jean. *L'Acte Unique Européen: Commentaire.* Brussels: Editions de l'Université de Bruxelles, 1987.

Dinan, Desmond, ed. *Encyclopedia of the European Union.* Boulder: Lynne Rienner, 1998.

Duchêne, François. *Jean Monnet: The First Statesman of Interdependence.* New York: Norton, 1994.

Duff, Andrew, John Pinder, and Roy Price, eds. *Maastricht and Beyond: Building the European Union.* London: Routledge, 1994.

Dyson, K., and Kevin Featherstone. *The Road to Maastricht: Negotiating Economic and Monetary Union.* Oxford: Oxford University Press, 1998.

Edwards, Geoffrey, and Alfred Pijpers, eds. *The Politics of European Treaty Reform: The 1996 Intergovernmental Conference and Beyond.* London: Pinter, 1997.

Edwards, Geoffrey, and David Spence, eds. *The European Commission.* London: Catermill, 1994.

Edwards, Geoffrey, and Helen Wallace. *The Council of Ministers of the EC and the President in Office.* London: Federal Trust, 1977.

Eeckhout, P. *The European Internal Market and International Trade: A Legal Analysis.* Oxford: Oxford University Press, 1994.

Eichengreen, B. *European Monetary Unification: Theory, Practice, and Analysis.* Boston: MIT Press, 1997.

Eichengreen, B., et al., eds. *Forging an Integrated Europe.* Michigan: University of Michigan Press, 1998.

Eichengreen, B., J. Frieden, and J. von Hagen. *Politics and Institutions in an Integrated Europe.* Heidelberg: Springer, 1995.

Emerson, Michael. *The Economics of 1992.* Oxford: Oxford University Press, 1988.

Emiliou, Nicholas, and David O'Keeffee, eds. *European and World Trade Law After the GATT Uruguay Round.* Chichester: John Wiley, 1996.

Estrin, Saul, and Peter Holmes, eds. *Competition and Economic Integration in Europe.* London: Edward Elgar, 1998.

Featherstone, Kevin, and Roy H. Ginsberg. *The United States and the European Union in the 1990s: Partners in Transition.* 2d ed. New York: St. Martin's Press, 1996.

Fennell, Rosemary. *The Common Agricultural Policy: Continuity and Change.* Oxford: Clarendon Press, 1997.

Flessdal, Andreas, ed. *Democracy and the European Union.* Berlin: Springer Verlag, 1997.

Fountas, S., and B. Kennelly. *European Integration and Regional Policy.* Galway: Center for Development Studies, 1994.

Frelleson, Thomas, and Roy H. Ginsberg. *EU-U.S. Foreign Policy Cooperation in the 1990s: Elements of Partnership*. Brussels: CEPS, 1994.

Frieden, Jeffry, Daniel Gros, and Erik Jones. *The New Political Economy of EMU*. Boston: Rowman & Littlefield, 1998.

Furlong, Paul, and Andrew Cox. *The European Union at the Crossroads: Problems in Implementing the Single Market Project*. Boston: Earlsgate Press, 1995.

Fursdon, Edward. *The European Defense Community: A History*. New York: St. Martin's Press, 1980.

Galtung, J. *Europe in the Making*. New York: Crane Russak, 1989.

Gardner, Brian. *European Agriculture: Policies, Production and Trade*. London: Routledge, 1996.

Gaynor, K. B., and E. Karakitsos. *Economic Convergence in a Multispeed Europe*. New York: St. Martin's Press, 1997.

Genscher, Hans-Dietrich. *Erinnerungen*. Berlin: Siedler Verlag, 1995.

George, Stephen. *Politics and Policy in the European Union*. 3d ed. Oxford: Oxford University Press, 1996.

———. *An Awkward Partner: Britain in the European Community*. 2d ed. Oxford: Clarendon Press, 1997.

Gillingham, John. *Coal, Steel and the Rebirth of Europe, 1945–1955: The Germans and French from Ruhr Conflict to Economic Community*. Cambridge: Cambridge University Press, 1991.

Gloeckler, Gabriel, et al., eds. *Guide to EU Policies*. London: Blackstone Press, 1998.

Goldsmith, M.J.F., and K. K. Klausen, eds. *European Integration and Local Government*. London: Edward Elgar, 1997.

Goodman, S. F. *The European Union*. 3d ed. Basingstoke: Macmillan, 1996.

Grant, Wynn. *The Common Agricultural Policy*. Basingstoke: Macmillan, 1997.

Greenwood, Justin, and Mark Aspinwall, eds. *Collective Action in the European Union: Interests and the New Politics of Associability*. London: Routledge, 1998.

Grosser, Alfred. *The Western Alliance: European-American Relations Since 1945*. New York: Vantage, 1982.

Hackett, Clifford. *Cautious Revolution: The European Community Arrives*. 2d ed. New York, Praeger, 1995.

Hall, S. *Nationality, Migration Rights and Citizenship of the Union*. Doordrecht: Nijhoff, 1995.

Hallstein, Walter. *Europe in the Making*. London: Allen & Unwin, 1972.

Hanrieder, Wolfram. *Germany, America, Europe: Forty Years of German Foreign Policy*. New Haven: Yale University Press, 1989.

Harrop, Jeffrey. *Structural Funding and Employment in the European Union: Financing the Path to Integration*. London: Edward Elgar, 1996.

Hauf, K., and Soetendorp, B., eds. *Adapting to European Integration: Small States and the European Union*. London: Addison-Wesley, 1998.

Hayes-Renshaw, Fiona, and Helen Wallace. *The Council of Ministers*. New York: St. Martin's Press, 1996.

Heinelt, Hubert, and Randall Smith, eds. *Policy Networks and European Structural Funds*. Brookfield, VT: Avebury, 1996.

Hix, S., and C. Lord. *Political Parties in the European Union*. Basingstoke: Macmillan, 1997.

Hogan, Michael. *The Marshall Plan: America, Britain and the Reconstruction of Western Europe, 1947–1952*. Cambridge: Cambridge University Press, 1987.

Holland, Martin. *European Union Common Foreign and Security Policy: From EPC to CFSP Joint Action and South Africa*. Basingstoke: Macmillan, 1995.

———. *Common Foreign and Security Policy: The Record and Reforms*. London: Pinter, 1997.

Hooghe, Liesbet, ed. *Cohesion Policy and European Integration: Building Multi-Level Governance*. Oxford: Oxford University Press, 1996.

Hurwitz, Leon, and Christian Lequesne. *The State of the European Community: Policies, Institutions and Debates in the Transition Years*. Boulder: Lynne Rienner, 1991.

Ingersent, K. A., A. J. Rayner, and R. C. Hine. *The Reform of the Common Agricultural Policy*. Basingstoke: Macmillan, 1998.

Isaacson, Walter. *The Wise Men: Six Friends and the World They Made*. New York: Simon & Schuster, 1986.

Jacquemin, Alexis, and Lucio Pench. *Europe Competing in the Global Economy*. London: Edward Elgar, 1997.

Jans, Jan. *European Environmental Law*. London: Kluwer, 1995.

Jansen, Thomas. *The European People's Party: Origins and Development*. New York: St. Martin's Press, 1998.

Jenkins, Roy. *European Diary, 1977–1981*. London: Collins, 1989.

———. *A Life at the Centre*. London: Macmillan, 1991.

Jones, Erik. *The Politics and Economics of Monetary Union*. Boston: Rowman & Littlefield, 1999.

Jones, Robert A. *The Politics and Economics of the European Union: An Introductory Text*. London: Edward Elgar, 1996.

Jovanovic, Miroslav N. *European Economic Integration: Limits and Prospects*. London: Routledge, 1997.

Kaiser, Karl, et al. *The European Community: Progress or Decline?* London: Royal Institute of International Affairs (RIIA), 1983.

Keating, Michael. *The New Regionalism in Western Europe: Territorial Restructuring and Regional Change*. London: Edward Elgar, 1998.

Kenen, Peter B. *Economic and Monetary Union in Europe: Moving Beyond Maastricht*. Cambridge: Cambridge University Press, 1995.

Keohane, Robert, and Stanley Hoffmann, eds. *The European Community: Decisionmaking and Institutional Change*. Boulder: Westview Press, 1991.

Kolodziej, Edward. *French International Policy Under de Gaulle and Pompidou: The Politics of Grandeur*. Ithaca: Cornell University Press, 1974.

Laffan, Brigid. *The Finances of the European Union*. Basingstoke: Macmillan, 1997.

Lankowski, Carl, ed. *Germany and the European Community: Beyond Hegemony and Containment?* New York: St. Martin's Press, 1993.

Laurent, Pierre-Henri, and Marc Maresceau, eds. *The State of the European Union*, vol. 4, *Deepening and Widening*. Boulder: Lynne Rienner, 1998.

Laursen, Finn, ed. *The Political Economy of European Integration*. The Hague: Kluwer, 1995.

Laursen, Finn, and Sophie Vanhoonacker, eds. *The Intergovernmental Conference on Political Union*. Maastricht: European Institute of Public Administration (EIPA), 1992.

———. *The Ratification of the Maastricht Treaty: Issues, Debates, and Future Implications*. Maastricht: EIPA, 1994.

Lindberg, Leon. *The Political Dynamics of European Integration*. Stanford: Stanford University Press, 1963.

Lindberg, Leon, and Stuart Scheingold. *Europe's Would-Be Polity*. Englewood Cliffs, NJ: Prentice-Hall, 1970.

Lipgens, Walter. *History of European Integration*, 2 vols. London: Oxford University Press, 1981 and 1986.

Lodge, Juliet, ed. *The European Community and the Challenge of the Future*. London: Pinter, 1989.

———. *The 1994 Elections to the European Parliament*. London: Pinter, 1996.

Lord, Christopher. *Democracy in the European Union*. Sheffield: Sheffield Academic Press, 1998.

Ludlow, Peter. *The Making of the European Monetary System: A Case Study in the Politics of the European Community*. London: Butterworths Scientific, 1982.

Majone, Giandomenico. *Regulating Europe*. London: Routledge, 1996.

Maresceau, Marc, ed. *Enlargement and the European Union: Relations Between the European Union and Central and Eastern Europe*. London: Longman, 1997.

Marjolin, Robert. *Architect of European Unity: Memoirs: 1911–1986*. London: Weidenfeld & Nicolson, 1989.

Marks, Gary, et al. *Governance in the European Union*. New York: Sage, 1996.

Mayes, David G., ed. *The Evolution of the Single European Market*. London: Edward Elgar, 1997.

Mazey, S., and C. Rhodes. *The State of the European Union*, vol. 3, *Building a European Policy*. Boulder: Lynne Rienner, 1996.

Mazzuchelli, Colette. *France and Germany at Maastricht: Politics and Negotiations to Create the European Union*. New York: Garland, 1997.

McCormick, John. *The European Union: Politics and Policies*. Boulder: Westview Press, 1996.

McGoldrick, Dominic. *International Relations Law of the European Union*. Harlow: Longman, 1997.

McLeod, I. D. Hendry, and Stephen Hyett. *The External Relations of the European Communities*. Oxford: Oxford University Press, 1996.

McNamara, Kathleen R. *The Currency of Ideas: Monetary Policy in the European Union*. Ithaca: Cornell University Press, 1998.

Meny, Yves, Pierre Muller, and Jean-Louis Quermone. *Adjusting to Europe: The Impact of the European Union on National Institutions and Policies*. London: Routledge, 1996.

Miall, Hugh, ed. *Redefining Europe: New Patterns of Conflict and Cooperation*. London: Pinter, 1994.

Miles, Lee, ed. *The European Union and the Nordic Countries*. New York: Routledge, 1996.

Milward, Alan. *The Reconstruction of Western Europe*. London: Methuen, 1984.

———. *The European Rescue of the Nation-State*. Berkeley: University of California Press, 1992.

Milward, Alan, et al. *The Frontier of National Sovereignty: History and Theory, 1945–1992*. London: Routledge, 1993.

Monar, J., and Roger Morgan, eds. *The Third Pillar of the European Union: Cooperation in the Fields of Justice and Home Affairs*. Brussels: Interuniversity Press, 1994.

Monnet, Jean. *Memoirs*. Garden City, NY: Doubleday, 1978.

Moravcsik, Andrew. *The Choice for Europe: Social Progress and State Power from Messina to Maastricht*. Ithaca: Cornell University Press, 1998.

Mullard, Maurice, and Simon Lee, eds. *The Politics of Social Policy in Europe*. London: Edward Elgar, 1997.

Neal, Larry, and Daniel Barbezat. *The Economics of the European Union and the Economies of Europe*. Oxford: Oxford University Press, 1998.

Neill, Patrick. *The European Court of Justice: A Case Study in Judicial Activism*. London: European Policy Forum, 1995.

Nelsen, Brent F., and Alexander C-G. Stubb, eds. *The European Union: Readings on the Theory and Practice of European Integration.* 2d ed. Boulder: Lynne Rienner, 1998.

Newhouse, John. *Europe Adrift.* New York: Pantheon, 1997.

Newman, Michael. *Democracy, Sovereignty, and the European Union.* New York: St. Martin's Press, 1996.

Nicholson, Frances, and Roger East. *From the Six to the Twelve: The Enlargement of the European Communities.* Chicago: St. James Press, 1987.

Nicolaides, Phedon, ed. *Industrial Policy in the European Community: A Necessary Response to European Integration?* Maastricht: EIPA, 1993.

Nicoll, William, and Trevor C. Salmon. *Building European Union: A Documentary History and Analysis.* Manchester: Manchester University Press, 1997.

Norton, Philip, ed. *National Parliaments and the European Union.* New York: Sage, 1996.

Nugent, Neill. *The Government and Politics of the European Union.* 3d ed. Basingstoke: Macmillan, 1994.

———, ed. *At the Heart of the Union: Studies of the European Commission.* Basingstoke: Macmillian, 1997.

Ovendale, Richard. *Foreign Policy of the British Labour Government, 1945–1951.* London: Pinter, 1984.

Overturf, Stephen F. *Money and European Union.* New York: St. Martin's Press, 1997.

Pappas, Spyros, and Sophie Vanhoonacker, eds. *The European Union's Common Foreign and Security Policy: The Challenges of the Future.* Maastricht: EIPA, 1996.

Paraskevopoulos, Christos C. *European Union at the Crossroads: A Critical Analysis of Monetary Union and Enlargement.* London: Edward Elgar, 1998.

Paraskevopoulos, Christos C., Ricardo Grinspun, and Theodore Georgakopoulos, eds. *Economic Integration and Public Policy in the European Union.* London: Edward Elgar, 1996.

Pelkmans, Jacques. *European Integration: Methods and Economic Analysis.* Harlow: Longman, 1997.

Peterson, John, and Helen Sjursen. *Common Foreign Policy for Europe? Competing Visions of the CFSP.* London: Routledge, 1998.

Piening, Christopher. *Global Europe: The European Union in World Affairs.* Boulder: Lynne Rienner, 1997.

Pinder, John. *European Community: The Building of a Union.* Oxford: Oxford University Press, 1991.

———. *The European Community and Eastern Europe.* London: RIIA, 1991.

Pitchford, Ruth, and Adam Cox, eds. *EMU Explained: Markets and Monetary Union.* London: Reuters, 1997.

Poidevin, Raymond. *Robert Schuman: Homme d'Etat, 1866–1963.* Paris: Imprimerie Nationale, 1986.

Preston, Christopher. *Enlargement and Integration in the European Union.* London: Routledge, 1997.

Pryce, Roy, ed. *The Dynamics of European Union.* London: Croom Helm, 1987.

Redmond, John, ed. *The 1995 Enlargement of the European Union.* Aldershot: Ashgate, 1997.

Redmond, John, and Glenda G. Rosenthal, eds. *The Expanding European Union: Past, Present, and Future.* Boulder: Lynne Rienner, 1997.

Regelsberger, Elfride, et al. *Foreign Policy of the European Union: From EPC to CFSP and Beyond.* Boulder: Lynne Rienner, 1997.

Rhodes, Carolyn, ed. *The European Union in the World Community.* Boulder: Lynne Rienner, 1998.

Richardson, Jeremy, ed. *European Union: Power and Policy-Making.* London: Routledge, 1996.

Roseman, Mark. *Recasting the Ruhr, 1945–1958: Manpower, Economic Recovery, and Labor Relations.* New York: Berg, 1992.

Ross, George. *Jacques Delors and European Integration.* Oxford: Oxford University Press, 1995.

Rudden, Bernard. *Basic Community Law.* Oxford: Clarendon Press, 1996.

Sauter, Wolf. *Competition Law and Industrial Policy in the European Union.* Oxford: Clarendon Press, 1998.

Sbragia, Alberta M., ed. *Europolitics: Institutions and Policymaking in the "New" European Community.* Washington, DC: Brookings Institution, 1992.

Schmidtchen, Dieter, and Robert Cooter, eds. *Constitutional Law and Economics of the European Union.* London: Edward Elgar, 1997.

Scobie, H. M., and Homa Motamen-Scobie, eds. *European Monetary Union: The Way Forward.* London: Routledge, 1998.

Scott, Dermot. *Ireland's Contribution to the European Union.* Dublin: Institute of International Affairs, 1994.

Simonian, Haig. *The Privileged Partnership: Franco-German Relations in the European Community, 1969–1984.* Oxford: Clarendon Press, 1985.

Smith, Karen Elizabeth. *The Making of European Union Foreign Policy.* New York: St. Martin's Press, 1998.

Smith, Michael, and Brian Hocking. *Beyond Foreign Economic Policy: The United States, the Single European Market, and the Changing World Economy.* London: Pinter, 1997.

Soveroski, Marie, ed. *Agenda 2000: An Appraisal of the Commission's Blueprint for Enlargement.* Maastricht: EIPA, 1997.

Springer, Beverly. *The Social Dimension of 1992.* New York: Praeger, 1992.

Stavridis, Stelios, and Roger Morgan. *New Challenges to the European Union: Policies and Policy Making.* Brookfield, VT: Ashgate, 1997.

Stirk, Peter. *European Unity in Context: The Interwar Period.* London: Pinter, 1989.

Swann, Dennis. *European Economic Integration: The Common Market, European Union and Beyond.* London: Edward Elgar, 1996.

Symes, Valerie, Carl Levy, and Jane Littlewood. *The Future of Europe: Problems and Issues for the Twenty-First Century.* Basingstoke: Macmillan, 1997.

Taylor, Paul. *The Limits of European Integration.* London: Croom Helm, 1983.

———. *The European Union in the 1990s.* Oxford: Oxford University Press, 1996.

Temperton, Paul, ed. *The Euro.* New York: John Wiley, 1997.

Thatcher, Margaret. *The Downing Street Years.* New York: HarperCollins, 1993.

Thody, Philip. *An Historical Introduction to the European Union.* London: Routledge, 1998.

Tiersky, Ronald. *Europe Today: National Politics, European Integration, and European Security.* Boston: Rowman & Littlefield, 1998.

Tsoukalis, Loukas. *The New European Economy Revisited: The Politics and Economics of Integration.* 3d ed. Oxford: Oxford University Press, 1977.

Ungerer, Horst. *A Concise History of European Monetary Integration: From EPU to EMU.* Westport, CT: Greenwood Press, 1997.

Van der Eijk, Cees, and Mark N. Franklin, eds. *Choosing Europe? The European Electorate and National Politics in the Face of Union.* Ann Arbor: University of Michigan Press, 1996.

Van Dijck, Pitou, and Gerrit Faber, eds. *The External Economic Dimension of the European Union*. The Hague: Kluwer, 1998.

Van Oudenaren, John. *Uniting Europe: European Integration and the Post–Cold War World*. Boston: Rowman & Littlefield, 1999.

Van Tartwijk-Novey, Louise B., and Christopher Mark. *The European House of Cards? Towards a United States of Europe?* New York: St. Martin's Press, 1995.

Von der Groeben, Hans. *The European Community: The Formative Years: The Struggle to Establish the Common Market and the Political Union (1958–66)*. European Perspectives Series. Luxembourg: Office for Official Publications of the European Communities (OOP), 1985.

Wallace, Helen, and William Wallace, eds. *Policy-Making in the European Union*. 3d ed. Oxford: Oxford University Press, 1996.

Wallace, William. *The Transformation of Western Europe*. London: RIIA, 1990.

Watson, Alison. *Aspects of European Integration: The Politics of Convergence*. New York: St. Martin's Press, 1998.

Weidenfeld, Werner, and Wolfgang Wessels. *Europe from A to Z: Guide to European Integration*. Luxembourg: Office for Official Publications of the European Communities, 1997.

Welsh, Michael. *Europe United? The European Union and the Retreat from Federalism*. New York: St. Martin's Press, 1996.

Werts, Jan. *The European Council*. Amsterdam: North-Holland, 1992.

Westlake, Martin. *The Commission and the Parliament: Partners and Rivals in the European Policy-Making System*. London: Butterworth, 1994.

———. *A Modern Guide to the European Parliament*. London: Pinter, 1994.

———. *The Council of the European Union*. London: Catermill, 1995.

Wexler, Imanuel. *The Marshall Plan Revisited: The European Recovery Program in Economic Perspective*. Westport, CT: Greenwood Press, 1983.

Whitman, Richard G. *From Civilian Power to Superpower? The International Identity of the European Union*. New York: St. Martin's Press, 1998.

Williams, Allan M. *The European Community: The Contradictions of Integration*. 2d ed. Oxford: Blackwell, 1994.

Wood, David M., and Birol Yesilada. *The Emerging European Union*. White Plains, NY: Longman, 1996.

Wyllie, James H. *European Security in the New Political Environment*. London: Longman, 1997.

Index

About the Book

Writing in an accessible, engaging style, Desmond Dinan cuts through the complexities of the European Union to explain clearly the evolution of European integration from the 1950s to the present.

This new edition of his widely acclaimed book retains the familiar three-part structure—history, institutions, and policies—but includes two entirely new chapters: one on key developments in the 1993–1999 period (e.g., the 1995 enlargement, the 1996–1997 intergovernmental conference, the Amsterdam Treaty, and preparations and prospects for EU enlargement into Central and Eastern Europe) and one exploring the increasingly complicated political and economic relationship between the United States and the EU, the world's leading trading powers. The road to the single European currency, launched on January 1, 1999, is examined in a thoroughly revised chapter on Economic and Monetary Union, and the other chapters in the second and third parts of the book also have been extensively rewritten to incorporate recent issues, developments, and debates affecting EU institutions and policies.

Other new material includes short chronologies in the history chapters, synopses of major treaties, results of key referendums, and charts of institutional structures and decisionmaking procedures.

Desmond Dinan is associate professor in the Institute for Public Policy at George Mason University, visiting fellow at the Netherlands Institute of International Relations, Clingendael, and a professor at the College of Europe, Bruges. He is editor of the *Encyclopedia of the European Union*.

About the Book